Books are

FUZZY SETS AND FUZZY LOGIC
Theory and Applications

GEORGE J. KLIR AND BO YUAN

For book and bookstore information

http://www.prenhall.com
gopher to gopher.prenhall.com

Prentice Hall P T R
Upper Saddle River, New Jersey 07458

Library of Congress Cataloging-in-Publication Data
Klir, George J., 1932–
     Fuzzy sets and fuzzy logic: theory and applications / George J.
Klir, Bo Yuan.
        p. cm.
     Includes bibliographical references and index.
     ISBN 0-13-101171-5
     1. Fuzzy sets. 2. Fuzzy logic. I. Yuan, Bo. II. Title.
QA248.K487 1995
511.3--dc20   94-36398
                                               CIP

Editorial/production supervision: *Patti Guerrieri*
Manufacturing buyer: *Alexis R. Heydt*
Acquisitions editor: *Paul Becker*
Editorial assistant: *Maureen Diana*
Cover Design: *Bo Yuan and Milena Klir*
Photographs: *Milena Klir*

Published by Prentice Hall PTR
Prentice-Hall Inc.
A Simon & Schuster Company
Upper Saddle River, NJ 07458

The publisher offers discounts on this book when ordered in bulk quantities.
For more information, contact:

    Corporate Sales Department
    Prentice Hall PTR
    One Lake Street
    Upper Saddle River, NJ 07458
    Phone: 800-382-3419
    Fax: 201-236-7141
    e-mail: corpsales@prenhall.com

Printed in the United States of America
10 9 8 7 6 5 4 3 2 1

ISBN   0-13-101171-5

Prentice-Hall International (UK) Limited, *London*
Prentice-Hall of Australia Pty. Limited, *Sydney*
Prentice-Hall of Canada Inc., *Toronto*
Prentice-Hall Hispanoamericana, S.A., *Mexico*
Prentice-Hall of India Private Limited, *New Delhi*
Prentice-Hall of Japan, Inc., *Tokyo*
Simon & Schuster Asia Pte. Ltd., *Singapore*
Editora Prentice-Hall do Brasil, Ltda., *Rio de Janeiro*

To Lotfi Zadeh,
Who had the courage and the gift
To begin the grand paradigm shift,
And to the many others,
Whose hard work and healthy thinking
Have contributed to the shifting.

CONTENTS

FOREWORD

Fuzzy Sets and Fuzzy Logic is a true magnum opus. An enlargement of *Fuzzy Sets, Uncertainty, and Information*—an earlier work of Professor Klir and Tina Folger—*Fuzzy Sets and Fuzzy Logic* addresses practically every significant topic in the broad expanse of the union of fuzzy set theory and fuzzy logic. To me *Fuzzy Sets and Fuzzy Logic* is a remarkable achievement; it covers its vast territory with impeccable authority, deep insight and a meticulous attention to detail.

To view *Fuzzy Sets and Fuzzy Logic* in a proper perspective, it is necessary to clarify a point of semantics which relates to the meanings of fuzzy sets and fuzzy logic.

A frequent source of misunderstanding has to do with the interpretation of fuzzy logic. The problem is that the term fuzzy logic has two different meanings. More specifically, in a narrow sense, fuzzy logic, FL_n, is a logical system which may be viewed as an extension and generalization of classical multivalued logics. But in a wider sense, fuzzy logic, FL_w, is almost synonymous with the theory of fuzzy sets. In this context, what is important to recognize is that: (a) FL_w is much broader than FL_n and subsumes FL_n as one of its branches; (b) the agenda of FL_n is very different from the agendas of classical multivalued logics; and (c) at this juncture, the term fuzzy logic is usually used in its wide rather than narrow sense, effectively equating fuzzy logic with FL_w.

In *Fuzzy Sets and Fuzzy Logic*, fuzzy logic is interpreted in a sense that is close to FL_w. However, to avoid misunderstanding, the title refers to both fuzzy sets and fuzzy logic.

Underlying the organization of *Fuzzy Sets and Fuzzy Logic* is a fundamental fact, namely, that any field X and any theory Y can be fuzzified by replacing the concept of a crisp set in X and Y by that of a fuzzy set. In application to basic fields such as arithmetic, topology, graph theory, probability theory and logic, fuzzification leads to fuzzy arithmetic, fuzzy topology, fuzzy graph theory, fuzzy probability theory and FL_n. Similarly, in application to applied fields such as neural network theory, stability theory, pattern recognition and mathematical programming, fuzzification leads to fuzzy neural network theory, fuzzy stability theory, fuzzy pattern recognition and fuzzy mathematical programming. What is gained through fuzzification is greater generality, higher expressive power, an enhanced ability to model real-world problems and, most importantly, a methodology for exploiting the tolerance for imprecision—a methodology which serves to achieve tractability, robustness and lower solution cost.

What we are witnessing today—and what is reflected in *Fuzzy Sets and Fuzzy Logic*—is a growing number of fields and theories which are undergoing fuzzification. This is what underlines the basic paradigm shift which is discussed so insightfully in the first chapter of *Fuzzy Sets and*

Fuzzy Logic. The driving force behind this paradigm shift is the realization that traditional two-valued logical systems, crisp set theory and crisp probability theory are inadequate for dealing with imprecision, uncertainty and complexity of the real world. It is this realization that motivates the evolution of fuzzy set theory and fuzzy logic and shapes their role in restructuring the foundations of scientific theories and their applications. And it is in this perspective that the contents of *Fuzzy Sets and Fuzzy Logic* should be viewed.

The first part of *Fuzzy Sets and Fuzzy Logic* provides a very carefully crafted introduction to the basic concepts and techniques of fuzzy set theory. The exposition is authoritative, rigorous and up-to-date. An important issue which receives a great deal of attention is that of the relationship between fuzzy set theory and alternative methods of dealing with uncertainty. This is a complex, controversial issue that is close to the heart of Professor Klir and which he treats with authority and insight.

There is a minor point relating to possibility theory that deserves a brief comment. In *Fuzzy Sets and Fuzzy Logic*, the concept of possibility measure is introduced via Dempster-Shafer's theory of evidence. This is motivated by the observation that in the case of nested focal sets in the Dempster-Shafer theory, possibility measure coincides with plausibility measure. I view this as merely a point of tangency between the Dempster-Shafer theory and possibility theory, since the two theories have altogether different agendas. Although the authors note that possibility theory can also be introduced via fuzzy set theory, their choice of the theory of evidence as the point of departure makes possibility theory less intuitive and harder to understand.

The second part of *Fuzzy Sets and Fuzzy Logic* is, in the main, applications oriented, but it also contains compact and yet insightful expositions of the calculi of fuzzy rules and fuzzy relations. The applications cover a wide spectrum of topics ranging from fuzzy control and expert systems to information retrieval, pattern recognition and decision analysis. The discussion of applications is thorough and up-to-date. The book closes with a valuable bibliography of over 1,700 papers and books dealing with various issues relating to fuzzy sets and fuzzy logic. To say that *Fuzzy Sets and Fuzzy Logic* is a major contribution to the literature is an understatement.

In most of the current applications of fuzzy logic in the realms of industrial systems and consumer products, what is used is a small subset of fuzzy logic centering on the methodology of fuzzy rules and their induction from observations. By focusing on this and only this methodology, it is possible to acquire—with a low expenditure of time and effort—a working knowledge of fuzzy logic techniques. This is not the route chosen by Professor Klir and Bo Yuan. Their goals are loftier; they have produced a volume that presents an exceptionally thorough, well-organized, authoritative and reader-friendly exposition of the methodology of fuzzy sets and fuzzy logic. Their book is eminently suitable both as a textbook and as a reference. It should be on the desk of everyone who is interested in acquiring a solid understanding of the foundations of fuzzy sets and fuzzy logic and the competence that is needed to apply them to the solution of real-world problems.

Lotfi A. Zadeh
December 16, 1994

PREFACE

This book is a natural outgrowth of *Fuzzy Sets, Uncertainty, and Information* by George J. Klir and Tina A. Folger (Prentice Hall, 1988). It reflects the tremendous advances that have taken place in the areas of fuzzy set theory and fuzzy logic during the period 1988–1995. Captured in the book are not only theoretical advances in these areas, but a broad variety of applications of fuzzy sets and fuzzy logic as well.

The primary purpose of the book is to facilitate education in the increasingly important areas of fuzzy set theory and fuzzy logic. It is written as a text for a course at the graduate or upper-division undergraduate level. Although there is enough material in the text for a two-semester course, relevant material may be selected, according to the needs of each individual program, for a one-semester course. The text is also suitable for self-study and for short, intensive courses of continuing education.

No previous knowledge of fuzzy set theory or fuzzy logic is required for an understanding of the material in this text. Although we assume that the reader is familiar with the basic notions of classical (nonfuzzy) set theory, classical (two-valued) logic, and probability theory, fundamentals of these subject areas are briefly overviewed in the book. Basic ideas of neural networks, genetic algorithms, and rough sets, which are occasionally needed in the text, are provided in Appendices A–C. This makes the book virtually self-contained.

Theoretical aspects of fuzzy set theory and fuzzy logic are covered in the first nine chapters, which are designated Part I of the text. Elementary concepts, including basic types of fuzzy sets, are introduced in Chapter 1, which also contains a discussion of the meaning and significance of the emergence of fuzzy set theory. Connections between fuzzy sets and crisp sets are examined in Chapter 2. It shows how fuzzy sets can be represented by families of crisp sets and how classical mathematical functions can be fuzzified. Chapter 3 deals with the various aggregation operations on fuzzy sets. It covers general fuzzy complements, fuzzy intersections (*t*-norms), fuzzy unions (*t*-conorms), and averaging operations. Fuzzy numbers and arithmetic operations on fuzzy numbers are covered in Chapter 4, where also the concepts of linguistic variables and fuzzy equations are introduced and examined. Basic concepts of fuzzy relations are introduced in Chapter 5 and employed in Chapter 6 for the study of fuzzy relation equations, an important tool for many applications of fuzzy set theory.

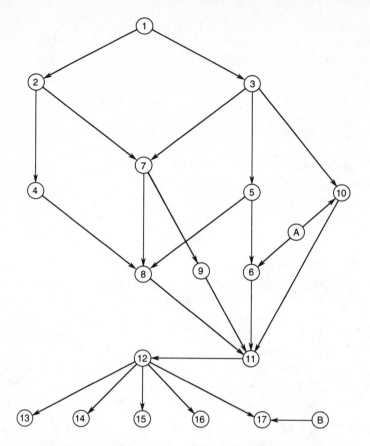

Figure P.1 Prerequisite dependencies among chapters of this book.

Chapter 7 deals with possibility theory and its intimate connection with fuzzy set theory. The position of possibility theory within the broader framework of fuzzy measure theory is also examined. Chapter 8 overviews basic aspects of fuzzy logic, including its connection to classical multivalued logics, the various types of fuzzy propositions, and basic types of fuzzy inference rules. Chapter 9, the last chapter in Part I, is devoted to the examination of the connection between uncertainty and information, as represented by fuzzy sets, possibility theory, or evidence theory. The chapter shows how relevant uncertainty and uncertainty-based information can be measured and how these uncertainty measures can be utilized. A Glossary of Key Concepts (Appendix E) and A Glossary of Symbols (Appendix F) are included to help the reader to quickly find the meaning of a concept or a symbol.

Part II, which is devoted to applications of fuzzy set theory and fuzzy logic, consists of the remaining eight chapters. Chapter 10 examines various methods for constructing membership functions of fuzzy sets, including the increasingly popular use of neural networks. Chapter 11 is devoted to the use of fuzzy logic for approximate reasoning in expert systems. It includes a thorough examination of the concept of a fuzzy implication. Fuzzy systems are covered in Chapter 12, including fuzzy controllers, fuzzy automata, and fuzzy neural networks. Fuzzy techniques in the related areas of clustering, pattern recognition, and image processing are overviewed in Chapter 13. Fuzzy databases, a well-developed application area of fuzzy set theory, and the related area of fuzzy retrieval systems are covered in Chapter 14. Basic ideas of the various types of fuzzy decision making are summarized in Chapter 15. Engineering applications other than fuzzy control are touched upon in Chapter 16, and applications in various other areas (medicine, economics, etc.) are overviewed in Chapter 17.

The prerequisite dependencies among the individual chapters and some appendices are expressed by the diagram in Fig. P.1. Following the diagram, the reader has ample flexibility in studying the material. For example, Chapters 3, 5 and 6 may be studied prior to Chapters 2 and 4; Chapter 10 and Appendix A may be studies prior to Chapter 2 and Chapters 4 through 9; etc.

In order to avoid interruptions in the main text, virtually all bibliographical, historical, and other remarks are incorporated in the notes that follow each individual chapter. These notes are uniquely numbered and are only occasionally referred to in the text. The notes are particularly important in Part II, where they contain ample references, allowing the interested reader to pursue further study in the application area of concern.

When the book is used at the upper-division undergraduate level, coverage of some or all proofs of the various mathematical theorems may be omitted, depending on the background of the students. At the graduate level, on the other hand, we encourage coverage of most of these proofs in order to effect a deeper understanding of the material. In all cases, the relevance of the material to the specific area of student interest can be emphasized with additional application-oriented readings guided by relevant notes in Part II of the text.

Each chapter is followed by a set of exercises, which are intended to enhance an understanding of the material presented in the chapter. The solutions to a selected subset of these exercises are provided in the instructor's manual, which also contains further suggestions for use of the text under various circumstances.

The book contains an extensive bibliography, which covers virtually all relevant books and significant papers published prior to 1995. It also contains a Bibliographical Index, which consists of reference lists for selected application areas and theoretical topics. This index should be particularly useful for graduate, project-oriented courses, as well as for both practitioners and researchers. Each book in the bibliography is emphasized by printing its year of publication in bold.

A few excellent quotes and one figure from the literature are employed in the text and we are grateful for permissions from the copyright owners to use them; they are: Williams & Wilkins, pp. 30–31; IEEE (The Institute of Electrical and Electronics Engineers), pp. 31, 329–330, 376 (Fig. 13.8); Academic Press, pp. 380; Cambridge University Press, pp. 391, 451; and Kluwer, pp. 451.

George J. Klir and Bo Yuan
Binghamton, New York

PART ONE: THEORY

1

FROM ORDINARY (CRISP) SETS TO FUZZY SETS: A GRAND PARADIGM SHIFT

1.1 INTRODUCTION

Among the various paradigmatic changes in science and mathematics in this century, one such change concerns the concept of *uncertainty*. In science, this change has been manifested by a gradual transition from the traditional view, which insists that uncertainty is undesirable in science and should be avoided by all possible means, to an alternative view, which is tolerant of uncertainty and insists that science cannot avoid it. According to the traditional view, science should strive for certainty in all its manifestations (precision, specificity, sharpness, consistency, etc.); hence, uncertainty (imprecision, nonspecificity, vagueness, inconsistency, etc.) is regarded as unscientific. According to the alternative (or modern) view, uncertainty is considered essential to science; it is not only an unavoidable plague, but it has, in fact, a great utility.

The first stage of the transition from the traditional view to the modern view of uncertainty began in the late 19th century, when physics became concerned with processes at the molecular level. Although precise laws of *Newtonian mechanics* were relevant to the study of these processes, their actual application to the enormous number of entities involved would have resulted in computational demands that were far beyond existing computational capabilities and, as we realize now, exceed even fundamental computational limits. That is, these precise laws are denied applicability in this domain not only in practice (based on existing computer technology) but in principle.

The need for a fundamentally different approach to the study of physical processes at the molecular level motivated the development of relevant statistical methods, which turned out to be applicable not only to the study of molecular processes (statistical mechanics), but to a host of other areas such as the actuarial profession, design of large telephone exchanges, and the like. In statistical methods, specific manifestations of microscopic entities (molecules, individual telephone sites, etc.) are replaced with their statistical averages, which are connected with appropriate macroscopic variables. The role played in Newtonian mechanics by the calculus, which involves no uncertainty, is replaced in statistical mechanics by *probability theory*, a theory whose very purpose is to capture uncertainty of a certain type.

While analytic methods based upon the calculus are applicable only to problems involving a very small number of variables that are related to one another in a predictable way, the applicability of statistical methods has exactly opposite characteristics: they require a very large number of variables and a very high degree of randomness. These two types of methods are thus highly complementary. When one type excels, the other totally fails. Despite their complementarity, these types of methods cover, unfortunately, only problems that are clustered around the two extremes of complexity and randomness scales. In his well-known paper, Warren Weaver [1948] refers to them as problems of *organized simplicity* and *disorganized complexity*. He argues that these types of problems represent only a tiny fraction of all systems problems. Most problems are somewhere between these two extremes: they involve nonlinear systems with large numbers of components and rich interactions among the components, which are usually nondeterministic, but not as a result of randomness that could yield meaningful statistical averages. Weaver calls them problems of *organized complexity*; they are typical in life, cognitive, social, and environmental sciences, as well as in applied fields such as modern technology or medicine.

The emergence of computer technology in World War II and its rapidly growing power in the second half of this century made it possible to deal with increasingly complex problems, some of which began to resemble the notion of organized complexity. Initially, it was the common belief of many scientists that the level of complexity we can handle is basically a matter of the level of computational power at our disposal. Later, in the early 1960s, this naive belief was replaced with a more realistic outlook. We began to understand that there are definite limits in dealing with complexity, which neither our human capabilities nor any computer technology can overcome. One such limit was determined by Hans Bremermann [1962] by simple considerations based on quantum theory. The limit is expressed by the proposition: "No data processing system, whether artificial or living, can process more than 2×10^{47} bits per second per gram of its mass." To process a certain number of bits means, in this statement, to transmit that many bits over one or several channels within the computing systems.

Using the limit of information processing obtained for one gram of mass and one second of processing time, Bremermann then calculates the total number of bits processed by a hypothetical computer the size of the Earth within a time period equal to the estimated age of the Earth. Since the mass and age of the Earth are estimated to be less than 6×10^{27} grams and 10^{10} years, respectively, and each year contains approximately 3.14×10^7 sec, this imaginary computer would not be able to process more than 2.56×20^{92} bits or, when rounding up to the nearest power of ten, 10^{93} bits. The last number—10^{93}—is usually referred to as *Bremermann's limit*, and problems that require processing more than 10^{93} bits of information are called *transcomputational problems*.

Bremermann's limit seems at first sight rather discouraging, even though it is based on overly optimistic assumptions (more reasonable assumptions would result in a number smaller than 10^{93}). Indeed, many problems dealing with systems of even modest size exceed the limit in their information-processing demands. The nature of these problems has been extensively studied within an area referred to as the theory of computational complexity, which emerged in the 1960s as a branch of the general theory of algorithms.

In spite of the insurmountable computational limits, we continue to pursue the many problems that possess the characteristics of organized complexity. These problems are too important for our well being to give up on them. The main challenge in pursuing these problems narrows down fundamentally to one question: how to deal with systems and associated problems whose complexities are beyond our information processing limits? That is, how can we deal with these problems if no computational power alone is sufficient?

In general, we deal with problems in terms of systems that are constructed as models of either some aspects of reality or some desirable man-made objects. The purpose of constructing models of the former type is to understand some phenomenon of reality, be it natural or man-made, making adequate predictions or retrodictions, learning how to control the phenomenon in any desirable way, and utilizing all these capabilities for various ends; models of the latter type are constructed for the purpose of prescribing operations by which a conceived artificial object can be constructed in such a way that desirable objective criteria are satisfied within given constraints.

In constructing a model, we always attempt to maximize its usefulness. This aim is closely connected with the relationship among three key characteristics of every systems model: *complexity, credibility*, and *uncertainty*. This relationship is not as yet fully understood. We only know that uncertainty (predictive, prescriptive, etc.) has a pivotal role in any efforts to maximize the usefulness of systems models. Although usually (but not always) undesirable when considered alone, uncertainty becomes very valuable when considered in connection to the other characteristics of systems models: in general, allowing more uncertainty tends to reduce complexity and increase credibility of the resulting model. Our challenge in systems modelling is to develop methods by which an optimal level of allowable uncertainty can be estimated for each modelling problem.

Uncertainty is thus an important commodity in the modelling business, which can be traded for gains in the other essential characteristics of models. This trade-off can then be utilized for constructing models that are maximally useful with respect to the purpose for which they are constructed. A recognition of this important role of uncertainty by some researchers, which became quite explicit in the literature of the 1960s, began the second stage of the transition from the traditional view to the modern view of uncertainty. This stage is characterized by the emergence of several new theories of uncertainty, distinct from probability theory. These theories challenge the seemingly unique connection between uncertainty and probability theory, which had previously been taken for granted. They show that probability theory is capable of representing only one of several distinct types of uncertainty.

It is generally agreed that an important point in the evolution of the modern concept of uncertainty was the publication of a seminal paper by Lotfi A. Zadeh [1965b], even though some ideas presented in the paper were envisioned some 30 years earlier by the American philosopher Max Black [1937]. In his paper, Zadeh introduced a theory whose objects—*fuzzy sets*—are sets with boundaries that are not precise. The membership in a fuzzy set is not a matter of affirmation or denial, but rather a matter of a *degree*.

The significance of Zadeh's paper was that it challenged not only probability theory as the sole agent for uncertainty, but the very foundations upon which probability theory is based: Aristotelian two-valued logic. When A is a fuzzy set and x is a relevant object, the proposition "x is a member of A" is not necessarily either true or false, as required by two-valued logic, but it may be true only to some degree, the degree to which x is actually a member of A. It is most common, but not required, to express degrees of membership in fuzzy sets as well as degrees of truth of the associated propositions by numbers in the closed unit interval $[0, 1]$. The extreme values in this interval, 0 and 1, then represent, respectively, the total denial and affirmation of the membership in a given fuzzy set as well as the falsity and truth of the associated proposition.

The capability of fuzzy sets to express gradual transitions from membership to nonmembership and vice versa has a broad utility. It provides us not only with a meaningful and powerful representation of measurement uncertainties, but also with a meaningful representation of vague concepts expressed in natural language. For instance, instead of describing the weather today in terms of the exact percentage of cloud cover, we can just say that it is sunny. While the latter description is vague and less specific, it is often more useful. In order for a term such as *sunny* to accomplish the desired introduction of vagueness, however, we cannot use it to mean precisely 0% cloud cover. Its meaning is not totally arbitrary, however; a cloud cover of 100% is not sunny, and neither, in fact, is a cloud cover of 80%. We can accept certain intermediate states, such as 10% or 20% of cloud cover, as sunny. But where do we draw the line? If, for instance, any cloud cover of 25% or less is considered sunny, does this mean that a cloud cover of 26% is not? This is clearly unacceptable, since 1% of cloud cover hardly seems like a distinguishing characteristic between sunny and not sunny. We could, therefore, add a qualification that any amount of cloud cover 1% greater than a cloud cover already considered to be sunny (that is, 25% or less) will also be labeled as sunny. We can see, however, that this definition eventually leads us to accept all degrees of cloud cover as sunny, no matter how gloomy the weather looks! In order to resolve this paradox, the term *sunny* may introduce vagueness by allowing some sort of gradual transition from degrees of cloud cover that are considered to be sunny and those that are not. This is, in fact, precisely the basic concept of the *fuzzy set*, a concept that is both simple and intuitively pleasing and that forms, in essence, a generalization of the classical or *crisp set*.

The crisp set is defined in such a way as to dichotomize the individuals in some given universe of discourse into two groups: members (those that certainly belong in the set) and nonmembers (those that certainly do not). A sharp, unambiguous distinction exists between the members and nonmembers of the set. However, many classification concepts we commonly employ and express in natural language describe sets that do not exhibit this characteristic. Examples are the set of tall people, expensive cars, highly contagious diseases, close driving distances, modest profits, numbers much greater than one, or sunny days. We perceive these sets as having imprecise boundaries that facilitate gradual transitions from membership to nonmembership and vice versa.

A fuzzy set can be defined mathematically by assigning to each possible individual in the universe of discourse a value representing its grade of membership in the fuzzy set. This grade corresponds to the degree to which that individual is similar or compatible with the concept represented by the fuzzy set. Thus, individuals may belong in the fuzzy set to a greater or lesser degree as indicated by a larger or smaller membership grade. As already mentioned, these membership grades are very often represented by real-number values ranging in the closed interval between 0 and 1. Thus, a fuzzy set representing our concept of sunny might assign a degree of membership of 1 to a cloud cover of 0%, .8 to a cloud cover of 20%, .4 to a cloud cover of 30%, and 0 to a cloud cover of 75%. These grades signify the degree to which each percentage of cloud cover approximates our subjective concept of *sunny*, and the set itself models the semantic flexibility inherent in such a common linguistic term. Because full membership and full nonmembership in the fuzzy set can still be indicated by the values of 1 and 0, respectively, we can consider the concept of a crisp set to be a restricted case of the more general concept of a fuzzy set for which only these two grades of membership are allowed.

Research on the theory of fuzzy sets has been growing steadily since the inception of the theory in the mid-1960s. The body of concepts and results pertaining to the theory is now quite impressive. Research on a broad variety of applications has also been very active and has produced results that are perhaps even more impressive. In this book, we present an introduction to the major developments of the theory as well as to some of the most successful applications of the theory.

1.2 CRISP SETS: AN OVERVIEW

The aim of this text is to introduce the main components of fuzzy set theory and to overview some of its applications. To distinguish between fuzzy sets and classical (nonfuzzy) sets, we refer to the latter as *crisp sets*. This name is now generally accepted in the literature.

In our presentation, we assume that the reader is familiar with fundamentals of the theory of crisp sets. We include this section into the text solely to refresh the basic concepts of crisp sets and to introduce notation and terminology useful in our discussion of fuzzy sets.

The following general symbols are employed, as needed, throughout the text:

$\mathbb{Z} = \{\ldots, -2, -1, 0, 1, 2, \ldots\}$ (the set of all integers),

$\mathbb{N} = \{1, 2, 3, \ldots\}$ (the set of all positive integers or natural numbers),

$\mathbb{N}_0 = \{0, 1, 2, \ldots\}$ (the set of all nonnegative integers),

$\mathbb{N}_n = \{1, 2, \ldots, n\}$,

$\mathbb{N}_{0,n} = \{0, 1, \ldots, n\}$,

$\mathbb{R}$: the set of all real numbers,

$\mathbb{R}^+$: the set of all nonnegative real numbers,

$[a, b], (a, b], [a, b), (a, b)$: closed, left-open, right-open, open interval of real numbers between a and b, respectively,

$\langle x_1, x_2, \ldots, x_n \rangle$: ordered n-tuple of elements $x_1, x_2, \ldots, x_n$.

In addition, we use "iff" as a shorthand expression of "if and only if," and the standard symbols $\exists$ and $\forall$ are used for the existential quantifier and the universal quantifier, respectively.

Sets are denoted in this text by upper-case letters and their members by lower-case letters. The letter X denotes the universe of discourse, or *universal set*. This set contains all the possible elements of concern in each particular context or application from which sets can be formed. The set that contains no members is called the *empty set* and is denoted by $\varnothing$.

To indicate that an individual object x is a *member* or *element* of a set A, we write

$$x \in A.$$

Whenever x is not an element of a set A, we write

$$x \notin A.$$

There are three basic methods by which sets can be defined within a given universal set X:

1. A set is defined by naming all its members (the list method). This method can be used only for finite sets. Set A, whose members are $a_1, a_2, \ldots, a_n$, is usually written as

$$A = \{a_1, a_2, \ldots, a_n\}.$$

2. A set is defined by a property satisfied by its members (the rule method). A common notation expressing this method is

$$A = \{x | P(x)\},$$

where the symbol $|$ denotes the phrase "such that," and $P(x)$ designates a proposition of the form "x has the property P." That is, A is defined by this notation as the set of all elements of X for which the proposition $P(x)$ is true. It is required that the property P be such that for any given $x \in X$, the proposition $P(x)$ is either true of false.

3. A set is defined by a function, usually called a *characteristic function*, that declares which elements of X are members of the set and which are not. Set A is defined by its characteristic function, χ_A, as follows:

$$\chi_A(x) = \begin{cases} 1 & \text{for } x \in A \\ 0 & \text{for } x \notin A. \end{cases}$$

That is, the characteristic function maps elements of X to elements of the set $\{0, 1\}$, which is formally expressed by

$$\chi_A : X \to \{0, 1\}.$$

For each $x \in X$, when $\chi_A(x) = 1$, x is declared to be a member of A; when $\chi_A(x) = 0$, x is declared as a nonmember of A.

A set whose elements are themselves sets is often referred to as a *family of sets*. It can be defined in the form

$$\{A_i | i \in I\},$$

where i and I are called the *set index* and the *index set*, respectively. Because the index i is used to reference the sets A_i, the family of sets is also called an *indexed set*. In this text, families of sets are usually denoted by script capital letters. For example,

$$\mathcal{A} = \{A_1, A_2, \ldots, A_n\}.$$

If every member of set A is also a member of set B (i.e., if $x \in A$ implies $x \in B$), then A is called a *subset* of B, and this is written as

$$A \subseteq B.$$

Every set is a subset of itself, and every set is a subset of the universal set. If $A \subseteq B$ and $B \subseteq A$, then A and B contain the same members. They are then called *equal sets*; this is denoted by

$$A = B.$$

To indicate that A and B are not equal, we write

$$A \neq B.$$

If both $A \subseteq B$ and $A \neq B$, then B contains at least one individual that is not a member of A. In this case, A is called a *proper subset* of B, which is denoted by

$$A \subset B.$$

When $A \subseteq B$, we also say that A is *included* in B.

The family of *all subsets* of a given set A is called the *power set* of A, and it is usually denoted by $\mathcal{P}(A)$. The family of all subsets of $\mathcal{P}(A)$ is called a *second order power set of* A; it is denoted by $\mathcal{P}^2(A)$, which stands for $\mathcal{P}(\mathcal{P}(A))$. Similarly, *higher order power sets* $\mathcal{P}^3(A)$, $\mathcal{P}^4(A), \ldots$ can be defined.

The number of members of a *finite set* A is called the *cardinality* of A and is denoted by $|A|$. When A is finite, then

$$|\mathcal{P}(A)| = 2^{|A|}, \ |\mathcal{P}^2(A)| = 2^{2^{|A|}}, \ \text{etc.}$$

The *relative complement* of a set A with respect to set B is the set containing all the members of B that are not also members of A. This can be written $B - A$. Thus,

$$B - A = \{x \mid x \in B \ \text{and} \ x \notin A\}.$$

If the set B is the universal set, the complement is absolute and is usually denoted by $\overline{A}$. The absolute complement is always *involutive*; that is, taking the complement of a complement yields the original set, or

$$\overline{\overline{A}} = A.$$

The absolute complement of the empty set equals the universal set, and the absolute complement of the universal set equals the empty set. That is,

$$\overline{\varnothing} = X$$

and

$$\overline{X} = \varnothing.$$

The *union* of sets A and B is the set containing all the elements that belong either to set A alone, to set B alone, or to both set A and set B. This is denoted by $A \cup B$. Thus,

$$A \cup B = \{x \mid x \in A \ \text{or} \ x \in B\}.$$

The union operation can be generalized for any number of sets. For a family of sets $\{A_i \mid i \in I\}$, this is defined as

$$\bigcup_{i \in I} A_i = \{x \mid x \in A_i \ \text{for some} \ i \in I\}.$$

The *intersection* of sets A and B is the set containing all the elements belonging to both set A and set B. It is denoted by $A \cap B$. Thus,

$$A \cap B = \{x \mid x \in A \ \text{and} \ x \in B\}.$$

The generalization of the intersection for a family of sets $\{A_i \mid i \in I\}$ is defined as

$$\bigcap_{i \in I} A_i = \{x \,|\, x \in A_i \text{ for all } i \in I\}.$$

The most fundamental properties of the set operations of absolute complement, union, and intersection are summarized in Table 1.1, where sets A, B, and C are assumed to be elements of the power set $\mathcal{P}(X)$ of a universal set X. Note that all the equations in this table that involve the set union and intersection are arranged in pairs. The second equation in each pair can be obtained from the first by replacing $\varnothing$, $\cup$, and $\cap$ with X, $\cap$, and $\cup$, respectively, and vice versa. We are thus concerned with pairs of dual equations. They exemplify a *general principle of duality*: for each valid equation in set theory that is based on the union and intersection operations, there corresponds a dual equation, also valid, that is obtained by the above-specified replacement.

TABLE 1.1   FUNDAMENTAL PROPERTIES OF CRISP SET OPERATIONS

Involution	$\overline{\overline{A}} = A$
Commutativity	$A \cup B = B \cup A$
	$A \cap B = B \cap A$
Associativity	$(A \cup B) \cup C = A \cup (B \cup C)$
	$(A \cap B) \cap C = A \cap (B \cap C)$
Distributivity	$A \cap (B \cup C) = (A \cap B) \cup (A \cap C)$
	$A \cup (B \cap C) = (A \cup B) \cap (A \cup C)$
Idempotence	$A \cup A = A$
	$A \cap A = A$
Absorption	$A \cup (A \cap B) = A$
	$A \cap (A \cup B) = A$
Absorption by X and $\varnothing$	$A \cup X = X$
	$A \cap \varnothing = \varnothing$
Identity	$A \cup \varnothing = A$
	$A \cap X = A$
Law of contradiction	$A \cap \overline{A} = \varnothing$
Law of excluded middle	$A \cup \overline{A} = X$
De Morgan's laws	$\overline{A \cap B} = \overline{A} \cup \overline{B}$
	$\overline{A \cup B} = \overline{A} \cap \overline{B}$

Elements of the power set $\mathcal{P}(X)$ of a universal set X (or any subset of X) can be ordered by the set inclusion $\subseteq$. This ordering, which is only partial, forms a lattice in which the *join* (least upper bound, supremum) and *meet* (greatest lower bound, infimum) of any pair of sets A, $B \in \mathcal{P}(X)$ is given by $A \cup B$ and $A \cap B$, respectively. This lattice is *distributive* (due to the distributive properties of $\cup$ and $\cap$ listed in Table 1.1) and *complemented* (since each set in $\mathcal{P}(X)$ has its complement in $\mathcal{P}(X)$); it is usually called a *Boolean lattice* or a *Boolean algebra*. The connection between the two formulations of this lattice, $\langle \mathcal{P}(X), \subseteq \rangle$ and $\langle \mathcal{P}(X), \cup, \cap \rangle$, is facilitated by the following equivalence:

$$A \subseteq B \text{ iff } A \cup B = B \text{ (or } A \cap B = A) \text{ for any } A, B \in \mathcal{P}(X).$$

Any two sets that have no common members are called *disjoint*. That is, every pair of disjoint sets, A and B, satisfies the equation

$$A \cap B = \emptyset.$$

A family of pairwise disjoint nonempty subsets of a set A is called a *partition* on A if the union of these subsets yields the original set A. We denote a partition on A by the symbol $\pi(A)$. Formally,

$$\pi(A) = \{A_i | i \in I, A_i \subseteq A\},$$

where $A_i \neq \emptyset$, is a partition on A iff

$$A_i \cap A_j = \emptyset$$

for each pair $i, j \in I, i \neq j$, and

$$\bigcup_{i \in I} A_i = A.$$

Members of a partition $\pi(A)$, which are subsets of A, are usually referred to as *blocks* of the partition. Each member of A belongs to one and only one block of $\pi(A)$.

Given two partitions $\pi_1(A)$ and $\pi_2(A)$, we say that $\pi_1(A)$ is a *refinement* of $\pi_2(A)$ iff each block of $\pi_1(A)$ is included in some block of $\pi_2(A)$. The refinement relation on the set of all partitions of A, $\Pi(A)$, which is denoted by $\leq$ (i.e., $\pi_1(A) \leq \pi_2(A)$ in our case), is a partial ordering. The pair $\langle \Pi(A), \leq \rangle$ is a lattice, referred to as the *partition lattice* of A.

Let $\mathcal{A} = \{A_1, A_2, \ldots, A_n\}$ be a family of sets such that

$$A_i \subseteq A_{i+1} \text{ for all } i = 1, 2, \ldots, n - 1.$$

Then, $\mathcal{A}$ is called a *nested family*, and the sets A_1 and A_n are called the *innermost set* and the *outermost set*, respectively. This definition can easily be extended to infinite families.

The *Cartesian product* of two sets—say, A and B (in this order)—is the set of all ordered pairs such that the first element in each pair is a member of A, and the second element is a member of B. Formally,

$$A \times B = \{\langle a, b \rangle | a \in A, b \in B\},$$

where $A \times B$ denotes the Cartesian product. Clearly, if $A \neq B$ and A, B are nonempty, then $A \times B \neq B \times A$.

The Cartesian product of a family $\{A_1, A_2, \ldots, A_n\}$ of sets is the set of all n-tuples $\langle a_1, a_2, \ldots, a_n \rangle$ such that $a_i \in A_i (i = 1, 2, \ldots, n)$. It is written as either $A_1 \times A_2 \times \ldots \times A_n$ or $\underset{1 \leq i \leq n}{\times} A_i$. Thus,

$$\underset{1 \leq i \leq n}{\times} A_i = \{\langle a_1, a_2, \ldots, a_n \rangle | a_i \in A_i \text{ for every } i = 1, 2, \ldots, n\}.$$

The Cartesian products $A \times A, A \times A \times A, \ldots$ are denoted by $A^2, A^3, \ldots$, respectively.

Subsets of Cartesian products are called *relations*. They are the subject of Chapter 5.

A set whose members can be labelled by the positive integers is called a *countable* set. If such labelling is not possible, the set is called *uncountable*. For instance, the set $\{a | a$ is a real number, $0 \leq a \leq 1\}$ is uncountable. Every uncountable set is *infinite*; countable sets are classified into *finite* and *countably infinite* (also called *denumerable*).

An important and frequently used universal set is the set of all points in the n-dimensional Euclidean vector space $\mathbb{R}^n$ for some $n \in \mathbb{N}$ (i.e., all n-tuples of real numbers).

Sets defined in terms of $\mathbb{R}^n$ are often required to possess a property referred to as convexity. A set A in $\mathbb{R}^n$ is called *convex* iff, for every pair of points

$$\mathbf{r} = \langle r_i | i \in \mathbb{N}_n \rangle \text{ and } \mathbf{s} = \langle s_i | i \in \mathbb{N}_n \rangle$$

in A and every real number $\lambda \in [0, 1]$, the point

$$\mathbf{t} = \langle \lambda r_i + (1 - \lambda)s_i | i \in \mathbb{N}_n \rangle$$

is also in A. In other words, a set A in $\mathbb{R}^n$ is convex iff, for every pair of points $\mathbf{r}$ and $\mathbf{s}$ in A, all points located on the straight-line segment connecting $\mathbf{r}$ and $\mathbf{s}$ are also in A. Examples of convex and nonconvex sets in $\mathbb{R}^2$ are given in Fig. 1.1.

In $\mathbb{R}$, any set defined by a single interval of real numbers is convex; any set defined by more than one interval that does not contain some points between the intervals is not convex. For example, the set $A = [0, 2] \cup [3, 5]$ is not convex, as can be shown by producing one of an infinite number of possible counter-examples: let $r = 1, s = 4$, and $\lambda = 0.4$; then, $\lambda r + (1 - \lambda)s = 2.8$ and $2.8 \notin A$.

Let R denote a set of real numbers ($R \subseteq \mathbb{R}$). If there is a real number r (or a real number s) such that $x \leq r$ (or $x \geq s$, respectively) for every $x \in R$, then r is called an *upper bound* of R (or a *lower bound* of R), and we say that A is *bounded above* by r (or *bounded below* by s).

For any set of real numbers R that is bounded above, a real number r is called the *supremum* of R iff:

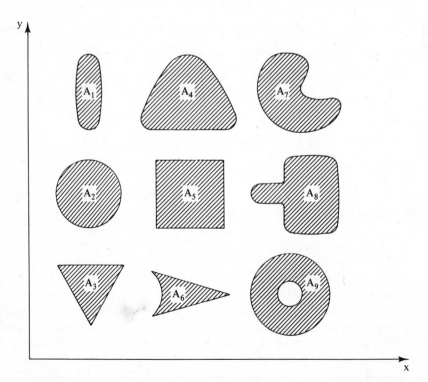

Figure 1.1 Example of sets in $\mathbb{R}^2$ that are convex (A_1–A_5) or nonconvex (A_6–A_9).

(a) r is an upper bound of R;

(b) no number less than r is an upper bound of R.

If r is the supremum of R, we write $r = \sup R$.

For any set of real numbers R that is bounded below, a real number s is called the *infimum* of R iff:

(a) s is a lower bound of R;

(b) no number greater than s is a lower bound of R.

If s is the infimum of R, we write $s = \inf R$.

1.3   FUZZY SETS: BASIC TYPES

As defined in the previous section, the characteristic function of a crisp set assigns a value of either 1 or 0 to each individual in the universal set, thereby discriminating between members and nonmembers of the crisp set under consideration. This function can be generalized such that the values assigned to the elements of the universal set fall within a specified range and indicate the membership grade of these elements in the set in question. Larger values denote higher degrees of set membership. Such a function is called a *membership function*, and the set defined by it a *fuzzy set*.

The most commonly used range of values of membership functions is the unit interval $[0, 1]$. In this case, each membership function maps elements of a given *universal set X*, which is *always a crisp set*, into real numbers in $[0, 1]$.

Two distinct notations are most commonly employed in the literature to denote membership functions. In one of them, the membership function of a fuzzy set A is denoted by μ_A; that is,

$$\mu_A : X \to [0, 1].$$

In the other one, the function is denoted by A and has, of course, the same form:

$$A : X \to [0, 1].$$

According to the first notation, the symbol (label, identifier, name) of the fuzzy set (A) is distinguished from the symbol of its membership function (μ_A). According to the second notation, this distinction is not made, but no ambiguity results from this double use of the same symbol. Each fuzzy set is completely and uniquely defined by one particular membership function; consequently, symbols of membership functions may also be used as labels of the associated fuzzy sets.

In this text, we use the second notation. That is, each fuzzy set and the associated membership function are denoted by the same capital letter. Since crisp sets and the associated characteristic functions may be viewed, respectively, as special fuzzy sets and membership functions, the same notation is used for crisp sets as well.

As discussed in Sec. 1.1, fuzzy sets allow us to represent vague concepts expressed in natural language. The representation depends not only on the concept, but also on the context in which it is used. For example, applying the concept of *high temperature* in one context to weather and in another context to a nuclear reactor would necessarily be represented by very different fuzzy sets. That would also be the case, although to a lesser degree, if the concept were applied to weather in different seasons, at least in some climates.

Even for similar contexts, fuzzy sets representing the same concept may vary considerably. In this case, however, they also have to be similar in some key features. As an example, let us consider four fuzzy sets whose membership functions are shown in Fig. 1.2. Each of these fuzzy sets expresses, in a particular form, the general conception of a class of real numbers that are close to 2. In spite of their differences, the four fuzzy sets are similar in the sense that the following properties are possessed by each $A_i (i \in \mathbb{N}_4)$:

  (i) $A_i(2) = 1$ and $A_i(x) < 1$ for all $x \neq 2$;
 (ii) A_i is symmetric with respect to $x = 2$, that is $A_i(2 + x) = A_i(2 - x)$ for all $x \in \mathbb{R}$;
(iii) $A_i(x)$ decreases monotonically from 1 to 0 with the increasing difference $|2 - x|$.

These properties are necessary in order to properly represent the given conception. Any additional fuzzy sets attempting to represent the same conception would have to possess them as well.

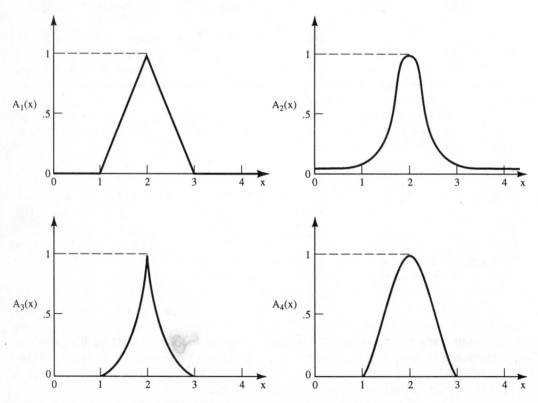

Figure 1.2 Examples of membership functions that may be used in different contexts for characterizing fuzzy sets of real numbers close to 2.

The four membership functions in Fig. 1.2 are also similar in the sense that numbers outside the interval $[1, 3]$ are virtually excluded from the associated fuzzy sets, since their membership grades are either equal to 0 or negligible. This similarity does not reflect the conception itself, but rather the context in which it is used. The functions are manifested by very different shapes of their graphs. Whether a particular shape is suitable or not can be determined only in the context of a particular application. It turns out, however, that many applications are not overly sensitive to variations in the shape. In such cases, it is convenient to use a simple shape, such as the triangular shape of A_1.

Each function in Fig. 1.2 is a member of a parametrized family of functions. The following are general formulas describing the four families of membership functions, where r denotes the real number for which the membership grade is required to be one ($r = 2$ for all functions in Fig. 1.2), and $p_i (i \in \mathbb{N}_4)$ is a parameter that determines the rate at which, for each x, the function decreases with the increasing difference $|r - x|$:

$$A_1(x) = \begin{cases} p_1(x - r) + 1 & \text{when } x \in [r - 1/p_1, r] \\ p_1(r - x) + 1 & \text{when } x \in [r, r + 1/p_1] \\ 0 & \text{otherwise} \end{cases}$$

$$A_2(x) = \frac{1}{1 + p_2(x - r)^2}$$

$$A_3(x) = e^{-|p_3(x-r)|}$$

$$A_4(x) = \begin{cases} (1 + \cos(p_4\pi(x - r)))/2 & \text{when } x \in [r - 1/p_4, r + 1/p_4] \\ 0 & \text{otherwise} \end{cases}$$

For each $i \in \mathbb{N}_4$, when p_i increases, the graph of A_i becomes narrower. Functions in Fig. 1.2 exemplify these classes of functions for $p_1 = 1$, $p_2 = 10$, $p_3 = 5$, $p_4 = 2$, and $r = 2$.

Fuzzy sets in Fig. 1.2 are defined within the set of real numbers. Let us consider now, as a simple example, three fuzzy sets defined within a finite universal set that consists of seven levels of education:

0 – no education
1 – elementary school
2 – high school
3 – two-year college degree
4 – bachelor's degree
5 – master's degree
6 – doctoral degree

Membership functions of the three fuzzy sets, which attempt to capture the concepts of little-educated, highly educated, and very highly educated people are defined in Fig. 1.3 by the symbols ○, ●, and □, respectively. Thus, for example, a person who has a bachelor's degree but no higher degree is viewed, according to these definitions, as highly educated to the degree of 0.8 and very highly educated to the degree of 0.5.

Several fuzzy sets representing linguistic concepts such as low, medium, high, and so on are often employed to define states of a variable. Such a variable is usually called a

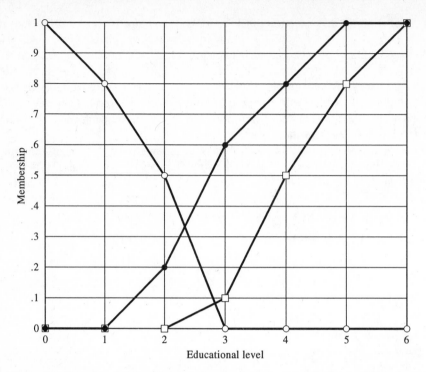

Figure 1.3 Examples of fuzzy sets expressing the concepts of people that are little educated (○), highly educated (●), and very highly educated (□).

fuzzy variable. In Fig. 1.4a, for example, temperature within a range $[T_1, T_2]$ is characterized as a fuzzy variable, and it is contrasted in Fig. 1.4b with comparable traditional (nonfuzzy) variable. States of the fuzzy variable are fuzzy sets representing five linguistic concepts: very low, low, medium, high, very high. They are all defined by membership functions of the form

$$[T_1, T_2] \rightarrow [0, 1].$$

Graphs of these functions have *trapezoidal shapes*, which, together with *triangular shapes* (such as A_1 in Fig. 1.2), are most common in current applications. States of the corresponding traditional variable are crisp sets defined by the right-open intervals of real numbers shown in Fig. 1.4b.

The significance of fuzzy variables is that they facilitate gradual transitions between states and, consequently, possess a natural capability to express and deal with observation and measurement uncertainties. Traditional variables, which we may refer to as *crisp variables*, do not have this capability. Although the definition of states by crisp sets is mathematically correct, it is unrealistic in the face of unavoidable measurement errors. A measurement that falls into a close neighborhood of each precisely defined border between states of a crisp variable is taken as evidential support for only one of the states, in spite of the inevitable uncertainty involved in this decision. The uncertainty reaches its maximum at each border, where any measurement should be regarded as equal evidence for the two states on either side of the border. When dealing with crisp variables,

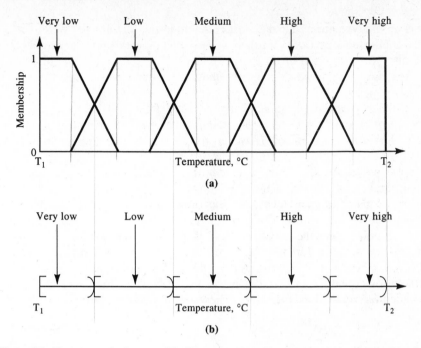

Figure 1.4 Temperature in the range $[T_1, T_2]$ conceived as: (a) a fuzzy variable; (b) a traditional (crisp) variable.

however, the uncertainty is ignored even in this extreme case; the measurement is regarded as evidence for one of the states, the one that includes the border point by virtue of an arbitrary mathematical definition.

Since fuzzy variables capture measurement uncertainties as part of experimental data, they are more attuned to reality than crisp variables. It is an interesting paradox that data based on fuzzy variables provide us, in fact, with more accurate evidence about real phenomena than data based upon crisp variables. This important point can hardly be expressed better than by the following statement made by Albert Einstein in 1921: *So far as laws of mathematics refer to reality, they are not certain. And so far as they are certain, they do not refer to reality.*

Although mathematics based on fuzzy sets has far greater expressive power than classical mathematics based on crisp sets, its usefulness depends critically on our capability to construct appropriate membership functions for various given concepts in various contexts. This capability, which was rather weak at the early stages of fuzzy set theory, is now well developed for many application areas. However, the problem of constructing meaningful membership functions is a difficult one, and a lot of additional research work will have to be done on it to achieve full satisfaction. We discuss the problem and overview currently available construction methods in Chapter 10.

Thus far, we introduced only one type of fuzzy set. Given a relevant universal set X, any arbitrary fuzzy set of this type (say, set A) is defined by a function of the form

$$A : X \rightarrow [0, 1]. \tag{1.1}$$

Fuzzy sets of this type are by far the most common in the literature as well as in the various successful applications of fuzzy set theory. However, several more general types of fuzzy sets have also been proposed in the literature. Let fuzzy sets of the type thus far discussed be called *ordinary fuzzy sets* to distinguish them from fuzzy sets of the various generalized types.

The primary reason for generalizing ordinary fuzzy sets is that their membership functions are often overly precise. They require that each element of the universal set be assigned a particular real number. However, for some concepts and contexts in which they are applied, we may be able to identify appropriate membership functions only approximately. For example, we may only be able to identify meaningful lower and upper bounds of membership grades for each element of the universal set. In such cases, we may basically take one of two possible approaches. We may either suppress the identification uncertainty by choosing reasonable values between the lower and upper bounds (e.g., the middle values), or we may accept the uncertainty and include it in the definition of the membership function. A membership function based on the latter approach does not assign to each element of the universal set one real number, but a closed interval of real numbers between the identified lower and upper bounds. Fuzzy sets defined by membership functions of this type are called *interval-valued fuzzy sets*. These sets are defined formally by functions of the form

$$A : X \rightarrow \mathcal{E}([0, 1]), \tag{1.2}$$

where $\mathcal{E}([0, 1])$ denotes the family of all closed intervals of real numbers in $[0, 1]$; clearly,

$$\mathcal{E}([0, 1]) \subset \mathcal{P}([0, 1]).$$

An example of a membership function of this type is given in Fig. 1.5. For each x, $A(x)$ is represented by the segment between the two curves, which express the identified lower and upper bounds. Thus, $A(a) = [\alpha_1, \alpha_2]$ for the example in Fig. 1.5.

Membership functions of interval-valued fuzzy sets are not as specific as their counter-

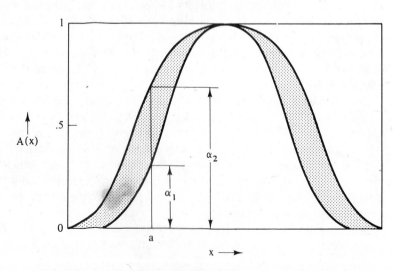

Figure 1.5   An example of an interval-valued fuzzy set ($A(a) = [\alpha_1, \alpha_2]$).

parts of ordinary fuzzy sets, but this lack of specificity makes them more realistic in some applications. Their advantage is that they allow us to express our uncertainty in identifying a particular membership function. This uncertainty is involved when interval-valued fuzzy sets are processed, making results of the processing less specific but more credible.

The primary disadvantage of interval-valued fuzzy sets is that this processing, when compared with ordinary fuzzy sets, is computationally more demanding. Since most current applications of fuzzy set theory do not seem to be overly sensitive to minor changes in relevant membership functions, this disadvantage of interval-valued fuzzy sets usually outweighs their advantages.

Interval-valued fuzzy sets can further be generalized by allowing their intervals to be fuzzy. Each interval now becomes an ordinary fuzzy set defined within the universal set $[0, 1]$. Since membership grades assigned to elements of the universal set by these generalized fuzzy sets are ordinary fuzzy sets, these sets are referred to as *fuzzy sets of type 2*. Their membership functions have the form

$$A : X \rightarrow \mathcal{F}([0, 1]), \tag{1.3}$$

where $\mathcal{F}([0, 1])$ denotes the set of all ordinary fuzzy sets that can be defined within the universal set $[0, 1]$; $\mathcal{F}([0, 1])$ is also called a *fuzzy power set* of $[0, 1]$.

The concept of a type 2 fuzzy set is illustrated in Fig. 1.6, where fuzzy intervals assigned to $x = a$ and $x = b$ are explicitly shown. It is assumed here that membership functions of all fuzzy intervals involved are of trapezoidal shapes and, consequently, each of them is fully defined by four numbers. For each x, these numbers are produced by four functions, represented in Fig. 1.6 by the four curves. Thus, for example, if $x = a$, we obtain numbers $\alpha_1, \alpha_2, \alpha_3$, and α_4, by which the fuzzy interval assigned to a (shown on the left-hand side) is uniquely determined. Similarly, if $x = b$, we obtain numbers $\beta_1, \beta_2, \beta_3$, and β_4, and the assigned fuzzy interval is shown on the right-hand side.

Fuzzy sets of type 2 possess a great expressive power and, hence, are conceptually quite appealing. However, computational demands for dealing with them are even greater than those for dealing with interval-valued fuzzy sets. This seems to be the primary reason why they have almost never been utilized in any applications.

Assume now that the membership grades assigned by a type 2 fuzzy set (e.g., the fuzzy

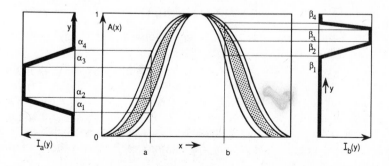

Figure 1.6   Illustration of the concept of a fuzzy set of type 2.

intervals in Fig. 1.6) are themselves type 2 fuzzy sets. Then, we obtain a *fuzzy set of type 3*, and it is easy to see that fuzzy sets of still higher types could be obtained recursively in the same way. However, there is little rationale for further pursuing this line of generalization, at least for the time being, since computational complexity increases significantly for each higher type.

When we relax the requirement that membership grades must be represented by numbers in the unit interval [0, 1] and allow them to be represented by symbols of an arbitrary set L that is at least partially ordered, we obtain fuzzy sets of another generalized type. They are called *L-fuzzy sets*, and their membership functions have the form

$$A : X \to L. \tag{1.4}$$

Since set L with its ordering is most frequently a lattice, letter L was initially chosen to signify this fact.

By allowing only a partial ordering among membership grades, L-fuzzy sets are very general. In fact, they capture all the other types introduced thus far as special cases.

A different generalization of ordinary fuzzy sets involves fuzzy sets defined within a universal set whose elements are ordinary fuzzy sets. These fuzzy sets are known as *level 2 fuzzy sets*. Their membership functions have the form

$$A : \mathcal{F}(X) \to [0, 1], \tag{1.5}$$

where $\mathcal{F}(X)$ denotes the fuzzy power set of X (the set of all ordinary fuzzy sets of X).

Level 2 fuzzy sets allow us to deal with situations in which elements of the universal set cannot be specified precisely, but only approximately, for example, by fuzzy sets expressing propositions of the form "*x* is close to *r*," where x is a variable whose values are real numbers, and r is a particular real number. In order to determine the membership grade of some value of x in an ordinary fuzzy set A, we need to specify the value (say, r) precisely. On the other hand, if A is a level 2 fuzzy set, it allows us to obtain the membership grade for an approximate value of x. Assuming that the proposition "*x* is close to *r*" is represented by an ordinary fuzzy set B, the membership grade of a value of x that is known to be close to r in the level 2 fuzzy set A is given by $A(B)$.

Level 2 fuzzy sets can be generalized into level 3 fuzzy sets by using a universal set whose elements are level 2 fuzzy sets. Higher-level fuzzy sets can be obtained recursively in the same way. We can also conceive of fuzzy sets that are of type 2 and also of level 2. Their membership functions have the form

$$A : \mathcal{F}(X) \to \mathcal{F}([0, 1]). \tag{1.6}$$

Other combinations are also possible, which may involve L-fuzzy sets as well as fuzzy sets of higher types and higher levels.

A formal treatment of fuzzy sets of type 2 and level 2 (as well as higher types and levels) is closely connected with methods of fuzzification, which are discussed in Sec. 2.3.

Except for this brief overview of the various types of generalized fuzzy sets, we do not further examine their properties and the procedures by which they are manipulated. Their detailed coverage is beyond the scope of this text. Since these generalized types of fuzzy sets have not as yet played a significant role in applications of fuzzy set theory, this omission is currently of no major consequence.

The generalized fuzzy sets are introduced in this section for two reasons. First, we want the reader to understand that fuzzy set theory does not stand or fall with ordinary fuzzy sets. Second, we feel that the practical significance of at least some of the generalized types will gradually increase, and it is thus advisable that the reader be familiar with the basic ideas and terminology pertaining to them.

We may occasionally refer to some of the generalized types of fuzzy sets later in the text. By and large, however, the rest of the text is devoted to the study of ordinary fuzzy sets. Unless otherwise stated, the term "fuzzy set" refers in this text to ordinary fuzzy sets. For the sake of completeness, let us mention that ordinary fuzzy sets may also be viewed as fuzzy sets of type 1 and level 1.

1.4 FUZZY SETS: BASIC CONCEPTS

In this section, we introduce some basic concepts and terminology of fuzzy sets. To illustrate the concepts, we consider three fuzzy sets that represent the concepts of a young, middle-aged, and old person. A reasonable expression of these concepts by trapezoidal membership functions A_1, A_2, and A_3 is shown in Fig. 1.7. These functions are defined on the interval $[0, 80]$ as follows:

$$A_1(x) = \begin{cases} 1 & \text{when } x \leq 20 \\ (35 - x)/15 & \text{when } 20 < x < 35 \\ 0 & \text{when } x \geq 35 \end{cases}$$

$$A_2(x) = \begin{cases} 0 & \text{when either } x \leq 20 \text{ or } \geq 60 \\ (x - 20)/15 & \text{when } 20 < x < 35 \\ (60 - x)/15 & \text{when } 45 < x < 60 \\ 1 & \text{when } 35 \leq x \leq 45 \end{cases}$$

$$A_3(x) = \begin{cases} 0 & \text{when } x \leq 45 \\ (x - 45)/15 & \text{when } 45 < x < 60 \\ 1 & \text{when } x \geq 60 \end{cases}$$

A possible discrete approximation, D_2, of function A_2, is also shown in Fig. 1.7; its explicit definition is given in Table 1.2. Such approximations are important because they are typical in computer representations of fuzzy sets.

One of the most important concepts of fuzzy sets is the concept of an α-*cut* and its variant, a *strong α-cut*. Given a fuzzy set A defined on X and any number $\alpha \in [0, 1]$, the α-cut, $^{\alpha}A$, and the strong α-cut, $^{\alpha+}A$, are the crisp sets

$$^{\alpha}A = \{x | A(x) \geq \alpha\} \tag{1.7}$$

$$^{\alpha+}A = \{x | A(x) > \alpha\}. \tag{1.8}$$

That is, the α-cut (or the strong α-cut) of a fuzzy set A is the crisp set $^{\alpha}A$ (or the crisp set $^{\alpha+}A$) that contains all the elements of the universal set X whose membership grades in A are greater than or equal to (or only greater than) the specified value of α.

As an example, the following is a complete characterization of all α-cuts and all strong α-cuts for the fuzzy sets A_1, A_2, A_3 given in Fig. 1.7:

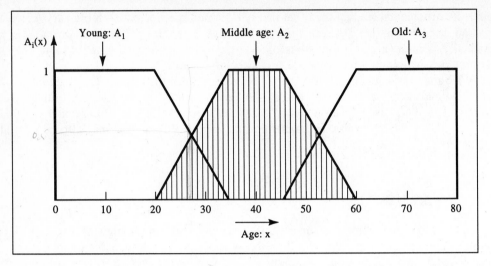

Figure 1.7 Membership functions representing the concepts of a young, middle-aged, and old person. Shown discrete approximation D_2 of A_2 is defined numerically in Table 1.2.

TABLE 1.2   DISCRETE APPROXIMATION
OF MEMBERSHIP FUNCTION A_2 (FIG. 1.7)
BY FUNCTION D_2 OF THE FORM:
$D_2 : \{0, 2, 4, \ldots, 80\} \to [0, 1]$

x	$D_2(x)$
$x \notin \{22, 24, \ldots, 58\}$	0.00
$x \in \{22, 58\}$	0.13
$x \in \{24, 56\}$	0.27
$x \in \{26, 54\}$	0.40
$x \in \{28, 52\}$	0.53
$x \in \{30, 50\}$	0.67
$x \in \{32, 48\}$	0.80
$x \in \{34, 46\}$	0.93
$x \in \{36, 38, \ldots, 44\}$	1.00

$^0A_1 = {}^0A_2 = {}^0A_3 = [0, 80] = X;$

$^\alpha A_1 = [0, 35 - 15\alpha], {}^\alpha A_2 = [15\alpha + 20, 60 - 15\alpha], {}^\alpha A_3 = [15\alpha + 45, 80]$ for all $\alpha \in (0, 1];$

$^{\alpha+}A_1 = (0, 35 - 15\alpha), {}^{\alpha+}A_2 = (15\alpha + 20, 60 - 15\alpha), {}^{\alpha+}A_3 = (15\alpha + 45, 80)$ for all $\alpha \in [0, 1);$

$^{1+}A_1 = {}^{1+}A_2 = {}^{1+}A_3 = \varnothing.$

The set of all levels $\alpha \in [0, 1]$ that represent distinct α-cuts of a given fuzzy set A is called a *level set* of A. Formally,

$$\Lambda(A) = \{\alpha | A(x) = \alpha \text{ for some } x \in X\},$$

where Λ denotes the level set of fuzzy set A defined on X. For our examples, we have:

$\Lambda(A_1) = \Lambda(A_2) = \Lambda(A_3) = [0, 1]$, and
$\Lambda(D_2) = \{0, 0.13, 0.27, 0.4, 0.53, 0.67, 0.8, 0.93, 1\}$.

An important property of both α-cuts and strong α-cuts, which follows immediately from their definitions, is that the total ordering of values of α in $[0, 1]$ is inversely preserved by set inclusion of the corresponding α-cuts as well as strong α-cuts. That is, for any fuzzy set A and pair $\alpha_1, \alpha_2 \in [0, 1]$ of distinct values such that $\alpha_1 < \alpha_2$, we have

$$^{\alpha_1}A \supseteq {}^{\alpha_2}A \quad \text{and} \quad {}^{\alpha_1+}A \supseteq {}^{\alpha_2+}A. \tag{1.9}$$

This property can also be expressed by the equations

$$^{\alpha_1}A \cap {}^{\alpha_2}A = {}^{\alpha_2}A, \, {}^{\alpha_1}A \cup {}^{\alpha_2}A = {}^{\alpha_1}A, \tag{1.10}$$

and

$$^{\alpha_1+}A \cap {}^{\alpha_2+}A = {}^{\alpha_2+}A, \, {}^{\alpha_1+}A \cup {}^{\alpha_2+}A = {}^{\alpha_1+}A. \tag{1.11}$$

An obvious consequence of this property is that all α-cuts and all strong α-cuts of any fuzzy set form two distinct families of *nested crisp sets*.

Notice, for example, that the intervals representing the α-cuts and the strong α-cuts of the fuzzy sets A_1, A_2, and A_3 in Fig. 1.7 shorten with increasing α. Since level sets of A_1, A_2, and A_3 are all $[0, 1]$, clearly, the families of all α-cuts and all strong α-cuts are in this case infinite for each of the sets. To see the nested families more explicitly, let us consider the discrete approximation D_2 of fuzzy set A_2, which is shown in Fig. 1.7 and defined numerically in Table 1.2. The families of all α-cuts and all strong α-cuts of D_2 are shown for some convenient values of α in Fig. 1.8; for each of the discrete values of x, the inclusion in each α-cut or each strong α-cut is marked with a dot at the crossing of x and α.

The *support* of a fuzzy set A within a universal set X is the crisp set that contains all the elements of X that have nonzero membership grades in A. Clearly, the support of A is exactly the same as the strong α-cut of A for $\alpha = 0$. Although special symbols, such as $S(A)$ or supp(A), are often used in the literature to denote the support of A, we prefer to use the natural symbol ^{0+}A. The 1-cut, ^1A, is often called the *core* of A.

The *height*, $h(A)$, of a fuzzy set A is the largest membership grade obtained by any element in that set. Formally,

$$h(A) = \sup_{x \in X} A(x). \tag{1.12}$$

A fuzzy set A is called *normal* when $h(A) = 1$; it is called *subnormal* when $h(A) < 1$. The height of A may also be viewed as the supremum of α for which $^\alpha A \neq \varnothing$.

An important property of fuzzy sets defined on $\mathbb{R}^n$ (for some $n \in \mathbb{N}$) is their convexity. This property is viewed as a generalization of the classical concept of convexity of crisp sets. In order to make the generalized convexity consistent with the classical definition of convexity, it is required that α-cuts of a *convex fuzzy set* be convex for all $\alpha \in (0, 1]$ in the classical sense (0-cut is excluded here since it is always equal to $\mathbb{R}^n$ in this case and thus includes $-\infty$ to $+\infty$).

Fig. 1.9 illustrates a subnormal fuzzy set that is convex. Two of the α-cuts shown in the figure are clearly convex in the classical sense, and it is easy see that any other

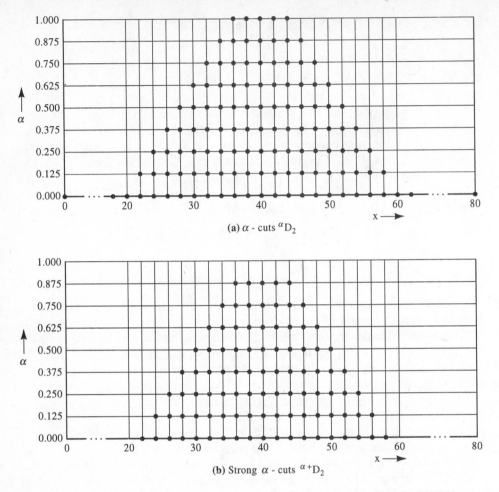

Figure 1.8 Complete families of α-cuts and strong α-cuts of the fuzzy set D_2 defined in Table 1.2: (a) α-cuts $^{\alpha}D_2$; (b) strong α-cuts $^{a+}D_2$.

α-cuts for $\alpha > 0$ are convex as well. Fig. 1.10 illustrates a normal fuzzy set that is not convex. The lack of convexity of this fuzzy set can be demonstrated by identifying some of its α-cuts ($\alpha > 0$) that are not convex; one such α-cut is shown in the figure. Fig. 1.11 illustrates a normal fuzzy set defined on $\mathbb{R}^2$ by all its α-cuts for $\alpha > 0$. Since all the α-cuts are convex, the resulting fuzzy set is also viewed as convex.

To avoid confusion, note that the definition of convexity for fuzzy sets does not mean that the membership function of a convex fuzzy set is a convex function. In fact, membership functions of convex fuzzy sets are functions that are, according to standard definitions, concave and not convex.

We now prove a useful theorem that provides us with an alternative formulation of convexity of fuzzy sets. For the sake of simplicity, we restrict the theorem to fuzzy sets on $\mathbb{R}$, which are of primary interest in this text.

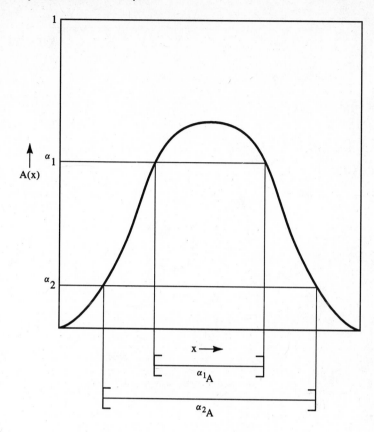

Figure 1.9 Subnormal fuzzy set that is convex.

Theorem 1.1.   A fuzzy set A on $\mathbb{R}$ is convex iff

$$A(\lambda x_1 + (1 - \lambda)x_2) \geq \min[A(x_1), A(x_2)] \tag{1.13}$$

for all $x_1, x_2 \in \mathbb{R}$ and all $\lambda \in [0, 1]$, where min denotes the minimum operator.

Proof: (i) Assume that A is convex and let $\alpha = A(x_1) \leq A(x_2)$. Then, $x_1, x_2 \in {}^{\alpha}A$ and, moreover, $\lambda x_1 + (1 - \lambda)x_2 \in {}^{\alpha}A$ for any $\lambda \in [0, 1]$ by the convexity of A. Consequently,

$$A(\lambda x_1 + (1 - \lambda)x_2) \geq \alpha = A(x_1) = \min[A(x_1), A(x_2)].$$

(ii) Assume that A satisfies (1.13). We need to prove that for any $\alpha \in (0, 1]$, ${}^{\alpha}A$ is convex. Now for any $x_1, x_2 \in {}^{\alpha}A$ (i.e., $A(x_1) \geq \alpha$, $A(x_2) \geq \alpha$), and for any $\lambda \in [0, 1]$, by (1.13)

$$A(\lambda x_1 + (1 - \lambda)x_2) \geq \min[A(x_1), A(x_2)] \geq \min(\alpha, \alpha) = \alpha;$$

i.e., $\lambda x_1 + (1 - \lambda)x_2 \in {}^{\alpha}A$. Therefore, ${}^{\alpha}A$ is convex for any $\alpha \in (0, 1]$. Hence, A is convex. ∎

Any property generalized from classical set theory into the domain of fuzzy set theory that is preserved in all α-cuts for $\alpha \in (0, 1]$ in the classical sense is called a *cutworthy*

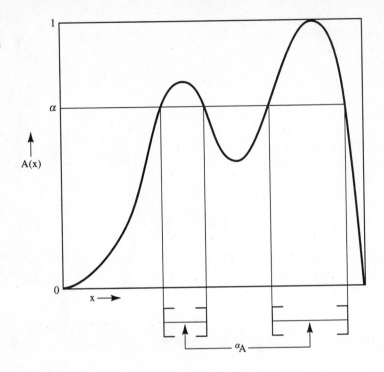

Figure 1.10   Normal fuzzy set that is not convex.

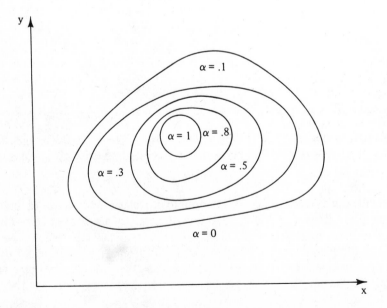

Figure 1.11   Normal and convex fuzzy set A defined by its α-cuts $^{.1}A$, $^{.3}A$, $^{.5}A$, $^{.8}A$, ^{1}A.

property; if it is preserved in all strong α-cuts for $\alpha \in [0, 1]$, it is called a *strong cutworthy property*. Convexity of fuzzy sets, as defined above, is an example of a cutworthy property and, as can be proven, also a strong cutworthy property.

The three basic operations on crisp sets—the complement, intersection and union—can be generalized to fuzzy sets in more than one way. However, one particular generalization, which results in operations that are usually referred to as *standard fuzzy set operations*, has a special significance in fuzzy set theory. In the following, we introduce only the standard operations. The full treatment of possible operations on fuzzy sets is in Chapter 3, where the special significance of the standard operations is also explained.

The *standard complement*, $\overline{A}$, of fuzzy set A with respect to the universal set X is defined for all $x \in X$ by the equation

$$\overline{A}(x) = 1 - A(x). \qquad (1.14)$$

Elements of X for which $A(x) = \overline{A}(x)$ are called *equilibrium points* of A. For the standard complement, clearly, membership grades of equilibrium points are 0.5. For example, the equilibrium points of A_2 in Fig. 1.7 are 27.5 and 52.5.

Given two fuzzy sets, A and B, their *standard intersection*, $A \cap B$, and *standard union*, $A \cup B$, are defined for all $x \in X$ by the equations

$$(A \cap B)(x) = \min[A(x), B(x)], \qquad (1.15)$$

$$(A \cup B)(x) = \max[A(x), B(x)], \qquad (1.16)$$

where min and max denote the minimum operator and the maximum operator, respectively. Due to the associativity of min and max, these definitions can be extended to any finite number of fuzzy sets.

Applying these standard operations to the fuzzy sets in Fig. 1.7, we can find, for example, that

$$A_2 = \overline{A}_1 \cap \overline{A}_3.$$

The construction of $\overline{A}_1 \cap \overline{A}_3$ is shown in Fig. 1.12. The equation makes good sense: a person who is not young and not old is a middle-aged person. Another example based on the same sets is shown in Fig. 1.13, where $B = A_1 \cap A_2$ and $C = A_2 \cap A_3$. Observe that both B and C are subnormal even though A_1, A_2, and A_3 are normal. Furthermore, $B \cup C$ and $\overline{B \cup C}$ are not convex even though B and C are convex. Normality and convexity may thus be lost when we operate on fuzzy sets by the standard operations of intersection and complement.

Any fuzzy power set $\mathcal{F}(X)$ can be viewed as a lattice, in which the standard fuzzy intersection and fuzzy union play the roles of the meet (infimum) and the join (supremum), respectively. The lattice is distributed and complemented under the standard fuzzy complement. It satisfies all the properties of the Boolean lattice listed in Table 1.1 except the law of contradiction and the law of excluded middle. Such a lattice is often referred to as a *De Morgan lattice* or a *De Morgan algebra*.

To verify, for example, that the law of contradiction is violated for fuzzy sets, we need only to show that the equation

$$\min[A(x), 1 - A(x)] = 0$$

is violated for at least one $x \in X$. This is easy since the equation is obviously violated for any

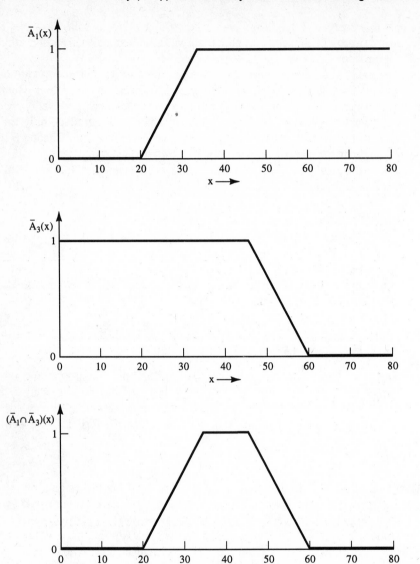

Figure 1.12   Illustration of standard operations on fuzzy sets (A_1, A_2, A_3 are given in Fig. 1.7).

value $A(x) \in (0, 1)$ and is satisfied only for $A(x) \in \{0, 1\}$. Hence, the law of contradiction is satisfied only for crisp sets.

As another example, let us verify the law of absorption,

$$A \cup (A \cap B) = A.$$

This requires showing that the equation

$$\max[A(x), \min[A(x), B(x)]] = A(x)$$

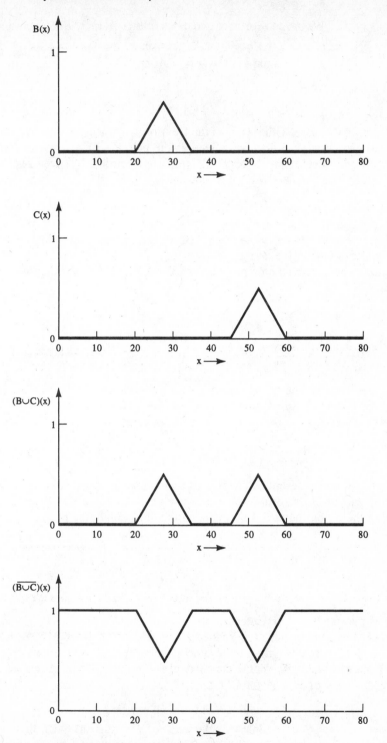

Figure 1.13 Illustration of standard operation on fuzzy sets $B = A_1 \cap A_2$ and $C = A_2 \cap A_3$ (A_1, A_2, A_3 are given in Fig. 1.7).

is satisfied for all $x \in X$. We have to consider two cases: either $A(x) \leq B(x)$ or $A(x) > B(x)$. In the first case, we obtain

$$\max[A(x), A(x)] = A(x);$$

in the second case, we have

$$\max[A(x), B(x)] = A(x)$$

since $A(x) > B(x)$ in this case. Other laws of the De Morgan lattice can be verified similarly.

The De Morgan lattice can also be defined as the pair $\langle \mathcal{F}(X), \subseteq \rangle$, where $\subseteq$ denotes a *fuzzy set inclusion* by which elements of $\mathcal{F}(X)$ are partially ordered. Given two fuzzy sets $A, B \in \mathcal{F}(X)$, we say that A is a *subset* of B and write $A \subseteq B$ iff

$$A(x) \leq B(x) \tag{1.17}$$

for all $x \in X$. It is easy to see that, under the standard fuzzy set operations, $A \subseteq B$ iff $A \cap B = A$ and $A \cup B = B$ for any $A, B \in \mathcal{F}(X)$. This equivalence makes a connection between the two definitions of the lattice.

For any fuzzy set A defined on a finite universal set X, we define its *scalar cardinality*, $|A|$, by the formula

$$|A| = \sum_{x \in X} A(x). \tag{1.18}$$

For example, the scalar cardinality of the fuzzy set D_2 defined in Table 1.2 is

$$|D_2| = 2(.13 + .27 + .4 + .53 + .67 + .8 + .93) + 5 = 12.46.$$

Some authors refer to $|A|$ as the *sigma count* of A.

For any pair of fuzzy subsets defined on a finite universal set X, the *degree of subsethood*, $S(A, B)$, of A in B is defined by the formula

$$S(A, B) = \frac{1}{|A|} \left(|A| - \sum_{x \in X} \max[0, A(x) - B(x)] \right). \tag{1.19}$$

The Σ term in this formula describes the sum of the degrees to which the subset inequality $A(x) \leq B(x)$ is violated, the difference describes the lack of these violations, and the cardinality $|A|$ in the denominator is a normalizing factor to obtain the range

$$0 \leq S(A, B) \leq 1. \tag{1.20}$$

It is easy to convert (1.19) to the more convenient formula

$$S(A, B) = \frac{|A \cap B|}{|A|}, \tag{1.21}$$

where $\cap$ denotes the standard fuzzy intersection.

To conclude this section, let us introduce a special notation that is often used in the literature for defining fuzzy sets with a finite support. Given a fuzzy set A defined on a finite universal set X, let $x_1, x_2, \ldots, x_n$ denote elements of the support ^{0+}A of A and let a_i denote the grade of membership of x_i in A for all $i \in \mathbb{N}_n$. Then, A is written as

$$A = a_1/x_1 + a_2/x_2 + \ldots + a_n/x_n,$$

where the slash is employed to link the elements of the support with their grades of membership in A, and the plus sign indicates, rather than any sort of algebraic addition, that the listed pairs of elements and membership grades collectively form the definition of the set A. For the case in which a fuzzy set A is defined on a universal set that is finite or countable, we may write, respectively,

$$A = \sum_{i=1}^{n} a_i/x_i \text{ or } A = \sum_{i=1}^{\infty} a_i/x_i.$$

Similarly, when X is an interval of real numbers, a fuzzy set A is often written in the form

$$A = \int_X A(x)/x.$$

Again, the integral sign does not have, in this notation, the usual meaning; it solely indicates that all the pairs of x and $A(x)$ in the interval X collectively form A.

It is interesting and conceptually useful to interpret ordinary fuzzy subsets of a finite universal set X with n elements as points in the n-dimensional unit cube $[0, 1]^n$. That is, the entire cube represents the fuzzy power set $\mathcal{F}(X)$, and its vertices represent the crisp power set $\mathcal{P}(X)$. This interpretation suggests that a suitable distance be defined between fuzzy sets. Using, for example, the concept of the Hamming distance, we have

$$d(A, B) = \sum_{x \in X} |A(x) - B(x)|. \tag{1.22}$$

The cardinality $|A|$ of a fuzzy set A, given by (1.18), can be then viewed as the distance $d(A, \varnothing)$ of A from the empty set. Observe that probability distributions are represented by sets whose cardinality is 1. Hence, the set of all probability distributions that can be defined on X is represented by an $(n-1)$-dimensional simplex of the n-dimensional unit cube. Examples of this simplex are shown in Fig. 1.14.

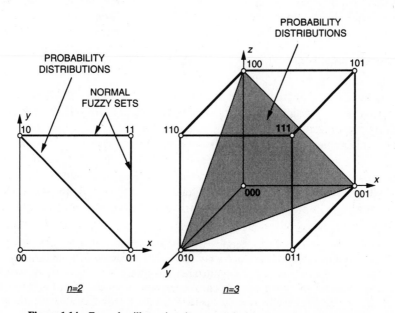

Figure 1.14   Examples illustrating the geometrical interpretation of fuzzy sets.

1.5 CHARACTERISTICS AND SIGNIFICANCE
OF THE PARADIGM SHIFT

Before embarking on deeper study of fuzzy sets, let us reflect a little more on the transition from the traditional view to the modern view of uncertainty, which is briefly mentioned in Sec. 1.1. It is increasingly recognized that this transition has characteristics typical of processes, usually referred to as *paradigm shifts*, which appear periodically throughout the history of science.

The concept of a *scientific paradigm* was introduced by Thomas Kuhn in his important and highly influential book *The Structure of Scientific Revolutions* (Univ. of Chicago Press, 1962); it is defined as a set of theories, standards, principles, and methods that are taken for granted by the scientific community in a given field. Using this concept, Kuhn characterizes scientific development as a process in which periods of *normal science*, based upon a particular paradigm, are interwoven with periods of paradigm shifts, which are referred to by Kuhn as *scientific revolutions*.

In his book, Kuhn illustrates the notion of a paradigm shift by many well-documented examples from the history of science. Some of the most visible paradigm shifts are associated with the names of Copernicus (astronomy), Newton (mechanics), Lavoisier (chemistry), Darwin (biology), Maxwell (electromagnetism), Einstein (mechanics), and Gödel (mathematics).

Although paradigm shifts vary from one another in their scope, pace, and other features, they share a few general characteristics. Each paradigm shift is initiated by emerging problems that are difficult or impossible to deal with in the current paradigm (paradoxes, anomalies, etc.). Each paradigm, when proposed, is initially rejected in various forms (it is ignored, ridiculed, attacked, etc.) by most scientists in the given field. Those who usually support the new paradigm are either very young or very new to the field and, consequently, not very influential. Since the paradigm is initially not well-developed, the position of its proponents is weak. The paradigm eventually gains its status on pragmatic grounds by demonstrating that it is more successful than the existing paradigm in dealing with problems that are generally recognized as acute. As a rule, the greater the scope of a paradigm shift, the longer it takes for the new paradigm to be generally accepted.

The paradigm shift initiated by the concept of a fuzzy set and the idea of mathematics based upon fuzzy sets, which is currently ongoing, has similar characteristics to other paradigm shifts recognized in the history of science. It emerged from the need to bridge the gap between mathematical models and their empirical interpretations. This gap has become increasingly disturbing, especially in the areas of biological, cognitive, and social sciences, as well as in applied sciences, such as modern technology and medicine.

The need to bridge the gap between a mathematical model and experience is well characterized in a penetrating study by the American philosopher Max Black [1937]:

> It is a paradox, whose importance familiarity fails to diminish, that the most highly developed and useful scientific theories are ostensibly expressed in terms of objects never encountered in experience. The line traced by a draftsman, no matter how accurate, is seen beneath the microscope as a kind of corrugated trench, far removed from the ideal line of pure geometry. And the "point-planet" of astronomy, the "perfect gas" of thermodynamics, or the "pure species" of genetics are equally remote from exact realization. Indeed the unintelligibility at the atomic

or subatomic level of the notion of a rigidly demarcated boundary shows that such objects not merely are not but could not be encountered. While the mathematician constructs a theory in terms of "perfect" objects, the experimental scientist observes objects of which the properties demanded by theory are and can, in the very nature of measurement, be only approximately true. Mathematical deduction is not useful to the physicist if interpreted rigorously. It is necessary to know that its validity is unaltered when the premise and conclusion are only "approximately true." But the indeterminacy thus introduced, it is necessary to add in criticism, will invalidate the deduction unless the permissible limits of variation are specified. To do so, however, replaces the original mathematical deduction by a more complicated mathematical theory in respect of whose interpretation the same problem arises, and whose exact nature is in any case unknown. This lack of exact correlation between a scientific theory and its empirical interpretation can be blamed either upon the world or upon the theory. We can regard the shape of an orange or a tennis ball as imperfect copies of an ideal form of which perfect knowledge is to be had in pure geometry, or we can regard the geometry of spheres as a simplified and imperfect version of the spatial relations between the members of a certain class of physical objects. On either view there remains a gap between scientific theory and its application which ought to be, but is not, bridged. To say that all language (symbolism, or thought) is vague is a favorite method for evading the problems involved and lack of analysis has the disadvantage of tempting even the most eminent thinkers into the appearance of absurdity. We shall not assume that "laws" of logic or mathematics prescribe modes of existence to which intelligible discourse must necessarily conform. It will be argued, on the contrary, that deviations from the logical or mathematical standards of precision are all pervasive in symbolism; that to label them as subjective aberrations sets an impassable gulf between formal laws and experience and leaves the usefulness of the formal sciences an insoluble mystery.

The same need was expressed by Zadeh [1962], three years before he actually proposed the new paradigm of mathematics based upon the concept of a fuzzy set:

> ...there is a fairly wide gap between what might be regarded as "animate" system theorists and "inanimate" system theorists at the present time, and it is not at all certain that this gap will be narrowed, much less closed, in the near future. There are some who feel this gap reflects the fundamental inadequacy of the conventional mathematics—the mathematics of precisely-defined points, functions, sets, probability measures, etc.—for coping with the analysis of biological systems, and that to deal effectively with such systems, which are generally orders of magnitude more complex than man-made systems, we need a radically different kind of mathematics, the mathematics of fuzzy or cloudy quantities which are not describable in terms of probability distributions. Indeed, the need for such mathematics is becoming increasingly apparent even in the realm of inanimate systems, for in most practical cases the a priori data as well as the criteria by which the performance of a man-made system is judged are far from being precisely specified or having accurately known probability distributions.

When the new paradigm was proposed [Zadeh, 1965b], the usual process of a paradigm shift began. The concept of a fuzzy set, which underlies this new paradigm, was initially ignored, ridiculed, or attacked by many, while it was supported only by a few, mostly young and not influential. In spite of the initial lack of interest, skepticism, or even open hostility, the new paradigm persevered with virtually no support in the 1960s, matured significantly and gained some support in the 1970s, and began to demonstrate its superior pragmatic utility in the 1980s.

The paradigm shift is still ongoing, and it will likely take much longer than usual to complete it. This is not surprising, since the scope of the paradigm shift is enormous. The new paradigm does not affect any particular field of science, but the very foundations of science. In fact, it challenges the most sacred element of the foundations—the Aristotelian two-valued logic, which for millennia has been taken for granted and viewed as inviolable. The acceptance of such a radical challenge is surely difficult for most scientists; it requires an open mind, enough time, and considerable effort to properly comprehend the meaning and significance of the paradigm shift involved.

At this time, we can recognize at least four features that make the new paradigm superior to the classical paradigm:

1. The new paradigm allows us to express *irreducible observation and measurement uncertainties* in their various manifestations and make these uncertainties intrinsic to empirical data. Such data, which are based on graded distinctions among states of relevant variables, are usually called *fuzzy data*. When fuzzy data are processed, their intrinsic uncertainties are processed as well, and the results obtained are more meaningful, in both epistemological and pragmatic terms, than their counterparts obtained by processing the usual crisp data.

2. For the reasons briefly discussed in Sec. 1.1, the new paradigm offers far greater resources for *managing complexity and controlling computational cost*. The general experience is that the more complex the problem involved, the greater the superiority of fuzzy methods.

3. The new paradigm has considerably *greater expressive power*; consequently, it can effectively deal with a broader class of problems. In particular, it has the capability to capture and deal with meanings of sentences expressed in natural language. This capability of the new paradigm allows us to deal in mathematical terms with problems that require *the use of natural language*.

4. The new paradigm has a greater capability to capture human common-sense reasoning, decision making, and other aspects of human cognition. When employed in machine design, the resulting machines are *human-friendlier*.

The reader may not be able at this point to comprehend the meaning and significance of the described features of the new paradigm. This hopefully will be achieved after his or her study of this whole text is completed.

NOTES

1.1. For a general background on crisp sets and classical two-valued logic, we recommend the book *Set Theory and Related Topics* by S. Lipschutz (Shaum, New York, 1964). The book covers all topics that are needed for this text and contains many solved examples. For a more advanced treatment of the topics, we recommend the book *Set Theory and Logic* by R. R. Stoll (W. H. Freeman, San Francisco, 1961).

1.2. The concept of *L-fuzzy sets* was introduced by Goguen [1967]. A thorough investigation of properties of *fuzzy sets of type 2* and higher types was done by Mizumoto and Tanaka [1976,

1981b]. The concept of *fuzzy sets of level k*, which is due to Zadeh [1971b], was investigated by Gottwald [1979]. Convex fuzzy sets were studied in greater detail by Lowen [1980] and Liu [1985].

1.3. The geometric interpretation of ordinary fuzzy sets as points in the n-dimensional unit cube was introduced and pursued by Kosko [1990, 1991, 1993a].

1.4. An alternative set theory, which is referred to as the *theory of semisets*, was proposed and developed by Vopěnka and Hájek [1972] to represent sets with imprecise boundaries. Unlike fuzzy sets, however, semisets may be defined in terms of vague properties and not necessarily by explicit membership grade functions. While semisets are more general than fuzzy sets, they are required to be approximated by fuzzy sets in practical situations. The relationship between semisets and fuzzy sets is well characterized by Novák [1992]. The concept of semisets leads into a formulation of an *alternative (nonstandard) set theory* [Vopěnka, 1979].

EXERCISES

1.1. Explain the difference between randomness and fuzziness.

1.2. Find some examples of prospective fuzzy variables in daily life.

1.3. Describe the concept of a fuzzy set in your own words.

1.4. Find some examples of interval-valued fuzzy sets, L-fuzzy sets, level 2 fuzzy sets, and type 2 fuzzy sets.

1.5. Explain why we need fuzzy set theory.

1.6. Explain why the law of contradiction and the law of exclusive middle are violated in fuzzy set theory under the standard fuzzy sets operations. What is the significance of this?

1.7. Compute the scalar cardinalities for each of the following fuzzy sets:
   (a) $A = .4/v + .2/w + .5/x + .4/y + 1/z$;
   (b) $B = 1/x + 1/y + 1/z$;
   (c) $C(x) = \frac{x}{x+1}$ for $x \in \{0, 1 \ldots, 10\} = X$;
   (d) $D(x) = 1 - x/10$ for $x \in \{0, 1, \ldots, 10\} = X$.

1.8. Let A, B be fuzzy sets defined on a universal set X. Prove that

$$|A| + |B| = |A \cup B| + |A \cap B|,$$

where $\cap, \cup$ are the standard fuzzy intersection and union, respectively.

1.9. Order the fuzzy sets defined by the following membership grade functions (assuming $x \geq 0$) by the inclusion (subset) relation:

$$A(x) = \frac{1}{1 + 10x}, B(x) = \left(\frac{1}{1 + 10x}\right)^{1/2}, C(x) = \left(\frac{1}{1 + 10x}\right)^2.$$

1.10. Consider the fuzzy sets $A, B,$ and C defined on the interval $X = [0, 10]$ of real numbers by the membership grade functions

$$A(x) = \frac{x}{x + 2}, B(x) = 2^{-x}, C(x) = \frac{1}{1 + 10(x - 2)^2}.$$

Determine mathematical formulas and graphs of the membership grade functions of each of the following sets:
   (a) $\overline{A}, \overline{B}, \overline{C}$;

(b) $A \cup B, A \cup C, B \cup C$;

(c) $A \cap B, A \cap C, B \cap C$;

(d) $A \cup B \cup C, A \cap B \cap C$;

(e) $A \cap \overline{C}, \overline{B \cap C}, \overline{A \cup C}$.

1.11. Calculate the α-cuts and strong α-cuts of the three fuzzy sets in Exercise 1.10 for some values of α, for example, $\alpha = 0.2, 0.5, 0.8, 1$.

1.12. Restricting the universal set to $[0, 10]$, determine which fuzzy sets in Exercise 1.10 are convex.

1.13. Let A, B be two fuzzy sets of a universal set X. The *difference* of A and B is defined by

$$A - B = A \cap \overline{B};$$

and the *symmetric difference* of A and B is defined by

$$A \triangle B = (A - B) \cup (B - A).$$

Prove that:

(a) $(A \triangle B) \triangle C = A \triangle (B \triangle C)$;

(b) $A \triangle B \triangle C = (\overline{A} \cap \overline{B} \cap C) \cup (\overline{A} \cap B \cap \overline{C}) \cup (A \cap \overline{B} \cap \overline{C}) \cup (A \cap B \cap C)$.

1.14. Given Equation (1.19), derive Equation (1.21).

1.15. Calculate the degrees of subsethood $S(C, D)$ and $S(D, C)$ for the fuzzy sets in Exercise 1.7 c, d.

2

Fuzzy Sets Versus Crisp Sets

2.1 ADDITIONAL PROPERTIES OF α-CUTS

The concepts of α-cuts and strong α-cuts, which are introduced in Sec. 1.4, play a principal role in the relationship between fuzzy sets and crisp sets. They can be viewed as a bridge by which fuzzy sets and crisp sets are connected. Before examining this connection, we first overview some additional properties of α-cuts of the two types. All these properties involve the standard fuzzy set operations and the standard fuzzy set inclusion, as defined in Sec. 1.4.

The various properties of α-cuts covered in this section are expressed in terms of four theorems. The first one covers some fairly elementary properties.

Theorem 2.1. Let $A, B \in \mathcal{F}(X)$. Then, the following properties hold for all $\alpha, \beta \in [0, 1]$:

(i) $^{\alpha+}A \subseteq {}^{\alpha}A$;
(ii) $\alpha \leq \beta$ implies $^{\alpha}A \supseteq {}^{\beta}A$ and $^{\alpha+}A \supseteq {}^{\beta+}A$;
(iii) $^{\alpha}(A \cap B) = {}^{\alpha}A \cap {}^{\alpha}B$ and $^{\alpha}(A \cup B) = {}^{\alpha}A \cup {}^{\alpha}B$;
(iv) $^{\alpha+}(A \cap B) = {}^{\alpha+}A \cap {}^{\alpha+}B$ and $^{\alpha+}(A \cup B) = {}^{\alpha+}A \cup {}^{\alpha+}B$;
(v) $^{\alpha}(\overline{A}) = {}^{(1-\alpha)+}\overline{A}$ (see a notational remark on p. 36).

Proof: We prove only (iii) and (v); the rest is left to the reader as an exercise.

(iii) *First equality.* For any $x \in {}^{\alpha}(A \cap B)$, we have $(A \cap B)(x) \geq \alpha$ and, hence, $\min[A(x), B(x)] \geq \alpha$. This means that $A(x) \geq \alpha$ and $B(x) \geq \alpha$. This implies that $x \in {}^{\alpha}A \cap {}^{\alpha}B$ and, consequently, $^{\alpha}(A \cap B) \subseteq {}^{\alpha}A \cap {}^{\alpha}B$. Conversely, for any $x \in {}^{\alpha}A \cap {}^{\alpha}B$, we have $x \in {}^{\alpha}A$ and $x \in {}^{\alpha}B$; that is $A(x) \geq \alpha$ and $B(x) \geq \alpha$. Hence, $\min[A(x), B(x)] \geq \alpha$, which means that $(A \cap B)(x) \geq \alpha$. This implies that $x \in {}^{\alpha}(A \cap B)$ and, consequently, $^{\alpha}A \cap {}^{\alpha}B \subseteq {}^{\alpha}(A \cap B)$. This concludes the proof that $^{\alpha}(A \cap B) = {}^{\alpha}A \cap {}^{\alpha}B$.

Second equality. For any $x \in {}^{\alpha}(A \cup B)$, we have $\max[A(x), B(x)] \geq \alpha$ and, hence, $A(x) \geq \alpha$ or $B(x) \geq \alpha$. This implies that $x \in {}^{\alpha}A \cup {}^{\alpha}B$ and, consequently, $^{\alpha}(A \cup B) \subseteq {}^{\alpha}A \cup {}^{\alpha}B$. Conversely, for any $x \in {}^{\alpha}A \cup {}^{\alpha}B$, we have $x \in {}^{\alpha}A$ or $x \in {}^{\alpha}B$; that is $A(x) \geq \alpha$ or

$B(x) \geq \alpha$. Hence, $\max[A(x), B(x)] \geq \alpha$, which means that $(A \cup B)(x) \geq \alpha$. This implies that $x \in {}^{\alpha}(A \cup B)$ and, consequently, ${}^{\alpha}A \cup {}^{\alpha}B \subseteq {}^{\alpha}(A \cup B)$. This concludes the proof that ${}^{\alpha}(A \cup B) = {}^{\alpha}A \cup {}^{\alpha}B$.

(v) For any $x \in {}^{\alpha}(\overline{A})$, we have $1 - A(x) = \overline{A}(x) \geq \alpha$; that is, $A(x) \leq 1 - \alpha$. This means that $x \notin {}^{(1-\alpha)+}A$ and, clearly, $x \in {}^{(1-\alpha)+}\overline{A}$; consequently, ${}^{\alpha}(\overline{A}) \subseteq {}^{(1-\alpha)+}\overline{A}$. Conversely, for any $x \in {}^{(1-\alpha)+}\overline{A}$, we have $x \notin {}^{(1-\alpha)+}A$. Hence, $A(x) \leq 1 - \alpha$ and $1 - A(x) \geq \alpha$. That is, $\overline{A}(x) \geq \alpha$, which means that $x \in {}^{\alpha}(\overline{A})$. Therefore, ${}^{(1-\alpha)+}\overline{A} \subseteq {}^{\alpha}(\overline{A})$ and, consequently, ${}^{\alpha}(\overline{A}) = {}^{(1-\alpha)+}\overline{A}$. ■

Let us examine the significance of the properties stated in Theorem 2.1. Property (i) is rather trivial, expressing that the strong α-cut is always included in the α-cut of any fuzzy set and for any $\alpha \in [0, 1]$; the property follows directly from the definitions of the two types of α-cuts. Property (ii) means that the set sequences $\{{}^{\alpha}A | \alpha \in [0, 1]\}$ and $\{{}^{\alpha+}A | \alpha \in [0, 1]\}$ of α-cuts and strong α-cuts, respectively, are always *monotonic decreasing* with respect to α; consequently, they are *nested families of sets*. Properties (iii) and (iv) show that the standard fuzzy intersection and fuzzy union are both cutworthy and strong cutworthy when applied to two fuzzy sets or, due to the associativity of min and max, to any finite number of fuzzy sets. However, we must be cautious when these operations are applied to an infinite family of fuzzy sets; this case is covered by Theorem 2.2.

To make sure that the reader understands the meaning of property (v), let us make a small notational remark. Observe that we denote the α-cut of the complement of A by ${}^{\alpha}(\overline{A})$, while the complement of the α-cut of A is denoted by ${}^{\overline{\alpha}A}$ (and we use an analogous notation for the strong α-cuts). Two distinct symbols must be used here since the two sets are, in general, not equal, as illustrated in Fig. 2.1. The symbol ${}^{\overline{\alpha}A}$ is a convenient simplification of the symbol $\overline{({}^{\alpha}A)}$, which more accurately captures the meaning of the set for which it stands. This simplification is justified since it does not introduce any ambiguity.

Proposition (v) shows that the standard fuzzy complement is neither cutworthy nor strong cutworthy. That is,

$$ {}^{\alpha}(\overline{A}) \neq {}^{\overline{\alpha}A} \text{ and } {}^{\alpha+}(\overline{A}) \neq {}^{\overline{\alpha+}A} $$

in general. This is not surprising since fuzzy sets violate, by definition, the two basic properties of the complement of crisp sets, the law of contradiction and the law of excluded middle. In spite of its negative connotation, property (v) describes an interesting feature of the standard fuzzy complement: the α-cut of the complement of A is always the same as the complement of the strong $(1 - \alpha)$-cut of A.

Theorem 2.2.   Let $A_i \in \mathcal{F}(X)$ for all $i \in I$, where I is an index set. Then,

(vi) $\displaystyle\bigcup_{i \in I} {}^{\alpha}A_i \subseteq {}^{\alpha}\left(\bigcup_{i \in I} A_i\right)$ and $\displaystyle\bigcap_{i \in I} {}^{\alpha}A_i = {}^{\alpha}\left(\bigcap_{i \in I} A_i\right)$;

(vii) $\displaystyle\bigcup_{i \in I} {}^{\alpha+}A_i = {}^{\alpha+}\left(\bigcup_{i \in I} A_i\right)$ and $\displaystyle\bigcap_{i \in I} {}^{\alpha+}A_i \subseteq {}^{\alpha+}\left(\bigcap_{i \in I} A_i\right)$.

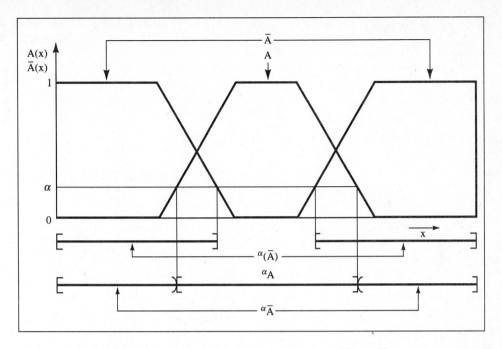

Figure 2.1 Illustration of the difference between $^\alpha(\overline{A})$ and $^\alpha\overline{A}$.

Proof: We prove only (vii) and leave (vi) to the reader. First, we prove the equality for set unions. For all $x \in X$,

$$x \in \bigcup_{i \in I} {}^{\alpha+}A_i$$

iff there exists some $i_0 \in I$ such that $x \in {}^{\alpha+}A_{i_0}$ (i.e., $A_{i_0}(x) > \alpha$). This inequality is satisfied iff

$$\sup_{i \in I} A_i(x) > \alpha,$$

which is equivalent to

$$\left(\bigcup_{i \in I} A_i \right)(x) > \alpha.$$

That is,

$$x \in {}^{\alpha+}\left(\bigcup_{i \in I} A_i \right).$$

Hence, the equality in (vii) is satisfied.

We prove now the second proposition in (vii). For all

$$x \in {}^{\alpha+}\left(\bigcap_{i \in I} A_i \right),$$

we have

$$\left(\bigcap_{i\in I} A_i \right)(x) > \alpha;$$

that is,

$$\inf_{i\in I} A_i(x) > \alpha.$$

Hence, for any $i \in I$, $A_i(x) > \alpha$ (i.e., $x \in {}^{\alpha+}A_i$). Therefore,

$$x \in \bigcap_{i\in I} {}^{\alpha+}A_i,$$

which concludes the proof. ∎

To show that the set inclusions in (vi) and (vii) cannot be replaced with equalities, it is sufficient to find examples in which the presumed equalities are violated. The following example applies only to (vi); a similar example can easily be found for (vii).

Given an arbitrary universal set X, let $A_i \in \mathcal{F}(X)$ be defined by

$$A_i(x) = 1 - \frac{1}{i}$$

for all $x \in X$ and all $i \in \mathbb{N}$. Then, for any $x \in X$,

$$\left(\bigcup_{i\in\mathbb{N}} A_i \right)(x) = \sup_{i\in\mathbb{N}} A_i(x) = \sup_{i\in\mathbb{N}} \left(1 - \frac{1}{i} \right) = 1.$$

Let $\alpha = 1$; then,

$${}^1\left(\bigcup_{i\in\mathbb{N}} A_i \right) = X.$$

However, for any $i \in \mathbb{N}$, ${}^1A_i = \varnothing$ because, for any $x \in X$,

$$A_i(x) = 1 - \frac{1}{i} < 1.$$

Hence,

$$\bigcup_{i\in\mathbb{N}} {}^1A_i = \bigcup_{i\in\mathbb{N}} \varnothing = \varnothing \neq X = {}^1\left(\bigcup_{i\in\mathbb{N}} A_i \right).$$

Theorem 2.2 establishes that the standard fuzzy intersection on infinite sets is cutworthy (but not strong cutworthy), while the standard fuzzy union on infinite sets is strong cutworthy (but not cutworthy).

Theorem 2.3. Let $A, B \in \mathcal{F}(X)$. Then, for all $\alpha \in [0, 1]$,

(viii) $A \subseteq B$ iff ${}^{\alpha}A \subseteq {}^{\alpha}B$;

   $A \subseteq B$ iff ${}^{\alpha+}A \subseteq {}^{\alpha+}B$;

 (ix) $A = B$ iff ${}^{\alpha}A = {}^{\alpha}B$;

   $A = B$ iff ${}^{\alpha+}A = {}^{\alpha+}B$.

Proof: We prove only (viii). To prove the first proposition in (viii), assume that there exists $\alpha_0 \in [0, 1]$ such that $^{\alpha_0}A \not\subseteq {}^{\alpha_0}B$; that is, there exists $x_0 \in X$ such that $x_0 \in {}^{\alpha_0}A$ and $x_0 \notin {}^{\alpha_0}B$. Then, $A(x_0) \geq \alpha_0$ and $B(x_0) < \alpha_0$. Hence, $B(x_0) < A(x_0)$, which contradicts with $A \subseteq B$. Now, assume $A \not\subseteq B$; that is, there exists $x_0 \in X$ such that $A(x_0) > B(x_0)$. Let $\alpha = A(x_0)$; then $x_0 \in {}^{\alpha}A$ and $x_0 \notin {}^{\alpha}B$, which demonstrates that $^{\alpha}A \subseteq {}^{\alpha}B$ is not satisfied for all $\alpha \in [0, 1]$.

Now we prove the second proposition in (viii). The first part is similar to the previous proof. For the second part, assume that $A \not\subseteq B$. Then, there exists $x_0 \in X$ such that $A(x_0) > B(x_0)$. Let α be any number between $A(x_0)$ and $B(x_0)$. Then, $x_0 \in {}^{\alpha+}A$ and $x_0 \notin {}^{\alpha+}B$. Hence, $^{\alpha+}A \not\subseteq {}^{\alpha+}B$, which demonstrates that $^{\alpha+}A \subseteq {}^{\alpha+}B$ is not satisfied for all $\alpha \in [0, 1]$. ∎

Theorem 2.3 establishes that the properties of fuzzy set inclusion and equality are both cutworthy and strong cutworthy.

Theorem 2.4.   For any $A \in \mathcal{F}(X)$, the following properties hold:

(x) $^{\alpha}A = \displaystyle\bigcap_{\beta < \alpha} {}^{\beta}A = \bigcap_{\beta < \alpha} {}^{\beta+}A$;

(xi) $^{\alpha+}A = \displaystyle\bigcup_{\alpha < \beta} {}^{\beta}A = \bigcup_{\alpha < \beta} {}^{\beta+}A$.

Proof: We prove only (x), leaving the proof of (xi) to the reader. For any $\beta < \alpha$, clearly $^{\alpha}A \subseteq {}^{\beta}A$. Hence,

$$^{\alpha}A \subseteq \bigcup_{\beta < \alpha} {}^{\beta}A.$$

Now, for all $x \in \displaystyle\bigcap_{\beta < \alpha} {}^{\beta}A$ and any $\varepsilon > 0$, we have $x \in {}^{\alpha - \varepsilon}A$ (since $\alpha - \varepsilon < \alpha$), which means that $A(x) \geq \alpha - \varepsilon$. Since ε is an arbitrary positive number, let $\varepsilon \to 0$. This results in $A(x) \geq \alpha$ (i.e., $x \in {}^{\alpha}A$). Hence,

$$\bigcap_{\beta < \alpha} {}^{\beta}A \subseteq {}^{\alpha}A,$$

which concludes the proof of the first equation of (x); the proof of the second equation is analogous. ∎

2.2   REPRESENTATIONS OF FUZZY SETS

The principal role of α-cuts and strong α-cuts in fuzzy set theory is their capability to represent fuzzy sets. We show in this section that each fuzzy set can uniquely be represented by either the family of all its α-cuts or the family of all its strong α-cuts. Either of these representations allows us to extend various properties of crisp sets and operations on crisp sets to their fuzzy counterparts. In each extension, a given classical (crisp) property or operation is required to be valid for each crisp set involved in the representation. As already mentioned, such extended properties or operations are called either cutworthy or strong cutworthy, depending on the type of representation employed.

As explained in detail later in the text, not all properties and operations involving fuzzy sets are cutworthy or strong cutworthy. In fact, properties or operations that are either cutworthy or strong cutworthy are rather rare. However, they are of special significance since they bridge fuzzy set theory with classical set theory. They are sort of reference points from which other fuzzy properties or operations deviate to various degrees.

To explain the two representations of fuzzy sets by crisp sets, let us begin by illustrating one of them by a simple example. Considering the fuzzy set

$$A = .2/x_1 + .4/x_2 + .6/x_3 + .8/x_4 + 1/x_5$$

as our example, let us show how this set can be represented by its α-cuts.

The given fuzzy set A is associated with only five distinct α-cuts, which are defined by the following characteristic functions (viewed here as special membership functions):

$$^{.2}A = 1/x_1 + 1/x_2 + 1/x_3 + 1/x_4 + 1/x_5,$$

$$^{.4}A = 0/x_1 + 1/x_2 + 1/x_3 + 1/x_4 + 1/x_5,$$

$$^{.6}A = 0/x_1 + 0/x_2 + 1/x_3 + 1/x_4 + 1/x_5,$$

$$^{.8}A = 0/x_1 + 0/x_2 + 0/x_3 + 1/x_4 + 1/x_5,$$

$$^{1}A = 0/x_1 + 0/x_2 + 0/x_3 + 0/x_4 + 1/x_5.$$

We now convert each of the α-cuts to a special fuzzy set, $_\alpha A$, defined for each $x \in X = \{x_1, x_2, x_3, x_4, x_5\}$ as follows:

$$_\alpha A(x) = \alpha \cdot {}^\alpha A(x). \tag{2.1}$$

We obtain

$$_{.2}A = .2/x_1 + .2/x_2 + .2/x_3 + .2/x_4 + .2/x_5,$$

$$_{.4}A = 0/x_1 + .4/x_2 + .4/x_3 + .4/x_4 + .4/x_5,$$

$$_{.6}A = 0/x_1 + 0/x_2 + .6/x_3 + .6/x_4 + .6/x_5,$$

$$_{.8}A = 0/x_1 + 0/x_2 + 0/x_3 + .8/x_4 + .8/x_5,$$

$$_{1}A = 0/x_1 + 0/x_2 + 0/x_3 + 0/x_4 + 1/x_5.$$

It is now easy to see that the standard fuzzy union of these five special fuzzy sets is exactly the original fuzzy set A. That is,

$$A = {}_{.2}A \cup {}_{.4}A \cup {}_{.6}A \cup {}_{.8}A \cup {}_{1}A.$$

Our aim in this section is to prove that the representation of fuzzy sets of their α-cuts, as illustrated by this example, is universal. It applies to every fuzzy set, regardless of whether it is based on a finite or infinite universal set. Furthermore, we also prove the universality of an alternative representation, which is based upon strong α-cuts.

The representation of an arbitrary fuzzy set A in terms of the special fuzzy sets $_\alpha A$, which are defined in terms of the α-cuts of A by (2.1), is usually referred to as a *decomposition* of A. In the following, we formulate and prove three basic *decomposition theorems of fuzzy sets*.

Theorem 2.5 (First Decomposition Theorem).   For every $A \in \mathcal{F}(X)$,

$$A = \bigcup_{\alpha \in [0,1]} {}_\alpha A, \tag{2.2}$$

where ${}_\alpha A$ is defined by (2.1) and $\cup$ denotes the standard fuzzy union.

Proof: For each particular $x \in X$, let $a = A(x)$. Then,

$$\left(\bigcup_{\alpha \in [0,1]} {}_\alpha A \right)(x) = \sup_{\alpha \in [0,1]} {}_\alpha A(x)$$

$$= \max[\, \sup_{\alpha \in [0,a]} {}_\alpha A(x), \; \sup_{\alpha \in (a,1]} {}_\alpha A(x)\,].$$

For each $\alpha \in (a, 1]$, we have $A(x) = a < \alpha$ and, therefore, ${}_\alpha A(x) = 0$. On the other hand, for each $\alpha \in [0, a]$, we have $A(x) = a \geq \alpha$, therefore, ${}_\alpha A(x) = \alpha$. Hence,

$$\left(\bigcup_{\alpha \in [0,1]} {}_\alpha A \right)(x) = \sup_{\alpha \in [0,a]} \alpha = a = A(x).$$

Since the same argument is valid for each $x \in X$, the validity of (2.2) is established. ∎

To illustrate the application of this theorem, let us consider a fuzzy set A with the following membership function of triangular shape (Fig. 2.2):

$$A(x) = \begin{cases} x - 1 & \text{when } x \in [1, 2] \\ 3 - x & \text{when } x \in [2, 3] \\ 0 & \text{otherwise.} \end{cases}$$

For each $\alpha \in (0, 1]$, the α-cut of A is in this case the closed interval

$${}^\alpha A = [\alpha + 1, 3 - \alpha],$$

and the special fuzzy set ${}_\alpha A$ employed in (2.2) is defined by the membership function

$${}_\alpha A = \begin{cases} \alpha & \text{when } x \in [\alpha + 1, 3 - \alpha] \\ 0 & \text{otherwise.} \end{cases}$$

Examples of sets ${}^\alpha A$ and ${}_\alpha A$ for three values of α are shown in Fig. 2.2. According to Theorem 2.5, A is obtained by taking the standard fuzzy union of sets ${}_\alpha A$ for all $\alpha \in [0, 1]$.

Theorem 2.6 (Second Decomposition Theorem).   For every $A \in \mathcal{F}(X)$,

$$A = \bigcup_{\alpha \in [0,1]} {}_{\alpha+} A, \tag{2.3}$$

where ${}_{\alpha+} A$ denotes a special fuzzy set defined by

$${}_{\alpha+} A(x) = \alpha \cdot {}^{\alpha+} A(x) \tag{2.4}$$

and $\cup$ denotes the standard fuzzy union.

Proof: Since the proof is analogous to the proof of Theorem 2.5, we express it in a more concise form. For each particular $x \in X$, let $a = A(x)$. Then,

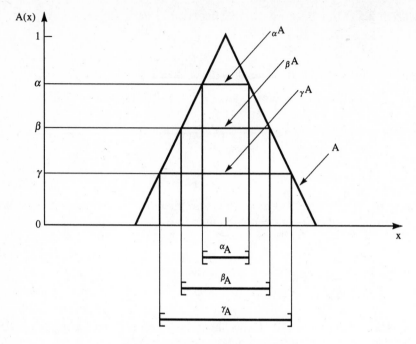

Figure 2.2   Illustration of Theorem 2.5.

$$\left(\bigcup_{\alpha \in [0,1]} {}_{\alpha +}A \right)(x) = \sup_{\alpha \in [0,1]} {}_{\alpha +}A(x)$$

$$= \max[\sup_{\alpha \in [0,a)} {}_{\alpha +}A(x),\ \sup_{\alpha \in [a,1]} {}_{\alpha +}A(x)]$$

$$= \sup_{\alpha \in [0,a)} \alpha = a = A(x). \quad \blacksquare$$

Theorem 2.7 (Third Decomposition Theorem).   For every $A \in \mathcal{F}(X)$,

$$A = \bigcup_{\alpha \in \Lambda(A)} {}_{\alpha}A, \tag{2.5}$$

where $\Lambda(A)$ is the level set of A, ${}_{\alpha}A$ is defined by (2.1), and $\cup$ denotes the standard fuzzy union.

Proof: Analogous to the proofs of the other decomposition theorems.   ∎

The meaning of this theorem is illustrated in Fig. 2.3 by the decomposition of a fuzzy set A defined by a simple stepwise membership function shown in Fig. 2.3a. Since $\Lambda(A) = \{0, .3, .6, 1\}$ and ${}_{0}A = \varnothing$, A is fully represented by the three special fuzzy sets ${}_{.3}A$, ${}_{.6}A$, and ${}_{1}A$; shown in Fig. 2.3b.

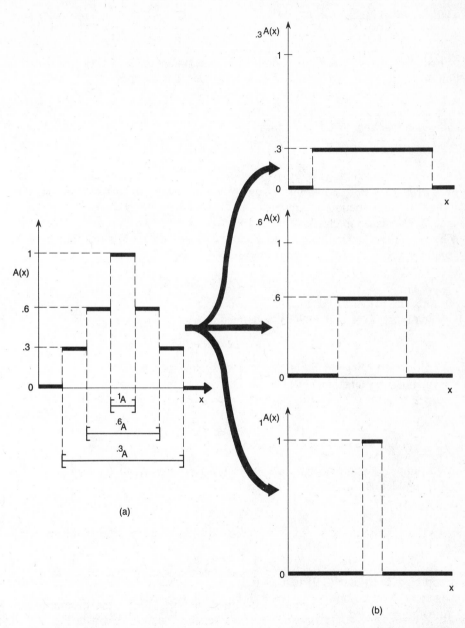

Figure 2.3 Illustration of Theorem 2.7: (a) given fuzzy set A; (b) decomposition of A into $_{.3}A$, $_{.6}A$, $_{1}A$.

2.3   EXTENSION PRINCIPLE FOR FUZZY SETS

We say that a crisp function

$$f : X \to Y$$

is fuzzified when it is extended to act on fuzzy sets defined on X and Y. That is, the fuzzified function, for which the same symbol f is usually used, has the form

$$f : \mathcal{F}(X) \to \mathcal{F}(Y),$$

and its inverse function, f^{-1}, has the form

$$f^{-1} : \mathcal{F}(Y) \to \mathcal{F}(X).$$

A principle for fuzzifying crisp functions (or, possibly, crisp relations) is called an *extension principle*. Before introducing this principle, let us first discuss its special case, in which the extended functions are restricted to crisp power sets $\mathcal{P}(X)$ and $\mathcal{P}(Y)$. This special case is well established in classical set theory.

Given a crisp function from X to Y, its extended version is a function from $\mathcal{P}(X)$ to $\mathcal{P}(Y)$ that, for any $A \in \mathcal{P}(X)$, is defined by

$$f(A) = \{y \mid y = f(x), x \in A\}. \tag{2.6}$$

Furthermore, the extended version of the inverse of f, denoted by f^{-1}, is a function from $\mathcal{P}(Y)$ to $\mathcal{P}(X)$ that, for any $B \in \mathcal{P}(Y)$, is defined by

$$f^{-1}(B) = \{x \mid f(x) \in B\}. \tag{2.7}$$

Expressing the sets $f(A)$ and $f^{-1}(B)$ by their characteristic functions (viewed here as special cases of membership functions), we obtain

$$[f(A)](y) = \sup_{x \mid y = f(x)} A(x), \tag{2.8}$$

$$\left[f^{-1}(B)\right](x) = B(f(x)). \tag{2.9}$$

As a simple example illustrating the meaning of these equations, let $X = \{a, b, c\}$ and $Y = \{1, 2\}$, and let us consider the function

$$f : \ a \to 1$$

$$b \to 1$$

$$c \to 2$$

When applying (2.8) and (2.9) to this function, we obtain the extension of f shown in Fig. 2.4a and the extension of f^{-1} shown in Fig. 2.4b, respectively.

Allowing now sets A and B in (2.8) and (2.9) to be fuzzy sets and replacing the characteristic functions in these equations with membership functions, we arrive at the following extension principle by which any crisp function can be fuzzified.

Extension Principle.   Any given function $f : X \to Y$ induces two functions,

$$f : \ \mathcal{F}(X) \to \mathcal{F}(Y),$$

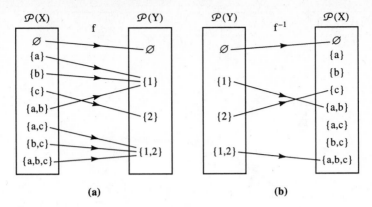

Figure 2.4   An example of the classical extensions of function $f : a \to 1, b \to 1, c \to 2$ and its inverse, f^{-1}.

$$f^{-1}: \quad \mathcal{F}(Y) \to \mathcal{F}(X),$$

which are defined by

$$[f(A)](y) = \sup_{x|y=f(x)} A(x) \tag{2.10}$$

for all $A \in \mathcal{F}(X)$ and

$$[f^{-1}(B)](x) = B(f(x)) \tag{2.11}$$

for all $B \in \mathcal{F}(Y)$.

The extension principle is illustrated in Fig. 2.5 (f continuous) and Fig. 2.6 (f discrete), which are self-explanatory. When sets X and Y are finite (as in Fig. 2.6), we can replace sup in (2.10) with max.

Fuzzifications based on the extension principle satisfy numerous properties. We select only properties that we consider most important and cluster them into three natural groups, which are expressed by the following three theorems. To save space, we present proofs of only some of the properties; to check his or her understanding of the extension principle, the reader should produce some of the proofs omitted here.

Theorem 2.8.   Let $f : X \to Y$ be an arbitrary crisp function. Then, for any $A_i \in \mathcal{F}(X)$ and any $B_i \in \mathcal{F}(Y)$, $i \in I$, the following properties of functions obtained by the extension principle hold:

(i) $f(A) = \varnothing$ iff $A = \varnothing$;

(ii) if $A_1 \subseteq A_2$, then $f(A_1) \subseteq f(A_2)$;

(iii) $f(\bigcup_{i \in I} A_i) = \bigcup_{i \in I} f(A_i)$;

(iv) $f(\bigcap_{i \in I} A_i) \subseteq \bigcap_{i \in I} f(A_i)$;

(v) if $B_1 \subseteq B_2$, then $f^{-1}(B_1) \subseteq f^{-1}(B_2)$;

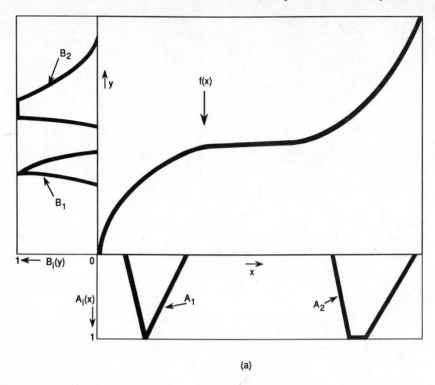

(a)

Figure 2.5   Illustration of the extension principle when f is continuous.

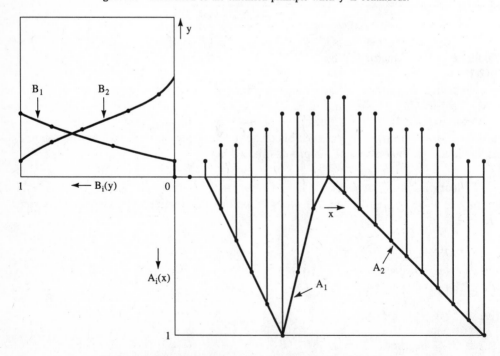

Figure 2.6   Illustration of the extension principle when f is discrete.

(vi) $f^{-1}(\bigcup\limits_{i\in I} B_i) = \bigcup\limits_{i\in I} f^{-1}(B_i)$;

(vii) $f^{-1}(\bigcap\limits_{i\in I} B_i) = \bigcap\limits_{i\in I} f^{-1}(B_i)$;

(viii) $\overline{f^{-1}(B)} = f^{-1}(\overline{B})$;

(ix) $A \subseteq f^{-1}(f(A))$;

(x) $B \supseteq f(f^{-1}(B))$.

Proof: Left to the reader. ∎

The following theorem shows that the extension principle is strong cutworthy, but not cutworthy.

Theorem 2.9.   Let $f : X \to Y$ be an arbitrary crisp function. Then, for any $A \in \mathcal{F}(X)$ and all $\alpha \in [0, 1]$ the following properties of f fuzzified by the extension principle hold:

(xi) $^{\alpha+}[f(A)] = f(^{\alpha+}A)$;

(xii) $^{\alpha}[f(A)] \supseteq f(^{\alpha}A)$.

Proof: (xi) For all $y \in Y$,

$$y \in {}^{\alpha+}[f(A)] \Leftrightarrow [f(A)](y) > \alpha$$

$$\Leftrightarrow \sup_{x|y=f(x)} A(x) > \alpha$$

$$\Leftrightarrow (\exists x_0 \in X)(y = f(x_0) \text{ and } A(x_0) > \alpha)$$

$$\Leftrightarrow (\exists x_0 \in X)(y = f(x_0) \text{ and } x_0 \in {}^{\alpha+}A)$$

$$\Leftrightarrow y \in f(^{\alpha+}A).$$

Hence, $^{\alpha+}[f(A)] = f(^{\alpha+}A)$.

(xii) If $y \in f(^{\alpha}A)$, then there exists $x_0 \in {}^{\alpha}A$ such that $y = f(x_0)$. Hence,

$$[f(A)](y) = \sup_{x|y=f(x)} A(x) \geq A(x_0) \geq \alpha$$

and, consequently, $y \in {}^{\alpha}[f(A)]$. Therefore, $f(^{\alpha}A) \subseteq {}^{\alpha}[f(A)]$. ∎

To show that $^{\alpha}[f(A)] \neq f(^{\alpha}A)$ in general, we can use the following example. Let $X = \mathbb{N}, Y = \{a, b\}$,

$$f(n) = \begin{cases} a & \text{when } n \leq 10 \\ b & \text{when } n > 10, \end{cases}$$

and

$$A(n) = 1 - \frac{1}{n}$$

for all $n \in \mathbb{N}$. Then,

$$[f(A)](a) = \sup_{n|a=f(n)} A(n) = \frac{9}{10},$$

$$[f(A)](b) = \sup_{n|b=f(n)} A(n) = 1.$$

Taking now $\alpha = 1$, we can see that $^1[f(A)] = \{b\}$ while $f(^1A) = \varnothing$ (since $^1A = \varnothing$). Hence, $f(^\alpha A) \neq {}^\alpha[f(A)]$ in this case.

As can be easily proven, $^\alpha[f(A)] = f(^\alpha A)$ for all $\alpha \in [0, 1]$ when X is finite. However, this is not a necessary condition for obtaining the equality.

Theorem 2.10.   Let $f : X \to Y$ be an arbitrary crisp function.   Then, for any $A \in \mathcal{F}(X)$, f fuzzified by the extension principle satisfies the equation

$$f(A) = \bigcup_{\alpha \in [0,1]} f(_{\alpha+}A). \tag{2.12}$$

Proof: Applying the Second Decomposition Theorem (Theorem 2.6) to $f(A)$, which is a fuzzy set on Y, we obtain

$$f(A) = \bigcup_{\alpha \in [0,1]} {}_{\alpha+}[f(A)].$$

By definition,

$$_{\alpha+}[f(A)] = \alpha \cdot {}^{\alpha+}[f(A)]$$

and, due to (xi) of Theorem 2.9, we have

$$f(A) = \bigcup_{\alpha \in [0,1]} \alpha \cdot f(^{\alpha+}A).$$

Equation (2.12) follows now immediately.   ■

The significance of Theorem 2.10 is that it provides us with an efficient procedure for calculating $f(A)$: first we calculate all images of strong α-cuts (i.e., crisp sets) under function f, convert them to the special fuzzy sets $_{\alpha+}A$, and then employ (2.12).

When a given function is defined on a Cartesian product (i.e., when $X = X_1 \times X_2 \times \ldots \times X_n$), the extension principle is still applicable. The only change is that symbols x in (2.10) and (2.11) stand now for the n-tuples $\mathbf{x} = \langle x_1, x_2, \ldots, x_n \rangle$, where $x_i \in X_i, i \in \mathbb{N}_n$, and, hence, fuzzy sets in (2.10) are defined on the Cartesian product. Such fuzzy sets are referred to as *fuzzy relations*; they are a subject of Chapter 5, where some additional aspects of the extension principle are discussed.

NOTES

2.1. A representation of fuzzy sets in terms of their α-cuts was introduced by Zadeh [1971c] in the form of the first decomposition theorem.

2.2. The *extension principle* was introduced by Zadeh [1975b].   A further elaboration of the principle was presented by Yager [1986a].

2.3. The extension principle is an important tool by which classical mathematical theories can be fuzzified. Fuzzy extensions of some mathematical theories are beyond the scope of this introductory text and are thus not covered here. They include, for example, *fuzzy topological spaces* [Chang, 1968; Wong, 1975; Lowen, 1976], *fuzzy metric spaces* [Kaleva and Seikkala, 1984], and various fuzzy algebraic structures such as groups, semigroups, and so on.

EXERCISES

2.1. What are the roles of α-cuts and strong α-cuts in fuzzy set theory? What is the difference between them? Describe these concepts in your own words.

2.2. Prove (iv) in Theorem 2.1.

2.3. Explain why the standard complement is not cutworthy and strong cutworthy.

2.4. Let A be a fuzzy set defined by

$$A = .5/x_1 + .4/x_2 + .7/x_3 + .8/x_4 + 1/x_5.$$

List all α-cuts and strong α-cuts of A.

2.5. Prove (vi) in Theorem 2.2. Find an example to show that the set inclusion in (vii) cannot be replaced with equality.

2.6. Prove (xi) in Theorem 2.4.

2.7. Prove Theorem 2.7.

2.8. Let the membership grade functions of fuzzy sets A, B, and C in Exercise 1.10 be defined on the universal set $X = \{0, 1, 2, \ldots, 10\}$, and let $f(x) = x^2$ for all $x \in X$. Use the extension principle to derive $f(A)$, $f(B)$, and $f(C)$. Given a fuzzy set D defined on $\{0, 1, 4, 9, 16, \ldots, 100\}$ by

$$D = .5/4 + .6/16 + .7/25 + 1/100,$$

find $f^{-1}(D)$.

2.9. Prove Theorem 2.8.

2.10. Show that the set inclusions in (ix) and (x) cannot be replaced with the equalities.

2.11. Let A and B be fuzzy sets defined on the universal set $X = \mathbb{Z}$ whose membership functions are given by

$$A(x) = .5/(-1) + 1/0 + .5/1 + .3/2 \text{ and}$$

$$B(x) = .5/2 + 1/3 + .5/4 + .3/5.$$

Let a function $f : X \times X \to X$ be defined for all $x_1, x_2 \in X$ by $f(x_1, x_2) = x_1 \cdot x_2$. Calculate $f(A, B)$.

2.12. Let f in the previous exercise be replaced with $f(x_1, x_2) = x_1 + x_2$. Calculate $f(A, B)$.

3

OPERATIONS ON FUZZY SETS

3.1 TYPES OF OPERATIONS

In Sec. 1.4, the following special operations of fuzzy complement, intersection, and union are introduced:

$$\overline{A}(x) = 1 - A(x), \tag{3.1}$$

$$(A \cap B)(x) = \min[A(x), B(x)], \tag{3.2}$$

$$(A \cup B)(x) = \max[A(x), B(x)] \tag{3.3}$$

for all $x \in X$. These operations are called the *standard fuzzy operations*.

As the reader can easily see, the standard fuzzy operations perform precisely as the corresponding operations for crisp sets when the range of membership grades is restricted to the set $\{0, 1\}$. That is, the standard fuzzy operations are generalizations of the corresponding classical set operations. It is now well understood, however, that they are not the only possible generalizations. For each of the three operations, there exists a broad class of functions whose members qualify as fuzzy generalizations of the classical operations as well. These three classes of functions are examined in Secs. 3.2 through 3.4, where each of the classes is characterized by properly justified axioms. Functions that qualify as fuzzy intersections and fuzzy unions are usually referred to in the literature as *t-norms* and *t-conorms*, respectively.

Since the fuzzy complement, intersection, and union are not unique operations, contrary to their crisp counterparts, different functions may be appropriate to represent these operations in different contexts. That is, not only membership functions of fuzzy sets but also operations on fuzzy sets are context-dependent. The capability to determine appropriate membership functions and meaningful fuzzy operations in the context of each particular application is crucial for making fuzzy set theory practically useful. This fundamental issue is addressed in Chapter 10.

Among the great variety of fuzzy complements, intersections, and unions, the standard fuzzy operations possess certain properties that give them a special significance. For example, they are the only operations that satisfy the cutworthy and strong cutworthy properties expressed by Theorems 2.1 and 2.2. Furthermore, the standard fuzzy intersection (min operator) produces for any given fuzzy sets the largest fuzzy set from among those produced by all possible fuzzy intersections (*t*-norms). The standard fuzzy union (max operator) produces, on the contrary, the smallest fuzzy set among the fuzzy sets produced by all possible fuzzy unions (*t*-conorms). That is, the standard fuzzy operations occupy specific positions in the whole spectrum of fuzzy operations: the standard fuzzy intersection is the weakest fuzzy intersection, while the standard fuzzy union is the strongest fuzzy union.

A desirable feature of the standard fuzzy operations is their inherent prevention of the compounding of errors of the operands. If any error *e* is associated with the membership grades $A(x)$ and $B(x)$, then the maximum error associated with the membership grade of x in $\overline{A}, A \cap B$, and $A \cup B$ remains *e*. Most of the alternative fuzzy set operations lack this characteristic.

Fuzzy intersections (*t*-norms) and fuzzy unions (*t*-conorms) do not cover all operations by which fuzzy sets can be aggregated, but they cover all aggregating operations that are associative. Due to the lack of associativity, the remaining aggregating operations must be defined as functions of *n* arguments for each $n > 2$. Aggregation operations that, for any given membership grades $a_1, a_2, \ldots, a_n$, produce a membership grade that lies between $\min(a_1, a_2, \ldots, a_n)$ and $\max(a_1, a_2, \ldots, a_n)$ are called *averaging operations*. For any given fuzzy sets, each of the averaging operations produces a fuzzy set that is larger than any fuzzy intersection and smaller than any fuzzy union. The class of averaging operations is examined in Sec. 3.6.

3.2 FUZZY COMPLEMENTS

Let A be a fuzzy set on X. Then, by definition, $A(x)$ is interpreted as *the degree to which x belongs to A*. Let cA denote a fuzzy *complement* of A of type c. Then, $cA(x)$ may be interpreted not only as the degree to which x belongs to cA, but also as *the degree to which x does not belong to A*. Similarly, $A(x)$ may also be interpreted as the degree to which x does not belong to cA.

As a notational convention, let a complement cA be defined by a function

$$c : [0, 1] \rightarrow [0, 1],$$

which assigns a value $c(A(x))$ to each membership grade $A(x)$ of any given fuzzy set A. The value $c(A(x))$ is interpreted as the value of $cA(x)$. That is,

$$c(A(x)) = cA(x) \tag{3.4}$$

for all $x \in X$ by definition. Given a fuzzy set A, we obtain cA by applying function c to values $A(x)$ for all $x \in X$.

Observe that function c is totally independent of elements x to which values $A(x)$ are assigned; it depends only on the values themselves. In the following investigation of its formal properties, we may thus ignore x and assume that the argument of c is an arbitrary number $a \in [0, 1]$. However, to use the function for determining a complement of a given fuzzy set A, we have to keep track of elements x to make the connection between $A(x)$ and $cA(x)$ expressed by (3.4).

It is obvious that function c must possess certain properties to produce fuzzy sets that qualify, on intuitive grounds, as meaningful complements of given fuzzy sets.   To characterize functions c that produce meaningful fuzzy complements, we may state any intuitively justifiable properties in terms of axiomatic requirements, and then examine the class of functions that satisfy these requirements.

To produce meaningful fuzzy complements, function c must satisfy at least the following two axiomatic requirements:

Axiom c1. $c(0) = 1$ and $c(1) = 0$ (*boundary conditions*).

Axiom c2.   For all $a, b \in [0, 1]$, if $a \leq b$, then $c(a) \geq c(b)$ (*monotonicity*).

According to Axiom c1, function c is required to produce correct complements for crisp sets. According to Axiom c2, it is required to be *monotonic decreasing*: when a membership grade in A increases (by changing x), the corresponding membership grade in cA must not increase as well; it may decrease or, at least, remain the same.

There are many functions that satisfy both Axioms c1 and c2. For any particular fuzzy set A, different fuzzy sets cA can be said to constitute its complement, each being produced by a distinct function c. All functions that satisfy the axioms form the most general class of fuzzy complements.   It is rather obvious that the exclusion or weakening of either of these axioms would add to this class some functions totally unacceptable as complements. Indeed, a violation of Axiom c1 would include functions that do not conform to the ordinary complement for crisp sets. Axiom c2 is essential since we intuitively expect that an increase in the degree of membership in a fuzzy set must result in either a decrease or, in the extreme case, no change in the degree of membership in its complement. Let Axioms c1 and c2 be called the *axiomatic skeleton for fuzzy complements*.

In most cases of practical significance, it is desirable to consider various additional requirements for fuzzy complements.   Each of them reduces the general class of fuzzy complements to a special subclass. Two of the most desirable requirements, which are usually listed in the literature among axioms of fuzzy complements, are the following:

Axiom c3. c is a continuous function.

Axiom c4. c is *involutive*, which means that $c(c(a)) = a$ for each $a \in [0, 1]$.

It turns out that the four axioms are not independent, as expressed by the following theorem.

Theorem 3.1.   Let a function $c : [0, 1] \rightarrow [0, 1]$ satisfy Axioms c2 and c4. Then, c also satisfies Axioms c1 and c3. Moreover, c must be a bijective function.

Proof:

(i) Since the range of c is $[0, 1]$, $c(0) \leq 1$ and $c(1) \geq 0$. By Axiom c2, $c(c(0)) \geq c(1)$; and, by Axiom c4, $0 = c(c(0)) \geq c(1)$. Hence, $c(1) = 0$. Now, again by Axiom c4, we have $c(0) = c(c(1)) = 1$. That is, function c satisfies Axiom c1.

(ii) To prove that c is a bijective function, we observe that for all $a \in [0, 1]$ there exists $b = c(a) \in [0, 1]$ such that $c(b) = c(c(a)) = a$. Hence, c is an onto function. Assume now that $c(a_1) = c(a_2)$; then, by Axiom c4,

$$a_1 = c(c(a_1)) = c(c(a_2)) = a_2.$$

That is, c is also a one-to-one function; consequently, it is a bijective function.

(iii) Since c is bijective and satisfies Axiom c2, it cannot have any discontinuous points. To show this, assume that c has a discontinuity at a_0, as illustrated in Fig. 3.1. Then, we have

$$b_0 = \lim_{a \to a_0-} c(a) > c(a_0)$$

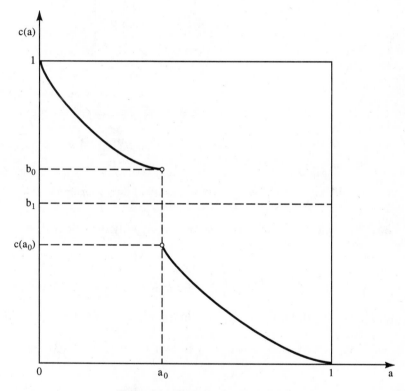

Figure 3.1 Illustration to Theorem 3.1.

and, clearly, there must exist $b_1 \in [0, 1]$ such that $b_0 > b_1 > c(a_0)$ for which no $a_1 \in [0, 1]$ exists such that $c(a_1) = b_1$. This contradicts the fact that c is a bijective function. ∎

It follows from Theorem 3.1 that all involutive complements form a special subclass of all continuous complements, which in turn forms a special subclass of all fuzzy complements. This nested structure of the three types of fuzzy complements is expressed in Fig. 3.2.

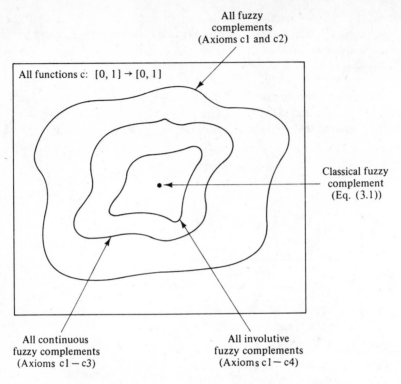

Figure 3.2   Nested structure of the basic classes of fuzzy complements.

Examples of general fuzzy complements that satisfy only the axiomatic skeleton are the threshold-type complements defined by

$$c(a) = \begin{cases} 1 & \text{for } a \leq t \\ 0 & \text{for } a > t, \end{cases}$$

where $a \in [0, 1]$ and $t \in [0, 1)$; t is called the threshold of c. This function is illustrated in Fig. 3.3a.

An example of a fuzzy complement that is continuous (Axiom c3) but not involutive (Axiom c4) is the function

$$c(a) = \frac{1}{2}(1 + \cos \pi a),$$

which is illustrated in Fig. 3.3b. The failure of this function to satisfy the property of involution can be seen by noting, for example, that $c(.33) = .75$ but $c(.75) = .15 \neq .33$.

One class of involutive fuzzy complements is the *Sugeno class* defined by

$$c_\lambda(a) = \frac{1 - a}{1 + \lambda a}, \tag{3.5}$$

where $\lambda \in (-1, \infty)$. For each value of the parameter λ, we obtain one particular involutive fuzzy complement. This class is illustrated in Fig. 3.4a for several different values of λ. Note

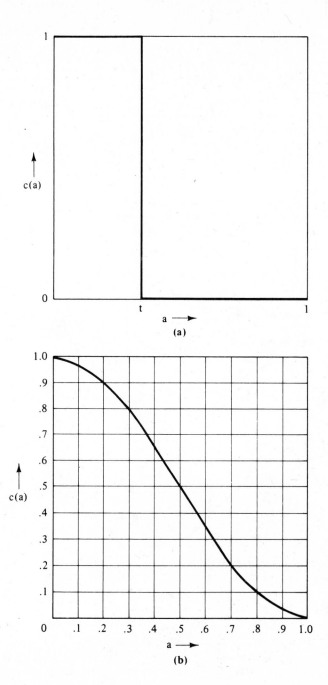

Figure 3.3 Examples of fuzzy complements: (a) a general complement of the threshold type; (b) a continuous fuzzy complement $c(a) = \dfrac{1}{2}(1 + \cos \pi a)$.

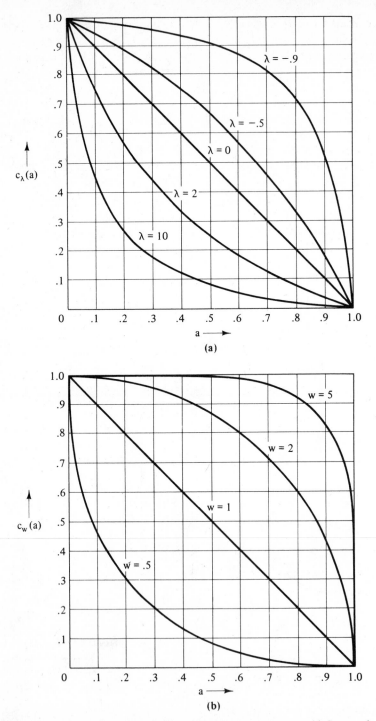

Figure 3.4 Examples from two classes of involutive fuzzy complements: (a) Sugeno class; (b) Yager class.

that the shape of the function is affected as the value of λ is changed. For $\lambda = 0$, the function becomes the classical fuzzy complement defined by (3.1).

Another example of a class of involutive fuzzy complements is defined by

$$c_w(a) = (1 - a^w)^{1/w}, \tag{3.6}$$

where $w \in (0, \infty)$; let us refer to it as the *Yager class* of fuzzy complements. Figure 3.4b illustrates this class of functions for various values of w. Here again, changing the value of the parameter w results in a deformation of the shape of the function. When $w = 1$, this function becomes the classical fuzzy complement of $c(a) = 1 - a$.

Several important properties are shared by all fuzzy complements. These concern the *equilibrium* of a fuzzy complement c, which is defined as any value a for which $c(a) = a$. In other words, the equilibrium of a complement c is that degree of membership in a fuzzy set A which equals the degree of membership in the complement cA. For instance, the equilibrium value for the classical fuzzy complement given by (2.1) is .5, which is the solution of the equation $1 - a = a$.

Theorem 3.2.   Every fuzzy complement has at most one equilibrium.

Proof: Let c be an arbitrary fuzzy complement. An equilibrium of c is a solution of the equation

$$c(a) - a = 0,$$

where $a \in [0, 1]$. We can demonstrate that any equation $c(a) - a = b$, where b is a real constant, must have at most one solution, thus proving the theorem. In order to do so, we assume that a_1 and a_2 are two different solutions of the equation $c(a) - a = b$ such that $a_1 < a_2$. Then, since $c(a_1) - a_1 = b$ and $c(a_2) - a_2 = b$, we get

$$c(a_1) - a_1 = c(a_2) - a_2. \tag{3.7}$$

However, because c is monotonic nonincreasing (by Axiom c2), $c(a_1) \geq c(a_2)$ and, since $a_1 < a_2$,

$$c(a_1) - a_1 > c(a_2) - a_2.$$

This inequality contradicts (3.7), thus demonstrating that the equation must have at most one solution. ∎

Theorem 3.3.   Assume that a given fuzzy complement c has an equilibrium e_c, which by Theorem 3.2 is unique. Then

$$a \leq c(a) \text{ iff } a \leq e_c$$

and

$$a \geq c(a) \text{ iff } a \geq e_c.$$

Proof: Let us assume that $a < e_c, a = e_c$, and $a > e_c$, in turn. Then, since c is monotonic nonincreasing by Axiom c2, $c(a) \geq c(e_c)$ for $a < e_c, c(a) = c(e_c)$ for $a = e_c$, and $c(a) \leq c(e_c)$ for $a > e_c$. Because $c(e_c) = e_c$, we can rewrite these expressions as $c(a) \geq e_c, c(a) = e_c$, and $c(a) \leq e_c$, respectively. In fact, due to our initial assumption we can further rewrite these as $c(a) > a$, $c(a) = a$, and $c(a) < a$, respectively. Thus, $a \leq e_c$ implies $c(a) \geq a$ and $a \geq e_c$ implies $c(a) \leq a$. The inverse implications can be shown in a similar manner. ∎

Theorem 3.4.   If c is a continuous fuzzy complement, then c has a unique equilibrium.

Proof: The equilibrium e_c of a fuzzy complement c is the solution of the equation $c(a) - a = 0$. This is a special case of the more general equation $c(a) - a = b$, where $b \in [-1, 1]$ is a constant. By Axiom c1, $c(0) - 0 = 1$ and $c(1) - 1 = -1$. Since c is a continuous complement, it follows from the intermediate value theorem for continuous functions that for each $b \in [-1, 1]$, there exists at least one a such that $c(a) - a = b$. This demonstrates the necessary existence of an equilibrium value for a continuous function, and Theorem 3.2 guarantees its uniqueness. ∎

The equilibrium for each individual fuzzy complement c_λ of the Sugeno class is given by

$$e_{c_\lambda} = \begin{cases} ((1 + \lambda)^{1/2} - 1)/\lambda & \text{for } \lambda \neq 0, \\ 1/2 & \text{for } \lambda = 0 \end{cases}$$

This is clearly obtained by selecting the positive solution of the equation

$$\frac{1 - e_{c_\lambda}}{1 + \lambda e_{c_\lambda}} = e_{c_\lambda}.$$

The dependence of the equilibrium e_{c_λ} on the parameter λ is shown in Fig. 3.5.

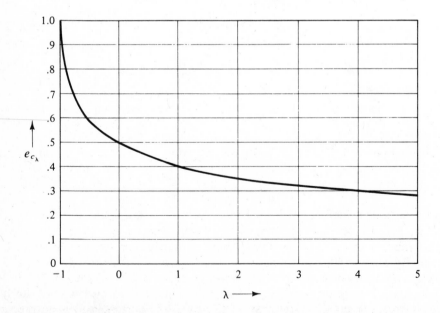

Figure 3.5   Equilibria for the Sugeno class of fuzzy complements.

If we are given a fuzzy complement c and a membership grade whose value is represented by a real number $a \in [0, 1]$, then any membership grade represented by the real number $^da \in [0, 1]$ such that

$$c(^da) - {}^da = a - c(a) \qquad (3.8)$$

is called a *dual point* of a with respect to c.

It follows directly from the proof of Theorem 3.2 that (3.8) has at most one solution for ^da given c and a. There is, therefore, at most one dual point for each particular fuzzy complement c and membership grade of value a. Moreover, it follows from the proof of Theorem 3.4 that a dual point exists for each $a \in [0, 1]$ when c is a continuous complement.

Theorem 3.5.   If a complement c has an equilibrium e_c, then

$$^de_c = e_c.$$

Proof: If $a = e_c$, then by our definition of equilibrium, $c(a) = a$ and thus $a - c(a) = 0$. Additionally, if $^da = e_c$, then $c(^da) = {}^da$ and $c(^da) - {}^da = 0$. Therefore,

$$c(^da) - {}^da = a - c(a).$$

This satisfies (3.8) when $a = {}^da = e_c$. Hence, the equilibrium of any complement is its own dual point. ∎

Theorem 3.6.   For each $a \in [0, 1]$, $^da = c(a)$ iff $c(c(a)) = a$, that is, when the complement is involutive.

Proof: Let $^da = c(a)$. Then, substitution of $c(a)$ for ^da in (3.8) produces

$$c(c(a)) - c(a) = a - c(a).$$

Therefore, $c(c(a)) = a$. For the reverse implication, let $c(c(a)) = a$. Then substitution of $c(c(a))$ for a in (3.8) yields the functional equation

$$c(^da) - {}^da = c(c(a)) - c(a).$$

for ^da whose solution is $^da = c(a)$. ∎

Thus, the dual point of any membership grade is equal to its complemented value whenever the complement is involutive. If the complement is not involutive, either the dual point does not exist or it does not coincide with the complement point.

These results associated with the concepts of the equilibrium and the dual point of a fuzzy complement are referenced in the discussion of measures of fuzziness contained in Chapter 9.

Since involutive fuzzy complements play by far the most important role in practical applications, let us restrict our further discussion to complements of this type. Perhaps the most important property of involutive complements is expressed by the following two theorems. By either of these theorems, we can generate an unlimited number of fuzzy complements or classes of fuzzy complements, such as the Sugeno class or the Yager class.

Theorem 3.7 (First Characterization Theorem of Fuzzy Complements).   Let c be a function from $[0, 1]$ to $[0, 1]$. Then, c is a fuzzy complement (involutive) iff there exists a continuous function g from $[0, 1]$ to $\mathbb{R}$ such that $g(0) = 0$, g is strictly increasing, and

$$c(a) = g^{-1}(g(1) - g(a)) \tag{3.9}$$

for all $a \in [0, 1]$.

   Proof: See Appendix D. ■

   Functions g defined in Theorem 3.7 are usually called *increasing generators*. Each function g that qualifies as an increasing generator determines a fuzzy complement by (3.9).
   For the standard fuzzy complement, the increasing generator is $g(a) = a$. For the Sugeno class of fuzzy complements, the increasing generators are

$$g_\lambda(a) = \frac{1}{\lambda} \ln(1 + \lambda a) \tag{3.10}$$

for $\lambda > -1$. Note that we have to take

$$\lim_{\lambda \to 0} g_\lambda(a) = a$$

for $\lambda = 0$; that is, the standard fuzzy complement can be generated by this limit. For the Yager class, the increasing generators are

$$g_w(a) = a^w \tag{3.11}$$

for $w > 0$.
   It is interesting that by taking the class of two-parameter increasing generators

$$g_{\lambda,w}(a) = \frac{1}{\lambda} \ln(1 + \lambda a^w)$$

for $\lambda > -1$ and $w > 0$, we obtain a class of fuzzy complements,

$$c_{\lambda,w}(a) = \left(\frac{1 - a^w}{1 + \lambda a^w} \right)^{1/w} \quad (\lambda > -1, w > 0), \tag{3.12}$$

which contains the Sugeno class (for $w = 1$) as well as the Yager class (for $\lambda = 0$) as special subclasses.
   As one additional example, let us consider the class of the increasing generators

$$g_\gamma(a) = \frac{a}{\gamma + (1 - \gamma)a} \quad (\gamma > 0), \tag{3.13}$$

which produce the class of fuzzy complements

$$c_\gamma(a) = \frac{\gamma^2(1 - a)}{a + \gamma^2(1 - a)} \quad (\gamma > 0). \tag{3.14}$$

We suggest that the reader plot function c_γ for several values of γ.
   As expressed by the following theorem, fuzzy complements can also be produced by *decreasing generators*.

   Theorem 3.8 (Second Characterization Theorem of Fuzzy Complements).   Let c be a function from $[0, 1]$ to $[0, 1]$. Then c is a fuzzy complement iff there exists a continuous function f from $[0, 1]$ to $\mathbb{R}$ such that $f(1) = 0$, f is strictly decreasing, and

$$c(a) = f^{-1}(f(0) - f(a)) \tag{3.15}$$

for all $a \in [0, 1]$.

Proof: According to Theorem 3.7, function c is a fuzzy complement iff there exists an increasing generator g such that $c(a) = g^{-1}(g(1) - g(a))$. Now, let $f(a) = g(1) - g(a)$. Then, $f(1) = 0$ and, since g is strictly increasing, f is strictly decreasing. Moreover,

$$f^{-1}(a) = g^{-1}(g(1) - a)$$
$$= g^{-1}(f(0) - a)$$

since $f(0) = g(1) - g(0) = g(1)$, $f(f^{-1}(a)) = g(1) - g(f^{-1}(a)) = g(1) - g(g^{-1}(g(1) - a)) = a$, and $f^{-1}(f(a)) = g^{-1}(g(1) - f(a)) = g^{-1}(g(1) - (g(1) - g(a))) = g^{-1}(g(a)) = a$. Now,

$$c(a) = g^{-1}(g(1) - g(a))$$
$$= f^{-1}(g(a))$$
$$= f^{-1}(g(1) - (g(1) - g(a)))$$
$$= f^{-1}(f(0) - f(a)).$$

If a decreasing generator f is given, we can define an increasing generator g as

$$g(a) = f(0) - f(a).$$

Then, (3.15) can be rewritten as

$$c(a) = f^{-1}(f(0) - f(a))$$
$$= g^{-1}(g(1) - g(a)).$$

Hence, c defined by (3.15) is a fuzzy complement. ∎

For example, applying (3.15) to any of the strictly decreasing functions

$$f(a) = -ka + k,$$

where $k > 0$, generates the standard fuzzy complement, and applying it to the functions

$$f(a) = 1 - a^w,$$

where $w > 0$, generates the Yager class of fuzzy complements.

Functions f defined in Theorem 3.8 are usually called *decreasing generators*. Each function f that qualifies as a decreasing generator also determines a fuzzy complement by (3.15).

3.3 FUZZY INTERSECTIONS: t-NORMS

The intersection of two fuzzy sets A and B is specified in general by a binary operation on the unit interval; that is, a function of the form

$$i : [0, 1] \times [0, 1] \to [0, 1].$$

For each element x of the universal set, this function takes as its argument the pair consisting of the element's membership grades in set A and in set B, and yield the membership grade of the element in the set constituting the intersection of A and B. Thus,

$$(A \cap B)(x) = i[A(x), B(x)] \tag{3.16}$$

for all $x \in X$.

In order for any function i of this form to qualify as a fuzzy intersection, it must possess appropriate properties, which ensure that fuzzy sets produced by i are intuitively acceptable as meaningful fuzzy intersections of any given pair of fuzzy sets. It turns out that functions known as t-norms, which have extensively been studied in the literature, do possess such properties. In fact, the class of t-norms is now generally accepted as equivalent to the class of fuzzy intersections. We may thus use the terms "t-norms" and "fuzzy intersections" interchangeably.

Given a t-norm i and fuzzy sets A and B, we have to apply (3.16) for each $x \in X$ to determine the intersection of A and B based upon i. This requires keeping track of each element x. However, the function i is totally independent of x; it depends only on the values $A(x)$ and $B(x)$. Hence, we may ignore x and assume that the arguments of i are arbitrary numbers $a, b \in [0, 1]$ in the following examination of formal properties of t-norms.

A *fuzzy intersection/t-norm* i is a binary operation on the unit interval that satisfies at least the following axioms for all $a, b, d \in [0, 1]$:

Axiom i1. $i(a, 1) = a$ *(boundary condition)*.

Axiom i2. $b \leq d$ implies $i(a, b) \leq i(a, d)$ *(monotonicity)*.

Axiom i3. $i(a, b) = i(b, a)$ *(commutativity)*.

Axiom i4. $i(a, i(b, d)) = i(i(a, b), d)$ *(associativity)*.

Let us call this set of axioms the *axiomatic skeleton for fuzzy intersections/t-norms*.

It is easy to see that the first three axioms ensure that the fuzzy intersection defined by (3.16) becomes the classical set intersection when sets A and B are crisp: $i(0, 1) = 0$ and $i(1, 1) = 1$ follow directly from the boundary condition; $i(1, 0) = 0$ follows then from commutativity, while $i(0, 0) = 0$ follows from monotonicity. When one argument of i is 1 (expressing a full membership), the boundary condition and commutativity also ensure, as our intuitive conception of fuzzy intersection requires, that the membership grade in the intersection is equal to the other argument.

Monotonicity and commutativity express the natural requirement that a decrease in the degree of membership in set A or B cannot produce an increase in the degree of membership in the intersection. Commutativity ensures that the fuzzy intersection is symmetric, that is, indifferent to the order in which the sets to be combined are considered. The last axiom, associativity, ensures that we can take the intersection of any number of sets in any order of pairwise grouping desired; this axiom allows us to extend the operation of fuzzy intersection to more than two sets.

It is often desirable to restrict the class of fuzzy intersections (t-norms) by considering various additional requirements. Three of the most important requirements are expressed by the following axioms:

Axiom i5. i is a continuous function (*continuity*).

Axiom i6. $i(a, a) < a$ (*subidempotency*).

Axiom i7. $a_1 < a_2$ and $b_1 < b_2$ implies $i(a_1, b_1) < i(a_2, b_2)$ (*strict monotonicity*).

The axiom of continuity prevents a situation in which a very small change in the membership grade of either set A or set B would produce a large (discontinuous) change in the membership grade is $A \cap B$. Axiom i6 deals with a special case in which both membership grades in A and B (for some x) have the same value a. The axiom expresses the requirement that the membership grade in $A \cap B$ in this special case must not exceed a. Since this requirement is weaker than *idempotency*, the requirement that $i(a, a) = a$, we call it *subidempotency*. Axiom i7 just expresses a stronger form of monotonicity.

A continuous t-norm that satisfies subidempotency is called an *Archimedean t-norm*; if it also satisfies strict monotonicity, it is called a *strict Archimedean t-norm*. The following theorem reveals another significant property of the standard fuzzy intersection.

Theorem 3.9.   The standard fuzzy intersection is the only idempotent t-norm.

Proof: Clearly, $\min(a, a) = a$ for all $a \in [0, 1]$. Assume that there exists a t-norm such that $i(a, a) = a$ for all $a \in [0, 1]$. Then, for any $a, b \in [0, 1]$, if $a \leq b$, then

$$a = i(a, a) \leq i(a, b) \leq i(a, 1) = a$$

by monotonicity and the boundary condition. Hence, $i(a, b) = a = \min(a, b)$. Similarly, if $a \geq b$, then

$$b = i(b, b) \leq i(a, b) \leq i(1, b) = b$$

and, consequently, $i(a, b) = b = \min(a, b)$. Hence, $i(a, b) = \min(a, b)$ for all $a, b \in [0, 1]$. ∎

The following are examples of some t-norms that are frequently used as fuzzy intersections (each defined for all $a, b \in [0, 1]$).

Standard intersection : $i(a, b) = \min(a, b)$.
Algebraic product : $i(a, b) = ab$.
Bounded difference : $i(a, b) = \max(0, a + b - 1)$.
Drastic intersection : $i(a, b) = \begin{cases} a & \text{when } b = 1 \\ b & \text{when } a = 1 \\ 0 & \text{otherwise.} \end{cases}$

Graphs of these four fuzzy intersections are shown in Fig. 3.6. We can see from these graphs that

$$i_{\min}(a, b) \leq \max(0, a + b - 1) \leq ab \leq \min(a, b)$$

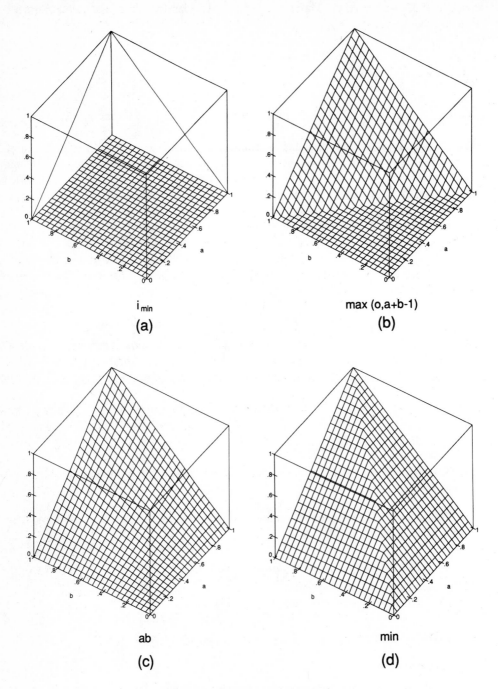

Figure 3.6 Graphs of fuzzy intersections.

for all $a, b \in [0, 1]$, where i_{min} denotes the drastic intersection. These inequalities can also be proven mathematically. The full range of all fuzzy intersections is specified in the next theorem.

Theorem 3.10.   For all $a, b \in [0, 1]$,

$$i_{min}(a, b) \leq i(a, b) \leq \min(a, b), \tag{3.17}$$

where i_{min} denotes the drastic intersection.

Proof: Upper bound. By the boundary condition and monotonicity,

$$i(a, b) \leq i(a, 1) = a$$

and, by commutativity,

$$i(a, b) = i(b, a) \leq i(b, 1) = b.$$

Hence, $i(a, b) \leq a$ and $i(a, b) \leq b$; that is, $i(a, b) \leq \min(a, b)$.

Lower bound. From the boundary condition, $i(a, b) = a$ when $b = 1$, and $i(a, b) = b$ when $a = 1$. Since $i(a, b) \leq \min(a, b)$ and $i(a, b) \in [0, 1]$, clearly,

$$i(a, 0) = i(0, b) = 0.$$

By monotonicity,

$$i(a, b) \geq i(a, 0) = i(0, b) = 0.$$

Hence, the drastic intersection $i_{min}(a, b)$ is the lower bound of $i(a, b)$ for any $a, b \in [0, 1]$. ∎

We proceed now to one of the fundamental theorems of t-norms, which provides us with a method for generating Archimedean t-norms or classes of t-norms. Before formulating the theorem, let us discuss relevant definitions. A *decreasing generator*, introduced in Theorem 3.8, is a continuous and strictly decreasing function f from $[0, 1]$ to $\mathbb{R}$ such that $f(1) = 0$. The pseudo-inverse of a decreasing generator f, denoted by $f^{(-1)}$, is a function from $\mathbb{R}$ to $[0, 1]$ given by

$$f^{(-1)}(a) = \begin{cases} 1 & \text{for } a \in (-\infty, 0) \\ f^{-1}(a) & \text{for } a \in [0, f(0)] \\ 0 & \text{for } a \in (f(0), \infty) \end{cases}$$

where f^{-1} is the ordinary inverse of f. The concept of a decreasing generator and its pseudo-inverse is illustrated in Fig. 3.7. Specific examples of decreasing generators are:

$$f_1(a) = 1 - a^p, \text{ for any } a \in [0, 1] \quad (p > 0),$$

$$f_2(a) = -\ln a \text{ for any } a \in [0, 1] \text{ with } f_2(0) = \infty.$$

Their pseudo-inverses are, respectively,

$$f_1^{(-1)}(a) = \begin{cases} 1 & \text{for } a \in (-\infty, 0) \\ (1 - a)^{1/p} & \text{for } a \in [0, 1] \\ 0 & \text{for } a \in (1, \infty), \end{cases}$$

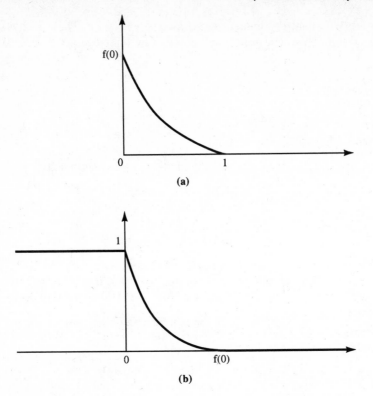

Figure 3.7 Example of (a) a decreasing generator and (b) its pseudo-inverse.

$$f_2^{(-1)}(a) = \begin{cases} 1 & \text{for } a \in (-\infty, 0) \\ e^{-a} & \text{for } a \in (0, \infty). \end{cases}$$

A decreasing generator f and its pseudo-inverse $f^{(-1)}$ satisfy $f^{(-1)}(f(a)) = a$ for any $a \in [0, 1]$, and

$$f(f^{(-1)}(a)) = \begin{cases} 0 & \text{for } a \in (-\infty, 0) \\ a & \text{for } a \in [0, f(0)] \\ f(0) & \text{for } a \in (f(0), \infty). \end{cases}$$

An *increasing generator*, introduced in Theorem 3.7, is a continuous and strictly increasing function g from $[0, 1]$ to $\mathbb{R}$ such that $g(0) = 0$. The pseudo-inverse of an increasing generator g, denoted by $g^{(-1)}$, is a function from $\mathbb{R}$ to $[0, 1]$ defined by

$$g^{(-1)}(a) = \begin{cases} 0 & \text{for } a \in (-\infty, 0) \\ g^{-1}(a) & \text{for } a \in [0, g(1)] \\ 1 & \text{for } a \in (g(1), \infty) \end{cases}$$

where g^{-1} is the ordinary inverse of g.

Examples of increasing generators are:

$$g_1(a) = a^p \ (p > 0) \text{ for any } a \in [0, 1],$$

$$g_2(a) = -\ln(1 - a) \text{ for any } a \in [0, 1] \text{ with } g_2(1) = \infty.$$

Their pseudo-inverses are, respectively,

$$g_1^{(-1)}(a) = \begin{cases} 0 & \text{for } a \in (-\infty, 0) \\ a^{1/p} & \text{for } a \in [0, 1] \\ 1 & \text{for } a \in (1, \infty), \end{cases}$$

$$g_2^{(-1)}(a) = \begin{cases} 0 & \text{for } a \in (-\infty, 0) \\ 1 - e^{-a} & \text{for } a \in (0, \infty). \end{cases}$$

An increasing generator g and its pseudo-inverse $g^{(-1)}$ satisfy $g^{(-1)}(g(a)) = a$ for any $a \in [0, 1]$ and

$$g(g^{(-1)}(a)) = \begin{cases} 0 & \text{for } a \in (-\infty, 0) \\ a & \text{for } a \in [0, g(1)] \\ g(1) & \text{for } a \in (g(1), \infty). \end{cases}$$

As expressed by the following two lemmas, decreasing generators and increasing generators can also be converted to each other.

Lemma 3.1.   Let f be a decreasing generator. Then a function g defined by

$$g(a) = f(0) - f(a)$$

for any $a \in [0, 1]$ is an increasing generator with $g(1) = f(0)$, and its pseudo-inverse $g^{(-1)}$ is given by

$$g^{(-1)}(a) = f^{(-1)}(f(0) - a)$$

for any $a \in \mathbb{R}$.

Proof: Since f is a decreasing generator, f is continuous, strictly decreasing, and such that $f(1) = 0$. Then g must be continuous. For any $a, b \in [0, 1]$ such that $a < b$, clearly $f(a) > f(b)$ and $g(a) = f(0) - f(a) < f(0) - f(b) = g(b)$. Thus, g is strictly increasing and $g(0) = f(0) - f(0) = 0$. Therefore, g is continuous, strictly increasing, and such that $g(0) = 0$. Thus, g is an increasing generator. Moreover, $g(1) = f(0) - f(1) = f(0)$ since $f(1) = 0$. The pseudo-inverse of g is defined by

$$g^{(-1)}(a) = \begin{cases} 0 & \text{for } a \in (-\infty, 0) \\ g^{-1}(a) & \text{for } a \in [0, g(1)] \\ 1 & \text{for } a \in (g(1), \infty). \end{cases}$$

Let $b = g(a) = f(0) - f(a), a \in [0, g(1)] = [0, f(0)]$; then, we have $f(a) = f(0) - b$ and $a = f^{-1}(f(0) - b)$. Thus, for any $a \in [0, g(1)] = [0, f(0)]$, $g^{-1}(a) = f^{-1}(f(0) - a)$. On the other hand,

$$f^{(-1)}(f(0) - a) = \begin{cases} 1 & \text{for } f(0) - a \in (-\infty, 0) \\ f^{-1}(f(0) - a) & \text{for } f(0) - a \in [0, f(0)] \\ 0 & \text{for } f(0) - a \in (f(0), \infty) \end{cases}$$

$$= \begin{cases} 1 & \text{for } a \in (f(0), \infty) \\ f^{-1}(f(0) - a) & \text{for } a \in [0, f(0)] \\ 0 & \text{for } a \in (-\infty, 0) \end{cases}$$

$$= \begin{cases} 0 & \text{for } a \in (-\infty, 0) \\ g^{-1}(a) & \text{for } a \in [0, g(1)] \\ 1 & \text{for } a \in (g(1), \infty). \end{cases}$$

Therefore,

$$g^{(-1)}(a) = f^{(-1)}(f(0) - a).$$

This completes the proof. ■

Lemma 3.2.   Let g be an increasing generator. Then the function f defined by

$$f(a) = g(1) - g(a)$$

for any $a \in [0, 1]$ is a decreasing generator with $f(0) = g(1)$ and its pseudo-inverse $f^{(-1)}$ is given by

$$f^{(-1)}(a) = g^{(-1)}(g(1) - a)$$

for any $a \in \mathbb{R}$.

Proof: Analogous to the proof of Lemma 3.1. ■

Theorem 3.11 (Characterization Theorem of t-Norms).   Let i be a binary operation on the unit interval. Then, i is an Archimedean t-norm iff there exists a decreasing generator f such that

$$i(a, b) = f^{(-1)}(f(a) + f(b)) \tag{3.18}$$

for all $a, b \in [0, 1]$.

Proof: [Schweizer and Sklar, 1963; Ling, 1965]. ■

Given a decreasing generator f, we can construct a t-norm i by (3.18). The following are examples of three parametrized classes of decreasing generators and the corresponding classes of t-norms. In each case, the parameter is used as a subscript of f and i to distinguish different generators and t-norms in each class. Since these classes of t-norms are described in the literature, we identify them by their authors and relevant references.

1. [Schweizer and Sklar, 1963]: The class of decreasing generators distinguished by parameter p is defined by

$$f_p(a) = 1 - a^p \quad (p \neq 0).$$

Then

$$f_p^{(-1)}(z) = \begin{cases} 1 & \text{when } z \in (-\infty, 0) \\ (1-z)^{1/p} & \text{when } z \in [0,1] \\ 0 & \text{when } z \in (1, \infty) \end{cases}$$

and we obtain the corresponding class of t-norms by applying (3.18):

$$
\begin{aligned}
i_p(a, b) &= f_p^{(-1)}(f_p(a) + f_p(b)) \\
&= f_p^{(-1)}(2 - a^p - b^p) \\
&= \begin{cases} (a^p + b^p - 1)^{1/p} & \text{when } 2 - a^p - b^p \in [0,1] \\ 0 & \text{otherwise} \end{cases} \\
&= (\max(0, a^p + b^p - 1))^{1/p}.
\end{aligned}
$$

2. [Yager, 1980f]: Given a class of decreasing generators

$$f_w(a) = (1-a)^w \quad (w > 0),$$

we obtain

$$f_w^{(-1)}(z) = \begin{cases} 1 - z^{1/w} & \text{when } z \in [0,1] \\ 0 & \text{when } z \in (1, \infty) \end{cases}$$

and

$$
\begin{aligned}
i_w(a, b) &= f_w^{(-1)}(f_w(a) + f_w(b)) \\
&= f_w^{(-1)}((1-a)^w + (1-b)^w) \\
&= \begin{cases} 1 - ((1-a)^w + (1-b)^w)^{1/w} & \text{when } (1-a)^w + (1-b)^w \in [0,1] \\ 0 & \text{otherwise} \end{cases} \\
&= 1 - \min(1, [(1-a)^w + (1-b)^w]^{1/w}).
\end{aligned}
$$

3. [Frank, 1979]: This class of t-norms is based on the class of decreasing generators

$$f_s(a) = -\ln \frac{s^a - 1}{s - 1} \quad (s > 0, s \neq 1),$$

whose pseudo-inverses are given by

$$f_s^{(-1)}(z) = \log_s(1 + (s-1)e^{-z}).$$

Employing (3.18), we obtain

$$
\begin{aligned}
i_s(a, b) &= f_s^{(-1)}(f_s(a) + f_s(b)) \\
&= f_s^{(-1)}\left[-\ln \frac{(s^a - 1)(s^b - 1)}{(s - 1)^2} \right] \\
&= \log_s \left[1 + (s - 1)\frac{(s^a - 1)(s^b - 1)}{(s - 1)^2} \right] \\
&= \log_s \left[1 + \frac{(s^a - 1)(s^b - 1)}{s - 1} \right].
\end{aligned}
$$

Let us examine one of the three introduced classes of t-norms, the Yager class

$$i_w(a, b) = 1 - \min(1, [(1 - a)^w + (1 - b)^w]^{1/w}) \quad (w > 0). \tag{3.19}$$

It is significant that this class covers the whole range of t-norms expressed by (3.17). This property of i_w is stated in the following theorem.

Theorem 3.12.   Let i_w denote the class of Yager t-norms defined by (3.19). Then

$$i_{\min}(a, b) \leq i_w(a, b) \leq \min(a, b)$$

for all $a, b \in [0, 1]$.

Proof: *Lower bound.* It is trivial that $i_w(1, b) = b$ and $i_w(a, 1) = a$ independent of w. It is also easy to show that

$$\lim_{w \to 0} [(1 - a)^w + (1 - b)^w]^{1/w} = \infty;$$

hence,

$$\lim_{w \to 0} i_w(a, b) = 0$$

for all $a, b \in [0, 1)$.

Upper bound. From the proof of Theorem 3.17, we know that

$$\lim_{w \to \infty} \min[1, [(1 - a)^w + (1 - b)^w]^{1/w}] = \max[1 - a, 1 - b].$$

Thus, $i_\infty(a, b) = 1 - \max[1 - a, 1 - b] = \min(a, b)$, which concludes the proof. ■

The various t-norms of the Yager class, which are defined by different choices of the parameter w, may be interpreted as performing fuzzy intersections of various strengths. Table 3.1a and Fig. 3.8a illustrate how the Yager fuzzy intersections increase as the value of w increases. Thus, the value $1/w$ can be interpreted as the degree of strength of the intersection performed. Since the intersection is analogous to the logical AND (conjunction), it generally demands simultaneous satisfaction of the operands of A and B. The Yager intersection for which $w = 1$, which is the bounded difference, returns a positive value only when the summation of the membership grades in the two sets exceeds 1. Thus, it performs a strong intersection with a high demand for simultaneous set membership. In contrast to this, the Yager function for which $w \to \infty$, which is the standard fuzzy intersection, performs a weak intersection that allows the lowest degree of membership in either set to dictate the degree of membership in their intersection. In effect, then, this operation shows the least demand for simultaneous set membership.

The three classes of fuzzy intersections introduced in this section, as well as some other classes covered in the literature, are summarized in Table 3.2. They are identified by the references in which they were published. For each class, the table includes its definition, its decreasing generator (if applicable), the range of its parameter, and the resulting functions for the two extreme limits of the parameter. We can see that some classes cover the whole range of t-norms expressed by (3.17), while other classes cover only a part of the range.

As stated in the following theorem, new t-norms can also be generated on the basis of known t-norms.

TABLE 3.1   EXAMPLES OF FUZZY SET OPERATIONS FROM THE YAGER CLASS

(a) Fuzzy intersections

$b =$	0	.25	.5	.75	1
$a = 1$	0	.25	.5	.75	1
.75	0	0	.25	.5	,75
.5	0	0	0	.25	.5
.25	0	0	0	0	.25
0	0	0	0	0	0

$w = 1$ (strong)

$b =$	0	.25	.5	.75	1
$a = 1$	0	.25	.5	.75	1
.75	0	.21	.44	.65	.75
.5	0	.1	.29	.44	.5
.25	0	0	.1	.21	.25
0	0	0	0	0	0

$w = 2$

$b =$	0	.25	.5	.75	·1
$a = 1$	0	.25	.5	.75	1
.75	0	.25	.5	.73	.75
.5	0	.25	.46	.5	.5
.25	0	.20	.25	.25	.25
0	0	0	0	0	0

$w = 10$

$b =$	0	.25	.5	.75	1
$a = 1$	0	.25	.5	.75	1
.75	0	.25	.5	.75	.75
.5	0	.25	.5	.5	.5
.25	0	.25	.25	.25	.25
0	0	0	0	0	0

$w \to \infty$ (weak)

(b) Fuzzy unions

$b =$	0	.25	.5	.75	1
$a = 1$	1	1	1	1	1
.75	.75	1	1	1	1
.5	.5	.75	1	1	1
.25	.25	.5	.75	1	1
0	0	.25	.5	.75	1

$w = 1$ (weak)

$b =$	0	.25	.5	.75	1
$a = 1$	1	1	1	1	1
.75	.75	.79	.9	1	1
.5	.5	.56	.71	.9	1
.25	.25	.35	.56	.79	1
0	0	.25	.5	.75	1

$w = 2$

$b =$	0	.25	.5	.75	1
$a = 1$	1	1	1	1	1
.75	.75	.75	.75	.8	1
.5	.5	.5	.54	.75	1
.25	.25	.27	.5	.75	1
0	0	.25	.5	.75	1

$w = 10$

$b =$	0	.25	.5	.75	1
$a = 1$	1	1	1	1	1
.75	.75	.75	.75	.75	1
.5	.5	.5	.5	.75	1
.25	.25	.25	.5	.75	1
0	0	.25	.5	.75	1

$w \to \infty$ (strong)

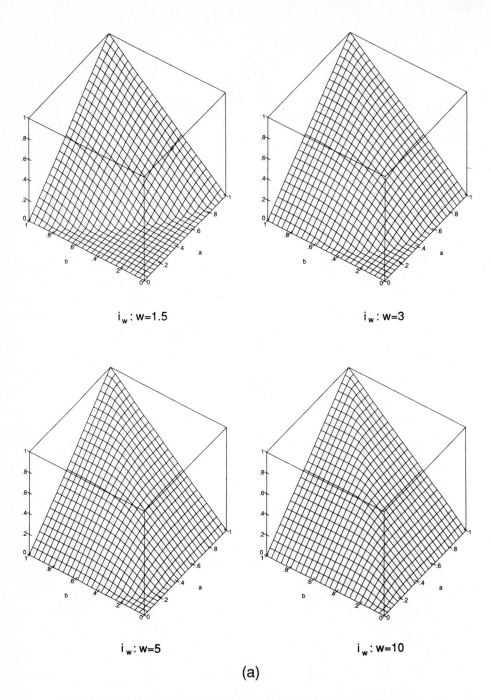

 (a)

Figure 3.8 Examples of fuzzy intersections and fuzzy unions from the Yager classes.

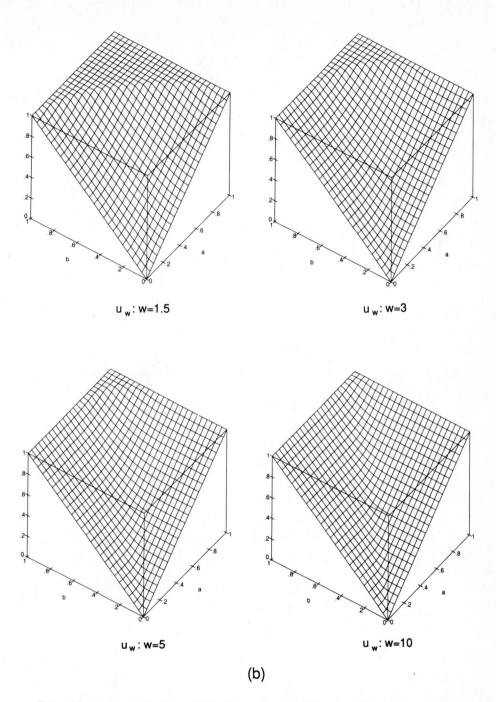

$u_w: w=1.5$ $u_w: w=3$

$u_w: w=5$ $u_w: w=10$

(b)

Figure 3.8 *(continued)*   Examples of fuzzy intersections and fuzzy unions from the Yager classes.

TABLE 3.2 SOME CLASSES OF FUZZY INTERSECTIONS (*t*-NORMS)

Reference	Formula $i(a,b)$	Decreasing generator $f(a)$	Parameter range	As parameter converges to 0	As parameter converges to 1 or −1	As parameter converges to ∞ or −∞
Dombi [1982]	$\left\{1 + \left[\left(\frac{1}{a}-1\right)^\lambda + \left(\frac{1}{b}-1\right)^\lambda\right]^{\frac{1}{\lambda}}\right\}^{-1}$	$\left(\frac{1}{a}-1\right)^\lambda$	$\lambda > 0$	$i_{\min}(a,b)$	$\frac{ab}{a+b-ab}$ when $\lambda = 1$	$\min(a,b)$
Frank [1979]	$\log_s\left[1 + \frac{(s^a-1)(s^b-1)}{s-1}\right]$	$-\ln\left(\frac{s^a-1}{s-1}\right)$	$s > 0, s \neq 1$	$\min(a,b)$	ab as $s \to 1$	$\max(0, a+b-1)$
Hamacher [1978]	$\frac{ab}{r+(1-r)(a+b-ab)}$	$-\ln\left(\frac{a}{r+(1-r)a}\right)$	$r > 0$	$\frac{ab}{a+b-ab}$	ab when $r = 1$	$i_{\min}(a,b)$
Schweizer & Sklar 1 [1963]	$\{\max(0,\, a^p + b^p - 1)\}^{\frac{1}{p}}$	$1 - a^p$	$p \neq 0$	ab	$\max(0, a+b-1)$, when $p=1$; $\frac{ab}{a+b-ab}$, when $p=-1$.	$i_{\min}(a,b)$ as $p \to \infty$; $\min(a,b)$ as $p \to -\infty$.
Schweizer & Sklar 2	$1 - [(1-a)^p + (1-b)^p - (1-a)^p(1-b)^p]^{\frac{1}{p}}$	$\ln[1-(1-a)^p]^{\frac{1}{p}}$	$p > 0$	$i_{\min}(a,b)$	ab when $p = 1$	$\min(a,b)$
Schweizer & Sklar 3	$\exp(-(|\ln a|^p + |\ln b|^p)^{\frac{1}{p}})$	$|\ln a|^p$	$p > 0$	$i_{\min}(a,b)$	ab when $p = 1$	$\min(a,b)$
Schweizer & Sklar 4	$\frac{ab}{[a^p + b^p - a^p b^p]^{\frac{1}{p}}}$	$a^{-p} - 1$	$p > 0$	ab	$\frac{ab}{a+b-ab}$, when $p = 1$	$\min(a,b)$
Yager [1980f]	$1 - \min\left\{1,\, [(1-a)^w + (1-b)^w]^{\frac{1}{w}}\right\}$	$(1-a)^w$	$w > 0$	$i_{\min}(a,b)$	$\max(0, a+b-1)$ when $w = 1$	$\min(a,b)$
Dubois & Prade [1980]	$\frac{ab}{\max(a,b,\alpha)}$		$\alpha \in [0,1]$	$\min(a,b)$	ab when $\alpha = 1$	
Weber [1983]	$\max\left(0,\, \frac{a+b+\lambda ab - 1}{1+\lambda}\right)$	$\frac{1}{\lambda}\ln[1 + \lambda(1-a)]$	$\lambda > -1$	$\max(0, a+b-1)$	$i_{\min}(a,b)$ as $\lambda \to -1$; $\max[0, (a+b+ab-1)/2]$ when $\lambda = 1$.	ab
Yu [1985]	$\max[0,\, (1+\lambda)(a+b-1) - \lambda ab]$	$\frac{1}{\lambda}\ln\frac{1+\lambda}{1+\lambda a}$	$\lambda > -1$	$\max(0, a+b-1)$	ab as $\lambda \to -1$; $\max[0, 2(a+b-ab/2-1)]$ when $\lambda = 1$.	$i_{\min}(a,b)$

Theorem 3.13.   Let i be a t-norm and let $g : [0, 1] \rightarrow [0, 1]$ be a function such that g is strictly increasing and continuous in $(0, 1)$ and $g(0) = 0$, $g(1) = 1$. Then, the function i^g defined by

$$i^g(a, b) = g^{(-1)}(i(g(a), g(b))) \tag{3.20}$$

for all $a, b \in [0, 1]$, where $g^{(-1)}$ denotes the pseudo-inverse of g, is also a t-norm.

Proof: See Appendix D. ∎

To illustrate the meaning of this theorem, let

$$g(a) = \begin{cases} \dfrac{a+1}{2} & \text{when } a \neq 0 \\ 0 & \text{when } a = 0. \end{cases}$$

The pseudo-inverse of g is the function

$$g^{(-1)}(z) = \begin{cases} 0 & \text{when } z \in [0, \tfrac{1}{2}) \\ 2z - 1 & \text{when } z \in [\tfrac{1}{2}, 1]. \end{cases}$$

Graphs of g and $g^{(-1)}$ are shown in Fig. 3.9a. Given now $i(a, b) = ab$, we readily obtain

$$i^g(a, b) = \max(0, (a + b + ab - 1)/2).$$

Considering now another increasing generator defined by

$$g(a) = \begin{cases} \dfrac{a}{2} & \text{when } a \neq 1 \\ 1 & \text{when } a = 1, \end{cases}$$

whose pseudo-inverse is the function

$$g^{(-1)}(z) = \begin{cases} 2z & \text{when } z \in [0, \tfrac{1}{2}] \\ 1 & \text{when } z \in (\tfrac{1}{2}, 1] \end{cases}$$

(Fig. 3.9b), we obtain

$$i^g(a, b) = \begin{cases} b & \text{when } a = 1 \\ a & \text{when } b = 1 \\ \dfrac{ab}{2} & \text{otherwise} \end{cases}$$

for the same t-norm $i(a, b) = ab$.

There are other methods for obtaining new t-norms from given t-norms, which are based on various ways of combining several t-norms into one t-norm, but we do not deem it necessary to cover them in this text.

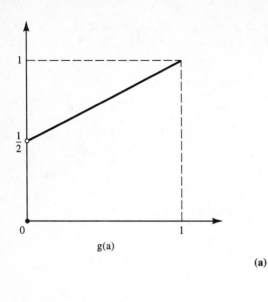

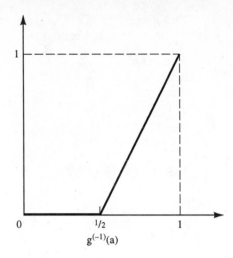

(a)

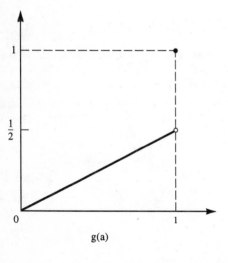

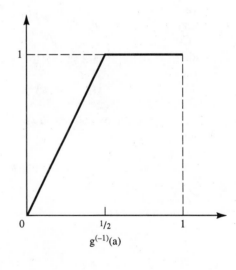

(b)

Figure 3.9 Illustration of Theorem 3.13.

3.4 *FUZZY UNIONS: t-CONORMS*

The discussion of fuzzy unions closely parallels that of fuzzy intersections. Like fuzzy intersection, the general fuzzy union of two fuzzy sets A and B is specified by a function

$$u : [0, 1] \times [0, 1] \to [0, 1].$$

The argument to this function is the pair consisting of the membership grade of some element x in fuzzy set A and the membership grade of that same element in fuzzy set B. The function returns the membership grade of the element in the set $A \cup B$. Thus,

$$(A \cup B)(x) = u[A(x), B(x)] \tag{3.21}$$

for all $x \in X$.

Properties that a function u must satisfy to be intuitively acceptable as a fuzzy union are exactly the same as properties of functions that are known in the literature as t-conorms. These functions, which are now well developed, capture exactly the full scope of fuzzy unions. We may thus use the terms "t-conorms" and "fuzzy unions" interchangeably.

A *fuzzy union/t-conorm u* is a binary operation on the unit interval that satisfies at least the following axioms for all $a, b, d \in [0, 1]$:

Axiom u1. $u(a, 0) = a$ (*boundary condition*).

Axiom u2. $b \leq d$ implies $u(a, b) \leq u(a, d)$ (*monotonicity*).

Axiom u3. $u(a, b) = u(b, a)$ (*commutativity*).

Axiom u4. $u(a, u(b, d)) = u(u(a, b), d)$ (*associativity*).

Since this set of axioms is essential for fuzzy unions, we call it the *axiomatic skeleton for fuzzy unions/t-conorms*.

Comparing Axioms u1–u4 with Axioms i1–i4, we can see that they differ only in the boundary condition. Axioms u1 through u3 ensure that the fuzzy union defined by (3.21) becomes the classical set union when sets A and B are crisp: $u(0, 0) = 0, u(0, 1) = u(1, 0) = u(1, 1) = 1$. Otherwise, the axioms are justified on the same grounds as those for fuzzy intersections.

The most important additional requirements for fuzzy unions are expressed by the following axioms:

Axiom u5. u is a continuous function (*continuity*).

Axiom u6. $u(a, a) > a$ (*superidempotency*).

Axiom u7. $a_1 < a_2$ and $b_1 < b_2$ implies $u(a_1, b_1) < u(a_2, b_2)$ (*strict monotonicity*).

These axioms are analogous to Axioms i5–i7 for fuzzy intersections, but observe that the requirement of subidempotency for fuzzy intersections is replaced here with the requirement of superidempotency.

Any continuous and superidempotent t-conorm is called *Archimedean*; if it is also strictly monotonic, it is called *strictly Archimedean*. The following theorem shows that the standard fuzzy union is significant with respect to idempotency.

Theorem 3.14.   The standard fuzzy union is the only idempotent t-conorm.

Proof: Analogous to the proof of Theorem 3.9.   ■

The following are examples of some t-conorms that are frequently used as fuzzy unions (each defined for all $a, b \in [0, 1]$):

Standard union: $u(a, b) = \max(a, b)$.

Algebraic sum: $u(a, b) = a + b - ab$.

Bounded sum: $u(a, b) = \min(1, a + b)$.

Drastic union: $u(a, b) = \begin{cases} a & \text{when } b = 0 \\ b & \text{when } a = 0 \\ 1 & \text{otherwise.} \end{cases}$

Graphs of these four fuzzy unions are shown in Fig. 3.10. We can see from the graphs that

$$\max(a, b) \leq a + b - ab \leq \min(1, a + b) \leq u_{\max}(a, b)$$

for all $a, b \in [0, 1]$, where $u_{\max}$ denotes the drastic union. These inequalities can also be proven mathematically. The full range of fuzzy unions is specified in the following theorem.

Theorem 3.15.   For all $a, b \in [0, 1]$,

$$\max(a, b) \leq u(a, b) \leq u_{\max}(a, b). \tag{3.22}$$

Proof: Analogous to the proof of Theorem 3.10. ■

We now proceed to a fundamental theorem of t-conorms, a counterpart of Theorem 3.11, which provides us with a method for generating Archimedean t-conorms or classes of t-conorms.

Theorem 3.16 (Characterization Theorem of t-Conorms).   Let u be a binary operation on the unit interval. Then, u is an Archimedean t-conorm iff there exists an increasing generator such that

$$u(a, b) = g^{(-1)}(g(a) + g(b)) \tag{3.23}$$

for all $a, b \in [0, 1]$.

Proof: [Schweizer and Sklar, 1963; Ling, 1965]. ■

Given an increasing generator g, we can construct a t-conorm u by (3.23). The following are examples of three parameterized classes of increasing generators and the corresponding classes of t-conorms, which are counterparts of the three classes of t-norms introduced in Sec. 3.3.

1. [Schweizer and Sklar, 1963]: The class of increasing generators is defined by

$$g_p(a) = 1 - (1 - a)^p \quad (p \neq 0).$$

Then,

$$g_p^{(-1)}(z) = \begin{cases} 1 - (1 - z)^{1/p} & \text{when } z \in [0, 1] \\ 1 & \text{when } z \in (1, \infty) \end{cases}$$

and we obtain the corresponding class of t-conorms by applying (3.23):

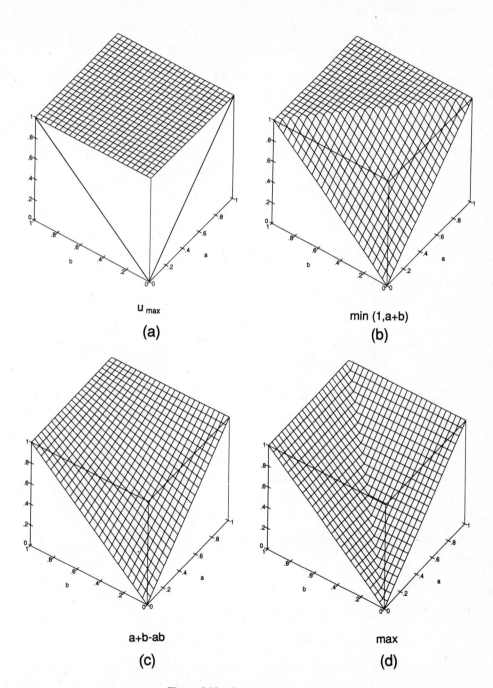

Figure 3.10   Graphs of fuzzy unions.

$$u_p(a, b) = g_p^{(-1)}(1 - (1-a)^p + 1 - (1-b)^p)$$

$$= \begin{cases} 1 - [(1-a)^p + (1-b)^p - 1]^{1/p} & \text{when } 2 - (1-a)^p - (1-b)^p \in [0, 1] \\ 1 & \text{otherwise} \end{cases}$$

$$= 1 - \{\max(0, (1-a)^p + (1-b)^p - 1)\}^{1/p}.$$

2. [Yager, 1980f]: Given a class of increasing generators

$$g_w(a) = a^w \quad (w > 0),$$

we obtain

$$g_w^{(-1)}(z) = \begin{cases} z^{1/w} & \text{when } z \in [0, 1] \\ 1 & \text{when } z \in (1, \infty) \end{cases}$$

and

$$u_w(a, b) = g_w^{(-1)}(a^w + b^w)$$
$$= \min(1, (a^w + b^w)^{1/w}).$$

3. [Frank, 1979]: Using the class of increasing generators

$$g_s(a) = -\ln \frac{s^{1-a} - 1}{s - 1} \quad (s > 0, s \neq 1)$$

whose pseudo-inverses are

$$g_s^{(-1)}(z) = 1 - \log_s(1 + (s-1)e^{-z}),$$

we obtain

$$u_s(a, b) = 1 - \log_s \left\{ 1 + \frac{(s^{1-a} - 1)(s^{1-b} - 1)}{s - 1} \right\}.$$

Let us further examine only the Yager class of t-conorms

$$u_w(a, b) = \min(1, (a^w + b^w)^{1/w}) \quad (w > 0). \tag{3.24}$$

As stated by the following theorem, this class covers the whole range of t-conorms.

Theorem 3.17.   Let u_w denote the class of Yager t-conorms defined by (3.24). Then,

$$\max(a, b) \leq u_w(a, b) \leq u_{\max}(a, b)$$

for all $a, b \in [0, 1]$.

Proof: *Lower bound.* We have to prove that

$$\lim_{w \to \infty} \min[1, (a^w + b^w)^{1/w}] = \max(a, b). \tag{3.25}$$

This is obvious whenever (1) a or b equal 0, or (2) $a = b$, because the limit of $2^{1/w}$ as $w \to \infty$ equals 1. If $a \neq b$ and the min equals $(a^w + b^w)^{1/w}$, the proof reduces to the demonstration that

$$\lim_{w \to \infty} (a^w + b^w)^{1/w} = \max(a, b).$$

Let us assume, with no loss of generality, that $a < b$, and let $Q = (a^w + b^w)^{1/w}$. Then

$$\lim_{w \to \infty} \ln Q = \lim_{w \to \infty} \frac{\ln(a^w + b^w)}{w}.$$

Using l'Hospital's rule, we obtain

$$\lim_{w \to \infty} \ln Q = \lim_{w \to \infty} \frac{a^w \ln a + b^w \ln b}{a^w + b^w}$$

$$= \lim_{w \to \infty} \frac{(a/b)^w \ln a + \ln b}{(a/b)^w + 1} = \ln b.$$

Hence,

$$\lim_{w \to \infty} Q = \lim_{w \to \infty} (a^w + b^w)^{1/w} = b \quad (= \max(a, b)).$$

It remains to show that (3.25) is still valid when the min equals 1. In this case,

$$(a^w + b^w)^{1/w} \geq 1$$

or

$$a^w + b^w \geq 1$$

for all $w \in (0, \infty)$. When $w \to \infty$, the last inequality holds if $a = 1$ or $b = 1$ (since $a, b \in [0, 1]$). Hence, (3.25) is again satisfied.

   Upper bound. It is trivial that $u(0, b) = b$ and $u(a, 0) = a$ independent of w. It is also easy to show that

$$\lim_{w \to 0} (a^w + b^w)^{1/w} = \infty;$$

hence,

$$\lim_{w \to 0} u_w(a, b) = 1$$

for all $a, b \in [0, 1]$. ■

   The various functions of the Yager class, which are defined by different choices of the parameter w, can be interpreted as performing union operations of various strengths. Table 3.1b and Fig. 3.8b illustrate how the values produced by the Yager functions for fuzzy unions decrease as the value of w increases. In fact, we may interpret the value $1/w$ as indicating the degree of interchangeability present in the union operation u_w. The notion of the set union operation corresponds to the logical OR (disjunction), in which some interchangeability between the two arguments of the statement "A or B" is assumed. The Yager t-conorm for which $w = 1$, which is the bounded sum, is very weak and indicates perfect interchangeability between the two arguments. On the other hand, the Yager t-conorm for which $w \to \infty$, which is the standard fuzzy union, represents the strongest fuzzy union. In this sense, the t-conorms of the Yager class represent fuzzy unions that increase in strength as the value of the parameter w increases.

   Various classes of fuzzy unions covered in the literature are summarized in Table 3.3; each of them is a counterpart of one of the classes of fuzzy intersections in Table 3.2.

TABLE 3.3   SOME CLASSES OF FUZZY UNIONS (t-CONORMS)

Reference	Formula $u(a,b)$	Increasing generator $g(a)$	Parameter range	As parameter converges to 0	As parameter converges to 1 or -1	As parameter converges to ∞ or -∞
Dombi [1982]	$\left\{1+\left[\left(\frac{1}{a}-1\right)^{\lambda}+\left(\frac{1}{b}-1\right)^{\lambda}\right]^{-\frac{1}{\lambda}}\right\}^{-1}$	$\left(\frac{1}{a}-1\right)^{-\lambda}$	$\lambda>0$	$u_{\max}(a,b)$	$\frac{a+b-2ab}{1-ab}$ when $\lambda=1$	$\max(a,b)$
Frank [1979]	$1-\log_s\left[1+\frac{(s^{1-a}-1)(s^{1-b}-1)}{s-1}\right]$	$-\ln\left(\frac{s^{1-a}-1}{s-1}\right)$	$s>0, s\neq 1$	$\max(a,b)$	$a+b-ab$ as $s\to 1$	$\min(1,a+b)$
Hamacher [1978]	$\frac{a+b+(r-2)ab}{r+(r-1)ab}$	$-\ln\left(\frac{1-a}{r+(1-r)(1-a)}\right)$	$r>0$	$\frac{a+b-2ab}{1-ab}$	$a+b-ab$ when $r=1$	$u_{\max}(a,b)$
Schweizer & Sklar 1 [1963]	$1-[\max(0,(1-a)^p+(1-b)^p-1)]^{\frac{1}{p}}$	$1-(1-a)^p$	$p\neq 0$	$a+b-ab$	$\min(1,a+b)$, when $p=1$; $\frac{a+b-2ab}{1-ab}$, when $p=-1$.	$u_{\max}(a,b)$ as $p\to\infty$; $\min(a,b)$ as $p\to-\infty$.
Schweizer & Sklar 2	$[a^p+b^p-a^pb^p]^{\frac{1}{p}}$	$\ln[1-a^p]^{\frac{1}{p}}$	$p>0$	$a+b-ab$	$a+b-ab$ when $p=1$	$\max(a,b)$
Schweizer & Sklar 3	$1-\exp(-(|\ln(1-a)|^p+|\ln(1-b)|^p)^{\frac{1}{p}})$	$|\ln(1-a)|^p$	$p>0$	$u_{\max}(a,b)$	$a+b-ab$ when $p=1$	$\max(a,b)$
Schweizer & Sklar 4	$1-\frac{(1-a)(1-b)}{[(1-a)^p+(1-b)^p-(1-a)^p(1-b)^p]^{\frac{1}{p}}}$	$(1-a)^{-p}-1$	$p>0$	$a+b-ab$	$\min\left(1,\frac{a+b}{1-ab}\right)$ when $p=1$	$\max(a,b)$
Yager [1980f]	$\min\left[1,(a^w+b^w)^{\frac{1}{w}}\right]$	a^w	$w>0$	$u_{\max}(a,b)$	$\min(1,a+b)$ when $w=1$	$\max(a,b)$
Dubois & Prade [1980]	$1-\frac{(1-a)(1-b)}{\max((1-a),(1-b),\alpha)}$		$\alpha\in[0,1]$	$\max(a,b)$	$a+b-ab$ when $\alpha=1$	
Weber [1983]	$\min\left(1,a+b-\frac{\lambda}{1-\lambda}ab\right)$	$\frac{1}{\lambda}\ln\frac{1+\lambda}{1+\lambda(1-a)}$	$\lambda>-1$	$\min(1,a+b)$	$u_{\max}(a,b)$ as $\lambda\to-1$; $\min(1,a+b-ab/2)$ when $\lambda=1$.	$a+b-ab$
Yu [1985]	$\min(1,a+b+\lambda ab)$	$\frac{1}{\lambda}\ln(1+\lambda a)$	$\lambda>-1$	$\min(1,a+b)$	$a+b-ab$ as $\lambda\to-1$; $\min(1,a+b+ab)$ when $\lambda=1$.	$u_{\max}(a,b)$

As stated by the following theorem, new t-conorms can also be generated on the basis of known t-conorms. The theorem is a counterpart of Theorem 3.13.

Theorem 3.18.   Let u be a t-conorm and let $g : [0, 1] \to [0, 1]$ be a function such that g is strictly increasing and continuous in $(0, 1)$ and $g(0) = 0, g(1) = 1$. Then, the function u^g defined by

$$u^g(a, b) = g^{(-1)}(u(g(a), g(b))) \tag{3.26}$$

for all $a, b \in [0, 1]$ is also a t-conorm.

Proof: Analogous to the proof of Theorem 3.13.   ∎

The construction of new t-conorms from given t-conorms by (3.26) is virtually the same as the construction of new t-norms from given t-norms by (3.20). Hence, we leave it to the reader as an exercise to try some of these constructions.

In analogy to t-norms, there are additional methods for constructing new t-conorms from given t-conorms, but they are not covered in this text due to space constraints.

3.5 COMBINATIONS OF OPERATIONS

In classical set theory, the operations of intersection and union are dual with respect to the complement in the sense that they satisfy the De Morgan laws

$$\overline{A \cap B} = \overline{A} \cup \overline{B} \quad \text{and} \quad \overline{A \cup B} = \overline{A} \cap \overline{B}.$$

It is desirable that this duality be satisfied for fuzzy sets as well. It is obvious that only some combinations of t-norms, t-conorms, and fuzzy complements can satisfy the duality. We say that a t-norm i and a t-conorm u are *dual with respect to a fuzzy complement c* iff

$$c(i(a, b)) = u(c(a), c(b)) \tag{3.27}$$

and

$$c(u(a, b)) = i(c(a), c(b)). \tag{3.28}$$

These equations describe the De Morgan laws for fuzzy sets. Let the triple $\langle i, u, c \rangle$ denote that i and u are dual with respect to c, and let any such triple be called a *dual triple*.

We can easily verify that the following are dual t-norms and t-conorms with respect to the standard complement c_s (i.e., dual triples):

$\langle \min(a, b), \max(a, b), c_s \rangle$
$\langle ab, a + b - ab, c_s \rangle$
$\langle \max(0, a + b - 1), \min(1, a + b), c_s \rangle$
$\langle i_{\min}(a, b), u_{\max}(a, b), c_s \rangle$

Several useful characteristics of the duality between t-norms and t-conorms are expressed by the following six theorems.

Theorem 3.19. The triples $\langle \min, \max, c \rangle$ and $\langle i_{\min}, u_{\max}, c \rangle$ are dual with respect to any fuzzy complement c.

Proof: Assume, without any loss of generality, that $a \leq b$. Then, $c(a) \geq c(b)$ for any fuzzy complement and, hence,

$$\max(c(a), c(b)) = c(a) = c(\min(a, b)),$$

$$\min(c(a), c(b)) = c(b) = c(\max(a, b)).$$

The proof for $i_{\min}$ and $u_{\min}$ is left to the reader as an exercise. ■

Theorem 3.20. Given a t-norm i and an involutive fuzzy complement c, the binary operation u on $[0, 1]$ defined by

$$u(a, b) = c(i(c(a), c(b))) \tag{3.29}$$

for all $a, b \in [0, 1]$ is a t-conorm such that $\langle i, u, c \rangle$ is a dual triple.

Proof: To prove that u given by (3.29) is a t-conorm, we have to show that it satisfies Axioms u1–u4.

(u1) For any $a \in [0, 1]$,

$$
\begin{aligned}
u(a, 0) &= c(i(c(a), c(0))) && \text{(by (3.29))} \\
&= c(i(c(a), 1)) && \text{(by Axiom c1)} \\
&= c(c(a)) && \text{(by Axiom i1)} \\
&= a && \text{(by Axiom c4).}
\end{aligned}
$$

Hence, u satisfies Axiom u1.

(u2) For any $a, b, d \in [0, 1]$, if $b \leq d$, then $c(b) \geq c(d)$. Moreover,

$$i(c(a), c(b)) \geq i(c(a), c(d))$$

by Axiom i2. Hence, by (3.29),

$$u(a, b) = c(i(c(a), c(b))) \leq c(i(c(a), c(d))) = u(a, d),$$

which shows that u satisfies Axiom u2.

(u3) For any $a, b, \in [0, 1]$, we have

$$u(a, b) = c(i(c(a), c(b))) = c(i(c(b), c(a))) = u(b, a)$$

by (3.29) and Axiom i3; that is, u satisfies Axiom u3.

(u4) For any $a, b, d \in [0, 1]$,

$$
\begin{aligned}
u(a, u(b, d)) &= c(i(c(a), c(u(b, d)))) & \text{(by (3.29))} \\
&= c(i(c(a), c(c(i(c(b), c(d)))))) & \text{(by (3.29))} \\
&= c(i(c(a), i(c(b), c(d)))) & \text{(by Axiom c4)} \\
&= c(i(i(c(a), c(b)), c(d))) & \text{(by Axiom i4)} \\
&= c(i(c(c(i(c(a), c(b)))), c(d))) & \text{(by Axiom c4)} \\
&= u(u(a, b), d) & \text{(by (3.29))}.
\end{aligned}
$$

Hence, u satisfies Axiom u4 and, consequently, it is a t-conorm.

By employing (3.29) and Axiom c4, we can now show that u satisfies the De Morgan laws:

$$
c(u(a, b)) = c(c(i(c(a), c(b)))) = i(c(a), c(b)),
$$

$$
u(c(a), c(b)) = c(i(c(c(a)), c(c(b)))) = c(i(a, b)).
$$

Hence, i and u are dual with respect to c. ∎

To illustrate the utility of this theorem, consider the t-norm $i(a, b) = ab$ and the Sugeno class of fuzzy complements

$$
c_\lambda(a) = \frac{1 - a}{1 + \lambda a} \quad (\lambda > -1).
$$

By applying these operations to (3.29), we obtain the class of t-conorms

$$
\begin{aligned}
u_\lambda(a, b) &= c_\lambda(i(c_\lambda(a), c_\lambda(b))) \\
&= c_\lambda \left[\frac{1 - a}{1 + \lambda a} \cdot \frac{1 - b}{1 + \lambda b} \right] \\
&= \frac{a + b + (\lambda - 1)ab}{1 + \lambda ab}.
\end{aligned}
$$

Now, taking $r = \lambda + 1$, we obtain the Hamacher class of t-conorms defined in Table 3.3:

$$
u_r(a, b) = \frac{a + b + (r - 2)ab}{1 + (r - 1)ab} \quad (r > 0).
$$

For $\lambda = 0$ (and $r = 1$), we obtain the standard fuzzy complement and the t-conorm $a + b - ab$. Hence, the t-norm ab and this t-conorm are dual with respect to the standard fuzzy complement. For $\lambda = 1$ (and $r = 2$) we obtain the t-conorm

$$
\frac{a + b}{1 + ab}
$$

and the fuzzy complement

$$
\frac{1 - a}{1 + a}.
$$

Hence,

$$\left\langle ab, \frac{a+b}{1+ab}, \frac{1-a}{1+a} \right\rangle.$$

Theorem 3.21. Given a t-conorm u and an involutive fuzzy complement c, the binary operation i on $[0, 1]$ defined by

$$i(a, b) = c(u(c(a), c(b))) \tag{3.30}$$

for all $a, b \in [0, 1]$ is a t-norm such that $\langle i, u, c \rangle$.

Proof: Analogous to the proof of Theorem 3.20. ■

The following theorem enables us to generate pairs of dual t-norms and t-conorms for any given involutive fuzzy complement c and an increasing generator of c.

Theorem 3.22. Given an involutive fuzzy complement c and an increasing generator g of c, the t-norm and t-conorm generated by g are dual with respect to c.

Proof: For any $a, b \in [0, 1]$, we have

$$c(a) = g^{-1}(g(1) - g(a)),$$

$$i(a, b) = g^{(-1)}(g(a) + g(b) - g(1)),$$

$$u(a, b) = g^{(-1)}(g(a) + g(b)).$$

Hence,

$$
\begin{aligned}
i(c(a), c(b)) &= g^{(-1)}(g(g^{-1}(g(1) - g(a))) + g(g^{-1}(g(1) - g(b))) - g(1)) \\
&= g^{(-1)}(g(1) - g(a) + g(1) - g(b) - g(1)) \\
&= g^{(-1)}(g(1) - g(a) - g(b)),
\end{aligned}
$$

$$
\begin{aligned}
c(u(a, b)) &= g^{-1}(g(1) - g(g^{(-1)}(g(a) + g(b)))) \\
&= g^{-1}(g(1) - \min(g(1), g(a) + g(b))) \\
&= g^{(-1)}(g(1) - g(a) - g(b)).
\end{aligned}
$$

That is,

$$c(u(a, b)) = i(c(a), c(b)). \quad ■$$

Applying this theorem to the Sugeno class of fuzzy complements, whose increasing generators g are defined by

$$g(a) = \frac{1}{\lambda} \ln(1 + \lambda a) \quad (\lambda > -1)$$

for all $a \in [0, 1]$, we obtain

$$i(a, b) = \max\left(0, \frac{a + b + \lambda ab}{1 + \lambda}\right),$$

which is the class of Weber t-norms (Table 3.2), and

$$u(a, b) = \min(1, a + b + \lambda ab),$$

which is the class of Yu t-conorms (Table 3.3). That is, the Weber t-norms and the Yu t-conorms are dual with respect to the Sugeno complements for any $\lambda > -1$. Observe, however, that the Weber and Yu t-norms and conorms are identical for the standard fuzzy complement ($\lambda = 0$). That is, t-norms and t-conorms of each of these classes are dual with respect to the standard fuzzy complement.

Note that each dual triple $\langle i, u, c \rangle$ obtained by Theorem 3.22 satisfies the law of excluded middle and the law of contraction, but they do not satisfy the distributive laws of the Boolean lattice (Table 1.1). These properties are formally expressed by the following two theorems.

Theorem 3.23.   Let $\langle i, u, c \rangle$ be a dual triple generated by Theorem 3.22. Then, the fuzzy operations i, u, c satisfy the law of excluded middle and the law of contraction.

Proof: According to Theorem 3.22, we have

$$c(a) = g^{-1}(g(1) - g(a)),$$

$$i(a, b) = g^{(-1)}(g(a) + g(b) - g(1)),$$

$$u(a, b) = g^{(-1)}(g(a) + g(b)).$$

Then,

$$
\begin{aligned}
u(a, c(a)) &= g^{(-1)}(g(a) + g(c(a))) \\
&= g^{(-1)}(g(a) + g(g^{-1}(g(1) - g(a)))) \\
&= g^{(-1)}(g(a) + g(1) - g(a)) \\
&= g^{(-1)}(g(1)) \\
&= 1
\end{aligned}
$$

for all $a \in [0, 1]$. That is, the law of excluded middle is satisfied. Moreover,

$$
\begin{aligned}
i(a, c(a)) &= g^{(-1)}(g(a) + g(c(a)) - g(1)) \\
&= g^{(-1)}(g(a) + g(g^{-1}(g(1) - g(a))) - g(1)) \\
&= g^{(-1)}(g(a) + g(1) - g(a) - g(1)) \\
&= g^{(-1)}(0) \\
&= 0
\end{aligned}
$$

for all $a \in [0, 1]$. Hence, the law of contradiction is also satisfied.   ∎

Theorem 3.24.   Let $\langle i, u, c \rangle$ be a dual triple that satisfies the law of excluded middle and the law of contradiction. Then, $\langle i, u, c \rangle$ does not satisfy the distributive laws.

Proof: Assume that the distributive law

$$i(a, u(b, d)) = u(i(a, b), i(a, d))$$

is satisfied for all $a, b, d \in [0, 1]$. Let e be the equilibrium of c. Clearly, $e \neq 0, 1$ since $c(0) = 1$ and $c(1) = 0$. By the law of excluded middle and the law of contradiction, we obtain

$$u(e, e) = u(e, c(e)) = 1,$$

$$i(e, e) = i(e, c(e)) = 0.$$

Now, applying e to the above distributive law, we have

$$i(e, u(e, e)) = u(i(e, e), i(e, e));$$

substituting for $u(e, e)$ and $i(e, e)$, we obtain

$$i(e, 1) = u(0, 0),$$

which results (by Axioms i1 and u1) in $e = 0$. This contradicts the requirement that $e \neq 0$. Hence, the distributive law does not hold. In an analogous way, we can prove that the dual distributive law does not hold either. ∎

3.6 AGGREGATION OPERATIONS

Aggregation operations on fuzzy sets are operations by which several fuzzy sets are combined in a desirable way to produce a single fuzzy set. Assume, for example, that a student's performance (expressed in %) in four courses taken in a particular semester is described as high, very high, medium, and very low, and each of these linguistic labels is captured by an appropriate fuzzy set defined on the interval $[0, 100]$. Then, an appropriate aggregation operation would produce a meaningful expression, in terms of a single fuzzy set, of the overall performance of the student in the given semester.

Formally, any *aggregation operation* on n fuzzy sets ($n \geq 2$) is defined by a function

$$h : [0, 1]^n \to [0, 1].$$

When applied to fuzzy sets $A_1, A_2, \dots, A_n$ defined on X, function h produces an aggregate fuzzy set A by operating on the membership grades of these sets for each $x \in X$. Thus,

$$A(x) = h(A_1(x), A_2(x), \dots, A_n(x))$$

for each $x \in X$.

In order to qualify as an intuitively meaningful aggregation function, h must satisfy at least the following three axiomatic requirements, which express the essence of the notion of aggregation:

Axiom h1. $h(0, 0, \dots, 0) = 0$ and $h(1, 1, \dots, 1) = 1$ (*boundary conditions*).

Axiom h2. For any pair $\langle a_1, a_2, \dots, a_n \rangle$ and $\langle b_1, b_2, \dots, b_n \rangle$ of n-tuples such that $a_i, b_i \in [0, 1]$ for all $i \in \mathbb{N}_n$, if $a_i \leq b_i$ for all $i \in \mathbb{N}_n$, then

$$h(a_1, a_2, \dots, a_n) \leq h(b_1, b_2, \dots, b_n);$$

that is, h is *monotonic increasing* in all its arguments.

Axiom h3. h is a *continuous* function.

Besides these essential and easily understood requirements, aggregating operations on fuzzy sets are usually expected to satisfy two additional axiomatic requirements.

Axiom h4. h is a *symmetric* function in all its arguments; that is,

$$h(a_1, a_2, \ldots, a_n) = h(a_{p(1)}, a_{p(2)}, \ldots, a_{p(n)})$$

for any permutation p on $\mathbb{N}_n$.

Axiom h5. h is an *idempotent* function; that is,

$$h(a, a, \ldots, a) = a$$

for all $a \in [0, 1]$.

Axiom h4 reflects the usual assumption that the aggregated fuzzy sets are equally important. If this assumption is not warranted in some application contexts, the symmetry axiom must be dropped. Axiom h5 expresses our intuition that any aggregation of equal fuzzy sets should result in the same fuzzy set. Observe that Axiom h5 subsumes Axiom h1.

We can easily see that fuzzy intersections and unions qualify as aggregation operations on fuzzy sets. Although they are defined for only two arguments, their property of associativity provides a mechanism for extending their definitions to any number of arguments. However, fuzzy intersections and unions are not idempotent, with the exception of the standard min and max operations.

It is significant that any aggregation operation h that satisfies Axioms h2 and h5 satisfies also the inequalities

$$\min(a_1, a_2, \ldots, a_n) \leq h(a_1, a_2, \ldots, a_n) \leq \max(a_1, a_2, \ldots, a_n) \qquad (3.31)$$

for all n-tuples $\langle a_1, a_2, \ldots, a_n \rangle \in [0, 1]^n$. To see this, let

$$a_* = \min(a_1, a_2, \ldots, a_n) \text{ and } a^* = \max(a_1, a_2, \ldots, a_n).$$

If h satisfies Axioms h2 and h5, then

$$a_* = h(a_*, a_*, \ldots, a_*) \leq h(a_1, a_2, \ldots, a_n) \leq h(a^*, a^*, \ldots, a^*) = a^*.$$

Conversely, if h satisfies (3.31), it must satisfy Axiom h5, since

$$a = \min(a, a, \ldots, a) \leq h(a, a, \ldots, a) \leq \max(a, a, \ldots, a) = a$$

for all $a \in [0, 1]$. That is, all aggregation operations between the standard fuzzy intersection and the standard fuzzy union are idempotent. Moreover, by Theorems 3.9 and 3.14, we may conclude that functions h that satisfy (3.31) are the only aggregation operations that are idempotent. These aggregation operations are usually called *averaging operations*.

One class of averaging operations that covers the entire interval between the min and max operations consists of *generalized means*. These are defined by the formula

$$h_\alpha(a_1, a_2, \ldots, a_n) = \left(\frac{a_1^\alpha + a_2^\alpha + \ldots + a_n^\alpha}{n} \right)^{1/\alpha}, \qquad (3.32)$$

where $\alpha \in \mathbb{R}$ ($\alpha \neq 0$) and $a_i \neq 0$ for all $i \in \mathbb{N}_n$ when $\alpha < 0$; α is a parameter by which different means are distinguished. For $\alpha < 0$ and $a_i \to 0$ for any $i \in \mathbb{N}_n$, it is easy to see that $h_\alpha(a_1, a_2, \ldots, a_n)$ converges to 0. For $\alpha \to 0$, the function h_α converges to the geometric mean, $(a_1 \cdot a_2 \cdots a_n)^{1/n}$. To show this, let us first determine the limit

$$\lim_{\alpha \to 0} \ln h_\alpha = \lim_{\alpha \to 0} \frac{\ln(a_1^\alpha + a_2^\alpha + \ldots + a_n^\alpha) - \ln n}{\alpha}.$$

Using l'Hospital's rule, we now have

$$\lim_{\alpha \to 0} \ln h_\alpha = \lim_{\alpha \to 0} \frac{a_1^\alpha \ln a_1 + a_2^\alpha \ln a_2 + \ldots + a_n^\alpha \ln a_n}{a_1^\alpha + a_2^\alpha + \ldots + a_n^\alpha}$$

$$= \frac{\ln a_1 + \ln a_2 + \ldots + \ln a_n}{n} = \ln(a_1 \cdot a_2 \cdots a_n)^{1/n}.$$

Hence,

$$\lim_{\alpha \to 0} h_\alpha = (a_1 \cdot a_2 \ldots a_n)^{1/n}.$$

Function h_α satisfies Axioms h1 through h5; consequently, it represents a parametrized class of continuous, symmetric, and idempotent aggregation operations. It also satisfies the inequalities (3.31) for all $\alpha \in \mathbb{R}$, with its lower bound

$$h_{-\infty}(a_1, a_2, \ldots, a_n) = \lim_{\alpha \to -\infty} h_\alpha(a_1, a_2, \ldots, a_n) = \min(a_1, a_2, \ldots, a_n)$$

and its upper bound

$$h_\infty(a_1, a_2, \ldots, a_n) = \lim_{\alpha \to \infty} h_\alpha(a_1, a_2, \ldots, a_n) = \max(a_1, a_2, \ldots, a_n).$$

For $\alpha = -1$,

$$h_{-1}(a_1, a_2, \ldots, a_n) = \frac{n}{\dfrac{1}{a_1} + \dfrac{1}{a_2} + \ldots + \dfrac{1}{a_n}},$$

which is the *harmonic mean*; for $\alpha = 1$,

$$h_1(a_1, a_2, \ldots, a_n) = \frac{1}{n}(a_1 + a_2 + \ldots + a_n),$$

which is the *arithmetic mean*.

Another class of aggregation operations that covers the entire interval between the min and max operations is called the class of *ordered weighted averaging operations*; the acronym *OWA* is often used in the literature to refer to these operations. Let

$$\mathbf{w} = \langle w_1, w_2, \ldots, w_n \rangle$$

be a *weighting vector* such that $w_i \in [0, 1]$ for all $i \in \mathbb{N}_n$ and

$$\sum_{i=1}^{n} w_i = 1.$$

Then, an *OWA* operation associated with $\mathbf{w}$ is the function

$$h_{\mathbf{w}}(a_1, a_2, \ldots, a_n) = w_1 b_1 + w_2 b_2 + \ldots + w_n b_n,$$

where b_i for any $i \in \mathbb{N}_n$ is the ith largest element in $a_1, a_2, \ldots, a_n$. That is, vector $\langle b_1, b_2, \ldots, b_n \rangle$ is a permutation of vector $\langle a_1, a_2, \ldots, a_n \rangle$ in which the elements are ordered: $b_i \geq b_j$ if $i < j$ for any pair $i, j \in \mathbb{N}_n$.

Given, for example, $\mathbf{w} = \langle .3, .1, .2, .4 \rangle$, we have $h_\mathbf{w}(.6, .9, .2, .7) = .3 \times .9 + .1 \times .7 + .2 \times .6 + .4 \times .2 = .54$.

It is easy to verify that the *OWA* operations $h_\mathbf{w}$ satisfy Axioms h1 through h5, and consequently, also the inequalities (3.31). The lower and upper bounds are obtained for

$$\mathbf{w}_* = \langle 0, 0, \ldots, 1 \rangle \text{ and } \mathbf{w}^* = \langle 1, 0, \ldots, 0 \rangle,$$

respectively. That is,

$$h_{\mathbf{w}_*}(a_1, a_2, \ldots, a_n) = \min(a_1, a_2, \ldots, a_n),$$
$$h_{\mathbf{w}^*}(a_1, a_2, \ldots, a_n) = \max(a_1, a_2, \ldots, a_n).$$

For $\mathbf{w} = (1/n, 1/n, \ldots, 1/n)$, $h_\mathbf{w}$ is the arithmetic mean. In general, by varying the assignment of weights from $\mathbf{w}_*$ to $\mathbf{w}^*$, we can cover the whole range between min and max.

Next, let us formulate three classes of aggregation operations, each of which satisfies a particular compositional property. These formulations are a subject of the following three theorems.

Theorem 3.25.   Let $h : [0, 1]^n \to \mathbb{R}^+$ be a function that satisfies Axiom h1, Axiom h2, and the property

$$h(a_1 + b_1, a_2 + b_2, \ldots, a_n + b_n) = h(a_1, a_2, \ldots, a_n) + h(b_1, b_2, \ldots, b_n) \qquad (3.33)$$

where $a_i, b_i, a_i + b_i \in [0, 1]$ for all $i \in \mathbb{N}_n$. Then,

$$h(a_1, a_2, \ldots, a_n) = \sum_{i=1}^{n} w_i a_i, \qquad (3.34)$$

where $w_i > 0$ for all $i \in \mathbb{N}_n$.

Proof: Let $h_i(a_i) = h(0, \ldots, 0, a_i, 0, \ldots, 0)$ for all $i \in \mathbb{N}_n$. Then, for any $a, b, a + b \in [0, 1]$,

$$h_i(a + b) = h_i(a) + h_i(b).$$

This is a well-investigated functional equation referred to as *Cauchy's functional equation*. Its solution is

$$h_i(a) = w_i a$$

for any $a \in [0, 1]$, where $w_i > 0$ [Aczél, 1966]. Therefore,

$$\begin{aligned} h(a_1, a_2, \ldots, a_n) &= h(a_1, 0, \ldots, 0) + h(0, a_2, 0, \ldots, 0) + \ldots + h(0, 0, \ldots, a_n) \\ &= h_1(a_1) + h_2(a_2) + \ldots + h_n(a_n) \\ &= w_1 a_1 + w_2 a_2 + \ldots + w_n a_n \\ &= \sum_{i=1}^{n} w_i a_i. \end{aligned}$$

This completes the proof.   ∎

It is easy to show that function h, defined in Theorem 3.25, becomes a *weighted average* if h also satisfies Axiom h5. In this case, when $a_1 = a_2 = \ldots = a_n = a \neq 0$, we have

$$a = h(a, a, \ldots, a) = \sum_{i=1}^{n} w_i a = a \sum_{i=1}^{n} w_i.$$

Hence, it is required that

$$\sum_{i=1}^{n} w_i = 1.$$

Theorem 3.26.   Let $h : [0, 1]^n \to [0, 1]$ be a function that satisfies Axiom h1, Axiom h3, and the properties

$$h(\max(a_1, b_1), \ldots, \max(a_n, b_n)) = \max(h(a_1, \ldots, a_n), h(b_1, \ldots, b_n)), \qquad (3.35)$$

$$h_i(h_i(a_i)) = h_i(a_i), \qquad (3.36)$$

where $h_i(a_i) = h(0, \ldots, 0, a_i, 0, \ldots, 0)$ for all $i \in \mathbb{N}_n$. Then,

$$h(a_1, \ldots, a_n) = \max(\min(w_1, a_1), \ldots, \min(w_n, a_n)), \qquad (3.37)$$

where $w_i \in [0, 1]$ for all $i \in \mathbb{N}_n$.

Proof: Observe that $h(a_1, a_2, \ldots, a_n) = h(\max(a_1, 0), \max(0, a_2), \ldots, \max(0, a_n))$, and by (3.35) we obtain $h(a_1, a_2, \ldots, a_n) = \max(h(a_1, 0, \ldots, 0), h(0, a_2, \ldots, a_n))$. We can now replace $h(0, a_2, a_3, \ldots, a_n)$ with $\max(h(0, a_2, 0, \ldots, 0), h(0, 0, a_3, \ldots, a_n))$ and repeating the same replacement with respect to $a_3, a_4, \ldots, a_n$, we eventually obtain

$$h(a_1, a_2, \ldots, a_n) = \max[h(a_1, 0, \ldots, 0), h(0, a_2, 0, \ldots, 0), \ldots, h(0, 0, \ldots, a_n)]$$

$$= \max[h_1(a_1), h_2(a_2), \ldots, h_n(a_n)].$$

It remains to prove that $h_i(a_i) = \min(w_i, a_i)$ for all $i \in \mathbb{N}_n$. Clearly, $h_i(a)$ is continuous, nondecreasing, and such that $h_i(0) = 0$ and $h_i(h_i(a_i)) = h_i(a_i)$. Let $h_i(1) = w_i$; then, the range of h_i is $[0, w_i]$. For any $a_i \in [0, w_i]$, there exists b_i such that $a_i = h_i(b_i)$ and hence, $h_i(a_i) = h_i(h_i(b_i)) = h_i(b_i) = a_i = \min(w_i, a_i)$ by (3.36); for any $a_i \in (w_i, 1]$, $w_i = h_i(1) = h_i(h_i(1)) = h_i(w_i) \leq h_i(a_i) \leq h(1) = w_i$ and, consequently, $h_i(a_i) = w_i = \min(w_i, a_i)$. ∎

Observe that function h, given by (3.37), may be viewed as a *weighted quasi-average*, in which the min and max operations replace, respectively, the arithmetic product and sum.

Theorem 3.27.   Let $h : [0, 1]^n \to [0, 1]$ be a function that satisfies Axiom h1, Axiom h3, and the properties

$$h(\min(a_1, b_1), \ldots, \min(a_n, b_n)) = \min(h(a_1, \ldots, a_n), h(b_1, \ldots, b_n)), \qquad (3.38)$$

$$h_i(ab) = h_i(a)h_i(b) \text{ and } h_i(0) = 0 \qquad (3.39)$$

for all $i \in \mathbb{N}_n$, where $h_i(a_i) = h(1, \ldots, 1, a_i, 1, \ldots, 1)$. Then, there exist numbers $\alpha_1, \alpha_2, \ldots, \alpha_n \in [0, 1]$ such that

$$h(a_1, a_2, \ldots, a_n) = \min(a_1^{\alpha_1}, a_2^{\alpha_2}, \ldots, a_n^{\alpha_n})$$

Proof: Left to the reader as an exercise. ∎

A special kind of aggregation operations are binary operations h on $[0, 1]$ that satisfy the properties of *monotonicity*, *commutativity*, and *associativity* of t-norms and t-conorms, but replace the boundary conditions of t-norms and t-conorms with *weaker boundary conditions*

$$h(0, 0) = 0 \text{ and } h(1, 1) = 1.$$

Let these aggregation operations be called *norm operations*.

Due to their associativity, norm operations can be extended to any finite member of arguments. When a norm operation also has the property $h(a, 1) = a$, it becomes a t-norm; when it has also the property $h(a, 0) = a$, it becomes a t-conorm. Otherwise, it is an *associative averaging operation*. Hence, norm operations cover the whole range of aggregating operations, from $i_{\min}$ to $u_{\max}$.

An example of a parametrized class of norm operations that are neither t-norms nor t-conorms is the class of binary operations on $[0, 1]$ defined by

$$h_\lambda(a, b) = \begin{cases} \min(\lambda, u(a, b)) & \text{when } a, b \in [0, \lambda] \\ \max(\lambda, i(a, b)) & \text{when } a, b \in [\lambda, 1] \\ \lambda & \text{otherwise} \end{cases}$$

for all $a, b \in [0, 1]$, where $\lambda \in (0, 1)$, i is a t-norm and u is a t-conorm. Let these operations be called λ-*averages*.

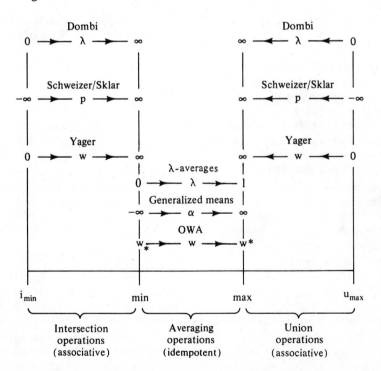

Figure 3.11 The full scope of fuzzy aggregation operations.

Special norms operations, referred in the literature as *medians*, are defined in the following theorem, by which their existence is established.

Theorem 3.28.   Let a norm operation h be continuous and idempotent. Then, there exists $\lambda \in [0, 1]$ such that

$$h(a, b) = \begin{cases} \max(a, b) & \text{when } a, b \in [0, \lambda] \\ \min(a, b) & \text{when } a, b \in [\lambda, 1] \\ \lambda & \text{otherwise} \end{cases}$$

for any $a, b \in [0, 1]$.

Proof: See Appendix D.   ■

The full scope of fuzzy aggregation operations is summarized in Fig. 3.11. Only some representative classes of t-norms, t-conorms, and averaging operations are shown in the figure. For each of these classes, the range of the respective parameter is indicated. Given one of these families of operations, the identification of a suitable operation for a specific application is equivalent to the estimation of the parameter involved.

NOTES

3.1. In the seminal paper by Zadeh [1965b], fuzzy set theory is formulated in terms of the standard operations of complement, union, and intersection, but other possibilities of combining fuzzy sets are also hinted at.

3.2. The first axiomatic treatment of fuzzy set operations was presented by Bellman and Giertz [1973]. They demonstrated the uniqueness of the max and min operators in terms of axioms that consist of our axiomatic skeleton for u and i, and the axioms of continuity, distributivity, strict increase of $u(a, a)$ and $i(a, a)$ in a, and lower and upper bounds $u(a, b) \geq \max(a, b)$ and $i(a, b) \leq \min(a, b)$. They concluded, however, that the operation of a fuzzy complement is not unique even when all reasonable requirements (boundary conditions, monotonicity, continuity, and involution) are employed as axioms. A thorough investigation of properties of the max and min operators was done by Voxman and Goetschel [1983].

3.3. The Sugeno class of fuzzy complements results from special measures (called λ-measures) introduced by Sugeno [1977]. The Yager class of fuzzy complements is derived from his class of fuzzy unions, defined by (3.24), by requiring that $A \cup cA = X$, where A is a fuzzy set defined on X. This requirement can be expressed more specifically by requiring that $u_w(a, c_w(a)) = 1$ for all $a \in [0, 1]$ and all $w > 0$.

3.4. Different approaches to the study of fuzzy complements were used by Lowen [1978], Esteva, Trillas, and Domingo [1981], and Ovchinnikov [1981a, 1983]. Yager [1979b, 1980g] investigated fuzzy complements for the purpose of developing useful measures of fuzziness (Sec. 9.4). Our presentation of fuzzy complements in Sec. 3.2 is based upon a paper by Higashi and Klir [1982], which is also motivated by the aim of developing measures of fuzziness.

3.5. The Yager class of fuzzy unions and intersections was introduced in a paper by Yager [1980f], which contains some additional characteristics of these classes. Yager [1982d] also addressed the question of the meaning of the parameter w in his class and the problem of selecting appropriate operations for various purposes.

3.6. The axiomatic skeletons that we use for characterizing fuzzy intersections and unions which are known in the literature as *triangular norms* (or *t-norms*) and *triangular conorms (or t-conorms*), respectively, were originally introduced by Menger [1942] in his study of statistical metric spaces. In current literature on fuzzy set theory, the terms "*t*-norms" and "*t*-conorms" are used routinely.

3.7. References to papers in which the various *t*-norms and *t*-conorms listed in Tables 3.2 and 3.3 were introduced are given directly in the tables. More general studies of *t*-norms and *t*-conorms, particularly studies of procedures by which classes of these functions can be generated, were undertaken by Schweizer and Sklar [1961, 1963, 1983], Ling [1965], Frank [1979], Alsina *et al.* [1983], and Fodor [1991a, 1993]. An overview of *t*-norms and *t*-conorms was prepared by Gupta and Qi [1991a].

3.8. The issue of which operations on fuzzy sets are suitable in various situations was studied by Zimmermann [1978a], Thole, Zimmermann, and Zysno [1979], Zimmermann and Zysno [1980], and Yager [1979a, 1982c].

3.9. One class of operators not covered in this chapter is the class of fuzzy implication operators. These are covered in Chapter 11 in the context of approximate reasoning.

3.10. An excellent overview of the whole spectrum of aggregation operations on fuzzy sets was prepared by Dubois and Prade [1985e]; it covers fuzzy unions and intersections as well as averaging operations. The class of generalized means defined by (3.32) is covered in a paper by Dyckhoff and Pedrycz [1984].

EXERCISES

3.1. Find the equilibrium of the fuzzy complement $c_{\lambda,w}$ given by (3.12).

3.2. Find the equilibrium of the fuzzy complement c_γ given by (3.14).

3.3. Does the function $c(a) = (1 - a)^w$ qualify for each $w > 0$ as a fuzzy complement? Plot the function for some values $w > 1$ and some values $w < 1$.

3.4. Show that $u_w(a, c_w(a)) = 1$ for $a \in [0, 1]$ and all $w > 0$, where u_w and c_w denote the Yager union and complement, respectively.

3.5. Give an example to show that for a discontinuous, strictly increasing function g from $[0, 1]$ to $\mathbb{R}$ such that $g(0) = 0$, the function c generated by (3.9) is not a fuzzy complement.

3.6. Determine whether each of the following functions is an increasing generator; if it is, find and plot the fuzzy complement, *t*-norm and *t*-conorm generated by it:
(a) $g(a) = \sin(a)$;
(b) $g(a) = \text{tg}(a)$;
(c) $g(a) = 1 + a$;

(d) $g(a) = \begin{cases} a & \text{for } 0 \le a \le \frac{1}{2} \\ \frac{1}{2} & \text{for } \frac{1}{2} < a \le 1; \end{cases}$

(e) $g(a) = \begin{cases} a & \text{for } 0 \le a \le \frac{1}{2} \\ \frac{1}{2}a + \frac{1}{4} & \text{for } \frac{1}{2} < a \le 1. \end{cases}$

3.7. Let i be a *t*-norm such that

$$i(a, b + c) = i(a, b) + i(a, c)$$

for all $a, b, c \in [0, 1]$, $b + c \leq 1$. Show that i must be the algebraic product; that is, $i(a, b) = a \cdot b$ for all $a, b \in [0, 1]$.

3.8. Show that the function

$$c(a) = \frac{\gamma^2(1 - a)}{a + \gamma^2(1 - a)}, \quad \forall a \in [0, 1], \gamma > 0$$

is a fuzzy complement. Plot the function for some values of γ. Find the generator of c.

3.9. Let u_w and c_w be the Yager fuzzy union and fuzzy complement, respectively. Find the dual fuzzy intersection of u_w with respect to c_w.

3.10. Prove Theorem 3.21.

3.11. Show that the generalized means defined by (3.32) become the min and max operations for $\alpha \to -\infty$ and $\alpha \to \infty$, respectively.

3.12. Show that an *OWA* operation h_w satisfies Axioms h_1 through h_5.

3.13. Show that the following operations satisfy the law of excluded middle and the law of contradiction:
  (a) $u_{\max}, i_{\min}, c(a) = 1 - a$;
  (b) $u(a, b) = \min(1, a + b), i(a, b) = \max(0, a + b - 1), c(a) = 1 - a$.

3.14. Show that the following operations on fuzzy sets satisfy De Morgan's laws:
  (a) $u_{\max}, i_{\min}, c(a) = 1 - a$;
  (b) max, min, c_λ is a Sugeno complement for some $\lambda \in (-1, \infty)$;
  (c) max, min, c_w is a Yager complement for some $w \in (0, \infty)$.

3.15. Demonstrate that the generalized means h_α defined by (3.32) are monotonic increasing with α for fixed arguments.

3.16. Prove Theorem 3.27.

4

Fuzzy Arithmetic

4.1 FUZZY NUMBERS

Among the various types of fuzzy sets, of special significance are fuzzy sets that are defined on the set $\mathbb{R}$ of real numbers. Membership functions of these sets, which have the form

$$A : \mathbb{R} \to [0, 1]$$

clearly have a quantitative meaning and may, under certain conditions, be viewed as fuzzy numbers or fuzzy intervals. To view them in this way, they should capture our intuitive conceptions of approximate numbers or intervals, such as "numbers that are close to a given real number" or "numbers that are around a given interval of real numbers." Such concepts are essential for characterizing states of fuzzy variables and, consequently, play an important role in many applications, including fuzzy control, decision making, approximate reasoning, optimization, and statistics with imprecise probabilities.

To qualify as a *fuzzy number*, a fuzzy set A on $\mathbb{R}$ must possess at least the following three properties:

  (i) A must be a normal fuzzy set;
 (ii) $^\alpha A$ must be a closed interval for every $\alpha \in (0, 1]$;
(iii) the support of A, ^{0+}A, must be bounded.

The fuzzy set must be normal since our conception of a set of "real numbers close to r" is fully satisfied by r itself; hence, the membership grade of r in any fuzzy set that attempts to capture this conception (i.e., a fuzzy number) must be 1. The bounded support of a fuzzy number and all its α-cuts for $\alpha \neq 0$ must be closed intervals to allow us to define meaningful arithmetic operations on fuzzy numbers in terms of standard arithmetic operations on closed intervals, well established in classical interval analysis.

Since α-cuts of any fuzzy number are required to be closed intervals for all $\alpha \in (0, 1]$, every fuzzy number is a convex fuzzy set. The inverse, however, is not necessarily true, since α-cuts of some convex fuzzy sets may be open or half-open intervals.

Special cases of fuzzy numbers include ordinary real numbers and intervals of real numbers, as illustrated in Fig. 4.1: (a) an ordinary real number 1.3; (b) an ordinary (crisp) closed interval [1.25, 1.35]; (c) a fuzzy number expressing the proposition "close to 1.3;" and (d) a fuzzy number with a flat region (a fuzzy interval).

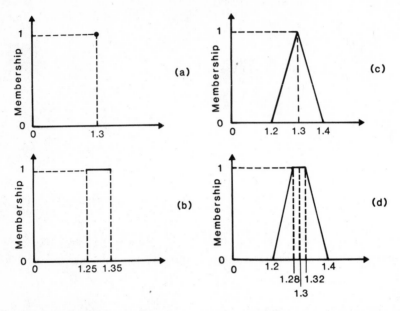

Figure 4.1 A comparison of a real number and a crisp interval with a fuzzy number and a fuzzy interval, respectively.

Although the triangular and trapezoidal shapes of membership functions shown in Fig. 4.1 are used most often for representing fuzzy numbers, other shapes may be preferable in some applications. Furthermore, membership functions of fuzzy numbers need not be symmetric as are those in Fig. 4.1. Fairly typical are so-called "bell-shaped" membership functions, as exemplified by the functions in Fig. 4.2a (symmetric) and 4.2b (asymmetric). Observe that membership functions which only increase (Fig. 4.2c) or only decrease (Fig. 4.2d) also qualify as fuzzy numbers. They capture our conception of a *large number* or a *small number* in the context of each particular application.

The following theorem shows that membership functions of fuzzy numbers may be, in general, piecewise-defined functions.

Theorem 4.1. Let $A \in \mathcal{F}(\mathbb{R})$. Then, A is a fuzzy number if and only if there exists a closed interval $[a, b] \neq \emptyset$ such that

$$A(x) = \begin{cases} 1 & \text{for } x \in [a, b] \\ l(x) & \text{for } x \in (-\infty, a) \\ r(x) & \text{for } x \in (b, \infty), \end{cases} \tag{4.1}$$

where l is a function from $(-\infty, a)$ to $[0, 1]$ that is monotonic increasing, continuous from the right, and such that $l(x) = 0$ for $x \in (-\infty, \omega_1)$; r is a function from (b, ∞) to

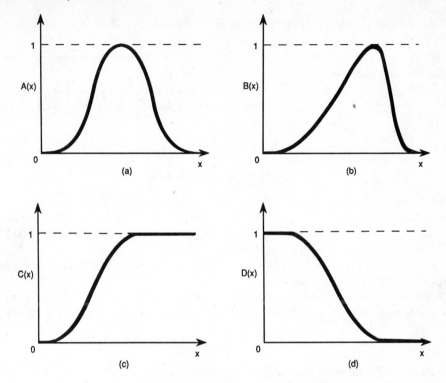

Figure 4.2   Basic types of fuzzy numbers.

$[0, 1]$ that is monotonic decreasing, continuous from the left, and such that $r(x) = 0$ for $x \in (\omega_2, \infty)$.

Proof: Necessity.   Since A is a fuzzy number, $^\alpha A$ is a closed interval for every $\alpha \in (0, 1]$. For $\alpha = 1$, ^1A is a nonempty closed interval because A is normal. Hence, there exists a pair $a, b \in \mathbb{R}$ such that $^1A = [a, b]$, where $a \le b$. That is, $A(x) = 1$ for $x \in [a, b]$ and $A(x) < 1$ for $x \notin [a, b]$. Now, let $l(x) = A(x)$ for any $x \in (-\infty, a)$. Then, $0 \le l(x) < 1$ since $0 \le A(x) < 1$ for every $x \in (-\infty, a)$. Let $x \le y < a$; then

$$A(y) \ge \min[A(x), A(a)] = A(x)$$

by Theorem 1.1 since A is convex and $A(a) = 1$. Hence, $l(y) \ge l(x)$; that is, l is monotonic increasing.

Assume now that $l(x)$ is not continuous from the right. This means that for some $x_0 \in (-\infty, a)$ there exists a sequence of numbers $\{x_n\}$ such that $x_n \ge x_0$ for any n and

$$\lim_{n \to \infty} x_n = x_0,$$

but

$$\lim_{n \to \infty} l(x_n) = \lim_{n \to \infty} A(x_n) = \alpha > l(x_0) = A(x_0).$$

Now, $x_n \in {}^\alpha A$ for any n since $^\alpha A$ is a closed interval and hence, also $x_0 \in {}^\alpha A$. Therefore, $l(x_0) = A(x_0) \ge \alpha$, which is a contradiction. That is, $l(x)$ is continuous from the right.

The proof that function r in (4.1) is monotonic decreasing and continuous from the left is similar.

Since A is a fuzzy number, ^{0+}A is bounded. Hence, there exists a pair $\omega_1, \omega_2 \in \mathbb{R}$ of finite numbers such that $A(x) = 0$ for $x \in (-\infty, \omega_1) \cup (\omega_2, \infty)$.

Sufficiency. Every fuzzy set A defined by (4.1) is clearly normal, and its support, ^{0+}A, is bounded, since $^{0+}A \subseteq [\omega_1, \omega_2]$. It remains to prove that $^{\alpha}A$ is a closed interval for any $\alpha \in (0, 1]$. Let

$$x_\alpha = \inf\{x | l(x) \geq \alpha, x < a\},$$

$$y_\alpha = \sup\{x | r(x) \geq \alpha, x > b\}$$

for each $\alpha \in (0, 1]$. We need to prove that $^{\alpha}A = [x_\alpha, y_\alpha]$ for all $\alpha \in (0, 1]$.

For any $x_0 \in {}^{\alpha}A$, if $x_0 < a$, then $l(x_0) = A(x_0) \geq \alpha$. That is, $x_0 \in \{x | l(x) \geq \alpha, x < a\}$ and, consequently, $x_0 \geq \inf\{x | l(x) \geq \alpha, x < a\} = x_\alpha$. If $x_0 > b$, then $r(x_0) = A(x_0) \geq \alpha$; that is, $x_0 \in \{x | r(x) \geq \alpha, x > b\}$ and, consequently, $x_0 \leq \sup\{x | r(x) \geq \alpha, x > b\} = y_\alpha$. Obviously, $x_\alpha \leq a$ and $y_\alpha \geq b$; that is, $[a, b] \subseteq [x_\alpha, y_\alpha]$. Therefore, $x_0 \in [x_\alpha, y_\alpha]$ and hence, $^{\alpha}A \subseteq [x_\alpha, y_\alpha]$. It remains to prove that $x_\alpha, y_\alpha \in {}^{\alpha}A$.

By the definition of x_α, there must exist a sequence $\{x_n\}$ in $\{x | l(x) \geq \alpha, x < a\}$ such that $\lim_{n \to \infty} x_n = x_\alpha$, where $x_n \geq x_\alpha$ for any n. Since l is continuous from the right, we have

$$l(x_\alpha) = l(\lim_{n \to \infty} x_n) = \lim_{n \to \infty} l(x_n) \geq \alpha.$$

Hence, $x_\alpha \in {}^{\alpha}A$. We can prove that $y_\alpha \in {}^{\alpha}A$ in a similar way. ■

The implication of Theorem 4.1 is that every fuzzy number can be represented in the form of (4.1). In general, this form allows us to define fuzzy numbers in a piecewise manner, as illustrated in Fig. 4.3.

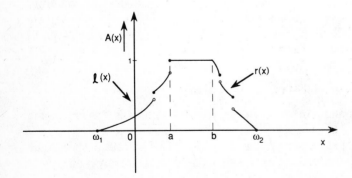

Figure 4.3 General fuzzy number A expressed in the form (4.1).

As an example, let us define the four fuzzy numbers in Fig. 4.1 in terms of (4.1):

(a) $\omega_1 = a = b = \omega_2 = 1.3, l(x) = 0$ for all $x \in (-\infty, 1.3), r(x) = 0$ for all $x \in (1.3, \infty)$.

(b) $\omega_1 = a = 1.25, b = \omega_2 = 1.35, l(x) = 0$ for all $x \in (-\infty, 1.25), r(x) = 0$ for all $x \in (1.35, \infty)$.

(c) $a = b = 1.3, \omega_1 = 1.2, \omega_2 = 1.4,$

$$l(x) = \begin{cases} 0 & \text{for } x \in (-\infty, 1.2) \\ 10(x - 1.3) + 1 & \text{for } x \in [1.2, 1.3), \end{cases}$$

$$r(x) = \begin{cases} 10(1.3 - x) + 1 & \text{for } x \in (1.3, 1.4] \\ 0 & \text{for } x \in (1.4, \infty). \end{cases}$$

(d) $a = 1.28, b = 1.32, \omega_1 = 1.2, \omega_2 = 1.4,$

$$l(x) = \begin{cases} 0 & \text{for } x \in (-\infty, 1.2) \\ 12.5(x - 1.28) + 1 & \text{for } x \in [1.2, 1.28), \end{cases}$$

$$r(x) = \begin{cases} 12.5(1.32 - x) + 1 & \text{for } x \in (1.32, 1.4] \\ 0 & \text{for } x \in (1.4, \infty). \end{cases}$$

Observe that (4.1) is also capable of expressing fuzzy numbers of the types depicted in Figs. 4.2c and d. For example, the fuzzy number by which we express the linguistic concept *very large*, as defined in Fig. 4.4, is expressed in terms of (4.1) as follows: $a = 90, b = 100, \omega_1 = 77.5, \omega_2 = 100,$

$$l(x) = \begin{cases} 0 & \text{for } x \in (-\infty, 77.5) \\ 0.08(x - 90) + 1 & \text{for } x \in [77.5, 90), \end{cases}$$

$$r(x) = 0 \quad \text{for } x \in (100, \infty).$$

Using fuzzy numbers, we can define the concept of a *fuzzy cardinality* for fuzzy sets that are defined on finite universal sets. Given a fuzzy set A defined on a finite universal set X, its fuzzy cardinality, $|\tilde{A}|$, is a fuzzy number defined on $\mathbb{N}$ by the formula

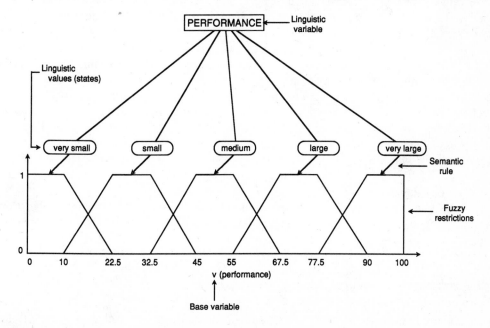

Figure 4.4 An example of a linguistic variable.

$$|\tilde{A}|(|^{\alpha}A|) = \alpha$$

for all $\alpha \in \Lambda(A)$. For example, the fuzzy cardinality of fuzzy set D_2 defined in Table 1.2, whose α-cuts are shown in Fig. 1.8a, is

$$|\tilde{D}_2| = .13/19 + .27/17 + .4/15 + .53/13 + .67/11 + .8/9 + .93/7 + 1/5.$$

4.2 LINGUISTIC VARIABLES

The concept of a fuzzy number plays a fundamental role in formulating *quantitative fuzzy variables*. These are variables whose states are fuzzy numbers. When, in addition, the fuzzy numbers represent linguistic concepts, such as *very small, small, medium*, and so on, as interpreted in a particular context, the resulting constructs are usually called *linguistic variables*.

Each linguistic variable the states of which are expressed by linguistic terms interpreted as specific fuzzy numbers is defined in terms of a *base variable*, the values of which are real numbers within a specific range. A base variable is a variable in the classical sense, exemplified by any physical variable (e.g., temperature, pressure, speed, voltage, humidity, etc.) as well as any other numerical variable, (e.g., age, interest rate, performance, salary, blood count, probability, reliability, etc.). In a linguistic variable, linguistic terms representing approximate values of a base variable, germane to a particular application, are captured by appropriate fuzzy numbers.

Each linguistic variable is fully characterized by a quintuple (v, T, X, g, m) in which v is the *name* of the variable, T is the set of *linguistic terms* of v that refer to a base variable whose values range over a universal set X, g is a *syntactic rule* (a grammar) for generating linguistic terms, and m is a *semantic rule* that assigns to each linguistic term $t \in T$ its *meaning*, $m(t)$, which is a fuzzy set on X (i.e., $m : T \rightarrow \mathcal{F}(X)$).

An example of a linguistic variable is shown in Fig. 4.4. Its name is performance. This variable expresses the performance (which is the base variable in this example) of a goal-oriented entity (a person, machine, organization, method, etc.) in a given context by five basic linguistic terms—*very small, small, medium, large, very large*—as well as other linguistic terms generated by a syntactic rule (not explicitly shown in Fig. 4.4), such as *not very small, large or very large, very very small*, and so forth. Each of the basic linguistic terms is assigned one of five fuzzy numbers by a semantic rule, as shown in the figure. The fuzzy numbers, whose membership functions have the usual trapezoidal shapes, are defined on the interval [0, 100], the range of the base variable. Each of them expresses a fuzzy restriction on this range.

To deal with linguistic variables, we need not only the various set-theoretic operations presented in Chapter 3, but also arithmetic operations on fuzzy numbers. The latter are examined in the rest of this chapter.

4.3 ARITHMETIC OPERATIONS ON INTERVALS

Fuzzy arithmetic is based on two properties of fuzzy numbers: (1) each fuzzy set, and thus also each fuzzy number, can fully and uniquely be represented by its α-cuts (Sec. 2.2); and

(2) α-cuts of each fuzzy number are closed intervals of real numbers for all $\alpha \in (0, 1]$. These properties enable us to define arithmetic operations on fuzzy numbers in terms of arithmetic operations on their α-cuts (i.e., arithmetic operations on closed intervals). The latter operations are a subject of *interval analysis*, a well-established area of classical mathematics; we overview them in this section to facilitate our presentation of fuzzy arithmetic in the next section.

Let $*$ denote any of the four arithmetic operations on closed intervals: *addition* $+$, *subtraction* $-$, *multiplication* $\cdot$, and *division* $/$. Then,

$$[a, b] * [d, e] = \{f * g | a \le f \le b, d \le g \le e\} \tag{4.2}$$

is a general property of all arithmetic operations on closed intervals, except that $[a, b]/[d, e]$ is not defined when $0 \in [d, e]$. That is, the result of an arithmetic operation on closed intervals is again a closed interval.

The four arithmetic operations on closed intervals are defined as follows:

$$[a, b] + [d, e] = [a + d, b + e], \tag{4.3}$$

$$[a, b] - [d, e] = [a - e, b - d], \tag{4.4}$$

$$[a, b] \cdot [d, e] = [\min(ad, ae, bd, be), \max(ad, ae, bd, be)], \tag{4.5}$$

and, provided that $0 \notin [d, e]$,

$$[a, b]/[d, e] = [a, b] \cdot [1/e, 1/d]$$
$$= [\min(a/d, a/e, b/d, b/e), \max(a/d, a/e, b/d, b/e)]. \tag{4.6}$$

Note that a real number r may also be regarded as a special (degenerated) interval $[r, r]$. When one of the intervals in (4.3)–(4.6) is degenerated, we obtain special operations; when both of them are degenerated, we obtain the standard arithmetic of real numbers.

The following are a few examples illustrating the interval-valued arithmetic operations defined by (4.3)–(4.6):

$$[2, 5] + [1, 3] = [3, 8] \qquad [0, 1] + [-6, 5] = [-6, 6],$$
$$[2, 5] - [1, 3] = [-1, 4] \qquad [0, 1] - [-6, 5] = [-5, 7],$$
$$[-1, 1] \cdot [-2, -0.5] = [-2, 2] \qquad [3, 4] \cdot [2, 2] = [6, 8],$$
$$[-1, 1]/[-2, -0.5] = [-2, 2] \qquad [4, 10]/[1, 2] = [2, 10].$$

Arithmetic operations on closed intervals satisfy some useful properties. To overview them, let $A = [a_1, a_2]$, $B = [b_1, b_2]$, $C = [c_1, c_2]$, $\mathbf{0} = [0, 0]$, $\mathbf{1} = [1, 1]$. Using these symbols, the properties are formulated as follows:

1. $A + B = B + A$,
   $A \cdot B = B \cdot A$ *(commutativity)*.
2. $(A + B) + C = A + (B + C)$
   $(A \cdot B) \cdot C = A \cdot (B \cdot C)$ *(associativity)*.
3. $A = \mathbf{0} + A = A + \mathbf{0}$
   $A = \mathbf{1} \cdot A = A \cdot \mathbf{1}$ *(identity)*.

4. $A \cdot (B + C) \subseteq A \cdot B + A \cdot C$ (*subdistributivity*).

5. If $b \cdot c \geq 0$ for every $b \in B$ and $c \in C$, then $A \cdot (B + C) = A \cdot B + A \cdot C$ (*distributivity*). Furthermore, if $A = [a, a]$, then $a \cdot (B + C) = a \cdot B + a \cdot C$.

6. $0 \in A - A$ and $1 \in A/A$.

7. If $A \subseteq E$ and $B \subseteq F$, then:

$$A + B \subseteq E + F,$$

$$A - B \subseteq E - F,$$

$$A \cdot B \subseteq E \cdot F,$$

$$A/B \subseteq E/F \ (\textit{inclusion monotonicity}).$$

Most of these properties follow directly from (4.3)–(4.6). As an example, we prove only the less obvious properties of subdistributivity and distributivity. First, we have

$$A \cdot (B + C) = \{a \cdot (b + c) | a \in A, b \in B, c \in C\}$$

$$= \{a \cdot b + a \cdot c | a \in A, b \in B, c \in C\}$$

$$\subseteq \{a \cdot b + a' \cdot c | a, a' \in A, b \in B, c \in C\}$$

$$= A \cdot B + A \cdot C.$$

Hence, $A \cdot (B + C) \subseteq A \cdot B + A \cdot C$.

Assume now, without any loss of generality, that $b_1 \geq 0$ and $c_1 \geq 0$. Then, we have to consider the following three cases:

1. If $a_1 \geq 0$, then

$$A \cdot (B + C) = [a_1 \cdot (b_1 + c_1), a_2 \cdot (b_2 + c_2)]$$

$$= [a_1 \cdot b_1, a_2 \cdot b_2] + [a_1 \cdot c_1 + a_2 \cdot c_2]$$

$$= A \cdot B + A \cdot C.$$

2. If $a_1 < 0$ and $a_2 \leq 0$, then $-a_2 \geq 0$, $(-A) = [-a_2, -a_1]$, and

$$(-A) \cdot (B + C) = (-A) \cdot B + (-A) \cdot C.$$

Hence, $A \cdot (B + C) = A \cdot B + A \cdot C$.

3. If $a_1 < 0$ and $a_2 > 0$, then

$$A \cdot (B + C) = [a_1 \cdot (b_2 + c_2), a_2 \cdot (b_2 + c_2)]$$

$$= [a_1 \cdot b_2, a_2 \cdot b_2] + [a_1 \cdot c_2, a_2 \cdot c_2]$$

$$= A \cdot B + A \cdot C.$$

To show that distributivity does not hold in general, let $A = [0, 1]$, $B = [1, 2]$, $C = [-2, -1]$. Then, $A \cdot B = [0, 2]$, $A \cdot C = [-2, 0]$, $B + C = [-1, 1]$, and

$$A \cdot (B + C) = [-1, 1] \subset [-2, 2] = A \cdot B + A \cdot C.$$

4.4 ARITHMETIC OPERATIONS ON FUZZY NUMBERS

In this section, we present two methods for developing fuzzy arithmetic. One method is based on interval arithmetic, which is overviewed in Sec. 4.3. The other method employs the extension principle, by which operations on real numbers are extended to operations on fuzzy numbers. We assume in this section that fuzzy numbers are represented by continuous membership functions.

Let A and B denote fuzzy numbers and let $*$ denote any of the four basic arithmetic operations. Then, we define a fuzzy set on $\mathbb{R}$, $A * B$, by defining its α-cut, $^{\alpha}(A * B)$, as

$$^{\alpha}(A * B) = {}^{\alpha}A * {}^{\alpha}B \tag{4.7}$$

for any $\alpha \in (0, 1]$. (When $* = /$, clearly, we have to require that $0 \notin {}^{\alpha}B$ for all $\alpha \in (0, 1]$.) Due to Theorem 2.5, $A * B$ can be expressed as

$$A * B = \bigcup_{\alpha \in [0,1]} {}_{\alpha}(A * B). \tag{4.8}$$

Since $^{\alpha}(A * B)$ is a closed interval for each $\alpha \in (0, 1]$ and A, B are fuzzy numbers, $A * B$ is also a fuzzy number.

As an example of employing (4.7) and (4.8), consider two triangular-shape fuzzy numbers A and B defined as follows:

$$A(x) = \begin{cases} 0 & \text{for } x \le -1 \text{ and } x > 3 \\ (x + 1)/2 & \text{for } -1 < x \le 1 \\ (3 - x)/2 & \text{for } 1 < x \le 3, \end{cases}$$

$$B(x) = \begin{cases} 0 & \text{for } x \le 1 \text{ and } x > 5 \\ (x - 1)/2 & \text{for } 1 < x \le 3 \\ (5 - x)/2 & \text{for } 3 < x \le 5. \end{cases}$$

Their α-cuts are:

$$^{\alpha}A = [2\alpha - 1, 3 - 2\alpha],$$
$$^{\alpha}B = [2\alpha + 1, 5 - 2\alpha].$$

Using (4.3)–(4.7), we obtain

$$^{\alpha}(A + B) = [4\alpha, 8 - 4\alpha] \quad \text{for } \alpha \in (0, 1],$$

$$^{\alpha}(A - B) = [4\alpha - 6, 2 - 4\alpha] \quad \text{for } \alpha \in (0, 1],$$

$$^{\alpha}(A \cdot B) = \begin{cases} [-4\alpha^2 + 12\alpha - 5, 4\alpha^2 - 16\alpha + 15] & \text{for } \alpha \in (0, .5] \\ [4\alpha^2 - 1, 4\alpha^2 - 16\alpha + 15] & \text{for } \alpha \in (.5, 1], \end{cases}$$

$$^{\alpha}(A/B) = \begin{cases} [(2\alpha - 1)/(2\alpha + 1), (3 - 2\alpha)/(2\alpha + 1)] & \text{for } \alpha \in (0, .5] \\ [(2\alpha - 1)/(5 - 2\alpha), (3 - 2\alpha)/(2\alpha + 1)] & \text{for } \alpha \in (.5, 1]. \end{cases}$$

The resulting fuzzy numbers are then:

$$(A + B)(x) = \begin{cases} 0 & \text{for } x \le 0 \quad \text{and } x > 8 \\ x/4 & \text{for } 0 < x \le 4 \\ (8 - x)/4 & \text{for } 4 < x \le 8, \end{cases}$$

$$(A - B)(x) = \begin{cases} 0 & \text{for } x \le -6 \text{ and } x > 2 \\ (x+6)/4 & \text{for } -6 < x \le -2 \\ (2-x)/4 & \text{for } -2 < x \le 2, \end{cases}$$

$$(A \cdot B)(x) = \begin{cases} 0 & \text{for } x < -5 \text{ and } x \ge 15 \\ \left[3 - (4-x)^{1/2}\right]/2 & \text{for } -5 \le x < 0 \\ (1+x)^{1/2}/2 & \text{for } 0 \le x < 3 \\ \left[4 - (1+x)^{1/2}\right]/2 & \text{for } 3 \le x < 15, \end{cases}$$

$$(A/B)(x) = \begin{cases} 0 & \text{for } x < -1 \text{ and } x \ge 3 \\ (x+1)/(2-2x) & \text{for } -1 \le x < 0 \\ (5x+1)/(2x+2) & \text{for } 0 \le x < 1/3 \\ (3-x)/(2x+2) & \text{for } 1/3 \le x < 3. \end{cases}$$

The four arithmetic operations performed in this example are illustrated in Fig. 4.5.

We now proceed to the second method for developing fuzzy arithmetic, which is based on the extension principle (Section 2.3). Employing this principle, standard arithmetic operations on real numbers are extended to fuzzy numbers.

Let $*$ denote any of the four basic arithmetic operations and let A, B denote fuzzy numbers. Then, we define a fuzzy set on $\mathbb{R}$, $A * B$, by the equation

$$(A * B)(z) = \sup_{z = x * y} \min[A(x), B(y)] \qquad (4.9)$$

for all $z \in \mathbb{R}$. More specifically, we define for all $z \in \mathbb{R}$:

$$(A + B)(z) = \sup_{z = x + y} \min[A(x), B(y)], \qquad (4.10)$$

$$(A - B)(z) = \sup_{z = x - y} \min[A(x), B(y)], \qquad (4.11)$$

$$(A \cdot B)(z) = \sup_{z = x \cdot y} \min[A(x), B(y)], \qquad (4.12)$$

$$(A/B)(z) = \sup_{z = x/y} \min[A(x), B(y)]. \qquad (4.13)$$

Although $A * B$ defined by (4.9) is a fuzzy set on $\mathbb{R}$, we have to show that it is a fuzzy number for each $* \in \{+, -, \cdot, /\}$. This is a subject of the following theorem.

Theorem 4.2. Let $* \in \{+, -, \cdot, /\}$, and let A, B denote continuous fuzzy numbers. Then, the fuzzy set $A * B$ defined by (4.9) is a continuous fuzzy number.

Proof: First, we prove (4.7) by showing that $^\alpha(A * B)$ is a closed interval for every $\alpha \in (0, 1]$. For any $z \in {}^\alpha A * {}^\alpha B$, there exist some $x_0 \in {}^\alpha A$ and $y_0 \in {}^\alpha B$ such that $z = x_0 * y_0$. Thus,

$$(A * B)(z) = \sup_{z = x * y} \min[A(x), B(y)]$$

$$\ge \min[A(x_0), B(y_0)]$$

$$\ge \alpha.$$

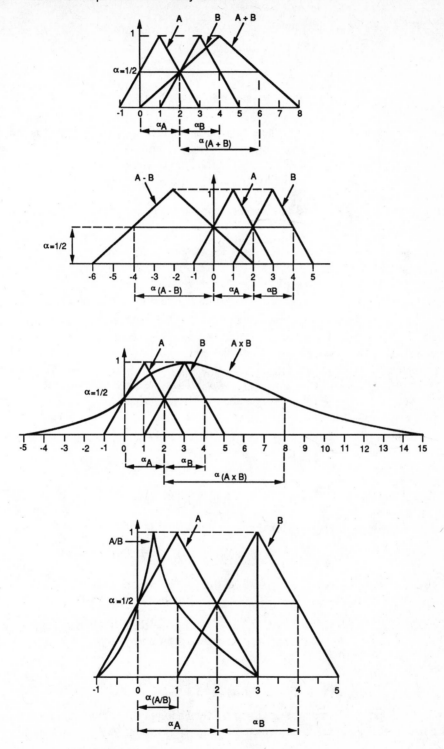

Figure 4.5 Illustration of arithmetic operations on fuzzy numbers.

Hence, $z \in {}^\alpha(A * B)$ and, consequently,

$$^\alpha A * {}^\alpha B \subseteq {}^\alpha(A * B).$$

For any $z \in {}^\alpha(A * B)$, we have

$$(A * B)(z) = \sup_{z=x*y} \min[A(x), B(y)] \geq \alpha.$$

Moreover, for any $n > [1/\alpha] + 1$, where $[1/\alpha]$ denotes the largest integer that is less than or equal to $1/\alpha$, there exist x_n and y_n such that $z = x_n * y_n$ and

$$\min[A(x_n), B(y_n)] > \alpha - \frac{1}{n}.$$

That is, $x_n \in {}^{\alpha - 1/n}A$, $y_n \in {}^{\alpha - 1/n}B$ and we may consider two sequences, $\{x_n\}$ and $\{y_n\}$. Since

$$\alpha - \frac{1}{n} \leq \alpha - \frac{1}{n+1},$$

we have

$$^{\alpha - 1/(n+1)}A \subseteq {}^{\alpha - 1/n}A, \quad {}^{\alpha - 1/(n+1)}B \subseteq {}^{\alpha - 1/n}B.$$

Hence, $\{x_n\}$ and $\{y_n\}$ fall into some ${}^{\alpha - 1/n}A$ and ${}^{\alpha - 1/n}B$, respectively. Since the latter are closed intervals, $\{x_n\}$ and $\{y_n\}$ are bounded sequences. Thus, there exists a convergent subsequence $\{x_{n,i}\}$ such that $x_{n,i} \to x_0$. To the corresponding subsequence $\{y_{n,i}\}$, there also exists a convergent subsequence $\{y_{n,i,j}\}$ such that $y_{n,i,j} \to y_0$. If we take the corresponding subsequence, $\{x_{n,i,j}\}$, from $\{x_{n,i}\}$, then $x_{n,i,j} \to x_0$. Thus, we have two sequences, $\{x_{n,i,j}\}$ and $\{y_{n,i,j}\}$, such that $x_{n,i,j} \to x_0$, $y_{n,i,j} \to y_0$, and $x_{n,i,j} * y_{n,i,j} = z$.

Now, since $*$ is continuous,

$$z = \lim_{j \to \infty} x_{n,i,j} * y_{n,i,j} = (\lim_{j \to \infty} x_{n,i,j}) * (\lim_{j \to \infty} y_{n,i,j}) = x_0 * y_0.$$

Also, since $A(x_{n,i,j}) > \alpha - \dfrac{1}{n_{i,j}}$ and $B(y_{n,i,j}) > \alpha - \dfrac{1}{n_{i,j}}$,

$$A(x_0) = A(\lim_{j \to \infty} x_{n,i,j}) = \lim_{j \to \infty} A(x_{n,i,j}) \geq \lim_{j \to \infty} (\alpha - \frac{1}{n_{i,j}}) = \alpha$$

and

$$B(y_0) = B(\lim_{j \to \infty} y_{n,i,j}) = \lim_{j \to \infty} B(y_{n,i,j}) \geq \lim_{j \to \infty} (\alpha - \frac{1}{n_{i,j}}) = \alpha.$$

Therefore, there exist $x_0 \in {}^\alpha A$, $y_0 \in {}^\alpha B$ such that $z = x_0 * y_0$. That is, $z \in {}^\alpha A * {}^\alpha B$. Thus,

$$^\alpha(A * B) \subseteq {}^\alpha A * {}^\alpha B,$$

and, consequently,

$$^\alpha(A * B) = {}^\alpha A * {}^\alpha B.$$

Now we prove that $A * B$ must be continuous. By Theorem 4.1, the membership function of $A * B$ must be of the general form depicted in Fig. 4.3. Assume $A * B$ is not continous at z_0; that is,

$$\lim_{z \to z_0^-} (A * B)(z) < (A * B)(z_0) = \sup_{z_0 = x*y} \min[A(x), B(y)].$$

Then, there must exist x_0 and y_0 such that $z_0 = x_0 * y_0$ and

$$\lim_{z \to z_0^-} (A * B)(z) < \min[A(x_0), B(y_0)]. \tag{4.14}$$

Since the operation $* \in \{+, -, \cdot, /\}$ is monotonic with respect to the first and the second arguments, respectively, we can always find two sequences $\{x_n\}$ and $\{y_n\}$ such that $x_n \to x_0$, $y_n \to y_0$ as $n \to \infty$, and $x_n * y_n < z_0$ for any n. Let $z_n = x_n * y_n$; then $z_n \to z_0$ as $n \to \infty$. Thus,

$$\lim_{z \to z_0^-} (A * B)(z) = \lim_{n \to \infty} (A * B)(z_n) = \lim_{n \to \infty} \sup_{z_n = x*y} \min[A(x), B(y)]$$

$$\geq \lim_{n \to \infty} \min[A(x_n), B(y_n)] = \min[A(\lim_{n \to \infty} x_n), B(\lim_{n \to \infty} y_n)] = \min[A(x_0), B(y_0)].$$

This contradicts (4.14) and, therefore, $A * B$ must be a continuous fuzzy number. This completes the proof. ■

4.5 LATTICE OF FUZZY NUMBERS

As is well known, the set $\mathbb{R}$ of real numbers is linearly ordered. For every pair of real numbers, x and y, either $x \leq y$ or $y \leq x$. The pair $(\mathbb{R}, \leq)$ is a lattice, which can also be expressed in terms of two lattice operations,

$$\min(x, y) = \begin{cases} x & \text{if } x \leq y \\ y & \text{if } y \leq x, \end{cases} \tag{4.15}$$

$$\max(x, y) = \begin{cases} y & \text{if } x \leq y \\ x & \text{if } y \leq x \end{cases} \tag{4.16}$$

for every pair $x, y \in \mathbb{R}$. The linear ordering of real numbers does not extend to fuzzy numbers, but we show in this section that fuzzy numbers can be ordered partially in a natural way and that this partial ordering forms a distributive lattice.

To introduce a meaningful ordering of fuzzy numbers, we first extend the lattice operations min and max on real numbers, as defined by (4.15) and (4.16), to corresponding operations on fuzzy numbers, MIN and MAX. For any two fuzzy numbers A and B, we define

$$\text{MIN} (A, B)(z) = \sup_{z = \min(x, y)} \min[A(x), B(y)], \tag{4.17}$$

$$\text{MAX} (A, B)(z) = \sup_{z = \max(x, y)} \min[A(x), B(y)] \tag{4.18}$$

for all $z \in \mathbb{R}$.

Observe that the symbols MIN and MAX, which denote the introduced operations on fuzzy numbers, must be distinguished from the symbols min and max, which denote the usual operations of minimum and maximum on real numbers, respectively. Since min and max are continuous operations, it follows from (4.17), (4.18), and the proof of Theorem 4.2 that MIN (A, B) and MAX (A, B) are fuzzy numbers.

.s important to realize that the operations MIN and MAX are totally different from
.. standard fuzzy intersection and union, min and max. This difference is illustrated in
Fig. 4.6, where

$$A(x) = \begin{cases} 0 & \text{for } x < -2 \text{ and } x > 4 \\ (x+2)/3 & \text{for } -2 \le x \le 1 \\ (4-x)/3 & \text{for } 1 \le x \le 4, \end{cases}$$

$$B(x) = \begin{cases} 0 & \text{for } x < 1 \text{ and } x > 3 \\ x-1 & \text{for } 1 \le x \le 2 \\ 3-x & \text{for } 2 \le x \le 3, \end{cases}$$

$$\text{MIN}(A,B)(x) = \begin{cases} 0 & \text{for } x < -2 \text{ and } x > 3 \\ (x+2)/3 & \text{for } -2 \le x \le 1 \\ (4-x)/3 & \text{for } 1 < x \le 2.5 \\ 3-x & \text{for } 2.5 < x \le 3, \end{cases}$$

$$\text{MAX}(A,B)(x) = \begin{cases} 0 & \text{for } x < 1 \text{ and } x > 4 \\ x-1 & \text{for } 1 \le x \le 2 \\ 3-x & \text{for } 2 < x \le 2.5 \\ (4-x)/3 & \text{for } 2.5 < x \le 4. \end{cases}$$

Let $\mathcal{R}$ denote the set of all fuzzy numbers. Then, operations MIN and MAX are clearly
functions of the form $\mathcal{R} \times \mathcal{R} \to \mathcal{R}$. The following theorem, which establishes basic properties
of these operations, ensures that the triple $\langle \mathcal{R}, \text{MIN}, \text{MAX} \rangle$ is a distributive lattice, in which
MIN and MAX represent the meet and join, respectively.

Theorem 4.3. Let MIN and MAX be binary operations on $\mathcal{R}$ defined by (4.17) and
(4.18), respectively. Then, for any $A, B, C \in \mathcal{R}$, the following properties hold:

(a) $\text{MIN}(A, B) = \text{MIN}(B, A)$,

  $\text{MAX}(A, B) = \text{MAX}(B, A)$ (*commutativity*).

(b) $\text{MIN}[\text{MIN}(A, B), C] = \text{MIN}[A, \text{MIN}(B, C)]$,

  $\text{MAX}[\text{MAX}(A, B), C] = \text{MAX}[A, \text{MAX}(B, C)]$ (*associativity*).

(c) $\text{MIN}(A, A) = A$,

  $\text{MAX}(A, A) = A$ (*idempotence*).

(d) $\text{MIN}[A, \text{MAX}(A, B)] = A$,

  $\text{MAX}[A, \text{MIN}(A, B)] = A$ (*absorption*).

(e) $\text{MIN}[A, \text{MAX}(B, C)] = \text{MAX}[\text{MIN}(A, B), \text{MIN}(A, C)]$,

  $\text{MAX}[A, \text{MIN}(B, C)] = \text{MIN}[\text{MAX}(A, B), \text{MAX}(A, C)]$ (*distributivity*).

Proof: We focus only on proving properties (b), (d), and (e); proving properties (a) and
(c) is rather trivial.
  (b) For all $z \in \mathbb{R}$,

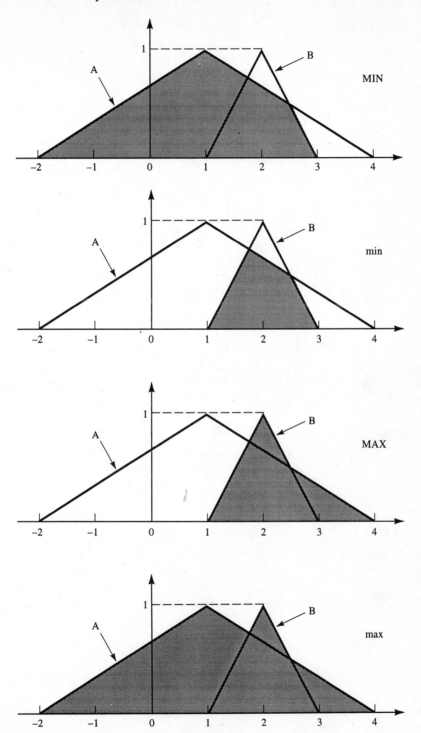

Figure 4.6 Comparison of the operations MIN, min, MAX, max.

$$MIN\,[A, MIN\,(B, C)](z) = \sup_{z=\min(x,y)} \min[A(x), MIN\,(B, C)(y)]$$

$$= \sup_{z=\min(x,y)} \min[A(x), \sup_{y=\min(u,v)} \min[B(u), C(v)]]$$

$$= \sup_{z=\min(x,y)\ y=\min(u,v)} \sup \min[A(x), B(u), C(v)]$$

$$= \sup_{z=\min(x,u,v)} \min[A(x), B(u), C(v)]$$

$$= \sup_{z=\min(s,v)\ s=\min(x,u)} \sup \min[A(x), B(u), C(v)]$$

$$= \sup_{z=\min(s,v)} \min[\sup_{s=\min(x,u)} \min[A(x), B(u)], C(v)]$$

$$= \sup_{z=\min(s,v)} \min[MIN\,(A, B)(s), C(v)]$$

$$= MIN\,[MIN\,(A, B), C](z).$$

The proof of the associativity of MAX is analogous.
(d) For all $z \in \mathbb{R}$,

$$MIN\,[A, MAX\,(A, B)](z) = \sup_{z=\min(x,y)} \min[A(x), MAX\,(A, B)(y)]$$

$$= \sup_{z=\min(x,y)} \min[A(x), \sup_{y=\max(u,v)} \min[A(u), B(v)]]$$

$$= \sup_{z=\min(x,\max(u,v))} \min[A(x), A(u), B(v)].$$

Let M denote the right-hand side of the last equation. Since B is a fuzzy number, there exists $v_0 \in \mathbb{R}$ such that $B(v_0) = 1$. By $z = \min[z, \max(z, v_0)]$, we have

$$M \geq \min[A(z), A(z), B(v_0)] = A(z).$$

On the other hand, since $z = \min[x, \max(u, v)]$, we have

$$\min(x, u) \leq z \leq x \leq \max(x, u).$$

By the convexity of fuzzy numbers,

$$A(z) \geq \min[A[\min(x, u)], A[\max(x, u)]]$$

$$= \min[A(x), A(u)]$$

$$\geq \min[A(x), A(u), B(v)].$$

Thus, $M = A(z)$ and, consequently, $MIN[A, MAX(B, C)] = A$. The proof of the other absorption property is similar.
(e) For any $z \in \mathbb{R}$, it is easy to see that

$$\text{MIN}\,[A, \text{MAX}\,(B, C)](z) = \sup_{z=\min[x,\max(u,v)]} \min[A(x), B(u), C(v)], \qquad (4.19)$$

$$\text{MAX}\,[\text{MIN}\,(A, B), \text{MIN}\,(A, C)](z) =$$

$$\sup_{z=\max[\min(m,n),\min(s,t)]} \min[A(m), B(n), A(s), C(t)]. \qquad (4.20)$$

To prove that (4.19) and (4.20) are equal, we first show that $E \subseteq F$, where

$$E = \{\min[A(x), B(u), C(v)]\,|\, \min[x, \max(u, v)] = z\},$$

$$F = \{\min[A(m), B(n), A(s), C(t)]\,|\, \max[\min(m, n), \min(s, t)] = z\}.$$

For every $a = \min[A(x), B(u), C(v)]$ such that $\min[x, \max(u, v)] = z$ (i.e., $a \in E$), there exists $m = s = x$, $n = u$, and $t = v$ such that

$$\max[\min(m, n), \min(s, t)] = \max[\min(x, u), \min(x, v)]$$

$$= \min[x, \max(u, v)] = z;$$

hence, $a = \min[A(x), B(u), A(x), C(v)] = \min[A(m), B(n), A(s), C(t)]$. That is, $a \in F$ and, consequently, $E \subseteq F$. This means that (4.20) is greater than or equal to (4.19). Next, we show that these two functions are equal by showing that for any number b in F, there exists a number a in E such that $b \le a$.

For any $b \in F$, there exist m, n, s, and t such that

$$\max[\min(m, n), \min(s, t)] = z,$$

$$b = \min[A(m), B(n), A(s), C(t)].$$

Hence, we have

$$z = \min[\max(s, m), \max(s, n), \max(t, m), \max(t, n)].$$

Let $x = \min[\max(s, m), \max(s, n), \max(t, m)]$, $u = n$, and $v = t$. Then, we have $z = \min[x, \max(u, v)]$. On the other hand, it is easy to see that

$$\min(s, m) \le x \le \max(s, m).$$

By convexity of A,

$$A(x) \ge \min[A(\min(s, m)), A(\max(s, m))]$$

$$= \min[A(s), A(m)].$$

Hence, there exists $a = \min[A(x), B(u), C(v)]$ with $\min[x, \max(u, v)] = z$ (i.e., $a \in F$), and

$$a = \min[A(x), B(u), C(v)] \ge \min[A(s), A(m), B(n), C(t)] = b.$$

That is, for any $b \in F$, there exists $a \in F$ such that $b \le a$. This implies that

$$\sup F \le \sup E.$$

This inequality, together with the previous result, ensure that (4.19) and (4.20) are equal. This concludes the proof of the first distributive law. The proof of the second distributive law is analogous. ■

The lattice $\langle \mathcal{R}, \text{MIN}, \text{MAX} \rangle$ can also be expressed as the pair $\langle \mathcal{R}, \preceq \rangle$, where $\preceq$ is a partial ordering defined as:

$A \preceq B$ iff $\text{MIN}(A, B) = A$ or, alternatively,
$A \preceq B$ iff $\text{MAX}(A, B) = B$

for any $A, B \in \mathcal{R}$. We can also define the partial ordering in terms of the relevant α-cuts:

$A \preceq B$ iff $\min({}^\alpha A, {}^\alpha B) = {}^\alpha A$,
$A \preceq B$ iff $\max({}^\alpha A, {}^\alpha B) = {}^\alpha B$

for any $A, B \in \mathcal{R}$ and $\alpha \in (0, 1]$, where ${}^\alpha A$ and ${}^\alpha B$ are closed intervals (say, ${}^\alpha A = [a_1, a_2], {}^\alpha B = [b_1, b_2]$). Then,

$$\min({}^\alpha A, {}^\alpha B) = [\min(a_1, b_1), \min(a_2, b_2)],$$

$$\max({}^\alpha A, {}^\alpha B) = [\max(a_1, b_1), \max(a_2, b_2)].$$

If we define the partial ordering of closed intervals in the usual way, that is,

$$[a_1, a_2] \leq [b_1, b_2] \text{ iff } a_1 \leq b_1 \text{ and } a_2 \leq b_2,$$

then for any $A, B \in \mathcal{R}$, we have

$$A \preceq B \text{ iff } {}^\alpha A \leq {}^\alpha B$$

for all $\alpha \in (0, 1]$. This means, for example, that the two fuzzy numbers, A and B, in Fig. 4.6 are not comparable. However, values of linguistic variables in most applications are defined by fuzzy numbers that are comparable. For example, the values of the linguistic variable "performance" defined in Fig. 4.4 form a chain:

$$\text{very small} \preceq \text{small} \preceq \text{medium} \preceq \text{large} \preceq \text{very large}.$$

Although the set $\mathcal{R}$ is not linearly ordered, contrary to the set $\mathbb{R}$, there are some subsets of $\mathcal{R}$ that are linearly ordered. Such subsets are most prevalent in common applications of fuzzy set theory.

4.6 FUZZY EQUATIONS

One area of fuzzy set theory in which fuzzy numbers and arithmetic operations on fuzzy numbers play a fundamental role are *fuzzy equations*. These are equations in which coefficients and unknowns are fuzzy numbers, and formulas are constructed by operations of fuzzy arithmetic. Such equations have a great potential applicability. Unfortunately, their theory has not been sufficiently developed as yet; moreover, some of the published work in this area is rather controversial. Due to the lack of a well-established theory of fuzzy equations, we only intend to characterize some properties of fuzzy equations by discussing equations of two very simple types: $A + X = B$ and $A \cdot X = B$, where A and B are fuzzy numbers, and X is an unknown fuzzy number for which either of the equations is to be satisfied.

Equation $A + X = B$

The difficulty of solving this fuzzy equation is caused by the fact that $X = B - A$ is not the solution. To see this, let us consider two closed intervals, $A = [a_1, a_2]$ and $B = [b_1, b_2]$, which may be viewed as special fuzzy numbers. Then, $B - A = [b_1 - a_2, b_2 - a_1]$ and

$$A + (B - A) = [a_1, a_2] + [b_1 - a_2, b_2 - a_1]$$
$$= [a_1 + b_1 - a_2, a_2 + b_2 - a_1]$$
$$\neq [b_1, b_2] = B,$$

whenever $a_1 \neq a_2$. Therefore, $X = B - A$ is not a solution of the equation.

Let $X = [x_1, x_2]$. Then, $[a_1 + x_1, a_2 + x_2] = [b_1, b_2]$ follows immediately from the equation. This results in two ordinary equations of real numbers,

$$a_1 + x_1 = b_1,$$
$$a_2 + x_2 = b_2,$$

whose solution is $x_1 = b_1 - a_1$ and $x_2 = b_2 - a_2$. Since X must be an interval, it is required that $x_1 \leq x_2$. That is, the equation has a solution iff $b_1 - a_1 \leq b_2 - a_2$. If this inequality is satisfied, the solution is $X = [b_1 - a_1, b_2 - a_2]$.

This example illustrates how to solve the equation when the given fuzzy numbers A and B are closed intervals. Since any fuzzy number is uniquely represented by its α-cuts (Theorem 2.5), which are closed intervals, the described procedure can be applied to α-cuts of arbitrary fuzzy numbers. The solution of our fuzzy equation can thus be obtained by solving a set of associated interval equations, one for each nonzero α in the level set $\Lambda_A \cup \Lambda_B$.

For any $\alpha \in (0, 1]$, let ${}^\alpha A = [{}^\alpha a_1, {}^\alpha a_2]$, ${}^\alpha B = [{}^\alpha b_1, {}^\alpha b_2]$, and ${}^\alpha X = [{}^\alpha x_1, {}^\alpha x_2]$ denote, respectively, the α-cuts of A, B, and X in our equation. Then, the equation has a solution iff:

(i) ${}^\alpha b_1 - {}^\alpha a_1 \leq {}^\alpha b_2 - {}^\alpha a_2$ for every $\alpha \in (0, 1]$, and
(ii) $\alpha \leq \beta$ implies ${}^\alpha b_1 - {}^\alpha a_1 \leq {}^\beta b_1 - {}^\beta a_1 \leq {}^\beta b_2 - {}^\beta a_2 \leq {}^\alpha b_2 - {}^\alpha a_2$.

Property (i) ensures that the interval equation

$$ {}^\alpha A + {}^\alpha X = {}^\alpha B $$

has a solution, which is ${}^\alpha X = [{}^\alpha b_1 - {}^\alpha a_1, {}^\alpha b_2 - {}^\alpha a_2]$. Property (ii) ensures that the solutions of the interval equations for α and β are nested; that is, if $\alpha \leq \beta$, then ${}^\beta X \subseteq {}^\alpha X$. If a solution ${}^\alpha X$ exists for every $\alpha \in (0, 1]$ and property (ii) is satisfied, then by Theorem 2.5, the solution X of the fuzzy equation is given by

$$X = \bigcup_{\alpha \in (0, 1]} {}_\alpha X.$$

To illustrate the solution procedure, let A and B in our equation be the following fuzzy numbers:

$$A = .2/[0, 1) + .6/[1, 2) + .8/[2, 3) + .9/[3, 4) + 1/4 + .5/(4, 5] + .1/(5, 6],$$
$$B = .1/[0, 1) + .2/[1, 2) + .6/[2, 3) + .7/[3, 4) + .8/[4, 5) + .9/[5, 6)$$
$$+ 1/6 + .5/(6, 7] + .4/(7, 8] + .2/(8, 9] + .1/(9, 10].$$

TABLE 4.1 α-CUTS ASSOCIATED WITH THE DISCUSSED FUZZY EQUATION OF TYPE $A + X = B$

α	$^{\alpha}A$	$^{\alpha}B$	$^{\alpha}X$
1.0	[4,4]	[6,6]	[2,2]
0.9	[3,4]	[5,6]	[2,2]
0.8	[2,4]	[4,6]	[2,2]
0.7	[2,4]	[3,6]	[1,2]
0.6	[1,4]	[2,6]	[1,2]
0.5	[1,5]	[2,7]	[1,2]
0.4	[1,5]	[2,8]	[1,3]
0.3	[1,5]	[2,8]	[1,3]
0.2	[0,5]	[1,9]	[1,4]
0.1	[0,6]	[0,10]	[0,4]

All relevant α-cuts of A, B, and X are given in Table 4.1. The solution of the equation is the fuzzy number

$$X = \bigcup_{\alpha \in (0,1]} {}_{\alpha}X = .1/[0, 1) + .7/[1, 2) + 1/2 + .4/(2, 3] + .2/(3, 4].$$

Equation $A \cdot X = B$

Let us assume, for the sake of simplicity, that A, B are fuzzy numbers on $\mathbb{R}^+$. It is easy to show that $X = B/A$ is not a solution of the equation. For each $\alpha \in (0, 1]$, we obtain the interval equation

$$^{\alpha}A \cdot {}^{\alpha}X = {}^{\alpha}B.$$

Our fuzzy equation can be solved by solving these interval equations for all $\alpha \in (0, 1]$. Let $^{\alpha}A = [^{\alpha}a_1, {}^{\alpha}a_2]$, $^{\alpha}B = [^{\alpha}b_1, {}^{\alpha}b_2]$, and $^{\alpha}X = [^{\alpha}x_1, {}^{\alpha}x_2]$. Then, the solution of the fuzzy equation exists iff:

(i) $^{\alpha}b_1/{}^{\alpha}a_1 \le {}^{\alpha}b_2/{}^{\alpha}a_2$ for each $\alpha \in (0, 1]$, and

(ii) $\alpha \le \beta$ implies $^{\alpha}b_1/{}^{\alpha}a_1 \le {}^{\beta}b_1/{}^{\beta}a_1 \le {}^{\beta}b_2/{}^{\beta}a_2 \le {}^{\alpha}b_2/{}^{\alpha}a_2$.

If the solution exists, it has the form

$$X = \bigcup_{\alpha \in (0,1]} {}_{\alpha}X.$$

As an example, let A and B in our equation be the following triangular-shape fuzzy numbers:

$$A(x) = \begin{cases} 0 & \text{for } x \le 3 \text{ and } x > 5 \\ x - 3 & \text{for } 3 < x \le 4 \\ 5 - x & \text{for } 4 < x \le 5 \end{cases}$$

$$B(x) = \begin{cases} 0 & \text{for } x \leq 12 \text{ and } x > 32 \\ (x-12)/8 & \text{for } 12 < x \leq 20 \\ (32-x)/12 & \text{for } 20 < x \leq 32. \end{cases}$$

Then, $^{\alpha}A = [\alpha + 3, 5 - \alpha]$ and $^{\alpha}B = [8\alpha + 12, 32 - 12\alpha]$. It is easy to verify that

$$\frac{8\alpha + 12}{\alpha + 3} \leq \frac{32 - 12\alpha}{5 - \alpha};$$

consequently,

$$^{\alpha}X = \left[\frac{8\alpha + 12}{\alpha + 3}, \frac{32 - 12\alpha}{5 - \alpha} \right]$$

for each $\alpha \in (0, 1]$. It is also easy to check that $\alpha \leq \beta$ implies $^{\beta}X \subseteq {}^{\alpha}X$ for each pair α, $\beta \in (0, 1]$. Therefore, the solution of our fuzzy equation is

$$X = \bigcup_{\alpha \in (0,1]} {}_{\alpha}X = \begin{cases} 0 & \text{for } x \leq 4 \text{ and } x \geq 32/5 \\ \dfrac{12 - 3x}{x - 8} & \text{for } 4 < x \leq 5 \\ \dfrac{32 - 5x}{12 - x} & \text{for } 5 \leq x \leq 32/5. \end{cases}$$

NOTES

4.1. Interval arithmetic is thoroughly covered in two books by Moore [1966, 1979]. A specialized book on fuzzy arithmetic was written by Kaufmann and Gupta [1985]; a good overview of fuzzy arithmetic was also prepared by Dubois and Prade [1987d].

4.2. Fuzzy equations were investigated by Buckley [1992d] and Buckley and Qu [1990]. A fuzzy differential calculus was initiated by Dubois and Prade [1982a].

EXERCISES

4.1. Determine which fuzzy sets defined by the following functions are fuzzy numbers:

(a) $A(x) = \begin{cases} \sin(x) & \text{for } 0 \leq x \leq \pi \\ 0 & \text{otherwise}; \end{cases}$

(b) $B(x) = \begin{cases} x & \text{for } 0 \leq x \leq 1 \\ 0 & \text{otherwise}; \end{cases}$

(c) $C(x) = \begin{cases} 1 & \text{for } 0 \leq x \leq 10 \\ 0 & \text{otherwise}; \end{cases}$

(d) $D(x) = \begin{cases} \min(1, x) & \text{for } x \geq 0 \\ 0 & \text{for } x < 0; \end{cases}$

(e) $E(x) = \begin{cases} 1 & \text{for } x = 5 \\ 0 & \text{otherwise.} \end{cases}$

4.2. Calculate the following:
   (a) $[-1, 2] + [1, 3]$;
   (b) $[-2, 4] - [3, 6]$;
   (c) $[-3, 4] \cdot [-3, 4]$;
   (d) $[-4, 6]/[1, 2]$.

4.3. Prove that $0 \in A - A$ and $1 \in A/A$ for $0 \notin A$, where A is a closed interval.

4.4. Prove that if $A \subseteq E$ and $B \subseteq F$, then $A + B \subseteq E + F$, $A - B \subseteq E - F$, $A \cdot B \subseteq E \cdot F$ and $A/B \subseteq E/F$ ($0 \notin F$, in this case), where A, B, E, and F are closed intervals.

4.5. Let A, B be two fuzzy numbers whose membership functions are given by

$$A(x) = \begin{cases} (x+2)/2 & \text{for } -2 < x \le 0 \\ (2-x)/2 & \text{for } 0 < x < 2 \\ 0 & \text{otherwise,} \end{cases}$$

$$B(x) = \begin{cases} (x-2)/2 & \text{for } 2 < x \le 4 \\ (6-x)/2 & \text{for } 0 < x \le 6 \\ 0 & \text{otherwise.} \end{cases}$$

   Calculate the fuzzy numbers $A + B$, $A - B$, $B - A$, $A \cdot B$, A/B, $\text{MIN}(A, B)$ and $\text{MAX}(A, B)$.

4.6. Let A, B be two fuzzy numbers given in Exercise 4.5 and let

$$C(x) = \begin{cases} (x-6)/2 & \text{for } 6 < x \le 8 \\ (10-x)/2 & \text{for } 8 < x \le 10 \\ 0 & \text{otherwise.} \end{cases}$$

   Solve the following equations for X:
   (a) $A + X = B$;
   (b) $B \cdot X = C$.

4.7. In the ordinary arithmetic of real numbers, the equation $a = a + b - b$ holds for any a, $b \in \mathbb{R}$. Does this equation hold for fuzzy numbers? Justify your answer and illustrate it by two symmetric triangular fuzzy numbers $A = (c_A, s_A)$ and $B = (c_B, s_B)$, where c_A, c_B are centers and s_A, s_B are spreads of A and B, respectively. That is, $c_A = {}^1A$, $c_B = {}^1B$, ${}^{0+}A = [c_A - s_A, c_A + s_A]$, ${}^{0+}B = [c_B - s_B, c_B + s_B]$. Is $A = A + B - B$?

4.8. Repeat Exercise 4.7 for the equation $A = A \cdot (B/B)$, where $0 \notin {}^{0+}B$.

4.9. Consider fuzzy sets A and B whose membership functions are defined by formulas

$$A(x) = x/(x+1) \text{ and } B(x) = 1 - x/10$$

for all $x \in \{0, 1, 2, \ldots, 10\} = X$. Calculate:
   (a) Scalar and fuzzy cardinalities of A and B (also plot the fuzzy cardinalities);
   (b) degrees of subsethood $S(|\tilde{A}|, |\tilde{B}|)$ and $S(|\tilde{B}|, |\tilde{A}|)$.

5

FUZZY RELATIONS

5.1 CRISP AND FUZZY RELATIONS

A *crisp relation* represents the presence or absence of association, interaction or interconnect-edness between the elements of two or more sets. This concept can be generalized to allow for various degrees or strengths of association or interaction between elements. Degrees of association can be represented by membership grades in a *fuzzy relation* in the same way as degrees of set membership are represented in the fuzzy set. In fact, just as the crisp set can be viewed as a restricted case of the more general fuzzy set concept, the crisp relation can be considered to be a restricted case of the fuzzy relation.

Throughout this chapter, the concepts and properties of crisp relations are briefly discussed as a refresher and in order to demonstrate their generalized application to fuzzy relations.

A *relation* among crisp sets $X_1, X_2, \ldots, X_n$ is a subset of the Cartesian product $\underset{i \in \mathbb{N}_n}{\times} X_i$. It is denoted either by $R(X_1, X_2, \ldots, X_n)$ or by the abbreviated form $R(X_i | i \in \mathbb{N}_n)$. Thus,

$$R(X_1, X_2, \ldots, X_n) \subseteq X_1 \times X_2 \times \ldots \times X_n,$$

so that for relations among sets $X_1, X_2, \ldots, X_n$, the Cartesian product $X_1 \times X_2 \times \ldots \times X_n$ represents the universal set. Because a relation is itself a set, the basic set concepts such as containment or subset, union, intersection, and complement can be applied without modification to relations.

Each crisp relation R can be defined by a characteristic function which assigns a value of 1 to every tuple of the universal set belonging to the relation and a 0 to every tuple not belonging to it. Denoting a relation and its characteristic function by the same symbol R, we have

$$R(x_1, x_2, \ldots, x_n) = \begin{cases} 1 & \text{iff } \langle x_1, x_2, \ldots, x_n \rangle \in R, \\ 0 & \text{otherwise} \end{cases}$$

The membership of a tuple in a relation signifies that the elements of the tuple are related to or associated with one another. For instance, let R represent the relation of marriage between the set of all men and the set of all women. Of all the possible pairings of men and women, then, only those pairs who are married to each other will be assigned a value of 1 indicating that they belong to this relation. A relation between two sets is called *binary*; if three, four, or five sets are involved, the relation is called *ternary, quaternary,* or *quinary,* respectively. In general, a relation defined on n sets is called *n-ary* or *n-dimensional.*

A relation can be written as a set of ordered tuples. Another convenient way of representing a relation $R(X_1, X_2, \ldots, X_n)$ involves an n-dimensional membership array: $\mathbf{R} = [r_{i_1, i_2, \ldots, i_n}]$. Each element of the first dimension i_1 of this array corresponds to exactly one member of X_1 and each element of dimension i_2 to exactly one member of X_2, and so on. If the n-tuple $\langle x_1, x_2, \ldots, x_n \rangle \in X_1 \times X_2 \times \ldots \times X_n$ corresponds to the element $r_{i_1, i_2, \ldots, i_n}$ of $\mathbf{R}$, then

$$r_{i_1, i_2, \ldots, i_n} = \begin{cases} 1 & \text{if and only if } \langle x_1, x_2, \ldots, x_n \rangle \in R, \\ 0 & \text{otherwise.} \end{cases}$$

Example 5.1

Let R be a relation among the three sets X = {English, French}, Y = {dollar, pound, franc, mark} and Z = {US, France, Canada, Britain, Germany}, which associates a country with a currency and language as follows:

$R(X, Y, Z) = $ {⟨English, dollar, US⟩, ⟨French, Franc, France⟩, ⟨English, dollar, Canada⟩, ⟨French, dollar, Canada⟩, ⟨English, pound, Britain⟩}.

This relation can also be represented with the following three-dimensional membership array:

	US	Fra	Can	Brit	Ger		US	Fra	Can	Brit	Ger
dollar	1	0	1	0	0	dollar	0	0	1	0	0
pound	0	0	0	1	0	pound	0	0	0	0	0
franc	0	0	0	0	0	franc	0	1	0	0	0
mark	0	0	0	0	0	mark	0	0	0	0	0
		English						*French*			

To illustrate the convenience of representing n-ary relations by n-dimensional arrays (especially important for computer processing), a possible structure for a five-dimensional array based on sets $X_i (i \in \mathbb{N}_5)$ is shown in Fig. 5.1. The full array (five-dimensional) can be viewed as a "library" that consists of $|X_1|$ "books" (four-dimensional arrays) distinguished from each other by elements of X_1. Each "book" consists of $|X_2|$ "pages" (three-dimensional arrays) distinguished from each other by elements of X_2. Each "page" consists of $|X_3|$ matrices (two-dimensional arrays) distinguished from each other by elements of X_3. Each matrix consists of $|X_4|$ rows (one-dimensional arrays) distinguished from each other by elements of X_4. Each row consists of $|X_5|$ individual entries distinguished from each other by elements of X_5.

Just as the characteristic function of a crisp set can be generalized to allow for degrees of set membership, the characteristic function of a crisp relation can be generalized to allow tuples to have degrees of membership within the relation. Thus, a *fuzzy relation* is a fuzzy set defined on the Cartesian product of crisp sets $X_1, X_2, \ldots, X_n$, where tuples $\langle x_1, x_2, \ldots, x_n \rangle$ may have varying degrees of membership within the relation. The membership grade indicates the strength of the relation present between the elements of the tuple.

A fuzzy relation can also be conveniently represented by an n-dimensional membership

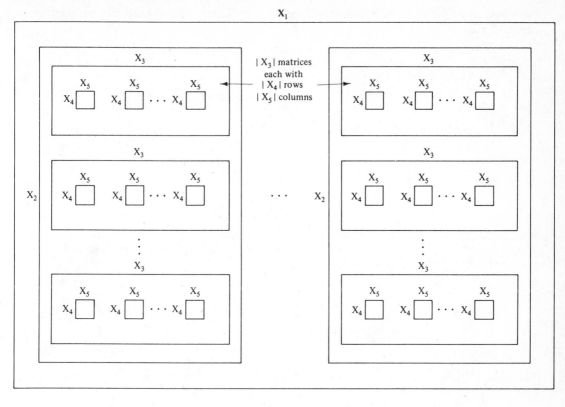

Figure 5.1 A possible representation of quinary relation by five-dimensional array.

array whose entries correspond to n-tuples in the universal set. These entries take values representing the membership grades of the corresponding n-tuples.

Example 5.2

Let R be a fuzzy relation between the two sets X = {New York City, Paris} and Y = {Beijing, New York City, London}, which represents the relational concept "very far." This relation can be written in list notation as

$$R(X, Y) = 1/\text{NYC, Beijing} + 0/\text{NYC, NYC} + .6/\text{NYC, London} +$$
$$.9/\text{Paris, Beijing} + .7/\text{Paris, NYC} + .3/\text{Paris, London}.$$

This relation can also be represented by the following two-dimensional membership array (matrix):

	NYC	*Paris*
Beijing	1	.9
NYC	0	.7
London	.6	.3

Ordinary fuzzy relations (with the valuation set [0, 1]) can obviously be extended to L-fuzzy relations (with an arbitrary ordered valuation set L) in the same way as fuzzy sets are extended to L-fuzzy sets. Similarly, type t, level k, and interval-valued fuzzy relations can be defined.

5.2 PROJECTIONS AND CYLINDRIC EXTENSIONS

Consider the Cartesian product of all sets in the family $\mathcal{X} = \{X_i | i \in \mathbb{N}_n\}$. For each sequence ($n$-tuple)

$$\mathbf{x} = \langle x_i | i \in \mathbb{N}_n \rangle \in \underset{i \in \mathbb{N}_n}{\times} X_i$$

and each sequence (r-tuple, $r \leq n$)

$$\mathbf{y} = \langle y_j | j \in J \rangle \in \underset{j \in J}{\times} X_j,$$

where $J \subseteq \mathbb{N}_n$ and $|J| = r$, let $\mathbf{y}$ be called a *subsequence* of $\mathbf{x}$ iff $y_j = x_j$ for all $j \in J$. Let $\mathbf{y} \prec \mathbf{x}$ denote that $\mathbf{y}$ is a subsequence of $\mathbf{x}$. More appropriate names may be used in various specific contexts. For example, if n-tuples $\mathbf{x}$ represent states of a system, $\mathbf{y}$ may be called a *substate* of $\mathbf{x}$; if they are strings of symbols in a formal language, $\mathbf{y}$ may be called a *substring* of $\mathbf{x}$.

Given a relation $R(X_1, X_2, \ldots, X_n)$, let $[R \downarrow \mathcal{Y}]$ denote the *projection* of R on $\mathcal{Y}$ that disregards all sets in X except those in the family

$$\mathcal{Y} = \{X_j | j \in J \subseteq \mathbb{N}_n\}.$$

Then, $[R \downarrow \mathcal{Y}]$ is a fuzzy relation whose membership function is defined on the Cartesian product of sets in $\mathcal{Y}$ by the equation

$$[R \downarrow \mathcal{Y}](\mathbf{y}) = \max_{\mathbf{x} \succ \mathbf{y}} R(\mathbf{x}). \tag{5.1}$$

Example 5.3

Consider the sets $X_1 = \{0, 1\}, X_2 = \{0, 1\}, X_3 = \{0, 1, 2\}$ and the ternary fuzzy relation on $X_1 \times X_2 \times X_3$ defined in Table 5.1. Let $R_{ij} = [R \downarrow \{X_i, X_j\}]$ and $R_i = [R \downarrow \{X_i\}]$ for all $i, j \in \{1, 2, 3\}$. Using this notation, all possible projections of R are given in Table 5.1. A detailed calculation of one of these projections, R_{12}, is shown in Table 5.2.

TABLE 5.1   TERNARY FUZZY RELATION AND ITS PROJECTIONS

$\langle x_1,$	$x_2,$	$x_3 \rangle$	$R(x_1, x_2, x_3)$	$R_{12}(x_1, x_2)$	$R_{13}(x_1, x_3)$	$R_{23}(x_2, x_3)$	$R_1(x_1)$	$R_2(x_2)$	$R_3(x_3)$
0	0	0	0.4	0.9	1.0	0.5	1.0	0.9	1.0
0	0	1	0.9	0.9	0.9	0.9	1.0	0.9	0.9
0	0	2	0.2	0.9	0.8	0.2	1.0	0.9	1.0
0	1	0	1.0	1.0	1.0	1.0	1.0	1.0	1.0
0	1	1	0.0	1.0	0.9	0.5	1.0	1.0	0.9
0	1	2	0.8	1.0	0.8	1.0	1.0	1.0	1.0
1	0	0	0.5	0.5	0.5	0.5	1.0	0.9	1.0
1	0	1	0.3	0.5	0.5	0.9	1.0	0.9	0.9
1	0	2	0.1	0.5	1.0	0.2	1.0	0.9	1.0
1	1	0	0.0	1.0	0.5	1.0	1.0	1.0	1.0
1	1	1	0.5	1.0	0.5	0.5	1.0	1.0	0.9
1	1	2	1.0	1.0	1.0	1.0	1.0	1.0	1.0

TABLE 5.2   CALCULATION OF THE PROJECTION R_{12} IN EXAMPLE 5.3

$\langle x_1,$	$x_2,$	$x_3 \rangle$	$R(x_1, x_2, x_3)$	$R_{12}(x_1, x_2)$
0	0	0	0.4	
0	0	1	0.9	$\max\,[R(0, 0, 0), R(0, 0, 1), R(0, 0, 2)] = 0.9$
0	0	2	0.2	
0	1	0	1.0	
0	1	1	0.0	$\max\,[R(0, 1, 0), R(0, 1, 1), R(0, 1, 2)] = 1.0$
0	1	2	0.8	
1	0	0	0.5	
1	0	1	0.3	$\max\,[R(1, 0, 0), R(1, 0, 1), R(1, 0, 2)] = 0.5$
1	0	2	0.1	
1	1	0	0.0	
1	1	1	0.5	$\max\,[R(1, 1, 0), R(1, 1, 1), R(1, 1, 2)] = 1.0$
1	1	2	1.0	

Under special circumstances, the projection defined by (5.1) can be generalized by replacing the max operator by another t-conorm.

Another operation on relations, which is in some sense an inverse to the projection, is called a *cylindric extension*. Let $\mathcal{X}$ and $\mathcal{Y}$ denote the same families of sets as employed in the definition of projection. Let R be a relation defined on the Cartesian product of sets in the family $\mathcal{Y}$, and let $[R \uparrow \mathcal{X} - \mathcal{Y}]$ denote the cylindric extension of R into sets $X_i (i \in \mathbb{N}_n)$ that are in $\mathcal{X}$ but are not in $\mathcal{Y}$. Then,

$$[R \uparrow \mathcal{X} - \mathcal{Y}](\mathbf{x}) = R(\mathbf{y}) \tag{5.2}$$

for each $\mathbf{x}$ such that $\mathbf{x} \succ \mathbf{y}$.

The cylindric extension clearly produces the *largest fuzzy relation* (in the sense of membership grades of elements of the extended Cartesian product) that is compatible with the given projection. Such a relation is the least specific of all relations compatible with the projection. The cylindric extension thus *maximizes the nonspecificity* (see Chapter 9) in deriving the n-dimensional relation from one of its r-dimensional projections ($r \leq n$). That is, it guarantees that no information not included in the projection is employed in determining the extended relation. Hence, the cylindric extension is totally *unbiased*.

Example 5.4

Membership functions of cylindric extensions of all the projections in Example 5.3 are actually those shown in Table 5.1 under the assumption that their arguments are extended to $\langle x_1, x_2, x_3 \rangle$. For instance:

$$[R_{23} \uparrow \{X_1\}](0, 0, 2) = [R_{23} \uparrow \{X_1\}](1, 0, 2) = R_{23}(0, 2) = 0.2.$$

We can see that none of the cylindric extensions (identical with the respective projections in Table 5.1) are equal to the original fuzzy relation from which the projections involved in the cylindric extensions were determined. This means that some information was lost when the given relation was replaced by any one of its projections in this example.

Relations that can be reconstructed from one of their projections by the cylindric extension exist, but they are rather rare. It is more common that a relation can be exactly reconstructed from several of its projections by taking the set intersection of their cylindric extensions. The resulting relation is usually called a *cylindric closure*. When projections are determined by the max operator (see Sec. 3.1), the min operator is normally used for the set intersection. Hence, given a set of projections $\{P_i | i \in I\}$ of a relation on X, the cylindric closure, cyl $\{P_i\}$, based on these projections is defined by the equation

$$\text{cyl}\{P_i\}(\mathbf{x}) = \min_{i \in I}[P_i \uparrow X - Y_i](\mathbf{x})$$

for each $\mathbf{x} \in X$ where Y_i denotes the family of sets on which P_i is defined.

Cylindric closures of three families of projections involved in Example 5.3 are shown in Table 5.3. We can see that none of them is the same as the original relation R. Hence, the relation is not fully reconstructible from its projections.

TABLE 5.3   CYLINDRIC CLOSURES OF THREE FAMILIES OF PROJECTIONS CALCULATED IN EXAMPLE 5.3

$\langle x_1,$	$x_2,$	$x_3 \rangle$	cyl$\{R_{12}, R_{13}, R_{23}\}$	cyl$\{R_1, R_2, R_3\}$	cyl$\{R_{12}, R_3\}$
0	0	0	0.5	0.9	0.9
0	0	1	0.9	0.9	0.9
0	0	2	0.2	0.9	1.0
0	1	0	1.0	1.0	1.0
0	1	1	0.5	0.9	0.9
0	1	2	0.8	1.0	1.0
1	0	0	0.5	0.9	0.5
1	0	1	0.5	0.9	0.5
1	0	2	0.2	0.9	0.5
1	1	0	0.5	1.0	1.0
1	1	1	0.5	0.9	0.9
1	1	2	1.0	1.0	1.0

5.3 BINARY FUZZY RELATIONS

Binary relations have a special significance among n-dimensional relations since they are, in some sense, generalized mathematical functions. Contrary to functions from X to Y, binary relations $R(X, Y)$ may assign to each element of X two or more elements of Y. Some basic operations on functions, such as the inverse and composition, are applicable to binary relations as well.

Given a fuzzy relation $R(X, Y)$, its *domain* is a fuzzy set on X, dom R, whose membership function is defined by

$$\text{dom } R(x) = \max_{y \in Y} R(x, y) \tag{5.3}$$

for each $x \in X$. That is, each element of set X belongs to the domain of R to the degree equal to the strength of its strongest relation to any member of set Y. The *range* of $R(X, Y)$ is a fuzzy relation on Y, ran R, whose membership function is defined by

$$\operatorname{ran} R(y) = \max_{x \in X} R(x, y) \tag{5.4}$$

for each $y \in Y$. That is, the strength of the strongest relation that each element of Y has to an element of X is equal to the degree of that element's membership in the range of R. In addition, the *height* of a fuzzy relation $R(X, Y)$ is a number, $h(R)$, defined by

$$h(R) = \max_{y \in Y} \max_{x \in X} R(x, y). \tag{5.5}$$

That is, $h(R)$ is the largest membership grade attained by any pair $\langle x, y \rangle$ in R.

A convenient representation of binary relation $R(X, Y)$ are *membership matrices* $\mathbf{R} = [r_{xy}]$, where $r_{xy} = R(x, y)$. Another useful representation of binary relations is a *sagittal diagram*. Each of the sets X, Y is represented by a set of nodes in the diagram; nodes corresponding to one set are clearly distinguished from nodes representing the other set. Elements of $X \times Y$ with nonzero membership grades in $R(X, Y)$ are represented in the diagram by lines connecting the respective nodes. These lines are labelled with the values of the membership grades. An example of the sagittal diagram of a binary fuzzy relation $R(X, Y)$ together with the corresponding membership matrix is shown in Fig. 5.2.

The *inverse* of a fuzzy relation $R(X, Y)$, which is denoted by $R^{-1}(Y, X)$, is a relation on $Y \times X$ defined by

$$R^{-1}(y, x) = R(x, y)$$

for all $x \in X$ and all $y \in Y$. A membership matrix $\mathbf{R}^{-1} = [r_{yx}^{-1}]$ representing $R^{-1}(Y, X)$ is the transpose of the matrix $\mathbf{R}$ for $R(X, Y)$, which means that the rows of $\mathbf{R}^{-1}$ equal the columns of $\mathbf{R}$ and the columns of $\mathbf{R}^{-1}$ equal the rows of $\mathbf{R}$. Clearly,

$$(\mathbf{R}^{-1})^{-1} = \mathbf{R} \tag{5.6}$$

for any binary fuzzy relation.

Consider now two binary fuzzy relations $P(X, Y)$ and $Q(Y, Z)$ with a common set Y. The *standard composition* of these relations, which is denoted by $P(X, Y) \circ Q(Y, Z)$, produces a binary relation $R(X, Z)$ on $X \times Z$ defined by

$$R(x, z) = [P \circ Q](x, z) = \max_{y \in Y} \min[P(x, y), Q(y, z)] \tag{5.7}$$

for all $x \in X$ and all $z \in Z$. This composition, which is based on the standard t-norm and t-conorm, is often referred to as the *max-min composition*. It follows directly from (5.7) that

$$[P(X, Y) \circ Q(Y, Z)]^{-1} = Q^{-1}(Z, Y) \circ P^{-1}(Y, X),$$

$$[P(X, Y) \circ Q(Y, Z)] \circ R(Z, W) = P(X, Y) \circ [Q(Y, Z) \circ R(Z, W)].$$

That is, the standard (or max-min) composition is associative and its inverse is equal to the reverse composition of the inverse relations. However, the standard composition is not commutative, because $Q(Y, Z) \circ P(X, Y)$ is not well-defined when $X \neq Z$. Even if $X = Z$ and $Q(Y, Z) \circ P(X, Y)$ are well-defined, we may have

$$P(X, Y) \circ Q(Y, Z) \neq Q(Y, Z) \circ P(X, Y).$$

Compositions of binary fuzzy relations can be performed conveniently in terms of membership matrices of the relations. Let $\mathbf{P} = [p_{ik}]$, $\mathbf{Q} = [q_{kj}]$, and $\mathbf{R} = [r_{ij}]$ be membership matrices of binary relations such that $R = P \circ Q$. We can then write, using this matrix notation,

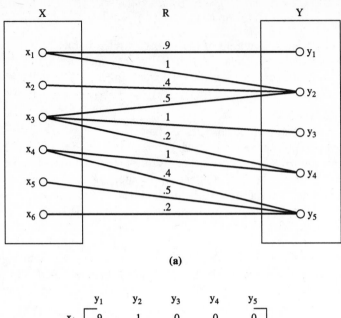

(a)

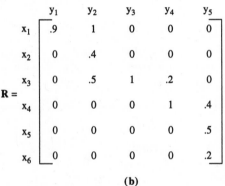

(b)

Figure 5.2 Examples of two convenient representations of a fuzzy binary relation: (a) sagittal diagram; (b) membership matrix.

$$[r_{ij}] = [p_{ik}] \circ [q_{kj}],$$

where

$$r_{ij} = \max_k \min(p_{ik}, q_{kj}). \tag{5.8}$$

Observe that the same elements of **P** and **Q** are used in the calculation of **R** as would be used in the regular multiplication of matrices, but the product and sum operations are here replaced with the min and max operations, respectively.

The following matrix equation illustrates the use of (5.8) to perform the standard composition of two binary fuzzy relations represented by their membership functions:

$$
\begin{bmatrix}
.3 & .5 & .8 \\
0 & .7 & 1 \\
.4 & .6 & .5
\end{bmatrix}
\circ
\begin{bmatrix}
.9 & .5 & .7 & .7 \\
.3 & .2 & 0 & .9 \\
1 & 0 & .5 & .5
\end{bmatrix}
=
\begin{bmatrix}
.8 & .3 & .5 & .5 \\
1 & .2 & .5 & .7 \\
.5 & .4 & .5 & .6
\end{bmatrix}.
$$

For example,

$$.8(= r_{11}) = \max[\min(.3, .9), \min(.5, .3), \min(.8, 1)]$$

$$= \max[\min(p_{11}, q_{11}), \min(p_{12}, q_{21}), \min(p_{13}, q_{31})],$$

$$.4(= r_{32}) = \max[\min(.4, .5), \min(.6, .2), \min(.5, 0)]$$

$$= \max[\min(p_{31}, q_{12}), \min(p_{32}, q_{22}), \min(p_{33}, q_{32})].$$

A similar operation on two binary relations, which differs from the composition in that it yields triples instead of pairs, is known as the *relational join*. For fuzzy relations $P(X, Y)$ and $Q(Y, Z)$, the relational join, $P * Q$, corresponding to the standard max-min composition is a ternary relation $R(X, Y, Z)$ defined by

$$R(x, y, z) = [P * Q](x, y, z) = \min[P(x, y), Q(y, z)] \qquad (5.9)$$

for each $x \in X$, $y \in Y$, and $z \in Z$.

The fact that the relational join produces a ternary relation from two binary relations is a major difference from the composition, which results in another binary relation. In fact, the max-min composition is obtained by aggregating appropriate elements of the corresponding

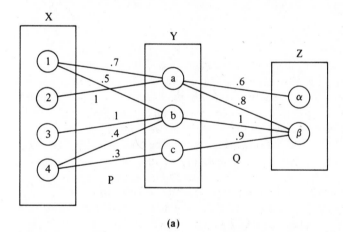

(a)

Join: S = P * Q			
x	y	z	$\mu_S(x, y, z)$
1	a	α	.6
1	a	β	.7
1	b	β	.5
2	a	α	.6
2	a	β	.8
3	b	β	1
4	b	β	.4
4	c	β	.3

Composition: R = P ∘ Q		
x	z	$\mu_R(x, z)$
1	α	.6
1	β	.7
2	α	.6
2	β	.8
3	β	1
4	β	.4

(b)   (c)

Figure 5.3 Composition and join of binary relation.

join by the max operator. Formally,

$$[P \circ Q](x, z) = \max_{y \in Y}[P * Q](x, y, z) \qquad (5.10)$$

for each $x \in X$ and $z \in Z$.

Example 5.5

The join $S = P * Q$ of relations P and Q given in Fig. 5.3a has the membership function given in Fig. 5.3b. To convert this join into the corresponding composition $R = P \circ Q$ by (5.10), the two indicated pairs of values of $S(x, y, z)$ in Fig. 5.3b are aggregated by the max operator. For instance,

$$R(1, \beta) = \max[S(1, a, \beta), S(1, b, \beta)]$$
$$= \max[.7, .5] = .7.$$

Although the standard max-min composition and the associated join are used most frequently in typical applications of fuzzy relations, some applications suggest broadening these concepts by employing general t-norms and t-conorms. The generalized compositions are covered in Secs. 5.9 and 5.10.

5.4 BINARY RELATIONS ON A SINGLE SET

In addition to defining a binary relation that exists between two different sets, it is also possible to define a crisp or fuzzy binary relation among the elements of a single set X. A binary relation of this type can be denoted by $R(X, X)$ or $R(X^2)$ and is a subset of $X \times X = X^2$. These relations are often referred to as *directed graphs* or *digraphs*.

Binary relations $R(X, X)$ can be expressed by the same forms as general binary relations (matrices, sagittal diagrams, tables). In addition, however, they can be conveniently expressed in terms of simple diagrams with the following properties: (1) each element of the set X is represented by a single node in the diagram; (2) directed connections between nodes indicate pairs of elements of X for which the grade of membership in R is nonzero; and (3) each connection in the diagram is labeled by the actual membership grade of the corresponding pair in R. An example of this diagram for a relation $R(X, X)$ defined on $X = \{1, 2, 3, 4\}$ is shown in Fig. 5.4, where it can be compared with the other forms of representation of binary relations.

Various significant types of relations $R(X, X)$ are distinguished on the basis of three different characteristic properties: reflexivity, symmetry, and transitivity. First, let us consider crisp relations.

A crisp relation $R(X, X)$ is *reflexive* iff $\langle x, x \rangle \in R$ for each $x \in X$, that is, if every element of X is related to itself. Otherwise, $R(X, X)$ is called *irreflexive*. If $\langle x, x \rangle \notin R$ for every $x \in X$, the relation is called *antireflexive*.

A crisp relation $R(X, X)$ is *symmetric* iff for every $\langle x, y \rangle \in R$, it is also the case that $\langle y, x \rangle \in R$, where $x, y, \in X$. Thus, whenever an element x is related to an element y through a symmetric relation, y is also related to x. If this is not the case for some x, y, then the relation is called *asymmetric*. If both $\langle x, y \rangle \in R$ and $\langle y, x \rangle \in R$ implies $x = y$, then the relation is called *antisymmetric*. If either $\langle x, y \rangle \in R$ or $\langle y, x \rangle \in R$, whenever $x \neq y$, then the relation is called *strictly antisymmetric*.

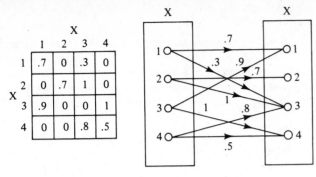

Membership matrix   Sagittal diagram

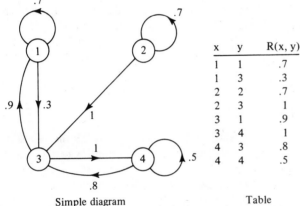

x	y	R(x, y)
1	1	.7
1	3	.3
2	2	.7
2	3	1
3	1	.9
3	4	1
4	3	.8
4	4	.5

Simple diagram   Table

Figure 5.4 Forms of representation of a fuzzy relation $R(X, X)$.

A crisp relation $R(X, X)$ is called *transitive* iff $\langle x, z \rangle \in R$ whenever both $\langle x, y \rangle \in R$ and $\langle y, z \rangle \in R$ for at least one $y \in X$. In other words, the relation of x to y and of y to z implies the relation of x to z in a transitive relation. A relation that does not satisfy this property is called *nontransitive*. If $\langle x, z \rangle \notin R$ whenever both $\langle x, y \rangle \in R$ and $\langle y, z \rangle \in R$, then the relation is called *antitransitive*.

The properties of reflexivity, symmetry, and transitivity are illustrated for crisp relations $R(X, X)$ in Fig. 5.5. We can readily see that these properties are preserved under inversion of the relation.

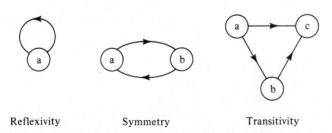

Reflexivity   Symmetry   Transitivity

Figure 5.5 Characteristic components of reflexive, symmetric, and transitive relations.

Example 5.6

Let R be a crisp relation defined on $X \times X$, where X is the set of all university courses and R represents the relation "is a prerequisite of." R is antireflexive because a course is never a prerequisite of itself. Further, if one course is a prerequisite of another, the reverse will never be true. Therefore, R is antisymmetric. Finally, if a course is a prerequisite for a second course that is itself a prerequisite for a third, then the first course is also a prerequisite for the third course. Thus, the relation R is transitive.

These three properties can be extended for fuzzy relations $R(X, X)$, by defining them in terms of the membership function of the relation. Thus, $R(X, X)$ is *reflexive* iff

$$R(x, x) = 1$$

for all $x \in X$. If this is not the case for some $x \in X$, the relation is called *irreflexive*; if it is not satisfied for all $x \in X$, the relation is called *antireflexive*. A weaker form of reflexivity, referred to as *ε-reflexivity*, is sometimes defined by requiring that

$$R(x, x) \geq \varepsilon,$$

where $0 < \varepsilon < 1$.

A fuzzy relation is *symmetric* iff

$$R(x, y) = R(y, x)$$

for all $x, y \in X$. Whenever this equality is not satisfied for some $x, y \in X$, the relation is called *asymmetric*. Furthermore, when $R(x, y) > 0$ and $R(y, x) > 0$ implies that $x = y$ for all $x, y \in X$, the relation R is called *antisymmetric*.

A fuzzy relation $R(X, X)$ is *transitive* (or, more specifically, *max-min transitive*) if

$$R(x, z) \geq \max_{y \in Y} \min[R(x, y), R(y, z)] \tag{5.11}$$

is satisfied for each pair $\langle x, z \rangle \in X^2$. A relation failing to satisfy this inequality for some members of X is called *nontransitive*, and if

$$R(x, z) < \max_{y \in Y} \min[R(x, y), R(y, z)],$$

for all $\langle x, z \rangle \in X^2$, then the relation is called *antitransitive*.

Example 5.7

Let R be the fuzzy relation defined on the set of cities and representing the concept *very near*. We may assume that a city is certainly (i.e., to a degree of 1) very near to itself. The relation is therefore reflexive. Furthermore, if city A is very near to city B, then B is certainly very near to A to the same degree. Therefore, the relation is also symmetric. Finally, if city A is very near to city B to some degree, say .7, and city B is very near to city C to some degree, say .8, it is possible (although not necessary) that city A is very near to city C to a smaller degree, say 0.5. Therefore, the relation is nontransitive.

Observe that the definition of the max-min transitivity (5.11) is based upon the max-min composition (5.7). Hence, alternative definitions of fuzzy transitivity, based upon other t-norms and t-conorms, are possible (Secs. 5.9 and 5.10) and useful in some applications.

By considering the four variants of reflexivity, three variants of symmetry, and three variants of transitivity defined for binary relations, we can distinguish $4 \times 3 \times 3 = 36$ different types of binary relations on a single set. Some of the most important of these types are discussed in Secs. 5.5 through 5.7; their names and properties are given in Fig. 5.6.

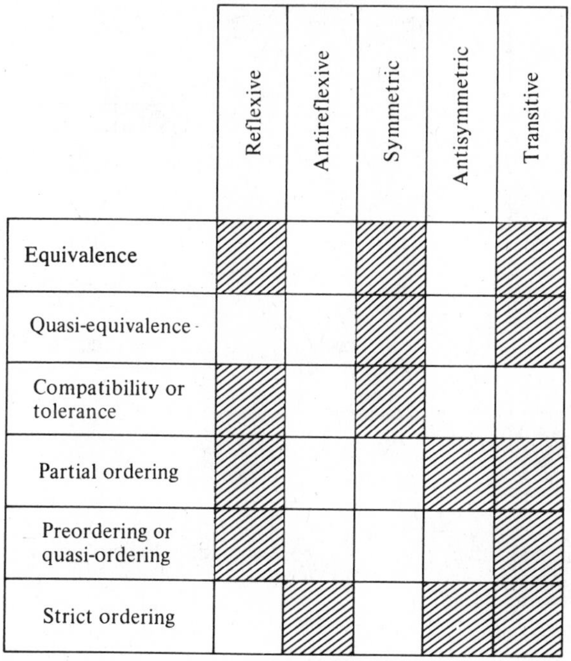

	Reflexive	Antireflexive	Symmetric	Antisymmetric	Transitive
Equivalence	▨		▨		▨
Quasi-equivalence			▨		▨
Compatibility or tolerance	▨		▨		
Partial ordering	▨			▨	▨
Preordering or quasi-ordering	▨				▨
Strict ordering		▨		▨	▨

Figure 5.6 Some important types of binary relations $R(X, X)$.

The *transitive closure* of a crisp relation $R(X, X)$ is defined as the relation that is transitive, contains $R(X, X)$, and has the fewest possible members. For fuzzy relations, this last requirement is generalized such that the elements of the transitive closure have the smallest possible membership grades that still allow the first two requirements to be met.

Given a relation $R(X, X)$, its transitive closure $R_T(X, X)$ can be determined by a simple algorithm that consists of the following three steps:

1. $R' = R \cup (R \circ R)$.
2. If $R' \neq R$, make $R = R'$ and go to Step 1.
3. Stop: $R' = R_T$.

This algorithm is applicable to both crisp and fuzzy relations. However, the type of composition and set union in Step 1 must be compatible with the definition of transitivity employed. When max-min composition and the max operator for set union are used, we call R_T the *transitive max-min closure*.

Example 5.8

Using the algorithm just given, we can determine the transitive max-min closure $R_T(X, X)$ for a fuzzy relation $R(X, X)$ defined by the membership matrix

$$\mathbf{R} = \begin{bmatrix} .7 & .5 & 0 & 0 \\ 0 & 0 & 0 & 1 \\ 0 & .4 & 0 & 0 \\ 0 & 0 & .8 & 0 \end{bmatrix}.$$

Applying Step 1 of the algorithm, we obtain

$$\mathbf{R} \circ \mathbf{R} = \begin{bmatrix} .7 & .5 & 0 & .5 \\ 0 & 0 & .8 & 0 \\ 0 & 0 & 0 & .4 \\ 0 & .4 & 0 & 0 \end{bmatrix} \qquad \mathbf{R} \cup (\mathbf{R} \circ \mathbf{R}) = \begin{bmatrix} .7 & .5 & 0 & .5 \\ 0 & 0 & .8 & 1 \\ 0 & .4 & 0 & .4 \\ 0 & .4 & .8 & 0 \end{bmatrix} = \mathbf{R'}.$$

Since $\mathbf{R'} \neq \mathbf{R}$, we take $\mathbf{R'}$ as a new matrix $\mathbf{R}$ and, repeating the previous procedure, we obtain

$$\mathbf{R} \circ \mathbf{R} = \begin{bmatrix} .7 & .5 & .5 & .5 \\ 0 & .4 & .8 & .4 \\ 0 & .4 & .4 & .4 \\ 0 & .4 & .4 & .4 \end{bmatrix} \qquad \mathbf{R} \cup (\mathbf{R} \circ \mathbf{R}) = \begin{bmatrix} .7 & .5 & .5 & .5 \\ 0 & .4 & .8 & .1 \\ 0 & .4 & .4 & .4 \\ 0 & .4 & .8 & .4 \end{bmatrix} = \mathbf{R'}.$$

Since $\mathbf{R'} \neq \mathbf{R}$ at this stage, we must again repeat the procedure with the new relation. If we do this, however, the last matrix does not change. Thus,

$$\begin{bmatrix} .7 & .5 & .5 & .5 \\ 0 & .4 & .8 & 1 \\ 0 & .4 & .4 & .4 \\ 0 & .4 & .8 & .4 \end{bmatrix}$$

is the membership matrix of the transitive closure R_T corresponding to the given relation $R(X, X)$.

5.5 FUZZY EQUIVALENCE RELATIONS

A crisp binary relation $R(X, X)$ that is reflexive, symmetric, and transitive is called an *equivalence relation*. For each element x in X, we can define a crisp set A_x, which contains all the elements of X that are related to x by the equivalence relation. Formally,

$$A_x = \{y | \langle x, y \rangle \in R(X, X)\}.$$

A_x is clearly a subset of X. The element x is itself contained in A_x due to the reflexivity of R; because R is transitive and symmetric, each member of A_x is related to all the other members of A_x. Furthermore, no member of A_x is related to any element of X not included in A_x. This set A_x is referred to as an *equivalence class* of $R(X, X)$ with respect to x. The members of each equivalence class can be considered equivalent to each other and only to each other under the relation R. The family of all such equivalence classes defined by the relation, which is usually denoted by X/R, forms a partition on X.

Example 5.9

Let $X = \{1, 2, \ldots, 10\}$. The Cartesian product $X \times Y$ contains 100 members: $\langle 1, 1 \rangle$, $\langle 1, 2 \rangle$, $\langle 1, 3 \rangle, \ldots, \langle 10, 10 \rangle$. Let $R(X, X) = \{\langle x, y \rangle | x \text{ and } y \text{ have the same remainder when divided by } 3\}$. The relation is easily shown to be reflexive, symmetric, and transitive and is therefore an equivalence relation on X. The three equivalence classes defined by this relation are:

$$A_1 = A_4 = A_7 = A_{10} = \{1, 4, 7, 10\},$$
$$A_2 = A_5 = A_8 = \{2, 5, 8\},$$
$$A_3 = A_6 = A_9 = \{3, 6, 9\}.$$

Hence, in this example, $X/R = \{\{1, 4, 7, 10\}, \{2, 5, 8\}, \{3, 6, 9\}\}$.

A fuzzy binary relation that is reflexive, symmetric, and transitive is known as a *fuzzy equivalence relation* or *similarity relation*. In the rest of this section, let us use the latter term. While the max-min form of transitivity is assumed in the following discussion, the concepts can be generalized to the alternative definitions of fuzzy transitivity.

While an equivalence relation clearly groups elements that are equivalent under the relation into disjoint classes, the interpretation of a similarity relation can be approached in two different ways. First, it can be considered to effectively group elements into crisp sets whose members are "similar" to each other to some specified degree. Obviously, when this degree is equal to 1, the grouping is an equivalence class. Alternatively, however, we may wish to consider the degree of similarity that the elements of X have to some specified element $x \in X$. Thus, for each $x \in X$, a *similarity class* can be defined as a fuzzy set in which the membership grade of any particular element represents the similarity of that element to the element x. If all the elements in the class are similar to x to the degree of 1 and similar to all elements outside the set to the degree of 0, then the grouping again becomes an equivalence class. The following discussion briefly elaborates on each of these approaches in turn.

Due to Theorem 2.5, every fuzzy relation R can be uniquely represented in terms of its α-cuts by the formula

$$R = \bigcup_{\alpha \in [0,1]} \alpha \cdot {}^{\alpha}R. \qquad (5.12)$$

It can easily be shown, if R is a similarity relation, then each α-cut ${}^{\alpha}R$ is a crisp equivalence relation. Effectively, then, we may use any similarity relation R and, by taking an α-cut ${}^{\alpha}R$ for any value $\alpha \in (0, 1]$, create a crisp equivalence relation that represents the presence of similarity between the elements to the degree α. Each of these equivalence relations forms a partition of X. Let $\pi({}^{\alpha}R)$ denote the partition corresponding to the equivalence relation ${}^{\alpha}R$. Clearly, two elements x and y belong to the same block of this partition iff $R(x, y) \geq \alpha$.

Each similarity relation is associated with the set

$$\Pi(R) = \{\pi({}^{\alpha}R) | \alpha \in (0, 1]\}$$

of partitions of X. These partitions are nested in the sense that $\pi({}^{\alpha}R)$ is a refinement of $\pi({}^{\beta}R)$ iff $\alpha \geq \beta$.

Example 5.10

The fuzzy relation $R(X, X)$ represented by the membership matrix

	a	b	c	d	e	f	g
a	1	.8	0	.4	0	0	0
b	.8	1	0	.4	0	0	0
c	0	0	1	0	1	.9	.5
d	.4	.4	0	1	0	0	0
e	0	0	1	0	1	.9	.5
f	0	0	.9	0	.9	1	.5
g	0	0	.5	0	.5	.5	1

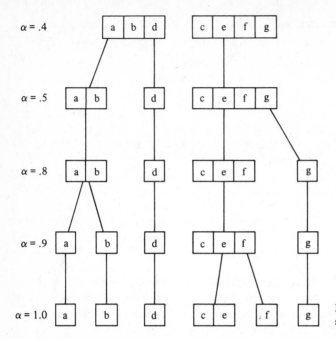

Figure 5.7 Partition tree for the similarity relation in Example 5.10.

is a similarity relation on $X = \{a, b, c, d, e, f, g\}$. To verify that R is reflexive and symmetric is trivial. To verify its transitivity, we may employ the algorithm for calculating transitive closures introduced in Sec. 5.4. If the algorithm is applied to R and terminates after the first iteration, then, clearly, R is transitive. The level set of R is $\Lambda_R = \{0, .4, .5, .8, .9, 1\}$. Therefore, R is associated with a sequence of five nested partitions $\pi(^\alpha R)$, for $\alpha \in \Lambda_R$ and $\alpha > 0$. Their refinement relationship can be conveniently diagrammed by a *partition tree*, as shown in Fig. 5.7.

The equivalence classes formed by the levels of refinement of a similarity relation can be interpreted as grouping elements that are similar to each other and only to each other to a degree not less than α. Thus, in Example 5.10, c, e, f, and g are all similar to each other to a degree of .5, but only c and e are similar to each other to a degree of 1.

Just as equivalence classes are defined by an equivalence relation, *similarity classes* are defined by a similarity relation. For a given similarity relation $R(X, X)$, the similarity class for each $x \in X$ is a fuzzy set in which the membership grade of each element $y \in X$ is simply the strength of that element's relation to x, or $R(x, y)$. Thus, the similarity class for an element x represents the degree to which all the other members of X are similar to x. Except in the restricted case of equivalence classes themselves, similarity classes are fuzzy, and therefore not generally disjoint.

Similarity classes are conveniently represented by membership matrices. Given a similarity relation R, the similarity class for each element is defined by the row of the membership matrix of R that corresponds to that element. For instance, the similarity classes for the element c and the element e of the similarity relation in Example 5.10 are equal. Therefore, the relation defines six different similarity classes.

Fuzzy equivalence is a cutworthy property of binary relations $R(X, X)$ since it is preserved in the classical sense in each α-cut of R. This implies that the properties of fuzzy reflexivity, symmetry, and max-min transitivity are also cutworthy.

Binary relations that are symmetric and transitive but not reflexive are usually referred to as *quasi-equivalence relations*. They are, however, of only marginal significance, and we omit a detailed discussion of them.

5.6   FUZZY COMPATIBILITY RELATIONS

A binary relation $R(X, X)$ that is reflexive and symmetric is usually called a *compatibility relation* or *tolerance relation*. When $R(X, X)$ is a reflexive and symmetric fuzzy relation, it is sometimes called a *proximity relation*.

An important concept associated with compatibility relations are compatibility classes (also tolerance classes). Given a crisp compatibility relation $R(X, X)$, a *compatibility class* is a subset A of X such that $\langle x, y \rangle \in R$ for all $x, y \in A$. A *maximal compatibility class* or *maximal compatible* is a compatibility class that is not properly contained within any other compatibility class. The family consisting of all the maximal compatibles induced by R on X is called a *complete cover* of X with respect to R.

When R is a fuzzy compatibility relation, compatibility classes are defined in terms of a specified membership degree α. An α-*compatibility class* is a subset A of X such that $R(x, y) \geq \alpha$ for all $x, y \in A$. *Maximal α-compatibles* and *complete α-cover* are obvious generalizations of the corresponding concepts for crisp compatibility relations.

Compatibility relations are often conveniently viewed as *reflexive undirected graphs*. In this context, reflexivity implies that each node of the graph has a loop connecting the node to itself; the loops are usually omitted from the visual representations of the graphs, although they are assumed to be present. Connections between nodes, as defined by the relation, are not directed, since the property of symmetry guarantees that all existing connections appear in both directions. Each connection is labeled with the value of the corresponding membership grade $R(x, y) = R(y, x)$.

Example 5.11

Consider a fuzzy relation $R(X, X)$ defined on $X = \mathbb{N}_9$ by the following membership matrix:

	1	2	3	4	5	6	7	8	9
1	1	.8	0	0	0	0	0	0	0
2	.8	1	0	0	0	0	0	0	0
3	0	0	1	1	.8	0	0	0	0
4	0	0	1	1	.8	.7	.5	0	0
5	0	0	.8	.8	1	.7	.5	.7	0
6	0	0	0	.7	.7	1	.4	0	0
7	0	0	0	.5	.5	.4	1	0	0
8	0	0	0	0	.7	0	0	1	0
9	0	0	0	0	0	0	0	0	1

Since the matrix is symmetric and all entries on the main diagonal are equal to 1, the relation represented is reflexive and symmetric; therefore, it is a compatibility relation. The graph of the relation is shown in Fig. 5.8; its complete α-covers for $\alpha > 0$ and $\alpha \in \Lambda_R = \{0, .4, .5, .7, .8, 1\}$ are depicted in Fig. 5.9.

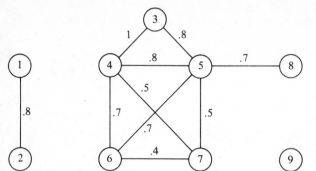

Figure 5.8 Graph of the compatibility relation in Example 5.11.

The complete α-covers of compatibility relations $R(X, X)$ may, for some values of α, form partitions of X; in general, however, this is not the case due to the lack of transitivity. For example, the complete α-covers illustrated in Fig. 5.9 form partitions of $\mathbb{N}_9$ for $\alpha \geq .8$. It is obvious that similarity relations are special cases of compatibility relations for which all complete α-covers form partitions of X. Since the lack of transitivity distinguishes compatibility relations from similarity relations, the transitive closures of compatibility relations are similarity relations.

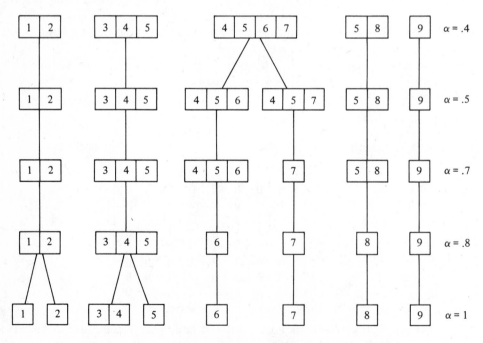

Figure 5.9 All complete α-covers for the compatibility relation R in Example 5.11.

5.7 FUZZY ORDERING RELATIONS

While similarity and compatibility relations are characterized by symmetry, ordering relations require asymmetry (or antisymmetry) and transitivity. There are several types of ordering relations.

A crisp binary relation $R(X, X)$ that is reflexive, antisymmetric, and transitive is called a *partial ordering*. The common symbol $\leq$ is suggestive of the properties of this class of relations. Thus, $x \leq y$ denotes $\langle x, y \rangle \in R$ and signifies that x *precedes* y. The inverse partial ordering $R^{-1}(X, X)$ is suggested by the symbol $\geq$. If $y \geq x$, indicating that $\langle y, x \rangle \in R^{-1}$, then we say that y *succeeds* x. When $x \leq y$, x is also referred to as a *predecessor* of y, while y is called a *successor* of x. When $x \leq y$ and there is no z such that $x \leq z$ and $z \leq y$, x is called an *immediate predecessor* of y, and y is called an *immediate successor* of x. If we need to distinguish several partial orderings, such as P, Q, and R, we use the symbols $\overset{P}{\leq}, \overset{Q}{\leq},$ and $\overset{R}{\leq}$, respectively.

Observe that a partial ordering $\leq$ on X does not guarantee that all pairs of elements x, y in X are comparable in the sense that either $x \leq y$ or $y \leq x$. Thus, for some $x, y \in X$, it is possible that x is neither a predecessor nor a successor of y. Such pairs are called *noncomparable* with respect to $\leq$.

The following are definitions of some fundamental concepts associated with partial orderings:

- If $x \in X$ and $x \leq y$ for every $y \in X$, then x is called the *first member* (or *minimum*) of X with respect to the relation denoted by $\leq$.
- If $x \in X$ and $y \leq x$ for every $y \in X$, then x is called the *last member* (or *maximum*) of X with respect to the partial ordering relation.
- If $x \in X$ and $y \leq x$ implies $x = y$, then x is called a *minimal member* of X with respect to the relation.
- If $x \in X$ and $x \leq y$ implies $x = y$, then x is called a *maximal member* of X with respect to the relation.

Using these concepts, every partial ordering satisfies the following properties:

1. There exists at most one first member and at most one last member.
2. There may exist several maximal members and several minimal members.
3. If a first member exists, then only one minimal member exists, and it is identical with the first member.
4. If a last member exists, then only one maximal member exists, and it is identical with the last member.
5. The first and last members of a partial ordering relation correspond to the last and first members of the inverse partial ordering, respectively.

Let X again be a set on which a partial ordering is defined, and let A be a subset of $X (A \subseteq X)$. If $x \in X$ and $x \leq y$ for every $y \in A$, then x is called a *lower bound* of A on X

with respect to the partial ordering. If $x \in X$ and $y \leq x$ for every $y \in A$, then x is called an *upper bound* of A on X with respect to the relation. If a particular lower bound succeeds every other lower bound of A, then it is called the *greatest lower bound*, or *infimum*, of A. If a particular upper bound precedes every other upper bound of A, then it is called the *least upper bound*, or *supremum*, of A.

A partial ordering on a set X that contains a greatest lower bound and a least upper bound for every subset of two elements of X is called a *lattice*.

A partial ordering $\leq$ on X is said to be *connected* iff for all $x, y \in X, x \neq y$ implies either $x \leq y$ or $y \leq x$. When a partial ordering is connected, all pairs of elements of X are comparable by the ordering. Such an ordering is usually called a *linear ordering*; some alternative names used in the literature are *total ordering*, *simple ordering*, and *complete ordering*.

Every partial ordering on a set X can be conveniently represented by a diagram in which each element of X is expressed by a single node that is connected only to the nodes representing its immediate predecessors and immediate successors. The connections are directed in order to distinguish predecessors from successors; the arrow $\leftarrow$ indicates the inequality $\leq$. Diagrams of this sort are called *Hasse diagrams*.

Example 5.12

Three crisp partial orderings P, Q, and R on the set $X = \{a, b, c, d, e\}$ are defined by their membership matrices (crisp) and their Hasse diagrams in Fig. 5.10. The underlined entries in each matrix indicate the relationship of the immediate predecessor and successor employed in the corresponding Hasse diagram. P has no special properties, Q is a lattice, and R is an example of a lattice that represents a linear ordering.

A fuzzy binary relation R on a set X is a *fuzzy partial ordering* iff it is reflexive, antisymmetric, and transitive under some form of fuzzy transitivity. Any fuzzy partial ordering based on max-min transitivity can be resolved into a series of crisp partial orderings in the same way in which this is done for similarity relations, that is, by taking a series of α-cuts that produce increasing levels of refinement.

When a fuzzy partial ordering is defined on a set X, two fuzzy sets are associated with each element x in X. The first is called the *dominating class* of x. It is denoted by $R_{\geq[x]}$ and is defined by

$$R_{\geq[x]}(y) = R(x, y),$$

where $y \in X$. In other words, the dominating class of x contains the members of X to the degree to which they dominate x.

The second fuzzy set of concern is the class *dominated* by x, which is denoted by $R_{\leq[x]}$ and defined by

$$R_{\leq[x]}(y) = R(y, x),$$

where $y \in X$. The class dominated by x contains the elements of X to the degree to which they are dominated by x.

An element $x \in X$ is *undominated* iff

$$R(x, y) = 0$$

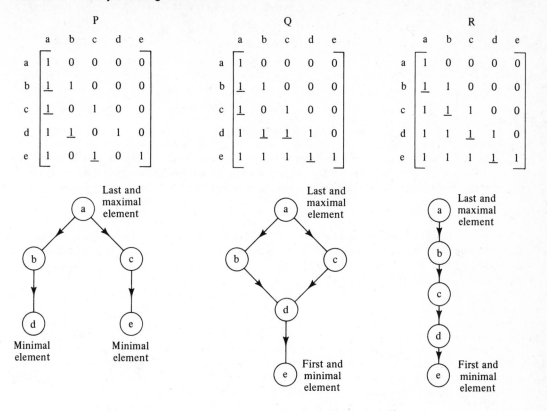

Figure 5.10   Examples of partial ordering (Example 5.12).

for all $y \in X$ and $x \neq y$; an element x is *undominating* iff

$$R(y, x) = 0$$

for all $y \in X$ and $y \neq x$.

For a crisp subset A of a set X on which a fuzzy partial ordering R is defined, the *fuzzy upper bound* for A is the fuzzy set denoted by $U(R, A)$ and defined by

$$U(R, A) = \bigcap_{x \in A} R_{\geq [x]},$$

where $\cap$ denotes an appropriate fuzzy intersection. This definition reduces to that of the conventional upper bound when the partial ordering is crisp. If a *least upper bound* of the set A exists, it is the unique element x in $U(R, A)$ such that

$$U(R, A)(x) > 0 \text{ and } R(x, y) > 0,$$

for all elements y in the support of $U(R, A)$.

Example 5.13

The following membership matrix defines a fuzzy partial ordering R on the set $X = \{a, b, c, d, e\}$:

$$
\begin{array}{c}
\begin{array}{ccccc} a & b & c & d & e \end{array} \\
\mathbf{R} = \begin{array}{c} a \\ b \\ c \\ d \\ e \end{array}
\left[\begin{array}{ccccc}
1 & .7 & 0 & 1 & .7 \\
0 & 1 & 0 & .9 & 0 \\
.5 & .7 & 1 & 1 & .8 \\
0 & 0 & 0 & 1 & 0 \\
0 & .1 & 0 & .9 & 1
\end{array}\right]
\end{array}
$$

The dominating class for each element is given by the row of the matrix corresponding to that element. The columns of the matrix give the dominated class for each element. Under this ordering, the element d is undominated, and the element c is undominating. For the subset $A = \{a, b\}$, the upper bound is the fuzzy set produced by the intersection of the dominating classes for a and b. Employing the min operator for fuzzy intersection, we obtain

$$U(R, \{a, b\}) = .7/b + .9/d.$$

The unique least upper bound for the set A is the element b. All distinct crisp orderings captured by the given fuzzy partial ordering R are shown in Fig. 5.11. We can see that the orderings became weaker with the increasing value of α.

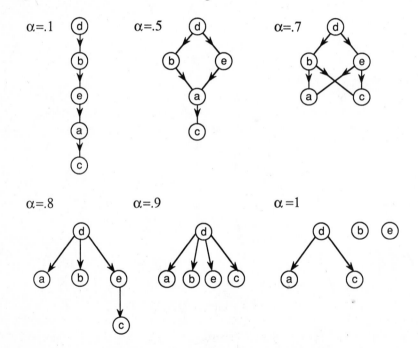

Figure 5.11 The set of all distinct crisp orderings captured by the fuzzy partial ordering R in Example 5.13.

Several other concepts of crisp orderings easily generalize to the fuzzy case. A *fuzzy preordering* is a fuzzy relation that is reflexive and transitive. Unlike a partial ordering, the preordering is not necessarily antisymmetric.

A *fuzzy weak ordering* R is an ordering satisfying all the properties of a fuzzy linear ordering except antisymmetry. Alternatively, it can be thought of as a fuzzy preordering

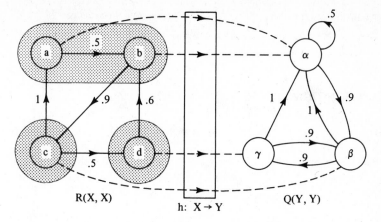

(a) Ordinary fuzzy homomorphism

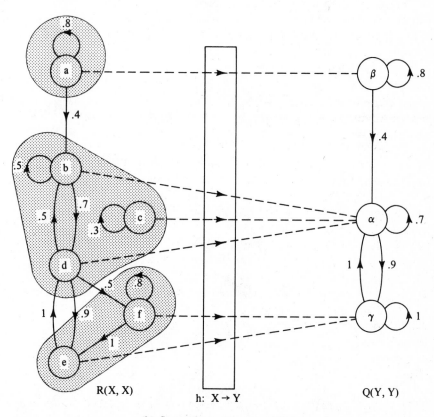

(b) Strong fuzzy homomorphism

Figure 5.12 Fuzzy homomorphisms (Example 5.14): (a) ordinary fuzzy homomorphism; (b) strong fuzzy homomorphism.

between two relations such as $R_1(X_1, Y_1)$ and $R_2(X_2, Y_2)$ would consist of two functions, $h_1 : X_1 \rightarrow X_2$ and $h_2 : Y_1 \rightarrow Y_2$. The properties described earlier must then be satisfied by each of these functions.

5.9 SUP-i COMPOSITIONS OF FUZZY RELATIONS

Sup-i compositions of binary fuzzy relations, where i refers to a t-norm, generalize the standard max-min composition. The need to study these generalizations emerges from some applications, such as approximate reasoning and fuzzy control. Given a particular t-norm i and two fuzzy relations $P(X, Y)$ and $Q(Y, Z)$, the sup-i composition of P and Q is a fuzzy relation $P \overset{i}{\circ} Q$ on $X \times Z$ defined by

$$[P \overset{i}{\circ} Q](x, z) = \sup_{y \in Y} i[P(x, y), Q(y, z)] \tag{5.13}$$

for all $x \in X, z \in Z$. When i is chosen to be the min operator, $P \overset{i}{\circ} Q$ becomes the standard composition $P \circ Q$.

Given fuzzy relations $P(X, Y)$, $P_j(X, Y)$, $Q(Y, Z)$, $Q_j(Y, Z)$, and $R(Z, V)$, where j takes values in an index set J, the following are basic properties of the sup-i composition under the standard fuzzy union and intersection:

$$(P \overset{i}{\circ} Q) \overset{i}{\circ} R = P \overset{i}{\circ} (Q \overset{i}{\circ} R), \tag{5.14}$$

$$P \overset{i}{\circ} (\bigcup_{j \in J} Q_j) = \bigcup_{j \in J} (P \overset{i}{\circ} Q_j), \tag{5.15}$$

$$P \overset{i}{\circ} (\bigcap_{j \in J} Q_j) \subseteq \bigcap_{j \in J} (P \overset{i}{\circ} Q_j), \tag{5.16}$$

$$(\bigcup_{j \in J} P_j) \overset{i}{\circ} Q = \bigcup_{j \in J} (P_j \overset{i}{\circ} Q), \tag{5.17}$$

$$(\bigcap_{j \in J} P_j) \overset{i}{\circ} Q \subseteq \bigcap_{j \in J} (P_j \overset{i}{\circ} Q), \tag{5.18}$$

$$(P \overset{i}{\circ} Q)^{-1} = Q^{-1} \overset{i}{\circ} P^{-1}. \tag{5.19}$$

These properties follow directly from the corresponding properties of t-norms, and their verification is left to the reader as an exercise. Sup-i composition is also monotonic increasing, that is, for any fuzzy relations $P(X, Y)$, $Q_1(Y, Z)$, $Q_2(Y, Z)$, and $R(Z, V)$, if $Q_1 \subseteq Q_2$, then

$$P \overset{i}{\circ} Q_1 \subseteq P \overset{i}{\circ} Q_2, \tag{5.20}$$

$$Q_1 \overset{i}{\circ} R \subseteq Q_2 \overset{i}{\circ} R. \tag{5.21}$$

The set of all binary fuzzy relations on X^2 forms a complete lattice-ordered monoid $\langle \mathcal{F}(X^2), \cap, \cup, \overset{i}{\circ} \rangle$, where $\cap$ and $\cup$ represent the meet and join of the lattice, respectively, and $\overset{i}{\circ}$

represents the semigroup operation of the monoid. The identity of $\overset{i}{\circ}$ is defined by the relations

$$E(x, y) = \begin{cases} 1 & \text{when } x = y \\ 0 & \text{when } x \neq y. \end{cases}$$

The concept of transitivity of a fuzzy relation, which is introduced in terms of the max-min composition in Sec. 5.4, can be generalized in terms of the sup-i compositions for the various t-norms i. We say that relation R on X^2 is i-*transitive* iff

$$R(x, z) \geq i[R(x, y), R(y, z)] \tag{5.22}$$

for all $x, y, z \in X$. It is easy to show that a fuzzy relation R on X^2 is i-transitive iff $R \overset{i}{\circ} R \subseteq R$, which may be used as an alternative definition of i-transitivity.

When a relation R is not i-transitive, we define its i-*transitive closure* as a relation $R_{T(i)}$ that is the smallest i-transitive relation containing R. To investigate properties of the i-transitive closure, let

$$R^{(n)} = R \overset{i}{\circ} R^{(n-1)},$$

for $n = 2, 3, \ldots,$ where R is a fuzzy relation on X^2 and $R^{(1)} = R$. Using this notation, we can now formulate two theorems regarding i-transitive closure.

Theorem 5.1.   For any fuzzy relation R on X^2, the fuzzy relation

$$R_{T(i)} = \bigcup_{n=1}^{\infty} R^{(n)} \tag{5.23}$$

is the i-transitive closure of R.

Proof: First, by (5.15) and (5.17),

$$R_{T(i)} \overset{i}{\circ} R_{T(i)} = (\bigcup_{n=1}^{\infty} R^{(n)}) \overset{i}{\circ} (\bigcup_{m=1}^{\infty} R^{(m)})$$

$$= \bigcup_{n=1}^{\infty} \bigcup_{m=1}^{\infty} (R^{(n)} \overset{i}{\circ} R^{(m)})$$

$$= \bigcup_{n,m=1}^{\infty} R^{(n+m)}$$

$$\subseteq \bigcup_{k=1}^{\infty} R^{(k)}$$

$$= R_{T(i)}.$$

This means that $R_{T(i)}$ is i-transitive.

Consider now a fuzzy relation S that is i-transitive and contains $R(R \subseteq S)$. Then,

$$R^{(2)} = R \overset{i}{\circ} R \subseteq S \overset{i}{\circ} S \subseteq S$$

and, moreover, if $R^{(n)} \subseteq S$, then

$$R^{(n+1)} = R \overset{i}{\circ} R^{(n)} \subseteq S \overset{i}{\circ} S \subseteq S.$$

Hence, $R^{(k)} \subseteq S$ for any $k \in \mathbb{N}$ and, therefore,

$$R_{T(i)} = \bigcup_{k=1}^{\infty} R^{(k)} \subseteq S.$$

That is, $R_{T(i)}$ is the smallest i-transitive fuzzy relation containing R. ∎

It follows directly from this theorem that any given fuzzy relation on X^2 is i-transitive iff $R = R_{T(i)}$. For finite and reflexive fuzzy relations, the i-transitive closure has a simpler form, as expressed by the following theorem.

Theorem 5.2.   Let R be a reflexive fuzzy relation on X^2, where $|X| = n \geq 2$. Then, $R_{T(i)} = R^{(n-1)}$.

Proof: Since R is reflexive, $E \subseteq R$ and $R = E \stackrel{i}{\circ} R \subseteq R \stackrel{i}{\circ} R = R^{(2)}$. Thus, $R^{(m)} \subseteq R^{(m+1)}$ for any $m \in \mathbb{N}$. Now, we prove that $R^{(n-1)} = R^{(n)}$. For any $x, y \in X$, if $x = y$, then $R^{(n)}(x, x) = R^{(n-1)}(x, x) = 1$; if $x \neq y$, then

$$R^{(n)}(x, y) = \sup_{z_1, \ldots, z_{n-1}} i[R(x, z_1), R(z_1, z_2), \ldots, R(z_{n-1}, y)].$$

Since $|X| = n$, the sequence $x = z_0, z_1, \ldots, z_{n-1}, z_n = y$ of $n + 1$ elements must contain at least two equal elements. Assume $z_r = z_s$, where $r < s$; then,

$$i[R(x, z_1), \ldots, R(z_{r-1}, z_r), \ldots, R(z_s, z_{s+1}), \ldots, R(z_{n-1}, y)]$$
$$\leq i[R(x, z_1), \ldots, R(z_{r-1}, z_r), R(z_s, z_{s+1}), \ldots, R(z_{n-1}, y)]$$
$$\leq R^{(k)}(x, y) \quad (k \leq n - 1)$$
$$\leq R^{(n-1)}(x, y).$$

Hence, $R^{(n)}(x, y) \leq R^{(n-1)}(x, y)$ for any $x, y \in X$ and, consequently, $R^{(n)} \subseteq R^{(n-1)}$. It follows that $R^{(n)} = R^{(n-1)}$ and, therefore, $R_{T(i)} = R^{(n-1)}$. ∎

The i-transitivity, together with reflexivity, symmetry, antisymmetry, and so on, can be used for defining fuzzy i-equivalence, i-compatibility, and other types of fuzzy relations, but the coverage of these generalizations is beyond the scope of this text.

5.10 INF-ω_i COMPOSITIONS OF FUZZY RELATIONS

Given a continuous t-norm i, let

$$\omega_i(a, b) = \sup\{x \in [0, 1] \mid i(a, x) \leq b\}$$

for every $a, b \in [0, 1]$. This operation, referred to as operation ω_i, plays an important role in fuzzy relation equations (Chapter 6). While the t-norm i may be interpreted as logical conjunction, the corresponding operation ω_i may be interpreted as logical implication. Basic properties of ω_i are expressed by the following theorem.

Theorem 5.3.   For any $a, a_j, b, d \in [0, 1]$, where j takes values from an index set J, operation ω_i has the following properties:

1. $i(a, b) \leq d$ iff $\omega_i(a, d) \geq b$;
2. $\omega_i[\omega_i(a, b), b] \geq a$;
3. $\omega_i[i(a, b), d] = \omega_i[a, \omega_i(b, d)]$;
4. $a \leq b$ implies $\omega_i(a, d) \geq \omega_i(b, d)$ and $\omega_i(d, a) \leq \omega_i(d, b)$;
5. $i[\omega_i(a, b), \omega_i(b, d)] \leq \omega_i(a, d)$;
6. $\omega_i[\inf_{j \in J} a_j, b] \geq \sup_{j \in J} \omega_i(a_j, b)$;
7. $\omega_i[\sup_{j \in J} a_j, b] = \inf_{j \in J} \omega_i(a_j, b)$;
8. $\omega_i[b, \sup_{j \in J} a_j] \geq \sup_{j \in J} \omega_i(b, a_j)$;
9. $\omega_i[b, \inf_{j \in J} a_j] = \inf_{j \in J} \omega_i(b, a_j)$;
10. $i[a, \omega_i(a, b)] \leq b$.

Proof: We illustrate the full proof by proving only properties **1**, **3**, and **7**, and leave the rest of the proof to the reader.

1. If $i(a, b) \leq d$, then $b \in \{x | i(a, x) \leq d\}$ and, consequently, $b \leq \sup\{x | i(a, x) \leq d\} = \omega_i(a, d)$. If $b \leq \omega_i(a, d)$, then

$$
\begin{aligned}
i(a, b) &\leq i[a, \omega_i(a, d)] \\
&= i[a, \sup\{x | i(a, x) \leq d\}] \\
&= \sup\{i(a, x) | i(a, x) \leq d\} \text{ (since } i \text{ is continuous)} \\
&\leq d.
\end{aligned}
$$

3. By property **1**, $i(a, x) \leq \omega_i(b, d) \Leftrightarrow i[b, i(a, x)] \leq d \Leftrightarrow i[i(a, b), x] \leq d \Leftrightarrow x \leq \omega_i[i(a, b), d]$. Hence,

$$
\begin{aligned}
\omega_i[a, \omega_i(b, d)] &= \sup\{x | i(a, x) \leq \omega_i(b, d)\} \\
&= \sup\{x | x \leq \omega_i[i(a, b), d]\} \\
&= \omega_i[i(a, b), d].
\end{aligned}
$$

7. Let $s = \sup_{j \in J} a_j$. Then, $a_j \leq s$ and $\omega_i(s, b) \leq \omega(a_j, b)$ for any $j \in J$ by property **4.** Hence, $\omega_i(s, b) \leq \inf_{j \in J} \omega_i(a_j, b)$. On the other hand, since $\inf_{j \in J} \omega_i(a_j, b) \leq \omega_i(a_{j_0}, b)$ for all $j_0 \in J$, by property **1** we have $i(a_{j_0}, \inf_{j \in J} \omega_i(a_j, b)) \leq b$ for all $j_0 \in J$. Thus, $i(s, \inf_{j \in J} \omega_i(a_j, b)) = \sup_{j_0 \in J} i(a_{j_0}, \inf_{j \in J} \omega_i(a_j, b)) \leq b$. Again by property **1**, we have

$$
\omega_i(s, b) \geq \inf_{j \in J} \omega_i(a_j, b);
$$

consequently,

$$
\omega_i(\sup_{j \in J} a_j, b) = \omega_i(s, b) = \inf_{j \in J} \omega_i(a_j, b),
$$

which completes the proof of property **7.** ■

Given a t-norm i and the associated operation ω_i, the inf-ω_i composition, $P \overset{\omega_i}{\circ} Q$, of fuzzy relation $P(X, Y)$ and $Q(Y, Z)$ is defined by the equation

$$(P \overset{\omega_i}{\circ} Q)(x, z) = \inf_{y \in Y} \omega_i[P(x, y), Q(y, z)] \tag{5.24}$$

for all $x \in X, z \in Z$.

Basic properties of the inf-ω_i composition are expressed by the following two theorems. Since these properties follow directly from the properties of operations ω_i expressed by Theorem 5.3, we omit their proofs.

Theorem 5.4. Let $P(X, Y)$, $Q(Y, Z)$, $R(X, Z)$, and $S(Z, V)$ be fuzzy relations. Then: (1) the following propositions are equivalent:

$$P \overset{i}{\circ} Q \subseteq R, \tag{5.25}$$

$$Q \subseteq P^{-1} \overset{\omega_i}{\circ} R, \tag{5.26}$$

$$P \subseteq (Q \overset{\omega_i}{\circ} R^{-1})^{-1}; \tag{5.27}$$

(2)
$$P \overset{\omega_i}{\circ} (Q \overset{\omega_i}{\circ} S) = (P \overset{i}{\circ} Q) \overset{\omega_i}{\circ} S. \tag{5.28}$$

Theorem 5.5. Let $P(X, Y)$, $P_j(X, Y)$, $Q(Y, Z)$, and $Q_j(Y, Z)$ be fuzzy relations, where j takes values in an index set J. Then,

$$(\bigcup_{j \in J} P_j) \overset{\omega_i}{\circ} Q = \bigcap_{j \in J} (P_j \overset{\omega_i}{\circ} Q), \tag{5.29}$$

$$(\bigcap_{j \in J} P_j) \overset{\omega_i}{\circ} Q \supseteq \bigcup_{j \in J} (P_j \overset{\omega_i}{\circ} Q), \tag{5.30}$$

$$P \overset{\omega_i}{\circ} (\bigcap_{j \in J} Q_j) = \bigcap_{j \in J} (P \overset{\omega_i}{\circ} Q_j), \tag{5.31}$$

$$P \overset{\omega_i}{\circ} (\bigcup_{j \in J} Q_j) \supseteq \bigcup_{j \in J} (P \overset{\omega_i}{\circ} Q_j). \tag{5.32}$$

This theorem is instrumental in proving the two properties of monotonicity of the inf-ω_i composition that are stated by the following theorem.

Theorem 5.6. Let $P(X, Y)$, $Q_1(Y, Z)$, $Q_2(Y, Z)$, and $R(Z, V)$ be fuzzy relations. If $Q_1 \subseteq Q_2$, then

$$P \overset{\omega_i}{\circ} Q_1 \subseteq P \overset{\omega_i}{\circ} Q_2 \text{ and } Q_1 \overset{\omega_i}{\circ} R \supseteq Q_2 \overset{\omega_i}{\circ} R.$$

Proof: $Q_1 \subseteq Q_2$ implies $Q_1 \cap Q_2 = Q_1$ and $Q_1 \cup Q_2 = Q_2$. Hence,

$$(P \overset{\omega_i}{\circ} Q_1) \cap (P \overset{\omega_i}{\circ} Q_2) = P \overset{\omega_i}{\circ} (Q_1 \cap Q_2) = P \overset{\omega_i}{\circ} Q_1$$

by (5.31), which implies that $P \overset{\omega_i}{\circ} Q_1 \subseteq P \overset{\omega_i}{\circ} Q_2$. Similarly,

$$(Q_1 \overset{\omega_i}{\circ} R) \cap (Q_2 \overset{\omega_i}{\circ} R) = (Q_1 \cup Q_2) \overset{\omega_i}{\circ} R = Q_2 \overset{\omega_i}{\circ} R$$

by (5.29), and this implies $Q_1 \overset{\omega_i}{\circ} R \supseteq Q_2 \overset{\omega_i}{\circ} R$. ∎

This theorem and its predecessors in this section enable us to prove another theorem, which plays an important role in fuzzy relation equations based on the inf-ω_i composition (Sec. 6.5).

Theorem 5.7.   Let $P(X, Y)$, $Q(Y, Z)$, and $R(X, Z)$ be fuzzy relations. Then,

$$P^{-1} \overset{i}{\circ} (P \overset{\omega_i}{\circ} Q) \subseteq Q, \tag{5.33}$$

$$R \subseteq P \overset{\omega_i}{\circ} (P^{-1} \overset{i}{\circ} R), \tag{5.34}$$

$$P \subseteq (P \overset{\omega_i}{\circ} Q) \overset{\omega_i}{\circ} Q^{-1}, \tag{5.35}$$

$$R \subseteq (R \overset{\omega_i}{\circ} Q^{-1}) \overset{\omega_i}{\circ} Q. \tag{5.36}$$

Proof: When the trivial proposition $P \overset{\omega_i}{\circ} Q \subseteq (P^{-1})^{-1} \overset{\omega_i}{\circ} Q$ is interpreted in terms of (5.26) and then replaced with the equivalent proposition (5.25), we directly obtain (5.33). Similarly, when the trivial proposition $P^{-1} \overset{i}{\circ} R \subseteq P^{-1} \overset{i}{\circ} R$ is interpreted in terms of (5.25) and then replaced with the equivalent proposition (5.26), we obtain (5.34). By (5.33), we have $Q^{-1} \supseteq [P^{-1} \overset{i}{\circ} (P \overset{\omega_i}{\circ} Q)]^{-1}$; hence, $Q^{-1} \supseteq (P \overset{\omega_i}{\circ} Q)^{-1} \overset{i}{\circ} P$. Interpreting the last proposition in terms of (5.25) and then replacing it with the equivalent proposition (5.26), we obtain (5.35). Proposition (5.36) follows then directly from (5.35).   ■

Note that (5.33) and (5.34) indicate that the sup-i composition and inf-ω_i composition are opposite compositions in the following weak sense: $P^{-1} \overset{i}{\circ} (P \overset{\omega_i}{\circ} Q) \subseteq Q$ instead of $P^{-1} \overset{i}{\circ} (P \overset{\omega_i}{\circ} Q) = Q$, and $R \subseteq P \overset{\omega_i}{\circ} (P^{-1} \overset{i}{\circ} R)$ instead of $R = P \overset{\omega_i}{\circ} (P^{-1} \overset{i}{\circ} R)$.

NOTES

5.1. The basic ideas of *fuzzy relations* and the concepts of *fuzzy equivalence, compatibility,* and *fuzzy orderings* were introduced by Zadeh [1971a]. Binary fuzzy relations were further investigated by Rosenfeld [1975], Yeh and Bang [1975], Yager [1981a], and Ovchinnikov [1984]; they are also extensively covered in one of the early books on fuzzy set theory [Kaufmann, 1975]. *Relational morphisms* were studied in great detail for both crisp and fuzzy relations by Bandler and Kohout [1986a, b].

5.2. The concepts of *projection, cylindric extension,* and *cylindric closure,* for n-dimensional crisp relations are due to Zadeh [1975a, b]; these concepts are essential for procedures of approximate reasoning.

EXERCISES

5.1. The fuzzy relation R is defined on sets $X_1 = \{a, b, c\}$, $X_2 = \{s, t\}$, $X_3 = \{x, y\}$, $X_4 = \{i, j\}$ as follows:

$$R(X_1, X_2, X_3, X_4) = .4/b, t, y, i + .6/a, s, x, i + .9/b, s, y, i + 1/b, s, y, j$$
$$+ .6/a, t, y, j + .2/c, s, y, i.$$

(a) Compute the projections $R_{1,2,4}$, $R_{1,3}$, and R_4.
(b) Compute the cylindric extensions $[R_{1,2,4} \uparrow \{X_3\}]$, $[R_{1,3} \uparrow \{X_2, X_4\}]$, $[R_4 \uparrow \{X_1, X_2, X_3\}]$.
(c) Compute the cylindric closure from the three cylindric extensions in (b).
(d) Is the cylindric closure from (c) equal to the original relation R?

5.2. Given any n-ary relation, how many different projections of the relation can be taken?

5.3. Express the relation defined in Exercise 5.1 in terms of a four-dimensional array.

5.4. Consider matrices M_1, M_2, M_3 in Table 5.4 as pages in a three-dimensional array that represents a fuzzy ternary relation. Determine:
(a) all two-dimensional projections;
(b) cylindric extensions and cylindric closure of the two-dimensional projections;
(c) all one-dimensional projections;
(d) cylindric extensions and cylindric closure of the one-dimensional projections;
(e) two three-dimensional arrays expressing the difference between each of the cylindric closures and the original ternary relation.

TABLE 5.4 MATRIX REPRESENTATIONS OF FUZZY BINARY RELATIONS
ON $X \times Y$ EMPLOYED IN EXERCISES (ASSUME EITHER
$X = \{x_i | i \in \mathbb{N}_n\}, Y = \{y_j | j \in \mathbb{N}_n\}$, OR $X = Y = \{x_i | i \in \mathbb{N}_n\}, n = 3, 4, 5, 7$)

$$M_1 = \begin{bmatrix} 1 & 0 & .7 \\ .3 & .2 & 0 \\ 0 & .5 & 1 \end{bmatrix} \quad M_2 = \begin{bmatrix} .6 & .6 & 0 \\ 0 & .6 & .1 \\ 0 & .1 & 0 \end{bmatrix} \quad M_3 = \begin{bmatrix} 1 & 0 & .7 \\ 0 & 1 & 0 \\ .7 & 0 & 1 \end{bmatrix}$$

$$M_4 = \begin{bmatrix} 1 & .2 & 0 & 0 \\ 0 & 0 & .4 & .3 \\ 1 & .2 & 0 & 0 \\ 0 & 0 & .4 & .3 \end{bmatrix} \quad M_5 = \begin{bmatrix} .3 & .6 & 0 & 1 \\ .7 & 0 & 1 & .5 \\ .5 & 0 & 0 & .2 \\ 0 & 0 & 1 & 0 \end{bmatrix}$$

$$M_6 = \begin{bmatrix} .7 & .4 & 0 & 1 \\ .7 & 0 & .6 & .2 \\ .5 & .2 & 0 & .2 \\ 0 & 0 & .6 & .3 \end{bmatrix} \quad M_7 = \begin{bmatrix} 0 & .5 & .5 & .4 \\ .3 & 0 & .8 & 0 \\ 1 & 0 & .5 & 0 \\ 0 & .3 & 0 & .1 \end{bmatrix}$$

$$M_8 = \begin{bmatrix} 0 & 0 & .5 & 0 & 0 \\ .6 & .2 & 0 & .3 & .7 \\ 0 & .7 & 0 & 0 & 0 \\ 0 & 0 & 1 & 0 & 1 \\ .1 & .9 & 0 & .9 & 0 \end{bmatrix} \quad M_9 = \begin{bmatrix} .3 & .4 & .5 & 1 & .7 \\ .7 & .3 & .2 & .3 & .6 \\ 0 & .6 & .7 & .3 & .5 \\ .2 & .6 & 1 & .1 & .1 \\ .8 & .1 & .2 & .9 & .4 \end{bmatrix}$$

$$M_{10} = \begin{bmatrix} 0 & .2 & 0 & .4 & .5 \\ .3 & 0 & 0 & .4 & 0 \\ 0 & 0 & .7 & 0 & 0 \\ 0 & .3 & 0 & 0 & .2 \\ .1 & 0 & 0 & .6 & 0 \end{bmatrix} \quad M_{11} = \begin{bmatrix} 1 & 1 & .8 & .4 & .9 \\ .5 & 1 & 1 & 1 & 1 \\ .7 & 0 & 1 & 0 & 0 \\ 0 & 0 & 0 & 1 & .6 \\ 1 & 0 & .7 & .4 & 1 \end{bmatrix}$$

$$M_{12} = \begin{bmatrix} 1 & 0 & .8 & 0 & .6 & .8 & 0 \\ 0 & 1 & 0 & .6 & 0 & .5 & 0 \\ .8 & 0 & 1 & .8 & 0 & 0 & 0 \\ 0 & .6 & .8 & 1 & 0 & 0 & .8 \\ .6 & 0 & 0 & 0 & 1 & .6 & 0 \\ .8 & .5 & 0 & 0 & .6 & 1 & 0 \\ 0 & 0 & 0 & .8 & 0 & 0 & 1 \end{bmatrix} \quad M_{13} = \begin{bmatrix} 0 & .8 & .7 & .1 & .2 & 0 & 0 \\ .3 & 0 & 1 & 0 & .7 & .3 & .2 \\ 0 & 0 & .5 & 1 & 0 & .9 & .2 \\ .1 & .2 & 0 & 1 & 1 & 0 & .7 \\ .3 & .2 & 1 & 0 & .5 & 1 & 1 \\ 0 & .7 & .6 & .2 & 0 & 1 & .5 \\ 1 & 1 & .5 & .7 & .3 & .2 & 1 \end{bmatrix}$$

5.5. Repeat Exercise 5.4 under the assumption that $\langle M_4, M_5 \rangle$ and $\langle M_6, M_7 \rangle$ are pages of a four-dimensional array that represents a fuzzy quaternary relation.

5.6. The fuzzy binary relation R is defined on sets $X = \{1, 2, \ldots, 100\}$ and $Y = \{50, 51, \ldots, 100\}$ and represents the relation "x is much smaller than y." It is defined by membership function

$$R(x, y) = \begin{cases} 1 - \dfrac{x}{y} & \text{for } x \le y \\[2mm] 0 & \text{otherwise,} \end{cases}$$

where $x \in X$ and $y \in Y$.
   (a) What is the domain of R?
   (b) What is the range of R?
   (c) What is the height of R?
   (d) Calculate R^{-1}.

5.7. For each of the following binary relations on a single set, state whether the relation is reflexive, irreflexive, or antireflexive, symmetric, asymmetric, antisymmetric, or strictly antisymmetric, and transitive, nontransitive, or antitransitive:
   (a) "is a sibling of";
   (b) "is a parent of";
   (c) "is smarter than";
   (d) "is the same height as";
   (e) "is at least as tall as."

5.8. For some of the binary relations given in Table 5.4, determine:
   (a) the domain, range, and height of the relation;
   (b) the inverse of the relation.

5.9. Prove that the max-min composition and min join are associative operations on binary fuzzy relations.

5.10. For some of the binary relations given in Table 5.4, draw each of the following:
   (a) a sagittal diagram of the relation;
   (b) a simple diagram of the relation under the assumption that $X = Y$.

5.11. Assuming $X = Y$, perform the max-min composition of some sequences of comparable relations given in Table 5.4. For example:
   (a) $M_1 \circ M_2, M_4 \circ M_5, M_8 \circ M_9, M_{12} \circ M_{13}$;
   (b) $M_1 \circ M_2 \circ M_3, M_4 \circ M_5 \circ M_6 \circ M_7$, etc.

5.12. Repeat Exercise 5.11 for some other max-i compositions.

5.13. Using binary relations given in Table 5.4, perform the following relational joins:
   (a) $M_1 * M_2$;
   (b) $M_4 * M_5$;
   (c) $M_8 * M_9$;
   (d) $M_{12} * M_{13}$.

5.14. Prove that the properties of symmetry, reflexivity, and transitivity (or the lack of these properties) are preserved under inversion for both crisp and fuzzy relations.

5.15. Assuming that $X = Y$ for binary relations given in Table 5.4, determine for some of the relations whether they are reflexive, ε-reflexive (for some $0 < \varepsilon < 1$), irreflexive, antireflexive, symmetric, asymmetric, antisymmetric, strictly antisymmetric, transitive, nontransitive, or antitransitive (assuming max-min transitivity).

5.16. Assuming that $X = Y$, determine the max-min transitive closure for some relations given in Table 5.4.

5.17. Repeat Exercise 5.16 for max-product transitive closure.

5.18. Given a fuzzy equivalence relation $R(X, X)$ and two partitions $\pi({}^{\alpha}R)$ and $\pi({}^{\beta}R)$, where ${}^{\alpha}R$ and ${}^{\beta}R$ are α-cuts and $\alpha \geq \beta$, prove that each element of $\pi({}^{\alpha}R)$ is contained in some element of $\pi({}^{\beta}R)$.

5.19. The transitive closure of the relation defined by matrix M_{12} in Table 5.4 (Exercise 5.16) is a equivalence relation. Determine its partition tree.

5.20. Relations defined by matrices M_3 and M_{12} in Table 5.4 are compatibility relations (assume $X = Y$). Determine:
   (a) simple diagrams of the relations;
   (b) all complete α-covers of the relations.

5.21. Prove the following proposition: When $R(X, X)$ is max-min transitive, then $R \circ R \subseteq R$.

5.22. Show that for every fuzzy partial ordering on X, the sets of undominated and undominating elements of X are nonempty.

5.23. Assuming $X = Y$, construct simplifications of some of the relations given in Table 5.4 under appropriate homomorphic mappings defined by you.

5.24. Let R be a reflexive fuzzy relation. Prove that $R_T = \lim_{k \to \infty} R^{(k)}$, where $R^{(k)}$ is defined recursively as $R^{(k)} = R \circ R^{(k-1)}$, for $k = 2, 3, \ldots,$ and $R^{(1)} = R$.

5.25. Repeat Exercise 5.11 for some inf-ω_i compositions based, for example, on the Yager t-norms i_ω for various values of the parameter ω.

5.26. Prove (5.14)–(5.19).

5.27. Prove Theorem 5.3.

5.28. Prove Theorem 5.4.

5.29. Prove Theorem 5.5.

6

Fuzzy Relation Equations

6.1 GENERAL DISCUSSION

The notion of fuzzy relation equations is associated with the concept of composition of binary relations. As explained in Sec. 5.3, the composition of two fuzzy binary relations $P(X, Y)$ and $Q(Y, Z)$ can be defined, in general, in terms of an operation on the membership matrices of P and Q that resembles matrix multiplication. This operation involves exactly the same combinations of matrix entries as in the regular matrix multiplication. However, the multiplications and additions that are applied to these combinations in the matrix multiplication are replaced with other operations; these alternative operations represent, in each given context, the appropriate operations of fuzzy set intersection and union, respectively. In the max-min composition, for example, the multiplications and additions are replaced with the min and max operations, respectively.

For the sake of simplicity and clarity, let our further discussion in this section be limited to the max-min form of composition. This form is not only viewed as the most fundamental composition of fuzzy relations, but it is also the form that has been studied most extensively and has the highest utility in numerous applications.

Consider three fuzzy binary relations $P(X, Y)$, $Q(Y, Z)$ and $R(X, Z)$, which are defined on the sets

$$X = \{x_i | i \in I\}, Y = \{y_j | j \in J\}, Z = \{z_k | k \in K\},$$

where we assume that $I = \mathbb{N}_n$, $J = \mathbb{N}_m$, and $K = \mathbb{N}_s$. Let the membership matrices of $\mathbf{P}, \mathbf{Q},$ and $\mathbf{R}$ be denoted by

$$\mathbf{P} = [p_{ij}], \quad \mathbf{Q} = [q_{jk}], \quad \mathbf{R} = [r_{ik}],$$

respectively, where

$$p_{ij} = P(x_i, y_j), \quad q_{jk} = Q(y_j, z_k), \quad r_{ik} = R(x_i, z_k)$$

for all $i \in I(= \mathbb{N}_n)$, $j \in J(= \mathbb{N}_m)$ and $k \in K(= \mathbb{N}_s)$. This means that all entries in the matrices $\mathbf{P}, \mathbf{Q},$ and $\mathbf{R}$ are real numbers in the unit interval $[0, 1]$.

Assume now that the three relations constrain each other in such a way that

$$\mathbf{P} \circ \mathbf{Q} = \mathbf{R}, \tag{6.1}$$

where $\circ$ denotes the max-min composition. This means that

$$\max_{j \in J} \min(p_{ij}, q_{jk}) = r_{ik} \tag{6.2}$$

for all $i \in I$ and $k \in K$. That is, the matrix equation (6.1) encompasses $n \times s$ simultaneous equations of the form (6.2). When two of the components in each of the equations are given and one is unknown, these equations are referred to as *fuzzy relation equations*.

When matrices $\mathbf{P}$ and $\mathbf{Q}$ are given and matrix $\mathbf{R}$ is to be determined from (6.1), the problem is trivial. It is solved simply by performing the max-min multiplication-like operation on $\mathbf{P}$ and $\mathbf{Q}$, as defined by (6.2). Clearly, the solution in this case exists and is unique. The problem becomes far from trivial when one of the two matrices on the left-hand side of (6.1) is unknown. In this case, the solution is guaranteed neither to exist nor to be unique.

Since $\mathbf{R}$ in (6.1) is obtained by composing $\mathbf{P}$ and $\mathbf{Q}$, it is suggestive to view the problem of determining $\mathbf{P}$ (or, alternatively, $\mathbf{Q}$) from $\mathbf{R}$ and $\mathbf{Q}$ (or, alternatively, $\mathbf{R}$ and $\mathbf{P}$) as a *decomposition* of $\mathbf{R}$ with respect to $\mathbf{Q}$ (or, alternatively, with respect to $\mathbf{P}$). Since many problems in various contexts can be formulated as problems of decomposition, the utility of any method for solving (6.1) is quite high. The use of fuzzy relation equations in some applications is illustrated in Part II of this text.

Assume that we have a method for solving (6.1) only for the first decomposition problem (given $\mathbf{Q}$ and $\mathbf{R}$). Then, we can indirectly utilize this method for solving the second decomposition problem as well. We simply rewrite (6.1) in the form

$$\mathbf{Q}^{-1} \circ \mathbf{P}^{-1} = \mathbf{R}^{-1}, \tag{6.3}$$

employing transposed matrices. We can now solve (6.3) for $\mathbf{Q}^{-1}$ by our method and, then, obtain the solution of (6.1) by

$$(\mathbf{Q}^{-1})^{-1} = \mathbf{Q}.$$

6.2 PROBLEM PARTITIONING

In the following discussion, let us assume that a pair of specific matrices $\mathbf{R}$ and $\mathbf{Q}$ from (6.1) is given and that we wish to determine the set of all particular matrices of the form $\mathbf{P}$ that satisfy (6.1). Let each particular matrix $\mathbf{P}$ that satisfies (6.1) be called its *solution*, and let

$$S(\mathbf{Q}, \mathbf{R}) = \{\mathbf{P} | \mathbf{P} \circ \mathbf{Q} = \mathbf{R}\} \tag{6.4}$$

denote the set of all solutions (the *solution set*).

It is easy to see that this problem can be partitioned, without loss of generality, into a set of simpler problems expressed by the matrix equations

$$\mathbf{p}_i \circ \mathbf{Q} = \mathbf{r}_i \tag{6.5}$$

for all $i \in I$, where

$$\mathbf{p}_i = [p_{ij} | j \in J] \quad \text{and} \quad \mathbf{r}_i = [r_{ik} | k \in K].$$

Indeed, each of the equations in (6.2) contains unknown p_{ij} identified only by one particular value of the index i; that is, the unknowns p_{ij} distinguished by different values of i do not appear together in any of the individual equations. Observe that $\mathbf{p}_i$, $\mathbf{Q}$, and $\mathbf{r}_i$ in (6.5) represent, respectively, a fuzzy set on Y, a fuzzy relation on $Y \times Z$, and a fuzzy set on Z.

Let

$$S_i(\mathbf{Q}, \mathbf{r}_i) = \{\mathbf{p}_i | \mathbf{p}_i \circ \mathbf{Q} = \mathbf{r}_i\} \tag{6.6}$$

denote, for each $i \in I$, the solution set of one of the simpler problems expressed by (6.5). Then, the matrices $\mathbf{P}$ in (6.4) can be viewed as one-column matrices

$$\mathbf{P} = \begin{bmatrix} \mathbf{p}_1 \\ \mathbf{p}_2 \\ \vdots \\ \mathbf{p}_n \end{bmatrix},$$

where $\mathbf{p}_i \in S_i(\mathbf{Q}, \mathbf{r}_i)$ for all $i \in I (= \mathbb{N}_n)$.

It follows immediately from (6.2) that if

$$\max_{j \in J} q_{jk} < r_{ik} \tag{6.7}$$

for some $i \in I$ and some $k \in K$, then no values $p_{ij} \in [0, 1]$ exist $(j \in J)$ that satisfy (6.1); therefore, no matrix $\mathbf{P}$ exists that satisfies the matrix equation. This proposition can be stated more concisely as follows: if

$$\max_{j \in J} q_{jk} < \max_{i \in I} r_{ik} \tag{6.8}$$

for some $k \in K$, then $S(\mathbf{Q}, \mathbf{R}) = \varnothing$. This proposition allows us, in certain cases, to determine quickly that (6.1) has no solution; its negation, however, is only a necessary, not sufficient, condition for the existence of a solution of (6.1), that is, for $S(\mathbf{Q}, \mathbf{R}) \neq \varnothing$.

Example 6.1

Consider the matrix equation

$$\begin{bmatrix} p_{11} & p_{12} & p_{13} \\ p_{21} & p_{22} & p_{23} \end{bmatrix} \circ \begin{bmatrix} .9 & .5 \\ .7 & .8 \\ 1 & .4 \end{bmatrix} = \begin{bmatrix} .6 & .3 \\ .2 & 1 \end{bmatrix}$$

whose general form is

$$[p_{ij}] \circ [q_{jk}] = [r_{ik}],$$

where $i \in \mathbb{N}_2$, $j \in \mathbb{N}_3$, and $k \in \mathbb{N}_2$. The first matrix in this equation is unknown, and our problem is to determine all particular configurations of its entries for which the equation is satisfied.

The given matrix represents the following four equations of the form (6.2):

$$\begin{array}{ll} \max\,[\min(p_{11}, .9), \min(p_{12}, .7), \min(p_{13}, 1)] \;=\; .6, & \text{(a)} \\ \max\,[\min(p_{11}, .5), \min(p_{12}, .8), \min(p_{13}, .4)] \;=\; .3, & \text{(b)} \\ \max\,[\min(p_{21}, .9), \min(p_{22}, .7), \min(p_{23}, 1)] \;=\; .2, & \text{(c)} \\ \max\,[\min(p_{21}, .5), \min(p_{22}, .8), \min(p_{23}, .4)] \;=\; 1. & \text{(d)} \end{array}$$

Observe that equations (a) and (b) contain only unknowns p_{11}, p_{12}, and p_{13}, whereas equations

(c) and (d) contain only unknowns p_{21}, p_{22}, p_{23}. This means that each of these pairs of equations can be solved independent of the other. Hence, as previously argued, the given set of four equations can be partitioned into two subsets, expressed by the matrix equations

$$[p_{11} \quad p_{12} \quad p_{13}] \circ \begin{bmatrix} .9 & .5 \\ .7 & .8 \\ 1 & .4 \end{bmatrix} = [.6 \quad .3]$$

and

$$[p_{21} \quad p_{22} \quad p_{23}] \circ \begin{bmatrix} .9 & .5 \\ .7 & .8 \\ 1 & .4 \end{bmatrix} = [.2 \quad 1].$$

We see, however, that the second matrix equation, which is associated with $i = 2$, satisfies the inequality (6.7) for $k = 2$ (and $i = 2$) and, therefore, has no solution. In fact,

$$\max(q_{12}, q_{22}, q_{32}) < r_{22},$$

or, specifically,

$$\max(.5, .8, .4) < 1.$$

Thus, the given matrix equation has no solution.

Since (6.1) can be partitioned without loss of generality into a set of equations of the form (6.5), we need only methods for solving equations of the latter form in order to arrive at a solution. We may therefore restrict our further discussion of matrix equations of the form (6.1) to matrix equations of the simpler form

$$\mathbf{p} \circ \mathbf{Q} = \mathbf{r}, \tag{6.9}$$

where

$$\mathbf{p} = [p_j | j \in J], \mathbf{Q} = [q_{jk} | j \in J, k \in K], \mathbf{r} = [r_k | k \in K].$$

6.3 SOLUTION METHOD

For the sake of consistency with our previous discussion, let us again assume that $\mathbf{p}, \mathbf{Q}$, and $\mathbf{r}$ represent, respectively, a fuzzy set on Y, a fuzzy relation on $Y \times Z$, and a fuzzy set on Z. Moreover, let $J = \mathbb{N}_m$ and $K = \mathbb{N}_s$ and let

$$S(\mathbf{Q}, \mathbf{r}) = \{\mathbf{p} | \mathbf{p} \circ \mathbf{Q} = \mathbf{r}\} \tag{6.10}$$

denote the solution set of (6.9).

In order to describe a method for solving (6.9), we need to introduce some additional concepts and convenient notation. First, let $\mathcal{P}$ denote the set of all possible vectors

$$\mathbf{p} = [p_j | j \in J]$$

such that $p_j \in [0, 1]$ for all $j \in J$, and let a partial ordering on $\mathcal{P}$ be defined as follows: for any pair ${}^1\mathbf{p}, {}^2\mathbf{p} \in \mathcal{P}$,

$${}^1\mathbf{p} \leq {}^2\mathbf{p} \text{ iff } {}^1p_j \leq {}^2p_j$$

for all $j \in J$. Given an arbitrary pair ${}^1\mathbf{p}, {}^2\mathbf{p} \in \mathcal{P}$ such that ${}^1\mathbf{p} \leq {}^2\mathbf{p}$, let

$$[{}^1\mathbf{p}, {}^2\mathbf{p}] = \{\mathbf{p} \in \mathcal{P} \mid {}^1\mathbf{p} \leq \mathbf{p} \leq {}^2\mathbf{p}\}.$$

For any pair ${}^1\mathbf{p}, {}^2\mathbf{p} \in \mathcal{P}$, $\langle[{}^1\mathbf{p}, {}^2\mathbf{p}], \leq\rangle$ is clearly a lattice.

Consider now some properties of the solution set $S(\mathbf{Q}, \mathbf{r})$. Employing the partial ordering on $\mathcal{P}$, let an element $\hat{\mathbf{p}}$ of $S(\mathbf{Q}, \mathbf{r})$ be called a *maximal solution* of (6.9) if, for all $\mathbf{p} \in S(\mathbf{Q}, \mathbf{r}), \mathbf{p} \geq \hat{\mathbf{p}}$ implies $\mathbf{p} = \hat{\mathbf{p}}$; if, for all $\mathbf{p} \in S(\mathbf{Q}, \mathbf{r}), \mathbf{p} \leq \hat{\mathbf{p}}$, then $\hat{\mathbf{p}}$ is the maximum solution. Similarly, let an element $\check{\mathbf{p}}$ of $S(\mathbf{Q}, \mathbf{r})$ be called a *minimal solution* of (6.9) if, for all $\mathbf{p} \in S(\mathbf{Q}, \mathbf{r}), \mathbf{p} \leq \check{\mathbf{p}}$ implies $\mathbf{p} = \check{\mathbf{p}}$; if, for all $\mathbf{p} \in S(\mathbf{Q}, \mathbf{r}), \check{\mathbf{p}} \leq \mathbf{p}$, then $\check{\mathbf{p}}$ is the minimum solution (unique).

It is well established that whenever the solution set $S(\mathbf{Q}, \mathbf{r})$ is not empty, it always contains a *unique maximum solution*, $\hat{\mathbf{p}}$, and it may contain several minimal solutions. Let $\check{S}(\mathbf{Q}, \mathbf{r})$ denote the set of all minimal solutions. It is known that the solution set $S(\mathbf{Q}, \mathbf{r})$ is fully characterized by the maximum and minimal solutions in the following sense: it consists exactly of the maximum solution $\hat{\mathbf{p}}$, all the minimal solutions, and all elements of $\mathcal{P}$ that are between $\hat{\mathbf{p}}$ and each of the minimal solutions. Formally,

$$S(\mathbf{Q}, \mathbf{r}) = \bigcup_{\check{\mathbf{p}}}[\check{\mathbf{p}}, \hat{\mathbf{p}}], \qquad (6.11)$$

where the union is taken for all $\check{\mathbf{p}} \in \check{S}(\mathbf{Q}, \mathbf{r})$. For quick orientation, the meaning of (6.11) is illustrated visually in Fig. 6.1.

Equation (6.11) enables us to solve (6.9) solely by determining its unique maximum solution $\hat{\mathbf{p}}$ and the set $\check{S}(\mathbf{Q}, \mathbf{r})$ of its minimal solutions.

When $S(\mathbf{Q}, \mathbf{r}) \neq \varnothing$, the maximum solution

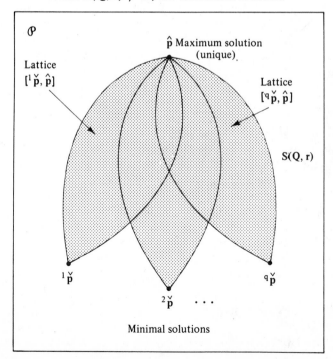

Figure 6.1 Structure of the solution set (shaded area) of (6.11).

$$\hat{\mathbf{p}} = [\hat{p}_j | j \in J]$$

of (6.9) is determined as follows:

$$\hat{p}_j = \min_{k \in K} \sigma(q_{jk}, r_k), \tag{6.12}$$

where

$$\sigma(q_{jk}, r_k) = \begin{cases} r_k & \text{if } q_{jk} > r_k, \\ 1 & \text{otherwise.} \end{cases}$$

When $\hat{\mathbf{p}}$ determined in this way does not satisfy (6.9), then $S(\mathbf{Q}, \mathbf{r}) = \varnothing$. That is, the existence of the maximum solution $\hat{\mathbf{p}}$, as determined by (6.12), is a necessary and sufficient condition for $S(\mathbf{Q}, \mathbf{r}) \neq \varnothing$. (This claim is justified in Sec. 6.4.)

Once $\hat{\mathbf{p}}$ is determined by (6.12), we must check to see if it satisfies the given matrix equation (6.9). If it does not, then the equation has no solution ($S(\mathbf{Q}, \mathbf{r}) = \varnothing$). Otherwise, $\hat{\mathbf{p}}$ is the maximum solution of the equation, and we next determine the set $\check{S}(\mathbf{Q}, \mathbf{r})$ of its minimal solutions.

The method we describe here for determining all minimal solutions of (6.9) is based on the assumption that the components of the vector $\mathbf{r}$ in (6.9) are ordered such that $r_1 \geq r_2 \geq \ldots \geq r_s$. If the components are not initially ordered in this way, we permute them appropriately and perform the same permutation on the columns of the matrix $\mathbf{Q}$. This procedure clearly yields an equivalent matrix equation, which has exactly the same set of solutions as the original equation.

Assume now that $\mathbf{Q}$ and $\mathbf{r}$ of (6.9) are given, and that we wish to determine the set $\check{S}(\mathbf{Q}, \mathbf{r})$ of all minimal solutions of the equation. Assume further that components of $\mathbf{r}$ are arranged in decreasing order, and that $\hat{\mathbf{p}}$ has been determined by (6.12) and has been verified as the maximum solution of (6.9). At this point, (6.9) may be reduced in some cases. When $\hat{p}_j = 0$ for some $j \in J$, we may eliminate this component from $\hat{\mathbf{p}}$ as well as the jth row from matrix $\mathbf{Q}$, since, clearly, $\hat{p}_j = 0$ implies $p_j = 0$ for each $\mathbf{p} \in S(\mathbf{Q}, \mathbf{r})$. Furthermore, when $r_k = 0$ for some $k \in K$, we may eliminate this component from $\mathbf{r}$ and the kth column from matrix $\mathbf{Q}$, since each $\mathbf{p} \leq \hat{\mathbf{p}}$ ($\mathbf{p} \in \mathcal{P}$) must satisfy, in this case, the max-min equation represented by $\mathbf{p}$, the kth column of $\mathbf{Q}$, and $r_k = 0$. Although this reduction is not necessary, the reduced equation is easier to deal with. When we obtain solutions of the reduced equation, we simply extend them by inserting zeros at the locations that were eliminated in the reduction step.

For convenience, assume for our further discussion that (6.9) is a reduced equation and $\hat{\mathbf{p}}$ is its maximum solution (i.e., $\hat{p}_j \neq 0$ for all $j \in J = \mathbb{N}_m$, and $r_k \neq 0$ for all $k \in K = \mathbb{N}_s$). Given $\mathbf{Q}$, $\mathbf{r}$, and $\hat{\mathbf{p}}$, the set $\check{S}(\mathbf{Q}, \mathbf{r})$ of all minimal solutions of (6.9) can be determined by the following procedure:

1. Determine the sets

$$J_k(\hat{\mathbf{p}}) = \{j \in J \,|\, \min(\hat{p}_j, q_{jk}) = r_k\}$$

for all $k \in K$ and construct their Cartesian product

$$J(\hat{\mathbf{p}}) = \underset{k \in K}{\times} J_k(\hat{\mathbf{p}}).$$

Denote elements (s-tuples) of $J(\hat{\mathbf{p}})$ by

$$\beta = [\beta_k | k \in K].$$

2. For each $\beta \in J(\hat{\mathbf{p}})$ and each $j \in J$, determine the set

$$K(\beta, j) = \{k \in K | \beta_k = j\}.$$

3. For each $\beta \in J(\hat{\mathbf{p}})$, generate the m-tuple

$$\mathbf{g}(\beta) = [g_j(\beta) | j \in J]$$

by taking

$$g_j(\beta) = \begin{cases} \max_{k \in K(\beta, j)} r_k & \text{if } K(\beta, j) \neq \varnothing, \\ 0 & \text{otherwise.} \end{cases}$$

4. From all the m-tuples $\mathbf{g}(\beta)$ generated in Step 3, select only the minimal ones by pairwise comparison. The resulting set of m-tuples is the set $\check{S}(\mathbf{Q}, \mathbf{r})$ of all minimal solutions of (6.9).

The described procedure is based on several nontrivial theorems, which we do not consider essential to present here. Appropriate references are given in Note 6.1.

Example 6.2

Given

$$\mathbf{Q} = \begin{bmatrix} .1 & .4 & .5 & .1 \\ .9 & .7 & .2 & 0 \\ .8 & 1 & .5 & 0 \\ .1 & .3 & .6 & 0 \end{bmatrix} \text{ and } \mathbf{r} = [.8\ .7\ .5\ 0],$$

determine all solutions of (6.9).

First, we determine the maximum solution $\hat{\mathbf{p}}$ by (6.12):

$$\hat{p}_1 = \min(1, 1, 1, 0) = 0,$$

$$\hat{p}_2 = \min(.8, 1, 1, 1) = .8,$$

$$\hat{p}_3 = \min(1, .7, 1, 1) = .7,$$

$$\hat{p}_4 = \min(1, 1, .5, 1) = .5.$$

Thus, $\hat{\mathbf{p}} = [0\ .8\ .7\ .5]$. We can easily check that $\hat{\mathbf{p}} \in S(\mathbf{Q}, \mathbf{r})$; hence, $S(\mathbf{Q}, \mathbf{r}) \neq \varnothing$.

Since $\hat{p}_1 = 0$, we may reduce the matrix equation by excluding p_1 and the first row of matrix $\mathbf{Q}$; since $r_4 = 0$, we may make a further reduction by excluding r_4 and the fourth column of $\mathbf{Q}$. The reduced equation has the form

$$[p_1\ p_2\ p_3] \circ \begin{bmatrix} .9 & .7 & .2 \\ .8 & 1 & .5 \\ .1 & .3 & .6 \end{bmatrix} = [.8\ .7\ .5].$$

We must remember that p_1, p_2, and p_3 in this reduced equation represent p_2, p_3, and p_4 of the original equation, respectively.

Next, we apply the four steps of the procedure for determining the set $\check{S}(\mathbf{Q}, \mathbf{r})$ of all minimal solutions of this reduced matrix equation:

1. Employing the maximum solution $\hat{\mathbf{p}} = [.8\ .7\ .5]$ of the reduced equation, we obtain $J_1(\hat{\mathbf{p}}) = \{1\}, J_2(\hat{\mathbf{p}}) = \{1, 2\}, J_3(\hat{\mathbf{p}}) = \{2, 3\}$; hence, $J(\hat{\mathbf{p}}) = \{1\} \times \{1, 2\} \times \{2, 3\}$.

2. The sets $K(\beta, j)$ that we must determine for all $\beta \in J(\hat{\mathbf{p}})$ and all $j \in J$ are listed in Table 6.1.

TABLE 6.1   ILLUSTRATION TO EXAMPLE 6.2

		j		
$K(\beta, j)$	1	2	3	$g(\beta)$
$\beta = 1\ 1\ 2$	$\{1, 2\}$	$\{3\}$	$\varnothing$	$\langle.8,\ .5,\ 0\rangle$
$1\ 1\ 3$	$\{1, 2\}$	$\varnothing$	$\{3\}$	$\langle.8,\ 0,\ .5\rangle$
$1\ 2\ 2$	$\{1\}$	$\{2, 3\}$	$\varnothing$	$\langle.8,\ .7,\ 0\rangle$
$1\ 2\ 3$	$\{1\}$	$\{2\}$	$\{3\}$	$\langle.8,\ .7,\ .5\rangle$

3. For each $\beta \in J(\hat{\mathbf{p}})$, we generate the triples $g(\beta)$, which are also listed in Table 6.1.

4. Two of the triples $g(\beta)$ in Table 6.1 are minimal: $\langle.8, .5, 0\rangle$ and $\langle.8, 0, .5\rangle$. These therefore comprise all the minimal solutions of the reduced matrix equation. By adding 0 as the first component to each of these triples, we obtain the minimal solutions of the original matrix equation. Hence,

$$\check{S}(\mathbf{Q}, \mathbf{r}) = \{^1\check{\mathbf{p}} = [0\ .8\ .5\ 0], {}^2\check{\mathbf{p}} = [0\ .8\ 0\ .5]\}.$$

The set $S(\mathbf{Q}, \mathbf{r})$ of all solutions of the given matrix equation is now fully captured by the maximum solution

$$\hat{\mathbf{p}} = [0\ .8\ .7\ .5],$$

and the two minimal solutions

$$^1\check{\mathbf{p}} = [0\ .8\ .5\ 0],$$

$$^2\check{\mathbf{p}} = [0\ .8\ 0\ .5].$$

According to (6.11), we have

$$S(\mathbf{Q}, \mathbf{r}) = \{\mathbf{p} \in \mathcal{P} | {}^1\check{\mathbf{p}} \le \mathbf{p} \le \hat{\mathbf{p}}\} \cup \{\mathbf{p} \in \mathcal{P} | {}^2\check{\mathbf{p}} \le \mathbf{p} \le \hat{\mathbf{p}}\}.$$

Let us now summarize concisely the described procedure for solving finite max-min fuzzy relation equations.

Basic Procedure

1. Partition (6.1) into equations of the form

$$\mathbf{p} \circ \mathbf{Q} = \mathbf{r}, \tag{a}$$

one for each row in $\mathbf{P}$ and $\mathbf{R}$ ($\mathbf{p}$ is associated with index j, $\mathbf{Q}$ with indices j and k, and $\mathbf{r}$ with index k).

2. For each equation (a), if

$$\max_{j \in J} q_{jk} < \max r_k$$

for some k, then the equation has no solution: $S(\mathbf{Q}, \mathbf{r}) = \varnothing$ and the procedure terminates; otherwise, proceed to Step 3.

3. Determine $\hat{\mathbf{p}}$ by Procedure 1.

4. If $\hat{\mathbf{p}}$ is not a solution of (a), then the equation has no solution: $S(\mathbf{Q}, \mathbf{r}) = \varnothing$ and the procedure terminates; otherwise, proceed to Step 5.

5. For each $\hat{p}_j = 0$ and $r_k = 0$, exclude these components as well as the corresponding rows j and columns k from matrix $\mathbf{Q}$ in (a): This results in the reduced equation

$$\mathbf{p}' \circ \mathbf{Q}' = \mathbf{r}', \tag{b}$$

where we assume $j \in J', k \in K'$.

6. Determine all minimal solutions of the reduced equation (b) by Procedure 2: this results in $\check{S}(\mathbf{Q}', \mathbf{r}')$.

7. Determine the solution set of the reduced equation (b):

$$S(\mathbf{Q}', \mathbf{r}') = \bigcup_{\check{\mathbf{p}}'} [\check{\mathbf{p}}', \hat{\mathbf{p}}'],$$

where the union is taken over all $\check{\mathbf{p}}' \in \check{S}(\mathbf{Q}', \mathbf{r}')$.

8. Extend all solutions in $S(\mathbf{Q}', \mathbf{r}')$ by zeros that were excluded in Step 5: this results in the solution set $S(\mathbf{Q}, \mathbf{r})$ of equation (a).

9. Repeat Steps 2–8 for all equations of type (a) that are embedded in (6.1): this results in all matrices $\mathbf{P}$ that satisfy (6.1).

Procedure 1

Form the vector $\hat{\mathbf{p}} = [\hat{p}_j | j \in J]$ in which

$$\hat{p}_j = \min_k \sigma(q_{jk}, r_k),$$

where

$$\sigma(q_{jk}, r_k) = \begin{cases} r_k & \text{if } q_{jk} > r_k, \\ 1 & \text{otherwise.} \end{cases}$$

Procedure 2

1. Permute elements of $\mathbf{r}'$ and the corresponding columns of $\mathbf{Q}'$ appropriately to arrange them in decreasing order.

2. Determine sets

$$J_k(\hat{\mathbf{p}}') = \{j \in J' | \min(\hat{p}'_j, q'_{jk}) = r'_k\}$$

for all $k \in K'$ and form

$$J(\hat{\mathbf{p}}') = \underset{k \in K'}{\times} J_k(\hat{\mathbf{p}}').$$

3. For each $\beta \in J(\hat{\mathbf{p}}')$ and each $j \in J'$, determine the set

$$K(\beta, j) = \{k \in K' | \beta_k = j\}.$$

4. For each $\beta \in J(\hat{p}')$, generate the tuple

$$\mathbf{g}(\beta) = [g_j(\beta) | j \in J']$$

by taking

$$g_j(\beta) = \begin{cases} \max r'_k & \text{if } K(\beta, j) \neq \emptyset, k \in K(\beta, j) \\ 0 & \text{otherwise.} \end{cases}$$

5. From all tuples $\mathbf{g}(\beta)$ generated in Step 4, select only the minimal ones: this results in $\check{S}(\mathbf{Q}', \mathbf{r}')$.

6.4 FUZZY RELATION EQUATIONS BASED ON SUP-i COMPOSITIONS

A matrix formulation of this kind of fuzzy relation equations, analogous to (6.1), has the form

$$\mathbf{P} \overset{i}{\circ} \mathbf{Q} = \mathbf{R}, \tag{6.13}$$

where $\overset{i}{\circ}$ denotes the sup-i composition, based upon a t-norm i, and $\mathbf{P}, \mathbf{Q}, \mathbf{R}$ are matrix representations of fuzzy relations on $X \times Y, Y \times Z$, and $X \times Z$, respectively. Let

$$\mathbf{P} = [p_{jk}], \mathbf{Q} = [q_{kl}], \mathbf{R} = [r_{jl}],$$

where $j \in \mathbb{N}_n, k \in \mathbb{N}_m$, and $l \in \mathbb{N}_s$. The matrix equation (6.13) represents the set of equations of the form

$$\max_{k \in \mathbb{N}_m} i(p_{jk}, q_{kl}) = r_{jl} \tag{6.14}$$

for all $j \in \mathbb{N}_n$ and $l \in \mathbb{N}_s$, where i is a continuous t-norm.

As in Sec. 6.1, we assume that $\mathbf{Q}$ and $\mathbf{R}$ are given and $\mathbf{P}$ that satisfies (6.13) is to be determined. Let

$$S(\mathbf{Q}, \mathbf{R}) = \{\mathbf{P} | \mathbf{P} \overset{i}{\circ} \mathbf{Q} = \mathbf{R}\}$$

denote the corresponding solution set.

The following theorem provides us with a procedure for determining the maximum solution of (6.13) provided that the equation is solvable at all.

Theorem 6.1. If $S(\mathbf{Q}, \mathbf{R}) \neq \emptyset$ for (6.13), then $\hat{\mathbf{P}} = (\mathbf{Q} \overset{\omega_i}{\circ} \mathbf{R}^{-1})^{-1}$ is the greatest member of $S(\mathbf{Q}, \mathbf{R})$.

Proof: Assume that $\mathbf{P}' \in S(\mathbf{Q}, \mathbf{R})$ (i.e., $\mathbf{P}' \overset{i}{\circ} \mathbf{Q} = \mathbf{R}$). By (5.27) of Theorem 5.4, we have

$$\mathbf{P}' \subseteq (\mathbf{Q} \overset{\omega_i}{\circ} \mathbf{R}^{-1})^{-1} = \hat{\mathbf{P}}.$$

It remains to show that $\hat{\mathbf{P}} \in S(\mathbf{Q}, \mathbf{R})$. Let

$$\mathbf{T} = (\mathbf{Q} \overset{\omega_i}{\circ} \mathbf{R}^{-1})^{-1} \overset{i}{\circ} \mathbf{Q} = \hat{\mathbf{P}} \overset{i}{\circ} \mathbf{Q}.$$

By (5.33) of Theorem 5.7, we have

$$\mathbf{T}^{-1} = \mathbf{Q}^{-1} \overset{i}{\circ} (\mathbf{Q} \overset{\omega_i}{\circ} \mathbf{R}^{-1}) \subseteq \mathbf{R}^{-1}$$

and, consequently, $\mathbf{T} \subseteq \mathbf{R}$. On the other hand,

$$\mathbf{T} = \hat{\mathbf{P}} \overset{i}{\circ} \mathbf{Q} \supseteq \mathbf{P}' \overset{i}{\circ} \mathbf{Q} = \mathbf{R}$$

and, hence, $\hat{\mathbf{P}} \overset{i}{\circ} \mathbf{Q} = \mathbf{R}$; that is, $\hat{\mathbf{P}} \in S(\mathbf{Q}, \mathbf{R})$. ∎

Theorem 6.1 can be utilized for testing whether (6.13) has a solution. The test is very simple: $S(\mathbf{Q}, \mathbf{R}) \neq \varnothing$ (i.e., (6.13) has a solution) iff

$$(\mathbf{Q} \overset{\omega_i}{\circ} \mathbf{R}^{-1})^{-1} \overset{i}{\circ} \mathbf{Q} = \mathbf{R}. \tag{6.15}$$

Example 6.3

Let the t-norm i employed in (6.13) be the product, and let

$$\mathbf{Q} = \begin{bmatrix} .1 \\ .2 \\ .3 \end{bmatrix} \text{ and } \mathbf{R} = \begin{bmatrix} .12 \\ .18 \\ .27 \end{bmatrix}.$$

Then,

$$\hat{\mathbf{P}}^{-1} = \begin{bmatrix} .1 \\ .2 \\ .3 \end{bmatrix} \overset{\omega_i}{\circ} [.12 \ .18 \ .27] \quad (= \mathbf{Q} \overset{\omega_i}{\circ} \mathbf{R}^{-1})$$

$$= \begin{bmatrix} 1 & 1 & 1 \\ .6 & .9 & 1 \\ .4 & .6 & .9 \end{bmatrix}$$

$$\hat{\mathbf{P}} = \begin{bmatrix} 1 & .6 & .4 \\ 1 & .9 & .6 \\ 1 & 1 & .9 \end{bmatrix}.$$

Since

$$\hat{\mathbf{P}} \overset{i}{\circ} \mathbf{Q} = \begin{bmatrix} 1 & .6 & .4 \\ 1 & .9 & .6 \\ 1 & 1 & .9 \end{bmatrix} \overset{i}{\circ} \begin{bmatrix} .1 \\ .2 \\ .3 \end{bmatrix} = \begin{bmatrix} .12 \\ .18 \\ .27 \end{bmatrix},$$

$\hat{\mathbf{P}}$ is the greatest solution of

$$\mathbf{P} \overset{i}{\circ} \begin{bmatrix} .1 \\ .2 \\ .3 \end{bmatrix} = \begin{bmatrix} .12 \\ .18 \\ .27 \end{bmatrix}.$$

Theorem 6.2. Let $\mathbf{P}_1, \mathbf{P}_2 \in S(\mathbf{Q}, \mathbf{R})$. Then, (i) $\mathbf{P}_1 \subseteq \mathbf{P} \subseteq \mathbf{P}_2$ implies that $\mathbf{P} \in S(\mathbf{Q}, \mathbf{R})$; (ii) $\mathbf{P}_1 \cup \mathbf{P}_2 \in S(\mathbf{Q}, \mathbf{R})$, where $\cup$ denotes the standard fuzzy union.

Proof: (i) Since $\mathbf{R} = \mathbf{P}_1 \overset{i}{\circ} \mathbf{Q} \subseteq \mathbf{P} \overset{i}{\circ} \mathbf{Q} \subseteq \mathbf{P}_2 \overset{i}{\circ} \mathbf{Q} = \mathbf{R}$, we have $\mathbf{P} \overset{i}{\circ} \mathbf{Q} = \mathbf{R}$; consequently, $\mathbf{P} \in S(\mathbf{Q}, \mathbf{R})$. (ii) Since, by (5.17), $(\mathbf{P}_1 \cup \mathbf{P}_2) \overset{i}{\circ} \mathbf{Q} = (\mathbf{P}_1 \overset{i}{\circ} \mathbf{Q}) \cup (\mathbf{P}_2 \overset{i}{\circ} \mathbf{Q}) = \mathbf{R} \cup \mathbf{R} = \mathbf{R}$, we have $(\mathbf{P}_1 \cup \mathbf{P}_2) \in S(\mathbf{Q}, \mathbf{R})$. ∎

Unfortunately, no general method for obtaining all minimal solutions of (6.13) has been developed as yet. However, employing the method described in Sec. 6.3, we can find minimal solutions for some particular equations.

6.5 FUZZY RELATION EQUATIONS BASED ON INF-ω_i COMPOSITIONS

Equations of this kind are expressed by the matrix form

$$\mathbf{P} \overset{\omega_i}{\circ} \mathbf{Q} = \mathbf{R}, \tag{6.16}$$

where $\overset{\omega_i}{\circ}$ denotes the inf-ω_i composition based upon a continuous t-norm i, and $\mathbf{P}, \mathbf{Q}, \mathbf{R}$ have the same meaning as in Sec. 6.4.

Given $\mathbf{Q}$ and $\mathbf{R}$, let $S(\mathbf{Q}, \mathbf{R})$ denote the solution set of (6.16) for $\mathbf{P}$. The maximum element of the solution set is given by the following theorem, but no method is currently known by which all minimal elements of $S(\mathbf{Q}, \mathbf{R})$ could be determined.

Theorem 6.3. If $S(\mathbf{Q}, \mathbf{R}) \neq \varnothing$, then $\hat{\mathbf{P}} = \mathbf{R} \overset{\omega_i}{\circ} \mathbf{Q}^{-1}$ is the greatest member of $S(\mathbf{Q}, \mathbf{R})$.

Proof: Assume that $\mathbf{P} \in S(\mathbf{Q}, \mathbf{R})$. Then, $\mathbf{P} \overset{\omega_i}{\circ} \mathbf{Q} = \mathbf{R}$ and, by (5.35) of Theorem 5.7, we have

$$\mathbf{R} \overset{\omega_i}{\circ} \mathbf{Q}^{-1} = (\mathbf{P} \overset{\omega_i}{\circ} \mathbf{Q}) \overset{\omega_i}{\circ} \mathbf{Q}^{-1} \supseteq \mathbf{P}. \tag{6.17}$$

Moreover, by Theorem 5.6 and (5.36) of Theorem 5.7, we have

$$\mathbf{R} \subseteq (\mathbf{R} \overset{\omega_i}{\circ} \mathbf{Q}^{-1}) \overset{\omega_i}{\circ} \mathbf{Q} \subseteq \mathbf{P} \overset{\omega_i}{\circ} \mathbf{Q} = \mathbf{R}.$$

Hence, $\hat{\mathbf{P}} \overset{\omega_i}{\circ} \mathbf{Q} = \mathbf{R}$ and, by (6.17), $\hat{\mathbf{P}}$ is the greatest element of $S(\mathbf{Q}, \mathbf{R})$. ∎

It follows directly from Theorem 6.3 that (6.16) has a solution for $\mathbf{P}$ iff

$$(\mathbf{R} \overset{\omega_i}{\circ} \mathbf{Q}^{-1}) \overset{\omega_i}{\circ} \mathbf{Q} = \mathbf{R}.$$

Example 6.4

Let the t-norm i employed in (6.16) be the product, and let

$$\mathbf{Q} = \begin{bmatrix} .1 & .6 \\ .8 & .9 \end{bmatrix} \text{ and } \mathbf{R} = \begin{bmatrix} .2 & 1 \\ .25 & 1 \end{bmatrix}.$$

Then,

$$\mathbf{R} \overset{\omega_i}{\circ} \mathbf{Q}^{-1} = \begin{bmatrix} .2 & 1 \\ .25 & 1 \end{bmatrix} \overset{\omega_i}{\circ} \begin{bmatrix} .1 & .8 \\ .6 & .9 \end{bmatrix}$$

$$= \begin{bmatrix} .5 & .9 \\ .4 & .9 \end{bmatrix}.$$

Since

$$\begin{bmatrix} .5 & .9 \\ .4 & .9 \end{bmatrix} \stackrel{\omega_i}{\circ} \begin{bmatrix} .1 & .6 \\ .8 & .9 \end{bmatrix} = \begin{bmatrix} .2 & 1 \\ .25 & 1 \end{bmatrix},$$

$$\hat{\mathbf{P}} = \begin{bmatrix} .5 & .9 \\ .4 & .9 \end{bmatrix} (= \mathbf{R} \stackrel{\omega_i}{\circ} \mathbf{Q}^{-1})$$

is the maximum solution of (6.16) for the given $\mathbf{Q}$ and $\mathbf{R}$.

Since $(\mathbf{P} \stackrel{\omega_i}{\circ} \mathbf{Q})^{-1} \neq \mathbf{Q}^{-1} \stackrel{\omega_i}{\circ} \mathbf{P}^{-1}$ for the inf-ω_i composition, the previous problem (determine $\mathbf{P}$ for given $\mathbf{Q}$ and $\mathbf{R}$) cannot be directly converted to the problem in which $\mathbf{P}$ and $\mathbf{R}$ are given and $\mathbf{Q}$ is to be determined. Denoting the solution set of the latter problem by $S(\mathbf{P}, \mathbf{R})$, the (unique) minimum element of this solution set is given by the following theorem, which is a counterpart of Theorem 6.3. Unfortunately, no method is known for determining all maximal elements of $S(\mathbf{P}, \mathbf{R})$.

Theorem 6.4.   If $S(\mathbf{P}, \mathbf{R}) \neq \varnothing$, then $\check{\mathbf{Q}} = \mathbf{P}^{-1} \stackrel{i}{\circ} \mathbf{R}$ is the smallest member of $S(\mathbf{P}, \mathbf{R})$.

Proof: Assume that $\mathbf{Q} \in S(\mathbf{P}, \mathbf{R})$. Then, $\mathbf{P} \stackrel{\omega_i}{\circ} \mathbf{Q} = \mathbf{R}$ and, by (5.33) of Theorem 5.7, we have

$$\mathbf{P}^{-1} \stackrel{i}{\circ} \mathbf{R} = \mathbf{P}^{-1} \stackrel{i}{\circ} (\mathbf{P} \stackrel{\omega_i}{\circ} \mathbf{Q}) \subseteq \mathbf{Q}. \tag{6.18}$$

Moreover, by Theorem 5.6 and (5.34) of Theorem 5.7, we have

$$\mathbf{R} \subseteq \mathbf{P} \stackrel{\omega_i}{\circ} (\mathbf{P}^{-1} \stackrel{i}{\circ} \mathbf{R}) \subseteq \mathbf{P} \stackrel{\omega_i}{\circ} \mathbf{Q} = \mathbf{R}.$$

Hence, $\mathbf{P} \stackrel{\omega_i}{\circ} \check{\mathbf{Q}} = \mathbf{R}$ and, by (6.18), $\check{\mathbf{Q}}$ is the smallest element of $S(\mathbf{P}, \mathbf{R})$. ■

It follows directly from Theorem 6.4 that (6.16) has a solution for $\mathbf{Q}$ iff $\mathbf{P} \stackrel{\omega_i}{\circ} (\mathbf{P}^{-1} \stackrel{i}{\circ} \mathbf{R}) = \mathbf{R}$.

It is easy to verify the following properties of the solution sets $S(\mathbf{Q}, \mathbf{R})$ and $S(\mathbf{P}, \mathbf{R})$ of (6.16), when $\cup$ and $\cap$ denote, respectively, the standard fuzzy union (max) and intersection (min):

1. if $\mathbf{P}_1, \mathbf{P}_2 \in S(\mathbf{Q}, \mathbf{R})$, then $\mathbf{P}_1 \cup \mathbf{P}_2 \in S(\mathbf{Q}, \mathbf{R})$;
2. if $\mathbf{P}_1, \mathbf{P}_2 \in S(\mathbf{Q}, \mathbf{R})$ and $\mathbf{P}_1 \subseteq \mathbf{P} \subseteq \mathbf{P}_2$, then $\mathbf{P} \in S(\mathbf{Q}, \mathbf{R})$;
3. if $\mathbf{Q}_1, \mathbf{Q}_2 \in S(\mathbf{P}, \mathbf{R})$, then $\mathbf{Q}_1 \cap \mathbf{Q}_2 \in S(\mathbf{P}, \mathbf{R})$; and
4. if $\mathbf{Q}_1, \mathbf{Q}_2 \in S(\mathbf{Q}, \mathbf{R})$ and $\mathbf{Q}_1 \subseteq \mathbf{Q} \subseteq \mathbf{Q}_2$, then $\mathbf{Q} \in S(\mathbf{P}, \mathbf{R})$.

Example 6.5

Let again the t-norm i in (6.16) be the product, and let

$$\mathbf{P} = \begin{bmatrix} .5 & .9 \\ .4 & .9 \end{bmatrix} \text{ and } \mathbf{R} = \begin{bmatrix} .2 & 1 \\ .25 & 1 \end{bmatrix}.$$

Then,

$$\mathbf{P}^{-1} \overset{i}{\circ} \mathbf{R} = \begin{bmatrix} .5 & .4 \\ .9 & .9 \end{bmatrix} \overset{i}{\circ} \begin{bmatrix} .2 & 1 \\ .25 & 1 \end{bmatrix} = \begin{bmatrix} .1 & .5 \\ .225 & .9 \end{bmatrix}.$$

Since

$$\begin{bmatrix} .5 & .9 \\ .4 & .9 \end{bmatrix} \overset{\omega_i}{\circ} \begin{bmatrix} .1 & .5 \\ .225 & .9 \end{bmatrix} = \begin{bmatrix} .2 & 1 \\ .25 & 1 \end{bmatrix},$$

$$\check{\mathbf{Q}} = \begin{bmatrix} .1 & .5 \\ .225 & .9 \end{bmatrix} (= \mathbf{P}^{-1} \overset{i}{\circ} \mathbf{R})$$

is the minimum solution of (6.16) for the given $\mathbf{P}$ and $\mathbf{R}$.

6.6 APPROXIMATE SOLUTIONS

It is quite common that fuzzy relation equations of the general form

$$\mathbf{P} \overset{i}{\circ} \mathbf{Q} = \mathbf{R}, \tag{6.19}$$

in which $\mathbf{Q}$ and $\mathbf{R}$ are given, have no solutions for $\mathbf{P}$. Since a solution is essential in some applications, it is important to consider the notion of approximate solutions.

Given (6.19) that has no solution for $\mathbf{P}$, we may slightly modify $\mathbf{Q}$ and $\mathbf{R}$ into $\mathbf{Q}'$ and $\mathbf{R}'$, respectively, such that the equation

$$\mathbf{P}' \overset{i}{\circ} \mathbf{Q}' = \mathbf{R}' \tag{6.20}$$

has a solution $\mathbf{P}'$. It is reasonable to view any solution of (6.20) as an approximate solution of (6.19) provided that $\mathbf{Q}'$ and $\mathbf{R}'$ satisfy the requirements specified in the following definition.

Definition 6.1. A fuzzy relation $\tilde{\mathbf{P}}$ is called an approximate solution of (6.19) if the following requirements are satisfied:

1. there exist $\mathbf{Q}' \supseteq \mathbf{Q}$ and $\mathbf{R}' \subseteq \mathbf{R}$ such that

$$\tilde{\mathbf{P}} \overset{i}{\circ} \mathbf{Q}' = \mathbf{R}'; \tag{6.21}$$

2. if there exist $\mathbf{P}'', \mathbf{Q}''$, and $\mathbf{R}''$ such that $\mathbf{Q} \subseteq \mathbf{Q}'' \subseteq \mathbf{Q}', \mathbf{R}' \subseteq \mathbf{R}'' \subseteq \mathbf{R}, \mathbf{P}'' \overset{i}{\circ} \mathbf{Q}'' = \mathbf{R}''$, then $\mathbf{Q}'' = \mathbf{Q}'$ and $\mathbf{R}'' = \mathbf{R}'$.

Requirement **1** means that we pursue the approximate solution of (6.19), making $\mathbf{Q}$ larger and $\mathbf{R}$ smaller; requirement **2** means that $\mathbf{Q}'$ and $\mathbf{R}'$ in (6.21) are the closest relations to $\mathbf{Q}$ and $\mathbf{R}$, respectively, for which a solution exists.

Example 6.6

Consider the equation

$$\mathbf{P} \overset{i}{\circ} \begin{bmatrix} .1 & .3 \\ .2 & .4 \end{bmatrix} = [.5 \quad .6],$$

where $\overset{i}{\circ}$ is the algebraic product. Then, by Theorem 6.1,

$$\hat{P} = \left[\left[\begin{array}{cc} .1 & .3 \\ .2 & .4 \end{array} \right] \overset{\omega i}{\circ} \left[\begin{array}{c} .5 \\ .6 \end{array} \right] \right]^{-1} = [\; 1 \quad 1 \;]$$

and, since

$$[\; 1 \quad 1 \;] \overset{i}{\circ} \left[\begin{array}{cc} .1 & .3 \\ .2 & .4 \end{array} \right] = [\; .2 \quad .4 \;] \neq [\; .5 \quad .6 \;],$$

the equation has no solution. To pursue approximate solutions of the equation, let us reduce $\mathbf{R} = [.5 \quad .6]$ to $\mathbf{R}' = [.2 \quad .4]$. Then, $(\mathbf{Q} \overset{\omega i}{\circ} \mathbf{R}^{-1})^{-1} = [1 \; 1]$ and

$$[\; 1 \quad 1 \;] \overset{i}{\circ} \left[\begin{array}{cc} .1 & .3 \\ .2 & .4 \end{array} \right] = [\; .2 \quad .4 \;].$$

Assume that there exists $\mathbf{R}''$ such that $\mathbf{R}' \subseteq \mathbf{R}'' \subseteq \mathbf{R}$, and the equation

$$\mathbf{P}'' \overset{i}{\circ} \left[\begin{array}{cc} .1 & .3 \\ .2 & .4 \end{array} \right] = \mathbf{R}''$$

has a solution for $\mathbf{P}''$. Then,

$$\max(.1p_1, .2p_2) = r_1,$$

$$\max(.3p_1, .4p_2) = r_2,$$

where $\mathbf{P}'' = [p_1 \; p_2]$ and $\mathbf{R}'' = [r_1 \; r_2]$. These equations can be satisfied only when $r_1 \leq .2$ and $r_2 \leq .4$. That means that $\mathbf{R}' \subseteq \mathbf{R}''$ and, hence, $\mathbf{R}'' = \mathbf{R}'$. This implies that, by Def. 6.1, $\hat{\mathbf{P}} = [1 \; 1]$ is an approximate solution of the original equation. Furthermore, we can easily see that $[a \; 1]$ for any $a \in [0, 1]$ is also an approximate solution of the equation. That is, approximate solutions are not unique.

Let us pursue now approximate solutions of the given equation by increasing $\mathbf{Q}$ to

$$\mathbf{Q}' = \left[\begin{array}{cc} .1 & .3 \\ .5 & .6 \end{array} \right].$$

Then,

$$(\mathbf{Q}' \overset{\omega i}{\circ} \mathbf{R}^{-1})^{-1} = \left[\left[\begin{array}{cc} .1 & .3 \\ .5 & .6 \end{array} \right] \overset{\omega i}{\circ} \left[\begin{array}{c} .5 \\ .6 \end{array} \right] \right]^{-1} = [\; 1 \quad 1 \;],$$

and $[1 \; 1]$ is a solution of the equation $\mathbf{P}' \overset{i}{\circ} \mathbf{Q}' = \mathbf{R}$ since

$$[\; 1 \quad 1 \;] \overset{i}{\circ} \left[\begin{array}{cc} .1 & .3 \\ .5 & .6 \end{array} \right] = [\; .5 \quad .6 \;].$$

If there is $\mathbf{Q}''$ such that $\mathbf{Q} \subseteq \mathbf{Q}'' \subseteq \mathbf{Q}'$ and there exists a solution for $\mathbf{P}''$, then

$$\mathbf{P}'' \overset{i}{\circ} \mathbf{Q}'' = [\; .5 \quad .6 \;].$$

Let $\mathbf{P}'' = [p_1 \; p_2]$ and $\mathbf{Q}'' = [q_{jk}]$. Then, $.1 \leq q_{11} \leq .1, .3 \leq q_{12} \leq .3, .2 \leq q_{21} \leq .5$, and $.4 \leq q_{22} \leq .6$. This means that $q_{11} = .1, q_{12} = .3, q_{21} \in [.2, .5]$, and $q_{22} \in [.4, .6]$. The previous equation now has the form

$$[\; p_1 \quad p_2 \;] \overset{i}{\circ} \left[\begin{array}{cc} .1 & .3 \\ q_{21} & q_{22} \end{array} \right] = [\; .5 \quad .6 \;],$$

which represents the simple equations

$$\max(.1p_1, q_{21}p_2) = .5,$$

$$\max(.3p_1, q_{22}p_2) = .6.$$

Clearly, $q_{21}p_2 = .5$ and $q_{22}p_2 = .6$, which implies that $q_{21} \geq .5$ and $q_{22} \geq .6$. Hence, $\mathbf{Q}'' \supseteq \mathbf{Q}'$ and, therefore, $\mathbf{Q}'' = \mathbf{Q}'$. Again, by Def. 6.1, $\check{\mathbf{P}}$ is an approximate solution of the original equation.

We can see from Example 6.6 that not only are approximate solutions of fuzzy relation equations (in the sense of Def. 6.1) not unique, but also the modified relations $\mathbf{Q}'$ and $\mathbf{R}'$ that facilitate the approximate solutions are not unique. The following theorem guarantees that approximate solutions of (6.19) always exist.

Theorem 6.5. $\check{\mathbf{P}} = (\mathbf{Q} \overset{\omega_i}{\circ} \mathbf{R}^{-1})^{-1}$ is the greatest approximate solution of (6.19).

Proof: First, we need to verify that $\check{\mathbf{P}}$ satisfies requirements **1** and **2** of Def. 6.1. Let $\mathbf{Q}' = \mathbf{Q}, \mathbf{R}' = (\mathbf{Q} \overset{\omega_i}{\circ} \mathbf{R}^{-1})^{-1} \overset{i}{\circ} \mathbf{Q}$. Then, clearly, $\check{\mathbf{P}} \overset{i}{\circ} \mathbf{Q}' = \mathbf{R}'$. However, we also have to show that $\mathbf{R}' \supseteq \mathbf{R}$. It follows from (5.33) of Theorem 5.7 that

$$\mathbf{R}' = [\mathbf{Q}^{-1} \overset{i}{\circ} (\mathbf{Q} \overset{\omega_i}{\circ} \mathbf{R}^{-1})]^{-1} \subseteq (\mathbf{R}^{-1})^{-1} = \mathbf{R};$$

hence, requirement **1** of Def. 6.1 is satisfied.

Assume now that there exist $\mathbf{P}''$ and $\mathbf{R}''$ such that $\mathbf{R}' \subseteq \mathbf{R}'' \subseteq \mathbf{R}$ and $\mathbf{P}'' \overset{i}{\circ} \mathbf{Q} = \mathbf{R}''$. Then $(\mathbf{Q} \overset{\omega_i}{\circ} \mathbf{R}''^{-1})^{-1} \in S(\mathbf{Q}, \mathbf{R}'')$, which by Theorem 6.1 is the greatest element in $S(\mathbf{Q}, \mathbf{R}'')$. Thus, $(\mathbf{Q} \overset{\omega_i}{\circ} \mathbf{R}''^{-1})^{-1} \overset{i}{\circ} \mathbf{Q} = \mathbf{R}''$. Since $\mathbf{R}' \subseteq \mathbf{R}'' \subseteq \mathbf{R}$, we have

$$\mathbf{Q} \overset{\omega_i}{\circ} \mathbf{R}'^{-1} \subseteq \mathbf{Q} \overset{\omega_i}{\circ} \mathbf{R}''^{-1} \subseteq \mathbf{Q} \overset{\omega_i}{\circ} \mathbf{R}^{-1},$$

and, moreover,

$$\mathbf{Q} \overset{\omega_i}{\circ} \mathbf{R}'^{-1} = \mathbf{Q} \overset{\omega_i}{\circ} [\mathbf{Q}^{-1} \overset{i}{\circ} (\mathbf{Q} \overset{\omega_i}{\circ} \mathbf{R}^{-1})] \supseteq \mathbf{Q} \overset{\omega_i}{\circ} \mathbf{R}^{-1}.$$

Therefore,

$$\mathbf{Q} \overset{\omega_i}{\circ} \mathbf{R}^{-1} \subseteq \mathbf{Q} \overset{\omega_i}{\circ} \mathbf{R}'^{-1} \subseteq \mathbf{Q} \overset{\omega_i}{\circ} \mathbf{R}''^{-1} \subseteq \mathbf{Q} \overset{\omega_i}{\circ} \mathbf{R}^{-1}.$$

We may now conclude that $\mathbf{Q} \overset{\omega_i}{\circ} \mathbf{R}''^{-1} = \mathbf{Q} \overset{\omega_i}{\circ} \mathbf{R}^{-1}$ and, consequently,

$$\mathbf{R}'' = (\mathbf{Q} \overset{\omega_i}{\circ} \mathbf{R}''^{-1})^{-1} \overset{i}{\circ} \mathbf{Q} = (\mathbf{Q} \overset{\omega_i}{\circ} \mathbf{R}^{-1})^{-1} \overset{i}{\circ} \mathbf{Q} = \mathbf{R}'.$$

Thus, requirement **2** of Def. 6.1 is verified.

It remains to show that $\check{\mathbf{P}}$ is the greatest approximate solution of (6.19). Assume that $\check{\mathbf{P}}'$ is another approximate solution; that is, there exist $\mathbf{Q}'$ and $\mathbf{R}'$ such that $\mathbf{Q}' \supseteq \mathbf{Q}, \mathbf{R}' \subseteq \mathbf{R}$, and $\check{\mathbf{P}}' \overset{i}{\circ} \mathbf{Q}' = \mathbf{R}'$. Then, by Theorem 6.1, $\check{\mathbf{P}}' \subseteq (\mathbf{Q}' \overset{\omega_i}{\circ} \mathbf{R}'^{-1})^{-1}$; moreover,

$$(\mathbf{Q}' \overset{\omega_i}{\circ} \mathbf{R}'^{-1})^{-1} \subseteq (\mathbf{Q} \overset{\omega_i}{\circ} \mathbf{R}^{-1})^{-1} = \check{\mathbf{P}}$$

by Theorem 5.6. Hence, $\check{\mathbf{P}}' \subseteq \check{\mathbf{P}}$. ∎

Although Theorem 6.5 provides us with a method for obtaining the greatest approximate solution of (6.19), it does not give us any indication of how good an approximation it is. We need a suitable index to characterize how well given fuzzy relation equations are approximated by a calculated approximate solution. To formulate such an index, we need to measure, in a justifiable way, the extent to which two given fuzzy sets are regarded as equal.

Let $\|P\|$ denote the degree of truth of a fuzzy proposition P (see Chapter 8). Then, for any given fuzzy sets A and B on the same universal set X, let $\|A = B\|$ be called an *equality index*. This index, which may be viewed as a reasonable measure of the degree to which the two sets are equal, should be determined (in analogy with crisp sets) by the formula

$$\|A = B\| = \min(\|A \subseteq B\|, \|A \supseteq B\|). \tag{6.22}$$

However, to utilize this formula, we have to determine the meaning of $\|A \subseteq B\|$ and $\|A \supseteq B\|$ first.

It seems essential, on intuitive grounds, that $\|A \subseteq B\|$ must satisfy at least the following conditions:

1. $\|A \subseteq B\| \in [0, 1]$ (*desirable range*);
2. $\|A \subseteq B\| = 1$ iff $A(x) \le B(x)$ for all $x \in X$, that is, iff $A \subseteq B$ (*boundary condition*);
3. if $C \subseteq B$, then $\|A \subseteq B\| \ge \|A \subseteq C\|$ and $\|C \subseteq A\| \ge \|B \subseteq A\|$ (*monotonicity*).

Although these conditions are necessary for an acceptable definition of $\|A \subseteq B\|$, they are not sufficient to determine it uniquely.

One possible definition of $\|A \subseteq B\|$, which is often used in the literature, is

$$\|A \subseteq B\| = \frac{|A \cap B|}{|A|}, \tag{6.23}$$

where $|A \cap B|$ and $|A|$ denote the sigma counts (scalar cardinalities) of the respective fuzzy sets, and $\cap$ denotes the standard fuzzy intersection.

It is easy to verify that $\|A \subseteq B\|$ defined by (6.23) satisfies the three conditions. However, this definition is applicable only when X is finite. Hence, we prefer to use the definition

$$\|A \subseteq B\| = \inf_{x \in X} \omega_i[A(x), B(x)], \tag{6.24}$$

which also satisfies the three conditions and is applicable to infinite sets as well.

When $\|A \subseteq B\|$ defined by (6.24) is applied to the definition of $\|A = B\|$ given by (6.22), it is easy to verify that $\|A = B\|$ satisfies the following properties, analogous to the required conditions 1–3 for $\|A \subseteq B\|$:

(a) $\|A = B\| \in [0, 1]$ (*range*);
(b) $\|A = B\| = 1$ iff $A = B$ (*boundary value*);
(c) if $C \subseteq B \subseteq A$, then $\|A = B\| \ge \|A = C\|$ and $\|C = B\| \ge \|C = A\|$ (*monotonicity*).

These properties are essential, on intuitive grounds, for any acceptable definition of $\|A = B\|$. Moreover, substituting to (6.22) from (6.24), we obtain

$$\begin{aligned}
\|A = B\| &= \min(\inf_{x \in X} \omega_i[A(x), B(x)], \inf_{x \in X} \omega_i[B(x), A(x)]) \\
&= \inf_{x \in X} \min(\omega_i[A(x), B(x)], \omega_i[(B(x), A(x)]).
\end{aligned} \tag{6.25}$$

Let $\|A = B\|$ given by this equation be called an *equality index*. It is obvious that the index may have different values for different t-norms i.

The equality index plays a key role in measuring the goodness of approximate solutions of fuzzy relation equations. Assuming that $\mathbf{P}'$ is an approximate solution of (6.19), a meaningful *goodness index* of $\mathbf{P}'$, $G(\mathbf{P}')$, is defined by the equation

$$G(\mathbf{P}') = \|\mathbf{P}' \overset{i}{\circ} \mathbf{Q} = \mathbf{R}\|, \tag{6.26}$$

where $\mathbf{P}' \overset{i}{\circ} \mathbf{Q}$ and $\mathbf{R}$ are matrix representations of fuzzy relations on $X \times Z$. That is, the goodness of $\mathbf{P}'$ is expressed in terms of the degree of equality of the left-hand side of (6.19), when $\mathbf{P}'$ is employed in the composition, and its right-hand side. According to $G(\mathbf{P}')$, the greater the equality degree, the better $\mathbf{P}'$ approximates (6.19). Furthermore, $G(\mathbf{P}') = 1$ iff $\mathbf{P}'$ is an exact solution of (6.19).

Employing the goodness index defined by (6.26) the following theorem shows that the greatest approximate solution $\tilde{\mathbf{P}}$ is the best approximation of (6.19).

Theorem 6.6. The fuzzy relation $\tilde{\mathbf{P}} = (\mathbf{Q} \overset{\omega_i}{\circ} \mathbf{R}^{-1})^{-1}$ is the best approximation (in terms of the goodness index G defined by (6.26)) of fuzzy relation equations (6.19).

Proof: To prove this theorem, we have to show that $G(\mathbf{P}') \leq G(\tilde{\mathbf{P}})$ for any approximate solution $\mathbf{P}'$ of (6.19). By (6.22) and (6.26), we have

$$G(\tilde{\mathbf{P}}) = \|\tilde{\mathbf{P}} \overset{i}{\circ} \mathbf{Q} = \mathbf{R}\| = \min(\|\tilde{\mathbf{P}} \overset{i}{\circ} \mathbf{Q} \subseteq \mathbf{R}\|, \|\tilde{\mathbf{P}} \overset{i}{\circ} \mathbf{Q} \supseteq \mathbf{R}\|).$$

Since $\tilde{\mathbf{P}} \overset{i}{\circ} \mathbf{Q} \subseteq \mathbf{R}$ (see the proof of Theorem 6.5), $\|\tilde{\mathbf{P}} \overset{i}{\circ} \mathbf{Q} \subseteq \mathbf{R}\| = 1$. Hence,

$$G(\tilde{\mathbf{P}}) = \|\tilde{\mathbf{P}} \overset{i}{\circ} \mathbf{Q} \supseteq \mathbf{R}\|.$$

Assume now that $\mathbf{P}'$ is any approximate solution of (6.19). Then, $\mathbf{P}' \subseteq \tilde{\mathbf{P}}$ by Theorem 6.5 and, consequently,

$$\mathbf{P}' \overset{i}{\circ} \mathbf{Q} \subseteq \tilde{\mathbf{P}} \overset{i}{\circ} \mathbf{Q} \subseteq \mathbf{R}.$$

It follows, then, from condition 3 of $\|A \subseteq B\|$, that

$$\|\tilde{\mathbf{P}} \overset{i}{\circ} \mathbf{Q} \supseteq \mathbf{R}\| \geq \|\mathbf{P}' \overset{i}{\circ} \mathbf{Q} \supseteq \mathbf{R}\|.$$

Hence,

$$G(\tilde{\mathbf{P}}) = \|\tilde{\mathbf{P}} \overset{i}{\circ} \mathbf{Q} \supseteq \mathbf{R}\| \geq \|\mathbf{P}' \overset{i}{\circ} \mathbf{Q} \supseteq \mathbf{R}\|$$

$$\geq \min(\|\mathbf{P}' \overset{i}{\circ} \mathbf{Q} \supseteq \mathbf{R}\|, \|\mathbf{P}' \overset{i}{\circ} \mathbf{Q} \subseteq \mathbf{R}\|)$$

$$= G(\mathbf{P}'). \qquad \blacksquare$$

Let us introduce another useful index, called a *solvability index*, which characterizes the ease in solving fuzzy relation equations of the general form (6.19). The solvability index, δ, is defined by the formula

$$\delta = \sup_{\mathbf{P} \in \mathcal{F}(X \times Y)} \{\|\mathbf{P} \overset{i}{\circ} \mathbf{Q} = \mathbf{R}\|\}. \tag{6.27}$$

It is obvious that $\delta \in [0, 1]$. Moreover, if (6.19) is solvable exactly, then $\delta = 1$. Unfortunately, the inverse implication is still an open question. When $\delta < 1$, the given equations have no exact solution. The smaller the value of δ, the more difficult it is to solve the equations approximately.

It follows directly from the definition of δ and from property (c) of the equality index that $\delta \geq G(\tilde{\mathbf{P}})$. That is, $G(\tilde{\mathbf{P}})$ is the lower bound of δ; its upper bound is stated by the following theorem.

Theorem 6.7.   Let δ be the solvability index of (6.19) defined by (6.27). Then

$$\delta \leq \inf_{z \in Z} \omega_i (\sup_{x \in X} \mathbf{R}(x, z), \sup_{y \in Y} \mathbf{Q}(y, z)). \tag{6.28}$$

Proof: For all $\mathbf{P} \in \mathcal{F}(X \times Y)$,

$$\|\mathbf{P} \overset{i}{\circ} \mathbf{Q} = \mathbf{R}\| = \min(\|\mathbf{P} \overset{i}{\circ} \mathbf{Q} \subseteq \mathbf{R}\|, \|\mathbf{R} \subseteq \mathbf{P} \overset{i}{\circ} \mathbf{Q}\|)$$

$$\leq \|\mathbf{R} \subseteq \mathbf{P} \overset{i}{\circ} \mathbf{Q}\|$$

$$= \inf_{z \in Z} \inf_{x \in X} \omega_i [\mathbf{R}(x, z), (\mathbf{P} \overset{i}{\circ} \mathbf{Q})(x, z)]$$

$$\leq \inf_{z \in Z} \inf_{x \in X} \omega_i [\mathbf{R}(x, z), (\mathbf{1} \overset{i}{\circ} \mathbf{Q})(x, z)]$$

$$= \inf_{z \in Z} \inf_{x \in X} \omega_i [\mathbf{R}(x, z), \sup_{y \in Y} \mathbf{Q}(y, z)]$$

$$= \inf_{z \in Z} \omega_i [\sup_{x \in X} \mathbf{R}(x, z), \sup_{y \in Y} \mathbf{Q}(y, z)].$$

The inequality (6.28) then follows immediately from the definition of δ.   ■

6.7 *THE USE OF NEURAL NETWORKS*

Fuzzy relation equations play a fundamental role in fuzzy set theory. They provide us with a rich framework within which many problems emerging from practical applications of the theory can be formulated. These problems can then be solved by solving the corresponding fuzzy relation equations.

This great utility of fuzzy relation equations is somewhat hampered by the rather high computational demands of all known solution methods. To overcome this difficulty, the possibility of using neural networks (see Appendix A) for solving fuzzy relation equations has lately been explored. While the feasibility of this approach has already been established, a lot of research is needed to develop its full potential.

Our aim in this section is rather modest: to illustrate the way in which fuzzy relation equations can be represented by neural networks. Our discussion is restricted to the form

$$\mathbf{P} \circ \mathbf{Q} = \mathbf{R}, \tag{6.29}$$

where $\circ$ is the max-product composition. Let $\mathbf{P} = [p_{ij}], \mathbf{Q} = [q_{jk}], \mathbf{R} = [r_{ik}]$, where $i \in \mathbb{N}_n, j \in \mathbb{N}_m, k \in \mathbb{N}_s$. We assume that relations $\mathbf{Q}$ and $\mathbf{R}$ are given, and we want to determine **P**. Equation (6.29) represents the set of equations

$$\max_{j \in \mathbb{N}_m} p_{ij} q_{jk} = r_{ik} \tag{6.30}$$

for all $i \in \mathbb{N}_n, k \in \mathbb{N}_s$.

To solve (6.30) for $p_{ij} (i \in \mathbb{N}_n, j \in \mathbb{N}_m)$, we can use a feedforward neural network with m inputs and only one layer with n neurons, shown in Fig. 6.2. Observe that, contrary to the analogous one-layer neural network discussed in Appendix A (Fig. A.3), we do not employ the extra input x_0 by which biases of individual neurons are defined. For our purpose, we assume no biases. There are two deviations of the neural network considered here other than the one introduced in Appendix A. First, the activation function employed by the neurons is not the sigmoid function, as in Appendix A, but the so-called linear activation function f defined for all $a \in \mathbb{R}$ by

$$f(a) = \begin{cases} 0 & \text{if } a < 0 \\ a & \text{if } a \in [0, 1] \\ 1 & \text{if } a > 1. \end{cases}$$

Second, the output y_i of neuron i is defined by

$$y_i = f(\max_{j \in \mathbb{N}_m} W_{ij} x_j) \quad (i \in \mathbb{N}_n). \tag{6.31}$$

Given (6.29), the training set consists of columns $\mathbf{q}_k$ of matrix $\mathbf{Q}$ as inputs ($x_j = q_{jk}$ for each $j \in \mathbb{N}_m, k \in \mathbb{N}_s$) and columns $\mathbf{r}_k$ of matrix $\mathbf{R}$ as expected outputs ($y_i = r_{ik}$ for each $i \in \mathbb{N}_n, k \in \mathbb{N}_s$). Applying this training set to the learning algorithm described in Appendix A, we obtain a solution to (6.29) when the error function reaches 0. The solution is then expressed by the weights W_{ij} as

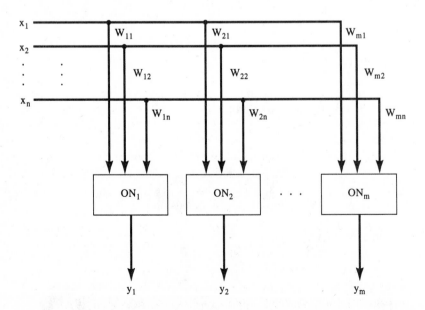

Figure 6.2 The structure of neural networks used for solving fuzzy relation equations.

$$p_{ij} = W_{ij} \tag{6.32}$$

for all $i \in \mathbb{N}_n$, $j \in \mathbb{N}_m$.

When (6.29) has no solution, the error function does not reach zero. In this case, any set of weights for which the error function reaches its minimum is not necessarily an approximate solution of (6.29) in the sense defined in Sec. 6.6.

Example 6.7

To illustrate the described procedure, let us consider the same fuzzy relation equation as in Example 6.3. That is,

$$\mathbf{P} \circ \begin{bmatrix} .1 \\ .2 \\ .3 \end{bmatrix} = \begin{bmatrix} .12 \\ .18 \\ .27 \end{bmatrix}.$$

We form a neural network with three inputs and three neurons in the output layer. The training set consists of only one input $\langle .1, .2, .3 \rangle$ and one expected output $\langle .12, .18, .27 \rangle$. This training pair is applied to the learning algorithm repeatedly until the error function reaches zero. The speed of convergence depends on the choice of initial values of the weights and on the chosen learning rate. In our experiment, the cost function reached zero after 109 cycles. The final weights are shown in Fig. 6.3. Hence, the solution is

$$\mathbf{P} = \begin{bmatrix} .1324 & .2613 & .4 \\ .2647 & .404 & .6 \\ .2925 & .5636 & .9 \end{bmatrix}.$$

Observe that this solution is not the maximum solution obtained in Example 6.3.

As already mentioned, this unorthodox way of solving fuzzy relation equations is not fully developed as yet, but it seems to have great potential.

NOTES

6.1. The notion of *fuzzy relation equations* based upon the max-min composition was first proposed and investigated by Sanchez [1976]. A comprehensive coverage of fuzzy relation equations is in a book by Di Nola *et al.* [1989]. The method for solving fuzzy relation equations described in Sec. 6.3 is based on the paper by Higashi and Klir [1984a]; all theorems by which the method is justified can be found in this paper. Fuzzy relation equations for other types of composition were studied by Pedrycz [1983b], Sanchez [1984b], and Miyakoshi and Shimbo [1985]. Generalizations to L-fuzzy relations were explored by numerous authors, for example, Di Nola and Sessa [1983], and Sessa [1984].

6.2. Existing methods for obtaining approximate solutions of fuzzy relation equations are reviewed by Di Nola *et al.* [1984, 1989]. Investigations of this topic were initiated by Pedrycz [1983c]. They were further pursued by Wu [1986], Gottwald and Pedrycz [1986], and Pedrycz [1988]. The solvability index employed in Sec. 6.6 was introduced by Gottwald [1985]. The way in which we define approximate solutions (Def. 6.1) was originally proposed by Wu [1986].

6.3. Solving fuzzy relation equations by neural networks was proposed by Pedrycz [1991b], and Wang [1993b].

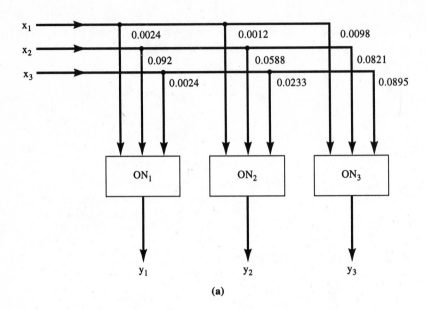

(a)

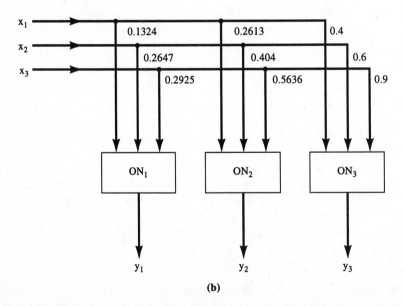

(b)

Figure 6.3 Illustration to Example 6.7: (a) neural network with initial weights; (b) neural network representing a solution.

EXERCISES

6.1. Solve the following fuzzy relation equations for the max-min composition.

(a) $\mathbf{p} \circ \begin{bmatrix} .9 & .6 & 1 \\ .8 & .8 & .5 \\ .6 & .4 & .6 \end{bmatrix} = \begin{bmatrix} .6 & .6 & .5 \end{bmatrix};$

(b) $\mathbf{p} \circ \begin{bmatrix} .5 & .7 & 0 & .2 \\ .4 & .6 & 1 & 0 \\ .2 & .4 & .5 & .6 \\ 0 & .2 & 0 & .8 \end{bmatrix} = \begin{bmatrix} .5 & .5 & .4 & .2 \end{bmatrix};$

(c) $\mathbf{P} \circ \begin{bmatrix} .5 & 0 & .3 & 0 \\ .4 & 1 & .3 & 0 \\ 0 & .1 & 1 & .1 \\ .4 & .3 & .3 & .5 \end{bmatrix} = \begin{bmatrix} .5 & .3 & .3 & .1 \\ .5 & .4 & .4 & .2 \end{bmatrix};$

(d) $\mathbf{P} \circ \begin{bmatrix} .5 & .4 & .6 & .7 \\ .2 & 0 & .6 & .8 \\ .1 & .4 & .6 & .7 \\ 0 & .3 & 0 & 1 \end{bmatrix} = \begin{bmatrix} .2 & .4 & .5 & .7 \\ .1 & .2 & .2 & .2 \end{bmatrix}.$

6.2. Let i be a t-norm in the equation

$$\mathbf{P} \overset{i}{\circ} \begin{bmatrix} .2 & .4 & .5 \\ 0 & .3 & .9 \\ .8 & 0 & .2 \\ 1 & .7 & 0 \end{bmatrix} = \begin{bmatrix} .7 & .4 & .8 \\ .3 & .4 & .9 \\ 1 & .7 & .2 \end{bmatrix}$$

Determine if the above equation has a solution for $i = $ min, product, and bounded difference, respectively.

6.3. Given two fuzzy relation equations

$$P \overset{i}{\circ} Q = R$$

$$P^{-1} \overset{i}{\circ} R = \overline{Q}$$

on a finite universal set with a continuous t-norm i, where $\overline{R}$ and $\overline{Q}$ are the standard fuzzy complements of R and Q, respectively, prove the proposition: if there is a common solution for both equations, then

$$(Q \overset{\omega_i}{\circ} R^{-1}) \cap (\overline{R} \overset{\omega_i}{\circ} \overline{Q}^{-1})$$

is the greatest solution for both equations, where $\cap$ stands for the standard fuzzy intersection.

6.4. Let i be the min, product, and bounded difference, respectively. Determine if each of the following fuzzy relation equations has a solution. If it has, find the maximum or minimum solution.

(a) $\mathbf{P} \overset{\omega_i}{\circ} \begin{bmatrix} .2 \\ .6 \end{bmatrix} = \begin{bmatrix} .2 \\ 1 \end{bmatrix},$

(b) $\begin{bmatrix} 1 & .9 \\ .2 & .6 \end{bmatrix} \overset{\omega_i}{\circ} Q = \begin{bmatrix} .2 \\ 1 \end{bmatrix}$.

6.5. Let i be the min, product, and bounded difference, respectively. Find an approximate solution for each of the following fuzzy relation equations:

(a) $P \overset{i}{\circ} \begin{bmatrix} .2 & .3 \\ .2 & .5 \end{bmatrix} = [.6 \quad .7]$;

(b) $\begin{bmatrix} .6 & .4 \\ .8 & .2 \end{bmatrix} \overset{i}{\circ} Q = \begin{bmatrix} .8 \\ 1 \end{bmatrix}$.

Using the goodness index (6.26), express the goodness of the solution obtained. Also try to find approximate solutions other than the maximum solutions and compare them by the goodness index.

7

POSSIBILITY THEORY

7.1 FUZZY MEASURES

The fuzzy set provides us with an intuitively pleasing method of representing one form of uncertainty. Consider, however, the jury members for a criminal trial who are uncertain about the guilt or innocence of the defendant. The uncertainty in this situation seems to be of a different type; the set of people who are guilty of the crime and the set of innocent people are assumed to have very distinct boundaries. The concern, therefore, is not with the degree to which the defendant is guilty, but with the degree to which the evidence proves his membership in either the crisp set of guilty people or the crisp set of innocent people. We assume that perfect evidence would point to full membership in one and only one of these sets. However, our evidence, is rarely, if ever, perfect, and some uncertainty usually prevails. In order to represent this type of uncertainty, we could assign a value to each possible crisp set to which the element in question might belong. This value would indicate the degree of evidence or certainty of the element's membership in the set. Such a representation of uncertainty is known as a *fuzzy measure*. Note how this method differs from the assignment of membership grades in fuzzy sets. In the latter case, a value is assigned to each element of the universal set, signifying its degree of membership in a particular set with unsharp boundaries. The fuzzy measure, on the other hand, assigns a value to each crisp set of the universal set, signifying the degree of evidence or belief that a particular element belongs in the set.

Fuzzy measure theory, which is now well developed [Wang and Klir, 1992], is not of primary interest in this text. However, we need to introduce the concept of a fuzzy measure for at least two reasons. First, the concept will provide us with a broad framework within which it is convenient to introduce and examine possibility theory, a theory that is closely connected with fuzzy set theory and plays an important role in some of its applications. Second, it will allow us to explicate differences between fuzzy set theory and probability theory.

Definition 7.1. Given a universal set X and a nonempty family $\mathcal{C}$ of subsets of X, a *fuzzy measure* on $\langle X, \mathcal{C} \rangle$ is a function

$$g : \mathcal{C} \to [0, 1]$$

that satisfies the following requirements:

(g1) $g(\varnothing) = 0$ and $g(X) = 1$ (*boundary requirements*);

(g2) for all $A, B \in \mathcal{C}$, if $A \subseteq B$, then $g(A) \leq g(B)$ (*monotonicity*);

(g3) for any increasing sequence $A_1 \subset A_2 \subset \dots$ in $\mathcal{C}$, if $\bigcup_{i=1}^{\infty} A_i \in \mathcal{C}$, then

$$\lim_{i \to \infty} g(A_i) = g\left(\bigcup_{i=1}^{\infty} A_i\right)$$

(*continuity from below*);

(g4) for any decreasing sequence $A_1 \supset A_2 \supset \dots$ in $\mathcal{C}$, if $\bigcap_{i=1}^{\infty} A_i \in \mathcal{C}$, then

$$\lim_{i \to \infty} g(A_i) = g\left(\bigcap_{i=1}^{\infty} A_i\right)$$

(*continuity from above*).

The boundary requirements (g1) state that, regardless of our evidence, we always know that the element in question definitely does not belong to the empty set and definitely does belong to the universal set. The empty set, by definition, does not contain any element; hence, it cannot contain the element of our interest, either; the universal set, on the other hand, contains all elements under consideration in each particular context; therefore, it must contain our element as well.

Requirement (g2) states that the evidence of the membership of an element in a set must be at least as great as the evidence that the element belongs to any subset of that set. Indeed, when we know with some degree of certainty that the element belongs to a set, then our degree of certainty that it belongs to a larger set containing the former set can be greater or equal, but it cannot be smaller.

Requirements (g3) and (g4) are clearly applicable only to an infinite universal set. They can therefore be disregarded when the universal set is finite. The requirements state that for every infinite sequence $A_1, A_2, \dots$ of nested (monotonic) subsets of X which converge to the set A, where $A = \bigcup_{i=1}^{\infty} A_i$ for increasing sequences and $A = \bigcap_{i=1}^{\infty} A_i$ for decreasing sequences, the sequence of numbers $g(A_1), g(A_2), \dots$ must converge to the number $g(A)$. That is, g is required to be a continuous function. Requirements (g3) and (g4) may also be viewed as requirements of *consistency*: calculation of $g(A)$ in two different ways, either as the limit of $g(A_i)$ for $i \to \infty$ or by application of the function g to the limit of A_i for $i \to \infty$, is required to yield the same value.

Fuzzy measures are usually defined on families $\mathcal{C}$ that satisfy appropriate properties (rings, semirings, σ-algebras, etc.). In some cases, $\mathcal{C}$ consists of the full power set $\mathcal{P}(X)$.

Three additional remarks regarding this definition are needed. First, functions that satisfy (g1), (g2), and either (g3) or (g4) are equally important in fuzzy measure theory as functions that satisfy all four requirements (g1)–(g4). These functions are called *semicontinuous fuzzy measures*; they are either *continuous from below* (satisfy (g3)) or *continuous from above* (satisfy (g4)). Second, it is sometimes needed to generalize fuzzy measures by extending the range of function g from $[0, 1]$ to the set of nonnegative real numbers and by excluding the second boundary requirement, $g(X) = 1$. These generalizations are not desirable for our purpose. Third, we can easily see that fuzzy measures, as defined here, are generalizations of probability measures or, when conceived in the broader sense, generalizations of classical measures. In either case, the generalization is obtained by replacing the additivity requirement with the weaker requirements of monotonicity and continuity or, at least, semincontinuity.

The number $g(A)$ assigned to a set $A \in \mathcal{C}$ by a fuzzy measure g signifies the total available evidence that a given element of X, whose characterization is deficient in some respect, belongs to A. The set in $\mathcal{C}$ to which we assign the highest value represents our best guess concerning the particular element in question. For instance, suppose we are trying to diagnose an ill patient. In simplified terms, we may be trying to determine whether this patient belongs to the set of people with, say, pneumonia, bronchitis, emphysema, or a common cold. A physical examination may provide us with helpful yet inconclusive evidence. For example, we might assign a high value, say 0.75, to our best guess, bronchitis, and a lower value to the other possibilities, such as 0.45 for the set consisting of pneumonia and emphysema and 0 for a common cold. These values reflect the degrees to which the patient's symptoms provide evidence for the individual diseases or sets of diseases; their collection constitutes a fuzzy measure representing the uncertainty associated with several well-defined alternatives. It is important to realize that this type of uncertainty, which results from information deficiency, is fundamentally different from fuzziness, which results from the lack of sharp boundaries.

The difference between these two types of uncertainty is also exhibited in the context of scientific observation or measurement. Observing attributes such as "a type of cloud formation" in meteorology, "a characteristic posture of an animal" in ethology, or "a degree of defect of a tree" in forestry clearly involves situations in which it is not practical to draw sharp boundaries; such observations or measurements are inherently fuzzy and, consequently, their connection with the concept of the fuzzy set is suggestive. In most measurements in physics, on the other hand, such as the measurement of length, weight, electric current, or light intensity, we define classes with sharp boundaries. Given a measurement range, usually represented by an interval of real numbers $[a, b]$, we partition this interval into n disjoint subintervals

$$[a, a_1), [a_1, a_2), [a_2, a_3), \ldots, [a_{n-1}, b]$$

according to the desired (or feasible) accuracy. Then, theoretically, each observed magnitude fits exactly into one of the intervals. In practice, however, this would be warranted only if no observational errors were involved. Since measurement errors are unavoidable in principle, each observation that coincides with or is in close proximity to one of the boundaries $a_1, a_2, \ldots, a_{n-1}$ between two neighboring intervals involves uncertainty regarding its membership in the two crisp intervals (crisp subsets of the set of real numbers). This uncertainty clearly has all the characteristics of a fuzzy measure.

Since both $A \cap B \subseteq A$ and $A \cap B \subseteq B$ for any two sets A and B, it follows from the monotonicity of fuzzy measures that every fuzzy measure g satisfies the inequality

$$g(A \cap B) \leq \min[g(A), g(B)] \tag{7.1}$$

for any three sets $A, B, A \cap B \in \mathcal{C}$. Similarly, since both $A \subseteq A \cup B$ and $B \subseteq A \cup B$ for any two sets, the monotonicity of fuzzy measures implies that every fuzzy measure g satisfies the inequality

$$g(A \cup B) \geq \max[g(A), g(B)] \tag{7.2}$$

for any three sets $A, B, A \cup B \in \mathcal{C}$.

Since fuzzy measure theory is not of interest in this text, we restrict our further consideration in this chapter to only three of its special branches: evidence theory, possibility theory, and probability theory. Although our principal interest is in possibility theory and its comparison with probability theory, evidence theory will allow us to examine and compare the two theories from a broader perspective.

Before concluding this section, one additional remark should be made. Fuzzy measure theory, as well as any of its branches, may be combined with fuzzy set theory. That is, function g characterizing a fuzzy measure may be defined on fuzzy sets rather than crisp sets.

7.2 EVIDENCE THEORY

Evidence theory is based on two dual nonadditive measures: belief measures and plausibility measures. Given a universal set X, assumed here to be finite, a *belief measure* is a function

$$\text{Bel} : \mathcal{P}(X) \to [0, 1]$$

such that $\text{Bel}(\varnothing) = 0$, $\text{Bel}(X) = 1$, and

$$\text{Bel}(A_1 \cup A_2 \cup \ldots \cup A_n) \geq \sum_j \text{Bel}(A_j) - \sum_{j<k} \text{Bel}(A_j \cap A_k)$$
$$+ \ldots + (-1)^{n+1} \text{Bel}(A_1 \cap A_2 \cap \ldots \cap A_n) \tag{7.3}$$

for all possible families of subsets of X. Due to the inequality (7.3), belief measures are called *superadditive*. When X is infinite, function Bel is also required to be *continuous from above*.

For each $A \in \mathcal{P}(X)$, $\text{Bel}(A)$ is interpreted as the *degree of belief* (based on available evidence) that a given element of X belongs to the set A. We may also view the subsets of X as answers to a particular question. We assume that some of the answers are correct, but we do not know with full certainty which ones they are.

When the sets $A_1, A_2, \ldots, A_n$ in (7.3) are pair-wise disjoint, the inequality requires that the degree of belief associated with the union of the sets is not smaller than the sum of the degrees of belief pertaining to the individual sets. This basic property of belief measures is thus a weaker version of the additivity property of probability measures. This implies that probability measures are special cases of belief measures for which the equality in (7.3) is always satisfied.

We can easily show that (7.3) implies the monotonicity requirement (g2) of fuzzy measures. Let $A \subseteq B(A, B \in \mathcal{P}(X))$ and let $C = B - A$. Then, $A \cup C = B$ and $A \cap C = \varnothing$. Applying now A and C to (7.3) for $n = 2$, we obtain

$$\text{Bel}(A \cup C) = \text{Bel}(B) \geq \text{Bel}(A) + \text{Bel}(C) - \text{Bel}(A \cap C).$$

Since $A \cap C = \varnothing$ and $\text{Bel}(\varnothing) = 0$, we have

$$\text{Bel}(B) \geq \text{Bel}(A) + \text{Bel}(C)$$

and, consequently, $\text{Bel}(B) \geq \text{Bel}(A)$.

Let $A_1 = A$ and $A_2 = \overline{A}$ in (7.3) for $n = 2$. Then, we can immediately derive the following fundamental property of belief measures:

$$\text{Bel}(A) + \text{Bel}(\overline{A}) \leq 1. \tag{7.4}$$

Associated with each belief measure is a *plausibility measure*, Pl, defined by the equation

$$\text{Pl}(A) = 1 - \text{Bel}(\overline{A}) \tag{7.5}$$

for all $A \in \mathcal{P}(X)$. Similarly,

$$\text{Bel}(A) = 1 - \text{Pl}(\overline{A}). \tag{7.6}$$

Belief measures and plausibility measures are therefore mutually dual. Plausibility measures, however, can also be defined independent of belief measures.

A plausibility measure is a function

$$\text{Pl} : \mathcal{P}(X) \rightarrow [0, 1]$$

such that $\text{Pl}(\varnothing) = 0$, $\text{Pl}(X) = 1$, and

$$\text{Pl}(A_1 \cap A_2 \cap \ldots \cap A_n) \leq \sum_j \text{Pl}(A_j) - \sum_{j<k} \text{Pl}(A_j \cup A_k)$$
$$+ \ldots + (-1)^{n+1} \text{Pl}(A_1 \cup A_2 \cup \ldots \cup A_n) \tag{7.7}$$

for all possible families of subsets of X. Due to (7.7), plausibility measures are called *subadditive*. When X is infinite, function Pl is also required to be *continuous from below*.

Let $n = 2, A_1 = A$, and $A_2 = \overline{A}$ in (7.7). Then, we immediately obtain the following basic inequality of plausibility measures:

$$\text{Pl}(A) + \text{Pl}(\overline{A}) \geq 1. \tag{7.8}$$

Belief and plausibility measures can conveniently be characterized by a function

$$m : \mathcal{P}(X) \rightarrow [0, 1],$$

such that $m(\varnothing) = 0$ and

$$\sum_{A \in \mathcal{P}(X)} m(A) = 1. \tag{7.9}$$

This function is called a *basic probability assignment*. For each set $A \in \mathcal{P}(X)$, the value $m(A)$ expresses the proportion to which all available and relevant evidence supports the claim that a particular element of X, whose characterization in terms of relevant attributes is deficient, belongs to the set A. This value, $m(A)$, pertains solely to one set, set A; it does not imply any additional claims regarding subsets of A. If there is some additional evidence supporting the claim that the element belongs to a subset of A, say $B \subseteq A$, it must be expressed by another value $m(B)$.

Although (7.9) resembles a similar equation for probability distribution functions, there is a fundamental difference between probability distribution functions and basic probability assignments: the former are defined on X, while the latter are defined on $\mathcal{P}(X)$.

Upon careful examination of the definition of the basic assignment, we observe the following:

1. it is not required that $m(X) = 1$;
2. it is not required that $m(A) \leq m(B)$ when $A \subseteq B$; and
3. no relationship between $m(A)$ and $m(\overline{A})$ is required.

It follows from these observations that the basic assignments are not fuzzy measures. However, given a basic assignment m, a belief measure and a plausibility measure are uniquely determined for all set $A \in \mathcal{P}(X)$ by the formulas

$$\text{Bel}(A) = \sum_{B|B \subseteq A} m(B), \tag{7.10}$$

$$\text{Pl}(A) = \sum_{B|A \cap B \neq \varnothing} m(B). \tag{7.11}$$

The inverse procedure is also possible. Given, for example, a belief measure Bel, the corresponding basic probability assignment m is determined for all $A \in \mathcal{P}(X)$ by the formula

$$m(A) = \sum_{B|B \subseteq A} (-1)^{|A-B|} \text{Bel}(B). \tag{7.12}$$

If a plausibility measure is given, it can be converted to the associated belief measure by (7.6), and (7.12) is then applicable to make a conversion to function m. Hence, each of the three functions, m, Bel and Pl, is sufficient to determine the other two.

The relationship between $m(A)$ and $\text{Bel}(A)$, expressed by (7.10), has the following meaning: while $m(A)$ characterizes the degree of evidence or belief that the element in question belongs to the set A alone (i.e., exactly to set A), $\text{Bel}(A)$ represents the total evidence or belief that the element belongs to A as well as to the various special subsets of A. The plausibility measure $\text{Pl}(A)$, as defined by (7.11), has a different meaning: it represents not only the total evidence or belief that the element in question belongs to set A or to any of its subsets, but also the additional evidence or belief associated with sets that overlap with A. Hence,

$$\text{Pl}(A) \geq \text{Bel}(A) \tag{7.13}$$

for all $A \in \mathcal{P}(X)$.

Every set $A \in \mathcal{P}(X)$ for which $m(A) > 0$ is usually called a *focal element* of m. As this name suggests, focal elements are subsets of X on which the available evidence focuses. When X is finite, m can be fully characterized by a list of its focal elements A with the corresponding values $m(A)$. The pair $\langle \mathcal{F}, m \rangle$, where $\mathcal{F}$ and m denote a set of focal elements and the associated basic assignment, respectively, is often called a *body of evidence*.

Total ignorance is expressed in terms of the basic assignment by $m(X) = 1$ and $m(A) = 0$ for all $A \neq X$. That is, we know that the element is in the universal set, but we have no evidence about its location in any subset of X. It follows from (7.10) that the expression of total ignorance in terms of the corresponding belief measure is exactly the same: Bel $(X) = 1$ and Bel $(A) = 0$ for all $A \neq X$. However, the expression of total ignorance in terms of the associated plausibility measure (obtained from the belief measure by (7.5)) is quite different: $\text{Pl}(\varnothing) = 0$ and $\text{Pl}(A) = 1$ for all $A \neq \varnothing$. This expression follows directly from (7.11).

Evidence obtained in the same context from two independent sources (for example, from two experts in the field of inquiry) and expressed by two basic assignments m_1 and m_2 on some power set $\mathcal{P}(X)$ must be appropriately combined to obtain a joint basic assignment $m_{1,2}$. In general, evidence can be combined in various ways, some of which may take into consideration the reliability of the sources and other relevant aspects. The standard way of combining evidence is expressed by the formula

$$m_{1,2}(A) = \frac{\sum\limits_{B \cap C = A} m_1(B) \cdot m_2(C)}{1 - K} \tag{7.14}$$

for all $A \neq \varnothing$, and $m_{1,2}(\varnothing) = 0$, where

$$K = \sum_{B \cap C = \varnothing} m_1(B) \cdot m_2(C). \tag{7.15}$$

Formula (7.14) is referred to as *Dempster's rule of combination*. According to this rule, the degree of evidence $m_1(B)$ from the first source that focuses on set $B \in \mathcal{P}(X)$ and the degree of evidence $m_2(C)$ from the second source that focuses on set $C \in \mathcal{P}(X)$ are combined by taking the product $m_1(B) \cdot m_2(C)$, which focuses on the intersection $B \cap C$. This is exactly the same way in which the joint probability distribution is calculated from two independent marginal distributions; consequently, it is justified on the same grounds. However, since some intersections of focal elements from the first and second source may result in the same set A, we must add the corresponding products to obtain $m_{1,2}(A)$. Moreover, some of the intersections may be empty. Since it is required that $m_{1,2}(\varnothing) = 0$, the value K expressed by (7.15) is not included in the definition of the joint basic assignment $m_{1,2}$. This means that the sum of products $m_1(B) \cdot m_2(C)$ for all focal elements B of m_1 and all focal elements C of m_2 such that $B \cap C \neq \varnothing$ is equal to $1 - K$. To obtain a normalized basic assignment $m_{1,2}$, as required (see (7.9)), we must divide each of these products by this factor $1 - K$, as indicated in (7.14).

Example 7.1

Assume that an old painting was discovered which strongly resembles paintings by Raphael. Such a discovery is likely to generate various questions regarding the status of the painting. Assume the following three questions:

1. Is the discovered painting a genuine painting by Raphael?
2. Is the discovered painting a product of one of Raphael's many disciples?
3. Is the discovered painting a counterfeit?

Let R, D, and C denote subsets of our universal set X—the set of all paintings—which contain the set of all paintings by Raphael, the set of all paintings by disciples of Raphael, and the set of all counterfeits of Raphael's paintings, respectively.

Assume now that two experts performed careful examinations of the painting and subsequently provided us with basic assignments m_1 and m_2, specified in Table 7.1. These are the degrees of evidence which each expert obtained by the examination and which support the various claims that the painting belongs to one of the sets of our concern. For example, $m_1(R \cup D) = .15$ is the degree of evidence obtained by the first expert that the painting was done by Raphael himself or that the painting was done by one of his disciples. Using (7.10), we can easily calculate the total evidence, Bel_1 and Bel_2, in each set, as shown in Table 7.1.

TABLE 7.1   COMBINATION OF DEGREES OF EVIDENCE
FROM TWO INDEPENDENT SOURCES (EXAMPLE 7.1)

Focal elements	Expert 1		Expert 2		Combined evidence	
	m_1	Bel_1	m_2	Bel_2	$m_{1,2}$	$\text{Bel}_{1,2}$
R	.05	.05	.15	.15	.21	.21
D	0	0	0	0	.01	.01
C	.05	.05	.05	.05	.09	.09
$R \cup D$	.15	.2	.05	.2	.12	.34
$R \cup C$	.1	.2	.2	.4	.2	.5
$D \cup C$	.05	.1	.05	.1	.06	.16
$R \cup D \cup C$	.6	1	.5	1	.31	1

Applying Dempster's rule (7.14) to m_1 and m_2, we obtain the joint basic assignment $m_{1,2}$, which is also shown in Table 7.1. To determine the values of $m_{1,2}$, we calculate the normalization factor $1 - K$ first. Applying (7.15), we obtain

$$K = m_1(R) \cdot m_2(D) + m_1(R) \cdot m_2(C) + m_1(R) \cdot m_2(D \cup C) + m_1(D) \cdot m_2(R)$$
$$+ \ m_1(D) \cdot m_2(C) + m_1(D) \cdot m_2(R \cup C) + m_1(C) \cdot m_2(R) + m_1(C) \cdot m_2(D)$$
$$+ \ m_1(C) \cdot m_2(R \cup D) + m_1(R \cup D) \cdot m_2(C) + m_1(R \cup C) \cdot m_2(D)$$
$$+ \ m_1(D \cup C) \cdot m_2(R)$$
$$= .03.$$

The normalization factor is then $1 - K = .97$. Values of $m_{1,2}$ are calculated by (7.14). For example,

$$m_{1,2}(R) = [m_1(R) \cdot m_2(R) + m_1(R) \cdot m_2(R \cup D) + m_1(R) \cdot m_2(R \cup C)$$
$$+ \ m_1(R) \cdot m_2(R \cup D \cup C) + m_1(R \cup D) \cdot m_2(R)$$
$$+ \ m_1(R \cup D) \cdot m_2(R \cup C) + m_1(R \cup C) \cdot m_2(R)$$
$$+ \ m_1(R \cup C) \cdot m_2(R \cup D) + m_1(R \cup D \cup C) \cdot m_2(R)]/.97$$
$$= .21,$$

$$m_{1,2}(D) = [m_1(D) \cdot m_2(D) + m_1(D) \cdot m_2(R \cup D) + m_1(D) \cdot m_2(D \cup C)$$
$$+ \ m_1(D) \cdot m_2(R \cup D \cup C) + m_1(R \cup D) \cdot m_2(D)$$
$$+ \ m_1(R \cup D) \cdot m_2(D \cup C) + m_1(D \cup C) \cdot m_2(D)$$
$$+ \ m_1(D \cup C) \cdot m_2(R \cup D) + m_1(R \cup D \cup C) \cdot m_2(D)]/.97$$
$$= .01,$$

$$m_{1,2}(R \cup C) = [m_1(R \cup C) \cdot m_2(R \cup C) + m_1(R \cup C) \cdot m_2(R \cup D \cup C)$$
$$+ m_1(R \cup D \cup C) \cdot m_2(R \cup C)]/.97$$
$$= .2,$$
$$m_{1,2}(R \cup D \cup C) = [m_1(R \cup D \cup C) \cdot m_2(R \cup D \cup C)]/.97$$
$$= .31,$$

and similarly for the remaining focal elements C, $R \cup D$, and $D \cup C$. The joint basic assignment can now be used to calculate the joint belief $\text{Bel}_{1,2}$ (Table 7.1) and joint plausibility $\text{Pl}_{1,2}$.

Consider now a basic assignment m defined on the Cartesian product $Z = X \times Y$; that is,

$$m : \mathcal{P}(X \times Y) \to [0, 1].$$

Each focal element of m is, in this case, a binary relation R on $X \times Y$. Let R_X denote the *projection* of R on X. Then,

$$R_X = \{x \in X | \langle x, y \rangle \in R \text{ for some } y \in Y\}.$$

Similarly,

$$R_Y = \{y \in Y | \langle x, y \rangle \in R \text{ for some } x \in X\}$$

defines the projection of R on Y. We can now define the projection m_X of m on X by the formula

$$m_X(A) = \sum_{R|A=R_X} m(R) \text{ for all } A \in \mathcal{P}(X). \tag{7.16}$$

To calculate $m_X(A)$ according to this formula, we add the values of $m(R)$ for all focal elements R whose projection on X is A. This is appropriate since all the focal elements R whose projection on X is A are represented in m_X by A. Similarly,

$$m_Y(B) = \sum_{R|B=R_Y} m(R) \text{ for all } B \in \mathcal{P}(Y) \tag{7.17}$$

defines the projection of m on Y. Let m_X and m_Y be called *marginal basic assignments*, and let $\langle \mathcal{F}_X, m_X \rangle$ and $\langle \mathcal{F}_Y, m_Y \rangle$ be the associated *marginal bodies of evidence*.

Two marginal bodies of evidence $\langle \mathcal{F}_X, m_X \rangle$ and $\langle \mathcal{F}_Y, m_Y \rangle$ are said to be *noninteractive* iff for all $A \in \mathcal{F}_X$ and all $B \in \mathcal{F}_Y$

$$m(A \times B) = m_X(A) \cdot m_Y(B) \tag{7.18}$$

and

$$m(R) = 0 \quad \text{for all } R \neq A \times B.$$

That is, two marginal bodies of evidence are noninteractive iff the only focal elements of the joint body of evidence are Cartesian products of focal elements of the marginal bodies and if the joint basic assignment is determined by the product of the marginal basic assignments.

Example 7.2

Consider the body of evidence given in Table 7.2a. Focal elements are subsets of the Cartesian product $X \times Y$, where $X = \{1, 2, 3\}$ and $Y = \{a, b, c\}$; they are defined in the table by their characteristic functions. To emphasize that each focal element is, in fact, a binary relation on $X \times Y$, they are labeled $R_1, R_2, \ldots, R_{12}$. Employing (7.16) and (7.17), we obtain the marginal bodies of evidence shown in Table 7.2b. For example,

$$m_X(\{2,3\}) = m(R_1) + m(R_2) + m(R_3) = .25,$$

$$m_X(\{1,2\}) = m(R_5) + m(R_8) + m(R_{11}) = .3,$$

$$m_Y(\{a\}) = m(R_2) + m(R_7) + m(R_8) + m(R_9) = .25,$$

$$m_Y(\{a,b,c\}) = m(R_3) + m(R_{10}) + m(R_{11}) + m(R_{12}) = .5,$$

TABLE 7.2 JOINT AND MARGINAL BODIES OF EVIDENCE: ILLUSTRATION OF INDEPENDENCE (EXAMPLE 7.2)

(a) Joint body of evidence

	$X \times Y$									
	$1a$	$1b$	$1c$	$2a$	$2b$	$2c$	$3a$	$3b$	$3c$	$m(R_i)$
$R_1 =$	0	0	0	0	1	1	0	1	1	.0625
$R_2 =$	0	0	0	1	0	0	1	0	0	.0625
$R_3 =$	0	0	0	1	1	1	1	1	1	.125
$R_4 =$	0	1	1	0	0	0	0	1	1	.0375
$R_5 =$	0	1	1	0	1	1	0	0	0	.075
$R_6 =$	0	1	1	0	1	1	0	1	1	.075
$R_7 =$	1	0	0	0	0	0	1	0	0	.375
$R_8 =$	1	0	0	1	0	0	0	0	0	.075
$R_9 =$	1	0	0	1	0	0	1	0	0	.075
$R_{10} =$	1	1	1	0	0	0	1	1	1	.075
$R_{11} =$	1	1	1	1	1	1	0	0	0	.15
$R_{12} =$	1	1	1	1	1	1	1	1	1	.15

$m : \mathcal{P}(X \times Y) \to [0, 1]$

(b) Marginal bodies of evidence

	X			
	1	2	3	$m_X(A)$
$A =$	0	1	1	.25
	1	0	1	.15
	1	1	0	.3
	1	1	1	.3

$m_X : \mathcal{P}(X) \to [0, 1]$

	Y			
	a	b	c	$m_Y(B)$
$B =$	0	1	1	.25
	1	0	0	.25
	1	1	1	.5

$m_Y : \mathcal{P}(Y) \to [0, 1]$

and similarly for the remaining sets A and B. We can easily verify that the joint basic assignment m is uniquely determined in this case by the marginal basic assignments through (7.18). The marginal bodies of evidence are thus noninteractive. For example,

$$m(R_1) = m_X(\{2,3\}) \cdot m_Y(\{b,c\})$$
$$= .25 \times .25 = .0625.$$

Observe that $\{2,3\} \times \{b,c\} = \{2b, 2c, 3b, 3c\} = R_1$. Similarly,

$$m(R_{10}) = m_X(\{1,3\}) \cdot m_Y(\{a,b,c\})$$
$$= .15 \times .5 = .075,$$

where $R_{10} = \{1,3\} \times \{a,b,c\} = \{1a, 1b, 1c, 3a, 3b, 3c\}$.

In addition to the basic probability assignment, belief measure, and plausibility measure, it is also sometimes convenient to use the function

$$Q(A) = \sum_{B|A \subseteq B} m(B),$$

which is called a *commonality function*. For each $A \in \mathcal{P}(X)$, the value $Q(A)$ represents the total portion of belief that can move freely to every point of A. Each commonality function defined on the power set of X is a unique representation of a body of evidence on the power set. All conversion formulas between m, Bel, Pl, and Q are given in Table 7.3.

TABLE 7.3   CONVERSION FORMULAS IN THE EVIDENCE THEORY

	m	Bel	Pl	Q
$m(A) =$	$m(A)$	$\sum_{B \subseteq A}(-1)^{|A-B|}\text{Bel}(B)$	$\sum_{B \subseteq A}(-1)^{|A-B|}[1-\text{Pl}(\overline{B})]$	$\sum_{A \subseteq B}(-1)^{|B-A|}Q(B)$
$\text{Bel}(A) =$	$\sum_{B \subseteq A} m(B)$	$\text{Bel}(A)$	$1-\text{Pl}(\overline{A})$	$\sum_{B \subseteq \overline{A}}(-1)^{|B|}Q(B)$
$\text{Pl}(A) =$	$\sum_{B \cap A \neq \varnothing} m(B)$	$1-\text{Bel}(\overline{A})$	$\text{Pl}(A)$	$\sum_{\varnothing \neq B \subseteq \overline{A}}(-1)^{|B|+1}Q(B)$
$Q(A) =$	$\sum_{A \subseteq B} m(B)$	$\sum_{B \subseteq A}(-1)^{|B|}\text{Bel}(\overline{B})$	$\sum_{\varnothing \neq B \subseteq \overline{A}}(-1)^{|B|+1}\text{Pl}(B)$	$Q(A)$

7.3   POSSIBILITY THEORY

A special branch of evidence theory that deals only with bodies of evidence whose focal elements are nested is referred to as *possibility theory*. Special counterparts of belief measures and plausibility measures in possibility theory are called *necessity measures* and *possibility measures*, respectively.

The requirement that focal elements be nested (also called *consonant*) restricts belief and plausibility measures in a way that is characterized by the following theorem.

Theorem 7.1.   Let a given finite body of evidence $\langle \mathcal{F}, m \rangle$ be nested. Then, the associated belief and plausibility measures have the following properties for all $A, B \in \mathcal{P}(X)$:

(i) $\text{Bel}(A \cap B) = \min [\text{Bel}(A), \text{Bel}(B)]$;
(ii) $\text{Pl}(A \cup B) = \max [\text{Bel}(A), \text{Bel}(B)]$.

Proof: (i) Since the focal elements in $\mathcal{F}$ are nested, they may be linearly ordered by the subset relationship. Let $\mathcal{F} = \{A_1, A_2, \ldots, A_n\}$, and assume that $A_i \subset A_j$ whenever $i < j$. Consider now arbitrary subsets A and B of X. Let i_1 be the largest integer i such that $A_i \subseteq A$, and let i_2 be the largest integer i such that $A_i \subseteq B$. Then, $A_i \subseteq A$ and $A_i \subseteq B$ iff $i \leq i_1$ and $i \leq i_2$, respectively. Moreover, $A_i \subseteq A \cap B$ iff $i \leq \min(i_1, i_2)$. Hence,

$$\text{Bel}\,(A \cap B) = \sum_{i=1}^{\min(i_1, i_2)} m(A_i) = \min\left[\sum_{i=1}^{i_1} m(A_i), \sum_{i=1}^{i_2} m(A_i)\right]$$

$$= \min[\,\text{Bel}\,(A),\,\text{Bel}\,(B)].$$

(ii) Assume that (i) holds. Then, by (7.5),

$$\text{Pl}\,(A \cup B) = 1 - \text{Bel}\,(\overline{A \cup B}) = 1 - \text{Bel}\,(\overline{A} \cap \overline{B})$$

$$= 1 - \min[\,\text{Bel}\,(\overline{A}),\,\text{Bel}\,(\overline{B})]$$

$$= \max[1 - \text{Bel}\,(\overline{A}),\,1 - \text{Bel}\,(\overline{B})]$$

$$= \max[\,\text{Pl}\,(A),\,\text{Pl}\,(B)]$$

for all $A, B \in \mathcal{P}(X)$. ∎

Let necessity measures and possibility measures be denoted by the symbols Nec and Pos, respectively. Then, Theorem 7.1 provides us directly with the following basic equations of possibility theory, which hold for every $A, B \in \mathcal{P}(X)$:

$$\text{Nec}\,(A \cap B) = \min[\,\text{Nec}\,(A),\,\text{Nec}\,(B)], \tag{7.19}$$

$$\text{Pos}\,(A \cup B) = \max[\,\text{Pos}\,(A),\,\text{Pos}\,(B)]. \tag{7.20}$$

When we compare these equations with the general properties (7.1) and (7.2) of fuzzy measures, we can see that possibility theory is based on the extreme values of fuzzy measures with respect to set intersections and unions. From this point of view, necessity and possibility measures are sometimes defined axiomatically by (7.19) and (7.20), and their underlying nested structure can then be proven as a theorem in the theory. This approach allows us to define necessity and possibility measures for arbitrary universal sets, not necessarily finite. This general formulation of necessity and possibility measures is given by the following two definitions.

Definition 7.2. Let Nec denote a fuzzy measure on $\langle X, \mathcal{C} \rangle$. Then, Nec is called a *necessity measure* iff

$$\text{Nec}\left(\bigcap_{k \in K} A_k\right) = \inf_{k \in K} \text{Nec}\,(A_k) \tag{7.21}$$

for any family $\{A_k | k \in K\}$ in $\mathcal{C}$ such that $\bigcap_{k \in K} A_k \in \mathcal{C}$, where K is an arbitrary index set.

Definition 7.3. Let Pos denote a fuzzy measure on $\langle X, \mathcal{C} \rangle$. Then, Pos is called a *possibility measure* iff

$$\text{Pos}\left(\bigcup_{k \in K} A_k\right) = \sup_{k \in K} \text{Pos}\,(A_k) \tag{7.22}$$

for any family $\{A_k | k \in K\}$ in $\mathcal{C}$ such that $\bigcup_{k \in K} A_k \in \mathcal{C}$, where K is an arbitrary index set.

Since necessity measures are special belief measures and possibility measures are special plausibility measures, they satisfy (7.4)–(7.6) and (7.8). Hence,

$$\text{Nec}\,(A) + \text{Nec}\,(\overline{A}) \le 1, \tag{7.23}$$

$$\text{Pos}\,(A) + \text{Pos}\,(\overline{A}) \ge 1, \tag{7.24}$$

$$\text{Nec}\,(A) = 1 - \text{Pos}\,(\overline{A}). \tag{7.25}$$

Furthermore, it follows immediately from (7.19) and (7.20) that

$$\min[\,\text{Nec}\,(A),\, \text{Nec}\,(\overline{A})] = 0, \tag{7.26}$$

$$\max[\,\text{Pos}\,(A),\, \text{Pos}\,(\overline{A})] = 1. \tag{7.27}$$

In addition, possibility measures and necessity measures constrain each other in a strong way, as expressed by the following theorem.

Theorem 7.2.   For every $A \in \mathcal{P}(X)$, any necessity measure, Nec, on $\mathcal{P}(X)$ and the associated possibility measure, Pos, satisfy the following implications:

(i) $\text{Nec}\,(A) > 0 \Rightarrow \text{Pos}\,(A) = 1$;
(ii) $\text{Pos}\,(A) < 1 \Rightarrow \text{Nec}\,(A) = 0.$

Proof: (i) Let $\text{Nec}\,(A) > 0$ for some $A \in \mathcal{P}(X)$. Then, $\text{Nec}\,(\overline{A}) = 0$ by (7.26), and $\text{Pos}\,(A) = 1 - \text{Nec}\,(\overline{A}) = 1$. (ii) Let $\text{Pos}\,(A) < 1$ for some $A \in \mathcal{P}(X)$. Then, $\text{Pos}\,(\overline{A}) = 1$ by (7.27), and $\text{Nec}\,(A) = 1 - \text{Pos}\,(\overline{A}) = 0$. ∎

Given a possibility measure Pos on $\mathcal{P}(X)$, let function $r : X \to [0, 1]$ such that $r(x) = \text{Pos}\,(\{x\})$ for all $x \in X$ be called a *possibility distribution function* associated with Pos. An important property of possibility theory is that every possibility measure is uniquely represented by the associated possibility distribution function. For finite universal sets, the property is formally expressed by the following theorem.

Theorem 7.3.   Every possibility measure Pos on a finite power set $\mathcal{P}(X)$ is uniquely determined by a *possibility distribution function*

$$r : X \to [0, 1]$$

via the formula

$$\text{Pos}\,(A) = \max_{x \in A} r(x) \tag{7.28}$$

for each $A \in \mathcal{P}(X)$.

Proof: We prove the theorem by induction on the cardinality of set A. Let $|A| = 1$. Then, $A = \{x\}$, where $x \in X$, and (7.28) is trivially satisfied. Assume now that (7.28) is satisfied for $|A| = n - 1$, and let $A = \{x_1, x_2, \ldots, x_n\}$. Then, by (7.20),

$$\begin{aligned}
\text{Pos}\,(A) &= \max[\text{Pos}\,(\{x_1, x_2, \ldots, x_{n-1}\}), \text{Pos}\,(\{x_n\})] \\
&= \max[\max[\text{Pos}\,(\{x_1\}), \text{Pos}\,(\{x_2\}), \ldots, \text{Pos}\,(\{x_{n-1}\})], \text{Pos}\,(\{x_n\})] \\
&= \max[\text{Pos}\,(\{x_1\}), \text{Pos}\,(\{x_2\}), \ldots, \text{Pos}\,(\{x_n\})] \\
&= \max_{x \in A} r(x). \quad \blacksquare
\end{aligned}$$

When X is not finite, (7.28) must be replaced with the more general equation

$$\text{Pos}(A) = \sup_{x \in A} r(x). \tag{7.29}$$

Let us now introduce a convenient notation applicable to finite universal sets. Assume that a possibility distribution function r is defined on the universal set $X = \{x_1, x_2, \ldots, x_n\}$. Then, the n-tuple

$$\mathbf{r} = \langle r_1, r_2, \ldots, r_n \rangle,$$

where $r_i = r(x_i)$ for all $x_i \in X$, is called a *possibility distribution* associated with the function r. The number of components in a possibility distribution is called its *length*.

It is convenient to order possibility distribution in such a way that $r_i \geq r_j$ when $i < j$. Let $^n\mathcal{R}$ denote the set of all ordered possibility distributions of length n, and let

$$\mathcal{R} = \bigcup_{n \in \mathbb{N}} {}^n\mathcal{R}.$$

Given two possibility distributions,

$$^1\mathbf{r} = \langle {}^1r_1, {}^1r_2, \ldots, {}^1r_n \rangle \in {}^n\mathcal{R}$$

and

$$^2\mathbf{r} = \langle {}^2r_1, {}^2r_2, \ldots, {}^2r_n \rangle \in {}^n\mathcal{R},$$

for some $n \in \mathbb{N}$, we define

$$^1\mathbf{r} \leq {}^2\mathbf{r} \text{ iff } {}^1r_i \leq {}^2r_i \text{ for all } i \in \mathbb{N}_n.$$

This ordering on $^n\mathcal{R}$ is partial and forms a lattice whose join, $\vee$, and meet, $\wedge$, are defined, respectively, as

$$^i\mathbf{r} \vee {}^j\mathbf{r} = \langle \max({}^ir_1, {}^jr_1), \max({}^ir_2, {}^jr_2), \ldots, \max({}^ir_n, {}^jr_n) \rangle$$

and

$$^i\mathbf{r} \wedge {}^j\mathbf{r} = \langle \min({}^ir_1, {}^jr_1), \min({}^ir_2, {}^jr_2), \ldots, \min({}^ir_n, {}^jr_n) \rangle$$

for all $^i\mathbf{r}, {}^j\mathbf{r} \in {}^n\mathcal{R}$. For each $n \in \mathbb{N}$, let $\langle {}^n\mathcal{R}, \leq \rangle$ be called a *lattice of possibility distributions of length n*.

Consider again $X = \{x_1, x_2, \ldots, x_n\}$ and assume that a possibility measure Pos is defined on $\mathcal{P}(X)$ in terms of its basic assignment m. This requires (by the definition of possibility measures) that all focal elements be nested. Assume, without any loss of generality, that the focal elements are some or all of the subsets in the complete sequence of nested subsets

$$A_1 \subset A_2 \subset \ldots \subset A_n (= X),$$

where $A_i = \{x_1, \ldots, x_i\}, i \in \mathbb{N}_n$, as illustrated in Fig. 7.1a. That is, $m(A) = 0$ for each $A \neq A_i (i \in \mathbb{N})$ and

$$\sum_{i=1}^{n} m(A_i) = 1. \tag{7.30}$$

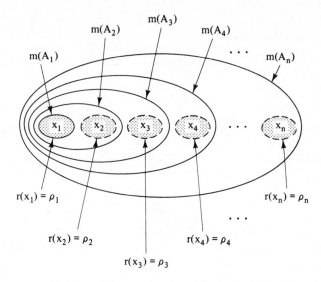

(a) Complete sequence of nested subsets of X

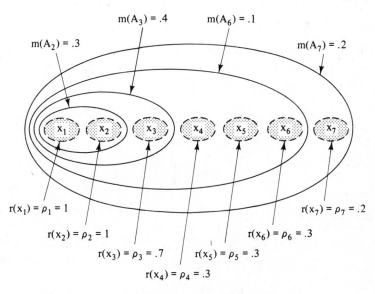

(b) A possibility measure defined on X

Figure 7.1 Nested focal elements of possibility measure on $\mathcal{P}(X)$, where $X = \{x_1, x_2, \ldots, x_n\}$: (a) complete sequence of nested subsets of X; (b) a possibility measure defined on X.

It is not required, however, that $m(A_i) \neq 0$ for all $i \in \mathbb{N}_n$, as illustrated by an example in Fig. 7.1b.

It follows from the previous discussion that every possibility measure on a finite universal set can be uniquely characterized by the n-tuple

$$\mathbf{m} = \langle m_1, m_2, \ldots, m_n \rangle$$

for some finite $n \in \mathbb{N}$, where $m_i = m(A_i)$ for all $i \in \mathbb{N}_n$. Clearly,

$$\sum_{i=1}^{n} m_i = 1 \tag{7.31}$$

and $m_i \in [0, 1]$ for all $i \in \mathbb{N}_n$. Let $\mathbf{m}$ be called a *basic distribution*. Let $^n\mathcal{M}$ denote the set of all basic distributions with n components (distributions of length n), and let

$$\mathcal{M} = \bigcup_{n \in \mathbb{N}} {}^n\mathcal{M}.$$

Using the introduced notation, let us demonstrate now that each basic distribution $\mathbf{m} \in \mathcal{M}$ represents exactly one possibility distribution $\mathbf{r} \in \mathcal{R}$, and vice versa. First, it follows from (7.28) and from the definition of possibility measures as special plausibility measures that

$$r_i = r(x_i) = \mathrm{Pos}\,(\{x_i\}) = \mathrm{Pl}\,(\{x_i\})$$

for all $x_i \in X$. Hence, we can apply (7.11) to $\mathrm{Pl}(\{x_i\})$ and thus obtain a set of equations

$$r_i = \mathrm{Pl}\,(\{x_i\}) = \sum_{k=i}^{n} m(A_k) = \sum_{k=i}^{n} m_k, \tag{7.32}$$

with one equation for each $i \in \mathbb{N}_n$. Written more explicitly, these equations are:

$$
\begin{aligned}
r_1 &= m_1 + m_2 + m_3 + \ldots + m_i + m_{i+1} + \ldots + m_n \\
r_2 &= \quad\quad\ m_2 + m_3 + \ldots + m_i + m_{i+1} + \ldots + m_n \\
&\ \ \vdots \\
r_i &= \quad\quad\quad\quad\quad\quad\quad\quad\quad m_i + m_{i+1} + \ldots + m_n \\
&\ \ \vdots \\
r_n &= \quad\quad\quad\quad\quad\quad\quad\quad\quad\quad\quad\quad\quad\quad\ m_n
\end{aligned}
$$

Solving these equations for $m_i (i \in \mathbb{N}_n)$, we obtain

$$m_i = r_i - r_{i+1} \tag{7.33}$$

for all $i \in \mathbb{N}_n$, where $r_{n+1} = 0$ by convention. Equations (7.32) and (7.33) define a one-to-one correspondence

$$t : \mathcal{R} \leftrightarrow \mathcal{M}$$

between possibility distributions and the underlying basic distributions. Given

$$\mathbf{r} = \langle r_i, r_2, \ldots, r_n \rangle \in \mathcal{R} \text{ and } \mathbf{m} = \langle m_1, m_2, \ldots, m_n \rangle \in \mathcal{M}$$

for some $n \in \mathbb{N}$, $t(\mathbf{r}) = \mathbf{m}$ iff (7.33) is satisfied; similarly, $t^{-1}(\mathbf{m}) = \mathbf{r}$ iff (7.32) is satisfied.

Function t enables us to define a partial ordering on set $\mathcal{M}$ in terms of the partial ordering defined on set $\mathcal{R}$. For all $^1\mathbf{m}, {}^2\mathbf{m} \in \mathcal{M}$, we define

$$^1\mathbf{m} \leq {}^2\mathbf{m} \text{ if and only if } t^{-1}(^1\mathbf{m}) \leq t^{-1}(^2\mathbf{m}).$$

Example 7.3

Consider the basic assignment m specified in Fig. 7.1b. We observe that (7.30) is satisfied, but $m(A_i) = 0$ in this case for some subsets of the complete sequence

$$A_1 \subset A_2 \subset \ldots \subset A_7$$

of nested subsets. For example, $m(A_1) = m(\{x_1\}) = 0$ and $m(A_4) = m(\{x_1, x_2, x_3, x_4\}) = 0$. The basic distribution is

$$\mathbf{m} = \langle 0, .3, .4, 0, 0, .1, .2 \rangle.$$

Applying (7.32) to this basic distribution for all $i \in \mathbb{N}_7$, we obtain the possibility distribution

$$\mathbf{r} = \langle 1, 1, .7, .3, .3, .3, .2 \rangle,$$

as shown in Fig. 7.1b. For instance,

$$r_3 = \sum_{k=3}^{7} m_k = .4 + 0 + 0 + .1 + .2 = .7,$$

$$r_5 = \sum_{k=5}^{7} m_k = 0 + .1 + .2 = .3.$$

Degrees of possibility $\text{Pos}(A)$ can now be calculated for any subset A of $X = \{x_1, x_2, \ldots, x_7\}$ from components of the possibility distribution $\mathbf{r}$ by (7.28). For instance,

$$\text{Pos}(\{x_1, \ldots, x_k\}) = \max(r_1, \ldots, r_k) = \max(1, \ldots, r_k) = 1$$

for each $k \in \mathbb{N}_7$; similarly,

$$\text{Pos}(\{x_3, x_4, x_5\}) = \max(r_3, r_4, r_5) = \max(.7, .3, .3) = .7.$$

It follows from (7.31) and (7.32) that $r_1 = 1$ for each possibility distribution

$$\mathbf{r} = \langle r_1, r_2, \ldots, r_n \rangle \in {}^n\mathcal{R}.$$

Hence, the *smallest possibility distribution* $\check{\mathbf{r}}_n$ of length n has the form

$$\check{\mathbf{r}}_n = \langle 1, 0, 0, \ldots, 0 \rangle$$

with $n - 1$ zeros. This possibility distribution, whose basic assignment

$$t(\check{\mathbf{r}}_n) = \langle 1, 0, \ldots, 0, 0 \rangle$$

has the same form, represents *perfect evidence* with no uncertainty involved. The *largest possibility distribution* $\hat{\mathbf{r}}_n$ of length n consists of all 1's, and

$$t(\hat{\mathbf{r}}_n) = \langle 0, 0, \ldots, 0, 1 \rangle$$

with $n - 1$ zeros. This distribution represents *total ignorance*, that is, a situation in which no relevant evidence is available. In general, the larger the possibility distribution, the less specific the evidence and, consequently, the more ignorant we are.

Let us consider now *joint possibility distributions* **r** defined on the Cartesian product $X \times Y$. Projections $\mathbf{r}_X$ and $\mathbf{r}_Y$ of **r**, which are called *marginal possibility distributions*, are defined by the formulas

$$r_X(x) = \max_{y \in Y} r(x, y) \qquad (7.34)$$

for each $x \in X$ and

$$r_Y(y) = \max_{x \in X} r(x, y) \qquad (7.35)$$

for each $y \in Y$. These formulas follow directly from (7.28). To see this, note that each particular element x of X, for which the marginal distribution $\mathbf{r}_X$ is defined, stands for the set $\{\langle x, y \rangle | y \in Y\}$ of pairs in $X \times Y$ for which the joint distribution is defined. Hence, it must be that

$$\text{Pos}_X(\{x\}) = \text{Pos}(\{\langle x, y \rangle \mid y \in Y\}),$$

where Pos_X and Pos are possibility measures corresponding to r_X and r, respectively. Applying (7.28) to the left-hand side of this equation, we obtain

$$\text{Pos}_X(\{x\}) = r_X(x);$$

and applying it to the right-hand side of the equation yields

$$\text{Pos}(\{\langle x, y \rangle \mid y \in Y\}) = \max_{y \in Y} r(x, y).$$

Hence, (7.34) is obtained. We can argue similarly for (7.35).

Nested bodies of evidence on X and Y represented by possibility distribution functions r_X and r_Y, respectively, are called *noninteractive* (in the possibilistic sense) iff

$$r(x, y) = \min[r_X(x), r_Y(y)] \qquad (7.36)$$

for all $x \in X$ and all $y \in Y$. An example of noninteractive nested bodies of evidence is given in Fig. 7.2, which is self-explanatory. Observe that for each joint possibility r_{ij} in Fig. 7.2b, we have

$$r_{ij} = \min(r_i, r_j'),$$

where r_i, r_j' are the respective marginal possibilities given in Fig. 7.2a. For instance,

$$r_{32} = \min(r_3, r_2') = \min(.6, 1) = .6$$

or

$$r_{43} = \min(r_4, r_3') = \min(.5, .3) = .3.$$

This definition of possibilistic noninteraction (see (7.36)) is clearly not based upon the product rule of evidence theory. Consequently, it does not conform to the general definition of noninteractive bodies of evidence as expressed by (7.18). The product rule cannot be used for defining possibilistic noninteraction because it does not preserve the nested structure of focal elements. This is illustrated by the following example.

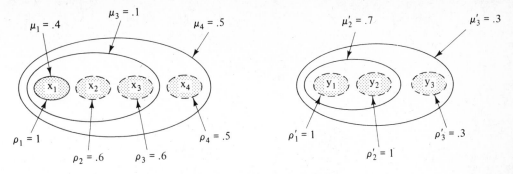

(a) Marginal consonant (nested) bodies of evidence

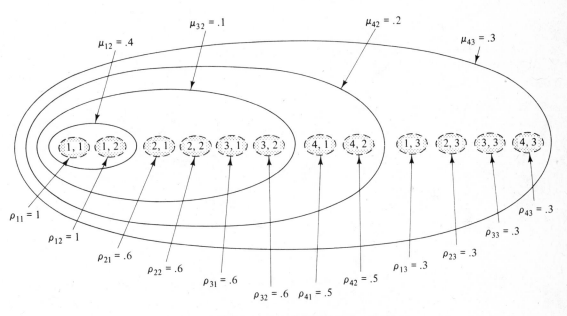

(b) Joint consonant (nested) body of evidence

Figure 7.2 Example of noninteractive sets with possibility measure: (a) marginal consonant bodies of evidence; (b) joint consonant body of evidence.

Example 7.4

Consider the marginal possibility distributions and basic distributions specified in Fig. 7.3a, which represent two nested bodies of evidence. When we combine them by (7.36), we obtain the joint possibility distribution shown in Fig. 7.3b. That is, the result of combining two nested bodies of evidence by the min operator is again nested so that we remain in the domain of possibility theory. In contrast to this, when the product rule is employed, we obtain the joint basic assignment shown in Fig. 7.3c. This basic assignment does not represent a nested body of evidence; consequently, it is not a subject of possibility theory. It follows directly from (7.34) and (7.35) that

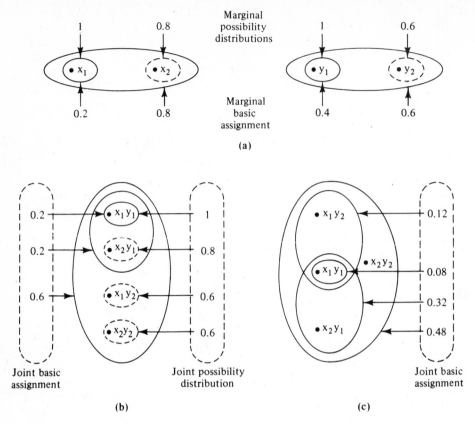

Figure 7.3 Combinations of consonant (nested) bodies of evidence by the minimum operator versus Dempster's rule (Example 7.4).

$$r(x, y) \leq r_X(x) \text{ and } r(x, y) \leq r_Y(y).$$

Hence,

$$r(x, y) \leq \min[r_X(x), r_Y(y)]. \tag{7.37}$$

This means that the joint possibility distribution defined by (7.36) is the largest joint distribution (or, equivalently, the least constrained joint distribution) that satisfies the given marginal distributions. As such, it represents the least specific claim about the actual joint distribution. It is certainly desirable, at least on intuitive grounds, to define noninteraction in terms of this extreme condition.

Let r_X and r_Y be marginal possibility distribution functions on X and Y, respectively, and let r be the joint possibility distribution function on $X \times Y$ defined in terms of r_X and r_Y by (7.36). Then, assuming that Pos_X, Pos_Y, and Pos denote the possibility measures corresponding to $r_X, r_Y,$ and r, Pos can be calculated from Pos_X and Pos_Y by the equation

$$\text{Pos}(A \times B) = \min[\text{Pos}_X(A), \text{Pos}_Y(B)] \tag{7.38}$$

for all $A \in \mathcal{P}(X)$ and all $B \in \mathcal{P}(Y)$, where

$$\text{Pos}_X(A) = \max_{x \in A} r_X(x),$$

$$\text{Pos}_Y(B) = \max_{y \in B} r_Y(y),$$

$$\text{Pos}\,(A \times B) = \max_{x \in A, y \in B} r(x, y).$$

Furthermore,

$$\text{Nec}\,(A + B) = \max[\text{Nec}_X(A), \text{Nec}_Y(B)] \qquad (7.39)$$

for all $A \in \mathcal{P}(X)$ and all $B \in \mathcal{P}(Y)$, where Nec, Nec_X, and Nec_Y are the necessity measures associated with possibility measures Pos, Pos_X, Pos_Y, respectively, by (7.25), and $A + B$ is the Cartesian coproduct $\overline{\overline{A} \times \overline{B}}$. This equation can easily have been derived by using (7.25) and (7.38):

$$\max[\text{Nec}_X(A), \text{Nec}_Y(B)] = \max[1 - \text{Pos}_X(\overline{A}), 1 - \text{Pos}_Y(\overline{B})]$$

$$= 1 - \min[\text{Pos}_X(\overline{A}), \text{Pos}_Y(\overline{B})]$$

$$= 1 - \text{Pos}\,(\overline{A} \times \overline{B})$$

$$= \text{Nec}\,(A + B).$$

Let us now discuss the concept of a *conditional possibility distribution function*, which is essential for defining possibilistic independence. We say that two marginal possibilistic bodies of evidence are *independent* iff the conditional possibilities do not differ from the corresponding marginal possibilities. This is expressed by the equations

$$r_{X|Y}(x|y) = r_X(x), \qquad (7.40)$$

$$r_{Y|X}(y|x) = r_Y(y) \qquad (7.41)$$

for all $x \in X$ and all $y \in Y$, where $r_{X|Y}(x|y)$ and $r_{Y|X}(y|x)$ denote conditional possibilities on $X \times Y$.

Observe that possibilistic independence, expressed by (7.40) and (7.41), is distinguished from possibilistic noninteraction, which is expressed by (7.36). To show that these concepts are not equivalent, contrary to their probabilistic counterparts, we employ the basic equations

$$r(x, y) = \min[r_Y(y), r_{X|Y}(x|y)], \qquad (7.42)$$

$$r(x, y) = \min[r_X(x), r_{Y|X}(y|x)], \qquad (7.43)$$

which must be satisfied for any two marginal possibilistic bodies of evidence and the associated joint body of evidence, regardless of their status with respect to independence.

Assume first that (7.40) is satisfied (independence). Then, substituting $r_X(x)$ for $r_{X|Y}(x|y)$ in (7.42), we obtain (7.36) (noninteraction). Similarly, assuming (7.41) and substituting $r_Y(y)$ for $r_{Y|X}(y|x)$ in (7.43), we obtain (7.36). Hence, the property of possibilistic independence implies the property of possibilistic noninteraction.

Assume now that (7.36) is satisfied (noninteraction). Then, substituting $\min[r_X(x), r_Y(y)]$ for $r(x, y)$ in (7.42), we obtain the equation

$$\min[r_X(x), r_Y(y)] = \min[r_Y(y), r_{X|Y}(x|y)].$$

Solving this equation for $r_{X|Y}(x|y)$, we obtain

$$r_{X|Y}(x|y) = \begin{cases} r_X(x) & \text{for } r_X(x) < r_Y(y) \\ [r_Y(y), 1] & \text{for } r_X(x) \geq r_Y(y). \end{cases} \tag{7.44}$$

In a similar way, we can obtain

$$r_{Y|X}(y|x) = \begin{cases} r_Y(y) & \text{for } r_Y(y) < r_X(x) \\ [r_X(x), 1] & \text{for } r_Y(y) \geq r_X(x). \end{cases} \tag{7.45}$$

Hence, the property of possibilistic noninteraction does not imply the property of possibilistic independence. The two concepts are thus not equivalent; possibilistic independence is stronger than possibilistic noninteraction.

We can see from (7.44) and (7.45) that conditional possibilities are not uniquely determined solely by the constraints of possibility theory. The choices of one value of $r_{X|Y}(x|y)$ from the interval $[r_Y(y), 1]$ or one value of $r_{Y|X}(y|x)$ from the interval $[r_X(x), 1]$ depend on some additional conditions. Several distinct conditions proposed for this purpose in the literature are still subjects of debate. We overview these proposals in Note 7.8.

As explained in this section, possibility theory is based on two dual functions: necessity measures, Nec, and possibility measures, Pos. The two functions, whose range is $[0, 1]$, can be converted to a single combined function, C, whose range is $[-1, 1]$. For each $A \in \mathcal{P}(X)$, function C is defined by the equation

$$C(A) = \text{Nec}(A) + \text{Pos}(A) - 1. \tag{7.46}$$

Conversely, for each $A \in \mathcal{P}(X)$,

$$\text{Nec}(A) = \begin{cases} 0 & \text{when } C(A) \leq 0 \\ C(A) & \text{when } C(A) > 0, \end{cases} \tag{7.47}$$

$$\text{Pos}(A) = \begin{cases} C(A) + 1 & \text{when } C(A) \leq 0 \\ 1 & \text{when } C(A) > 0. \end{cases} \tag{7.48}$$

Positive values of $C(A)$ indicate the *degree of confirmation* of A by the evidence available, while its negative values express the *degree of disconfirmation* of A by the evidence.

7.4 FUZZY SETS AND POSSIBILITY THEORY

Possibility theory can be formulated not only in terms of nested bodies of evidence, but also in terms of fuzzy sets. This alternative formulation of possibility theory is suggestive since fuzzy sets, similar to possibilistic bodies of evidence, are also based on families of nested sets, the appropriate α-cuts.

Possibility measures are directly connected with fuzzy sets via the associated possibility distribution functions. To explain this connection, let $\mathcal{V}$ denote a variable that takes values in a universal set V, and let the equation $\mathcal{V} = v$, where $v \in V$, be used for describing the fact that the value of $\mathcal{V}$ is v.

Consider now a fuzzy set F on V that expresses an elastic constraint on values that may be assigned to $\mathcal{V}$. Then, given a particular value $v \in V$, $F(v)$ is interpreted as the *degree of compatibility* of v with the concept described by F. On the other hand, given the proposition "$\mathcal{V}$ is F" based upon F, it is more meaningful to interpret $F(v)$ as the *degree of possibility* that $\mathcal{V} = v$. That is, given a fuzzy set F on V and the proposition "$\mathcal{V}$ is F," the possibility,

$r_F(v)$, of $\mathcal{V} = v$ for each $v \in V$ is numerically equal to the degree $F(v)$ to which v belongs to F. Formally,

$$r_F(v) = F(v) \tag{7.49}$$

for all $v \in V$.

Function r_F: $V \to [0, 1]$ defined by (7.49) is clearly a possibility distribution function on V. Given r_F, the associated possibility measure, Pos_F, is defined for all $A \in \mathcal{P}(V)$ by the equation

$$\mathrm{Pos}_F(A) = \sup_{v \in A} r_F(v), \tag{7.50}$$

which is a counterpart of (7.29). This measure expresses the uncertainty regarding the actual value of variable $\mathcal{V}$ under incomplete information given in terms of the proposition "$\mathcal{V}$ is F." For normal fuzzy sets, the associated necessity measure, Nec_F, can then be calculated for all $A \in \mathcal{P}(V)$ by the equation

$$\mathrm{Nec}_F(A) = 1 - \mathrm{Pos}_F(\overline{A}), \tag{7.51}$$

which is a counterpart of (7.25).

As an example, let variable $\mathcal{V}$ be temperature measured in °C and assume that only its integer values are recognized (i.e., $V = \mathbb{Z}$). Let information about the actual value of $\mathcal{V}$ be given in terms of the proposition "$\mathcal{V}$ is around 21°C" in which the concept *around* 21°C is expressed by the fuzzy set F given in Fig. 7.4a. This incomplete information induces a possibility distribution function r_F that, according to (7.49), is numerically identical with the membership function F. The α-cuts of F, which are nested as shown in Fig. 7.4b, play the same role as the focal elements in possibilistic bodies of evidence formulated within evidence theory. That is, focal elements and α-cuts correspond to each other in the two formulations of possibility theory. In our example, the α-cuts (or focal elements) are $A_1 = \{21\}, A_2 = \{20, 21, 22\}, A_3 = \{19, 20, 21, 22, 23\}$. Using (7.50), we can readily find that $\mathrm{Pos}(A_1) = \mathrm{Pos}(A_2) = \mathrm{Pos}(A_3) = 1$ and $\mathrm{Pos}(\overline{A_1}) = 2/3$, $\mathrm{Pos}(\overline{A_2}) = 1/3$, $\mathrm{Pos}(\overline{A_3}) = 0$. Then, using (7.51), we obtain $\mathrm{Nec}(A_1) = 1/3$,

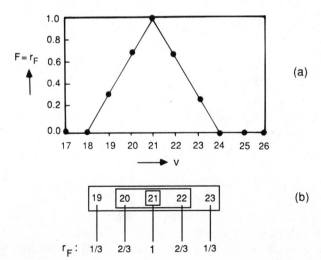

(a)

(b)

Figure 7.4 Possibility distribution for a fuzzy proposition.

Nec $(A_2) = 2/3$, Nec $(A_3) = 1$. We can also easily see that Nec $(A) = 0$ for any set A that contains no α-cut. Furthermore, using (7.33), we can calculate the basic probability assignment: $m(A_1) = 1 - 2/3 = 1/3, m(A_2) = 2/3 - 1/3 = 1/3, m(A_3) = 1/3 - 0 = 1/3$, and $m(A) = 0$ for any set A that is not an α-cut. Converting functions Pos and Nec into the combined function C, we obtain: $C(A_1) = 1/3, C(A_2) = 2/3, C(A_3) = 1, C(\overline{A_1}) = -1/3, C(\overline{A_2}) = -2/3, C(\overline{A_3}) = 0$.

When r_F is derived from a normal set F, as in our example, the two formulations of possibility theory are equivalent. The full equivalence breaks when F is not normal. In this case, the basic probability assignment function, which is defined in terms of the differences in values of function r_F, is not directly applicable. The reason is that the differences do not add to 1 when F is not normal. However, all other properties of possibility theory remain equivalent in both formulations.

We can see that possibility theory is a measure-theoretic counterpart of fuzzy set theory based upon the standard fuzzy operations. It provides us with appropriate tools for processing incomplete information expressed in terms of fuzzy propositions; consequently, it plays a major role in fuzzy logic (Chapter 8) and approximate reasoning (Chapter 11).

7.5 POSSIBILITY THEORY VERSUS PROBABILITY THEORY

The purpose of this section is to compare probability theory with possibility theory, and to use this comparison in comparing probability theory with fuzzy set theory. It is shown that probability theory and possibility theory are distinct theories, and neither is subsumed under the other.

The best way of comparing probabilistic and possibilistic conceptualizations of uncertainty is to examine the two theories from a broader perspective. Such a perspective is offered by evidence theory, within which probability theory and possibility theory are recognized as special branches. While the various characteristics of possibility theory within the broader framework of evidence theory are expounded in Sec. 7.3, we need to introduce their probabilistic counterparts to facilitate our discussion.

As is well known, a *probability measure*, Pro, is required to satisfy the equation

$$\text{Pro} \, (A \cup B) = \text{Pro} \, (A) + \text{Pro} \, (B) \tag{7.52}$$

for all sets $A, B \in \mathcal{P}(X)$ such that $A \cap B = \varnothing$.

This requirement is usually referred to as the *additivity axiom* of probability measures. Observe that this axiom is stronger than the superadditivity axiom of belief measures expressed by (7.3). This implies that probability measures are a special type of belief measures. This relationship between belief measures and probability measures is more precisely characterized by the following theorem.

Theorem 7.4. A belief measure Bel on a finite power set $\mathcal{P}(X)$ is a probability measure if and only if the associated basic probability assignment function m is given by $m(\{x\}) = \text{Bel}(\{x\})$ and $m(A) = 0$ for all subsets of X that are not singletons.

Proof: Assume that Bel is a probability measure. For the empty set $\varnothing$, the theorem trivially holds, since $m(\varnothing) = 0$ by definition of m. Let $A \neq \varnothing$ and assume $A = \{x_1, x_2, \ldots, x_n\}$. Then, by repeated application of the additivity axiom (7.52), we obtain

$$\text{Bel}(A) = \text{Bel}(\{x_1\}) + \text{Bel}(\{x_2, x_3, \ldots, x_n\})$$
$$= \text{Bel}(\{x_1\}) + \text{Bel}(\{x_2\}) + \text{Bel}(\{x_3, x_4, \ldots, x_n\})$$
$$= \ldots = \text{Bel}(\{x_1\}) + \text{Bel}(\{x_2\}) + \ldots + \text{Bel}(\{x_n\}).$$

Since $\text{Bel}(\{x\}) = m(\{x\})$ for any $x \in X$ by (7.10), we have

$$\text{Bel}(A) = \sum_{i=1}^{n} m(\{x_i\}).$$

Hence, Bel is defined in terms of a basic assignment that focuses only on singletons. Assume now that a basic probability assignment function m is given such that

$$\sum_{x \in X} m(\{x\}) = 1.$$

Then, for any sets $A, B \in \mathcal{P}(X)$ such that $A \cap B = \varnothing$, we have

$$\text{Bel}(A) + \text{Bel}(B) = \sum_{x \in A} m(\{x\}) + \sum_{x \in B} m(\{x\})$$
$$= \sum_{x \in A \cup B} m(\{x\}) = \text{Bel}(A \cup B);$$

consequently, Bel is a probability measure. This completes the proof. ∎

According to Theorem 7.4, probability measures on finite sets are thus fully represented by a function

$$p : X \rightarrow [0, 1]$$

such that $p(x) = m(\{x\})$. This function is usually called a *probability distribution function*. Let $\mathbf{p} = \langle p(x) | x \in X \rangle$ be referred to as a *probability distribution* on X.

When the basic probability assignment function focuses only on singletons, as required for probability measures, then the right-hand sides of (7.10) and (7.11) become equal. Hence,

$$\text{Bel}(A) = \text{Pl}(A) = \sum_{x \in A} m(\{x\})$$

for all $A \in \mathcal{P}(X)$; this can also be written, by utilizing the notion of a probability distribution function, as

$$\text{Bel}(A) = \text{Pl}(A) = \sum_{x \in A} p(x).$$

This means that the dual belief and plausibility measures merge under the additivity axiom of probability measures. It is therefore convenient, in this case, to denote them by a single symbol. Let us denote probability measures by Pro. Then,

$$\text{Pro}(A) = \sum_{x \in A} p(x) \tag{7.53}$$

for all $A \in \mathcal{P}(X)$.

Within probability measures, total ignorance is expressed by the uniform probability distribution

$$p(x) = \frac{1}{|X|} \quad (= m(\{x\}))$$

for all $x \in X$. This follows directly from the fact that basic assignments of probability measures are required to focus only on singletons (Theorem 7.4).

Probability measures, which are the subject of probability theory, have been studied at length. The literature of probability theory, including textbooks at various levels, is abundant. We therefore assume that the reader is familiar with the fundamentals of probability theory; consequently, we do not attempt a full coverage of probability theory in this book. However, we briefly review a few concepts from probability theory that are employed later in the text.

When a probability distribution $\mathbf{p}$ is defined on the Cartesian product $X \times Y$, it is called a *joint probability distribution*. Projections $\mathbf{p}_X$ and $\mathbf{p}_Y$ of $\mathbf{p}$ on X and Y, respectively, are called *marginal probability distributions*; they are defined by the formulas

$$p_X(x) = \sum_{y \in Y} p(x, y) \tag{7.54}$$

for each $x \in X$ and

$$p_Y(y) = \sum_{x \in X} p(x, y) \tag{7.55}$$

for each $y \in Y$. The marginal distributions are called *noninteractive* (in the probabilistic sense) with respect to $\mathbf{p}$ iff

$$p(x, y) = p_X(x) \cdot p_Y(y) \tag{7.56}$$

for all $x \in X$ and all $y \in Y$. This definition is a special case of the general definition of noninteractive bodies of evidence expressed by (7.18).

Two conditional probability distributions, $\mathbf{p}_{X|Y}$ and $\mathbf{p}_{Y|X}$ are defined in terms of a joint distribution $\mathbf{p}$ by the formulas

$$p_{X|Y}(x|y) = \frac{p(x, y)}{p_Y(y)} \tag{7.57}$$

and

$$p_{Y|X}(y|x) = \frac{p(x, y)}{p_X(x)} \tag{7.58}$$

for all $x \in X$ and all $y \in Y$. The value $p_{X|Y}(x|y)$ represents the probability that x occurs provided that y is known; similarly, $p_{Y|X}(y|x)$ designates the probability of y given x.

The two marginal distributions are called *independent* iff

$$p_{X|Y}(x|y) = p_X(x), \tag{7.59}$$

$$p_{Y|X}(y|x) = p_Y(y) \tag{7.60}$$

for all $x \in X$ and all $y \in Y$. Since the joint probability distribution is defined by

$$p(x, y) = p_{X|Y}(x|y) \cdot p_Y(y) = p_{Y|X}(y|x) \cdot p_X(x), \tag{7.61}$$

we can immediately see that the marginal distributions are independent if and only if they are noninterative.

We are now in a position to discuss similarities and differences between probability theory and possibility theory. Basic mathematical properties of both theories are summarized and contrasted in Table 7.4 to facilitate our discussion.

The two theories are similar in the sense that they both are subsumed not only under fuzzy measure theory, but also under the more restricted evidence theory. The inclusion relationship among the six types of measures employed in these theories is depicted in Fig. 7.5.

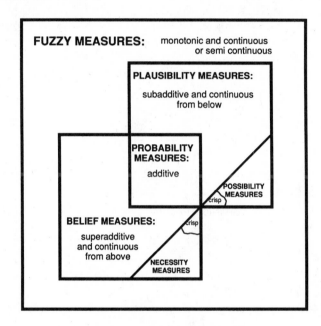

Figure 7.5 Inclusion relationship among the discussed types of measures.

As obvious from their mathematical properties, possibility, necessity, and probability measures do not overlap with one another except for one very special measure, which is characterized by only one focal element, a singleton. The two distribution functions that represent probabilities and possibilities become equal for this measure: one element of the universal set is assigned the value of 1, with all other elements being assigned a value of 0. This is clearly the only measure that represents perfect evidence.

Let us examine now some aspects of the relationship between probability theory and possibility theory in more detail. While possibility theory is based on two dual measures, which are special versions of belief and plausibility measures, probability theory coincides with that subarea of evidence theory in which belief measures and plausibility measures are equal. This results from a fundamental difference in the structure of respective bodies of evidence. While probabilistic bodies of evidence consist of singletons, possibilistic bodies of evidence are families of nested sets. Both probability and possibility measures are uniquely represented by distribution functions, but their normalization requirements are very different. Values of each probability distribution are required to add to 1, while for possibility distributions the largest values are required to be 1. Moreover, the latter requirement may even be abandoned when possibility theory is formulated in terms of fuzzy sets.

These differences in mathematical properties of the two theories make each theory suitable for modeling certain types of uncertainty and less suitable for modeling other types.

TABLE 7.4 PROBABILITY THEORY VERSUS POSSIBILITY THEORY:
COMPARISON OF MATHEMATICAL PROPERTIES FOR FINITE SETS

Probability Theory	Possibility Theory
Based on measures of *one type*: probability measures, Pro	Based on measures of *two types*: possibility measures, Pos, and necessity measures, Nec
Body of evidence consists of *singletons*	Body of evidence consists of a *family of nested subsets*
Unique representation of Pro by a *probability distribution function* $$\mathbf{p}: X \to [0,1]$$ via the formula $$\mathrm{Pro}(A) = \sum_{x \in A} p(x)$$	Unique representation of Pos by a *possibility distribution function* $$\mathbf{r}: X \to [0,1]$$ via the formula $$\mathrm{Pos}(A) = \max_{x \in A} r(x)$$
Normalization: $$\sum_{x \in X} p(x) = 1$$	*Normalization*: $$\max_{x \in X} r(x) = 1$$
Additivity: $$\mathrm{Pro}(A \cup B) = \mathrm{Pro}(A) + \mathrm{Pro}(B) - \mathrm{Pro}(A \cap B)$$	*Max/Min rules*: $$\mathrm{Pos}(A \cup B) = \max[\mathrm{Pos}(A), \mathrm{Pos}(B)]$$ $$\mathrm{Nec}(A \cap B) = \min[\mathrm{Nec}(A), \mathrm{Nec}(B)]$$
Not applicable	$$\mathrm{Nec}(A) = 1 - \mathrm{Pos}(\overline{A})$$ $$\mathrm{Pos}(A) < 1 \Rightarrow \mathrm{Nec}(A) = 0$$ $$\mathrm{Nec}(A) > 0 \Rightarrow \mathrm{Pos}(A) = 1$$
$$\mathrm{Pro}(A) + \mathrm{Pro}(\overline{A}) = 1$$	$$\mathrm{Pos}(A) + \mathrm{Pos}(\overline{A}) \geq 1$$ $$\mathrm{Nec}(A) + \mathrm{Nec}(\overline{A}) \leq 1$$ $$\max[\mathrm{Pos}(A), \mathrm{Pos}(\overline{A})] = 1$$ $$\min[\mathrm{Nec}(A), \mathrm{Nec}(\overline{A})] = 0$$
Total ignorance: $$p(x) = 1/|X| \text{ for all } x \in X$$	*Total ignorance*: $$r(x) = 1 \text{ for all } x \in X$$
Conditional probabilities: $$p_{X|Y}(x|y) = \frac{p(x,y)}{p_Y(y)}$$ $$p_{Y|X}(y|x) = \frac{p(x,y)}{p_X(x)}$$	*Conditional possibilities*: $$r_{X|Y}(x|y) = \begin{cases} r_X(x) & \text{for } r_X(x) < r_Y(y) \\ [r_Y(y), 1] & \text{for } r_X(x) \geq r_Y(y) \end{cases}$$ $$r_{Y|X}(y|x) = \begin{cases} r_Y(y) & \text{for } r_Y(y) < r_X(x) \\ [r_X(x), 1] & \text{for } r_Y(y) \geq r_X(x) \end{cases}$$
Probabilistic noninteraction: $$p(x,y) = p_X(x) \cdot p_Y(y) \qquad (a)$$ *Probabilistic independence*: $$p_{X|Y}(x|y) = p_X(x)$$ $$p_{Y|X}(y|x) = p_Y(y) \qquad (b)$$ $$(a) \Leftrightarrow (b)$$	*Possibilistic noninteraction*: $$r(x,y) = \min[r_X(x), r_Y(y)] \qquad (\alpha)$$ *Possibilistic independence*: $$r_{X|Y}(x|y) = r_X(x)$$ $$r_{Y|X}(y|x) = r_Y(y) \qquad (\beta)$$ $$(\beta) \Rightarrow (\alpha), \text{ but } (\alpha) \not\Rightarrow (\beta)$$

As is well known, for example, probability theory is an ideal tool for formalizing uncertainty in situations where class frequencies are known or where evidence is based on outcomes of a sufficiently long series of independent random experiments. Possibility theory, on the other hand, is ideal for formalizing incomplete information expressed in terms of fuzzy propositions, as explained in Sec. 7.4.

A fundamental difference between the two theories is in their expressions of total ignorance. In possibility theory, total uncertainty is expressed in the same way as in evidence theory: $m(X) = 1$ and $m(A) = 0$ for all $A \neq X$ or, equivalently, $r(x) = 1$ for all $x \in X$. In probability theory, on the contrary, it is expressed by the uniform probability distribution on the universal set: $m(\{x\}) = 1/|X|$ for all x. This choice is justified on several grounds within probability theory, where it is required that every uncertainty situation be characterized by a single probability distribution. On purely intuitive grounds, however, this requirement is too strong to allow us to obtain an honest characterization of total ignorance. If no information is available about the situation under consideration, then no distribution is supported by any evidence and, hence, a choice of one particular distribution does not make any sense. Total ignorance should be expressed in terms of the full set of possible probability distributions on X. This means, in turn, that the probability of each element of X should be allowed to take any value in $[0, 1]$: in face of total ignorance, we know, by definition, that the value of each probability is in $[0, 1]$, but we have no rationale to narrow down this range. However, such a formulation, which is based on imprecise probabilities, is foreign to probability theory.

It is significant that the mathematical structure of evidence theory allows us to describe and deal with interval-valued probabilities. Due to their properties, belief measures and plausibility measures may be interpreted as lower and upper probability estimates. In this interpretation, the two dual measures, Bel and Pl, are employed to form intervals [Bel (A), Pl (A)] for each $A \in \mathcal{P}(X)$, which are viewed as imprecise estimates of probabilities. These estimates are derived from coarse evidence expressed by the basic probability assignment function.

Possibility theory may also be interpreted in terms of interval-valued probabilities, provided that the normalization requirement is applied. Due to the nested structure of evidence, the intervals of estimated probabilities are not totally arbitrary. If Pos $(A) < 1$, then the estimated probabilities are in the interval $[0, \text{Pl}(A)]$; if Bel $(A) > 0$, then the estimated probabilities are in the interval [Bel (A), 1].

As is well known, there are multiple interpretations of probability theory. Similarly, there are multiple interpretations of possibility theory. Viewing necessity and possibility measures as lower and upper probabilities opens a bridge between the two theories, which allows us to adjust some of the interpretations of probability theory to the interval-valued probabilities of possibilistic type. However, other interpretations of possibility theory, totally devoid of any connection to probability theory, appear to be even more fundamental.

An important interpretation of possibility theory is based on the concept of similarity. In this interpretation, the possibility $r(x)$ reflects the degree of similarity between x and an ideal prototype, x_i, for which the possibility degree is 1. That is, $r(x)$ is expressed by a suitable distance between x and x_i defined in terms of relevant attributes of the elements involved. The closer x is to x_i according to the chosen distance, the more possible we consider it in this interpretation of possibility theory. In some cases, the closeness may be determined objectively by a defined measurement procedure. In other cases, it may be based on a subjective judgement of a person (e.g., an expert in the application area involved).

Another interpretation of possibility theory, distinct from the similarity-based interpretation, is founded on special orderings, $\leq_{\text{Pos}}$, defined on the power set $\mathcal{P}(X)$. For any $A, B \in \mathcal{P}(X)$, $A \leq_{\text{Pos}} B$ means that B is at least as possible as A. When $\leq_{\text{Pos}}$ satisfies the requirement

$$A \leq_{\text{Pos}} B \Rightarrow A \cup C \leq_{\text{Pos}} B \cup C \qquad (7.62)$$

for all $A, B, C \in \mathcal{P}(X)$, it is called a *comparative possibility relation*. It is known that the only measures which conform to comparative possibility ordering are possibility measures. It is also known that for each ordering $\leq_{\text{Pos}}$ there exists a dual ordering, $\leq_{\text{Nec}}$, defined by the equivalence

$$A \leq_{\text{Pos}} B \Leftrightarrow \overline{A} \leq_{\text{Nec}} \overline{B}. \qquad (7.63)$$

These dual orderings are called *comparative necessity relations*; the only measures that conform to them are necessity measures.

Although interpretations of possibility theory are still less developed than their probabilistic counterparts, it is already well established that possibility theory provides a link between fuzzy sets and probability theory. While some interpretations of possibility theory are connected with probability theory, other interpretations are not. The growing literature on interpretations of possibility theory is overviewed in Note 7.7.

When information regarding some phenomenon is given in both probabilistic and possibilistic terms, the two descriptions should be in some sense consistent. That is, given a probability measure, Pro, and a possibility measure, Pos, both defined on $\mathcal{P}(X)$, the two measures should satisfy some consistency condition. Although various consistency conditions may be required, the weakest one acceptable on intuitive grounds can be expressed as follows: an event that is probable to some degree must be possible at least to the same degree. That is, the weakest consistency condition is expressed formally by the inequality

$$\text{Pro}\,(A) \leq \text{Pos}\,(A) \qquad (7.64)$$

for all $A \in \mathcal{P}(X)$. The strongest consistency condition would require, on the other hand, that any event with nonzero probability must be fully possible. Formally,

$$\text{Pro}\,(A) > 0 \Rightarrow \text{Pos}\,(A) = 1 \qquad (7.65)$$

for all $A \in \mathcal{P}(X)$. Other consistency conditions may also be formulated that are stronger than (7.64) and weaker than (7.65).

The degree of *probability-possibility consistency*, c, between Pro and Pos can be measured in terms of the associated probability distribution function $\mathbf{p}$ and possibility distribution function $\mathbf{r}$ by the formula

$$c(\mathbf{p}, \mathbf{r}) = \sum_{x \in X} p(x) \cdot r(x). \qquad (7.66)$$

Probability-possibility consistency, at least in its weakest form (7.64), is an essential requirement in any probability-possibility transformation. The motivation to study probability-possibility transformations has arisen not only from our desire to comprehend the relationship between the two theories of uncertainty, but also from some practical problems. Examples of these problems are: constructing a membership grade function of a fuzzy set from statistical data, constructing a probability measure from a given possibility measure in the context of decision making or systems modeling, combining probabilistic and possibilistic information in expert systems, or transforming probabilities to possibilities to reduce computational complexity. To deal with these problems, various probability-possibility transformations have been suggested in the literature. Except for the normalization requirements, they differ from one another substantially, ranging from simple ratio scaling to more sophisticated transformations based upon various principles.

To discuss these various possibility-probability transformations, let us introduce convenient notational assumptions first. Let $X = \{x_1, x_2, \ldots, x_n\}$ and let $p_i = p(x_i), r_i = r(x_i)$. Assume that elements of X are ordered in such a way that possibility distributions,

$$\mathbf{r} = \langle r_1, r_2, \ldots, r_n \rangle,$$

and probability distributions,

$$\mathbf{p} = \langle p_1, p_2, \ldots, p_n \rangle,$$

are always nonincreasing sequences. That is, $r_i \geq r_{i+1}$ and $p_i \geq p_{i+1}$ for all $i = 1, 2, \ldots, n-1$. Furthermore, we have

$$r_1 = 1 \text{ and } \sum_{i=1}^{n} p_i = 1$$

as possibilistic and probabilistic normalizations, respectively.

The most common transformations $\mathbf{p} \leftrightarrow \mathbf{r}$ are based on the *ratio scale*: $r_i = p_i \alpha$ for all i, where α is a positive constant. They are expressed by the equations

$$r_i = \frac{p_i}{p_1}, \tag{7.67}$$

$$p_i = \frac{r_i}{r_1 + r_2 + \ldots + r_n}. \tag{7.68}$$

Another type of transformations, less common, is based on the *interval scale*: $r_i = p_1 \alpha + \beta$ for all i, where α and β are positive constants. These transformations are defined by the equations:

$$r_i = 1 - \alpha(p_1 - p_i), \tag{7.69}$$

$$p_i = \frac{1}{\alpha}(r_i - \bar{r}) + \frac{1}{n}, \tag{7.70}$$

where $\bar{r}$ denotes the arithmetic mean of the given possibilities r_i. This transformation type depends on the value of α and, hence, it is not unique; the value can be determined by adding a requirement regarding the relationship between $\mathbf{p}$ and $\mathbf{r}$.

Transformations defined by the equations

$$r_i = \sum_{j=1}^{n} \min(p_i, p_j), \tag{7.71}$$

$$p_i = \sum_{j=i}^{n} \frac{(r_j - r_{j+1})}{j}, \tag{7.72}$$

are often cited in the literature. Equation (7.71) is based on the view that the degree of necessity of event $A \subseteq X$ is the extra amount of probability of elementary events in A over the amount of probability assigned to the most frequent elementary event outside A. Equation (7.72) expresses a probabilistic approximation of the given possibilistic body of evidence obtained by distributing values of the basic probability assignment equally among singletons of the respective focal elements. It was also suggested to replace (7.71) in these transformations with the formula

$$r_i = \sum_{j=i}^{n} p_j, \tag{7.73}$$

which yields the smallest possibility distribution that satisfies the weak probability-possibility consistency (7.64). However, when (7.73) is combined with (7.72), then $\mathbf{p} \to \mathbf{r}$ and $\mathbf{r} \to \mathbf{p}'$, where $\mathbf{p}' \neq \mathbf{p}$. Observe that $\mathbf{p}' = \mathbf{p}$ in each of the other pairs of transformations. Additional probability-possibility transformations, which employ relevant information measures, were proposed in the literature. These transformations, referred to as information-preserving transformations, are discussed in Sec. 9.7.

NOTES

7.1. The concept of a fuzzy measure was introduced by Sugeno [1974, 1977]. A graduate textbook on fuzzy measure theory was written by Wang and Klir [1992].

7.2. The *mathematical theory of evidence* that is based on the complementary *belief and plausibility measures* was originated and developed by Glenn Shafer [1976]. It was motivated by previous work on upper and lower probabilities by Dempster [1967], as well as by Shafer's historical reflection upon the concept of probability [Shafer, 1978] and his critical examination of the Bayesian approach to evidence [Shafer, 1976, 1981]. Although Shafer's book [1976] is still the best introduction to evidence theory, the two-volume book by Guan and Bell [1991, 1992] is more up-to-date and covers the rapidly growing literature dealing with this theory.

7.3. Derivations of the conversion formulas in Table 7.3 are given in the books by Shafer [1976] and Guan and Bell [1991, 1992].

7.4. Given a body of evidence $\langle \mathcal{F}, m \rangle$, the corresponding functions Pl and Bel can be viewed as *upper and lower probabilities* that characterize a set of probability measures. Individual probability measures in the set can be defined by the following allocation procedure:
  1. Choose a particular $x_A \in A$ for each $A \in \mathcal{F}$.
  2. Set $\text{Pro}(\{x\}) = p(x) = \sum_{A|x_A=x} m(A)$ for all $x \in X$.
For all probability measures Pro that can be assigned in this way, the inequalities

$$\text{Bel}(A) \leq \text{Pro}(A) \leq \text{Pl}(A) \tag{7.74}$$

are known to hold for all $A \in \mathcal{F}$. This explains the interpretation of Pl and Bel as upper and lower probabilities, respectively. A body of evidence thus represents for each $A \in \mathcal{P}(X)$, the range $[\text{Bel}(A), \text{Pl}(A)]$ of feasible probabilities; this range is clearly $[0, 1]$ for all $A \neq \emptyset$ and $A \neq X$ in the face of total ignorance.

  Lower and upper probabilities were first investigated by Dempster [1967] independent of the concepts of belief and plausibility measures.

7.5. Evidence theory is only one mathematical tool for dealing with imprecise probabilities. A general coverage of statistical reasoning and decision making with imprecise probabilities, not restricted to evidence theory, was prepared by Walley [1991].

7.6. Possibility theory was originally introduced in the context of fuzzy sets by Zadeh [1978b]. A book by Dubois and Prade [1988a] is the most comprehensive coverage of possibility theory. It is interesting that the need for possibility theory in economics was perceived by the British economist Shackle [1961] well before it emerged from fuzzy set theory [Zadeh, 1978b] or from evidence theory [Shafer, 1976].

7.7. Connections between probability theory, possibility theory, and fuzzy set theory are explored in a paper by Dubois and Prade [1993b]. Some interpretations of possibility theory are also overviewed in the paper. Other publications that deal with various interpretations of possibility theory include [Ruspini, 1989, 1991b; Shafer, 1987; Klir and Harmanec, 1994; Zadeh, 1978b; Shackle, 1961].

7.8. Equations (7.44) and (7.45) for conditional possibilities were derived by Hisdal [1978]. Various proposals for choosing one value from the interval of conditional possibilities were presented by Dubois and Prade [1985a, 1986b, 1990a, 1991a], Nguyen [1978c], Ramer [1989], and Cavallo and Klir [1982].

7.9. Various forms of probability-possibility consistency are overviewed in a paper by Delgado and Moral [1987].

EXERCISES

7.1. Compare the concepts of fuzzy sets and fuzzy measures in some situations connected with, for example, the degree of education of a person, the age of a painting or a collector's coin, the size of a city or a country, the degree of inflation or unemployment in a country, the distance between two cities, and so on.

7.2. Let $X = \{a, b, c, d\}$. Given the basic assignment $m(\{a, b, c\}) = .5$, $m(\{a, b, d\}) = .2$, and $m(X) = .3$, determine the corresponding belief and plausibility measures.

7.3. Repeat Exercise 7.2 for some of the basic assignments given in Table 7.5, where subsets of X are defined by their characteristic functions.

7.4. Show that the function Bel determined by (7.10) for any given basic assignment m is a belief measure.

7.5. Show that the function Pl determined by (7.11) for any given basic assignment m is a plausibility measure.

7.6. Let $X = \{a, b, c, d\}$. Given the belief measure Bel $(\{b\}) = .1$, Bel $(\{a, b\}) = .2.$, Bel $(\{b, c\}) = .3$, Bel $(\{b, d\}) = 1$, determine the corresponding basic assignment.

7.7. Using (7.5) and (7.12), derive a formula by which the basic assignment for a given plausibility measure can be determined.

7.8. Calculate the joint basic assignment $m_{1,2}$ for the focal elements $C, R \cup D$, and $D \cup C$ in Example 7.1. Also determine Bel$_{1,2}$ for these focal elements.

7.9. For each of the focal elements in Example 4.1 (Raphael's paintings), determine the ranges $[\text{Bel}_1(A), \text{Pl}_1(A)]$, $[\text{Bel}_2(A), \text{Pl}_2(A)]$, $[\text{Bel}_{1,2}(A), \text{Pl}_{1,2}(A)]$, which can be viewed as ranges of feasible probabilites corresponding to these bodies of evidence (Note 7.4).

7.10. Repeat Exercise 7.9 for some of the basic assignments given in Table 7.5.

7.11. Calculate $m_x(\{1, 3\})$, $m_x(X)$, and $m_y(\{b, c\})$ in Example 7.2.

TABLE 7.5   BASIC ASSIGNMENTS EMPLOYED IN EXERCISES

a	b	c	d	m_1	m_2	m_3	m_4	m_5	m_6	m_7	m_8	m_9	m_{10}
0	0	0	0	0	0	0	0	0	0	0	0	0	0
0	0	0	1	.2	0	0	.2	.2	.3	0	.1	0	.7
0	0	1	0	0	.4	0	0	.2	0	0	.1	0	.1
0	0	1	1	0	0	0	.1	0	.3	0	.1	0	0
0	1	0	0	0	.5	0	0	.3	0	0	.1	0	0
0	1	0	1	0	0	0	0	0	0	.4	.1	0	0
0	1	1	0	.3	0	0	0	0	0	.2	.1	.1	0
0	1	1	1	0	0	0	0	0	.3	.1	.1	.1	.2
1	0	0	0	.1	.1	.2	0	.3	0	.3	.1	.1	0
1	0	0	1	0	0	0	0	0	0	0	.1	.1	0
1	0	1	0	.1	0	.3	0	0	0	0	.1	.1	0
1	0	1	1	0	0	0	0	0	0	0	0	.1	0
1	1	0	0	0	0	0	0	0	0	0	0	.1	0
1	1	0	1	.2	0	0	0	0	0	0	0	.1	0
1	1	1	0	.1	0	.4	0	0	0	0	0	.1	0
1	1	1	1	0	0	.1	.7	0	.1	0	0	.1	0

7.12. Verify completely that the marginal bodies of evidence given in Table 7.2b, which were obtained as projections of the joint body of evidence given in Table 7.2a, are noninteractive.

7.13. Determine whether each of the basic assignments given in Table 7.5 represents a probability measure, possibility measure, or neither of these.

7.14. Given two noninteractive marginal possibility distributions $r_X = \langle 1, .8, .5 \rangle$ and $r_Y = \langle 1, .7 \rangle$ on sets $X = \{a, b, c\}$ and $Y = \{\alpha, \beta\}$, respectively, determine the corresponding basic distributions. Then, calculate the joint basic distribution in two different ways:
(a) by the rules of possibility theory;
(b) by the rules of evidence theory.
Show visually (as in Fig. 7.3) the focal elements of the marginal and joint distributions.

7.15. Repeat Exercise 7.14 for the following marginal possibility distributions:
(a) $r_X = \langle 1, .7, .2 \rangle$ on $X = \{a, b, c\}$ and $r_Y = \langle 1, 1, .4 \rangle$ on $Y = \{\alpha, \beta, \gamma\}$;
(b) $r_X = \langle 1, .9, .6, .2 \rangle$ on $X = \{a, b, c, d\}$ and $r_Y = \langle 1, .6 \rangle$ on $Y = \{\alpha, \beta\}$.

7.16. Show that a belief measure that satisfies (7.19) is based on nested focal elements.

7.17. Show that a plausibility measure that satisfies (7.20) is based on nested focal elements.

7.18. Determine the basic assignment, possibility measure, and necessity measure for each of the following possibility distributions defined on $X = \{x_i | i \in \mathbb{N}_n\}$ for appropriate values of n:
(a) $^1r = \langle 1, .8, .8, .5, .2 \rangle$;
(b) $^2r = \langle 1, 1, 1, .7, .7, .7, .7 \rangle$;
(c) $^3r = \langle 1, .9, .8, .6, .5, .3, .3 \rangle$;
(d) $^4r = \langle 1, .5, .4, .3, .2, .1 \rangle$;
(e) $^5r = \langle 1, 1, .8, .8, .5, .5, .5, .1 \rangle$.
Assume in each case that $r_i = r(x_i)$, $i \in \mathbb{N}_n$.

7.19. Determine the possibility distribution, possibility measure, and necessity measure for each of the following basic distributions defined on $X = \{x_i | i \in \mathbb{N}_n\}$ for appropriate values of n:
(a) $^1m = \langle 0, 0, .3, .2, 0, .4, .1 \rangle$;
(b) $^2m = \langle .1, .1, .1, 0, .1, .2, .2, .2 \rangle$;
(c) $^3m = \langle 0, 0, 0, 0, .5, .5 \rangle$;
(d) $^4m = \langle 0, .2, 0, .2, 0, .3, 0, .3 \rangle$;

(e) $^5\mathbf{m} = \langle .1, .2, .3, .4 \rangle$;

(f) $^6\mathbf{m} = \langle .4, .3, .2, .1 \rangle$.

Assume in each case that $m_i = m(\{x_1, x_2, \ldots, x_i\}), i \in \mathbb{N}_n$.

7.20. Calculate the commonality numbers for some of the basic assignments given in Table 7.5.

7.21. Let basic probability assignments m_1 and m_2 on $X = \{a, b, c, d\}$, which are obtained from two independent sources, be defined as follows: $m_1(\{a, b\}) = .2, m_1(\{a, c\}) = .3, m_1(\{b, d\}) = .5; m_2(\{a, d\}) = .2, m_2(\{b, c\}) = .5, m_2(\{a, b, c\}) = .3$. Calculate the combined basic probability assignment $m_{1,2}$ by using the Dempster rule of combination.

7.22. Let $X = \{a, b, c, d, e\}$ and $Y = \mathbb{N}_8$. Using a joint possibility distribution on $X \times Y$ given in terms of the matrix

$$\begin{bmatrix} 1 & 0 & 0 & .3 & .5 & .2 & .4 & .1 \\ 0 & .7 & 0 & .6 & 1 & 0 & .4 & .3 \\ 0 & .5 & 0 & 0 & 1 & 0 & 1 & .5 \\ 1 & 1 & 1 & .5 & 0 & 0 & 1 & .4 \\ .8 & 0 & .9 & 0 & 1 & .7 & 1 & .2 \end{bmatrix}$$

where rows are assigned to elements a, b, c, d, e, and columns are assigned to numbers $1, 2, \ldots, 8$, determine:

(a) marginal possibilities;

(b) joint and marginal basic assignments;

(c) both conditional possibilities given by (7.44) and (7.45);

(d) hypothetical joint possibility distribution based on the assumption of noninteraction.

7.23. Determine values of function C given by (7.46) for the bodies of evidence defined by m_3, m_4, and m_6 in Table 7.5.

7.24. Let $C(A)$ for all subsets of $X = \{a, b, c, d\}$ be the numbers 0, .4, .6, .7, $-.7$, .4, .6, .9, $-.9$, .4, .6, .7, $-.7$, .4, $-.4$, and 1 (listed in the same order as in Table 7.5). Determine Nec (A) and Pos (A) for all A.

7.25. Let a fuzzy set F be defined on $\mathbb{N}$ by $F = .4/1 + .7/2 + 1/3 + .8/4 + .5/5$ and $A(x) = 0$ for all $x \notin \{1, 2, 3, 4, 5\}$. Determine Nec (A) and Pos (A) induced by F for all $A \in \mathcal{P}(\{1, 2, 3, 4, 5\})$.

8

FUZZY LOGIC

8.1 CLASSICAL LOGIC: AN OVERVIEW

We assume that the reader of this text is familiar with the fundamentals of classical logic. Therefore, this section is solely intended to provide a brief overview of the basic concepts of classical logic and to introduce terminology and notation employed in our discussion of fuzzy logic.

Logic is the study of the methods and principles of *reasoning* in all its possible forms. Classical logic deals with *propositions* that are required to be either *true* or *false*. Each proposition has its opposite, which is usually called a *negation* of the proposition. A proposition and its negation are required to assume opposite truth values.

One area of logic, referred to as *propositional logic*, deals with combinations of variables that stand for arbitrary propositions. These variables are usually called *logic variables* (or propositional variables). As each variable stands for a hypothetical proposition, it may assume either of the two truth values; the variable is not committed to either truth value unless a particular proposition is substituted for it.

One of the main concerns of propositional logic is the study of rules by which new logic variables can be produced as functions of some given logic variables. It is not concerned with the internal structure of the propositions that the logic variables represent.

Assume that n logic variables $v_1, v_2, \ldots, v_n$ are given. A new logic variable can then be defined by a function that assigns a particular truth value to the new variable for each combination of truth values of the given variables. This function is usually called a *logic function*. Since n logic variables may assume 2^n prospective truth values, there are 2^{2^n} possible logic functions of these variables. For example, all the logic functions of two variables are listed in Table 8.1, where falsity and truth are denoted by 0 and 1, respectively, and the resulting 16 logic variables are denoted by $w_1, w_2, \ldots, w_{16}$. Logic functions of one or two variables are usually called *logic operations*.

The key issue of propositional logic is the expression of all the logic functions of n variables ($n \in \mathbb{N}$), the number of which grows extremely rapidly with increasing values of n, with the aid of a small number of simple logic functions. These simple functions are

TABLE 8.1   LOGIC FUNCTIONS OF TWO VARIABLES

v_2	1	1	0	0	Adopted name	Adopted	Other names used	Other symbols used
v_1	1	0	1	0	of function	symbol	in the literature	in the literature
w_1	0	0	0	0	Zero function	**0**	Falsum	$F, \perp$
w_2	0	0	0	1	Nor function	$v_1 \curlyvee v_2$	Pierce function	$v_1 \downarrow v_2$, NOR(v_1, v_2)
w_3	0	0	1	0	Inhibition	$v_1 \Leftarrow\!\!\!| \, v_2$	Proper inequality	$v_1 > v_2$
w_4	0	0	1	1	Negation	$\overline{v}_2$	Complement	$\neg v_2, \sim v_2, v_2^0$
w_5	0	1	0	0	Inhibition	$v_1 |\!\!\!\Rightarrow v_2$	Proper inequality	$v_1 < v_2$
w_6	0	1	0	1	Negation	$\overline{v}_1$	Complement	$\neg v_1, \sim v_1, v_1^0$
w_7	0	1	1	0	Exclusive-or function	$v_1 \otimes v_2$	Nonequivalence	$v_1 \not\equiv v_2, v_1 \oplus v_2$
w_8	0	1	1	1	Nand function	$v_1 \barwedge v_2$	Sheffer stroke	$v_1|v_2$, NAND(v_1, v_2)
w_9	1	0	0	0	Conjunction	$v_1 \wedge v_2$	And function	$v_1 \& v_2, v_1 v_2$
w_{10}	1	0	0	1	Biconditional	$v_1 \Leftrightarrow v_2$	Equivalence	$v_1 \equiv v_2$
w_{11}	1	0	1	0	Assertion	v_1	Identity	v_1^1
w_{12}	1	0	1	1	Implication	$v_1 \Leftarrow v_2$	Conditional, inequality	$v_1 \subset v_2, v_1 \geq v_2$
w_{13}	1	1	0	0	Assertion	v_2	Identity	v_2^1
w_{14}	1	1	0	1	Implication	$v_1 \Rightarrow v_2$	Conditional, inequality	$v_1 \supset v_2, v_1 \leq v_2$
w_{15}	1	1	1	0	Disjunction	$v_1 \vee v_2$	Or function	$v_1 + v_2$
w_{16}	1	1	1	1	One function	**1**	Verum	T, I

preferably logic operations of one or two variables, which are called *logic primitives*. It is known that this can be accomplished only with some sets of logic primitives. We say that a set of primitives is *complete* if any logic function of variables $v_1, v_2, \ldots, v_n$ (for any finite n) can be composed by a finite number of these primitives.

Two of the many complete sets of primitives have been predominant in propositional logic: (i) negation, conjunction, and disjunction; and (ii) negation and implication. By combining, for example, negations, conjunctions, and disjunctions (employed as primitives) in appropriate algebraic expressions, referred to as *logic formulas*, we can form any other logic function. Logic formulas are then defined recursively as follows:

1. if v denotes a logic variable, then v and $\overline{v}$ are logic formulas;
2. if a and b denote logic formulas, then $a \wedge b$ and $a \vee b$ are also logic formulas;
3. the only logic formulas are those defined by the previous two rules.

Every logic formula of this type defines a logic function by composing it from the three primary functions. To define a unique function, the order in which the individual compositions are to be performed must be specified in some way. There are various ways in which this order can be specified. The most common is the usual use of parentheses as in any other algebraic expressions.

Other types of logic formulas can be defined by replacing some of the three operations in this definition with other operations or by including some additional operations. We may replace, for example, $a \wedge b$ and $a \vee b$ in the definition with $a \Rightarrow b$, or we may simply add $a \Rightarrow b$ to the definition.

While each proper logic formula represents a single logic function and the associated logic variable, different formulas may represent the same function and variable. If they do, we consider them equivalent. When logic formulas a and b are equivalent, we write $a = b$. For example,

$$(\overline{v}_1 \wedge \overline{v}_2) \vee (v_1 \wedge \overline{v}_3) \vee (v_2 \wedge v_3) = (\overline{v}_2 \wedge \overline{v}_3) \vee (\overline{v}_1 \wedge v_3) \vee (v_1 \wedge v_2),$$

as can be easily verified by evaluating each of the formulas for all eight combinations of truth values of the logic variables v_1, v_2, v_3.

When the variable represented by a logic formula is always true regardless of the truth values assigned to the variables participating in the formula, it is called a *tautology*; when it is always false, it is called a *contradiction*. For example, when two logic formulas a and b are equivalent, then $a \Leftrightarrow b$ is a tautology, while the formula $a \wedge \overline{b}$ is a contradiction. Tautologies are important for deductive reasoning because they represent logic formulas that, due to their form, are true on logical grounds alone.

Various forms of tautologies can be used for making deductive inferences. They are referred to as *inference rules*. Examples of some tautologies frequently used as inference rules are

$$(a \wedge (a \Rightarrow b)) \Rightarrow b \ (modus \ ponens),$$

$$(\overline{b} \wedge (a \Rightarrow b)) \Rightarrow \overline{a} \ (modus \ tollens),$$

$$((a \Rightarrow b) \wedge (b \Rightarrow c)) \Rightarrow (a \Rightarrow c) \ (hypothetical \ syllogism).$$

Modus ponens, for instance, states that given two true propositions, "a" and "$a \Rightarrow b$" (the premises), the truth of the proposition "b" (the conclusion) may be inferred.

Every tautology remains a tautology when any of its variables is replaced with any arbitrary logic formula. This property is another example of a powerful rule of inference, referred to as a *rule of substitution*.

It is well established that propositional logic based on a finite set of logic variables is isomorphic to finite set theory under a particular correspondence between components of these two mathematical systems. Furthermore, both of these systems are isomorphic to a finite Boolean algebra, which is a mathematical system defined by abstract (interpretation-free) entities and their axiomatic properties.

A *Boolean algebra* on a set B is defined as the quadruple

$$\mathcal{B} = \langle B, +, \cdot, - \rangle,$$

where the set B has at least two elements (bounds) $\mathbf{0}$ and $\mathbf{1}$; $+$ and $\cdot$ are binary operations on B, and $-$ is a unary operation on B for which the properties listed in Table 8.2 are satisfied. Not all of these properties are necessary for an axiomatic characterization of Boolean algebras; we present this larger set of properties in order to emphasize the relationship between Boolean algebras, set theory, and propositional logic.

Properties (B1)–(B4) are common to all lattices. Boolean algebras are therefore lattices that are distributive (B5), bounded (B6), and complemented (B7)–(B9). This means that each Boolean algebra can also be characterized in terms of a partial ordering on a set, which is defined as follows: $a \leq b$ if $a \cdot b = a$ or, alternatively, if $a + b = b$.

The isomorphisms between finite Boolean algebra, set theory, and propositional logic guarantee that every theorem in any one of these theories has a counterpart in each of the

TABLE 8.2   PROPERTIES OF BOOLEAN ALGEBRAS

(B1)	Idempotence	$a + a = a$
		$a \cdot a = a$
(B2)	Commutativity	$a + b = b + a$
		$a \cdot b = b \cdot a$
(B3)	Associativity	$(a + b) + c = a + (b + c)$
		$(a \cdot b) \cdot c = a \cdot (b \cdot c)$
(B4)	Absorption	$a + (a \cdot b) = a$
		$a \cdot (a + b) = a$
(B5)	Distributivity	$a \cdot (b + c) = (a \cdot b) + (a \cdot c)$
		$a + (b \cdot c) = (a + b) \cdot (a + c)$
(B6)	Universal bounds	$a + 0 = a, a + 1 = 1$
		$a \cdot 1 = a, a \cdot 0 = 0$
(B7)	Complementarity	$a + \bar{a} = 1$
		$a \cdot \bar{a} = 0$
		$\bar{1} = 0$
(B8)	Involution	$\bar{\bar{a}} = a$
(B9)	Dualization	$\overline{a + b} = \bar{a} \cdot \bar{b}$
		$\overline{a \cdot b} = \bar{a} + \bar{b}$

TABLE 8.3   CORRESPONDENCES DEFINING
ISOMORPHISMS BETWEEN SET THEORY,
BOOLEAN ALGEBRA, AND PROPOSITIONAL LOGIC

Set theory	Boolean algebra	Propositional logic
$\mathcal{P}(X)$	B	$\mathcal{L}(V)$
$\cup$	$+$	$\vee$
$\cap$	$\cdot$	$\wedge$
$-$	$-$	$-$
X	1	1
$\varnothing$	0	0
$\subseteq$	$\leq$	$\Rightarrow$

other two theories. These counterparts can be obtained from one another by applying the substitutional correspondences in Table 8.3. All symbols used in this table are previously defined in the text except for the symbols V and $\mathcal{L}(V)$, which denote here, respectively, a set of logic variables and the set of all combinations of truth values of these variables. The combination containing only truths is denoted by **1**; the one containing only falsities is denoted by **0**. It is required that the cardinalities of sets $\mathcal{P}(X)$, B, and $\mathcal{L}(V)$ be equal. These isomorphisms allow us, in effect, to cover all these theories by developing only one of them.

Propositional logic is concerned only with those logic relationships that depend on the way in which propositions are composed from other propositions by logic operations. These latter propositions are treated as unanalyzed wholes. This is not adequate for many instances of deductive reasoning for which the internal structure of propositions cannot be ignored.

Propositions are sentences expressed in some language. Each sentence representing a proposition can fundamentally be broken down into a *subject* and a *predicate*. In other words, a simple proposition can be expressed, in general, in the canonical form

$$x \text{ is } P,$$

where x is a symbol of a subject, and P designates a predicate that characterizes a property. For example, "Austria is a German-speaking country" is a proposition in which "Austria" stands for a subject (a particular country) and "a German-speaking country" is a predicate that characterizes a specific property, namely, the property of being a country whose inhabitants speak German. This proposition is true.

Instead of dealing with particular propositions, we may use the general form "x is P," where x now stands for any subject from a designated universe of discourse X. The predicate P then plays the role of a function defined on X, which for each value of x forms a proposition. This function is usually called a *predicate* and is denoted by $P(x)$. Clearly, a predicate becomes a proposition which is either true or false when a particular subject from X is substituted for x.

It is useful to extend the concept of a predicate in two ways. First, it is natural to extend it to more than one variable. This leads to the notion of an n-ary predicate $P(x_1, x_2, \ldots, x_n)$, which for $n = 1$ represents a property and for $n \geq 2$ an n-ary relation among subjects from designated universal sets $X_i (i \in \mathbb{N}_n)$. For example,

$$x_1 \text{ is a citizen of } x_2$$

is a binary predicate, where x_1 stands for individual persons from a designated population X_1 and x_2 stands for individual countries from a designated set X_2 of countries. Here, elements of X_2 are usually called *objects* rather than subjects. For convenience, n-ary predicates for $n = 0$ are defined as propositions in the same sense as in propositional logic.

Another way of extending the scope of a predicate is to quantify its applicability with respect to the domain of its variables. Two kinds of quantification have been predominantly used for predicates; they are referred to as existential quantification and universal quantification.

Existential quantification of a predicate $P(x)$ is expressed by the form

$$(\exists x)P(x),$$

which represents the sentence "There exists an individual x (in the universal set X of the variable x) such that x is P" (or the equivalent sentence "Some $x \in X$ are P"). The symbol $\exists$ is called an *existential quantifier*. We have the following equality:

$$(\exists x)P(x) = \bigvee_{x \in X} P(x). \tag{8.1}$$

Universal quantification of a predicate $P(x)$ is expressed by the form

$$(\forall x)P(x),$$

which represents the sentence "For every individual x (in the designated universal set), x is P" (or the equivalent sentence, "All $x \in X$ are P"). The symbol $\forall$ is called a *universal quantifier*. Clearly, the following equality holds:

$$(\forall x)P(x) = \bigwedge_{x \in X} P(x). \tag{8.2}$$

For n-ary predicates, we may use up to n quantifiers of either kind, each applying to one variable. For instance,

$$(\exists x_1)(\forall x_2)(\exists x_3)P(x_1, x_2, x_3)$$

stands for the sentence "there exists an $x_1 \in X_1$ such that for all $x_2 \in X_2$ there exists $x_3 \in X_3$ such that $P(x_1, x_2, x_3)$." For example, if $X_1 = X_2 = X_3 = [0, 1]$ and $P(x_1, x_2, x_3)$ means $x_1 \le x_2 \le x_3$, then the sentence is true (assume $x_1 = 0$ and $x_3 = 1$).

The standard existential and universal quantification of predicates can be conveniently generalized by conceiving a quantifier Q applied to a predicate $P(x), x \in X$, as a binary relation

$$Q \subseteq \{(\alpha, \beta)|\alpha, \beta \in \mathbb{N}, \alpha + \beta = |X|\},$$

where α, β specify the number of elements of X for which $P(x)$ is true or false, respectively. Formally,

$$\alpha = |\{x \in X|P(x) \text{ is true}\}|,$$

$$\beta = |\{x \in X|P(x) \text{ is false}\}|,$$

For example, when Q is defined by the condition $\alpha \ne 0$, we obtain the standard existential quantifier; when $\beta = 0$, Q becomes the standard universal quantifier; when $\alpha > \beta$, we obtain the so-called plurality quantifier, expressed by the word "most."

New predicates (quantified or not) can be produced from given predicates by logic formulas in the same way as new logic variables are produced by logic formulas in propositional logic. These formulas, which are called *predicate formulas*, are the essence of *predicate logic*.

8.2 MULTIVALUED LOGICS

The basic assumption upon which classical logic (or two-valued logic) is based—that every proposition is either true or false—has been questioned since Aristotle. In his treatise *On Interpretation*, Aristotle discusses the problematic truth status of matters that are future-contingent. Propositions about future events, he maintains, are neither actually true nor actually false, but potentially either; hence, their truth value is undetermined, at least prior to the event.

It is now well understood that propositions whose truth status is problematic are not restricted to future events. As a consequence of the Heisenberg principle of uncertainty, for example, it is known that truth values of certain propositions in quantum mechanics are inherently indeterminate due to fundamental limitations of measurement. In order to deal with such propositions, we must relax the true/false dichotomy of classical two-valued logic by allowing a third truth value, which may be called *indeterminate*.

The classical two-valued logic can be extended into *three-valued logic* in various ways. Several three-valued logics, each with its own rationale, are now well established. It is common in these logics to denote the truth, falsity, and indeterminacy by 1, 0, and 1/2, respectively. It is also common to define the negation $\bar{a}$ of a proposition a as $1 - a$; that is, $\bar{1} = 0, \bar{0} = 1$, *and* $\overline{1/2} = 1/2$. Other primitives, such as $\wedge, \vee, \Rightarrow$, and $\Leftrightarrow$, differ from one three-valued logic to another. Five of the best-known three-valued logics, labelled by the names of their originators, are defined in terms of these four primitives in Table 8.4.

TABLE 8.4   PRIMITIVES OF SOME THREE-VALUED LOGICS

a	b	Łukasiewicz $\wedge$	$\vee$	$\Rightarrow$	$\Leftrightarrow$	Bochvar $\wedge$	$\vee$	$\Rightarrow$	$\Leftrightarrow$	Kleene $\wedge$	$\vee$	$\Rightarrow$	$\Leftrightarrow$	Heyting $\wedge$	$\vee$	$\Rightarrow$	$\Leftrightarrow$	Reichenbach $\wedge$	$\vee$	$\Rightarrow$	$\Leftrightarrow$
0	0	0	0	1	1	0	0	1	1	0	0	1	1	0	0	1	1	0	0	1	1
0	½	0	½	1	½	½	½	½	½	0	½	1	½	0	½	1	0	0	½	1	½
0	1	0	1	1	0	0	1	1	0	0	1	1	0	0	1	1	0	0	1	1	0
½	0	0	½	½	½	½	½	½	½	0	½	½	½	0	½	0	0	0	½	½	½
½	½	½	½	1	1	½	½	½	½	½	½	½	½	½	½	1	1	½	½	1	1
½	1	½	1	1	½	½	½	½	½	½	1	1	½	½	1	1	½	½	1	1	½
1	0	0	1	0	0	0	1	0	0	0	1	0	0	0	1	0	0	0	1	0	0
1	½	½	1	½	½	½	½	½	½	½	1	½	½	½	1	½	½	½	1	½	½
1	1	1	1	1	1	1	1	1	1	1	1	1	1	1	1	1	1	1	1	1	1

We can see from Table 8.4 that all the logic primitives listed for the five three-valued logics fully conform to the usual definitions of these primitives in the classical logic for $a, b \in \{0, 1\}$, and that they differ from each other only in their treatment of the new truth value 1/2. We can also easily verify that none of these three-valued logics satisfies the law of contradiction ($a \wedge \bar{a} = 0$), the law of excluded middle ($a \vee \bar{a} = 1$), and some other tautologies of two-valued logic. The Bochvar three-valued logic, for example, clearly does not satisfy any of the tautologies of two-valued logic, since each of its primitives produces the truth value 1/2 whenever at least one of the propositions a and b assumes this value. Therefore, it is common to extend the usual concept of the tautology to the broader concept of a *quasi-tautology*. We say that a logic formula in a three-valued logic which does not assume the truth value 0 (falsity) regardless of the truth values assigned to its proposition variables is a quasi-tautology. Similarly, we say that a logic formula which does not assume the truth value 1 (truth) is a *quasi-contradiction*.

Once the various three-valued logics were accepted as meaningful and useful, it became desirable to explore generalizations into *n-valued logics* for an arbitrary number of truth values ($n \geq 2$). Several n-valued logics were, in fact, developed in the 1930s. For any given n, the truth values in these generalized logics are usually labelled by rational numbers in the unit interval $[0, 1]$. These values are obtained by evenly dividing the interval between 0 and 1 exclusive. The set T_n of truth values of an n-valued logic is thus defined as

$$T_n = \left\{ 0 = \frac{0}{n-1}, \frac{1}{n-1}, \frac{2}{n-1}, \cdots, \frac{n-2}{n-1}, \frac{n-1}{n-1} = 1 \right\}.$$

These values can be interpreted as *degrees of truth*.

The first series of n-valued logics for which $n \geq 2$ was proposed by Lukasiewicz in the early 1930s as a generalization of his three-valued logic. It uses truth values in T_n and defines the primitives by the following equations:

$$\bar{a} = 1 - a,$$
$$a \wedge b = \min(a, b),$$
$$a \vee b = \max(a, b), \tag{8.3}$$
$$a \Rightarrow b = \min(1, 1 + b - a),$$
$$a \Leftrightarrow b = 1 - |a - b|.$$

Lukasiewicz, in fact, used only negation and implication as primitives and defined the other logic operations in terms of these two primitives as follows:

$$a \vee b = (a \Rightarrow b) \Rightarrow b,$$

$$a \wedge b = \overline{\overline{a} \vee \overline{b}},$$

$$a \Leftrightarrow b = (a \Rightarrow b) \wedge (b \Rightarrow a).$$

It can be easily verified that (8.3) subsumes the definitions of the usual primitives of two-valued logic when $n = 2$, and defines the primitives of Lukasiewicz's three-valued logic as given in Table 8.4.

For each $n \geq 2$, the n-valued logic of Lukasiewicz is usually denoted in the literature by L_n. The truth values of L_n are taken from T_n, and its primitives are defined by (8.3). The sequence $(L_2, L_3, \ldots, L_\infty)$ of these logics contains two extreme cases—logics L_2 and L_∞. Logic L_2 is clearly the classical two-valued logic discussed in Sec. 8.1. Logic L_∞ is an *infinite-valued logic* whose truth values are taken from the countable set T_∞ of all rational numbers in the unit interval $[0, 1]$.

When we do not insist on taking truth values only from the set T_∞, but rather accept as truth values any real numbers in the interval $[0, 1]$, we obtain an alternative infinite-valued logic. Primitives of both of these infinite-valued logics are defined by (8.3); they differ in their sets of truth values. While one of these logics uses the set T_∞ as truth values, the other employs the set of all real numbers in the interval $[0,1]$. In spite of this difference, these two infinite-valued logics are established as essentially equivalent in the sense that they represent exactly the same tautologies. However, this equivalence holds only for logic formulas involving propositions; for predicate formulas with quantifiers, some fundamental differences between the two logics emerge.

Unless otherwise stated, the term *infinite-valued logic* is usually used in the literature to indicate the logic whose truth values are represented by all the real numbers in the interval $[0, 1]$. This is also quite often called the *standard Lukasiewicz logic* L_1, where the subscript 1 is an abbreviation for $\aleph_1$ (read aleph 1), which is the symbol commonly used to denote the cardinality of the continuum.

We can see that the standard Lukasiewicz logic L_1 is isomorphic to fuzzy set theory based on the standard fuzzy operators, in the same way as the two-valued logic is isomorphic to the crisp set theory. In fact, the membership grades $A(x)$ for $x \in X$, by which a fuzzy set A on the universal set X is defined, can be interpreted as the truth values of the proposition "x is a member of set A" in L_1. Conversely, the truth values for all $x \in X$ of any proposition "x is P" in L_1, where P is a vague (fuzzy) predicate (such as tall, young, expensive, dangerous, etc.), can be interpreted as the membership degrees $P(x)$ by which the fuzzy set characterized by the property P is defined on X. The isomorphism follows then from the fact that the logic operations of L_1, defined by (8.3), have exactly the same mathematical form as the corresponding standard operations on fuzzy sets.

The standard Lukasiewicz logic L_1 is only one of a variety of infinite-valued logics in the same sense that the standard fuzzy set theory is only one of a variety of fuzzy set theories which differ from one another by the set operations they employ. For each particular infinite-valued logic, we can derive the isomorphic fuzzy set theory.

The insufficiency of any single infinite-valued logic (and therefore the desirability of a variety of these logics) is connected with the notion of a complete set of logic primitives. It is known that there exists no finite complete set of logic primitives for any one infinite-valued logic. Hence, using a finite set of primitives that defines an infinite-valued logic, we can obtain only a subset of all the logic functions of the given primary logic variables. Because some applications require functions outside this subset, it may become necessary to resort to alternative logics.

8.3 FUZZY PROPOSITIONS

The fundamental difference between classical propositions and fuzzy propositions is in the range of their truth values. While each classical proposition is required to be either true or false, the truth or falsity of fuzzy propositions is a matter of degree. Assuming that truth and falsity are expressed by values 1 and 0, respectively, the degree of truth of each fuzzy proposition is expressed by a number in the unit interval [0, 1].

In this section, we focus on simple fuzzy propositions, which we classify into the following four types:

1. unconditional and unqualified propositions;
2. unconditional and qualified propositions;
3. conditional and unqualified propositions;
4. conditional and qualified propositions.

For each type, we introduce relevant canonical forms and discuss their interpretations.

Unconditional and Unqualified Fuzzy Propositions

The canonical form of fuzzy propositions of this type, p, is expressed by the sentence

$$p : \mathcal{V} \text{ is } F, \tag{8.4}$$

where $\mathcal{V}$ is a variable that takes values v from some universal set V, and F is a fuzzy set on V that represents a fuzzy predicate, such as tall, expensive, low, normal, and so on. Given a particular value of $\mathcal{V}$ (say, v), this value belongs to F with membership grade $F(v)$. This membership grade is then interpreted as the degree of truth, $T(p)$, of proposition p. That is,

$$T(p) = F(v) \tag{8.5}$$

for each given particular value v of variable $\mathcal{V}$ in proposition p. This means that T is in effect a fuzzy set on [0, 1], which assigns the membership grade $F(v)$ to each value v of variable $\mathcal{V}$.

To illustrate the introduced concepts, let variable $\mathcal{V}$ be the air temperature at some particular place on the Earth (measured in °F) and let the membership function shown in Fig. 8.1a represent, in a given context, the predicate *high*. Then, assuming that all relevant measurement specifications regarding the temperature are given, the corresponding fuzzy proposition, p, is expressed by the sentence

$$p : temperature \ (\mathcal{V}) \text{ is } high \ (F).$$

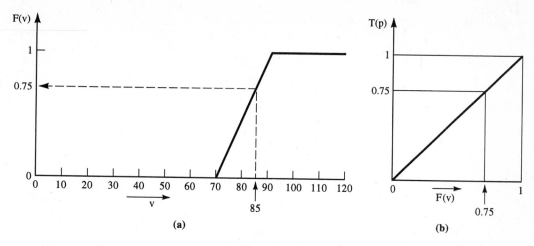

Figure 8.1 Components of the fuzzy proposition p: Temperature (V) is high (F).

The degree of truth, $T(p)$, depends on the actual value of the temperature and on the given definition (meaning) of the predicate *high*; it is defined by the membership function T in Fig. 8.1b, which represents (8.5). For example, if $v = 85$, then $F(85) = 0.75$ and $T(p) = 0.75$.

We can see that the role of function T is to provide us with a bridge between fuzzy sets and fuzzy propositions. Although the connection between grades of membership in F and degrees of truth of the associated fuzzy proposition p, as expressed by (8.5), is numerically trivial for unqualified propositions, it has a conceptual significance.

In some fuzzy propositions, values of variable V in (8.4) are assigned to individuals in a given set I. That is, variable V becomes a function $V : I \rightarrow V$, where $V(i)$ is the value of V for individual i in V. The canonical form (8.4) must then be modified to the form

$$p : V(i) \text{ is } F, \tag{8.6}$$

where $i \in I$.

Consider, for example, that I is a set of persons, each person is characterized by his or her *Age*, and a fuzzy set expressing the predicate *Young* is given. Denoting our variable by *Age* and our fuzzy set by *Young*, we can exemplify the general form (8.6) by the specific fuzzy proposition

$$p : Age(i) \text{ is } Young.$$

The degree of truth of this proposition, $T(p)$, is then determined for each person i in I via the equation

$$T(p) = Young\,(Age(i)).$$

As explained in Sec. 7.4, any proposition of the form (8.4) can be interpreted as a possibility distribution function r_F on V that is defined by the equation

$$r_F(v) = F(v)$$

for each value $v \in V$. Clearly, this interpretation applies to propositions of the modified form (8.6) as well.

Unconditional and Qualified Propositions

Propositions p of this type are characterized by either the canonical form

$$p : \mathcal{V} \text{ is } F \text{ is } S, \tag{8.7}$$

or the canonical form

$$p : \text{Pro} \{\mathcal{V} \text{ is } F\} \text{ is } P, \tag{8.8}$$

where $\mathcal{V}$ and F have the same meaning as in (8.4), $\text{Pro} \{\mathcal{V} \text{ is } F\}$ is the probability of fuzzy event "$\mathcal{V}$ is F," S is a fuzzy truth qualifier, and P is a fuzzy probability qualifier. If desired, $\mathcal{V}$ may be replaced with $\mathcal{V}(i)$, which has the same meaning as in (8.6). We say that the proposition (8.7) is *truth-qualified*, while the proposition (8.8) is *probability-qualified*. Both S and P are represented by fuzzy sets on $[0,1]$.

An example of a truth-qualified proposition is the proposition "Tina is young is very true," where the predicate *young* and the truth qualifier *very true* are represented by the respective fuzzy sets shown in Fig. 8.2. Assuming that the age of Tina is 26, she belongs to the set representing the predicate *young* with the membership grade 0.87. Hence, our proposition belongs to the set of propositions that are very true with membership grade 0.76, as illustrated in Fig. 8.2b. This means, in turn, that the degree of truth of our truth-qualified proposition is also 0.76. If the proposition were modified by changing the predicate (e.g., to *very young*) or the truth qualifier (e.g., to *fairly true, very false*, etc.), we would obtain the respective degrees of truth of these propositions by the same method.

In general, the degree of truth, $T(p)$, of any truth-qualified proposition p is given for each $v \in V$ by the equation

$$T(p) = S(F(v)). \tag{8.9}$$

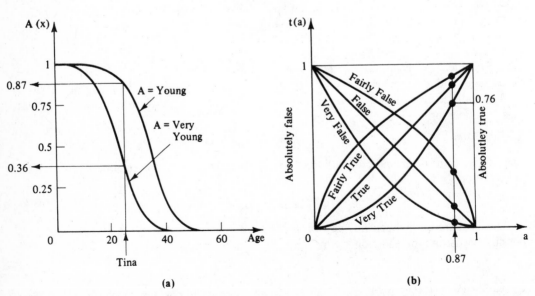

Figure 8.2 Truth values of a fuzzy proposition.

Viewing the membership function $G(v) = S(F(v))$, where $v \in V$, as a simple predicate, we can interpret any truth-qualified proposition of the form (8.7) as the unqualified proposition "$\mathcal{V}$ is G."

Observe that unqualified propositions are, in fact, special truth-qualified propositions, in which the truth qualifier S is assumed to be *true*. As shown in Figs. 8.1b and 8.2b, the membership function representing this qualifier is the identity function. That is, $S(F(v)) = F(v)$ for unqualified propositions; hence, S may be ignored for the sake of simplicity.

Let us discuss now probability-qualified propositions of the form (8.8). Each proposition of this type describes an elastic restriction on possible probability distributions on V. For any given probability distribution f on V, we have

$$\text{Pro}\{\mathcal{V} \text{ is } F\} = \sum_{v \in V} f(v) \cdot F(v); \tag{8.10}$$

and, then, the degree $T(p)$ to which proposition p of the form (8.8) is true is given by the formula

$$T(p) = P(\sum_{v \in V} f(v) \cdot F(v)). \tag{8.11}$$

As an example, let variable $\mathcal{V}$ be the average daily temperature t in °F at some place on the Earth during a certain month. Then, the probability-qualified proposition

p : Pro {temperature t (at given place and time) is around 75°F} is likely

may provide us with a meaningful characterization of one aspect of climate at the given place and time and may be combined with similar propositions regarding other aspects, such as humidity, rainfall, wind speed, and so on. Let in our example the predicate "around 75°F" be represented by the fuzzy set A on $\mathbb{R}$ specified in Fig. 8.3a and the qualifier "likely" be expressed by the fuzzy set on $[0, 1]$ defined in Fig. 8.3b.

Assume now that the following probability distribution (obtained, e.g., from relevant statistical data over many years) is given:

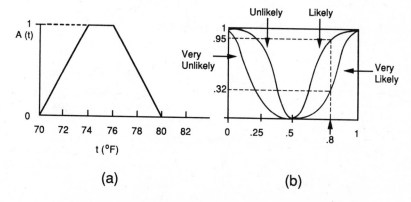

(a)   (b)

Figure 8.3   Example of a probability-qualified proposition.

t	68	69	70	71	72	73	74	75	76	77	78	79	80	81	82	83
$f(t)$	.002	.005	.005	.01	.04	.11	.15	.21	.16	.14	.11	.04	.01	.005	.002	.001

Then, using (8.10), we obtain

$$\text{Pro } (t \text{ is close to } 75°F) = .01 \times .25 + .04 \times .5 + .11 \times .75 + .15 \times 1 + .21 \times 1$$
$$+ .16 \times 1 + .14 \times .75 + .11 \times .5 + .04 \times .25 = .8,$$

and, applying this result to the fuzzy probability *likely* in Fig. 8.3b (according to (8.11)), we find that $T(p) = .95$ for our proposition. That is, given the definitions of *around 75* and *likely* in Fig. 8.3, it is true with the degree of .95 that it is *likely* that the temperature (at a given place, time, etc.) is *around* 75°F. Due to this high degree of truth, we may conclude that our proposition is a good characterization of the actual situation. However, if we replaced the qualification *likely* in our proposition with *very likely* (as also defined in Fig. 8.3b), the degree of truth of the new proposition would be only .32. This low degree of truth would not make the new proposition a good description of the actual situation.

Observe that the degree of truth depends on the predicate F, the qualifier P, and the given probability distribution. Replacing, for example, our fuzzy predicate *around 75* with a crisp predicate *in the 70s*, we obtain

$$\text{Pro } \{t \text{ is in the 70s}\} = \sum_{t=70}^{79} f(t) = .98,$$

and $T(p)$ becomes practically equal to 1 even if we apply the stronger qualifier *very likely*.

Conditional and Unqualified Propositions

Propositions p of this type are expressed by the canonical form

$$p: \text{ If } \mathcal{X} \text{ is } A, \text{ then } \mathcal{Y} \text{ is } B, \tag{8.12}$$

where $\mathcal{X}, \mathcal{Y}$ are variables whose values are in sets X, Y, respectively, and A, B are fuzzy sets on X, Y, respectively. These propositions may also be viewed as propositions of the form

$$\langle \mathcal{X}, \mathcal{Y} \rangle \text{ is } R, \tag{8.13}$$

where R is a fuzzy set on $X \times Y$ that is determined for each $x \in X$ and each $y \in Y$ by the formula

$$R(x, y) = \mathcal{J}[A(x), B(y)],$$

where $\mathcal{J}$ denotes a binary operation on $[0, 1]$ representing a suitable *fuzzy implication*.

Fuzzy implications are discussed in detail in the context of approximate reasoning in Secs. 11.2 and 11.3. Here, let us only illustrate the connection between (8.13) and (8.12) for one particular fuzzy implication, the Lukasiewicz implication

$$\mathcal{J}(a, b) = \min(1, 1 - a + b). \tag{8.14}$$

Let $A = .1/x_1 + .8/x_2 + 1/x_3$ and $B = .5/y_1 + 1/y_2$. Then

$$R = 1/x_1, y_1 + 1/x_1, y_2 + .7/x_2, y_1 + 1/x_2, y_2 + .5/x_3, y_1 + 1/x_3, y_2.$$

This means, for example, that $T(p) = 1$ when $X = x_1$ and $\mathcal{Y} = y_1$; $T(p) = .7$ when $X = x_2$ and $\mathcal{Y} = y_1$; and so on.

Conditional and Qualified Propositions

Propositions of this type can be characterized by either the canonical form

$$p: \text{ If } X \text{ is } A, \text{ then } \mathcal{Y} \text{ is } B \text{ is } S \tag{8.15}$$

or the canonical form

$$p: \text{Pro}\{X \text{ is } A|\mathcal{Y} \text{ is } B\} \text{ is } P, \tag{8.16}$$

where $\text{Pro}\{X \text{ is } A|\mathcal{Y} \text{ is } B\}$ is a conditional probability.

Since methods introduced for the other types of propositions can be combined to deal with propositions of this type, we do not deem it necessary to discuss them further.

8.4 FUZZY QUANTIFIERS

Similar to how the scope of classical predicates can be extended by quantifying their applicability, we can extend the scope of the fuzzy predicates by the use of *fuzzy quantifiers*. In general, fuzzy quantifiers are fuzzy numbers that take part in fuzzy propositions. They are of two kinds. Fuzzy quantifiers of the first kind are defined on $\mathbb{R}$ and characterize linguistic terms such as *about 10, much more than 100, at least about 5*, and so on. Fuzzy quantifiers of the second kind are defined on [0,1] and characterize linguistic terms such as *almost all, about half, most*, and so on.

There are two basic forms of propositions that contain fuzzy quantifiers of the first kind. One of them is the form

$$p: \text{ There are } Q \text{ } i\text{'s in } I \text{ such that } \mathcal{V}(i) \text{ is } F, \tag{8.17}$$

where $\mathcal{V}$ is a variable that for each individual i in a given set I assumes a value $\mathcal{V}(i)$, F is a fuzzy set defined on the set of values of variable $\mathcal{V}$, and Q is a fuzzy number on $\mathbb{R}$. In general, I is an index set by which distinct measurements of variable V are distinguished.

An example of this form is the proposition: "There are about 10 students in a given class whose fluency in English is high." Given a set of students, I, the value $\mathcal{V}(i)$ of variable $\mathcal{V}$ represents in this proposition the degree of fluency in English of student i (expressed, e.g., by numbers in $[0, 1]$), F is a fuzzy set defined on the set of values of variable $\mathcal{V}$ that expresses the linguistic term *high*, and Q is a fuzzy number expressing the linguistic term *about 10*.

Any proposition p of the form (8.17) can be converted into another proposition, p', of a simplified form,

$$p': \text{ There are } Q \text{ } E\text{'s}, \tag{8.18}$$

where Q is the same quantifier as in (8.17), and E is a fuzzy set on a given set I that is defined by the composition

$$E(i) = F(\mathcal{V}(i)) \tag{8.19}$$

for all $i \in I$. Thus, for example, the proposition

p : "There are about 10 students in a given class whose fluency in English is high"

can be replaced with the proposition

p' : "There are about 10 high-fluency English-speaking students in a given class."

Here, E is the fuzzy set of "high-fluency English-speaking students in a given class."

Proposition p' of the form (8.18) may be viewed as a simplified expression of proposition p of the form (8.17). It is common in natural language to use the simplified form in lieu of the full form. For the sake of simplicity, we adopt this usage. Then, proposition p' of the form (8.18) may be rewritten in the form

$$p' : \mathcal{W} \text{ is } Q, \qquad (8.20)$$

where $\mathcal{W}$ is a variable taking values in $\mathbb{R}$ that represents the scalar cardinality (sigma count) of fuzzy set E (i.e., $\mathcal{W} = |E|$). Obviously,

$$|E| = \sum_{i \in I} E(i) = \sum_{i \in I} F(\mathcal{V}(i))$$

and, for each given fuzzy set E, we have

$$T(p) = T(p') = Q(|E|). \qquad (8.21)$$

As explained in Sec. 7.4, any given proposition "$\mathcal{W}$ is Q" induces a possibility distribution function, r_Q, that is defined for each $|E| \in \mathbb{R}$ by the equation

$$r_Q(|E|) = Q(|E|). \qquad (8.22)$$

This possibility distribution acts as an elastic constraint on values of variable $\mathcal{W}$; that is $r_Q(|E|)$ expresses the degree of possibility that $\mathcal{W} = |E|$.

As an example, let us discuss the proposition

p : There are about three students in I whose fluency in English, $\mathcal{V}(i)$, is high.

Assume that $I = \{$Adam, Bob, Cathy, David, Eve$\}$, and $\mathcal{V}$ is a variable with values in the interval [0, 100] that express degrees of fluency in English. Comparing this proposition with its general counterpart (8.17), we can see that Q is, in our case, a fuzzy quantifier "about 3," and F is a fuzzy set on [0, 100] that captures the linguistic term "high fluency." Both Q and F are defined in Fig. 8.4. Assume now that the following scores are given: $\mathcal{V}$(Adam) = 35, $\mathcal{V}$(Bob) = 20, $\mathcal{V}$(Cathy) = 80, $\mathcal{V}$(David) = 95, $\mathcal{V}$(Eve) = 70. The truth value of the proposition is then determined as follows. First, we construct the fuzzy set defined by (8.19):

$$E = 0/\text{Adam} + 0/\text{Bob} + .75/\text{Cathy} + 1/\text{David} + .5/\text{Eve}.$$

Next, we calculate the cardinality of E:

$$|E| = \sum_{i \in I} E(i) = 2.25.$$

Finally, we use (8.21) to obtain the truth value of our proposition:

$$T(p) = Q(2.25) = 0.625.$$

Assuming, on the other hand, that the students' scores are not known, we are not able to construct the set E. The proposition provides us, in this case, with information about the

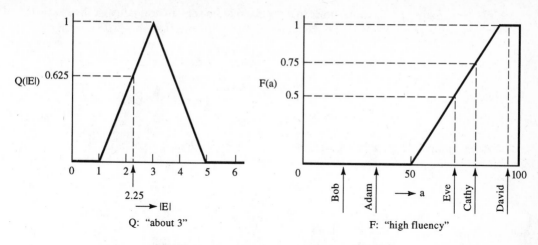

Figure 8.4 Fuzzy sets in a quantified fuzzy proposition.

degrees of possibility of various values of the cardinality of E. For instance, since $Q(3) = 1$, the possibility of $|E| = 3$ is 1; since $Q(5) = 0$, it is impossible that $|E| = 5$, and so on.

Fuzzy quantifiers of the first kind may also appear in fuzzy propositions of the form

$$p : \text{There are } Q \ i\text{'s in } I \text{ such that } \mathcal{V}_1(i) \text{ is } F_1 \text{ and } \mathcal{V}_2(i) \text{ is } F_2, \qquad (8.23)$$

where $\mathcal{V}_1, \mathcal{V}_2$ are variables that take values from sets V_1, V_2, respectively, I is an index set by which distinct measurements of variables $\mathcal{V}_1, \mathcal{V}_2$ are identified (e.g., measurements on a set of individuals or measurements at distinct time instants), Q is a fuzzy number on $\mathbb{R}$, and F_1, F_2 are fuzzy sets on V_1, V_2, respectively.

An example of this form of a quantified fuzzy proposition is the proposition "There are about 10 students in a given class whose fluency in English is high and who are young." In this proposition, I is an index set by which students in the given class are labelled, variables $\mathcal{V}_1$ and $\mathcal{V}_2$ characterize *fluency in English* and *age* of the students, Q is a fuzzy number that captures the linguistic term "about 10," and F_1, F_2 are fuzzy sets that characterize the linguistic terms "high" and "young," respectively.

Any proposition p of the form (8.23) can be expressed in a simplified form,

$$p' : QE_1\text{'s } E_2\text{'s}, \qquad (8.24)$$

where Q is the same quantifier as in (8.23), and E_1, E_2 are fuzzy sets on I that are defined by the compositions

$$\begin{aligned} E_1(i) &= F_1(\mathcal{V}_1(i)) \\ E_2(i) &= F_2(\mathcal{V}_2(i)) \end{aligned} \qquad (8.25)$$

for all $i \in I$. Moreover, (8.24) may be interpreted as

$$p' : \text{There are } Q(E_1 \text{ and } E_2)\text{'s}. \qquad (8.26)$$

Comparing now (8.26) with (8.18), we may rewrite (8.26) in the form

$$p' : \mathcal{W} \text{ is } Q, \qquad (8.27)$$

where W is a variable taking values in $\mathbb{R}$ that represents the scalar cardinality of the fuzzy set $E_1 \cap E_2$ (i.e., $W = |E_1 \cap E_2|$). Using the standard fuzzy intersection and (8.25), we have

$$W = \sum_{i \in I} \min[F_1(\mathcal{V}_1(i)), F_2(\mathcal{V}_2(i))]. \tag{8.28}$$

Now, for any given sets E_1 and E_2,

$$T(p) = T(p') = Q(W). \tag{8.29}$$

Furthermore, proposition p' (and, hence, also the equivalent proposition p) induces a possibility distribution function, r_Q, that is defined for each $W = |E_1 \cap E_2|$ by the equation

$$r_Q(W) = Q(W). \tag{8.30}$$

Let us now discuss fuzzy propositions with quantifiers of the second kind. These are quantifiers such as "almost all," "about half," "most," and so on. They are represented by fuzzy numbers on the unit interval [0, 1]. Examples of some quantifiers of this kind are shown in Fig. 8.5.

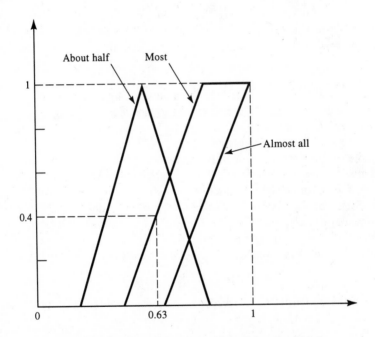

Figure 8.5 Examples of fuzzy quantifiers of the second kind.

Fuzzy propositions with quantifiers of the second kind have the general form

$$p : \text{Among } i\text{'s in } I \text{ such that } \mathcal{V}_1(i) \text{ is } F_1 \text{ there are } Qi\text{'s in } I \text{ such that} \tag{8.31}$$
$$\mathcal{V}_2(i) \text{ is } F_2,$$

where Q is a fuzzy number on [0, 1], and the meaning of the remaining symbols is the same as previously defined. An example of a proposition of this form is the proposition "Among students in a given class that are young, there are almost all whose fluency in English is high."

As previously explained, any proposition of the form (8.31) may be written in a simplified form,

$$p' : QE_1\text{'s are } E_2\text{'s,} \tag{8.32}$$

where Q is the same quantifier used in (8.31), and E_1, E_2 are fuzzy sets on X defined by

$$\begin{aligned} E_1(i) &= F_1(\mathcal{V}_1(i)), \\ E_2(i) &= F_2(\mathcal{V}_2(i)) \end{aligned} \tag{8.33}$$

for all $i \in I$. In this form, the previous example is modified as follows: "Almost all young students in a given class are students whose fluency in English is high."

Comparing (8.32) with (8.24), we can see that both these propositions have the same form, but the quantifiers involved are different. By analogy of the two forms, we may rewrite (8.32) in the form

$$p' : \mathcal{W} \text{ is } Q, \tag{8.34}$$

where $\mathcal{W}$ is a variable that represents the degree of subsethood of E_2 in E_1; that is,

$$\mathcal{W} = \frac{|E_1 \cap E_2|}{|E_1|}.$$

Using the standard fuzzy intersection and (8.33), we obtain

$$\mathcal{W} = \frac{\sum\limits_{i \in I} \min[F_1(\mathcal{V}_1(i)), F_2(\mathcal{V}_2(i))]}{\sum\limits_{i \in I} F_1(\mathcal{V}_1(i))} \tag{8.35}$$

for any given sets E_1 and E_2. Clearly, $T(p)$ is obtained by (8.29). On the other hand, given a proposition p of the form (8.31), we obtain a possibility distribution r_Q defined by (8.30).

Quantifiers of the first kind are also called *absolute quantifiers*, while quantifiers of the second kind are called *relative quantifiers*. This terminology makes sense when we compare the definitions of variable $\mathcal{W}$ for quantifiers of the first kind, given by (8.28), and the second kind, given by (8.35).

8.5   LINGUISTIC HEDGES

Linguistic hedges (or simply hedges) are special linguistic terms by which other linguistic terms are modified. Linguistic terms such as *very, more or less, fairly,* or *extremely* are examples of hedges. They can be used for modifying fuzzy predicates, fuzzy truth values, and fuzzy probabilities. For example, the proposition "x is young," which is assumed to mean "x is young is true," may be modified by the hedge *very* in any of the following three ways:

"x is very young is true,"
"x is young is very true,"
"x is very young is very true."

Similarly, the proposition "x is young is likely" may be modified to "x is young is very likely," and so forth.

In general, given a fuzzy proposition

$$p : x \text{ is } F$$

and a linguistic hedge, H, we can construct a modified proposition,

$$Hp : x \text{ is } HF,$$

where HF denotes the fuzzy predicate obtained by applying the hedge H to the given predicate F. Additional modifications can be obtained by applying the hedge to the fuzzy truth value or fuzzy probability employed in the given proposition.

It is important to realize that linguistic hedges are not applicable to crisp predicates, truth values, or probabilities. For example, the linguistic terms *very horizontal*, *very pregnant*, *very teenage*, or *very rectangular* are not meaningful. Hence, hedges do not exist in classical logic.

Any linguistic hedge, H, may be interpreted as a unary operation, h, on the unit interval $[0, 1]$. For example, the hedge *very* is often interpreted as the unary operation $h(a) = a^2$, while the hedge *fairly* is interpreted as $h(a) = \sqrt{a}$ ($a \in [0, 1]$). Let unary operations that represent linguistic hedges be called *modifiers*.

Given a fuzzy predicate F on X and a modifier h that represents a linguistic hedge H, the modified fuzzy predicate HF is determined for each $x \in X$ by the equation

$$HF(x) = h(F(x)). \tag{8.36}$$

This means that properties of linguistic hedges can be studied by studying properties of the associated modifiers.

Any modifier h is an increasing bijection. If $h(a) < a$ for all $a \in [0, 1]$, the modifier is called *strong*; if $h(a) > a$ for all $a \in [0, 1]$, the modifier is called *weak*. The special (vacuous) modifier for which $h(a) = a$ is called an *identity modifier*.

A strong modifier strengthens a fuzzy predicate to which it is applied and, consequently, it reduces the truth value of the associated proposition. A weak modifier, on the contrary, weakens the predicate and, hence, the truth value of the proposition increases. For example, consider three fuzzy propositions:

p_1 : John is young,

p_2 : John is very young,

p_3 : John is fairly young,

and let the linguistic hedges *very* and *fairly* be represented by the strong modifier a^2 and the weak modifier $\sqrt{a}$. Assume now that John is 26 and, according to the fuzzy set YOUNG representing the fuzzy predicate *young*, YOUNG (26) = 0.8. Then, VERY YOUNG (26) = 0.8^2 = 0.64 and FAIRLY YOUNG (26) = $\sqrt{0.8}$ = 0.89. Hence, $T(p_1)$ = 0.8, $T(p_2)$ = 0.64, and $T(p_3)$ = 0.89. These values agree with our intuition: the stronger assertion is less true and vice versa.

It is easy to prove that every modifier h satisfies the following conditions, which are self-explanatory:

1. $h(0) = 0$ and $h(1) = 1$;
2. h is a continuous function;
3. if h is strong, then h^{-1} is weak and vice versa;
4. given another modifier g, compositions of g with h and h with g are also modifiers and, moreover, if both h and g are strong (weak), then so are the compositions.

A convenient class of functions that satisfy these conditions is the class

$$h_\alpha(a) = a^\alpha, \tag{8.37}$$

where $\alpha \in \mathbb{R}^+$ is a parameter by which individual modifiers in this class are distinguished and $a \in [0, 1]$. When $\alpha < 1$, h_α is a weak modifier; when $\alpha > 1$, h_α is a strong modifier; h_1 is the identity modifier. This class of modifiers (as well as any other acceptable class) enables us to capture the meaning of each relevant linguistic hedge in a particular context by determining an appropriate value of the parameter α. This is a similar problem as the problem of constructing a membership function, which is discussed in Chapter 10.

In representing modifiers of linguistic hedges, we should avoid various ambiguities of natural language. For example, the linguistic term *not very* may be viewed as the negation of the hedge *very*, but it may also be viewed (as some authors argue) as a new hedge that is somewhat weaker than the hedge *very*. In our further considerations, we always view any linguistic term *not H*, where H is an arbitrary hedge, as the negation of H.

8.6   *INFERENCE FROM CONDITIONAL FUZZY PROPOSITIONS*

As explained in Sec. 8.1, inference rules in classical logic are based on the various tautologies. These inference rules can be generalized within the framework of fuzzy logic to facilitate approximate reasoning. In this section, we describe generalizations of three classical inference rules, *modus ponens*, *modus tollens*, and *hypothetical syllogism*. These generalizations are based on the so-called compositional rule of inference.

Consider variables $\mathcal{X}$ and $\mathcal{Y}$ that take values from sets X and Y, respectively, and assume that for all $x \in X$ and all $y \in Y$ the variables are related by a function $y = f(x)$. Then, given $\mathcal{X} = x$, we can infer that $\mathcal{Y} = f(x)$, as shown in Fig. 8.6a. Similarly, knowing that the value of $\mathcal{X}$ is in a given set A, we can infer that the value of $\mathcal{Y}$ is in the set $B = \{y \in Y | y = f(x), x \in A\}$, as shown in Fig. 8.6b.

Assume now that the variables are related by an arbitrary relation on $X \times Y$, not necessarily a function. Then, given $\mathcal{X} = u$ and a relation R, we can infer that $\mathcal{Y} \in B$, where $B = \{y \in Y | \langle x, y \rangle \in R\}$, as illustrated in Fig. 8.7a. Similarly, knowing that $\mathcal{X} \in A$, we can infer that $\mathcal{Y} \in B$, where $B = \{y \in Y | \langle x, y \rangle \in R, x \in A\}$, as illustrated in Fig. 8.7b. Observe that this inference may be expressed equally well in terms of characteristic functions χ_A, χ_B, χ_R of sets A, B, R respectively, by the equation

$$\chi_B(y) = \sup_{x \in X} \min[\chi_A(x), \chi_R(x, y)] \tag{8.38}$$

for all $y \in Y$.

Let us proceed now one step further and assume that R is a fuzzy relation on $X \times Y$, and A', B' are fuzzy sets on X and Y, respectively. Then, if R and A' are given, we can obtain B' by the equation

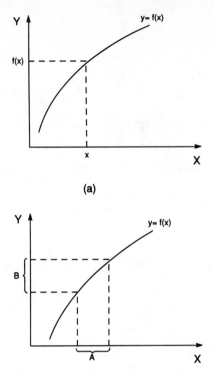

Figure 8.6 Functional relation between two variables: (a) $x \to y$, where $y = f(x)$; (b) $A \to B$, where $B = \{y \in Y | y = f(x), x \in A\}$.

$$B'(y) = \sup_{x \in X} \min[A'(x), R(x, y)] \tag{8.39}$$

for all $y \in Y$, which is a generalization of (8.38) obtained by replacing the characteristic functions in (8.38) with the corresponding membership functions. This equation, which can also be written in the matrix form as

$$\mathbf{B'} = \mathbf{A'} \circ \mathbf{R},$$

is called the *compositional rule of inference*. This rule is illustrated in Fig. 8.8.

The fuzzy relation employed in (8.39) is usually not given directly, but in some other form. In this section, we consider the case in which the relation is embedded in a single conditional fuzzy proposition. A more general case, in which the relation emerges from several conditional fuzzy propositions, is discussed in Chapter 11.

As explained in Sec. 8.3, relation R that is embedded in a conditional fuzzy proposition p of the form

$$p : \text{If } \mathcal{X} \text{ is A, then } \mathcal{Y} \text{ is } B$$

is determined for all $x \in X$ and all $y \in Y$ by the formula

$$R(x, y) = \mathfrak{J}[A(x), B(y)], \tag{8.40}$$

where $\mathfrak{J}$ denotes a fuzzy implication (Chapter 11).

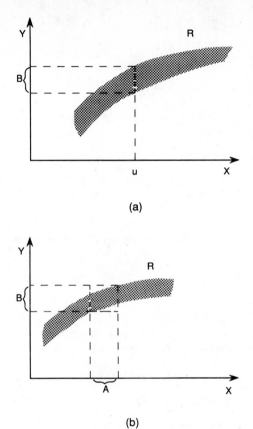

(a)

(b)

Figure 8.7 Inference expressed by (8.38).

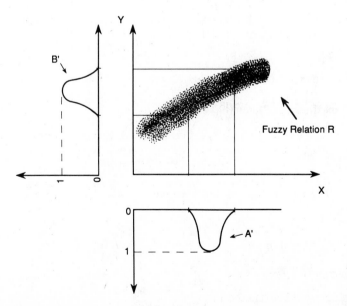

Fuzzy Relation R

Figure 8.8 Compositional rule of inference expressed by (8.39).

Using relation R obtained from given proposition p by (8.40), and given another proposition q of the form

$$q : \mathcal{X} \text{ is } A',$$

we may conclude that $\mathcal{Y}$ is B' by the compositional rule of inference (8.39). This procedure is called a *generalized modus ponens*.

Viewing proposition p as a rule and proposition q as a fact, the generalized modus ponens is expressed by the following schema:

Rule :   If $\mathcal{X}$ is A, then $\mathcal{Y}$ is B
Fact : $\mathcal{X}$ is A'

$\overline{\qquad\qquad\qquad\qquad\qquad\qquad\qquad\qquad\qquad\qquad}$ (8.41)

Conclusion : $\mathcal{Y}$ is B'

In this schema, B' is calculated by (8.39), and R in this equation is determined by (8.40). Observe that (8.41) becomes the classical modus ponens when the sets are crisp and $A' = A, B' = B$.

Example 8.1

Let sets of values of variables $\mathcal{X}$ and $\mathcal{Y}$ be $X = \{x_1, x_2, x_3\}$ and $Y = \{y_1, y_2\}$, respectively. Assume that a proposition "if $\mathcal{X}$ is A, then $\mathcal{Y}$ is B" is given, where $A = .5/x_1 + 1/x_2 + .6/x_3$ and $B = 1/y_1 + .4/y_2$. Then, given a fact expressed by the proposition "x is A'," where $A' = .6/x_1 + .9/x_2 + .7/x_3$, we want to use the generalized modus ponens (8.41) to derive a conclusion in the form "$\mathcal{Y}$ is B'."

Using, for example, the Lukasiewicz implication (8.14), we obtain

$$R = 1/x_1, y_1 + .9/x_1, y_2 + 1/x_2, y_1 + .4/x_2, y_2 + 1/x_3, y_1, + .8/x_3, y_2$$

by (8.40). Then, by the compositional rule of inference (8.39), we obtain

$$B'(y_1) = \sup_{x \in X} \min[A'(x), R(x, y_1)]$$

$$= \max[\min(.6, 1), \min(.9, 1), \min(.7, 1)]$$

$$= .9$$

$$B'(y_2) = \sup_{x \in X} \min[A'(x), R(x, y_2)]$$

$$= \max[\min(.6, .9), \min(.9, .4), \min(.7, .8)]$$

$$= .7$$

Thus, we may conclude that $\mathcal{Y}$ is B', where $B' = .9/y_1 + .7/y_2$.

Another inference rule in fuzzy logic, which is a *generalized modus tollens*, is expressed by the following schema:

Rule :   If $\mathcal{X}$ is A, then $\mathcal{Y}$ is B
Fact : $\mathcal{Y}$ is B'

$\overline{\qquad\qquad\qquad\qquad\qquad\qquad\qquad\qquad\qquad\qquad}$

Conclusion : $\mathcal{X}$ is A'

In this case, the compositional rule of inference has the form

$$A'(x) = \sup_{y \in Y} \min[B'(y), R(x, y)], \tag{8.42}$$

and R in this equation is again determined by (8.40). When the sets are crisp and $A' = \overline{A}, B' = \overline{B}$, we obtain the classical *modus tollens*.

Example 8.2

Let $X, Y, \mathcal{J}, A$, and B are the same as in Example 8.1. Then, R is also the same as in Example 8.1. Assume now that a fact expressed by the proposition "$\mathcal{Y}$ is B'" is given, where $B' = .9/y_1 + .7/y_2$. Then, by (8.42),

$$A'(x_1) = \sup_{y \in Y} \min[B'(y), R(x_1, y)]$$

$$= \max[\min(.9, 1), \min(.7, .9)] = .9,$$

$$A'(x_2) = \sup_{y \in Y} \min[B'(y), R(x_2, y)]$$

$$= \max[\min(.9, 1), \min(.7, .4)] = .9,$$

$$A'(x_3) = \sup_{y \in Y} \min[B'(y), R(x_3, y)]$$

$$= \max[\min(.9, 1), \min(.7, .8)] = .9.$$

Hence, we conclude that $\mathcal{X}$ is A' where $A' = .9/x_1 + .9/x_2 + .9/x_3$.

Finally, let us discuss a generalization of hypothetical syllogism, which is based on two conditional fuzzy propositions. The *generalized hypothetical syllogism* is expressed by the following schema:

Rule 1 :   If $\mathcal{X}$ is A, then $\mathcal{Y}$ is B
Rule 2 :   If $\mathcal{Y}$ is B, then $\mathcal{Z}$ is C

Conclusion :   If $\mathcal{X}$ is A, then $\mathcal{Z}$ is C $\tag{8.43}$

In this case, $\mathcal{X}, \mathcal{Y}, \mathcal{Z}$ are variables taking values in sets X, Y, Z, respectively, and A, B, C are fuzzy sets on sets X, Y, Z, respectively.

For each conditional fuzzy proposition in (8.43), there is a fuzzy relation determined by (8.40). These relations are determined for each $x \in X, y \in Y$, and $z \in Z$ by the equations

$$R_1(x, y) = \mathcal{J}[A(x), B(y)],$$

$$R_2(y, z) = \mathcal{J}[B(y), C(z)],$$

$$R_3(x, z) = \mathcal{J}[A(x), C(z)].$$

Given R_1, R_2, R_3, obtained by these equations, we say that the generalized hypothetical syllogism holds if

$$R_3(x, z) = \sup_{y \in Y} \min[R_1(x, y), R_2(y, z)], \tag{8.44}$$

which again expresses the compositional rule of inference. This equation may also be written in the matrix form

$$\mathbf{R}_3 = \mathbf{R}_1 \circ \mathbf{R}_2. \tag{8.45}$$

Example 8.3

Let X, Y be the same as in Example 8.1, and let $Z = \{z_1, z_2\}$. Moreover, let $A = .5/x_1 + 1/x_2 + .6/x_3$, $B = 1/y_1 + .4/y_2$, $C = .2/z_1 + 1/z_2$, and

$$\mathcal{J}(a, b) = \begin{cases} 1 & \text{if } a \le b \\ b & \text{if } a > b. \end{cases}$$

Then, clearly,

$$\mathbf{R}_1 = \begin{bmatrix} 1 & .4 \\ 1 & .4 \\ 1 & .4 \end{bmatrix}, \quad \mathbf{R}_2 = \begin{bmatrix} .2 & 1 \\ .2 & 1 \end{bmatrix}, \quad \mathbf{R}_3 = \begin{bmatrix} .2 & 1 \\ .2 & 1 \\ .2 & 1 \end{bmatrix}$$

The generalized hypothetical syllogism holds in this case since $\mathbf{R}_1 \circ \mathbf{R}_2 = \mathbf{R}_3$.

8.7 *INFERENCE FROM CONDITIONAL AND QUALIFIED PROPOSITIONS*

The inference rule of our concern in this section involves conditional fuzzy propositions with fuzzy truth qualifiers. Given a conditional and qualified fuzzy proposition p of the form

$$p : \text{If } X \text{ is } A, \text{ then } Y \text{ is } B \text{ is } S, \tag{8.46}$$

where S is a fuzzy truth qualifier, and a fact is in the form "X is A'," we want to make an inference in the form "Y is B'."

One method developed for this purpose, called a *method of truth-value restrictions*, is based on a manipulation of linguistic truth values. The method involves the following four steps.

Step 1. Calculate the relative fuzzy truth value of A' with respect to A, denoted by $RT(A'/A)$, which is a fuzzy set on the unit interval defined by

$$RT(A'/A)(a) = \sup_{x:A(x)=a} A'(x), \tag{8.47}$$

for all $a \in [0, 1]$. The relative fuzzy truth value $RT(A'/A)$ expresses the degree to which the fuzzy proposition (8.46) is true given the available fact "X is A'."

Step 2. Select a suitable fuzzy implication $\mathcal{J}$ by which the fuzzy proposition (8.46) is interpreted. This is similar to the selection of fuzzy implication in Sec. 8.6, whose purpose is to express a conditional but unqualified fuzzy proposition as a fuzzy relation.

Step 3. Calculate the relative fuzzy truth value $RT(B'/B)$ by the formula

$$RT(B'/B)(b) = \sup_{a \in [0,1]} \min[RT(A'/A)(a), S(\mathcal{J}(a, b))] \tag{8.48}$$

for all $b \in [0, 1]$, where S is the fuzzy qualifier in (8.46). Clearly, the role of the qualifier S is to modify the truth value of $\mathcal{J}(a, b)$. Note that when S stands for *true* (i.e., $S(a) = a$) for all $a \in [0, 1]$, then $S(\mathcal{J}(a, b)) = \mathcal{J}(a, b)$, and we obtain the case discussed in Sec. 8.6.

The relative fuzzy truth value $RT(B'/B)$ expresses the degree to which the conclusion of the fuzzy proposition (8.46) is true.

Step 4.   Calculate the set B' involved in the inference "$\mathcal{Y}$ is B'" by the equation

$$B'(y) = RT(B'/B)(B(y)),\qquad(8.49)$$

for all $y \in Y$.

Example 8.4

Suppose we have a fuzzy conditional and qualified proposition,

$$p:\text{ If }\mathcal{X}\text{ is }A\text{ then }\mathcal{Y}\text{ is }B\text{ is very true,}$$

where $A = 1/x_1 + .5/x_2 + .7/x_3$, $B = .6/y_1 + 1/y_2$, and S stands for *very true*; let $S(a) = a^2$ for all $a \in [0, 1]$. Given a fact "$\mathcal{X}$ is A'," where $A' = .9/x_1 + .6/x_2 + .7/x_3$, we conclude that "$\mathcal{Y}$ is B'," where B' is calculated by the following steps.

Step 1.   We calculate $RT(A'/A)$ by (8.47):

$$RT(A'/A)(1) = A'(x_1) = .9,$$

$$RT(A'/A)(.5) = A'(x_2) = .6,$$

$$RT(A'/A)(.7) = A'(x_3) = .7,$$

$$RT(A'/A)(a) = 0 \text{ for all } a \in [0, 1] - \{.5, .7, 1\}.$$

Step 2.   We select the Lukasiewicz fuzzy implication $\mathcal{J}$ defined by (8.14).

Step 3.   We calculate $RT(B'/B)$ by (8.48):

$$RT(B'/B)(b) = \max\{\min[.9, S(\mathcal{J}(.9, b))], \min[.6, S(\mathcal{J}(.6, b))],$$

$$\min[.7, S(\mathcal{J}(.7, b))]\}$$

$$= \begin{cases} (.4 + b)^2 & \text{for } b \in [0, .375) \\ .6 & \text{for } b \in [.375, .475) \\ (.3 + b)^2 & \text{for } b \in [.475, .537) \\ .7 & \text{for } b \in [.537, .737) \\ (.1 + b)^2 & \text{for } b \in [.737, .849) \\ .9 & \text{for } b \in [.849, 1] \end{cases}$$

A graph of this function $RT(B'/B)$ is shown in Fig. 8.9.

Step 4.   We calculate B' by (8.49):

$$B'(y_1) = RT(B'/B)(B(y_1)) = RT(B'/B)(.6) = .7,$$

$$B'(y_2) = RT(B'/B)(B(y_2)) = RT(B'/B)(1) = .9.$$

Hence, we make the inference "$\mathcal{Y}$ is B'," where $B' = .7/y_1 + .9/y_2$.

When S in (8.46) stands for *true* (i.e., S is the identity function), the method of truth-value restrictions is equivalent to the generalized modus ponens under a particular condition, as stated in the following theorem.

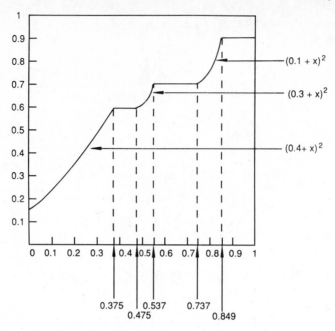

Figure 8.9   Function $RT(B/B')$ in Example 8.3.

Theorem 8.1.   Let a fuzzy proposition of the form (8.46) be given, where S is the identity function (i.e., S stands for *true*), and let a fact be given in the form "$\mathcal{X}$ is A'," where

$$\sup_{x:A(x)=a} A'(x) = A'(x_0) \tag{8.50}$$

for all $a \in [0, 1]$ and some x_0 such that $A(x_0) = a$. Then, the inference "$\mathcal{Y}$ is B'" obtained by the method of truth-value restrictions is equal to the one obtained by the generalized modus ponens (i.e., (8.41) and (8.49) define the same membership function B'), provided that we use the same fuzzy implication in both inference methods.

Proof: When $S(a) = a$ for all $a \in [0, 1]$, B', defined by (8.49), becomes

$$B'(y) = \sup_{a \in [0,1]} \min[RT(A'/A)(a), \mathcal{J}(a, B(y))] \tag{8.51}$$

for all $y \in Y$. Using the same fuzzy implication $\mathcal{J}$, B', defined by (8.41), becomes

$$B'(y) = \sup_{x \in X} \min[A'(x), \mathcal{J}(A(x), B(y))] \tag{8.52}$$

for all $y \in Y$. To prove the theorem, we have to show that (8.51) and (8.52) define the same membership function B'. To facilitate the proof, let B'_1, B'_2 denote the functions defined by (8.51) and (8.52), respectively. Since

$$A'(x) \leq \sup_{x':A(x')=A(x)} A'(x') = RT(A'/A)(A(x))$$

for all $x \in X$, we have

$$\min[A'(x), \mathcal{J}(A(x), B(y))] \leq \min[RT(A'/A)(A(x)), \mathcal{J}(A(x), B(y))]$$

for all $y \in Y$. Hence,

$$B_2'(y) = \sup_{x \in X} \min[A'(x), \mathcal{J}(A(x), B(y))]$$

$$\leq \sup_{x \in X} \min[RT(A'/A)(A(x)), \mathcal{J}(A(x), B(y))]$$

$$\leq \sup_{a \in [0,1]} \min[RT(A'/A)(a), \mathcal{J}(a, B(y))]$$

$$= B_1'(y)$$

for all $y \in Y$. On the other hand, by condition (8.50), we have

$$\min[RT(A'/A)(a), \mathcal{J}(a, B(y))] = \min[\sup_{x:A(x)=a} A'(x), \mathcal{J}(a, B(y))]$$

$$= \min[A'(x_0), \mathcal{J}(A(x_0), B(y))]$$

$$\leq \sup_{x \in X} \min[A'(x), \mathcal{J}(A(x), B(y))]$$

$$= B_2'(y)$$

for all $y \in Y$. Thus,

$$B_1'(y) = \sup_{a \in [0,1]} \min[RT(A'/A)(a), \mathcal{J}(a, B(y))] \leq B_2'(y)$$

for all $y \in Y$ and, consequently, $B_1' = B_2'$. ■

Observe that the condition (8.50) is rather weak and, hence, easy to satisfy. For example, it is satisfied whenever the universal set X is finite or the sets $\{x \in X | A(x) = a\}$, $a \in [0, 1]$, are finite. The significance of the theorem is that, under this weak condition, the two inference methods are equivalent when S stands for *true*. Under these circumstances, propositions (8.12) and (8.15) may be considered equivalent.

8.8 *INFERENCE FROM QUANTIFIED PROPOSITIONS*

As explained in Sec. 8.4, all quantified fuzzy propositions can be expressed in the form

$$p : \mathcal{W} \text{ is } Q,$$

where $\mathcal{W}$ is a variable whose values are specified either as $|E|$ (E defined by (8.19)), when Q is an absolute quantifier, or as $\text{Prop}(E_2/E_1) = |E_1 \cap E_2|/|E_1|$ (E_1, E_2 defined by (8.25)), when Q is a relative quantifier. Observe that $\text{Prop}(E_2/E_1) = S(E_1, E_2)$.

In general, the problem of inference from quantified fuzzy propositions may be stated as follows. Given n quantified fuzzy propositions of the form

$$p_i : \mathcal{W}_i \text{ is } Q_i \quad (i \in \mathbb{N}_n), \tag{8.53}$$

where Q_i is either an absolute quantifier or a relative quantifier, and $\mathcal{W}_i$ is a variable compatible with the quantifier Q_i for each $i \in \mathbb{N}_n$, what can we infer from these propositions?

One possible principle that addresses this question is known in the literature as the *quantifier extension principle*. To discuss this principle, let us assume that the prospective inference is expressed in terms of a quantified fuzzy proposition of the form

$$p : W \text{ is } Q. \tag{8.54}$$

The principle states the following: if there exists a function $f : \mathbb{R}^n \to \mathbb{R}$ such that $W = f(W_1, W_2, \ldots, W_n)$ and $Q = f(Q_1, Q_2, \ldots, Q_n)$, where the meaning of $f(Q_1, Q_2, \ldots, Q_n)$ is defined by the extension principle (Sec. 2.3), then we may conclude that p follows from $p_1, p_2, \ldots, p_n$. An alternative, more general formulation of the principle is: if there exist two functions $f : \mathbb{R}^n \to \mathbb{R}$ and $g : \mathbb{R}^n \to \mathbb{R}$ such that

$$f(W_1, W_2, \ldots, W_n) \leq W \leq g(W_1, W_2, \ldots, W_n),$$

then we may conclude that p follows from $p_1, p_2, \ldots, p_n$, where Q in proposition p is a special quantifier denoted by

$$Q = [\geq f(Q_1, Q_2, \ldots, Q_n)] \cap [\leq g(Q_1, Q_2, \ldots, Q_n)],$$

whose meaning is "at least $f(Q_1, Q_2, \ldots, Q_n)$ and at most $g(Q_1, Q_2, \ldots, Q_n)$." Fuzzy sets $f(Q_1, Q_2, \ldots, Q_n)$ and $g(Q_1, Q_2, \ldots, Q_n)$ are again obtained by the extension principle.

To illustrate the quantifier extension principle, let the following quantified fuzzy propositions be given:

p_1 : There are about 10 persons in the room.

p_2 : About half of the persons in the room are females.

If we want to make an inference in terms of the proposition

p : There are Q females in the room,

we need to determine Q. Let us discuss how this can be accomplished by the quantifier extension principle.

To facilitate our discussion, let the quantifiers "about 10" and "about half" be denoted by Q_1 and Q_2, respectively. Furthermore, let E, F denote, respectively, the set of persons and the set of females in the room. Using these symbols, we can now be given propositions in the form

$$p_1 : W_1 \text{ is } Q_1,$$
$$p_2 : W_2 \text{ is } Q_2,$$
$$p : W \text{ is } Q,$$

where W_1, W_2, W are variables with values $|E|, |E \cap F|/|E|, |F|$, respectively.

Now, there exists a function $f : \mathbb{R}^2 \to \mathbb{R}$ such that $f(W_1, W_2) = W$ for the variables in our example. It is the product function, $f(a, b) = ab$:

$$f(W_1, W_2) = W_1 W_2$$
$$= |E|\frac{|E \cap F|}{|E|}$$
$$= |E \cap F| = |F| = W.$$

Hence, by the quantifier extension principle, if $Q = Q_1 \cdot Q_2$ is the quantifier in proposition

p, where $Q_1 \cdot Q_2$ is the arithmetic product of fuzzy numbers Q_1 and Q_2 employed in the given propositions, then p is a correct inference from p_1 and p_2.

The quantifier extension principle can be used for deriving various inference rules for quantified fuzzy propositions. Let us mention two of them.

One of the inference rules is called the *intersection/product syllogism*. It is expressed by the following schema:

$$
\begin{array}{l}
p_1 : Q_1 \ E\text{'s are } F\text{'s} \\
p_2 : Q_2 \ (E \text{ and } F)\text{'s are } G\text{'s} \\
\hline
p \ : Q_1 \cdot Q_2 \ E\text{'s are } (F \text{ and } G)\text{'s}
\end{array}
\qquad (8.55)
$$

where E, F, G are fuzzy sets on a universal set X, Q_1 and Q_2 are relative quantifiers (fuzzy numbers on $[0, 1]$), and $Q_1 \cdot Q_2$ is the arithmetic product of the quantifiers.

As previously explained (Sec. 8.4), propositions p_1, p_2, and p may be expressed in the form

$$p_1 : \mathcal{W}_1 \text{ is } Q_1,$$

$$p_2 : \mathcal{W}_2 \text{ is } Q_2,$$

$$p : \mathcal{W} \text{ is } Q,$$

where $\mathcal{W}_1 = \text{Prop}\,(F/E)$, $\mathcal{W}_2 = \text{Prop}\,(G/E \cap F)$, and $\mathcal{W} = \text{Prop}\,(F \cap G/E)$. To prove that the inference schema (8.55) is valid, we have to demonstrate (according to the quantifier extension principle) that $\mathcal{W} = \mathcal{W}_1 \cdot \mathcal{W}_2$. This demonstration is rather simple:

$$
\begin{aligned}
\mathcal{W}_1 \cdot \mathcal{W}_2 &= \text{Prop}\,(F/E) \cdot \text{Prop}\,(G/E \cap F) \\
&= \frac{|E \cap F|}{|E|} \cdot \frac{|E \cap F \cap G|}{|E \cap F|} \\
&= \frac{|E \cap F \cap G|}{|E|} \\
&= \text{Prop}\,(F \cap G/E) = \mathcal{W}.
\end{aligned}
$$

Hence, the inference schema (8.55) is valid.

As an example, let us consider quantified fuzzy propositions

$$p_1 : \text{Most students are young.}$$

$$p_2 : \text{About half young students are males.}$$

Using the intersection/product syllogism (8.55), we may infer the proposition

$$p : Q \text{ of students are young and males,}$$

where Q is a quantifier obtained by taking the arithmetic product of fuzzy numbers that represent the quantifiers *most* and *about half*.

Another inference rule, which is called the *consequent conjunction syllogism*, is expressed by the following schema:

$$p_1 : Q_1 \; E\text{'s are } F\text{'s}$$
$$\underline{p_2 : Q_2 \; E\text{'s are } G\text{'s}} \qquad\qquad (8.56)$$
$$p \; : Q \; E\text{'s are } (F \text{ and } G)\text{'s}$$

where E, F, G are fuzzy sets on some universal set X, Q_1, Q_2 are relative quantifiers, and Q is a relative quantifier given by

$$Q = [\geq \text{MAX}(0, Q_1 + Q_2 - 1)] \cap [\leq \text{MIN}(Q_1, Q_2)];$$

that is, Q is at least $\text{MAX}(0, Q_1 + Q_2 - 1)$ and at most $\text{MIN}(Q_1, Q_2)$. Here, MIN and MAX are extensions of min and max operations on real numbers to fuzzy numbers (Sec. 4.5).

We leave the proof that inference schema (8.56) follows from the quantifier extension principle to the reader as an exercise.

NOTES

8.1. An excellent and comprehensive survey of multivalued logics was prepared by Rescher [1969], which also contains an extensive bibliography on the subject. A survey of more recent developments was prepared by Wolf [1977]. Various aspects of the relationship between multivalued logics and fuzzy logic are examined by numerous authors, including Bellman and Zadeh [1977], Giles [1977], Gaines [1978], Baldwin [1979a], Pavelka [1979], Gottwald [1980], Skala [1978], and Novák [1989, 1990].

8.2. Fuzzy propositions of the various types introduced in this chapter and the various fuzzy inference rules based on these propositions were introduced, by and large, by Zadeh in numerous articles. Most of these articles are included in [Yager *et al.*, 1987]. Important contributions to this subject were also made by Goguen [1968–69], Lee and Chang [1971], Dubois and Prade [1979b, 1984a, 1991a, b, 1992b], Baldwin [1979b], Baldwin and Guild [1980a, b], Mizumoto [1981], and Turksen and Yao [1984].

EXERCISES

8.1. Give an example from daily life of each type of fuzzy proposition introduced in this chapter, and express the proposition in its canonical form.

8.2. For each of the three-valued logics defined in Table 8.4, determine the truth values of each of the following logic expressions for all combinations of truth values of logic variables a, b, c (assume that negation $\bar{a}$ is defined by $1 - a$):
   (a) $(\bar{a} \wedge b) \Rightarrow c$;
   (b) $(\bar{a} \vee \bar{b}) \Leftrightarrow (\overline{a \wedge b})$;
   (c) $(a \Rightarrow b) \Rightarrow (\bar{c} \Rightarrow a)$.

8.3. Define in the form of a table (analogous to Table 8.4) the primitives $\wedge, \vee \Rightarrow$, and $\Leftrightarrow$ of the Lukasiewicz logics L_4 and L_5.

8.4. Assume four types of fuzzy predicates applicable to persons (age, height, weight, and level of education). Several specific fuzzy predicates for each of these types are represented by fuzzy sets whose membership functions are specified in Fig. 8.10. Apply these membership

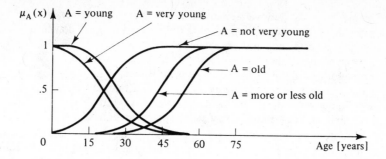

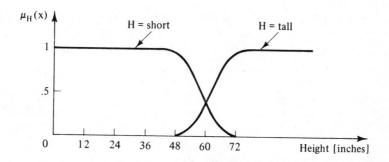

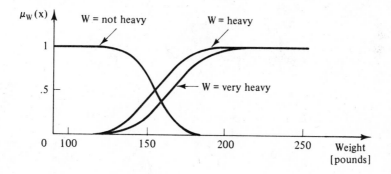

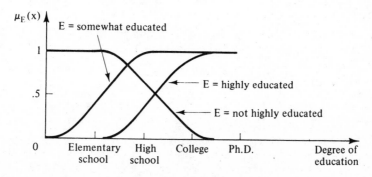

Figure 8.10   Fuzzy sets for Exercise 8.4.

functions and the fuzzy truth values defined in Fig. 8.2b to some person x (perhaps yourself) to determine the truth values of various propositions such as the following:

   x is highly educated and not very young is very true;

   x is very young, tall, not heavy, and somewhat educated is true;

   x is more or less old or highly educated is fairly true;

   x is very heavy or old or not highly educated is fairly true;

   x is short, not very young, and highly educated is very true.

In your calculations, use standard fuzzy set operators (min, max, $1 - a$).

8.5. Consider a fuzzy logic based on the standard logic operators (min, max, $1 - a$). For any two arbitrary propositions, A and B, in the logic, assume that we require that the equality

$$\overline{A \wedge B} = B \vee (\overline{A} \wedge \overline{B})$$

holds. Imposing such a requirement means that pairs of truth values of A and B become restricted to a subset of $[0, 1]^2$. Show exactly how they are restricted.

8.6. Solve the problem in Example 8.1 by using $A = .6/x_1 + 1/x_2 + .9/x_2$, $B = .6/y_1 + 1/y_2$, and $A' = .5/x_1 + .9/x_2 + 1/x_3$.

8.7. Use the method of truth-value restrictions to solve Exercise 8.6.

8.8. Assume that there are ten students in a class. About half of them are young girls. Most of those young girls are good students. Using the quantifiers specified in Fig. 8.5, answer the question: Approximately how many young girls in the class are good students?

8.9. Suppose there are five people in a women's figure skating competition. They are Anny, Bonnie, Cathy, Diana, and Eve. Assume that their relative goodness of performance is given by a fuzzy set $E = 1/\text{Anny} + .9/\text{Bonnie} + .5/\text{Cathy} + .9/\text{Diana} + .1/\text{Eve}$. Using the quantifiers specified in Figs. 8.4 and 8.5, determine the truth values of the following fuzzy propositions:

(a) There are about three persons who had good performances.

(b) Most of them have good performance.

(c) About half of them have good performance.

8.10. Consider some other linguistic hedges than those discussed in Section 8.5 and determine reasonable modifiers for them.

9

UNCERTAINTY-BASED INFORMATION

9.1 INFORMATION AND UNCERTAINTY

The concept of information, as a subject of this chapter, is intimately connected with the concept of uncertainty. The most fundamental aspect of this connection is that uncertainty involved in any problem-solving situation is a result of some information deficiency. Information (pertaining to the model within which the situation is conceptualized) may be incomplete, imprecise, fragmentary, not fully reliable, vague, contradictory, or deficient in some other way. In general, these various information deficiencies may result in different types of uncertainty.

Assume that we can measure the amount of uncertainty involved in a problem-solving situation conceptualized in a particular mathematical theory. Assume further that the amount of uncertainty can be reduced by obtaining relevant information as a result of some action (finding a relevant new fact, designing a relevant experiment and observing the experimental outcome, receiving a requested message, or discovering a relevant historical record). Then, the amount of information obtained by the action may be measured by the reduction of uncertainty that results from the action.

Information measured solely by the reduction of uncertainty does not capture the rich notion of information in human communication and cognition. It is not explicitly concerned with semantic and pragmatic aspects of information viewed in the broader sense. This does not mean, however, that information viewed in terms of uncertainty reduction ignores these aspects. It does not ignore them, but they are assumed to be fixed in each particular application. Furthermore, the notion of information as uncertainty reduction is sufficiently rich as a base for an additional treatment through which human communication and cognition can adequately be explicated.

It should be noted at this point that the concept of information has also been investigated in terms of the theory of computability, independent of the concept of uncertainty. In this approach, the amount of information represented by an object is measured by the length of the shortest possible program written in some standard language (e.g., a program for the standard Turing machine) by which the object is described in the sense that it can be computed. Information of this type is usually referred to as *descriptive information* or *algorithmic information*.

In this chapter, we are concerned solely with information conceived in terms of uncertainty reduction. To distinguish this conception of information from various other conceptions of information, let us call it *uncertainty-based information*.

The nature of uncertainty-based information depends on the mathematical theory within which uncertainty pertaining to various problem-solving situations is formalized. Each formalization of uncertainty in a problem-solving situation is a mathematical model of the situation. When we commit ourselves to a particular mathematical theory, our modeling becomes necessarily limited by the constraints of the theory. Clearly, a more general theory is capable of capturing uncertainties of some problem situations more faithfully than its less general competitors. As a rule, however, it involves greater computational demands.

Uncertainty-based information was first conceived in terms of classical set theory and, later, in terms of probability theory. The term *information theory* has almost invariably been used to refer to a theory based upon the well-known measure of probabilistic uncertainty established by Claude Shannon [1948]. Research on a broader conception of uncertainty-based information, liberated from the confines of classical set theory and probability theory, began in the early 1980s. The name *generalized information theory* was coined for a theory based upon this broader conception.

The ultimate goal of generalized information theory is to capture properties of uncertainty-based information formalized within any feasible mathematical framework. Although this goal has not been fully achieved as yet, substantial progress has been made in this direction since the early 1980s. In addition to classical set theory and probability theory, uncertainty-based information is now well understood in fuzzy set theory, possibility theory, and evidence theory.

When the seemingly unique connection between uncertainty and probability theory was broken, and uncertainty began to be conceived in terms of the much broader frameworks of fuzzy set theory and fuzzy measure theory, it soon became clear that uncertainty can be manifested in different forms. These forms represent distinct types of uncertainty. In probability theory, uncertainty is manifested only in one form.

Three types of uncertainty are now recognized in the five theories, in which measurement of uncertainty is currently well established. These three uncertainty types are: *nonspecificity* (or *imprecision*), which is connected with sizes (cardinalities) of relevant sets of alternatives; *fuzziness* (or *vagueness*), which results from imprecise boundaries of fuzzy sets; and *strife* (or *discord*), which expresses conflicts among the various sets of alternatives.

It is conceivable that other types of uncertainty will be discovered when the investigation of uncertainty extends to additional theories of uncertainty. Rather than speculating about this issue, this chapter is restricted to the three currently recognized types of uncertainty (and the associated information). It is shown, for each of the five theories of uncertainty, which uncertainty type is manifested in it and how the amount of uncertainty of that type can adequately be measured. The chapter is intended as a summary of existing results rather than a detailed exposition of the broad subject of uncertainty-based information. Hence, we do not cover axiomatic characterization of the various measures of uncertainty, proofs of their uniqueness, and other theoretical issues associated with them.

9.2 NONSPECIFICITY OF CRISP SETS

Measurement of uncertainty (and associated information) was first conceived in terms of classical set theory. It was shown by Hartley [1928] that using a function from the class of functions

$$U(A) = c \cdot \log_b |A|,$$

where $|A|$ denotes the cardinality of a finite nonempty set A, and b, c are positive constants ($b > 1, c > 0$), is the only sensible way to measure the amount of uncertainty associated with a finite set of possible alternatives. Each choice of values of the constants b and c determines the unit in which uncertainty is measured. When $b = 2$ and $c = 1$, which is the most common choice, uncertainty is measured in *bits*, and we obtain

$$U(A) = \log_2 |A|. \tag{9.1}$$

One bit of uncertainty is equivalent to the total uncertainty regarding the truth or falsity of one proposition.

Let the set function U defined by (9.1) be called a *Hartley function*. Its uniqueness as a measure of uncertainty (in bits) associated with sets of alternatives can also be proven axiomatically.

When the Hartley function U is applied to nonempty subsets of a given finite universal set X, it has the form

$$U : \mathcal{P}(X) - \{\varnothing\} \to \mathbb{R}^+.$$

In this case, its range is

$$0 \le U(A) \le \log_2 |X|.$$

The meaning of uncertainty measured by the Hartley function depends on the meaning of the set A. For example, when A is a set of predicted states of a variable (from the set X of all states defined for the variable), $U(A)$ is a measure of *predictive uncertainty*; when A is a set of possible diseases of a patient determined from relevant medical evidence, $U(A)$ is a measure of *diagnostic uncertainty*; when A is a set of possible answers to an unsettled historical question, $U(A)$ is a measure of *retrodictive uncertainty*; when A is a set of possible policies, $U(A)$ is a measure of *prescriptive uncertainty*.

Observe that uncertainty expressed in terms of sets of alternatives results from the nonspecificity inherent in each set. Large sets result in less specific predictions, retrodictions, and so forth than their smaller counterparts. Full specificity is obtained when all alternatives are eliminated except one. Hence, uncertainty expressed by sets of possible alternatives and measured by the Hartley function is well characterized by the term *nonspecificity*.

Consider now a situation characterized by a set A of possible alternatives (predictive, prescriptive, etc.). Assume that this set is reduced to its subset B by some action. Then, the amount of uncertainty-based information, $I(A, B)$, produced by the action, which is relevant to the situation, is equal to the amount of reduced uncertainty given by the difference $U(A) - U(B)$. That is,

$$I(A, B) = \log_2 \frac{|A|}{|B|}. \tag{9.2}$$

When the action eliminates all alternatives except one (i.e., when $|B| = 1$), we obtain $I(A, B) = \log_2 |A| = U(A)$. This means that $U(A)$ may also be viewed as the amount of information needed to characterize one element of set A.

Consider now two universal sets, X and Y, and assume that a relation $R \subseteq X \times Y$ describes a set of possible joint alternatives in some situation of interest. Assume further that the domain and range of R are sets $R_X \subseteq X$ and $R_Y \subseteq Y$, respectively. Then three distinct Hartley functions are applicable, defined on the power sets of X, Y, and $X \times Y$. To identify clearly which universal set is involved in each case, it is useful (and a common practice) to write $U(X)$, $U(Y)$, $U(X, Y)$ instead of $U(R_X)$, $U(R_Y)$, and $U(R)$, respectively. Functions

$$U(X) = \log_2 |R_X|, \tag{9.3}$$

$$U(Y) = \log_2 |R_Y| \tag{9.4}$$

are called *simple uncertainties*, while function

$$U(X, Y) = \log_2 |R| \tag{9.5}$$

is called a *joint uncertainty*.

Two additional Hartley functions are defined by the formulas

$$U(X|Y) = \log_2 \frac{|R|}{|R_Y|}, \tag{9.6}$$

$$U(Y|X) = \log_2 \frac{|R|}{|R_X|}, \tag{9.7}$$

which are called *conditional uncertainties*.

Observe that the ratio $|R|/|R_Y|$ in $U(X|Y)$ represents the average number of elements of X that are possible alternatives under the condition that an element of Y has already been selected. This means that $U(X|Y)$ measures the average nonspecificity regarding alternative choices from X for all particular choices from Y. Function $U(Y|X)$ clearly has a similar meaning, with the roles of sets X and Y exchanged. Observe also that the conditional uncertainties can be expressed in terms of the joint uncertainty and the two simple uncertainties:

$$U(X|Y) = U(X, Y) - U(Y), \tag{9.8}$$

$$U(Y|X) = U(X, Y) - U(X). \tag{9.9}$$

Furthermore,

$$U(X) - U(Y) = U(X|Y) - U(Y|X), \tag{9.10}$$

which follows immediately from (9.8) and (9.9).

If possible alternatives from X do not depend on selections from Y, and vice versa, then $R = X \times Y$ and the sets X and Y are called *noninteractive*. Then, clearly,

$$U(X|Y) = U(X), \tag{9.11}$$

$$U(Y|X) = U(Y), \tag{9.12}$$

$$U(X, Y) = U(X) + U(Y). \tag{9.13}$$

In all other cases, when sets X and Y are *interactive*, these equations become the inequalities

$$U(X|Y) < U(X), \tag{9.14}$$

$$U(Y|X) < U(Y), \tag{9.15}$$

$$U(X,Y) < U(X) + U(Y). \tag{9.16}$$

The following symmetric function, which is usually referred to as *information transmission*, is a useful indicator of the strength of constraint between sets X and Y:

$$T(X,Y) = U(X) + U(Y) - U(X,Y). \tag{9.17}$$

When the sets are noninteractive, $T(X,Y) = 0$; otherwise, $T(X,Y) > 0$. Using (9.8) and (9.9), $T(X,Y)$ can also be expressed in terms of the conditional uncertainties

$$T(X,Y) = U(X) - U(X|Y), \tag{9.18}$$

$$T(X,Y) = U(Y) - U(Y|X). \tag{9.19}$$

Information transmission can be generalized to express the constraint among more than two sets. It is always expressed as the difference between the total information based on the individual sets and the joint information. Formally,

$$T(X_1, X_2, \ldots, X_n) = \sum_{i=1}^{n} U(X_i) - U(X_1, X_2, \ldots, X_n). \tag{9.20}$$

Example 9.1

Consider two variables x and y whose values are taken from sets $X = \{\text{low, medium, high}\}$ and $Y = \{1, 2, 3, 4\}$, respectively. It is known that the variables are constrained by the relation R, expressed by the matrix

$$
\begin{array}{c}
\\
\text{Low} \\
\text{Medium} \\
\text{High}
\end{array}
\begin{array}{cccc}
1 & 2 & 3 & 4 \\
\left[\begin{array}{cccc}
1 & 1 & 1 & 1 \\
1 & 0 & 1 & 0 \\
0 & 1 & 0 & 0
\end{array}\right]
\end{array}
$$

We can see that the *low* value of x does not constrain y at all, the *medium* value of x constrains y partially, and the *high* value constrains it totally. The following types of Hartley information can be calculated in this example:

$$U(X) = \log_2 |X| = \log_2 3 = 1.6,$$

$$U(Y) = \log_2 |Y| = \log_2 4 = 2,$$

$$U(X,Y) = \log_2 |R| = \log_2 7 = 2.8,$$

$$U(X|Y) = U(X,Y) - U(Y) = 2.8 - 2 = .8,$$

$$U(Y|X) = U(X,Y) - U(X) = 2.8 - 1.6 = 1.2,$$

$$T(X,Y) = U(X) + U(Y) - U(X,Y) = 1.6 + 2 - 2.8 = .8.$$

The Hartley function in the form (9.1) is applicable only to finite sets. However, this form may be appropriately modified to infinite sets on $\mathbb{R}$ (or, more generally, $\mathbb{R}^k$ for some natural number k). Given a measurable and Lebesgue-integrable subset A of $\mathbb{R}$ (or $\mathbb{R}^k$), a meaningful counterpart of (9.1) for infinite sets takes the form

$$U(A) = \log[1 + \mu(A)], \tag{9.21}$$

where $\mu(A)$ is the measure of A defined by the Lebesgue integral of the characteristic function of A. For example, when A is an interval $[a, b]$ on $\mathbb{R}$, then $\mu(A) = b - a$ and

$$U([a, b]) = \log[1 + b - a].$$

The choice of the logarithm in (9.21) is less significant than in (9.1) since values $U(A)$ obtained for infinite sets by (9.21) do not yield any meaningful interpretation in terms of uncertainty regarding truth values of a finite number of propositions and, consequently, they are not directly comparable with values obtained for finite sets by (9.1). For its mathematical convenience, the natural logarithm is a suitable choice.

9.3 NONSPECIFICITY OF FUZZY SETS

A natural generalization of the Hartley function from classical set theory to fuzzy set theory was proposed in the early 1980s under the name *U-uncertainty*. For any nonempty fuzzy set A defined on a finite universal set X, the generalized Hartley function has the form

$$U(A) = \frac{1}{h(A)} \int_0^{h(A)} \log_2 |{}^\alpha A| d\alpha, \tag{9.22}$$

where $|{}^\alpha A|$ denotes the cardinality of the α-cut of A and $h(A)$ is the height of A. Observe that $U(A)$, which measures nonspecificity of A, is a weighted average of values of the Hartley function for all distinct α-cuts of the normalized counterpart of A, defined by $A(x)/h(A)$ for all $x \in X$. Each weight is a difference between the values of α of a given α-cut and the immediately preceding α-cut. For any $A, B \in \mathcal{F}(X) - \{\varnothing\}$, if $A(x)/h(A) = B(x)/h(B)$ for all $x \in X$, then $U(A) = U(B)$. That is, fuzzy sets that are equal when normalized have the same nonspecificity measured by function U.

Example 9.2

Consider a fuzzy set A on $\mathbb{N}$ whose membership function is defined by the dots in the diagram in Fig. 9.1; we assume that $A(x) = 0$ for all $x > 15$. Applying formula (9.22) to A, we obtain:

$$\int_0^1 \log_2 |{}^\alpha A| d\alpha = \int_0^{.1} \log_2 15 d\alpha + \int_{.1}^{.3} \log_2 12 d\alpha + \int_{.3}^{.4} \log_2 11 d\alpha$$

$$+ \int_{.4}^{.6} \log_2 9 d\alpha + \int_{.6}^{.7} \log_2 7 d\alpha + \int_{.7}^{.9} \log_2 5 d\alpha + \int_{.9}^1 \log_2 3 d\alpha$$

$$= .1 \log_2 15 + .2 \log_2 12 + .1 \log_2 11 + .2 \log_2 9 + .1 \log_2 7$$

$$+ .2 \log_2 5 + .1 \log_2 3 = 2.99.$$

The amount of nonspecifity associated with the given fuzzy set is thus approximately three bits. This is equivalent to the nonspecifity of a crisp set that contains eight elements, for example, the set $\{6, 7, \ldots, 13\}$, whose characteristic function is illustrated in Fig. 9.1 by the shaded area.

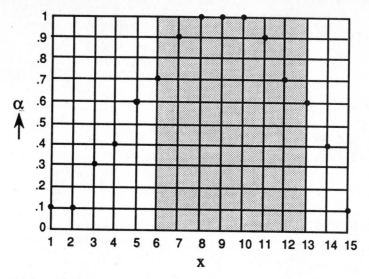

Figure 9.1 Membership functions of fuzzy set A (defined by the dots) and crisp set C (defined by the shaded area).

When a nonempty fuzzy set A is defined on $\mathbb{R}$ (or $\mathbb{R}^k$ for some $k \in \mathbb{N}$), and the α-cuts ${}^{\alpha}A$ are infinite sets (e.g., intervals of real numbers), we have to calculate $U(A)$ by the modified form

$$U(A) = \frac{1}{h(A)} \int_0^{h(A)} \log[1 + \mu({}^{\alpha}A)]d\alpha, \tag{9.23}$$

which is a generalization of (9.21). It is assumed that ${}^{\alpha}A$ is a measurable and Lebesgue-integrable function; $\mu({}^{\alpha}A)$ is the measure of ${}^{\alpha}A$ defined by the Lebesgue integral of the characteristic function of ${}^{\alpha}A$. As in the discrete case, defined by (9.22), fuzzy sets that are equal when normalized have the same nonspecificity.

Example 9.3

Consider fuzzy sets A_1, A_2, A_3 on $\mathbb{R}$, whose membership functions are depicted in Fig. 9.2. To calculate the nonspecificities of these fuzzy sets by (9.23), we have to determine for each set A_i ($i = 1, 2, 3$) the measure $\mu({}^{\alpha}A_i)$ as a function of α. In each case, the α-cuts ${}^{\alpha}A_i$ are intervals ${}^{\alpha}A_i = [a_i(\alpha), b_i(\alpha)]$, and hence, $\mu({}^{\alpha}A_i) = b_i(\alpha) - a_i(\alpha)$. For A_1,

$$A_1(x) = \begin{cases} x/2 & \text{for } x \in [0, 2] \\ 2 - x/2 & \text{for } x \in [2, 4] \\ 0 & \text{otherwise,} \end{cases}$$

and $a_1(\alpha)$ and $b_1(\alpha)$ are determined by the equations $\alpha = a_1(\alpha)/2$ and $\alpha = 2 - b_1(\alpha)/2$. Hence, ${}^{\alpha}A_1 = [2\alpha, 4 - 2\alpha]$ and $\mu({}^{\alpha}A_1) = 4 - 4\alpha$. Now applying (9.23) and choosing the natural logarithm for convenience, we obtain

$$U(A_1) = \int_0^1 \ln(5 - 4\alpha)d\alpha = \left[-\frac{1}{4}(5 - 4\alpha)\ln(5 - 4\alpha) - \alpha \right]_0^1$$

$$= \frac{5}{4}\ln 5 - 1 = 1.012.$$

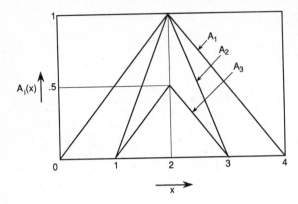

Figure 9.2 Fuzzy sets employed in Example 9.3.

Similarly, for the other two fuzzy sets, we have

$$U(A_2) = \int_0^1 \ln(3 - 2\alpha)d\alpha = \left[-\frac{1}{2}(3 - 2\alpha)\ln(3 - 2\alpha) - \alpha \right]_0^1$$

$$= \frac{3}{2}\ln 3 - 1 = 0.648,$$

$$U(A_3) = 2\int_0^{.5} \ln(3 - 4\alpha)d\alpha = 2\left[-\frac{1}{4}(3 - 4\alpha)\ln(3 - 4\alpha) - \alpha \right]_0^{.5}$$

$$= 2(\frac{3}{4}\ln 3 - \frac{1}{2}) = 0.648.$$

Observe that set A_3, which is not normal, can be normalized by replacing $A_3(x)$ with $2A_3(x)$ for each $x \in \mathbb{R}$. Since $2A_3(x) = A_2(x)$, set A_2 may be viewed as the normalized counterpart of A_3. These two sets have the same nonspecificity, which is true for any fuzzy set and its normal counterparts (the latter may, of course, be the set itself).

In general, given a normal fuzzy set $A \in \mathcal{F}(X)$, all fuzzy sets B in the infinite family

$$\mathcal{B}_A = \{B \in \mathcal{F}(X) - \{\varnothing\} \mid B(x) = h(B)A(x) \text{ for all } x \in X\} \qquad (9.24)$$

have the same nonspecificity, regardless whether X is finite or infinite and we apply (9.22) or (9.23), respectively. Although the sets in $\mathcal{B}_A$ are not distinguished by the nonspecificity, they are clearly distinguished by their heights $h(B)$. For each fuzzy set $B \in \mathcal{B}_A$, its height may be viewed as the degree of *validity* or *credibility* of information expressed by the fuzzy set. From this point of view, information expressed by the empty set has no validity. This explains why it is reasonable to exclude the empty set from the domain of function U.

The U-uncertainty was investigated more thoroughly within possibility theory, utilizing ordered possibility distributions. In this domain, function U has the form

$$U : \mathcal{R} \to \mathbb{R}^+,$$

where $\mathcal{R}$ denotes the set of all finite and ordered possibility distributions, each of which represents a normal fuzzy set. Given a possibility distribution

$$\mathbf{r} = \langle r_1, r_2, \dots, r_n \rangle \text{ such that } 1 = r_1 \geq r_2 \geq \dots \geq r_n,$$

the U-uncertainty of $\mathbf{r}$, $U(\mathbf{r})$, can be expressed by a convenient form,

$$U(\mathbf{r}) = \sum_{i=2}^{n} (r_i - r_{i+1}) \log_2 i, \qquad (9.25)$$

where $r_{n+1} = 0$ by convention.

Assume that the possibility distribution $\mathbf{r}$ in (9.25) represents a normal fuzzy set A in (9.22) in the way discussed in Sec. 7.4. Then it is easy to see that $U(\mathbf{r}) = U(A)$ whenever $r_i - r_{i+1} > 0$, i represents the cardinality of the α-cut with $\alpha = r_i$.

When terms on the right-hand side of (9.25) are appropriately combined, the U-uncertainty can be expressed by another formula:

$$U(\mathbf{r}) = \sum_{i=2}^{n} r_i \log_2 \frac{i}{i-1}. \qquad (9.26)$$

Furthermore, (9.25) can be written as

$$U(\mathbf{m}) = \sum_{i=2}^{n} m_i \log_2 i, \qquad (9.27)$$

where $\mathbf{m} = \langle m_1, m_2, \ldots, m_n \rangle$ represents the basic probability assignment corresponding to $\mathbf{r}$ in the sense of the convention introduced in Sec. 7.3.

Example 9.4

Calculate $U(\mathbf{r})$ for the possibility distribution

$$\mathbf{r} = \langle 1, 1, .8, .7, .7, .7, .4, .3, .2, .2 \rangle.$$

Let us use (9.27), which is particularly convenient for calculating the U-uncertainty. First, using the equation $m_i = r_i - r_{i+1}$ for all $i = 1, 2, \ldots, 10$, and assuming $r_{11} = 0$, we determine

$$\mathbf{m} = t(\mathbf{r}) = \langle 0, .2, .1, 0, 0, .3, .1, .1, 0, .2 \rangle.$$

Now, we apply components of $\mathbf{m}$ to (9.27) and obtain

$$U(\mathbf{r}) = 0 \log_2 1 + .2 \log_2 2 + .1 \log_2 3 + 0 \log_2 4 + 0 \log_2 5 + .3 \log_2 6$$
$$+ .1 \log_2 7 + .1 \log_2 8 + 0 \log_2 9 + .2 \log_2 10 = 2.18$$

Consider now two universal sets, X and Y, and a joint possibility distribution $\mathbf{r}$ defined on $X \times Y$. Adopting the notation introduced for the Hartley function, let $U(X, Y)$ denote the joint U-uncertainty, and let $U(X)$ and $U(Y)$ denote simple U-uncertainties defined on the marginal possibility distributions $\mathbf{r}_X$ and $\mathbf{r}_Y$, respectively. Then, we have

$$U(X) = \sum_{A \in \mathcal{F}_X} m_X(A) \log_2 |A|, \qquad (9.28)$$

$$U(Y) = \sum_{B \in \mathcal{F}_Y} m_Y(B) \log_2 |B|, \qquad (9.29)$$

$$U(X, Y) = \sum_{A \times B \in \mathcal{F}} m(A \times B) \log_2 |A \times B|, \qquad (9.30)$$

where $\mathcal{F}_X, \mathcal{F}_Y, \mathcal{F}$ are sets of focal elements induced by m_X, m_Y, m, respectively. Furthermore, we define conditional U-uncertainties, $U(X|Y)$ and $U(Y|X)$, as the following generalizations of the corresponding conditional Hartley functions:

$$U(X|Y) = \sum_{A \times B \in \mathcal{F}} m(A \times B) \log_2 \frac{|A \times B|}{|B|}, \qquad (9.31)$$

$$U(Y|X) \doteq \sum_{A \times B \in \mathcal{F}} m(A \times B) \log_2 \frac{|A \times B|}{|A|}. \qquad (9.32)$$

Observe that the term $|A \times B|/|B|$ in (9.31) represents for each focal element $A \times B$ in $\mathcal{F}$ the average number of elements of A that remain possible alternatives under the condition that an element of Y has already been selected. Expressing $U(X|Y)$ in the form of (9.22), we have

$$U(X|Y) = \int_0^1 \log_2 \frac{|^\alpha(E \times F)|}{|^\alpha F|} d\alpha$$

$$= \int_0^1 \log_2 |^\alpha(E \times F)| d\alpha - \int_0^1 \log_2 |^\alpha F| d\alpha \qquad (9.33)$$

$$= U(X, Y) - U(Y).$$

This equation is clearly a generalization of (9.8) from crisp sets to normal fuzzy sets, and by (9.22) to subnormal fuzzy sets. Observe that the focal elements A, B in (9.31) correspond to the α-cuts $^\alpha E, {}^\alpha F$ in (9.33), respectively. In a similar way, a generalization of (9.9) can be derived. Using these two generalized equations, it can easily be shown that (9.10)–(9.16) are also valid for the U-uncertainty. Furthermore, information transmission can be defined for the U-uncertainty by (9.17), and, then, (9.18) and (9.19) are also valid in the generalized framework.

9.4 FUZZINESS OF FUZZY SETS

The second type of uncertainty that involves fuzzy sets (but not crisp sets) is fuzziness (or vagueness). In general, a *measure of fuzziness* is a function

$$f : \mathcal{F}(X) \rightarrow \mathbb{R}^+,$$

where $\mathcal{F}(X)$ denotes the set of all fuzzy subsets of X (fuzzy power set). For each fuzzy set A, this function assigns a nonnegative real number $f(A)$ that expresses the degree to which the boundary of A is not sharp.

In order to qualify as a sensible measure of fuzziness, function f must satisfy some requirements that adequately capture our intuitive comprehension of the degree of fuzziness. The following three requirements are essential:

1. $f(A) = 0$ iff A is a crisp set;
2. $f(A)$ attains its maximum iff $A(x) = 0.5$ for all $x \in X$, which is intuitively conceived as the highest fuzziness;
3. $f(A) \leq f(B)$ when set A is undoubtedly sharper than set B, which, according to our intuition, means that

$$A(x) \le B(x) \text{ when } B(x) \le 0.5$$

and

$$A(x) \ge B(x) \text{ when } B(x) \ge 0.5$$

for all $x \in X$.

There are different ways of measuring fuzziness that all satisfy the three essential requirements. One way is to measure fuzziness of any set A by a metric distance between its membership grade function and the membership grade function (or characteristic function) of the nearest crisp set. Even when committing to this conception of measuring fuzziness, the measurement is not unique. To make it unique, we have to choose a suitable distance function.

Another way of measuring fuzziness, which seems more practical as well as more general, is to view the fuzziness of a set in terms of the lack of distinction between the set and its complement. Indeed, it is precisely the lack of distinction between sets and their complements that distinguishes fuzzy sets from crisp sets. The less a set differs from its complement, the fuzzier it is. Let us restrict our discussion to this view of fuzziness, which is currently predominant in the literature.

Measuring fuzziness in terms of distinctions between sets and their complements is dependent on the definition of a fuzzy complement (Sec. 3.2). This issue is not discussed here. For the sake of simplicity, we assume that only the standard fuzzy complement is employed. If other types of fuzzy complements were also considered, the second and third of the three properties required of function f would have to be generalized by replacing the value 0.5 with the equilibrium of the fuzzy complement employed.

Employing the standard fuzzy complement, we can still choose different distance functions to express the lack of distinction of a set and its complement. One that is simple and intuitively easy to comprehend is the Hamming distance, defined by the sum of absolute values of differences. Choosing the Hamming distance, the local distinction (one for each $x \in X$) of a given set A and its complement is measured by

$$|A(x) - (1 - A(x))| = |2A(x) - 1|,$$

and the lack of each local distinction is measured by

$$1 - |2A(x) - 1|.$$

The measure of fuzziness, $f(A)$, is then obtained by adding all these local measurements:

$$f(A) = \sum_{x \in X} (1 - |2A(x) - 1|). \tag{9.34}$$

The range of function f is $[0, |X|]$; $f(A) = 0$ iff A is a crisp set; $f(A) = |X|$ when $A(x) = 0.5$ for all $x \in X$.

Applying, for example, (9.34) to the fuzzy set A defined in Fig. 9.1, we obtain

$$f(A) = \sum_{i=1}^{15} (1 - |2A(x) - 1|)$$

$$= 15 - (.8 + .8 + .4 + .2 + .2 + .4 + .8 + 1 + 1 + 1 + .8 + .4 + .2 + .2 + .8)$$

$$= 15 - 9 = 6.$$

Formula (9.34) is applicable only to fuzzy sets defined on finite universal sets. However, it can be readily modified to fuzzy sets defined on infinite but bounded subsets of $\mathbb{R}$ (or $\mathbb{R}^k$ for some natural number k). Consider, for example, that $X = [a, b]$, which is perhaps the most practical case. Then, (9.34) needs to be modified by replacing the summation with integration. This replacement results in the formula

$$f(A) = \int_a^b (1 - |2A(x) - 1|)dx$$

$$= b - a - \int_a^b |2A(x) - 1|dx. \tag{9.35}$$

Example 9.5

Calculate the degrees of fuzziness of the three fuzzy sets defined in Fig. 9.2. Assuming that the sets are defined within the interval $[0, 4]$ and using (9.35), we obtain:

$$f(A_1) = 4 - \int_0^2 |x - 1|dx - \int_2^4 |3 - x|dx$$

$$= 4 - \int_0^1 (1 - x)dx - \int_1^2 (x - 1)dx - \int_2^3 (3 - x)dx - \int_3^4 (x - 3)dx$$

$$= 4 + \left[\frac{(1 - x)^2}{2}\right]_0^1 - \left[\frac{(x - 1)^2}{2}\right]_1^2 + \left[\frac{(3 - x)^2}{2}\right]_2^3 - \left[\frac{(x - 3)^2}{2}\right]_3^4$$

$$= 4 - .5 - .5 - .5 - .5 = 2,$$

$$f(A_2) = 4 - \int_0^1 dx - \int_1^2 |2x - 3|dx - \int_2^3 |5 - 2x|dx - \int_3^4 dx$$

$$= 4 - 1 - .5 - .5 - 1 = 1,$$

$$f(A_3) = 4 - \int_0^1 dx - \int_1^2 |x - 2|dx - \int_2^3 |2 - x|dx - \int_3^4 dx$$

$$= 4 - 1 - .5 - .5 - 1 = 1.$$

Although set A_3 and its normal counterpart, set A_2, happen to be equally fuzzy, this is not a general property, contrary to nonspecificity, of sets in a given family $\mathcal{B}_A$ defined by (9.24). To illustrate this difference between nonspecificity and fuzziness, let us calculate the degree of fuzziness for two additional fuzzy sets, A_4 and A_5, both of which belong to $\mathcal{B}_{A_2}$ with $h(A_4) = .4$ and $h(A_5) = .625$. That is,

$$A_k(x) = \begin{cases} h(A_k)(x - 1) & \text{for } x \in [1, 2] \\ h(A_k)(3 - x) & \text{for } x \in [2, 3] \\ 0 & \text{otherwise,} \end{cases}$$

where $k = 4, 5$, and we obtain:

$$f(A_4) = 4 - \int_0^1 dx - \int_1^2 (1.8 - .8x)dx - \int_2^3 (.8x - 1.4)dx - \int_3^4 dx$$

$$= 4 - 1 - .6 - .6 - 1 = .8,$$

$$f(A_5) = 4 - \int_0^1 dx - \int_1^2 |1.25x - 2.25|dx - \int_2^3 |2.75 - 1.25x|dx - \int_3^4 dx$$

$$= 4 - 1 - .425 - .425 - 1 = 1.15.$$

The meaning of the calculations in this example is illustrated in Fig. 9.3. For the universal set [0, 4] and each of the fuzzy sets A_1–A_5, the shaded areas indicate for each $x \in [0, 4]$ the difference between membership grades of the set and its complement. Since the degree of fuzziness is expressed in terms of the deficiency of these differences with respect to 1, it is measured by the total size of the unshaded areas in each diagram.

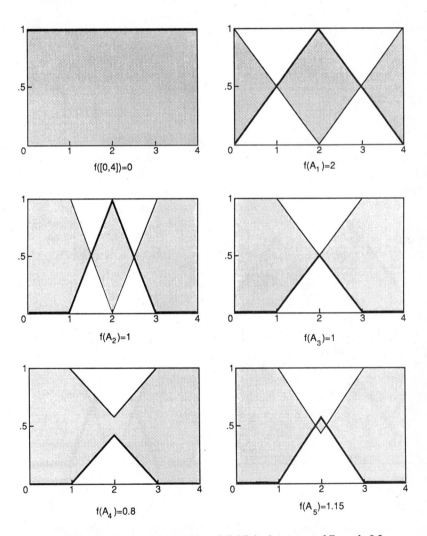

Figure 9.3 Illustration of the meaning of (9.35) in the context of Example 9.5.

It is important to realize that nonspecificity and fuzziness, which are both applicable to fuzzy sets, are distinct types of uncertainty. Moreover, they are totally independent of each other. Observe, for example, that the two fuzzy sets defined by their membership functions in Fig. 9.1 have almost the same nonspecificity (Example 9.2), but their degrees of fuzziness are quite different. On the other hand, fuzzy sets depicted in Fig. 9.4 have very different nonspecificities, but their degrees of fuzziness are exactly the same.

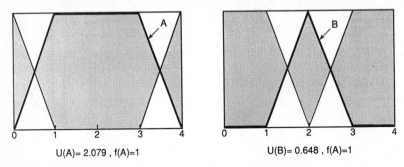

U(A)= 2.079 , f(A)=1   U(B)= 0.648 , f(A)=1

Figure 9.4   Example of a fuzzy set with very different nonspecificities, but equal fuzziness.

Fuzziness and nonspecificity are also totally different in their connections to information. When nonspecificity is reduced, we view the reduction as a gain in information, regardless of the associated change in fuzziness. The opposite, however, is not true. Whether it is meaningful to view a reduction in fuzziness as a gain in information depends on the accompanied change in nonspecificity. The view is reasonable when nonspecificity also decreases or remains the same, but it is questionable when nonspecificity increases. To illustrate this point, let us consider an integer-valued variable whose exact value is of interest, but the only available information regarding its value is given in terms of the fuzzy set A whose membership function is defined by the dots in Fig. 9.1. This information is incomplete; consequently, it results in uncertainty regarding the actual value of the variable: $U(A) = 2.99$, $f(A) = 6$. Assume now that we learn, as a result of some action, that the actual value of the variable is at least 6 and no more than 13. This defines a crisp set $B = \{6, 7, \ldots, 13\}$ whose characteristic function is illustrated in Fig. 9.1 by the shaded area. We have now $U(B) = 3$ and $f(B) = 0$. Although there is virtually no change in nonspecificity, the action helped us to completely eliminate fuzziness. It is reasonable to view the amount of eliminated fuzziness as a result of some proportional amount of information gained.

9.5   UNCERTAINTY IN EVIDENCE THEORY

Nonspecificity

The Hartley function, as a measure of nonspecificity, was first generalized from classical set theory to fuzzy set theory and possibility theory (Sec. 9.3). Once this generalized function, the U-uncertainty, was well established in possibility theory, a special branch of evidence theory, it was relatively easy to generalize it further and make it applicable within all of evidence theory.

To distinguish the U-uncertainty from its more general counterpart in evidence theory, let the latter be denoted by N. It is defined by the formula

$$N(m) = \sum_{A \in \mathcal{F}} m(A) \log_2 |A|, \tag{9.36}$$

where $\langle \mathcal{F}, m \rangle$ is an arbitrary body of evidence. This function was proven a unique measure of nonspecificity in evidence theory under well-justified axioms and the choice of bits as measurement units. When focal elements in $\mathcal{F}$ are nested, N becomes the U-uncertainty.

Function N is clearly a weighted average of the Hartley function for all focal elements. The weights are values of the basic probability assignment. For each focal element A, $m(A)$ indicates the degree of evidence focusing on A, while $\log_2 |A|$ indicates the lack of specificity of this evidential claim. The larger the value of $m(A)$, the stronger the evidence; the larger the set A (and $\log_2 |A|$), the less specific the evidence. Consequently, it is reasonable to view function N as a *measure of nonspecificity*.

The range of function N is, as expected, $[0, \log_2 |X|]$. The minimum, $N(m) = 0$, is obtained when $m(\{x\}) = 1$ for some $x \in X$ (no uncertainty); the maximum, $N(m) = \log_2 |X|$, is reached for $m(X) = 1$ (total ignorance). It can easily be shown that (9.8)–(9.19) for the Hartley function remain valid when it is generalized to the N-uncertainty.

Since focal elements in probability measures are singletons, $|A| = 1$ and $\log_2 |A| = 0$ for each focal element. Consequently, $N(m) = 0$ for every probability measure. That is, probability theory is not capable of incorporating nonspecificity, one of the basic types of uncertainty. All probability measures are fully specific and, hence, are not distinguished from one another by their nonspecificities. What, then, is actually measured by the Shannon entropy, which is a well-established measure of uncertainty in probability theory? Before attempting to answer this question, let us review the key properties of the Shannon entropy.

The Shannon Entropy

The *Shannon entropy*, H, which is applicable only to probability measures, assumes in evidence theory the form

$$H(m) = - \sum_{x \in X} m(\{x\}) \log_2 m(\{x\}). \tag{9.37}$$

This function, which forms the basis of *classical information theory*, measures the average uncertainty (in bits) associated with the prediction of outcomes in a random experiment; its range is $[0, \log_2 |X|]$. Clearly, $H(m) = 0$ when $m(\{x\}) = 1$ for some $x \in X$; $H(m) = \log_2 |X|$ when m defines the uniform probability distribution on X (i.e., $m(\{x\}) = 1/|X|$ for all $x \in X$).

As the name suggests, function H was proposed by Shannon [1948]. It was proven in numerous ways, from several well-justified axiomatic characterizations, that this function is the only sensible measure of uncertainty in probability theory. It is also well known that (9.8)–(9.19) are valid when function U is replaced with function H.

Since values $m(\{x\})$ are required to add to 1 for all $x \in X$, (9.37) can be rewritten as

$$H(m) = - \sum_{x \in X} m(\{x\}) \log_2 [1 - \sum_{y \neq x} m(\{y\})]. \tag{9.38}$$

The term

$$\text{Con}(\{x\}) = \sum_{y \neq x} m(\{y\}) \tag{9.39}$$

in (9.38) represents the total evidential claim pertaining to focal elements that are different with the focal element $\{x\}$. That is, $\text{Con}(\{x\})$ expresses the sum of all evidential claims that fully conflict with the one focusing on $\{x\}$. Clearly, $\text{Con}(\{x\}) \in [0, 1]$ for each $x \in X$. The function $-\log_2[1 - \text{Con}(\{x\})]$, which is employed in (9.38), is monotonic increasing with $\text{Con}(\{x\})$ and extends its range from $[0, 1]$ to $[0, \infty)$. The choice of the logarithmic function is a result of the axiomatic requirement that the joint uncertainty of several independent random variables be equal to the sum of their individual uncertainty.

It follows from these facts and from the form of (9.38) that the Shannon entropy is the mean (expected) value of the *conflict* among evidential claims within a given probabilistic body of evidence.

When a probability measure is defined on a real interval $[a, b]$ by a probability density function f, the Shannon entropy is not directly applicable as a measure of uncertainty. It can be employed only in a modified form,

$$D(f(x), g(x)|x \in [a, b]) = \int_a^b f(x) \log_2 \frac{f(x)}{g(x)} dx, \tag{9.40}$$

which involves two probability density functions, $f(x)$ and $g(x)$, defined on $[a, b]$. Its finite counterpart is the function

$$D(p(x), q(x)|x \in X) = \sum_{x \in X} p(x) \log_2 \frac{p(x)}{q(x)}, \tag{9.41}$$

which is known in information theory as the *Shannon cross-entropy* or *directed divergence*. Function D measures uncertainty in relative rather than absolute terms.

When $f(x)$ in (9.40) is replaced with a density function, $f(x, y)$, of a joint probability distribution on $X \times Y$, and $g(x)$ is replaced with the product of density functions of marginal distributions on X and Y, $f_X(x) \cdot f_Y(y)$, D becomes equivalent to the information transmission given by (9.17). This means that the continuous counterpart of the information transmission can be expressed as

$$D(f(x, y), f_X(x) \cdot f_Y(y)|x \in [a, b], y \in [c, d]) =$$

$$\int_c^d \int_a^b f(x, y) \log_2 \frac{f(x, y)}{f_X(x) \cdot f_Y(y)} dx dy. \tag{9.42}$$

Entropy-like Measure in Evidence Theory

What form should the generalized counterpart of the Shannon entropy take in evidence theory? The answer is by no means obvious, as exhibited by several proposed candidates for the entropy-like measure in evidence theory. Let us introduce and critically examine each of them.

Two of the candidates were proposed in the early 1980s. One of them is function E, defined by the formula

$$E(m) = -\sum_{A \in \mathcal{F}} m(A) \log_2 \text{Pl}(A),\tag{9.43}$$

which is usually called a measure of *dissonance*. The other one is function C, defined by the formula

$$C(m) = -\sum_{A \in \mathcal{F}} m(A) \log_2 \text{Bel}(A),\tag{9.44}$$

which is referred to as a measure of *confusion*. It is obvious that both of these functions collapse into the Shannon entropy when m defines a probability measure.

To decide if either of the two functions is an appropriate generalization of the Shannon entropy in evidence theory, we have to determine what these functions actually measure.

From (7.11) and the general property of basic assignments (satisfied for every $A \in \mathcal{P}(X)$),

$$\sum_{A \cap B = \varnothing} m(B) + \sum_{A \cap B \neq \varnothing} m(B) = 1,$$

we obtain

$$E(m) = -\sum_{A \in \mathcal{F}} m(A) \log_2 [1 - \sum_{A \cap B = \varnothing} m(B)].\tag{9.45}$$

The term

$$K(A) = \sum_{A \cap B = \varnothing} m(B)$$

in (9.45) represents the total evidential claim pertaining to focal elements that are disjoint with the set A. That is, $K(A)$ expresses the sum of all evidential claims that fully conflict with the one focusing on the set A. Clearly, $K(A) \in [0, 1]$. The function

$$-\log_2 [1 - K(A)],$$

which is employed in (9.45), is monotonic increasing with $K(A)$ and extends its range from $[0, 1]$ to $[0, \infty)$. The choice of the logarithmic function is motivated in the same way as in the classical case of the Shannon entropy.

It follows from these facts and the form of (9.45) that $E(m)$ is the mean (expected) value of the conflict among evidential claims within a given body of evidence $\langle \mathcal{F}, m \rangle$; it measures the conflict in bits, and its range is $[0, \log_2 |X|]$.

Function E is not fully satisfactory since we feel intuitively that $m(B)$ conflicts with $m(A)$ not only when $B \cap A = \varnothing$; but also when $B \not\subseteq A$. This broader view of conflict is expressed by the measure of confusion C given by (9.44). Let us demonstrate this fact.

From (7.10) and the general property of basic assignments (satisfied for every $A \in \mathcal{P}(X)$),

$$\sum_{B \subseteq A} m(B) + \sum_{B \not\subseteq A} m(B) = 1,$$

we get

$$C(m) = -\sum_{A \in \mathcal{F}} m(A) \log_2 [1 - \sum_{B \not\subseteq A} m(B)].\tag{9.46}$$

The term

$$L(A) = \sum_{B \not\subseteq A} m(B)$$

in (9.46) expresses the sum of all evidential claims that conflict with the one focusing on the set A according to the following broader view of conflict: $m(B)$ conflicts with $m(A)$ whenever $B \not\subseteq A$. The reason for using the function

$$- \log_2 [1 - L(A)]$$

instead of $L(A)$ in (9.46) is the same as already explained in the context of function E. The conclusion is that $C(m)$ is the mean (expected) value of the conflict, viewed in the broader sense, among evidential claims within a given body of evidence $\langle \mathcal{F}, m \rangle$.

Function C is also not fully satisfactory as a measure of conflicting evidential claims within a body of evidence, but for a different reason than function E. Although it employs the broader, and more satisfactory, view of conflict, it does not properly scale each particular conflict of $m(B)$ with respect to $m(A)$ according to the degree of violation of the subsethood relation $B \subseteq A$. It is clear that the more this subsethood relation is violated, the greater the conflict. In addition, function C also has some undesirable mathematical properties. For example, its maximum is greater than $\log_2 |X|$.

To overcome the deficiencies of function E and C as adequate measures of conflict in evidence theory, a new function, D, was proposed:

$$D(m) = - \sum_{A \in \mathcal{F}} m(A) \log_2 \left[1 - \sum_{B \in \mathcal{F}} m(B) \frac{|B - A|}{|B|} \right]. \tag{9.47}$$

Observe that the term

$$\text{Con}(A) = \sum_{B \in \mathcal{F}} m(B) \frac{|B - A|}{|B|} \tag{9.48}$$

in (9.47) expresses the sum of individual conflicts of evidential claims with respect to a particular set A, each of which is properly scaled by the degree to which the subsethood $B \subseteq A$ is violated. This conforms to the intuitive idea of conflict that emerged from the critical reexamination of functions E and C. Let function Con, whose application to probability measures is given by (9.39), be called a *conflict*. Clearly, $\text{Con}(A) \in [0, 1]$ and, furthermore,

$$K(A) \leq \text{Con}(A) \leq L(A). \tag{9.49}$$

The reason for using the function

$$- \log_2 [1 - \text{Con}(A)]$$

instead of Con in (9.47) is exactly the same as previously explained in the context of function E. This monotonic transformation extends the range of $\text{Con}(A)$ from $[0, 1]$ to $[0, \infty)$.

Function D, which is called a measure of *discord*, is clearly a measure of the mean conflict (expressed by the logarithmic transformation of function Con) among evidential claims within each given body of evidence. It follows immediately (9.47) that

$$E(m) \leq D(m) \leq C(m). \tag{9.50}$$

Observe that $|B - A| = |B| - |A \cap B|$; consequently, (9.47) can be rewritten as

$$D(m) = -\sum_{A \in \mathcal{F}} m(A) \log_2 \sum_{B \in \mathcal{F}} m(B) \frac{|A \cap B|}{|B|}. \tag{9.51}$$

It is obvious that

$$\text{Bel}\,(A) \le \sum_{B \in \mathcal{F}} m(B) \frac{|A \cap B|}{|B|} \le \text{Pl}\,(A). \tag{9.52}$$

Although function D is intuitively more appealing than functions E and C, further examination reveals a conceptual defect in it. To explain the defect, let sets A and B in (9.48) be such that $A \subseteq B$. Then, according to function Con, the claim $m(B)$ is taken to be in conflict with the claim $m(A)$ to the degree $|B - A|/|B|$. This, however, should not be the case: the claim focusing on B is implied by the claim focusing on A (since $A \subseteq B$), and hence, $m(B)$ should not be viewed in this case as contributing to the conflict with $m(A)$.

Consider, as an example, incomplete information regarding the age of a person, say, Joe. Assume that the information is expressed by two evidential claims pertaining to the age of Joe: "Joe is between 15 and 17 years old" with degree $m(A)$, where $A = [15, 17]$, and "Joe is a teenager" with degree $m(B)$, where $B = [13, 19]$. Clearly, the weaker second claim does not conflict with the stronger first claim.

Assume now that $A \supseteq B$. In this case, the situation is inverted: the claim focusing on B is not implied by the claim focusing on A and, consequently, $m(B)$ does conflict with $m(A)$ to a degree proportional to number of elements in A that are not covered by B. This conflict is not captured by function Con since $|B - A| = 0$ in this case.

It follows from these observations that the total conflict of evidential claims within a body of evidence $\langle \mathcal{F}, m \rangle$ with respect to a particular claim $m(A)$ should be expressed by function

$$\text{CON}\,(A) = \sum_{B \in \mathcal{F}} m(B) \frac{|A - B|}{|A|}$$

rather than function Con given by (9.48). Replacing Con(A) in (9.47) with CON(A), we obtain a new function, which is better justified as a measure of conflict in evidence theory than function D. This new function, which is called *strife* and denoted by S, is defined by the form

$$S(m) = -\sum_{A \in \mathcal{F}} m(A) \log_2 \left[1 - \sum_{B \in \mathcal{F}} m(B) \frac{|A - B|}{|A|} \right]. \tag{9.53}$$

It is trivial to convert this form into a simpler one,

$$S(m) = -\sum_{A \in \mathcal{F}} m(A) \log_2 \sum_{B \in \mathcal{F}} m(B) \frac{|A \cap B|}{|A|}, \tag{9.54}$$

where the term $|A \cap B|/|A|$ expresses the degree of subsethood of set A in set B. Equation (9.54) can also be rewritten as

$$S(m) = N(m) - \sum_{A \in \mathcal{F}} m(A) \log_2 \sum_{B \in \mathcal{F}} m(B)|A \cap B|, \tag{9.55}$$

where $N(m)$ is the nonspecificity measure given by (9.36). Furthermore, introducing

$$Z(m) = \sum_{A \in \mathcal{F}} m(A) \log_2 \sum_{B \in \mathcal{F}} m(B) |A \cap B|, \qquad (9.56)$$

we have

$$S(m) = N(m) - Z(m).$$

It is reasonable to conclude that function S is well justified on intuitive grounds. It also has some desirable mathematical properties: it is additive, its measurement units are bits, it becomes the Shannon entropy for probability measures, and its range is $[0, \log_2 |X|]$, where $S(m) = 0$ when $m(\{x\}) = 1$ for some $x \in X$ and $S(m) = \log_2 |X|$ when $m(\{x\}) = 1/|X|$ for all $x \in X$.

Strife in Possibility Theory

Employing ordered possibility distributions $1 = r_1 \geq r_2 \geq \ldots \geq r_n$, the form of function S (strife) in possibility theory is very simple:

$$S(\mathbf{r}) = U(\mathbf{r}) - \sum_{i=2}^{n} (r_i - r_{i+1}) \log_2 \sum_{j=1}^{i} r_j, \qquad (9.57)$$

where $U(\mathbf{r})$ is the measure of possibilistic nonspecificity (U-uncertainty) given by (9.25). Combining the two terms in (9.57), we can express $S(\mathbf{r})$ in a more compact form,

$$S(\mathbf{r}) = \sum_{i=2}^{n} (r_i - r_{i+1}) \log_2 \frac{i}{\displaystyle\sum_{j=1}^{i} r_j}. \qquad (9.58)$$

It turns out that the mathematical properties of this function are almost the same as those of possibilistic discord function D. In particular, the maximum of possibilistic strife, given by (9.57), depends on n in exactly the same way as the maximum value of possibilistic discord: it increases with n and converges to a constant, estimated as 0.892 as $n \to \infty$. However, the possibility distributions for which the maximum of possibilistic strife are obtained (one for each value of n) are different from those for possibilistic discord.

Maximum values of possibilistic discord and possibilistic strife are plotted in Fig. 9.5 for $n = 2, 3, \ldots, 21$ by the circles and diamonds, respectively. We can observe the perfect match of maxima of the two functions. In Fig. 9.6, values of $r_2, r_3, \ldots, r_n$ are shown for which the maxima are obtained ($2 \leq n \leq 21$).

We may conclude from these results that the measures of both discord and strife, whose range in evidence theory is $[0, \log_2 |X|]$, are severely constrained within the domain of possibility theory. We may say that possibility theory is almost conflict-free. For large bodies of evidence, at least, these measures can be considered negligible when compared with the other type of uncertainty, nonspecificity. Neglecting strife (or discord), when justifiable, may substantially reduce computational complexity in dealing with large possibilistic bodies of evidence.

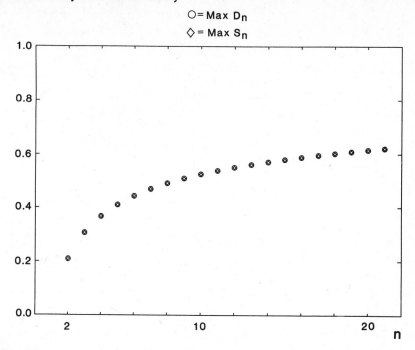

Figure 9.5 Maximum values of possibilistic discord (circles) and possibilistic strife (diamonds) for $n = 2, 3, \ldots, 21$.

Total Uncertainty

Since the two types of uncertainty, nonspecificity and strife, coexist in evidence theory, and both are measured in the same units, it is reasonable to consider the possibility of adding their individual measures to form a measure of total uncertainty. Following this idea and choosing the measure of strife defined by (9.54) as the best justified generalization of the Shannon entropy, the total uncertainty, NS, is defined by the equation

$$NS(m) = N(m) + S(m).$$

Substituting for $S(m)$ from (9.55) and for $N(m)$ from (9.36), we obtain

$$NS(m) = 2 \sum_{A \in \mathcal{F}} m(A) \log_2 |A| - \sum_{A \in \mathcal{F}} m(A) \log_2 \sum_{B \in \mathcal{F}} m(B)|A \cap B|$$

or, in a more compact form,

$$NS(m) = \sum_{A \in \mathcal{F}} m(A) \log_2 \frac{|A|^2}{\sum_{B \in \mathcal{F}} m(B)|A \cap B|}. \tag{9.59}$$

In possibility theory, the measure of total uncertainty clearly assumes the form

$$NS(\mathbf{r}) = \sum_{i=2}^{n} (r_i - r_{i+1}) \log_2 \frac{i^2}{\sum_{j=1}^{i} r_j}. \tag{9.60}$$

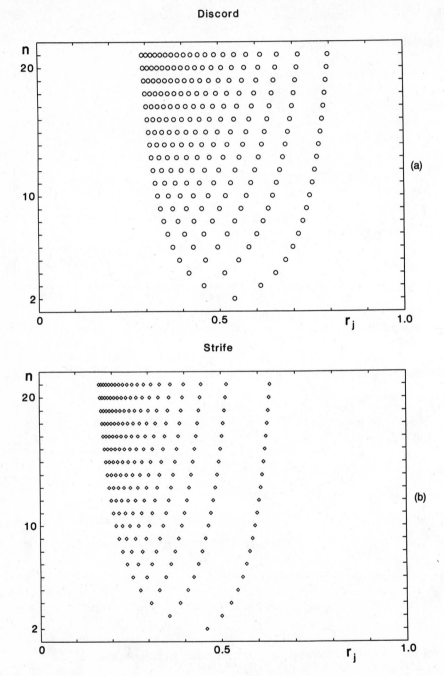

Figure 9.6 Values $r_1, r_2, \ldots, r_n$ for which the maxima shown in Fig. 9.5 are obtained: (a) discord; (b) strife.

The range of the total uncertainty NS is $[0, \log_2 |X|]$, which is the same as the range of each of its components. The minimum, $NS(m) = 0$, is obtained iff $m(\{x\}) = 1$ for some $x \in X$, which is the correct representation of complete certainty (full information). The maximum, $NS(m) = \log_2 |X|$, is not unique. Two significant maxima are obtained for $m(X) = 1$ (when $S(m) = 0$) and for $m(\{x\}) = 1/|X|$ for all $x \in X$ (when $N(m) = 0$).

Another measure of total uncertainty in evidence theory is based on the recognition that any given body of evidence defined on $\mathcal{P}(X)$ may be viewed as a set of constraints that define which probability distributions on X are acceptable. Among the acceptable probability distributions, one has the largest value of the Shannon entropy. It is reasonable to take this value as a measure of total uncertainty associated with the body of evidence. The measure, denoted by AU, is a function whose domain is the set of all belief measures. It is defined by

$$AU(\mathrm{Bel}) = \max\{-\sum_{x \in X} p_x \log_2 p_x\},$$

where the maximum is taken over all distributions $\langle p_x | x \in X \rangle$ that satisfy the constraints:

(a) $p_x \in [0, 1]$ for all $x \in X$ and $\sum_{x \in X} p_x = 1$;

(b) $\mathrm{Bel}(A) \leq \sum_{x \in A} p_x \leq 1 - \mathrm{Bel}(\overline{A})$ for all $A \subseteq X$.

This measure has even stronger justification in terms of mathematical properties than the measure NS, but it is computationally more cumbersome.

Fuzziness in Evidence Theory

Evidence theory normally operates with focal elements that are crisp subsets of a given universal set. However, the theory can be fuzzified, as can any other mathematical theory. Focal elements in fuzzified evidence theory are fuzzy sets, each of which has some degree of fuzziness. Given a body of evidence $\langle m, \mathcal{F} \rangle$ in which elements of $\mathcal{F}$ are fuzzy sets, it is reasonable to express the total degree of fuzziness, $F(m)$, of this body by the weighted average of the individual degrees of fuzziness, $f(A)$, of all focal elements ($A \in \mathcal{F}$), each weighted by $m(A)$. That is,

$$F(m) = \sum_{A \in \mathcal{F}} m(A) f(A), \tag{9.61}$$

where $f(A)$ is defined by (9.34).

Observe that the formulas for nonspecificity and strife, given by (9.36) and (9.54), remain unchanged when evidence theory is fuzzified, provided that the set cardinalities involved are interpreted as sigma counts of the respective fuzzy sets, and the standard fuzzy intersection is employed in (9.54).

9.6 SUMMARY OF UNCERTAINTY MEASURES

The three types of uncertainty whose measures are now well established in classical set theory, fuzzy set theory, probability theory, possibility theory, and evidence theory are summarized

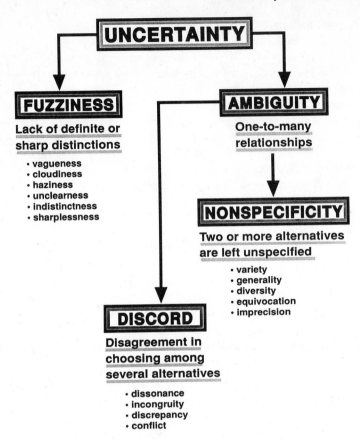

Figure 9.7 Three basic types of uncertainty.

in Fig. 9.7. Each type is depicted by a brief common-sense characterization and a group of pertinent synonyms. Two of the uncertainty types, *nonspecificity* and *strife*, are viewed as species of a higher uncertainty type, which seems well captured by the term *ambiguity*; the latter is associated with any situation in which it remains unclear which of several alternatives should be accepted as the genuine one. In general, ambiguity results from the lack of certain distinctions characterizing an object (nonspecificity), from conflicting distinctions, or from both of these. The third uncertainty type, *fuzziness*, is different from ambiguity; it results from the lack of sharpness of relevant distinctions.

Functions by which the various types of uncertainty are measured are summarized for finite sets in Table 9.1. For each function, four pieces of information are given in the table: the type of uncertainty measured by the function, the uncertainty theory to which the function applies, the year in which the function was proposed as a measure of the respective uncertainty, and the number of equation by which the function is defined. When dealing with infinite sets, no direct counterparts exist for some of these uncertainty measures, particularly in probability theory and evidence theory. However, for nonspecificity and fuzziness of fuzzy sets defined on bounded subsets of $\mathbb{R}$, such counterparts exist and are expressed by the formulas (9.21) and (9.35), respectively.

TABLE 9.1   SUMMARY OF BASIC UNCERTAINTY MEASURES FOR FINITE SETS

Uncertainty Theory	Uncertainty Measure	Equation	Uncertainty Type	Year
Classical set theory	$U(A) = \log_2 |A|$	(9.1)	Nonspecificity	1928
Fuzzy set theory	$U(A) = \dfrac{1}{h(A)} \displaystyle\int_0^{h(A)} \log_2 |^\alpha A| \, d\alpha$	(9.22)	Nonspecificity	1983
Possibility theory	$U(r) = \displaystyle\sum_{i=2}^{n} r_i \log_2 \dfrac{i}{i-1}$	(9.26)	Nonspecificity	1983
Evidence theory	$N(m) = \displaystyle\sum_{A \in \mathcal{F}} m(A) \log_2 |A|$	(9.36)	Nonspecificity	1985
Probability theory	$H(m) = -\displaystyle\sum_{x \in X} m(\{x\}) \log_2 m(\{x\})$	(9.37)	Strife	1948
Evidence theory	$S(m) = -\displaystyle\sum_{A \in \mathcal{F}} m(A) \log_2 \sum_{B \in \mathcal{F}} m(B) \dfrac{|A \cap B|}{|A|}$	(9.54)	Strife	1992
Possibility theory	$S(r) = \displaystyle\sum_{i=2}^{n} (r_i - r_{i+1}) \log_2 \dfrac{i}{\sum_{j=1}^{i} r_j}$	(9.58)	Strife	1992
Evidence theory	$NS(m) = \displaystyle\sum_{A \in \mathcal{F}} m(A) \log_2 \dfrac{|A|^2}{\sum_{B \in \mathcal{F}} m(B)|A \cap B|}$	(9.59)	Total: $N(m) + S(m)$	1992
Possibility theory	$NS(r) = \displaystyle\sum_{i=2}^{n} (r_i - r_{i+1}) \log_2 \dfrac{i^2}{\sum_{j=1}^{i} r_j}$	(9.60)	Total: $N(r) + S(r)$	1992
Fuzzy set theory	$f(A) = \displaystyle\sum_{x \in X} [1 - |2A(x) - 1|]$	(9.34)	Fuzziness	1979
Fuzzified evidence theory	$F(m) = \displaystyle\sum_{A \in \mathcal{F}} m(A) f(A)$	(9.61)	Fuzziness	1988

9.7 PRINCIPLES OF UNCERTAINTY

Once uncertainty (and information) measures become well justified, they can very effectively be utilized for managing uncertainty and the associated information. For example, they can be utilized for extrapolating evidence, assessing the strength of relationship between given groups of variables, assessing the influence of given input variables on given output variables, measuring the loss of information when a system is simplified, and the like. In many problem situations, the relevant measures of uncertainty are applicable only in their conditional or relative terms.

Although the utility of relevant uncertainty measures is as broad as the utility of any relevant measuring instrument, their role is particularly significant in three fundamental principles for managing uncertainty: the principle of minimum uncertainty, the principle of maximum uncertainty, and the principle of uncertainty invariance. Since types and measures of uncertainty substantially differ in different uncertainty theories, the principles result in considerably different mathematical problems when we move from one theory to another. In this section, we only explain the principal characteristics of each of these principles.

The Principle of Minimum Uncertainty

The *principle of minimum uncertainty* is basically an arbitration principle. It is used, in general, for narrowing down solutions in various systems problems that involve uncertainty. The principle states that we should accept only those solutions, from among all otherwise equivalent solutions, whose uncertainty (pertaining to the purpose concerned) is minimal.

A major class of problems for which the principle of minimum uncertainty is applicable are *simplification problems*. When a system is simplified, the loss of some information contained in the system is usually unavoidable. The amount of information that is lost in this process results in the increase of an equal amount of relevant uncertainty. Examples of relevant uncertainties are predictive, retrodictive, or prescriptive uncertainty. A sound simplification of a given system should minimize the loss of relevant information (or the increase in relevant uncertainty) while achieving the required reduction of complexity. That is, we should accept only such simplifications of a given system at any desirable level of complexity for which the loss of relevant information (or the increase in relevant uncertainty) is minimal. When properly applied, the principle of minimum uncertainty guarantees that no information is wasted in the process of simplification.

There are many simplification strategies, which can perhaps be classified into three main classes:

1. simplifications made by eliminating some entities from the system (variables subsystems, etc.);
2. simplifications made by aggregating some entities of the system (variables, states, etc.);
3. simplifications made by breaking overall systems into appropriate subsystems.

Regardless of the strategy employed, the principle of minimum uncertainty is utilized in the same way. It is an arbiter that decides which simplifications to choose at any given level of complexity.

Another application of the principle of minimum uncertainty is the area of *conflict-resolution problems*. For example, when we integrate several overlapping models into one larger model, the models may be locally inconsistent. It is reasonable, then, to require that each of the models be appropriately adjusted in such a way that the overall model becomes consistent. It is obvious that some information contained in the given models is inevitably lost by these adjustments. This is not desirable. Hence, we should minimize this loss of information. That is, we should accept only those adjustments for which the total loss of information (or total increase of uncertainty) is minimal. The total loss of information may be expressed, for example, by the sum of all individual losses or by a weighted sum, if the given models are valued differently.

The Principle of Maximum Uncertainty

The second principle, the *principle of maximum uncertainty*, is essential for any problem that involves *ampliative reasoning*. This is reasoning in which conclusions are not entailed in the given premises. Using common sense, the principle may be expressed by the following requirement: in any ampliative inference, use all information available, but make sure that no additional information is unwittingly added. That is, employing the connection between information and uncertainty, the principle requires that conclusions resulting from any ampliative inference maximize the relevant uncertainty within the constraints representing the premises. This principle guarantees that our ignorance be fully recognized when we try to enlarge our claims beyond the given premises and, at the same time, that all information contained in the premises be fully utilized. In other words, the principle guarantees that our conclusions are maximally noncommittal with regard to information not contained in the premises.

Ampliative reasoning is indispensable to science in a variety of ways. For example, whenever we utilize a scientific model for predictions, we employ ampliative reasoning. Similarly, when we want to estimate microstates from the knowledge of relevant macrostates and partial information regarding the microstates (as in image processing and many other problems), we must resort to ampliative reasoning. The problem of the identification of an overall system from some of its subsystems is another example that involves ampliative reasoning.

Ampliative reasoning is also common and important in our daily life, where, unfortunately, the principle of maximum uncertainty is not always adhered to. Its violation leads almost invariably to conflicts in human communication, as well expressed by Bertrand Russell in his *Unpopular Essays* (London, 1950): "...whenever you find yourself getting angry about a difference in opinion, be on your guard; you will probably find, on examination, that your belief is getting beyond what the evidence warrants."

The principle of maximum uncertainty is well developed and broadly utilized within classical information theory, where it is called the *principle of maximum entropy*. A general formulation of the principle of maximum entropy is: determine a probability distribution $\langle p(x)|x \in X \rangle$ that maximizes the Shannon entropy subject to given constraints $c_1, c_2, \ldots$, which express partial information about the unknown probability distribution, as well as general constraints (axioms) of probability theory. The most typical constraints employed in practical applications of the maximum entropy principle are mean (expected) values of one or more random variables or various marginal probability distributions of an unknown joint distribution.

As an example, consider a random variable x with possible (given) nonnegative real values $x_1, x_2, \ldots, x_n$. Assume that probabilities $p(x_i)$ are not known, but we know the mean (expected) value $E(x)$ of the variable, which is related to the unknown probabilities by the formula

$$E(x) = \sum_{i=1}^{n} x_i \, p(x_i).\tag{9.62}$$

Employing the maximum entropy principle, we estimate the unknown probabilities $p(x_i)$, $i = 1, 2, \ldots, n$, by solving the following optimization problem: maximize function

$$H(p(x_i)|i = 1, 2, \ldots, n) = - \sum_{i=1}^{n} p(x_i) \log_2 p(x_i)$$

subject to the axiomatic constraints of probability theory and an additional constraint expressed by (9.62), where $E(x)$ and $x_1, x_2, \ldots, x_n$ are given numbers. When solving this problem, we obtain

$$p(x_i) = \frac{e^{-\beta x_i}}{\displaystyle\sum_{k=1}^{n} e^{-\beta x_k}}, \tag{9.63}$$

for all $i = 1, 2, \ldots, n$, where β is a constant obtained by solving (numerically) the equation

$$\sum_{i=1}^{n} [x_i - E(x)] e^{-\beta[x_i - E(x)]} = 0. \tag{9.64}$$

Our only knowledge about the random variable x in this example is the knowledge of its expected value $E(x)$. It is expressed by (9.62) as a constraint on the set of relevant probability distributions. If $E(x)$ were not known, we would be totally ignorant about x, and the maximum entropy principle would yield the uniform probability distribution (the only distribution for which the entropy reaches its absolute maximum). The entropy of the probability distribution given by (9.63) is smaller than the entropy of the uniform distribution, but it is the largest entropy from among all the entropies of the probability distributions that conform to the given expected value $E(x)$.

A generalization of the principle of maximum entropy is the *principle of minimum cross-entropy*. It can be formulated as follows: given a prior probability distribution function q on a finite set X and some relevant new evidence, determine a new probability distribution function p that minimizes the cross-entropy D given by (9.41) subject to constraints $c_1, c_2, \ldots$, which represent the new evidence, as well as to the standard constraints of probability theory.

New evidence reduces uncertainty. Hence, uncertainty expressed by p is, in general, smaller than uncertainty expressed by q. The principle of minimum cross-entropy helps us to determine how much smaller it should be. It allows us to reduce the uncertainty of q in the smallest amount necessary to satisfy the new evidence. That is, the posterior probability distribution function p estimated by the principle is the largest among all other distribution functions that conform to the evidence.

Optimization problems that emerge from the maximum uncertainty principle outside classical information theory have yet to be properly investigated and tested in praxis. When several types of uncertainty are applicable, we must choose one from several possible optimization problems. In evidence theory, for example, the principle of maximum uncertainty yields four possible optimization problems, which are distinguished from one another by the objective function involved: nonspecificity, strife, total uncertainty, or both nonspecificity and strife viewed as two distinct objective functions.

As a simple example to illustrate the principle of maximum nonspecificity in evidence theory, let us consider a finite universal set X, three nonempty subsets of which are of interest to us: A, B, and $A \cap B$. Assume that the only evidence on hand is expressed in terms of two numbers, a and b, that represent the total beliefs focusing on A and B, respectively ($a, b \in [0, 1]$). Our aim is to estimate the degree of support for $A \cap B$ based on this evidence.

As a possible interpretation of this problem, let X be a set of diseases considered in an expert system designed for medical diagnosis in a special area of medicine, and let A and B be sets of diseases that are supported for a particular patient by some diagnostic tests to degrees a and b, respectively. Using this evidence, it is reasonable to estimate the degree of support for diseases in $A \cap B$ by using the principle of maximum nonspecificity. This principle is a safeguard which does not allow us to produce an answer (diagnosis) that is more specific than warranted by the evidence.

The use of the principle of maximum nonspecificity leads, in our example, to the following optimization problem:

Determine values $m(X)$, $m(A)$, $m(B)$, and $m(A \cap B)$ for which the function $m(X) \log_2 |X| + m(A) \log_2 |A| + m(B) \log_2 |B| + m(A \cap B) \log_2 |A \cap B|$ reaches its maximum subject to the constraints

$$m(A) + m(A \cap B) = a,$$

$$m(B) + m(A \cap B) = b,$$

$$m(X) + m(A) + m(B) + m(A \cap B) = 1,$$

$$m(X), m(A), m(B), m(A \cap B) \geq 0,$$

where $a, b \in [0, 1]$ are given numbers.

The constraints are represented in this case by three linear algebraic equations of four unknowns and, in addition, by the requirement that the unknowns be nonnegative real numbers. The first two equations represent our evidence; the third equation and the inequalities represent general constraints of evidence theory. The equations are consistent and independent. Hence, they involve one degree of freedom. Selecting, for example, $m(A \cap B)$ as the free variable, we readily obtain

$$m(A) = a - m(A \cap B),$$

$$m(B) = b - m(A \cap B), \tag{9.65}$$

$$m(X) = 1 - a - b + m(A \cap B).$$

Since all the unknowns must be nonnegative, the first two equations set the upper bound of $m(A \cap B)$, whereas the third equation specifies its lower bound; the bounds are

$$\max(0, a + b - 1) \leq m(A \cap B) \leq \min(a, b). \tag{9.66}$$

Using (9.65), the objective function can now be expressed solely in terms of the free variable $m(A \cap B)$. After a simple rearrangement of terms, we obtain

$$m(A \cap B)[\log_2 |X| - \log_2 |A| - \log_2 |B| + \log_2 |A \cap B|]$$

$$+ (1 - a - b) \log_2 |X| + a \log_2 |A| + b \log_2 |B|.$$

Clearly, only the first term in this expression can influence its value, so we may rewrite the expression as

$$m(A \cap B) \log_2 K_1 + K_2, \tag{9.67}$$

where

$$K_1 = \frac{|X| \cdot |A \cap B|}{|A| \cdot |B|}$$

and

$$K_2 = (1 - a - b) \log_2 |X| + a \log_2 |A| + b \log_2 |B|$$

are constant coefficients. The solution to the optimization problem depends only on the value of K_1. Since A, B, and $A \cap B$ are assumed to be nonempty subsets of X, $K_1 > 0$. If $K_1 < 1$, then $\log_2 K_1 < 0$, and we must minimize $m(A \cap B)$ to obtain the maximum of expression (9.67); hence, $m(A \cap B) = \max(0, a + b - 1)$ due to (9.66). If $K_1 > 1$, then $\log_2 K_1 > 0$, and we must maximize $m(A \cap B)$; hence, $m(A \cap B) = \min(a, b)$, as given by (9.66). When $K_1 = 1$, $\log_2 K_1 = 0$, and expression (9.67) is independent of $m(A \cap B)$; this implies that the solution is not unique or, more precisely, that any value of $m(A \cap B)$ in the range (9.66) is a solution to the optimization problem. The complete solution can thus be expressed by the following equations:

$$m(A \cap B) = \begin{cases} \max(0, a + b - 1) & \text{when } K_1 < 1 \\ [\max(0, a + b - 1), \min(a, b)] & \text{when } K_1 = 1 \\ \min(a, b) & \text{when } K_1 > 1. \end{cases} \quad (9.68)$$

The three types of solutions are exemplified in Table 9.2.

TABLE 9.2   EXAMPLES OF THE THREE TYPES OF SOLUTIONS OBTAINED BY THE PRINCIPLE OF MAXIMUM NONSPECIFICITY

	$|X|$	$|A|$	$|B|$	$|A \cap B|$	a	b	$m(X)$	$m(A)$	$m(B)$	$m(A \cap B)$
$K_1 < 1$	10	5	5	2	.7	.5	0	.5	.3	.2
$K_1 = 1$	10	5	4	2	.8	.6	[0, .2]	[.2, .4]	[0, .2]	[.4, .6]
$K_1 > 1$	20	10	12	4	.4	.5	.5	0	.1	.4

Observe that, due to the linearity of the measure of nonspecificity, the use of the principle of maximum nonspecificity leads to linear programming problems. This is a great advantage when compared with the maximum entropy principle. The use of the latter leads to nonlinear optimization problems, which are considerably more difficult computationally.

The use of the maximum nonspecificity principle does not always result in a unique solution, as demonstrated by the case of $K_1 = 1$ in (9.68). If the solution is not unique, this is a good reason to utilize the second type of uncertainty—strife. We may either add the measure of strife, given by (9.54), as a second objective function in the optimization problem, or use the measure of total uncertainty, given by (9.59), as a more refined objective function. These variations of the maximum uncertainty principle have yet to be developed.

Principle of Uncertainty Invariance

Our repertory of mathematical theories by which we can characterize and deal with situations under uncertainty is already quite respectable, and it is likely that additional theories will be added to it in the future. The theories differ from one another in their meaningful interpretations, generality, computational complexity, robustness, and other aspects. Furthermore, different theories may be appropriate at different stages of a problem-solving process or for different purposes at the same stage. Based on various studies, it is increasingly recognized that none of the theories is superior in all respects and for all purposes. In order to opportunistically utilize the advantages of the various theories of uncertainty, we need the capability of moving from one theory to another as appropriate. These moves, or transformations, from one theory to another should be based on some justifiable principle. When well-established measures of uncertainty are available in the theories involved, the following principle, called a *principle of uncertainty invariance*, is germane to this purpose.

To transform the representation of a problem-solving situation in one theory, T_1, into an equivalent representation in another theory, T_2, the principle of uncertainty invariance requires that:

1. the amount of uncertainty associated with the situation be preserved when we move from T_1 into T_2; and

2. the degrees of belief in T_1 be converted to their counterparts in T_2 by an appropriate scale, at least ordinal.

Requirement **1** guarantees that no uncertainty is added or eliminated solely by changing the mathematical theory by which a particular phenomenon is formalized. If the amount of uncertainty were not preserved, then either some information not supported by the evidence would unwittingly be added by the transformation (information bias), or some useful information contained in the evidence would unwittingly be eliminated (information waste). In either case, the model obtained by the transformation could hardly be viewed as equivalent to its original.

Requirement **2** guarantees that certain properties, which are considered essential in a given context (such as ordering or proportionality of relevant values), are preserved under the transformation. Transformations under which certain properties of a numerical variable remain invariant are known in the theory of measurement as scales.

Due to the unique connection between uncertainty and information, the principle of uncertainty invariance can also be conceived as a *principle of information invariance or information preservation*. Indeed, each model of a decision-making situation, formalized in some mathematical theory, contains information of some type and some amount. The amount is expressed by the difference between the maximum possible uncertainty associated with the set of alternatives postulated in the situation and the actual uncertainty of the model. When we approximate one model with another one, formalized in terms of a different mathematical theory, this basically means that we want to replace one type of information with an equal amount of information of another type. That is, we want to convert information from one type to another while, at the same time, preserving its amount. This expresses the spirit of the principle of information invariance or preservation: no information should be added or eliminated solely by converting one type of information to another. It seems reasonable to compare this principle, in a metaphoric way, with the principle of energy preservation in physics.

Let us illustrate the principle of uncertainty invariance by describing its use for formalizing transformations between probabilistic and possibilistic conceptualizations of uncertainty. The general idea is illustrated in Fig. 9.8, where only nonzero components of the probability distribution **p** and the possibility distribution **r** are listed. It is also assumed that the corresponding components of the distributions are ordered in the same way: $p_i \geq p_{i+1}$ and $r_i \geq r_{i+1}$ for all $i = 1, 2, \ldots, n - 1$. This is equivalent to the assumption that values p_i correspond to values r_i for all $i = 1, 2, \ldots, n$ by some scale, which must be at least ordinal.

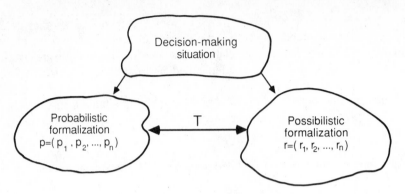

Figure 9.8 Probability-possibility transformations.

Thus far, the following results regarding uncertainty-invariant transformations $\mathbf{p} \leftrightarrow \mathbf{r}$ under different scales have been obtained: (1) transformations based on ratio and difference scales do not have enough flexibility to preserve uncertainty and, consequently, are not applicable; (2) for interval scales, uncertainty-invariant transformations $\mathbf{p} \rightarrow \mathbf{r}$ exist and are unique for all probability distributions, while the inverse transformations $\mathbf{r} \rightarrow \mathbf{p}$ that preserve uncertainty exist (and are unique) only for some possibility distributions; (3) for log-interval scales, uncertainty-invariant transformations exist and are unique in both directions; and (4) ordinal-scale transformations that preserve uncertainty always exist in both directions, but, in general, are not unique.

The log-interval scale is thus the strongest scale under which the uncertainty invariance transformations $\mathbf{p} \leftrightarrow \mathbf{r}$ always exist and are unique. A scheme of these transformations is shown in Fig. 9.9. First, a transformation coefficient α is determined by Equation II, which expresses the required equality of the two amounts of total uncertainty; then, the obtained value of α is substituted to the transformation formulas (Equation I for $\mathbf{p} \rightarrow \mathbf{r}$ and Equation III for $\mathbf{r} \rightarrow \mathbf{p}$). It is known that $0 < \alpha < 1$, which implies that the possibility-probability consistency condition ($r_i \geq p_i$ for all $i = 1, 2, \ldots, n$), is always satisfied by these transformations. When the transformations are simplified by excluding $S(\mathbf{r})$ in Equation II, which for large n is negligible, their basic properties (existence, uniqueness, consistency) remain intact.

For ordinal scales, uncertainty-invariant transformations $\mathbf{p} \leftrightarrow \mathbf{r}$ are not unique. They result, in general, in closed convex sets of probability or possibility distributions, which are obtained by solving appropriate linear inequalities constrained by the requirements of normalization and uncertainty invariance. From one point of view, the lack of uniqueness is a disadvantage of ordinal-scale transformations. From another point of view, it is an advantage since it allows us to impose additional requirements on the transformations. These additional requirements may be expressed, for example, in terms of second-order properties, such as projections, noninteraction, or conditioning.

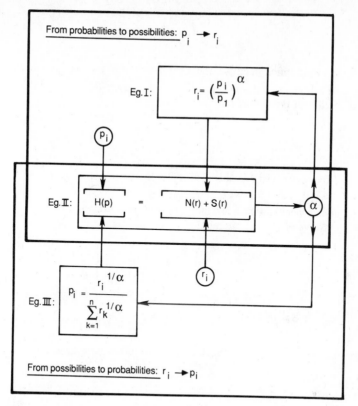

Figure 9.9 Uncertainty-invariant probability-possibility transformations based on log-interval scales.

NOTES

9.1. The Hartley function discussed in Sec. 9.2 was derived by Hartley [1928]; it was justified on axiomatic grounds by Rényi [1970].

9.2. Literature on information theory based on the Shannon entropy, which is abundant, is overviewed in [Klir and Folger, 1988]. The original paper by Shannon [1948] is also available in a book [Shannon and Weaver, 1964].

9.3. The developments regarding nonclassical measures of uncertainty and uncertainty-based information are overviewed in a paper by Klir [1993]; a chronology of the main events in these developments is also presented in a paper by Harmanec and Klir [1994], which introduces the well-justified measure AU of total uncertainty in evidence theory.

9.4. The principle of uncertainty invariance was introduced by Klir [1990b] and further developed by Geer and Klir [1992], Klir and Parviz [1992b], Jumarie [1994], and Wonneberger [1994].

EXERCISES

9.1. Calculate the nonspecificity and fuzziness for each of the following fuzzy sets:

(a) $A = .3/a + .5/b + .9/c + 1/d + .7/e + .4/f + .2/g$;

(b) fuzzy relation R defined by the matrix

$$R = \begin{bmatrix} 1 & .7 & 0 & .5 & 0 \\ .5 & 1 & .3 & .9 & .4 \\ 0 & .5 & 1 & 0 & .9 \end{bmatrix};$$

(c) some of the fuzzy relations specified in Table 5.4 (p. 150);

(d) fuzzy sets in Fig. 8.4 (pp. 227).

9.2. Calculate the nonspecificity and fuzziness for each fuzzy relation involved in the procedure for obtaining transitive closure of the relation R, defined by the matrix

$$R = \begin{bmatrix} .7 & .5 & 0 & 0 \\ 0 & 0 & 0 & 1 \\ 0 & .4 & 0 & 0 \\ 0 & 0 & .8 & 0 \end{bmatrix}.$$

9.3. For some relations on $X \times Y$ specified in Table 5.4 (p. 150), calculate $U(X)$, $U(Y)$, $U(X, Y)$, $U(X|Y)$, and $U(Y|X)$.

9.4. Calculate the nonspecificity and fuzziness for the following fuzzy sets defined on the interval $[0, 10]$:

(a) $A(x) = x/10$;

(b) $B(x) = 2^{-x}$;

(c) $C(x) = x/5$ for $x \leq 5$ and $C(x) = 2 - x/5$ for $x \geq 5$.

9.5. Consider the following basic assignments defined on $X = \{a, b, c\}$:

$$m_1(\{c\}) = .2, \qquad m_1(\{b, c\}) = .3, \qquad m_1(X) = .5;$$
$$m_2(\{a\}) = .5, \qquad m_2(\{b\}) = .2, \qquad m_2(\{c\}) = .3;$$
$$m_3(\{c\}) = .2, \qquad m_3(\{a, b\}) = .3, \qquad m_3(X) = .5.$$

Calculate $N(m_i)$, $E(m_i)$, $C(m_i)$, $S(m_i)$, and $NS(m_i)$ for each $i = 1, 2, 3$.

9.6. Six joint basic assignments on $X \times Y$, where $X = \{1, 2, 3\}$, and $Y = \{a, b, c\}$, are given in Table 9.3. Focal elements are specified in the table by their characteristic functions. Determine:

(a) which of the basic assignments represent probability or possibility measures;

(b) which of the basic assignments represent noninteractive marginal bodies of evidence;

(c) measures of strife, nonspecificity, and total uncertainty for all the given joint basic assignments as well as the associated marginal basic assignments (projections), and check the additivity properties of the three measures for basic assignments that represent noninteractive marginals;

(d) joint basic assignments reconstructed from their marginals on the assumption of noninteraction, and their measures of strife, nonspecificity, and total uncertainty.

9.7. Prove that the nonspecificity function N defined by (9.36) is subadditive and additive.

9.8. Calculate the U-uncertainty and strife for the following possibility distributions:

(a) $^1r = \langle 1, 1, .9, .8, .7, .6 \rangle$;

(b) $^2r = \langle 1, .9, .8, .7, .6, .5 \rangle$;

(c) $^3r = \langle 1, .7, .5, .3, .1, .1 \rangle$;

TABLE 9.3   JOINT BASIC ASSIGNMENTS FOR EXERCISE 9.6

R_i	1a	1b	1c	2a	2b	2c	3a	3b	3c	$m_1(R_i)$	$m_2(R_i)$	$m_3(R_i)$	$m_4(R_i)$	$m_5(R_i)$	$m_6(R_i)$
R_1	1	0	0	0	0	0	0	0	0	.2	.25	0	0	0	0
R_2	0	1	0	0	0	0	0	0	0	.05	.15	0	0	0	0
R_3	0	0	1	0	0	0	0	0	0	.1	.1	0	0	0	0
R_4	0	0	0	1	0	0	0	0	0	.05	.2	0	0	0	0
R_5	0	0	0	0	1	0	0	0	0	.25	.12	0	0	0	0
R_6	0	0	0	0	0	1	0	0	0	.04	.08	0	0	0	0
R_7	0	0	0	0	0	0	1	0	0	.25	.05	.3	0	.02	.05
R_8	0	0	0	0	0	0	0	1	0	.03	.03	0	0	0	0
R_9	0	0	0	0	0	0	0	0	1	.03	.02	0	0	0	0
R_{10}	0	0	0	1	0	0	1	0	0	0	0	.1	.02	.03	.03
R_{11}	0	0	0	0	0	0	1	0	1	0	0	0	0	.06	.10
R_{12}	0	0	1	0	0	1	0	0	0	0	0	0	0	0	0
R_{13}	1	0	0	1	0	0	0	0	0	0	0	0	.03	.025	.07
R_{14}	1	0	0	1	0	0	1	0	0	0	0	0	.05	.025	.05
R_{15}	0	0	0	0	0	0	1	1	1	0	0	0	0	.12	.12
R_{16}	1	1	1	0	0	0	0	0	0	0	0	0	0	0	0
R_{17}	0	0	0	0	1	1	0	1	1	0	0	0	.06	0	0
R_{18}	0	0	0	1	0	1	1	0	1	0	0	.2	.04	.09	.09
R_{19}	1	0	1	1	0	1	0	0	0	0	0	0	.06	.075	.02
R_{20}	0	1	1	0	1	1	0	0	0	0	0	0	.09	0	0
R_{21}	1	0	1	1	0	1	1	0	1	0	0	.1	.1	0	0
R_{22}	0	0	0	1	1	1	1	1	1	0	0	0	.08	.18	.07
R_{23}	1	1	1	1	1	1	0	0	0	0	0	0	.12	.15	.10
R_{24}	0	1	1	0	1	1	0	1	1	0	0	0	.15	0	0
R_{25}	1	1	1	0	0	0	1	1	1	0	0	0	0	.075	.17
R_{26}	1	1	1	1	1	1	1	1	1	0	0	.3	.2	.15	.13

  (d) ${}^4\mathbf{r} = \langle 1, .5, .4, .3, .2, .1 \rangle$;
  (e) ${}^5\mathbf{r} = \langle 1, .2, .2, .2, .2, .2 \rangle$.

9.9. Consider a universal set X, four nonempty subsets of which are of interest: $A \cap B$, $A \cap C$, $B \cap C$, and $A \cap B \cap C$. The only evidence we have is expressed by the equations

$$m(A \cap B) + m(A \cap B \cap C) = .2,$$

$$m(A \cap C) + m(A \cap B \cap C) = .5,$$

$$m(B \cap C) + m(A \cap B \cap C) = .1.$$

Estimate, using the maximum nonspecificity principle, the values of $m(A \cap B), m(A \cap C), m(B \cap C), m(A \cap B \cap C)$, and $m(X)$.

PART TWO: APPLICATIONS

10

CONSTRUCTING FUZZY SETS AND OPERATIONS ON FUZZY SETS

10.1 GENERAL DISCUSSION

Fuzzy set theory, as overviewed in Part I of this text, provides us with a respectable inventory of theoretical tools for dealing with concepts expressed in natural language. These tools enable us to represent linguistic concepts, most of which are inherently vague, by fuzzy sets of various types, and to manipulate them in a great variety of ways for various purposes; they enable us to express and deal with various relations, functions, and equations that involve linguistic concepts; and they allow us to fuzzify any desired area of classical mathematics to facilitate emerging applications. That is, we have at our disposal theoretical resources of great expressive power and, consequently, great utility.

Linguistic concepts are not only predominantly vague, but their meanings are almost invariably context-dependent as well. For example, the concept of *large distance* has different meanings in the contexts of walking, driving, or air travel; the concepts *cheap, expensive, very expensive*, and so on, depend not only on the items to which they are applied (e.g., a house versus a vacation trip), but also on the affluence of the buyer and a host of other circumstances; the meanings of *young* and *old* change when applied to different animal species, and they change even more drastically when applied to mountain formations in geology or stars in astronomy; the concept of *high temperature* has two very different meanings when applied to a patient or a nuclear reactor; concepts such as *beautiful, pleasing, painful*, or *talented* certainly have many different meanings, which may differ from person to person even under the same circumstances. We may go on and on; the examples are countless.

The context dependency involves not only meanings of linguistic terms, but also meanings of operations on linguistic terms. We have to determine, in each particular application, which of the available operations on fuzzy sets best represent the intended operations on the corresponding linguistic terms. It is now experimentally well established that the various connectives of linguistic terms, such as *and, or, not*, and *if-then*, have different meanings in different contents. We have to determine which of the *t*-norms, *t*-conorms, complements, or other operations on fuzzy sets best approximate the intended meanings of the connectives. The various linguistic hedges are context dependent as well.

While context dependency is not essential for developing theoretical resources for representing and processing linguistic concepts, it is crucial for applications of these tools to real-world problems. That is, a prerequisite to each application of fuzzy set theory are meanings of relevant linguistic concepts expressed in terms of appropriate fuzzy sets as well as meanings of relevant operations on fuzzy sets.

The problem of constructing membership functions that adequately capture the meanings of linguistic terms employed in a particular application, as well as the problem of determining meanings of associated operations on the linguistic terms, are not problems of fuzzy set theory *per se*. These problems belong to the general problem area of *knowledge acquisition* within the underlying framework of fuzzy set theory. That is, fuzzy set theory provides a framework within which the process of knowledge acquisition takes place and in which the elicited knowledge can effectively be represented. Knowledge acquisition is a subject of a relatively new field of study referred to as *knowledge engineering*.

We do not attempt to cover methods of knowledge acquisition comprehensively. However, we overview basic types of methods that are applicable to the construction of membership functions of fuzzy sets and to the selection of appropriate operations on fuzzy sets. In addition, we describe some representative methods in more detail.

10.2   METHODS OF CONSTRUCTION: AN OVERVIEW

Both fuzzy sets and operations on fuzzy sets are characterized by functions of the form $X \rightarrow [0, 1]$. For a fuzzy set, X is a given universal set; for a fuzzy set operation, $X = [0, 1]^k$ for some positive integer k. Both fuzzy sets and fuzzy set operations are also employed, in general, as approximators of meanings of relevant linguistic terms in given contexts. Therefore, the problem of constructing membership functions of fuzzy sets is essentially the same as the problem of constructing functions that represent fuzzy set operations. That is, methods developed for constructing membership functions are applicable for constructing fuzzy set operations as well. In our discussion, we focus primarily on the construction of membership functions.

The following is a general scenario within which the construction of fuzzy sets (or fuzzy set operations) takes place. The scenario involves a specific knowledge domain of interest, one or more experts in this domain, and a knowledge engineer. The role of the knowledge engineer is to elicit the knowledge of interest from the experts, who are assumed to possess it, and to express the knowledge in some operational form of a required type. In our case, the knowledge is supposed to be expressed in terms of propositions involving linguistic variables.

Knowledge can be elicited only through an interaction of the knowledge engineer with the expert(s). In the first stage, the knowledge engineer attempts to elicit knowledge in terms of propositions expressed in natural language. In the second stage, he or she attempts to determine the meaning of each linguistic term employed in these propositions. It is during this second stage of knowledge acquisition that functions representing fuzzy sets and operations on fuzzy sets are constructed.

Numerous methods for constructing membership functions, almost invariably based on experts' judgement, have been described in the literature. All these methods may usefully be classified, in the most fundamental way, into *direct methods* and *indirect methods*. In direct methods, experts are expected to give answers to questions of various kinds that explicitly pertain to the constructed membership function. In indirect methods, experts are required to answer simpler questions, easier to answer and less sensitive to the various biases of subjective judgement, which pertain to the constructed membership function only implicitly. The answers are subject to further processing based on various assumptions.

Both direct and indirect methods are further classified to methods that involve *one expert* and methods that require *multiple experts*. This results in four principal classes of methods for constructing membership functions: direct methods/one expert, direct methods/multiple experts, indirect methods/one expert, and indirect methods/multiple experts. In the following four sections, we describe representative methods in each of these four classes.

10.3   DIRECT METHODS WITH ONE EXPERT

In this category of methods, an expert is expected to assign to each given element $x \in X$ a membership grade $A(x)$ that, according to his or her opinion, best captures the meaning of the linguistic term represented by the fuzzy set A. This can be done by either defining the membership function completely in terms of a justifiable mathematical formula or exemplifying it for some selected elements of X.

The complete definition of the membership function in question by the expert is feasible for some linguistic concepts. It is feasible for any concept that satisfies two conditions: the concept is perfectly represented by some elements of the universal set, which are usually called *ideal prototypes* of the concept; and the compatibility of other elements of the universal set with these ideal prototypes can be expressed mathematically in terms of a meaningful similarity function.

For example, in pattern recognition of handwritten characters, the expert may define a fuzzy set of straight lines, S, in terms of the least square straight-line fitting with minimum error, $e(x)$, for each given line x. Then, the function

$$S(x) = \begin{cases} 1 - e(x)/e_t & \text{when } e(x) < e_t \\ 0 & \text{otherwise,} \end{cases}$$

where e_t is the largest acceptable least square error, is a meaningful membership function that captures quite well the linguistic concept *straightness* in the context of handwritten character recognition. The ideal prototypes are in these cases all perfect straight lines, that is, lines x for which $e(x) = 0$. Given a particular line x, $e(x)$ expresses the dissimilarity between x and its best straight-line approximation, and e_t expresses the largest dissimilarity (in the opinion of the expert) to capture the concept of lines that are approximately straight.

Although it is often not feasible to define the membership function that adequately captures a given linguistic term, the expert should be able to exemplify it for some representative elements of X. The exemplification may be facilitated by asking the expert questions of the form

"What is the degree of membership of x in A?"

or, alternatively,

"What is the degree of compatibility of x with L_A?"

where L_A is the linguistic term that we want to represent in a given context by fuzzy set A. If desirable, the questions may be formulated in reverse forms:

"Which elements x have the degree A(x) of membership in A?"

"Which elements x are compatible with L_A to degree A(x)?"

These questions, regardless of their form, result in a set of pairs $\langle x, A(x) \rangle$. This set is then used for constructing the membership function A of a given shape (triangular, trapezoidal, S-shaped, bell-shaped, etc.) by an appropriate curve-fitting method (Sec. 10.7).

The described procedure of direct exemplification and curve fitting is feasible only for linguistic terms that describe simple concepts such as *high temperature, close driving distance, normal blood pressure*, and the like. More elaborate procedures are needed to determine meanings of concepts that do not enjoy this simplicity, such as *high violence, depressed economy*, or *highly stressful situation*. One such procedure, referred to as the *method of a semantic differential*, is well developed and widely used. It is based on selecting a set of scales for polar adjectives (bad-good, usual-unusual, chaotic-ordered, etc.) that are relevant to the concept in question and evaluating the concept in terms of these scales for each given object of the universal set. This results, for each object, in a vector whose entries are values assigned to the object under the chosen scales. The degree of compatibility of a given object with the concept is then expressed by calculating a normalized distance of this vector from the vector $\langle 0, 0, \ldots, 0 \rangle$. This general method for measuring meanings of linguistic terms, the full description of which is beyond the scope of this text, is thoroughly covered in a monograph by Osgood *et al.* [1957].

10.4   *DIRECT METHODS WITH MULTIPLE EXPERTS*

When a direct method is extended from one expert to multiple experts, the opinions of individual experts must be appropriately aggregated. One of the most common methods is based on a probabilistic interpretation of membership functions. Assume that n experts (or, generally, subjects) are asked for some $x \in X$ to valuate the proposition "x belongs to A" as either true or false, where A is a fuzzy set on X that represent a linguistic term associated with a given linguistic variable. Given a particular element $x \in X$, let $a_i(x)$ denote the answer of expert $i (i \in \mathbb{N}_n)$. Assume that $a_i(x) = 1$ when the proposition is valued by expert i as true, and $a_i(x) = 0$ when it is valued as false. Then,

$$A(x) = \frac{\sum_{i=1}^{n} a_i(x)}{n} \tag{10.1}$$

may be viewed as a probabilistic interpretation of the constructed membership function. It is often useful to generalize this interpretation by allowing one to distinguish degrees of competence, c_i, of the individual experts ($i \in \mathbb{N}_n$). This results in the formula

$$A(x) = \sum_{i=1}^{n} c_i \cdot a_i(x), \tag{10.2}$$

where

$$\sum_{i=1}^{n} c_i = 1.$$

Consider now two fuzzy sets, A and B, defined on the same universal set X. Using (10.2), we can calculate $A(x)$ and $B(x)$ for each $x \in X$, and then choose appropriate fuzzy operators to calculate $\overline{A}, \overline{B}, A \cup B, A \cap B$, and so forth. Alternatively, we can combine valuations $a_i(x)$ and $b_i(x)$ for each expert i by relevant operations of classical logic ($\vee$ for $\cup$, $\vee$ for $\cap$, etc.), and then aggregate the resulting vector. By this procedure, each fuzzy operation is unique for each $x \in X$. Let

$$\mathbf{a}(x) = \langle a_i(x) | i \in \mathbb{N}_n \rangle \text{ and } \mathbf{b}(x) = \langle b_i(x) | i \in \mathbb{N}_n \rangle$$

be vectors of experts' valuations associated with fuzzy sets A and B, respectively, both defined on the same universal set X and constructed in the same context. Then, employing the generalized formula (10.2), we obtain

$$\overline{A}(x) = \sum_{i=1}^{n} c_i [1 - a_i(x)], \tag{10.3}$$

$$[A \cap B](x) = \sum_{i=1}^{n} c_i [a_i(x) \cdot b_i(x)], \tag{10.4}$$

$$[A \cup B](x) = \sum_{i=1}^{n} c_i [a_i(x) + b_i(x) - a_i(x) \cdot b_i(x)]. \tag{10.5}$$

Observe that fuzzy intersection and union defined in this way are unique, but they are not truth functional; that is, for all $x \in X$,

$$[A \cap B](x) \neq i[A(x), B(x)],$$
$$[A \cup B](x) \neq u[A(x), B(x)].$$

In general, different operations are used for different elements $x \in X$, depending on the vectors $\mathbf{a}(x)$ and $\mathbf{b}(x)$. However, it is easy to see that fuzzy intersections and unions defined by (10.4) and (10.5) satisfy the inequalities

$$0 \leq [A \cap B](x) \leq \min[A(x), B(x)],$$
$$\max[A(x), B(x)] \leq [A \cup B](x) \leq 1$$

for each $x \in X$. These inequalities are exactly the same as those for t-norms and t-conorms. This means that operations defined by (10.4) and (10.5) yield for each $x \in X$ values which coincide with the values of a particular t-norm and a particular t-conorm, respectively. These values are uniquely determined by the vectors $\mathbf{a}(x)$ and $\mathbf{b}(x)$. Moreover, they are such that all properties of the Boolean lattice are locally satisfied for each $x \in X$. We can thus obtain unique operations of fuzzy intersection, union, and complement that preserve the Boolean lattice at the cost of losing truth functionality. Observe also that a fuzzy complement defined in this way is always the standard fuzzy complement.

For some concepts (e.g., those involving aesthetic judgements), subjective perceptions of distinct subjects may be too different to justify their aggregation. Instead, the results may be summarized in terms of an appropriate interval-valued fuzzy set. This is reasonable since the graphs of membership functions elicited from different subjects tend to have the same shape.

As a specific example of eliciting membership functions that characterize subjective perceptions of a linguistic term by different subjects, let us describe two relevant experiments performed by Norwich and Turksen [1982 a–c, 1984].

The experiments to be described are based on the assumption that the interval scale is employed. Two techniques, referred to as direct rating and reverse rating, were used; these are described later. Experiments were performed with 30 subjects. Membership functions were constructed for each subject by randomly generating different stimuli (each one at least nine times) and then averaging the subject's responses. The following is a brief characterization of each of the two experiments:

1. The first experiment involves the subjective perception of each participant of the notion of tall persons. It uses a life-sized wooden figure of adjustable height.

2. The second experiment involves the notion of aesthetically pleasing houses among one-story houses of fixed width and variable heights. A cardboard model of a house is used, which consists of a chimney and a triangular roof sitting on a rectangle of width 12 inches and of height adjustable from 0 inches to 34 inches.

Membership ratings in both experiments are indicated with movable pointer along a horizontal line segment. The right-hand end of this segment corresponds to the membership degree of those persons who are definitely "tall" (or to those houses that are definitely "pleasing"), and the left-hand end to those persons felt to be definitely not tall (or to those houses that are definitely not pleasing). The distance at which the pointer is placed between these two endpoints is interpreted as the strength of agreement or truth of the classification of each person (or house) as tall (or pleasing). In the direct ratings procedure, the subject is presented with a random series of persons (houses) and asked to use this method of indicating membership degree to rate each one as tall (or pleasing). In the reverse rating procedure, the same method of depicting membership degree is used to give the subject a random membership rating; the subject is then presented with an ordered series of persons (houses) and asked to select the one person (house) that best seems to correspond to the indicated degree of membership in the category of tall persons (or pleasing houses).

An example of the membership functions obtained for the fuzzy sets of tall, very tall, not tall, and short persons, as perceived by a particular subject, is shown in Fig. 10.1. The plots in this figure represent the mean response to nine stimuli based on the direct rating procedure. An example of a membership function for the fuzzy set of pleasing houses, again representing the mean response of a particular subject to nine stimuli based on the direct rating procedure, is shown in Fig. 10.2.

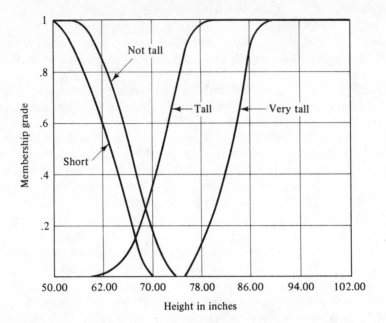

Figure 10.1 Membership grade functions of four fuzzy sets expressing the subjective perception of a particular subject related to the concept of tall persons (adopted from Norwich and Turksen [1984]).

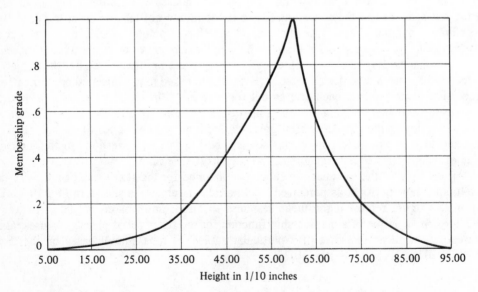

Figure 10.2 Membership grade function of the fuzzy set expressing the subjective perception of a particular subject of aesthetically pleasing houses (adopted from Norwich and Turksen [1984]).

10.5 *INDIRECT METHODS WITH ONE EXPERT*

Unless a membership function can be defined in terms of a suitable similarity function with respect to an ideal prototype (or a set of ideal prototypes), direct methods have one fundamental disadvantage. They require the expert (or experts) to give answers that are overly precise to capture subjective judgments. As a consequence, the answers are always somewhat arbitrary, which becomes critical for complex concepts, such as *beauty, talent, creativity,* and the like. Indirect methods attempt to reduce this arbitrariness by replacing direct estimates of membership grades with simpler tasks. As an example, let us describe a method in which direct estimates are replaced with pairwise comparisons.

Given a linguistic term in a particular context, let A denote a fuzzy set that is supposed to capture the meaning of this term. Let $x_1, x_2, \ldots, x_n$ be elements of the universal set X for which we want to estimate the grades of membership in A. That is, our problem is to determine the values $a_i = A(x_i)$ for all $i \in \mathbb{N}_n$. Instead of asking the expert to estimate values a_i directly, we ask him or her to compare elements $x_1, x_2, \ldots, x_n$ in pairs according to their relative weights of belonging to A. The pairwise comparisons, which are easier to estimate than the direct values, are conveniently expressed by the square matrix $\mathbf{P} = [p_{ij}], i, j \in \mathbb{N}_n$, which has positive entries everywhere.

Assume first that it is possible to obtain perfect values p_{ij}. In this case, $p_{ij} = a_i/a_j$, and matrix $\mathbf{P}$ is consistent in the sense that

$$p_{ik} = p_{ij} p_{jk} \tag{10.6}$$

for all $i, j, k \in \mathbb{N}_n$, which implies that $p_{ii} = 1$ and $p_{ij} = 1/p_{ji}$. Furthermore,

$$\sum_{j=1}^{n} p_{ij} a_j = \sum_{j=1}^{n} a_i = n a_i$$

for all $i \in \mathbb{N}_n$ or, in matrix form,

$$\mathbf{Pa} = n\mathbf{a}, \tag{10.7}$$

where

$$\mathbf{a} = [a_1\, a_2 \ldots a_n]^T.$$

Equation (10.7) means that n is an eigenvalue of $\mathbf{P}$ and $\mathbf{a}$ is the corresponding eigenvector. The equation may also be rewritten in the form

$$(\mathbf{P} - n\mathbf{I})\mathbf{a} = 0, \tag{10.8}$$

where $\mathbf{I}$ is the identity matrix. This matrix equation represents a system of homogeneous linear equations, which have a nonzero solution if the determinant of $(\mathbf{P} - n\mathbf{I})$ is zero (i.e., n is an eigenvalue of $\mathbf{P}$). If we assume that

$$\sum_{i=1}^{n} a_i = 1,$$

then a_j for any $j \in \mathbb{N}_n$ can be determined by the following simple procedure:

$$\sum_{i=1}^{n} p_{ij} = \sum_{i=1}^{n} a_i/a_j = \frac{1}{a_j} \sum_{i=1}^{n} a_i = \frac{1}{a_j};$$

hence,

$$a_j = \frac{1}{\sum\limits_{i=1}^{n} p_{ij}}.$$ (10.9)

In practice, the pairwise comparisons p_{ij} elicited from the user are usually not fully consistent. That is, (10.6) is violated to some degree. In this case, matrix $\mathbf{P}$ can be viewed as a perturbation of the ideal, fully consistent matrix. It is well known that when the values p_{ij} change slightly, the eigenvalues of $\mathbf{P}$ change in a similar way. As a consequence, the maximum eigenvalue remains close to n (always greater than n), while all the other eigenvalues are close to zero. The problem of estimating vector $\mathbf{a}$ from matrix $\mathbf{P}$ now becomes the problem of finding the largest eigenvalue $\lambda_{\max}$ and the associated eigenvector. That is, the estimated vector $\mathbf{a}$ must satisfy the equation

$$\mathbf{Pa} = \lambda_{\max}\mathbf{a},$$ (10.10)

where $\lambda_{\max}$ is usually close to n. In fact, the closer $\lambda_{\max}$ is to n, the more accurate is the estimate of $\mathbf{a}$. That is, the relative deviation of $\lambda_{\max}$ from n, $(\lambda_{\max} - n)/n$, may be employed as a measure of the accuracy of the obtained estimate.

Various numerical methods for obtaining the largest eigenvalue and the associated eigenvector are available, but coverage of them does not belong in this text. We should mention, however, that an initial estimate of $\mathbf{a}$ by (10.9) is in many cases sufficiently accurate, and no further procedure is needed.

Fuzzy sets obtained by the described method are not normal. We can normalize them by dividing each entry of the estimated vector $\mathbf{a}$ by its largest entry.

10.6 INDIRECT METHODS WITH MULTIPLE EXPERTS

Let us illustrate methods in this category by describing an interesting method, which enables us to determine degrees of competence of participating experts, which are then utilized, together with the experts' judgments, for calculating grades of membership of relevant elements in the fuzzy set that is supposed to represent a given linguistic concept. The method is based on the assumption that, in general, the concept in question is n-dimensional (based on n distinct features), each defined on $\mathbb{R}$. Hence, the universal set on which the concept is defined is $\mathbb{R}^n$.

Let $[\underline{x}_{ji}, \overline{x}_{ji}]$ denote the interval of values of feature j that, in the opinion of expert i, relate to the concept in question ($i \in \mathbb{N}_m, j \in \mathbb{N}_n$). The full opinion of expert i regarding the relevance of elements (n-tuples) of $\mathbb{R}^n$ to the concept is then expressed by the hyperparallelepiped

$$h_i = [\underline{x}_{1i}, \overline{x}_{1i}] \times [\underline{x}_{2i}, \overline{x}_{2i}] \times \ldots \times [\underline{x}_{ni}, \overline{x}_{ni}].$$

With m experts, we obtain m hyperparallelepipeds of this form, one for each expert. Membership function of the fuzzy set by which the concept is to be represented is then constructed by the following algorithmic procedure:

1. For each j, consider all intervals obtained from the experts, and construct a union of each subset of intervals that overlap. This results in a set of nonoverlapping intervals

$$[\underline{x}_{jt_j}, \overline{x}_{jt_j}] \quad (j \in \mathbb{N}_n, t_j \in \mathbb{N}_{m_j}),$$

where m_j is an appropriate integer for each j.

2. Employing the intervals obtained in Step 1, construct the hyperparallelepipeds

$$g_k = [\underline{x}_{1t_1}, \overline{x}_{1t_1}] \times [\underline{x}_{2t_2}, \overline{x}_{2t_2}] \times \ldots \times [\underline{x}_{nt_n}, \overline{x}_{nt_n}]$$

for all $k \in \{\langle t_1, t_2, \ldots, t_n\rangle | t_j \in \mathbb{N}_{m_j}, j \in \mathbb{N}_n\} = K$.

3. Evaluate for each $\mathbf{x} \in g_k$ the function

$$\varphi_i(\mathbf{x}) = \begin{cases} 1 & \text{when } g_k \cap h_i \neq \varnothing \\ 0 & \text{otherwise}, \end{cases}$$

where $i \in \mathbb{N}_m$.

4. Let $r = 1$ (r denotes the number of an iteration).

5. Define the initial coefficients of competence, ${}^r c_i$, the same for all experts:

$$^r c_i = \frac{1}{m} \text{ for all } i \in \mathbb{N}_m \quad (r = 1).$$

6. Calculate approximate grades of membership, ${}^r A(\mathbf{x})$, of elements (n-tuples) $\mathbf{x}$ in fuzzy set A that, according to experts' testimony, represent the given concept by the formula

$$^r A(\mathbf{x}) = \sum_{i=1}^m {}^r c_i \varphi_i(\mathbf{x})$$

for all $\mathbf{x} \in g_k$ and all $k \in K$, where values ${}^r c_i$ are assumed to be normalized in the sense that

$$\sum_{i=1}^m {}^r c_i = 1.$$

7. For each $i \in \mathbb{N}_m$, calculate the aggregated difference

$$^r \delta_i = \sum_{k \in K} \sum_{\mathbf{x} \in g_k} [{}^r A(\mathbf{x}) - \varphi_i(\mathbf{x})]^2$$

between the opinion of expert i and the opinion of the whole group of participating experts in iteration r.

8. Calculate $\Delta = \sum_{i=1}^m 1/{}^r \delta_i$.

9. Increase r by one.

10. Calculate ${}^r c_i = \Delta / {}^{r-1} \delta_i$.

11. If $\max |{}^{r-1} c_i - {}^r c_i| < \varepsilon$, where ε is a small positive number chosen by the knowledge engineer, then we take $A(\mathbf{x}) = {}^{r-1} A(\mathbf{x})$ for all $\mathbf{x} \in g_k$ and all $k \in K$ (assuming that $A(\mathbf{x}) = 0$ for all $\mathbf{x} \notin g_k$ for any $k \in K$); otherwise, go to Step 6.

10.7 CONSTRUCTIONS FROM SAMPLE DATA

In this section, we address the problem of constructing a membership function from samples of membership grades for some elements of the given universal set X. We restrict our discussions to the case $X = \mathbb{R}$.

Two approaches to this problem are overviewed. One of them is based on the mathematical theory of curve fitting, which is exemplified here by two methods, the method of Lagrange interpolation and the least-square error method. The other approach is based on learning through artificial neural networks and employs the method of backpropagation.

In each of the discussed methods, we assume that n sample data

$$\langle x_1, a_1 \rangle, \langle x_2, a_2 \rangle, \ldots, \langle x_n, a_n \rangle \tag{10.11}$$

are given, where $x_i \in X(= \mathbb{R})$ for each $i \in \mathbb{N}_n$, and a_i is a given grade of membership of x_i in a fuzzy set A (i.e., $a_i = A(x_i)$). The problem is to determine the whole membership function A.

Lagrange Interpolation

The method of Lagrange interpolation is a curve-fitting method in which the constructed function is assumed to be expressed by a suitable polynomial form. According to this method, the function f employed for the interpolation of given sample data (10.11) for all $x \in \mathbb{R}$ has the form

$$f(x) = a_1 L_1(x) + a_2 L_2(x) + \ldots + a_n L_n(x), \tag{10.12}$$

where

$$L_i(x) = \frac{(x - a_1) \ldots (x - a_{i-1})(x - a_{i+1}) \ldots (x - a_n)}{(x_i - a_1) \ldots (x_i - a_{i-1})(x_i - a_{i+1}) \ldots (x_i - a_n)} \tag{10.13}$$

for all $i \in \mathbb{N}_n$.

Since values $f(x)$ need not be in $[0, 1]$ for some $x \in \mathbb{R}$, function f cannot be directly considered as the sought membership function A. We may convert f to A for each $x \in \mathbb{R}$ by the formula

$$A(x) = \max[0, \min[1, f(x)]]. \tag{10.14}$$

An advantage of this method is that the membership function matches the sample data exactly. Its disadvantage is that the complexity of the resulting function (expressed by the degree of the polynomial involved) increases with the number of data samples. Furthermore, the method does not work well for values of x that are less than the smallest value in the set $\{x_1, x_2, \ldots, x_n\}$ or greater than the largest value in this set. Hence, the method requires that the sample data be well distributed over the estimated support of the constructed membership function. Another disadvantage of this method is that the data may be overfitted.

Example 10.1

To realize some difficulties involved in using this method for constructing membership functions, let us consider the following sample data:

$$\langle 0, 0 \rangle, \langle .5, .2 \rangle, \langle .8, .9 \rangle, \langle 1, 1 \rangle, \langle 1.2, .9 \rangle, \langle 1.5, .2 \rangle, \langle 2, 0 \rangle.$$

These data are shown graphically in Fig. 10.3a. Using (10.12) and (10.13), we obtain function

$$f(x) = 6.53x^6 - 39.17x^5 + 92.69x^4 - 109.65x^3 + 64.26x^2 - 13.66x,$$

whose graph is shown in Fig. 10.3b. Applying now (10.14), we obtain function A whose graph is given in Fig. 10.3c. We can see on intuitive grounds that this function is not a reasonable representation of the data outside the interval [0, 2]. It can be corrected by assuming that the estimated support of A is the interval [0, 2]. The corrected function is shown in Fig. 10.3d.

This example illustrates that the method of Lagrange interpolation requires that the resulting function be critically evaluated and appropriately corrected.   In particular, an

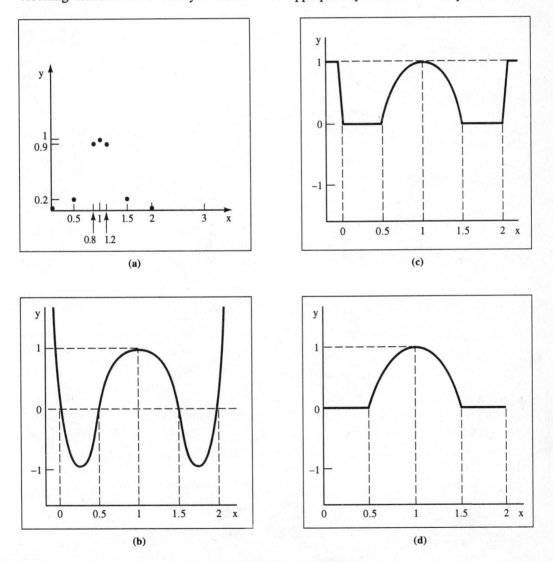

Figure 10.3   Illustration to Example 10.1.

estimate of the support of the constructed membership function plays an important role in this evaluation and correction.

Least-square Curve Fitting

Given sample data (10.11) and a suitable parametrized class of functions $f(x; \alpha, \beta, \ldots)$, where $\alpha, \beta, \ldots$ are parameters whose values distinguish functions in the class from one another, the method of least-square curve fitting selects that function $f(x; \alpha_0, \beta_0, \ldots)$ from the class for which

$$E = \sum_{i=1}^{n} [f(x_i; \alpha, \beta, \ldots) - a_i]^2 \tag{10.15}$$

reaches its minimum. Then,

$$A(x) = \max[0, \min(1, f(x; \alpha_0, \beta_0, \ldots))] \tag{10.16}$$

for all $x \in \mathbb{R}$.

The method of least-square curve fitting requires that a suitable parametrized class of functions be chosen. The choice may reflect the opinion of an expert or, alternatively, it may be based on some theory, previous experience, or experimental comparison with other classes.

An example of a class of functions that is frequently used for this purpose is the class of *bell-shaped functions*, $f(x; \alpha, \beta, \gamma)$, defined by the formula

$$f(x; \alpha, \beta, \gamma) = \gamma e^{-(x-\alpha)^2/\beta}, \tag{10.17}$$

where α controls the position of the center of the bell, $\sqrt{\beta/2}$ defines the inflection points, and γ control the height of the bell (Fig. 10.4a). Given sample data (10.11), we determine (by any effective optimization method) values $\alpha_0, \beta_0, \gamma_0$ of parameters α, β, γ, respectively, for which

$$E = \sum_{i=1}^{N} [\gamma e^{-(x_i - \alpha)^2/\beta} - a_i]^2 \tag{10.18}$$

reaches its minimum. Then, according to (10.16), the bell-shape membership function A that best conforms to the sample data is given by the formula

$$A(x) = \max[0, \min(1, \gamma_0 e^{-(x-\alpha_0)^2/\beta_0})] \tag{10.19}$$

for all $x \in \mathbb{R}$.

Another class of functions that is frequently used for representing linguistic terms is the class of trapezoidal-shaped functions, $f(x; \alpha, \beta, \gamma, \delta, \theta)$, defined in the following way:

$$f(x; \alpha, \beta, \gamma, \delta, \theta) = \begin{cases} 0 & \text{when } x < \alpha \text{ and } x > \delta \\ \dfrac{(\alpha - x)\theta}{\alpha - \beta} & \text{when } \alpha \leq x \leq \beta \\ \theta & \text{when } \beta \leq x \leq \gamma \\ \dfrac{(\delta - x)\theta}{\delta - \gamma} & \text{when } \gamma \leq x \leq \delta \end{cases} \tag{10.20}$$

The meaning of the five parameters is illustrated in Fig. 10.4b.

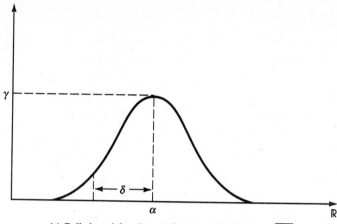

(a) Bell-shaped functions defined by (10.17) ($\delta = \sqrt{\beta/2}$).

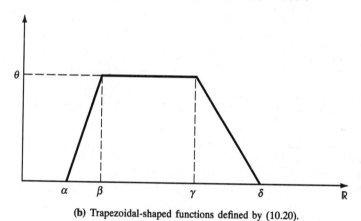

(b) Trapezoidal-shaped functions defined by (10.20).

Figure 10.4 Frequently used classes of functions in the least-square curve fitting method: (a) bell-shaped functions defined by (10.17) ($\delta = \sqrt{\beta/2}$); (b) trapezoidal-shaped functions defined by (10.20).

Example 10.2

To illustrate the least-square curve fitting method, let us apply it by using the class of bell-shaped functions to the sample data given in Example 10.1 (Fig. 10.3a). First, we find that, given the sample data, the minimum of function E defined by (10.18) is reached for $\alpha_0 = 1$, $\beta_0 = 0.164$, and $\gamma_0 = 1.074$. Hence, we obtain function

$$f(x) = 1.074e^{-(x-1)^2/0.164}$$

with $E(f) = 0.0146$. Now applying (10.19), we obtain function A, shown in Fig. 10.5a, and $E(A) = 0.0091$. This function is certainly acceptable as a membership function representing the given data.

Assume now that it is required that the constructed membership function A have only one maximum. This is a reasonable requirement when, for example, A is supposed to represent the concept *around one* or *approximately one*. To satisfy the requirement, we may constrain the

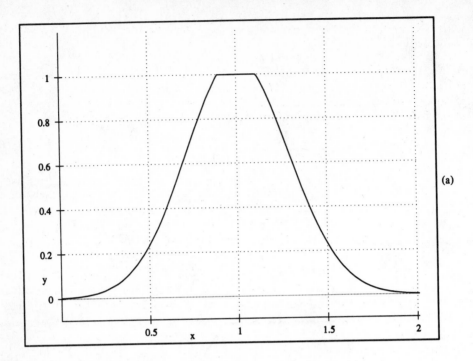

(a)

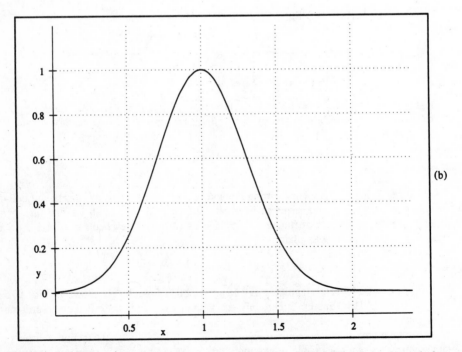

(b)

Figure 10.5 Two possible membership functions constructed from sample data by the method of least-square curve fitting.

class of bell-shaped functions by choosing $\gamma = 1$. Then, we directly obtain the membership function

$$A(x) = f(x) = e^{-(x-1)^2/0.18}$$

which is shown in Fig. 10.5b, and $E(A) = 0.0246$. Although this function does not fit the data as closely as the function in Fig. 10.5a (due to the imposed constraint on the class of acceptable functions), it keeps the bell shape and satisfies the requirement of a unique maximum.

Constructions by Neural Networks

Neural networks have lately been recognized as an important tool for constructing membership functions, operations on membership functions, fuzzy inference rules, and other context-dependent entities in fuzzy set theory. They are increasingly utilized for this purpose in many application areas. In this section, we discuss only the construction of membership functions.

In general, constructions by neural networks are based on learning patterns from sample data. For basic ideas of neural networks and associated learning algorithms, see Appendix A.

To explain the process of learning a membership function from sample data by a neural network, let us consider the two-layer network structure shown in Fig. 10.6. In describing this network and the learning process, we use master symbols that have the same meaning as symbols introduced in Appendix A.

The network has two inputs: input x, which accepts values $x^p (p \in \mathbb{N}_n)$ of the sample data, and input b, whose purpose is to represent the bias of each neuron and which is

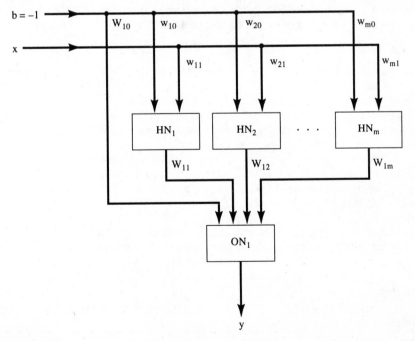

Figure 10.6 The structure of a neural network for constructing a membership function from sample data.

permanently set to -1. The output layer consists of one neuron, ON_1, whose output y is expected to produce value t^p for each input value x^p; the actual output value is denoted by y^p. The hidden layer consists of m neurons, $HN_1, HN_2, \ldots, HN_m$, which are connected to both inputs and the output neurons as shown in Fig. 10.6. The neurons operate under a suitable activation function (e.g., a particular sigmoid function).

Following the *backpropagation learning algorithm*, we first initialize the weights in the network. This means that we assign a small random number to each weight. Then, we apply pairs $\langle x^p, t^p \rangle$ of the training set

$$\{\langle x^p, t^p \rangle \mid p \in \mathbb{N}_n\}$$

to the learning algorithm in some order. For each x^p, we calculate the actual output y^p and calculate the *square error*

$$E_p = \frac{1}{2}(y^p - t^p)^2.$$

Using E_p (for each $p \in \mathbb{N}_n$), we update the weights in the network according to the backpropagation algorithm described in Appendix A. We also calculate a *cumulative cycle error*,

$$E = \frac{1}{2}\sum_{p=1}^{n}(y^p - t^p)^2.$$

At the end of each cycle, in which each sample in the training set is applied once, we compare the cumulative error with the largest acceptable error, E_{max}, specified by the user. When $E \leq E_{max}$, a solution is obtained, which means that the neural network represents the desired membership function; when $E > E_{max}$, we initiate a new cycle. The algorithm is terminated when either we obtain a solution or the number of cycles exceeds a number specified by the user.

Example 10.3

Let the sample data be the same as in Example 10.1 (Fig. 10.3a), and let the neural network employed have the structure specified in Fig. 10.6, with three neurons in the hidden layer ($m = 3$). Before applying the backpropagation algorithm, we have to select an activation function (or functions) under which the neurons will operate, initial weights, and various parameters required by the learning algorithm (maximum acceptable error, maximum number of iterations, learning rate, etc.).

Two neural networks that represent distinct solutions to our problem, which were obtained for different initial weights and different activation functions, are shown in Fig. 10.7. They are based on the sigmoid functions with $\beta = 1$ and $\beta = 2$, respectively. Graphs of the membership functions represented by these networks are shown in Fig. 10.7 under the respective block diagrams.

This example illustrates that, given the same training set, we are likely to obtain different solutions for different activation functions or different parameters in the backpropagation learning algorithm. However, the differences are, by and large, rather small and insignificant, provided that we stay within reasonable ranges of functions or parameters, as determined by previous experience.

Example 10.4

In this example, we want to illustrate how a neural network can learn from a training set a membership function that captures the conception of a "close driving distance" in a particular

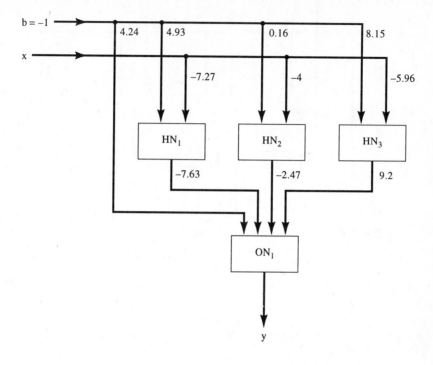

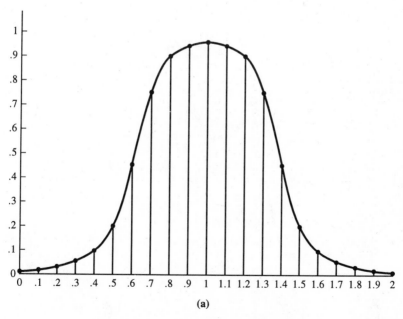

(a)

Figure 10.7   Illustration to Example 10.3: $\beta = 1$.

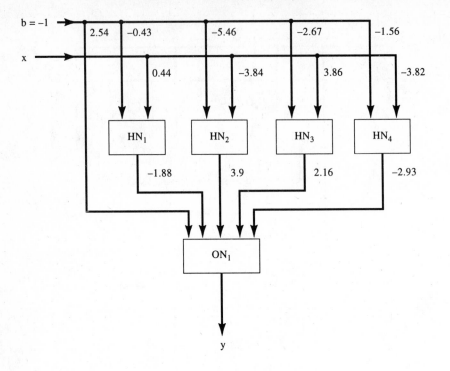

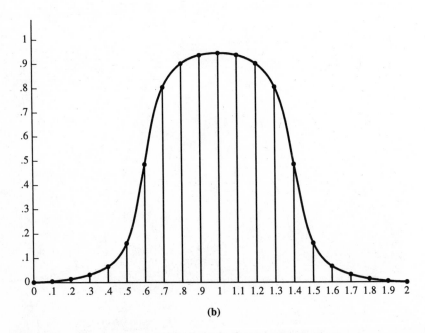

(b)

Figure 10.7 *(continued)* Illustration to Example 10.3: $\beta = 2$.

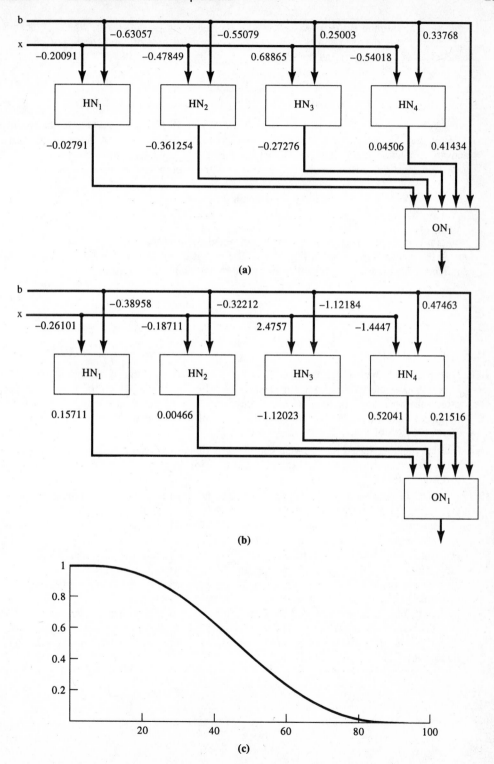

Figure 10.8 Illustration to Example 10.4.

context. The training set is given in terms of the following pairs $\langle x^p, t^p \rangle$, where x^p denotes a particular driving distance and t^p expresses the perceived degree of compatibility of x^p with the conception of a "close driving distance" in a given context:

x^p	0	10	20	30	40	50	60	70	80	90	100
t^p	1	1	1	.8	.6	.4	.2	.1	.05	0	0

A neural network with the structure shown in Fig. 10.6 is again suitable for our problem. Assume that the chosen network has four neurons in the hidden layer. Assume further that the activation function chosen for the hidden layer is the sigmoid function with $\beta = 1$, while the activation function chosen for the output neuron is the hyperbolic tangent function

$$h(a) = \text{tangh } a = \frac{e^a - e^{-a}}{e^a + e^{-a}}.$$

Then, starting with the initial weights specified in Fig. 10.8a (chosen randomly by the computer program employed), the resulting weights, obtained by the backpropagation learning algorithm for 10,000 cycles, are shown in Fig. 10.8b. The neural network with these weights represents a continuous function on $\mathbb{R}^+$, which is illustrated by the graph in Fig. 10.8c.

NOTES

10.1. Direct methods with multiple experts can be formulated in terms of models of modal logic based on possible worlds [Resconi *et al.*, 1992, 1993; Klir, 1994]. This formulation seems promising since other theories of uncertainty, such as evidence theory, possibility theory, and rough set theory, can also be interpreted in terms of models of modal logic [Harmanec *et al.*, 1994; Klir, 1994].

10.2. Indirect methods based on pairwise comparisons of relevant elements by experts (Sec. 10.5) were investigated by Saaty [1974, 1977, 1978, 1986], Chu *et al.*, [1979], and Triantaphyllou and Mann [1990].

10.3. Methods for constructing membership functions from statistical data were explored by Devi and Sarma [1985], Civanlar and Trussell [1986], and Dubois and Prade [1985c, 1986a]. The literature dealing with the use of neural networks for learning membership functions or inference rules is rapidly growing; the following are a few relevant references: [Takagi and Hayashi, 1991; Keller and Tahani, 1992; Wang and Mendel, 1992b; Hayashi *et al.*, 1992; Jang, 1992, 1993; Berenji, 1992; Berenji and Khedkar, 1992; Wang, 1994]. Overview papers of different methods for constructing membership functions were written by Chameau and Santamarina [1987] and Turksen [1991]. Experimental studies regarding fuzzy operation used by human beings were performed by Zimmermann [1978a], Zimmermann and Zysno [1980], and Kovalerchuk and Taliansky [1992]. More general studies regarding the measurement of fuzzy concepts, including the notion of context, were pursued by Nowakowska [1977], Smithson [1987], and Ezhkova [1989].

EXERCISES

10.1. In Sec. 10.3, a fuzzy set of straight lines is defined as an example of using the method of mathematically defined compatibility of given elements with ideal prototypes. Using this method, define fuzzy sets of straight lines that are horizontal, vertical, or diagonal (two kinds).

10.2. Consider $X = \{x_1, x_2, x_3, x_4, x_5\}$ and propositions "x_i belongs to A" and "x_i belongs to B" ($i \in \mathbb{N}_5$), where A and B are fuzzy sets. Given valuations of these propositions by 10 experts in Table 10.1, determine for each $x_i \in X$:

(a) $A(x_i), B(x_i)$ by (10.1) and $[A \cap B](x_i), [A \cup B](x_i)$ by the standard fuzzy operators (or some other t-norms and t-conorms);

(b) $A(x_i), B(x_i)$ by (10.1) and $[A \cap B](x_i), [A \cup B](x_i)$ by (10.4) and (10.5), respectively.

TABLE 10.1   EXAMPLE OF VALUATIONS OF TWO FUZZY PROPOSITIONS BY TEN EXPERTS (EXERCISE 10.2)

X	A	B
x_1	$a(x_1) = \langle 0\ 1\ 1\ 0\ 1\ 1\ 0\ 1\ 1\ 0 \rangle$	$b(x_1) = \langle 1\ 1\ 0\ 1\ 1\ 1\ 0\ 1\ 0\ 1 \rangle$
x_2	$a(x_2) = \langle 1\ 1\ 1\ 1\ 0\ 0\ 1\ 1\ 1\ 1 \rangle$	$b(x_2) = \langle 1\ 1\ 1\ 1\ 1\ 1\ 1\ 1\ 1\ 1 \rangle$
x_3	$a(x_3) = \langle 1\ 1\ 1\ 1\ 1\ 1\ 1\ 1\ 1\ 1 \rangle$	$b(x_3) = \langle 0\ 1\ 1\ 1\ 1\ 1\ 1\ 1\ 1\ 1 \rangle$
x_4	$a(x_4) = \langle 0\ 1\ 0\ 1\ 1\ 0\ 0\ 1\ 0\ 1 \rangle$	$b(x_4) = \langle 1\ 1\ 1\ 1\ 1\ 0\ 0\ 1\ 0\ 1 \rangle$
x_5	$a(x_5) = \langle 1\ 0\ 1\ 0\ 0\ 0\ 0\ 0\ 0\ 0 \rangle$	$b(x_5) = \langle 0\ 0\ 0\ 1\ 1\ 0\ 1\ 1\ 1\ 0 \rangle$

10.3. Apply the indirect method with one expert explained in Sec. 10.5 to the matrix of pairwise comparisons (matrix $\mathbf{P}$) given in Table 10.2 to determine the degrees of membership of the countries listed in the table in the fuzzy set of wealthy nations (adopted from [Chu *et al.*, 1979]).

TABLE 10.2   WEALTH-OF-RELATIONS MATRIX (MATRIX $\mathbf{P}$ IN EXERCISE 10.3)

Country	U.S.	USSR	China	France	U.K.	Japan	W. Germany
U.S.	1	4	9	6	6	5	5
USSR	1/4	1	7	5	5	3	4
China	1/9	1/7	1	1/5	1/5	1/7	1/5
France	1/6	1/5	5	1	1	1/3	1/3
U.K.	1/6	1/5	5	1	1	1/3	1/3
Japan	1/5	1/3	7	3	3	1	2
W. Germany	1/5	1/4	5	3	3	1/2	1

10.4. Suppose we have the following sample data,

$$\langle 0, 0 \rangle, \langle 1, .1 \rangle, \langle 2, .2 \rangle, \langle 3, .3 \rangle, \langle 4, .4 \rangle, \langle 5, .5 \rangle,$$

$$\langle 6, .6 \rangle, \langle 7, .7 \rangle, \langle 8, .8 \rangle, \langle 9, .9 \rangle, \langle 10, 1 \rangle, \langle 11, .9 \rangle,$$

$$\langle 12, .8 \rangle, \langle 13, .7 \rangle, \langle 14, .6 \rangle, \langle 15, .5 \rangle, \langle 16, .4 \rangle, \langle 17, .3 \rangle,$$

$$\langle 18, .2 \rangle, \langle 19, .1 \rangle, \langle 20, 0 \rangle$$

in the form of $\langle x^p, t^p \rangle$ for a fuzzy set A. Assume that the support of A is $[0, 20]$. Using some of the methods described in Sec. 10.7, determine the membership function of A, respectively. Compare results obtained by different methods.

11

APPROXIMATE REASONING

11.1 FUZZY EXPERT SYSTEMS: AN OVERVIEW

An expert system, as the name suggests, is a computer-based system that emulates the reasoning process of a human expert within a specific domain of knowledge. Expert systems are primarily built for the purpose of making the experience, understanding, and problem-solving capabilities of the expert in a particular subject area available to the nonexpert in this area. In addition, they may be designed for various specific activities, such as consulting, diagnosis, learning, decision support, design, planning, or research.

A typical architecture of an expert system is depicted by the block diagram in Fig. 11.1. Let us describe the role of each of the units shown in the diagram. Our focus is, of course, on fuzzy expert systems.

The kernel of any expert system consists of a knowledge base (also called a long-term memory), a database (also called a short-term memory or a blackboard interface), and an inference engine. These three units, together with some interface for communicating with the user, form the minimal configuration that may still be called an expert system.

The *knowledge base* contains general knowledge pertaining to the problem domain. In fuzzy expert systems, the knowledge is usually represented by a set of *fuzzy production rules*, which connect antecedents with consequences, premises with conclusions, or conditions with actions. They most commonly have the form *"If A, then B,"* where *A* and *B* are fuzzy sets.

The purpose of the *database* is to store data for each specific task of the expert system. The data may be obtained through a dialog between the expert system and the user. Typically, such data are parameters of the problem or other relevant facts. Other data may be obtained by the inference of the expert system.

The *inference engine* of a fuzzy expert system operates on a series of production rules and makes fuzzy inferences. There exist two approaches to evaluating relevant production rules. The first is data-driven and is exemplified by the generalized modus ponens. In this case, available data are supplied to the expert system, which then uses them to evaluate relevant production rules and draw all possible conclusions. An alternative method of evaluation is goal-driven; it is exemplified by the generalized modus tollens form of logical

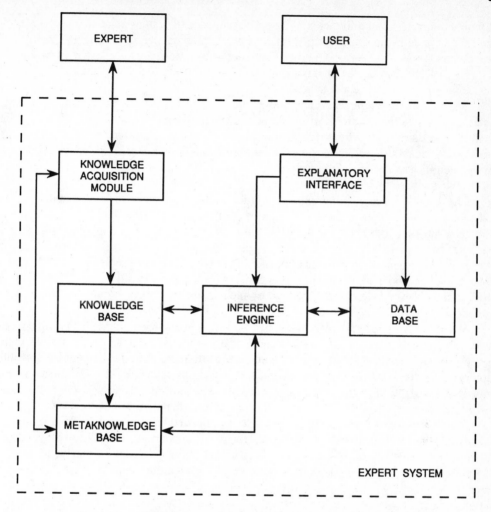

Figure 11.1   Architecture of an expert system.

inference. Here, the expert system searches for data specified in the *IF* clauses of production rules that will lead to the objective; these data are found either in the knowledge base, in the *THEN* clauses of other production rules, or by querying the user. Since the data-driven method proceeds from *IF* clauses to *THEN* clauses in the chain through the production rules, it is commonly called *forward chaining*. Similarly, since the goal-driven method proceeds backward, from the *THEN* clauses (objectives) to the *IF* clauses, in its search for the required data, it is commonly referred to as *backward chaining*. Backward chaining has the advantage of speed, since only the rules leading to the objective need to be evaluated. Moreover, if certain data are difficult to obtain, and these are only potentially necessary, then the backward-chaining method is clearly superior.

The inference engine may also use knowledge regarding the fuzzy production rules in the knowledge base. This type of knowledge, whose appropriate name is *metaknowledge*, is located in the unit called a *metaknowledge base*. This unit contains rules about the use of production rules in the knowledge base. These rules, or rather *metarules*, prescribe, for example, stopping criteria, require precedences in applying certain production rules under various conditions or whether a needed fact should be inferred or requested from the user. The primary purpose of the metaknowledge base is to simplify computation by pruning unnecessary paths in the search space.

The *explanatory interface* facilitates communication between the user and the expert system. It enables the user to determine how the expert system obtained various intermediate or final conclusions, or why specific information is being requested from the user. This capability is crucial for building user confidence in the expert system. It is also very important for the identification of errors, omissions, inconsistencies, and so on, during the debugging of the knowledge base or inference engine.

The *knowledge acquisition module*, which is included only in some expert systems, makes it possible to update the knowledge base or metaknowledge base through interaction with relevant human experts. In general, this unit must implement suitable algorithms for machine learning, such as algorithms conceptualized in terms of artificial neural networks (Appendix A) or genetic algorithms (Appendix B), by which fuzzy productions can be learned from examples obtained from human experts. This capability allows the expert system to expand or modify its knowledge base or metaknowledge base through feedback during operation.

When the knowledge domain is removed from an expert system, the remaining structure is usually referred to as an *expert system shell*. The applicability of an expert system shell is not necessarily restricted to one particular knowledge domain. An inference engine embedded in an appropriate expert system shell is thus, in principle, reusable for different domains of knowledge and, thus, for different expert systems.

The purpose of this chapter is to cover fundamentals of reasoning based on fuzzy production rules, which is usually referred to as *approximate reasoning*. This material is essential for the design of inference engines for fuzzy expert systems. The actual design of fuzzy expert systems or even inference engines for approximate reasoning is beyond the scope of this book. However, we guide the reader through the literature on this topic in Note 11.1.

11.2 FUZZY IMPLICATIONS

The logic operation of implication is as essential for approximate reasoning as it is for reasoning within classical two-valued logic. In general, a *fuzzy implication*, $\mathcal{J}$, is a function of the form

$$\mathcal{J} : [0, 1] \times [0, 1] \to [0, 1],$$

which for any possible truth values a, b of given fuzzy propositions p, q, respectively, defines the truth value, $\mathcal{J}(a, b)$, of the conditional proposition "if p, then q." This function should be an extension of the classical implication, $p \Rightarrow q$, from the restricted domain $\{0, 1\}$ to the full domain $[0, 1]$ of truth values in fuzzy logic.

In classical logic, where a, $b \in \{0, 1\}$, $\mathcal{J}$ can be defined in several distinct forms. While these forms are equivalent in classical logic, their extensions to fuzzy logic are not equivalent and result in distinct classes of fuzzy implications. This fact makes the concept of fuzzy implication somewhat complicated. The purpose of this section is to discuss the issues involved in a comprehensive manner and to overview the specific operators of fuzzy implications that are most common in the literature.

One way of defining $\mathfrak{I}$ in classical logic is to use the logic formula

$$\mathfrak{I}(a, b) = \overline{a} \vee b \tag{11.1}$$

for all $a, b \in \{0, 1\}$. When extending this formula to fuzzy logic, we interpret the disjunction and negation as a fuzzy union (t-conorm) and a fuzzy complement, respectively. This results in defining $\mathfrak{I}$ in fuzzy logic by the formula

$$\mathfrak{I}(a, b) = u(c(a), b) \tag{11.2}$$

for all $a, b \in [0, 1]$, where u and c denote a fuzzy union and a fuzzy complement, respectively.

Another way of defining $\mathfrak{I}$ in classical logic is to employ the formula

$$\mathfrak{I}(a, b) = \max\{x \in \{0, 1\} \mid a \wedge x \leq b\} \tag{11.3}$$

for all $a, b \in \{0, 1\}$. Interpreting the conjunction in this formula as a fuzzy intersection (t-norm), $\mathfrak{I}$ in fuzzy logic is then defined by the extended formula

$$\mathfrak{I}(a, b) = \sup\{x \in [0, 1] \mid i(a, x) \leq b\} \tag{11.4}$$

for all $a, b \in [0, 1]$, where i denotes a continuous fuzzy intersection.

While the definitions (11.1) and (11.3) of implication in classical logic are equivalent, their extensions (11.2) and (11.4) in fuzzy logic are not. Moreover, (11.1) may also be rewritten, due to the law of absorption of negation in classical logic, as either

$$\mathfrak{I}(a, b) = \overline{a} \vee (a \wedge b) \tag{11.5}$$

or

$$\mathfrak{I}(a, b) = (\overline{a} \wedge \overline{b}) \vee b. \tag{11.6}$$

The extensions of these equations in fuzzy logic are, respectively,

$$\mathfrak{I}(a, b) = u(c(a), i(a, b)), \tag{11.7}$$

$$\mathfrak{I}(a, b) = u(i(c(a), c(b)), b), \tag{11.8}$$

where u, i, c are required to satisfy the De Morgan laws (i.e., u and i are dual with respect to c). Again, while definitions (11.1), (11.5), and (11.6) pertaining to classical logic are equivalent, their counterparts in fuzzy logic—(11.2), (11.7), and (11.8), respectively— are distinct (the law of absorption of negation does not hold in fuzzy logic in general).

Equations (11.2), (11.4), (11.7), and (11.8) thus yield distinct classes of fuzzy implication operators. Specific implication operators are obtained by choosing specific t-norms, t- conorms, or fuzzy complements, as relevant in each class. Let us examine each of these classes by looking at a few examples and discussing some general properties of the class. To denote specific fuzzy implications, we adopt symbols that are usually used for them in the literature. We also adopt names that are commonly used for these implications.

First, let us examine fuzzy implications that are obtained from (11.2), which are usually referred to in the literature as S-implications (the symbol S is often used for denoting t-conorms). The following are examples of four well-known S-implications, all of which are based on the standard fuzzy complement and differ from one another by the chosen fuzzy unions:

1. When we choose the standard fuzzy union, we obtain a function $\mathcal{J}_b$ defined for all $a, b \in [0, 1]$ by the formula

$$\mathcal{J}_b(a, b) = \max(1 - a, b),$$

which is called a *Kleene-Dienes implication*.

2. Choosing the algebraic sum as a fuzzy union (i.e., $u(a, b) = a + b - ab$), we obtain

$$\mathcal{J}_r(a, b) = 1 - a + ab,$$

which is called a *Reichenbach implication*.

3. The choice of the bounded sum $u(a, b) = \min(1, a + b)$ results in the function

$$\mathcal{J}_a(a, b) = \min(1, 1 - a + b),$$

which is called a *Lukasiewicz implication*.

4. When we choose the drastic fuzzy union $u_{\max}$, which is the largest t-conorm, we obtain

$$\mathcal{J}_{LS}(a, b) = \begin{cases} b & \text{when } a = 1 \\ 1 - a & \text{when } b = 0 \\ 1 & \text{otherwise,} \end{cases}$$

which is the *largest S-implication*. This fact is a consequence of the following theorem, which establishes that S-implications based on the same fuzzy complement are ordered in the same way as the associated t-conorms.

Theorem 11.1. Let u_1, u_2 be t-conorms such that $u_1(a, b) \leq u_2(a, b)$ for all $a, b \in [0, 1]$, and let $\mathcal{J}_1, \mathcal{J}_2$ be S-implications based on the same fuzzy complement c and u_1, u_2, respectively. Then $\mathcal{J}_1(a, b) \leq \mathcal{J}_2(a, b)$ for all $a, b \in [0, 1]$.

Proof: For all $a, b \in [0, 1]$, we have $\mathcal{J}_1(a, b) = u_1(c(a), b) \leq u_2(c(a), b) = \mathcal{J}_2(a, b)$. ■

Since $u_{\max}$ is the largest t-conorm, $\mathcal{J}_{LS}$ is the largest S-implication by Theorem 11.1. Similarly, $\mathcal{J}_b$ is the smallest S-implication. Furthermore,

$$\mathcal{J}_b \leq \mathcal{J}_r \leq \mathcal{J}_a \leq \mathcal{J}_{LS}.$$

Let us proceed now to fuzzy implications that are characterized by (11.4). They are usually called *R-implications*, as they are closely connected with the so-called residuated semigroup. We do not deem it necessary to discuss this connection, which would require that we introduce the appropriate mathematical background first. The following are examples of four well-known R-implications.

1. When we choose the standard fuzzy intersection, we obtain

$$\mathcal{J}_g(a, b) = \sup\{x \mid \min(a, x) \leq b\} = \begin{cases} 1 & \text{when } a \leq b \\ b & \text{when } a > b, \end{cases}$$

which is called a *Gödel implication*.

2. Choosing $i(a, b) = ab$, we obtain

$$\mathcal{J}_\Delta(a, b) = \sup\{x \,|\, ax \leq b\} = \begin{cases} 1 & \text{when } a \leq b \\ b/a & \text{when } a > b, \end{cases}$$

which is called a *Goguen implication*.

3. The choice of $i(a, b) = \max(0, a+b-1)$ (bounded difference) results in the Lukasiewicz implication

$$\mathcal{J}_a(a, b) = \sup\{x \,|\, \max(0, a + x - 1) \leq b\}$$
$$= \min(1, 1 - a + b).$$

Hence, the Lukasiewicz implication is both S-implication and R-implication.

4. Another implication, defined by

$$\mathcal{J}_{LR}(a, b) = \begin{cases} b & \text{when } a = 1 \\ 1 & \text{otherwise}, \end{cases}$$

is actually the limit of all R-implications. It serves as the least upper bound of the class of R-implications. For this reason, we still categorize it as the largest R-implication, although it cannot be defined through (11.4).

Theorem 11.2.   Let i_1, i_2 be t-norms such that $i_1(a, b) \leq i_2(a, b)$ for all $a, b \in [0, 1]$, and let $\mathcal{J}_1, \mathcal{J}_2$ be R-implications based on i_1, i_2, respectively. Then $\mathcal{J}_1(a, b) \geq \mathcal{J}_2(a, b)$ for all $a, b \in [0, 1]$.

Proof: Since $i_1(a, b) \leq i_2(a, b)$ for all $a, b \in [0, 1]$, we have $i_1(a, x_0) \leq i_2(a, x_0) \leq b$ for all $x_0 \in \{x \,|\, i_2(a, x) \leq b\}$. Then, $x_0 \in \{x \,|\, i_1(a, x) \leq b\}$ and, consequently,

$$\{x \,|\, i_2(a, x) \leq b\} \subseteq \{x \,|\, i_1(a, x) \leq b\}.$$

Hence,

$$\mathcal{J}_2(a, b) = \sup\{x \,|\, i_2(a, x) \leq b\} \leq \sup\{x \,|\, i_1(a, x) \leq b\} = \mathcal{J}_1(a, b). \quad \blacksquare$$

It follows immediately from this theorem that $\mathcal{J}_g$ is the smallest R-implication and

$$\mathcal{J}_g \leq \mathcal{J}_\Delta \leq \mathcal{J}_a \leq \mathcal{J}_{LR}.$$

Next, let us examine fuzzy implications based on (11.7), where the t-norm i and t-conorm u are required to be dual with respect to the complement c. These fuzzy implications are called *QL-implications*, since they were originally employed in quantum logic. The following are four examples of *QL*-implications, in all of which the standard fuzzy complement is assumed.

1. When i and u are the standard min and max operations, we obtain

$$\mathcal{J}_m(a, b) = \max[1 - a, \min(a, b)],$$

which is sometimes called a *Zadeh implication*.

2. When i is the algebraic product and u is the algebraic sum, we obtain

$$\mathcal{J}_p(a, b) = 1 - a + a^2 b.$$

3. When i is the bounded difference and u is the bounded sum, we obtain the Kleene-Dienes implication $\mathcal{J}_b$.

4. When $i = i_{min}$ and $u = u_{max}$, we obtain

$$\mathcal{J}_q(a, b) = \begin{cases} b & \text{when } a = 1 \\ 1 - a & \text{when } a \neq 1, b \neq 1 \\ 1 & \text{when } a \neq 1, b = 1. \end{cases}$$

In addition to the three classes of fuzzy implications, which are predominant in the literature, other fuzzy implications are possible. For example, we may use (11.8) as a source of another class of fuzzy implications, but we leave it to the reader to explore this source. We may also form new fuzzy implications by combining existing ones (Table 11.1). The following combinations, for example, have been suggested in the literature:

$$\mathcal{J}_{sg}(a, b) = \min[\mathcal{J}_s(a, b), \mathcal{J}_g(1 - b, 1 - a)],$$

$$\mathcal{J}_{gs}(a, b) = \min[\mathcal{J}_g(a, b), \mathcal{J}_s(1 - b, 1 - a)],$$

$$\mathcal{J}_{ss}(a, b) = \min[\mathcal{J}_s(a, b), \mathcal{J}_s(1 - b, 1 - a)],$$

$$\mathcal{J}_{gg}(a, b) = \min[\mathcal{J}_g(a, b), \mathcal{J}_g(1 - b, 1 - a)],$$

$$\mathcal{J}_{\Delta\Delta}(a, b) = \min[\mathcal{J}_\Delta(a, b), \mathcal{J}_\Delta(1 - b, 1 - a)].$$

All fuzzy implications are obtained by generalizing the implication operator of classical logic. That is, they collapse to the classical implication when truth values are restricted to 0 and 1. Identifying various properties of the classical implication and generalizing them appropriately leads to the following properties, which may be viewed as reasonable axioms of fuzzy implications.

Axiom 1. $a \leq b$ implies $\mathcal{J}(a, x) \geq \mathcal{J}(b, x)$ (*monotonicity in first argument*). This means that the truth value of fuzzy implications increases as the truth value of the antecedent decreases.

Axiom 2. $a \leq b$ implies $\mathcal{J}(x, a) \leq \mathcal{J}(x, b)$ (*monotonicity in second argument*). This means that the truth value of fuzzy implications increases as the truth value of the consequent increases.

Axiom 3. $\mathcal{J}(0, a) = 1$ (*dominance of falsity*). This means that the falsity implies everything.

Axiom 4. $\mathcal{J}(1, b) = b$ (*neutrality of truth*). This means that the truth does not imply anything.

Axiom 5. $\mathcal{J}(a, a) = 1$ (*identity*). This means that fuzzy implications are true whenever the truth values of the antecedent and consequent are equal.

Axiom 6. $\mathcal{J}(a, \mathcal{J}(b, x)) = \mathcal{J}(b, \mathcal{J}(a, x))$ (*exchange property*). This is a generalization of the equivalence of $a \Rightarrow (b \Rightarrow x)$ and $b \Rightarrow (a \Rightarrow x)$ that holds for the classical implication.

Axiom 7. $\mathcal{J}(a, b) = 1$ iff $a \leq b$ (*boundary condition*). This means that fuzzy implications are true if and only if the consequent is at least as true as the antecedent.

TABLE 11.1 LIST OF FUZZY IMPLICATIONS

Name	Symbol	Class	Function $\mathfrak{I}(a,b)$	Axioms	Complement $c(a)$	Year
Early Zadeh	$\mathfrak{I}_m$	QL	$\max[1-a, \min(a,b)]$	1, 2, 3, 4, 9	$1-a$	1973
Gaines-Rescher	$\mathfrak{I}_s$		$\begin{cases} 1 & a \le b \\ 0 & a > b \end{cases}$	1, 2, 3, 4, 5, 6, 7, 8		1969
Gödel	$\mathfrak{I}_g$	R	$\begin{cases} 1 & a \le b \\ b & a > b \end{cases}$	1, 2, 3, 4, 5, 6, 7		1976
Goguen	$\mathfrak{I}_\Delta$	R	$\begin{cases} 1 & a \le b \\ b/a & a > b \end{cases}$	1, 2, 3, 4, 5, 6, 7, 9		1969
Kleene-Dienes	$\mathfrak{I}_b$	S, QL	$\max(1-a, b)$	1, 2, 3, 4, 6, 8, 9	$1-a$	1938, 1949
Lukasiewicz	$\mathfrak{I}_a$	R, S	$\min(1, 1-a+b)$	1, 2, 3, 4, 5, 6, 7, 8, 9	$1-a$	1920
Pseudo-Lukasiewicz 1	$\mathfrak{I}_\lambda$ $(\lambda > -1)$	R, S	$\min\left[1, \dfrac{1-a+(1+\lambda)b}{1+\lambda a}\right]$	1, 2, 3, 4, 5, 6, 7, 8, 9	$\dfrac{1-a}{1+\lambda a}$	1987
Pseudo-Lukasiewicz 2	$\mathfrak{I}_w$ $(w > 0)$	R, S	$\min\left[1, (1-a^w+b^w)^{\frac{1}{w}}\right]$	1, 2, 3, 4, 5, 6, 7, 8, 9	$(1-a^w)^{\frac{1}{w}}$	1987
Reichenbach	$\mathfrak{I}_r$	S	$1-a+ab$	1, 2, 3, 4, 6, 8, 9	$1-a$	1935
Willmott	$\mathfrak{I}_{wi}$		$\min[\max(1-a, b), \max(a, 1-a), \max(b, 1-b)]$	4, 6, 8, 9	$1-a$	1980
Wu	$\mathfrak{I}_{wu}$		$\begin{cases} 1 & a \le b \\ \min(1-a, b) & a > b \end{cases}$	1, 2, 3, 5, 7, 8	$1-a$	1986
Yager	$\mathfrak{I}_y$		$\begin{cases} 1 & a = b = 0 \\ b^a & \text{others} \end{cases}$	1, 2, 3, 4, 6		1980
Klir and Yuan 1	$\mathfrak{I}_p$	QL	$1-a+a^2 b$	2, 3, 4, 9	$1-a$	1994
Klir and Yuan 2	$\mathfrak{I}_q$	QL	$\begin{cases} b & a = 1 \\ 1-a & a \ne 1, b \ne 1 \\ 1 & a \ne 1, b = 1 \end{cases}$	2, 4	$1-a$	1994

Axiom 8. $\mathcal{J}(a, b) = \mathcal{J}(c(b), c(a))$ for a fuzzy complement c (*contraposition*). This means that fuzzy implications are equally true when the antecedent and consequent are exchanged and negated.

Axiom 9. $\mathcal{J}$ is a continuous function (*continuity*). This property ensures that small changes in the truth values of the antecedent or consequent do not produce large (discontinuous) changes in truth values of fuzzy implications.

These nine axioms are not independent of one another. For example, Axioms 3 and 5 can be derived from Axiom 7, but not vice versa. The reason for listing the weaker axioms as well is that some fuzzy implications suggested in the literature satisfy Axioms 3 and 5, but not the stronger Axiom 7. Fuzzy implications that satisfy all the listed axioms are characterized by the following theorem.

Theorem 11.3. A function $\mathcal{J} : [0, 1]^2 \to [0, 1]$ satisfies Axioms 1–9 of fuzzy implications for a particular fuzzy complement c iff there exists a strict increasing continuous function $f : [0, 1] \to [0, \infty)$ such that $f(0) = 0$,

$$\mathcal{J}(a, b) = f^{(-1)}(f(1) - f(a) + f(b)) \tag{11.9}$$

for all $a, b \in [0, 1]$, and

$$c(a) = f^{-1}(f(1) - f(a)) \tag{11.10}$$

for all $a \in [0, 1]$.

Proof: See [Smets and Magrez, 1987]. ■

Let us apply Theorem 11.3 to some functions f. In the simplest case, when f is the identity function, we obtain the Lukasiewicz implication and c is the standard fuzzy complement. This also means the following: given the standard fuzzy complement, the only fuzzy implication that satisfies Axioms 1–9 is the Lukasiewicz implication.

Consider now the function $f(a) = \ln(1 + a), a \in [0, 1]$. Its pseudo-inverse is

$$f^{(-1)}(a) = \begin{cases} e^a - 1 & \text{when } 0 \le a \le \ln 2 \\ 1 & \text{otherwise,} \end{cases}$$

and the fuzzy complement generated by f is given by

$$c(a) = \frac{1 - a}{1 + a}$$

for all $a \in [0, 1]$. The resulting fuzzy implication is defined by the formula

$$\mathcal{J}(a, b) = \min\left(1, \frac{1 - a + 2b}{1 + a}\right)$$

for all $a, b \in [0, 1]$.

This example can be generalized by using $f(a) = \ln(1 + \lambda a)$, where λ is a positive parameter ($\lambda > 0$). Then,

$$f^{(-1)}(a) = \begin{cases} \dfrac{e^a - 1}{\lambda} & \text{when } 0 \leq a \leq \ln(1 + \lambda) \\ 1 & \text{otherwise}, \end{cases}$$

and we obtain the Sugeno class of fuzzy complements,

$$c_\lambda(a) = \frac{1 - a}{1 + \lambda a},$$

and the parameterized class of fuzzy implications,

$$\mathcal{J}_\lambda(a, b) = \min[1, (1 - a + b + \lambda b)/(1 + \lambda a)].$$

Fuzzy implications in this class, which can be extended to $\lambda > -1$ by using $f(a) = -\ln(1 + \lambda a)$ for $\lambda \in (-1, 0)$, are called *pseudo-Lukasiewicz implications*. Observe that $\mathcal{J}_\lambda$ increases with increasing λ.

Given a particular Sugeno fuzzy complement for $\lambda \neq 0$, the associated pseudo-Lukasiewicz implication is not necessarily the only fuzzy implication that satisfies Axioms 1–9. To illustrate this point, let $f(a) = 2a/(1 + a)$, $a \in [0, 1]$. Then,

$$f^{(-1)}(a) = \begin{cases} \dfrac{a}{2 - a} & \text{when } 0 \leq a \leq 1 \\ 1 & \text{otherwise}, \end{cases}$$

and

$$c(a) = \frac{1 - a}{1 + 3a}$$

for all $a \in [0, 1]$. Under this fuzzy complement (Sugeno complement for $\lambda = 3$), the fuzzy implication

$$\mathcal{J}(a, b) = \min\left(1, \frac{1 - a + 3b + ab}{1 + 3a - b + ab}\right) (a, b \in [0, 1])$$

satisfies, according to Theorem 11.3, Axioms 1–9. However, it is not the pseudo-Lukasiewicz implication $\mathcal{J}_\lambda$ for $\lambda = 3$. The latter has the form

$$\mathcal{J}_3(a, b) = \min[1, (1 - a + 4b)/(1 + 3a)].$$

Another class of pseudo-Lukasiewicz implications, associated with the Yager class of fuzzy complements,

$$c_w(a) = (1 - a^w)^{1/w},$$

is defined by the formula

$$\mathcal{J}_w(a, b) = \min[1, (1 - a^w + b^w)^{1/w}],$$

where $w > 0$. Again, $\mathcal{J}_w$ increases with increasing w. This class of fuzzy implications is based on $f(a) = a^w$.

Some of the main fuzzy implications discussed in the literature are summarized in Table 11.1. In Fig. 11.2, we show ordering among some of these implications; the greatest fuzzy implication is on top of the diagram; $\supset$ denotes the classical implication.

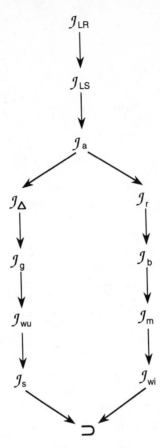

Figure 11.2 Ordering of fuzzy implications.

11.3 SELECTION OF FUZZY IMPLICATIONS

To select an appropriate fuzzy implication for approximate reasoning under each particular situation is a difficult problem. Although some theoretically supported guidelines are now available for some situations, we are still far from a general solution to this problem.

In this section, we discuss some of the issues involved in dealing with this problem, and we also examine some theoretical results pertaining to it. Our presentation is restricted to reasoning with unqualified fuzzy propositions.

We recall from Chapter 8 that any unqualified conditional fuzzy proposition p of the form

$$p : \text{If } X \text{ is } A, \text{ then } y \text{ is } B \tag{11.11}$$

is determined by

$$R(x, y) = \mathcal{J}(A(x), B(x)) \tag{11.12}$$

for all $x \in X$ and $y \in Y$, where $\mathcal{J}$ denotes a fuzzy implication, and R expresses the relationship between the variables X and Y involved in the given proposition. For each $x \in X$ and each $y \in Y$, the membership grade $R(x, y)$ represents the truth value of the proposition

$$p_{xy} : \text{If } X = x, \text{then } Y = y.$$

Now, the truth values of propositions "$X = x$" and "$Y = y$" are expressed by the membership grades $A(x)$ and $B(y)$, respectively. Consequently, the truth value of proposition p_{xy}, given by $R(x, y)$, involves a fuzzy implication in which $A(x)$ is the truth value of the antecedent and $B(y)$ is the truth value of the consequent. This is formally expressed by (11.12).

Since the meaning of fuzzy implication is not unique, contrary to classical logic, we have to resolve the following question to make (11.12) operational: which fuzzy implication should be used for calculating the fuzzy relation R? To answer this question, we need to identify meaningful criteria in terms of which distinct fuzzy implications could be evaluated and compared. It is obvious that these criteria must emerge from the various fuzzy inference rules. In the following, we examine criteria that emerge from the three fuzzy inference rules introduced in Sec. 8.6: the generalized rules of modus ponens, modus tollens, and hypothetical syllogism.

Let us begin with the generalized modus ponens. According to this fuzzy inference rule, given a fuzzy proposition of the form (11.11) and a fact "X is A'," we conclude that "Y is B'" by the compositional rule of inference

$$B' = A' \overset{i}{\circ} R,$$

where $\overset{i}{\circ}$ is the sup-i composition for a t-norm i. However, in the classical modus ponens, the fact is always given as the proposition "X is A" (i.e., it is tacitly assumed that $A' = A$), and we obtain the conclusion "Y is B" by (11.11) (i.e., $B' = B$). The generalized modus ponens should coincide with the classical one in the special case when $A' = A$. That is, the compositional rule of inference for this special case should be

$$B = A \overset{i}{\circ} R,$$

or, more specifically,

$$B(y) = \sup_{x \in X} i[A(x), \mathcal{J}(A(x), B(y))]. \tag{11.13}$$

This equation provides us with a meaningful criterion for selecting an appropriate fuzzy implication $\mathcal{J}$: any fuzzy implication suitable for approximate reasoning based on the generalized modus ponens should satisfy (11.13) for arbitrary fuzzy sets A and B. Although no general results regarding this criterion have been obtained as yet, some restricted but useful results are expressed by the following two theorems.

Theorem 11.4. Let A be a normal fuzzy set. For any continuous t-norm i and the associated ω_i operator, let $\mathcal{J} = \omega_i$; that is,

$$\mathcal{J}(A(x), B(y)) = \omega_i(A(x), B(y))$$

for all $x \in X, y \in Y$. Then, (11.13) holds.

Proof: Since $i[a, \omega_i(a, b)] \le b$ for all $a, b \in [0, 1]$, we have

$$i[A(x), \omega_i(A(x), B(y))] \le B(y)$$

for all $x \in X, y \in Y$. On the other hand, since A is normal, there exists $x_0 \in X$ such that $A(x_0) = 1$, and we have

$$i[A(x_0), \omega_i(A(x_0), B(y))] = \omega_i(1, B(y)) = B(y).$$

Hence,

$$\sup_{x \in X} i[A(x), \omega_i(A(x), B(y))] = B(y). \quad \blacksquare$$

Theorem 11.5. Let the range of the membership function A in (11.13) cover the whole interval $[0, 1]$. Then, the following fuzzy implications satisfy (11.13) for any t-norm i:

1. Gaines-Rescher implication $\mathcal{J}_s$;
2. Gödel implication $\mathcal{J}_g$;
3. Wu implication $\mathcal{J}_{wu}$.

Proof: We show the proof only for the Wu implication and leave the other two proofs to the reader as an exercise. For all $y \in Y$,

$$\sup_{x \in X} i[A(x), \mathcal{J}_{wu}(A(x), B(y))] = \sup_{a \in [0,1]} i[a, \mathcal{J}_{wu}(a, B(y))]$$

$$= \max\{ \sup_{a \leq B(y)} i[a, \mathcal{J}_{wu}(a, B(y))], \sup_{a > B(y)} i[a, \mathcal{J}_{wu}(a, B(y))]\}$$

$$= \max\{B(y), \sup_{a > B(y)} i[a, \min(1 - a, B(y))]\}$$

$$= B(y). \quad \blacksquare$$

Known results (including those stated in Theorem 11.5) regarding the outcome of the expression

$$\sup_{x \in X} i[A(x), \mathcal{J}(A(x), B(y))]$$

are summarized in Table 11.2 for some fuzzy implications and some t-norms. These results are based on the assumption that the ranges of membership functions A and B are $[0, 1]$.

Another criterion for selecting an appropriate fuzzy implication may be derived from the requirement that the generalized modus tollens coincide with the classical modus tollens. In this case, fuzzy implications suitable for approximate reasoning based upon the generalized modus tollens should satisfy the equation

$$c(A(x)) = \sup_{y \in Y} i[c(B(y)), \mathcal{J}(A(x), B(y))] \quad (11.14)$$

for all $x \in X$.

Known results regarding the outcome of the right-hand side of this equation for some fuzzy implications and some t-norms are summarized in Table 11.3. It is again assumed that the ranges of both membership functions A and B are $[0, 1]$.

It is now obvious that we can derive a criterion for the selection of fuzzy implications from each fuzzy inference rule that has a counterpart in classical logic, for example, from the

TABLE 11.2   GENERALIZED MODUS PONENS

Name	Standard intersection	Algebraic product	Bounded difference	Drastic intersection
Early Zadeh $\mathfrak{I}_m$	$\max\left[\dfrac{1}{2}, B\right]$	$\max\left[\dfrac{1}{4}, B\right]$	B	B
Gaines-Rescher $\mathfrak{I}_s$	B	B	B	B
Gödel $\mathfrak{I}_g$	B	B	B	B
Goguen $\mathfrak{I}_\Delta$	$B^{1/2}$	B	B	B
Kleene-Dienes $\mathfrak{I}_b$	$\max\left[\dfrac{1}{2}, B\right]$	$\max\left[\dfrac{1}{4}, B\right]$	B	B
Lukasiewicz $\mathfrak{I}_a$	$\dfrac{1}{2}(1 + B)$	$\dfrac{1}{4}(1 + B)^2$	B	B
Reichenbach $\mathfrak{I}_r$	$\dfrac{1}{2 - B}$	$\max\left[B, \dfrac{1}{4 - 4\min(B, 1/2)}\right]$	B	B
Willmott $\mathfrak{I}_{wi}$	$\max\left[\dfrac{1}{2}, B\right]$	$\max\left[\dfrac{1}{4}, B\right]$	B	B
Wu $\mathfrak{I}_{wu}$	B	B	B	B
$\mathfrak{I}_{ss}$	B	B	B	B
$\mathfrak{I}_{sg}$	B	B	B	B
$\mathfrak{I}_{gg}$	B	B	B	B
$\mathfrak{I}_{gs}$	B	B	B	B

generalized hypothetical syllogism. The derivation is analogous to the described derivations for modus ponens and modus tollens. For the generalized hypothetical syllogism, the counterpart of (11.13) and (11.14) is the equation

$$\mathfrak{I}(A(x), C(z)) = \sup_{y \in Y} i[\mathfrak{I}(A(x), B(y)), \mathfrak{I}(B(y), C(z))] \qquad (11.15)$$

for all $x \in X$ and $z \in Z$.

In Table 11.4, we indicate for some fuzzy implications and some t-norms whether (11.15) is satisfied (Y) or not (N). It is again assumed that the ranges of all membership functions involved are $[0, 1]$.

By examining Tables 11.2–11.4, we can see that the only fuzzy implications (among

TABLE 11.3   GENERALIZED MODUS TOLLENS

Name	Standard intersection	Algebraic product	Bounded difference	Drastic intersection
Early Zadeh $\mathfrak{I}_m$	$\max\left[\frac{1}{2}, \overline{A}\right]$	$\max\left[\frac{1}{4}, \overline{A}\right]$	$\overline{A}$	$\overline{A}$
Gaines-Rescher $\mathfrak{I}_s$	$\overline{A}$	$\overline{A}$	$\overline{A}$	$\overline{A}$
Gödel $\mathfrak{I}_g$	$\max\left[\frac{1}{2}, \overline{A}\right]$	$\max\left[\frac{1}{4}, \overline{A}\right]$	$\overline{A}$	$\overline{A}$
Goguen $\mathfrak{I}_\Delta$	$\dfrac{1}{1+A}$	$\max\left[\frac{1}{4A}, \overline{A}\right]$	$\overline{A}$	$\overline{A}$
Kleene-Dienes $\mathfrak{I}_b$	$\max\left[\frac{1}{2}, \overline{A}\right]$	$\max\left[\frac{1}{4}, \overline{A}\right]$	$\overline{A}$	$\overline{A}$
Lukasiewicz $\mathfrak{I}_a$	$1 - \dfrac{A}{2}$	$\dfrac{(A-2)^2}{4}$	$\overline{A}$	$\overline{A}$
Reichenbach $\mathfrak{I}_r$	$\dfrac{1}{1+A}$	$\begin{cases} \dfrac{1}{4A(x)} & A(x) \geq \dfrac{1}{2} \\[2mm] \overline{A}(x) & A(x) < \dfrac{1}{2} \end{cases}$	$\overline{A}$	$\overline{A}$
Willmott $\mathfrak{I}_{wi}$	$\max\left[\frac{1}{2}, \overline{A}\right]$	$\max\left[\frac{1}{4}, \overline{A}\right]$	$\overline{A}$	$\overline{A}$
Wu $\mathfrak{I}_{wu}$	$\overline{A}$	$\overline{A}$	$\overline{A}$	$\overline{A}$
$\mathfrak{I}_{ss}$	$\overline{A}$	$\overline{A}$	$\overline{A}$	$\overline{A}$
$\mathfrak{I}_{sg}$	$\overline{A}$	$\overline{A}$	$\overline{A}$	$\overline{A}$
$\mathfrak{I}_{gg}$	$\max\left[\frac{1}{2}, \overline{A}\right]$	$\max\left[\frac{1}{4}, \overline{A}\right]$	$\overline{A}$	$\overline{A}$
$\mathfrak{I}_{gs}$	$\max\left[\frac{1}{2}, \overline{A}\right]$	$\max\left[\frac{1}{4}, \overline{A}\right]$	$\overline{A}$	$\overline{A}$

those listed in the tables) which satisfy all the three derived criteria with respect to the four considered t-norms are the following four: $\mathfrak{I}_s, \mathfrak{I}_{wu}, \mathfrak{I}_{ss},$ and $\mathfrak{I}_{sg}$. This means that these four fuzzy implications are suitable for the generalized modus ponens, modus tollens, and hypothetical syllogisms. It does not mean, however, that these fuzzy implications are superior in general. Any general claims in this regard will have to be based on a comprehensive study, taking into account all feasible fuzzy inference rules (including qualified and quantified fuzzy propositions) and the whole continuum of t-norms.

TABLE 11.4   GENERALIZED HYPOTHETICAL SYLLOGISMS

Name	Standard intersection	Algebraic product	Bounded difference	Drastic intersection
Early Zadeh $\mathfrak{I}_m$	N	N	N	N
Gaines-Rescher $\mathfrak{I}_s$	Y	Y	Y	Y
Gödel $\mathfrak{I}_g$	Y	Y	Y	Y
Goguen $\mathfrak{I}_\Delta$	N	Y	Y	Y
Kleene-Dienes $\mathfrak{I}_b$	N	N	Y	Y
Lukasiewicz $\mathfrak{I}_a$	N	N	Y	Y
Reichenbach $\mathfrak{I}_r$	N	N	N	N
Willmott $\mathfrak{I}_{wi}$	N	N	N	N
Wu $\mathfrak{I}_{wu}$	Y	Y	Y	Y
$\mathfrak{I}_{ss}$	Y	Y	Y	Y
$\mathfrak{I}_{sg}$	Y	Y	Y	Y
$\mathfrak{I}_{gg}$	Y	Y	Y	Y
$\mathfrak{I}_{gs}$	Y	Y	Y	Y

11.4 MULTICONDITIONAL APPROXIMATE REASONING

The general schema of multiconditional approximate reasoning has the form:

$$
\begin{aligned}
&Rule\ 1: &&\text{If } \mathcal{X} \text{ is } A_1, \text{ then } \mathcal{Y} \text{ is } B_1 \\
&Rule\ 2: &&\text{If } \mathcal{X} \text{ is } A_2, \text{ then } \mathcal{Y} \text{ is } B_2 \\
&\quad\cdots\cdots\cdots\cdots\cdots\cdots\cdots\cdots\cdots \\
&Rule\ n: &&\text{If } \mathcal{X} \text{ is } A_n, \text{ then } \mathcal{Y} \text{ is } B_n \\
&Fact: &&\mathcal{X} \text{ is } A' \\
&\overline{\phantom{Conclusion: \mathcal{Y} \text{ is } B'}} \\
&Conclusion: &&\mathcal{Y} \text{ is } B'
\end{aligned}
$$

(11.16)

Given n *if-then* rules, rules 1 through n, and a fact "X is A'," we conclude that "Y is B'," where $A', A_j \in \mathcal{F}(X), B', B_j \in \mathcal{F}(Y)$ for all $j \in \mathbb{N}_n$, and X, Y are sets of values of variables $\mathcal{X}$ and $\mathcal{Y}$. This kind of reasoning is typical in fuzzy logic controllers (Chapter 12).

The most common way to determine B' in (11.16) is referred to as a *method of interpolation*. It consists of the following two steps:

Step 1. Calculate the degree of consistency, $r_j(A')$, between the given fact and the antecedent of each *if-then* rule j in terms of the height of intersection of the associated sets A' and A_j. That is, for each $j \in \mathbb{N}_n$,

$$r_j(A') = h(A' \cap A_j)$$

or, using the standard fuzzy intersection,

$$r_j(A') = \sup_{x \in X} \min[A'(x), A_j(x)]. \tag{11.17}$$

Step 2. Calculate the conclusion B' by truncating each set B_j by the value of $r_j(A')$, which expresses the degree to which the antecedent A_j is compatible with the given fact A', and taking the union of the truncated sets. That is,

$$B'(y) = \sup_{j \in \mathbb{N}_n} \min[r_j(A'), B_j(y)] \tag{11.18}$$

for all $y \in Y$.

An illustration of the method of interpolation for two *if-then* rules is given in Fig. 11.3, which is self-explanatory.

The interpolation method is actually a special case of the compositional rule of inference. To show this, assume that R is a fuzzy relation on $X \times Y$ defined by

$$R(x, y) = \sup_{j \in \mathbb{N}_n} \min[A_j(x), B_j(y)] \tag{11.19}$$

for all $x \in X, y \in Y$. Then, B' obtained by (11.18) is equal to $A' \circ R$, where $\circ$ denotes the sup-min composition. This equality can be easily demonstrated. Using (11.18) and (11.17), the following holds:

$$
\begin{aligned}
B'(y) &= \sup_{j \in \mathbb{N}_n} \min[r_j(A'), B_j(y)] \\
&= \sup_{j \in \mathbb{N}_n} \min[\sup_{x \in X} \min(A'(x), A_j(x)), B_j(y)] \\
&= \sup_{j \in \mathbb{N}_n, x \in X} \sup[\min(A'(x), A_j(x), B_j(y))] \\
&= \sup_{x \in X, j \in \mathbb{N}_n} \sup \min[A'(x), \min(A_j(x), B_j(y))] \\
&= \sup_{x \in X} \min[A'(x), \sup_{j \in \mathbb{N}_n} \min(A_j(x), B_j(y))] \\
&= \sup_{x \in X} \min[A'(x), R(x, y)] \\
&= (A' \circ R)(y).
\end{aligned}
$$

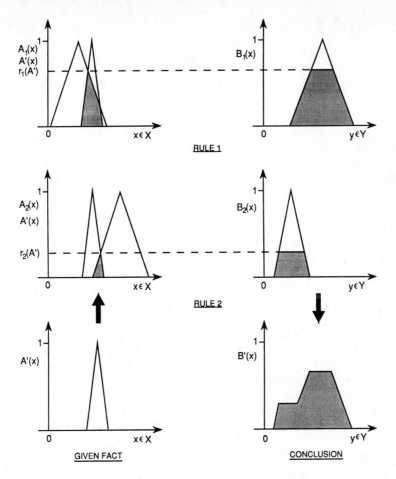

Figure 11.3   Illustration of the method of interpolation.

Hence, $B' = A' \circ R$.

Observe that the fuzzy relation R employed in the reasoning is obtained from the given *if-then* rules in (11.16) in the following way. For each rule j in (11.16), we determine a relation R_j by the formula

$$R_j(x, y) = \min[A_j(x), B_j(y)] \tag{11.20}$$

for all $x \in X, y \in Y$. Then, R is defined by the union of relations R_j for all rules in (11.16). That is,

$$R = \bigcup_{j \in \mathbb{N}_n} R_j. \tag{11.21}$$

In this case, we treat the *if-then* rules as *disjunctive*. This means that we obtain a conclusion for a given fact A' whenever $r_j(A') > 0$ for at least one rule j. When $r_j(A') > 0$, we say that rule j *fires* for the given fact A'.

The *if-then* rules in (11.16) may also be treated as *conjunctive*. In this case, we define

R by the intersection

$$R = \bigcap_{j \in \mathbb{N}_n} R_j. \tag{11.22}$$

We obtain a conclusion for a given fact A' only if $r_j(A') > 0$ for all $j \in \mathbb{N}_n$. That is, to obtain a conclusion, all rules in (11.16) must fire.

The interpretation of the rules in (11.16) as either disjunctive or conjunctive depends on their intended use and the way R_j is obtained. For either interpretation, there are two possible ways of applying the compositional rule of inference: the compositional rule is applied to the fuzzy relation R, after it is calculated by either (11.21) or (11.22); or the compositional rule is applied locally to each relation R_j, and then, the resulting fuzzy sets are combined in either disjunctive or conjunctive ways. Hence, we have the following four possible ways of calculating the conclusion B':

$$B_1' = A' \circ (\bigcup_{j \in \mathbb{N}_n} R_j), \tag{11.23}$$

$$B_2' = A' \circ (\bigcap_{j \in \mathbb{N}_n} R_j), \tag{11.24}$$

$$B_3' = \bigcup_{j \in \mathbb{N}_n} A' \circ R_j, \tag{11.25}$$

$$B_4' = \bigcap_{j \in \mathbb{N}_n} A' \circ R_j. \tag{11.26}$$

The four distinct fuzzy sets obtained by these formulas are ordered in the way stated in the following theorem.

Theorem 11.6. $B_2' \subseteq B_4' \subseteq B_1' = B_3'.$

Proof: First, we prove that $B_2' \subseteq B_4'$. For all $y \in Y$,

$$B_4'(y) = \inf_{j \in \mathbb{N}_n} (A' \circ R_j)(y)$$

$$= \inf_{j \in \mathbb{N}_n} \sup_{x \in X} \min[A'(x), R_j(x, y)]$$

$$\geq \sup_{x \in X} \inf_{j \in \mathbb{N}_n} \min[A'(x), R_j(x, y)]$$

$$= \sup_{x \in X} \min[A'(x), \inf_{j \in \mathbb{N}_n} R_j(x, y)]$$

$$= \sup_{x \in X} \min[A'(x), (\bigcap_{j \in \mathbb{N}_n} R_j)(x, y)]$$

$$= [A' \circ (\bigcap_{j \in \mathbb{N}_n} R_j)](y)$$

$$= B_2'(y).$$

Hence, $B_2' \subseteq B_4'$. Next, we prove that $B_4' \subseteq B_1'$. This is rather trivial, since

$$A' \circ R_j \subseteq A' \circ (\bigcup_{j \in \mathbb{N}_n} R_j)$$

for all $j \in \mathbb{N}_n$ and, hence,

$$B'_4 = \bigcap_{j \in \mathbb{N}_n} A' \circ R_j \subseteq A' \circ (\bigcup_{j \in \mathbb{N}_n} R_j) = B'_1.$$

Finally, we prove that $B'_1 = B'_3$. For all $y \in Y$,

$$B'_1(y) = \sup_{x \in X} \min[A'(x), \bigcup_{j \in \mathbb{N}_n} R_j(x, y)]$$

$$= \sup_{x \in X} \sup_{j \in \mathbb{N}_n} \min[A'(x), R_j(x, y)]$$

$$= \sup_{j \in \mathbb{N}_n} \sup_{x \in X} \min[A'(x), R_j(x, y)]$$

$$= (\bigcup_{j \in \mathbb{N}_n} A' \circ R_j)(y)$$

$$= B'_3(y).$$

Hence, $B'_1 = B'_3$, which completes the proof. ∎

Let us mention that this theorem is not restricted to the sup-min composition. It holds for any sup-i composition, provided that the t-norm i is continuous.

In general, R_j may be determined by a suitable fuzzy implication, as discussed in Sec. 11.3. That is,

$$R_j(x, y) = \mathfrak{J}[A_j(x), B_j(y)] \tag{11.27}$$

is a general counterpart of (11.20). Furthermore, R may be determined by solving appropriate fuzzy relation equations, as discussed in the next section, rather than by aggregating relations R_j.

11.5   *THE ROLE OF FUZZY RELATION EQUATIONS*

As previously explained, any conditional (*if-then*) fuzzy proposition can be expressed in terms of a fuzzy relation R between the two variables involved. One of the key issues in approximate reasoning is to determine this relation for each given proposition. Once it is determined, we can apply the compositional rule of inference to facilitate our reasoning process.

One way of determining R, which is discussed in Sec. 11.3, is to determine a suitable fuzzy implication $\mathfrak{J}$, which operates on fuzzy sets involved in the given proposition, and to express R in terms of $\mathfrak{J}$ (see, e.g., (11.12)). As criteria for determining suitable fuzzy implications, we require that the various generalized rules of inference coincide with their classical counterparts. For each rule of inference, this requirement is expressed by a fuzzy relation equation that fuzzy implications suitable for the rule must satisfy. However, the problem of determining R for a given conditional fuzzy proposition may be detached from fuzzy implications and viewed solely as a problem of solving the fuzzy relation equation for R.

As explained in Sec. 11.3, the equation to be solved for modus ponens has the form

$$B = A \overset{i}{\circ} R, \tag{11.28}$$

where A and B are given fuzzy sets that represent, respectively, the antecedent and consequent in the conditional fuzzy proposition involved, and i is a continuous t-norm. We recall from Chapter 6 that this equation is solvable for R if $A \overset{\omega_i}{\circ} B$ is a solution.

For modus tollens, the required equation has the form

$$c(A) = c(B) \overset{i}{\circ} R^{-1}, \tag{11.29}$$

where c denotes a fuzzy complement and R^{-1} is the inverse of R.

Suppose now that both modus ponens and modus tollens are required. Then, the problem of determining R for a given conditional fuzzy proposition with antecedent A and consequent B becomes the problem of solving the following system of fuzzy relation equation:

$$B = A \overset{i}{\circ} R,$$
$$c(A) = c(B) \overset{i}{\circ} R^{-1}. \tag{11.30}$$

The question of solvability of this system of equations is addressed by the following theorem.

Theorem 11.7. The system of fuzzy relation equations (11.30) has a solution for R if and only if

$$\hat{R} = (A \overset{\omega_i}{\circ} B) \cap [c(B) \overset{\omega_i}{\circ} c(A)]^{-1} \tag{11.31}$$

is the greatest solution, where $\cap$ is the standard fuzzy intersection.

Proof: The "*if*" part of the statement is trivial. To prove the "*only if*" part, let us assume that R is a solution to (11.30). Then, $R \subseteq A \overset{\omega_i}{\circ} B$ since $A \overset{i}{\circ} R = B$; furthermore, $R^{-1} \subseteq c(B) \overset{\omega_i}{\circ} c(A)$ or $R \subseteq [c(B) \overset{\omega_i}{\circ} c(A)]^{-1}$ since $c(B) \overset{i}{\circ} R^{-1} = c(A)$. Therefore,

$$R \subseteq (A \overset{\omega_i}{\circ} B) \cap [c(B) \overset{\omega_i}{\circ} c(A)]^{-1} = \hat{R}.$$

Since $R \subseteq \hat{R} \subseteq (A \overset{\omega_i}{\circ} B)$, $\hat{R}$ satisfies the first equation in (11.30). Similarly, since $R^{-1} \subseteq \hat{R}^{-1} \subseteq c(B) \overset{\omega_i}{\circ} c(A)$, $\hat{R}$ satisfies the second equation in (11.30). Hence, $\hat{R}$ is the greatest solution to (11.30). ∎

This theorem has at least two implications. First, it allows us to use formula (11.31) to test whether (11.30) has a solution. Second, if $\hat{R}$ given by (11.31) is not a solution to (11.30), then the system of equations (11.30) has no solution and, consequently, there are no fuzzy implications for the given conditional proposition that are suitable for both modus ponens and modus tollens.

When the equations in (11.30) have no solutions for R, we need to search for appropriate approximate solutions. We know from Chapter 6 that $A \overset{\omega_i}{\circ} B$ and $[c(B) \overset{\omega_i}{\circ} c(A)]^{-1}$ are, respectively, the greatest approximate solutions to the first and second equation in (11.30). Obviously, if

$$A \overset{\omega_i}{\circ} B = [c(B) \overset{\omega_i}{\circ} c(A)]^{-1}, \tag{11.32}$$

then $\hat{R} = A \overset{\omega_i}{\circ} B$ is also the greatest approximate solution to the system (11.30). The following theorem establishes one case in which (11.32) is satisfied.

Theorem 11.8.   Let $i(a, b) = \max(0, a + b - 1)$ for all $a, b \in [0, 1]$, and let $\mathcal{J}_a$ be the Lukasiewicz implication; that is,

$$\omega_i(a, b) = \mathcal{J}_a(a, b) = \min(1, 1 - a + b)$$

for all $a, b \in [0, 1]$.   Then, (11.32) holds for any fuzzy sets A, B and, consequently, $\hat{R} = A \overset{\omega_i}{\circ} B$ is the greatest approximate solution to (11.30) for the standard fuzzy complement c.

Proof: For all $x \in X, y \in Y$,

$$(A \overset{\omega_i}{\circ} B)(x, y) = \omega_i[A(x), B(y)] = \min[1, 1 - A(x) + B(y)]$$

and

$$
\begin{aligned}
[c(B) \overset{\omega_i}{\circ} c(A)]^{-1}(x, y) &= [c(B) \overset{\omega_i}{\circ} c(A)](y, x) = \omega_i[c(B(y)), c(A(x))] \\
&= \omega_i[1 - B(y), 1 - A(x)] \\
&= \min[1, 1 - (1 - B(y)) + (1 - A(x))] \\
&= \min[1, 1 - A(x) + B(y)].
\end{aligned}
$$

Hence, (11.32) holds.   ∎

It should be clear from the examples examined in this section that fuzzy relation equations play a fundamental role in approximate reasoning.   However, more research is needed to fully utilize their potential in this area.

11.6 INTERVAL-VALUED APPROXIMATE REASONING

Although this text is largely restricted to ordinary fuzzy sets, we occasionally explore some issues that involve other types of fuzzy sets. This section is one of those explorations. Its purpose is to characterize approximate reasoning with interval-valued fuzzy sets. This subject is important for the development of inference engines of expert systems in any application area in which it is not sensible to define exact membership grades.

Let A denote an *interval-valued fuzzy set*. Then,

$$A(x) = [L_A(x), U_A(x)] \subseteq [0, 1] \tag{11.33}$$

for each $x \in X$, where L_A, U_A are fuzzy sets that are called the *lower bound* of A and the *upper bound* of A, respectively. For convenience, (11.33) may be written in a shorthand notation as

$$A = [L_A, U_A]. \tag{11.34}$$

When $L_A = U_A$, clearly, A becomes an ordinary fuzzy set.

The basic issue of approximate reasoning with interval-valued fuzzy sets can be expressed as follows: given a conditional fuzzy proposition (*if-then* rule) of the form

$$\text{If } \mathcal{X} \text{ is } A, \text{ the } \mathcal{Y} \text{ is } B, \tag{11.35}$$

where A, B are interval-valued fuzzy sets defined on universal sets X and Y, respectively, and given a fact

$$\mathfrak{X} \text{ is } A', \tag{11.36}$$

how can we derive a conclusion in the form

$$\mathfrak{Y} \text{ is } B' \tag{11.37}$$

from (11.35) and (11.36)?

To address this question, we have to use some interpretation of the conditional fuzzy proposition (11.35). One possible interpretation is to view this conditional proposition as an interval-valued fuzzy relation $R = [L_R, U_R]$, where

$$L_R(x, y) = \mathfrak{I}[U_A(x), L_B(y)],$$
$$U_R(x, y) = \mathfrak{I}[L_A(x), U_B(y)] \tag{11.38}$$

for all $x \in X, y \in Y$; $\mathfrak{I}$ denotes a fuzzy implication satisfying at least Axioms 1 and 2 in Sec. 11.2. It is easy to prove that $L_R(x, y) \leq U_R(x, y)$ for all $x \in X$ and $y \in Y$ and, hence, R is well defined.

Once relation R is determined, it facilitates the reasoning process. Given $A' = [L_{A'}, U_{A'}]$, we derive a conclusion $B' = [L_{B'}, U_{B'}]$ by the compositional rule of inference

$$B' = A' \overset{i}{\circ} R, \tag{11.39}$$

where i is a t-norm and

$$L_{B'} = L_{A'} \overset{i}{\circ} L_R,$$
$$U_{B'} = U_{A'} \overset{i}{\circ} U_R. \tag{11.40}$$

The choice of the t-norm depends on the choice of fuzzy implication in (11.38) as well as other circumstances.

To illustrate the described reasoning procedure, let a proposition of the form (11.35) be given, where $X = \{x_1, x_2, x_3\}$, $Y = \{y_1, y_2\}$, $L_A = .5/x_1 + .6/x_2 + 1/x_3$, $U_A = .6/x_1 + .8/x_2 + 1/x_3$, $L_B = .4/y_1 + 1/y_2$, $U_B = .6/y_1 + 1/y_2$. Assuming that the Lukasiewicz implication

$$\mathfrak{I}(a, b) = \min(1, 1 - a + b) \quad (a, b \in [0, 1])$$

is chosen, we obtain the lower and bounds of relation R by (11.38):

$$L_R = .8/x_1, y_1 + 1/x_1, y_2 + .6/x_2, y_1 + 1/x_2, y_2 + .4/x_3, y_1 + 1/x_3, y_2,$$
$$U_R = 1/x_1, y_1 + 1/x_1, y_2 + 1/x_2, y_1 + 1/x_2, y_2 + .6/x_3, y_1 + 1/x_3, y_2.$$

Given now $L_{A'} = .4/x_1 + .8/x_2 + 1/x_3$ and $U_{A'} = .5/x_1 + .9/x_2 + 1/x_3$, and choosing $i(a, b) = \max[0, a + b - 1]$, we obtain the lower and upper bounds of the conclusion B' by (11.40):

$$L_{B'} = .4/y_1 + 1/y_2,$$
$$U_{B'} = .9/y_1 + 1/y_2.$$

NOTES

11.1. Literature dealing with fuzzy expert systems is quite extensive. To guide the reader, we deem it sufficient to refer only to books on the subject, each of which contains many additional references to papers in journals or conference proceedings. The key books on this subject were written or edited by Negoita [1985], Zemankova-Leech and Kandel [1984], Gupta *et al.* [1985], Hall and Kandel [1986], Verdegay and Delgado [1990], Kruse, Schwecke, and Heinsohn [1991], and Kandel [1991]. Thorough overviews of the role of fuzzy sets in approximate reasoning were prepared by Dubois and Prade [1991a, b] and Nakanishi *et al.* [1993].

11.2. This issue of fuzzy implication in approximate reasoning was addressed in an early paper by Gaines [1976]. The first systematic study of fuzzy implications was undertaken by Bandler and Kohout [1980a, b]. Important contributions related to the material in Secs. 11.2 and 11.3 were made by Willmott [1980], Weber [1983], Trillas and Valverde [1985], Wu [1986], Oh and Bandler [1987], Smets and Magrez [1987], and Fodor [1991b]. Perhaps the most comprehensive study of fuzzy implications was undertaken by Ruan and Kerre [1993] and Kerre [1991]. Numerous articles by Zadeh collected in [Yager *et al.*, 1987] are also relevant to this chapter. In fact, most ideas associated with approximate reasoning were first presented by Zadeh and later developed by other researchers. A few additional contributors to approximate reasoning should be mentioned: Baldwin [1979a, b, 1993a, b], Dubois and Prade [1991a, b, 1992b], Giles [1982], Gorzalczany [1987, 1989a, b], Koczy and Hirota [1993], Mizumoto [1981], Raha and Ray [1992], Thornber [1993a, b], Turksen [1989], Uehara and Fujise [1993a, b], and Whalen and Schott [1985b].

EXERCISES

11.1. Prove that (11.1) and (11.3) are equivalent in the sense of classical two-value logic.

11.2. Explore fuzzy implications defined by (11.7) and (11.8), respectively, in the following cases:
   (a) $i = \min,\ u = \max$;
   (b) $i = $ product, $u = $ algebraic sum;
   (c) $i = $ bounded difference, $u = $ bounded sum;
   (d) $i = i_{\min},\ u = u_{\max}$.
   Assume that c is always the standard fuzzy complement.

11.3. Determine, for each fuzzy implication obtained in Exercise 11.2, which axioms it satisfies.

11.4. Let i and u be the standard fuzzy intersection and fuzzy union, respectively. Suppose that $\mathfrak{J}$ is a fuzzy implication satisfying Axiom 1 and Axiom 2. Prove that the following equations hold for any $a, b, c \in [0, 1]$:
   (a) $\mathfrak{J}(a, i(b, c)) = i(\mathfrak{J}(a, b), \mathfrak{J}(a, c))$;
   (b) $\mathfrak{J}(a, u(b, c)) = u(\mathfrak{J}(a, b), \mathfrak{J}(a, c))$;
   (c) $\mathfrak{J}(i(a, b), c) = u(\mathfrak{J}(a, c), \mathfrak{J}(b, c))$;
   (d) $\mathfrak{J}(u(a, b), c) = i(\mathfrak{J}(a, c), \mathfrak{J}(b, c))$.

11.5. Prove that Axiom 7 implies Axiom 3 and Axiom 4.

11.6. Let f be a function defined by $f(a) = e^a$ for all $a \in [0, 1]$. Determine the fuzzy intersection, fuzzy union, fuzzy implication, and fuzzy complement generated by f.

11.7. Prove that the following fuzzy implications satisfy the generalized modus ponens, modus tollens, and hypothetical syllogism: **(a)** $\mathfrak{J}_s$; **(b)** $\mathfrak{J}_{wu}$; **(c)** $\mathfrak{J}_{ss}$; **(d)** $\mathfrak{J}_{sg}$;

11.8. Consider the *if-then* rules

   (1) If X is A_1, then Y is B_1,

   (2) If X is A_2, then Y is B_2,

   where $A_j \in \mathcal{F}(X), B_i \in \mathcal{F}(Y)$ $(j = 1, 2)$ are fuzzy sets

$$A_1 = 1/x_1 + .9/x_2 + .1/x_3; A_2 = .9/x_1 + 1/x_2 + .2/x_3;$$

$$B_1 = 1/y_1 + .2/y_2; B_2 = .2/y_1 + .9/y_2.$$

Given the fact

$$X \text{ is } A',$$

where $A' = .8/x_1 + .9/x_2 + .1/x_3$, use the method of interpolation to calculate the conclusion B'.

11.9. Let the Lukasiewicz implication $\mathcal{J}_a$ be employed to calculate fuzzy relation R_j in (11.12); that is, $R_j(x, y) = \mathcal{J}_a(A_j(x), B_j(y))$, for all $x \in X, y \in Y$. Calculate B'_2 and B'_4 in (11.24) and (11.26) for Exercise 11.8.

11.10. Prove that Theorem 11.6 holds for sup-i composition based on a continuous t-norm i.

11.11. If modus ponens is required, find fuzzy relation R for Rule (1) in Exercise 11.8.

11.12. If modus tollens is required, find fuzzy relation R for Rule (1) in Exercise 11.8.

11.13. If both modus ponens and modus tollens were required, what would happen to fuzzy relation R for Rule (1) in Exercise 11.8?

11.14. If modus ponens is required, find fuzzy relation R for both rules in Exercise 11.8.

11.15. Generalize Theorem 11.7 to multiconditional cases.

12

FUZZY SYSTEMS

12.1 GENERAL DISCUSSION

In general, a *fuzzy system* is any system whose variables (or, at least, some of them) range over states that are fuzzy sets. For each variable, the fuzzy sets are defined on some relevant universal set, which is often an interval of real numbers. In this special but important case, the fuzzy sets are fuzzy numbers, and the associated variables are linguistic variables (Sec. 4.2).

Representing states of variables by fuzzy sets is a way of quantizing the variables. Due to the finite resolution of any measuring instrument, appropriate quantization, whose coarseness reflects the limited measurement resolution, is inevitable whenever a variable represents a real-world attribute. For example, when measurements of values of a variable can be obtained only to an accuracy of one decimal digit, two decimal digits, and so on, a particular quantization takes place. The interval of real numbers that represents the range of values of the variable is partitioned into appropriate subintervals. Distinct values within each subinterval are indistinguishable by the measuring instrument involved and, consequently, are considered equivalent. The subintervals are labelled by appropriate real numbers (i.e., relevant real numbers with one significant digit, two significant digits, etc.), and these labels are viewed as *states* of the variable. That is, states of any quantized variable are representatives of equivalence classes of actual values of the variable. Each given state of a quantized variable is associated with uncertainty regarding the actual value of the variable. This uncertainty can be measured by the size of the equivalence class, as explained in Sec. 9.2.

To illustrate the usual quantization just described, let us consider a variable whose range is $[0, 1]$. Assume that the measuring instrument employed allows us to measure the variable to an accuracy of one decimal digit. That is, states of the variable are associated with intervals $[0, .05), [.05, .15), [.15, .25), \ldots, [.85, .95), [.95, 1]$ that are labelled, respectively, by their representatives $0, .1, .2, \ldots, .9, 1$. This example of quantization is shown in Fig. 12.1a.

Measurement uncertainty, expressed for each measuring instrument by a particular coarseness of states of the associated variable, is an example of *forced uncertainty*. In general, forced uncertainty is a result of information deficiency. Measurement uncertainty,

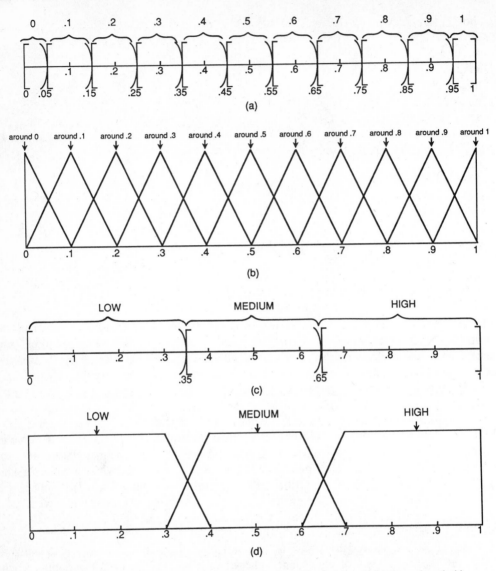

Figure 12.1 Examples of distinct types of quantization: (a) crisp forced; (b) fuzzy forced; (c) crisp opted; (d) fuzzy opted.

for example, results from the principal inability of any measuring instrument to overcome its limiting finite resolution.

Although the usual quantization of variables is capable of capturing limited resolutions of measuring instruments, it completely ignores the issue of measurement errors. While representing states of a variable by appropriate equivalence classes of its values is mathematically convenient, the ever-present measurement errors make this representation highly unrealistic. It can be made more realistic by expressing the states as fuzzy sets. This is illustrated for our previous example in Fig. 12.1b. Fuzzy sets are, in this example, fuzzy numbers with the shown triangular membership functions, and their representations are the linguistic labels *around* 0, *around* .1, *around* .2, and so forth. Fuzzy quantization is often called *granulation*.

Forced uncertainty must be distinguished from *opted uncertainty*. The latter is not a result of any information deficiency but, instead, results from the lack of need for higher certainty. Opted uncertainty is obtained, for example, by quantizing a variable beyond the coarseness induced by the measuring instrument involved. This additional quantization allows us to reduce information regarding the variable to a level desirable for a given task. Hence, while forced uncertainty is a subject of epistemology, opted uncertainty is of a pragmatic nature.

Considering our previous example, assume that we need to distinguish only three states of the variable instead of the eleven states that are made available by our measuring instrument. It is reasonable to label these states as *low, medium*, and *high*. A crisp definition of these states and its more meaningful fuzzy counterpart are shown in Figs. 12.1c and d, respectively.

One reason for eliminating unnecessary information in complex systems with many variables is to reduce the complexity when using the system for a given task. For example, to describe a procedure for parking a car in terms of a set of relevant variables (position of the car relative to other objects on the scene, direction of its movement, speed, etc.), it would not be practical to specify values of these variables with high precision. As is well known, a description of this procedure in approximate linguistic terms is quite efficient. This important role of uncertainty in reducing complexity is well characterized by Zadeh [1973]:

> Given the deeply entrenched tradition of scientific thinking which equates the understanding of a phenomenon with the ability to analyze it in quantitative terms, one is certain to strike a dissonant note by questioning the growing tendency to analyze the behavior of humanistic systems as if they were mechanistic systems governed by difference, differential, or integral equations.
>
> Essentially, our contention is that the conventional quantitative techniques of system analysis are intrinsically unsuited for dealing with humanistic systems or, for that matter, any system whose complexity is comparable to that of humanistic systems. The basis for this contention rests on what might be called the *principle of incompatibility*. Stated informally, the essence of this principle is that as the complexity of a system increases, our ability to make precise and yet significant statements about its behavior diminishes until a threshold is reached beyond which precision and significance (or relevance) become almost mutually exclusive characteristics. It is in this sense that precise analyses of the behavior of humanistic systems are not likely to have much relevance to the real-world societal, political, economic, and other types of problems which involve humans either as individuals or in groups.
>
> An alternative approach... is based on the premise that the key elements in human thinking are not numbers, but labels of fuzzy sets, that is, classes of objects in which the transition from membership to non-membership is gradual rather than abrupt. Indeed, the pervasiveness of fuzziness in human thought processes suggests that much of the logic behind human reasoning is not the traditional two-valued or even multivalued logic, but a logic with fuzzy truths, fuzzy connectives, and fuzzy rules of inference. In our view, it is this fuzzy, and as yet not well-understood, logic that plays a basic role in what may well be one of the most important facets of human thinking, namely, the ability to *summarize* information—to extract from the collection of masses of data impinging upon the human brain those and only those subcollections which are relevant to the performance of the task at hand.

By its nature, a summary is an approximation to what it summarizes. For many purposes, a very approximate characterization of a collection of data is sufficient because most of the basic tasks performed by humans do not require a high degree of precision in their execution. The human brain takes advantage of this tolerance for imprecision by encoding the "task-relevant" (or "decision-relevant") information into labels of fuzzy sets which bear an approximate relation to the primary data. In this way, the stream of information reaching the brain via the visual, auditory, tactile, and other senses is eventually reduced to the trickle that is needed to perform a specific task with a minimal degree of precision. Thus, the ability to manipulate fuzzy sets and the consequent summarizing capability constitute one of the most important assets of the human mind as well as a fundamental characteristic that distinguishes human intelligence from the type of machine intelligence that is embodied in present-day digital computers.

Viewed in this perspective, the traditional techniques of system analysis are not well suited for dealing with humanistic systems because they fail to come to grips with the reality of the fuzziness of human thinking and behavior. Thus to deal with such systems radically, we need approaches which do not make a fetish of precision, rigor, and mathematical formalism, and which employ instead a methodological framework which is tolerant of imprecision and partial truths.

A lot of work has already been done to explore the utility of fuzzy set theory in various subareas of systems analysis. However, the subject of systems analysis is too extensive to be covered here in a comprehensive fashion. Hence, we can cover only a few representative aspects and rely primarily on the Notes at the end of this chapter to overview the rapidly growing literature on this subject.

The most successful application area of fuzzy systems has undoubtedly been the area of fuzzy control. It is thus appropriate to cover fuzzy control in greater detail than other topics. Our presentation of fuzzy control includes a discussion of the connection between fuzzy controllers and neural networks, the importance of which has increasingly been recognized. Furthermore, we also discuss the issue of fuzzifying neural networks.

12.2 FUZZY CONTROLLERS: AN OVERVIEW

In general, fuzzy controllers are special expert systems (Sec. 11.1). Each employs a knowledge base, expressed in terms of relevant fuzzy inference rules, and an appropriate inference engine to solve a given control problem. Fuzzy controllers vary substantially according to the nature of the control problems they are supposed to solve. Control problems range from complex tasks, typical in robotics, which require a multitude of coordinated actions, to simple goals, such as maintaining a prescribed state of a single variable. Since specialized books on fuzzy controllers are now available (Note 12.2), we restrict our exposition to relatively simple control problems.

Fuzzy controllers, contrary to classical controllers, are capable of utilizing knowledge elicited from human operators. This is crucial in control problems for which it is difficult or even impossible to construct precise mathematical models, or for which the acquired models are difficult or expensive to use. These difficulties may result from inherent nonlinearities, the time-varying nature of the processes to be controlled, large unpredictable environmental disturbances, degrading sensors or other difficulties in obtaining precise and reliable measurements, and a host of other factors. It has been observed that experienced human operators are generally able to perform well under these circumstances.

The knowledge of an experienced human operator may be used as an alternative to a precise model of the controlled process. While this knowledge is also difficult to express in precise terms, an imprecise linguistic description of the manner of control can usually be articulated by the operator with relative ease. This linguistic description consists of a set of control rules that make use of fuzzy propositions. A typical form of these rules is exemplified by the rule

> IF the temperature is very high
> AND the pressure is slightly low
> THEN the heat change should be slightly negative,

where temperature and pressure are the observed state variables of the process, and heat change is the action to be taken by the controller. The vague terms *very high, slightly low,* and *slightly negative* can be conveniently represented by fuzzy sets defined on the universes of discourse of temperature values, pressure values, and heat change values, respectively. This type of linguistic rule has formed the basis for the design of a great variety of fuzzy controllers described in the literature.

A general fuzzy controller consists of four modules: a *fuzzy rule base*, a *fuzzy inference engine*, and *fuzzification/defuzzification modules*. The interconnections among these modules and the controlled process are shown in Fig. 12.2.

A fuzzy controller operates by repeating a cycle of the following four steps. First, measurements are taken of all variables that represent relevant conditions of the controlled process. Next, these measurements are converted into appropriate fuzzy sets to express measurement uncertainties. This step is called a *fuzzification*. The fuzzified measurements are then used by the inference engine to evaluate the control rules stored in the fuzzy rule base. The result of this evaluation is a fuzzy set (or several fuzzy sets) defined on the universe

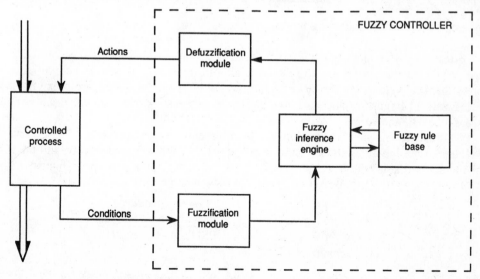

Figure 12.2 A general scheme of a fuzzy controller.

of possible actions. This fuzzy set is then converted, in the final step of the cycle, into a single (crisp) value (or a vector of values) that, in some sense, is the best representative of the fuzzy set (or fuzzy sets). This conversion is called a *defuzzification*. The defuzzified values represent actions taken by the fuzzy controller in individual control cycles.

To characterize the steps involved in designing a fuzzy controller, let us consider a very simple control problem, the problem of keeping a desired value of a single variable in spite of environmental disturbances. In this case, two conditions are usually monitored by the controller: an *error*, e, defined as the difference between the actual value of the controlled variable and its desired value, and the *derivative of the error*, $\dot{e}$, which expresses the rate of change of the error. Using values of e and $\dot{e}$, the fuzzy controller produces values of a controlling variable v, which represents relevant control actions.

Let us now discuss the basic steps involved in the design of fuzzy controllers and illustrate each of them by this simple control problem, expressed by the scheme in Fig. 12.3.

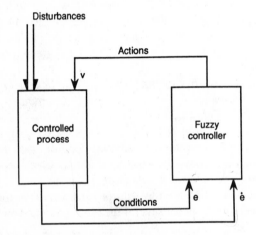

Figure 12.3 A general scheme for controlling a desired value of a single variable.

The design involves the following five steps.

Step 1. After identifying relevant input and output variables of the controller and ranges of their values, we have to select meaningful *linguistic states* for each variable and express them by appropriate fuzzy sets. In most cases, these fuzzy sets are fuzzy numbers, which represent linguistic labels such as *approximately zero, positive small, negative small, positive medium*, and so on.

To illustrate this step by the simple control problem depicted in Fig. 12.3, assume that the ranges of the input variables e and $\dot{e}$ are $[-a, a]$ and $[-b, b]$, respectively, and the range of the output variable v is $[-c, c]$. Assume further that the following seven linguistic states are selected for each of the three variables:

NL—*negative large*　　　　　PL—*positive large*
NM—*negative medium*　　　 PM—*positive medium*
NS—*negative small*　　　　　PS—*positive small*
AZ—*approximately zero*

Representing, for example, these linguistic states by triangular-shape fuzzy numbers that are equally spread over each range, we obtain the *fuzzy quantizations* exemplified for variable

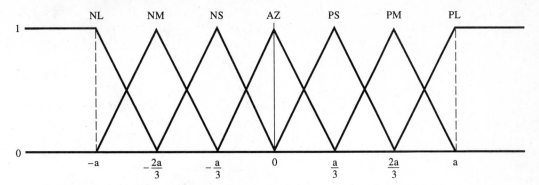

Figure 12.4 Possible fuzzy quantization of the range $[-a, a]$ by triangular-shaped fuzzy numbers.

e in Fig. 12.4; for variables $\dot{e}$ and v, value a in Fig. 12.4 is replaced with values b and c, respectively.

It is important to realize that the fuzzy quantization defined in Fig. 12.4 for the range $[-a, a]$ and the seven given linguistic labels are only a reasonable example. For various reasons, emerging from specific applications, other shapes of the membership functions might be preferable to the triangular shapes. The shapes need not be symmetric and need not be equally spread over the given ranges. Moreover, different fuzzy quantizations may be defined for different variables. Some intuitively reasonable definitions of the membership functions (e.g., those given in Fig. 12.4) are usually chosen only as preliminary candidates. They are later modified by appropriate learning methods, often implemented by neural networks.

Step 2.   In this step, a *fuzzification function* is introduced for each input variable to express the associated measurement uncertainty. The purpose of the fuzzification function is to interpret measurements of input variables, each expressed by a real number, as more realistic fuzzy approximations of the respective real numbers. Consider, as an example, a fuzzification function f_e applied to variable e. Then, the fuzzification function has the form

$$f_e : [-a, a] \to \mathcal{R},$$

where $\mathcal{R}$ denotes the set of all fuzzy numbers, and $f_e(x_0)$ is a fuzzy number chosen by f_e as a fuzzy approximation of the measurement $e = x_0$. A possible definition of this fuzzy number for any $x_0 \in [-a, a]$ is given in Fig. 12.5, where ε denotes a parameter that has to be determined in the context of each particular application. It is obvious that, if desirable, other shapes of membership functions may be used to represent the fuzzy numbers $f_e(x_0)$. For each measurement $e = x_0$, the fuzzy set $f_e(x_0)$ enters into the inference process (Step 4) as a fact.

In some fuzzy controllers, input variables are not fuzzified. That is, measurements of input variables are employed in the inference process directly as facts. In these cases, function f_e has, for each measurement $e = x_0$ the special form $f_e(x_0) = x_0$.

Step 3.   In this step, the knowledge pertaining to the given control problem is formulated in terms of a set of *fuzzy inference rules*. There are two principal ways in which

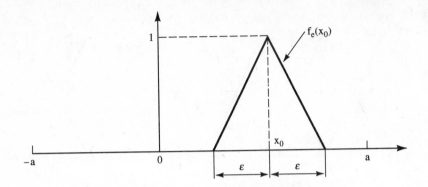

Figure 12.5 An example of the fuzzification function for variable e.

relevant inference rules can be determined. One way is to elicit them from experienced human operators. The other way is to obtain them from empirical data by suitable learning methods, usually with the help of neural networks.

In our example with variables e, $\dot{e}$, and v, the inference rules have the canonical form

$$\text{If } e = A \text{ and } \dot{e} = B, \text{ then } v = C, \qquad (12.1)$$

where A, B, and C are fuzzy numbers chosen from the set of fuzzy numbers that represent the linguistic states NL, NM, NS, AZ, PS, PM, and PL. Since each input variable has, in this example, seven linguistic states, the total number of possible nonconflicting fuzzy inference rules is $7^2 = 49$. They can conveniently be represented in a matrix form, as exemplified in Fig. 12.6. This matrix and the definitions of the linguistic states (Fig. 12.4) form the fuzzy rule base of our fuzzy controller. In practice, a small subset of all possible fuzzy inference rules is often sufficient to obtain acceptable performance of the fuzzy controller. Appropriate pruning of the fuzzy rule base may be guided, for example, by statistical data regarding the utility of the individual fuzzy inference rules under specified circumstances.

		$\dot{e}$						
	v	NL	NM	NS	AZ	PS	PM	PL
	NL			PL			PM	AZ
	NM			PL			PM	AZ
	NS			PM	PS	AZ		
e	AZ	PM		PS	AZ	NS		NM
	PS			AZ	NS	NM		
	PM	AZ		NM		NL		
	PL	AZ		NM		NL		

Figure 12.6 An example of a fuzzy rule base.

To determine proper fuzzy inference rules experimentally, we need a set of input-output data

$$\{\langle x_k, y_k, z_k \rangle | k \in K\},$$

where z_k is a desirable value of the output variable v for given values x_k and y_k of the input variables e and $\dot{e}$, respectively, and K is an appropriate index set. Let $A(x_k), B(y_k), C(z_k)$ denote the largest membership grades in fuzzy sets representing the linguistic states of variables $e, \dot{e}, v$, respectively. Then, it is reasonable to define a *degree of relevance* of the rule (12.1) by the formula

$$i_1[i_2(A(x_k), B(y_k)), C(z_k)],$$

where i_1, i_2 are t-norms. This degree, when calculated for all rules activated by the input-output data, allows us to avoid conflicting rules in the fuzzy rule base. Among rules that conflict with one another, we select the one with the largest degree of relevance.

Step 4.   Measurements of input variables of a fuzzy controller must be properly combined with relevant fuzzy information rules to make inferences regarding the output variables. This is the purpose of the *inference engine*. In designing inference engines, we can directly utilize some of the material covered in Chapters 8 and 11.

In our example with variables $e, \dot{e}, v$, we may proceed as follows. First, we convert given fuzzy inference rules of the form (12.1) into equivalent simple fuzzy conditional propositions of the form

$$\text{If } \langle e, \dot{e} \rangle \text{ is } A \times B, \text{ then } v \text{ is } C,$$

where

$$[A \times B](x, y) = \min[A(x), B(y)]$$

for all $x \in [-a, a]$ and all $y \in [-b, b]$. Similarly, we express the fuzzified input measurements $f_e(x_0)$ and $f_{\dot{e}}(y_0)$ as a single joint measurement,

$$\langle e_0, \dot{e}_0 \rangle = f_e(x_0) \times f_{\dot{e}}(y_0).$$

Then, the problem of inference regarding the output variable v becomes the problem of approximate reasoning with several conditional fuzzy propositions, which is discussed in Sec. 11.4. When the fuzzy rule base consists of n fuzzy inference rules, the reasoning schema has, in our case, the form

Rule 1 :	If $\langle e, \dot{e} \rangle$ is $A_1 \times B_1$, then v is C_1
Rule 2 :	If $\langle e, \dot{e} \rangle$ is $A_2 \times B_2$, then v is C_2
. . . .	
Rule n :	If $\langle e, \dot{e} \rangle$ is $A_n \times B_n$, then v is C_n
Fact :	$\langle e, \dot{e} \rangle$ is $f_e(x_0) \times f_{\dot{e}}(y_0)$

Conclusion : v is C

The symbols $A_j, B_j, C_j (j = 1, 2, \ldots, n)$ denote fuzzy sets that represent the linguistic states of variables $e, \dot{e}, v$, respectively.

For each rule in the fuzzy rule base, there is a corresponding relation R_j, which is determined as explained in Sec. 8.3. Since the rules are interpreted as disjunctive, we may use (11.25) to conclude that the state of variable v is characterized by the fuzzy set

$$C = \bigcup_{j} [f_e(x_0) \times f_{\dot{e}}(y_0)] \overset{i}{\circ} R_j, \tag{12.2}$$

where $\overset{i}{\circ}$ is the sup-i composition for a t-norm i. The choice of the t-norm is a matter similar to the choice of fuzzy sets for given linguistic labels. The t-norm can be either elicited from domain experts or determined from empirical data.

The method of interpolation explained in Sec. 11.4 and illustrated in Fig. 11.3 is the usual method employed in simple fuzzy controllers for determining the resulting fuzzy set C in the described reasoning schema. The formulation of the method in Sec. 11.4 can be applied to our case by taking $\mathcal{X} = \langle e, \dot{e} \rangle$ and $\mathcal{Y} = v$. Linguistic states of $\langle e, \dot{e} \rangle$ are fuzzy sets defined on $[-a, a] \times [-b, b]$, which are calculated from their counterparts for e and $\dot{e}$ by the minimum operator.

Step 5.   In this last step of the design process, the designer of a fuzzy controller must select a suitable *defuzzification method*. The purpose of defuzzification is to convert each conclusion obtained by the inference engine, which is expressed in terms of a fuzzy set, to a single real number. The resulting number, which defines the action taken by the fuzzy controller, is not arbitrary. It must, in some sense, summarize the elastic constraint imposed on possible values of the output variable by the fuzzy set. The set to be defuzzified in our example is, for any input measurements $e = x_0$ and $\dot{e} = y_0$, the set C defined by (12.2).

A number of defuzzification methods leading to distinct results were proposed in the literature. Each method is based on some rationale. The following three defuzzification methods have been predominant in the literature on fuzzy control.

Center of Area Method

In this method, which is sometimes called the *center of gravity method* or *centroid method*, the defuzzified value, $d_{CA}(C)$, is defined as the value within the range of variable v for which the area under the graph of membership function C is divided into two equal subareas. This value is calculated by the formula

$$d_{CA}(C) = \frac{\int_{-c}^{c} C(z)z\,dz}{\int_{-c}^{c} C(z)\,dz}. \tag{12.3}$$

For the discrete case, in which C is defined on a finite universal set $\{z_1, z_2, \ldots, z_n\}$, the formula is

$$d_{CA}(C) = \frac{\sum_{k=1}^{n} C(z_k)z_k}{\sum_{k=1}^{n} C(z_k)}. \tag{12.4}$$

If $d_{CA}(C)$ is not equal to any value in the universal set, we take the value closest to it. Observe that the values

$$\frac{C(z_k)}{\sum_{k=1}^{n} C(z_k)}$$

for all $k = 1, 2, \ldots, n$ form a probability distribution obtained from the membership function C by the ratio-scale transformation. Consequently, the defuzzified value $d_{CA}(C)$ obtained by formula (12.4) can be interpreted as an expected value of variable v.

Center of Maxima Method

In this method, the defuzzified value, $d_{CM}(C)$, is defined as the average of the smallest value and the largest value of v for which $C(z)$ is the height, $h(C)$, of C. Formally,

$$d_{CM}(C) = \frac{\inf M + \sup M}{2}, \tag{12.5}$$

where

$$M = \{z \in [-c, c] | C(z) = h(C)\}. \tag{12.6}$$

For the discrete case,

$$d_{CM}(C) = \frac{\min\{z_k | z_k \in M\} + \max\{z_k | z_k \in M\}}{2}, \tag{12.7}$$

where

$$M = \{z_k | C(z_k) = h(C)\}. \tag{12.8}$$

Mean of Maxima Method

In this method, which is usually defined only for the discrete case, the defuzzified value, $d_{MM}(C)$, is the average of all values in the crisp set M defined by (12.8). That is,

$$d_{MM}(C) = \frac{\sum\limits_{z_k \in M} z_k}{|M|}. \tag{12.9}$$

In the continuous case, when M is given by (12.6), $d_{MM}(C)$ may be defined as the arithmetic average of mean values of all intervals contained in M, including intervals of length zero. Alternatively, $d_{MM}(C)$ may be defined as a weighted average of mean values of the intervals, in which the weights are interpreted as the relative lengths of the intervals.

An application of the four defuzzification methods (d_{CA}, d_{CM}, d_{MM}, and d_{MM} weighted) to a particular fuzzy set is illustrated in Fig. 12.7.

It is now increasingly recognized that these defuzzification methods, as well as other methods proposed in the literature, may be viewed as special members of parametrized families of defuzzification methods. For the discrete case, an interesting family is defined by the formula

$$d_p(C) = \frac{\sum\limits_{k=1}^{n} C^p(z_k) z_k}{\sum\limits_{k=1}^{n} C^p(z_k)}, \tag{12.10}$$

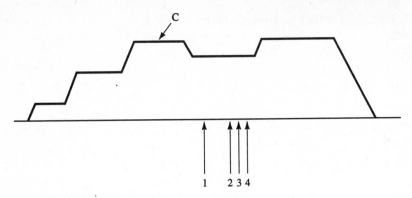

Figure 12.7 Illustration of the described defuzzification methods: $1 - d_{CA}$, $2 - d_{MM}$, $3 - d_{CM}$, $4 - d_{MM}$ (weighted).

where $p \in (0, \infty)$ is a parameter by which different defuzzification methods are distinguished. This parameter has an interesting interpretation. When $p = 1$, the center of area method is obtained. When $p \neq 1$, the parameter introduces a bias into the probability distribution obtained from C by the ratio-scale transformation. When $p < 1$, probabilities of values z_k for which $C(z_k) < h(C)$ are magnified. The magnification increases with decreasing value p and, for each given value of p, it increases with decreasing value of $C(z_k)$. When $p > 1$, the biasing effect is inversed; that is, probabilities of value z_k for which $C(z_k) < h(C)$ are reduced. The reduction increases with decreasing values $C(z_k)$ and increasing values p.

When $p \to 0$, all values in $\{z_1, z_2, \ldots, z_n\}$ are given equal probabilities and, hence, $d_0(C)$ is equal to their arithmetic average. In this case, the shape of the membership function C is totally discounted. Taking $d_0(C)$ as a value that represents a summary of fuzzy set C may be interpreted as an expression of very low confidence in the inference process. At the other extreme, when $p \to \infty$, we obtain the mean of maxima method, and taking $d_\infty(C) = d_{MM}(C)$ may be interpreted as the expression of full confidence in the reasoning process. Hence, the value of p of the chosen defuzzification may be interpreted as an indicator of the confidence placed by the designer in the reasoning process.

Observe that one particular value of p is obtained by the uncertainty invariance principle explained in Sec. 9.7. In this case, the probability distribution that is used for calculating the expected value of variable v preserves all information contained in the fuzzy set C. Hence, the defuzzification method based on this value is the only method fully justified in information-theoretic terms.

For the continuous case, the following formula is a counterpart of (12.10):

$$d_p(C) = \frac{\int_{-c}^{c} C^P(z) z \, dz}{\int_{-c}^{c} C^P(z) \, dz}. \tag{12.11}$$

The formula is not directly applicable for $p \to \infty$, but it is reasonable (in analogy with the discrete case) to define d_∞ as d_{MM} given by (12.9).

12.3 *FUZZY CONTROLLERS: AN EXAMPLE*

In this section, we describe a particular fuzzy controller of the simple type characterized in Fig. 12.3. We use only one example since descriptions of many other fuzzy controllers, designed for a great variety of control problems, can readily be found in the literature (Note 12.2).

We chose to describe a fuzzy controller whose control problem is to stabilize an inverted pendulum. This control problem, which has been quite popular in both classical control and fuzzy control, has a pedagogical value. It can easily be understood, due to its appeal to common sense, and yet it is not overly simple. We describe a very simple version, which consists of only seven fuzzy inference rules. It was designed and implemented by Yamakawa [1989]. He demonstrated that even such a simple fuzzy controller works reasonably well for poles that are not too short or too light, and under environmental disturbances that are not too severe. Although performance can be greatly improved by enlarging the fuzzy rule base, the simple version is preferable from the pedagogical point of view.

The problem of stabilizing an inverted pendulum, which is illustrated in Fig. 12.8, is described as follows. A movable pole is attached to a vehicle through a pivot, as shown in the figure. This situation can be interpreted as an inverted pendulum. The control problem is to keep the pole (pendulum) in the vertical position by moving the vehicle appropriately. The three variables involved in this control problem have the following meaning: e is the angle between the actual position of the pole and its desirable vertical position, $\dot{e}$ is the derivative (rate of change) of variable e, and v is proportional to the velocity, $\dot{w}$, of the vehicle. While variable e is directly measured by an appropriate angle sensor, its derivative $\dot{e}$ is calculated from successive measurements of e. When the pole is tilted toward left (or toward right), e is viewed as negative (or positive, respectively), and a similar convention applies to $\dot{e}$. Variable v is a suitable electrical quantity (electric current or voltage). Its values determine, through an electric motor driven by an appropriate servomechanism, the force applied to the vehicle. Again, the force is viewed as negative (or positive) when it causes the vehicle to move to the left (or to the right, respectively). For convenience, we may express v in a suitable scale for which it is numerically equal to the resulting force. Then, propositions about v may be directly interpreted in terms of the force applied to the vehicle.

Observe that this simplified formulation of the control problem does not include the requirement that the position of the vehicle also be stabilized. Two additional input variables would have to be included in the fuzzy controller to deal with this requirement: a variable defined by the distance (positive or negative) between the actual position of the vehicle and its desirable position, and the derivative of this variable expressing the velocity of the vehicle (positive or negative). Assuming that seven linguistic states were again recognized for each of the variables, the total number of possible nonconflicting fuzzy inference rules would become $7^4 = 2,401$. It turns out from experience that only a small fraction of these rules, say 20 or so, is sufficient to achieve a high performance of the resulting fuzzy controller.

To compare fuzzy control with classical control in dealing with the problem of stabilizing an inverted pendulum, we briefly describe a mathematical model of the mechanics involved by which proper movements of the vehicle would be determined in a classical controller. The model consists of a system of four differential equations, whose derivation is outside the scope of this text. The equations are

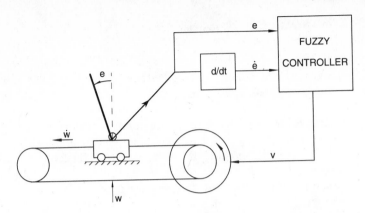

Figure 12.8 Fuzzy controller as a stabilizer of an inverted pendulum.

$$I\ddot{e} = VL\sin e - HL\cos e,$$

$$V - mg = -mL(\ddot{e}\sin e + \dot{e}^2\cos e),$$

$$H = m\ddot{w} + mL(\ddot{e}\cos e - \dot{e}^2\sin e),$$

$$U - H = M\ddot{w},$$

where $e, \dot{e}, \ddot{e}$ are the angle and its first and second derivatives, $2L$ is the length of the pendulum, $\ddot{w}$ is the second derivative of the position of the vehicle, m and M are masses of the pendulum and the vehicle, H and V are horizontal and vertical forces at the pivot, V is the driving force given to the vehicle, and $I = mL^2/3$ is the moment of inertia. It is clearly difficult to comprehend this model intuitively. Moreover, since the first three equations are nonlinear, the system is difficult, if not impossible, to solve analytically. Hence, we have to resort to computer simulation, which is not suitable for real-time control due to excessive computational demands. To overcome these difficulties, special assumptions are usually introduced to make the model linear. This, however, restricts the capabilities of the controller. Another difficulty of the model-based classical control is that the model must be modified whenever some parameters change, (e.g., when one pendulum is replaced with another of different size and weight). Fuzzy control, based on intuitively understandable linguistic control rules, is not subject to these difficulties.

Let us now discuss the main issues involved in the design of a fuzzy controller for stabilizing an inverted pendulum. The discussion is organized in terms of the five design steps described in Sec 12.2.

Step 1. It is typical to use seven linguistic states for each variable in fuzzy controllers designed for simple control problems such as the stabilization of an inverted pendulum. The linguistic states are usually represented by fuzzy sets with triangular membership functions, such as those defined in Fig. 12.4. Let us choose this representation for all three variables, each defined for the appropriate range.

Step 2. Assume, for the sake of simplicity, that measurements of input variables are employed directly in the inference process. However, the distinction made in the inference process by fuzzified inputs is illustrated in Fig. 12.11.

Step 3.   Following Yamakawa [1989], we select the seven linguistic inference rules defined by the matrix in Fig. 12.9. The complete representation of these linguistic rules by the fuzzy sets chosen in Step 1 is shown in Fig. 12.10. Observe that the linguistic states NL and PL do not even participate in this very restricted set of inference rules.

$\dot{e}$ \ e	NM	NS	AZ	PS	PM
NS		NS		AZ	
AZ	NM		AZ		PM
PS		AZ		PS	

Figure 12.9   Minimum set of linguistic inference rules to stabilize an inverted pendulum.

The inference rules can easily be understood intuitively. For example, if the angle is negative small ($e = NS$) and its rate of change is negative small ($\dot{e} = NS$), then it is quite natural that the velocity of the vehicle should be also negative small ($v = NS$) to make a correction in the way the pole is moving. On the other hand, when the angle is positive small ($e = PS$) and its rate of change is negative small ($\dot{e} = NS$), the movement of the pole is self-correcting; consequently, the velocity of the vehicle should be approximately zero ($v = AZ$). Other rules can be easily explained by similar common-sense reasoning.

Step 4.   To illustrate the inference engine, let us choose the interpolation method explained in Sec. 11.4 and extended as explained in Sec. 12.2. This method is frequently used in simple fuzzy controllers. For each pair of input measurements, $e = x_0$ and $\dot{e} = y_0$, or their fuzzified counterparts, $e = f_e(x_0)$ and $\dot{e} = f_{\dot{e}}(y_0)$, we first calculate the degree of their compatibility $r_j(x_0, y_0)$ with the antecedent (a fuzzy number) of each inference rule j. When $r_j(x_0, y_0) > 0$, we say that rule j fires for the measurements. We can see by a careful inspection of our fuzzy rule base, as depicted in Fig. 12.10, that: (a) at least one rule fires for all possible input measurements, crisp or fuzzified; (b) no more that two rules can fire when the measurements of input variables are crisp; (c) more than two rules (and perhaps as many as five) can fire when the measurements are fuzzified. For each pair of input measurements, the value of the output variable v is approximated by a fuzzy set $C(z)$ determined by (12.2), as illustrated in Fig. 12.11 for both crisp and fuzzified measurements. Observe that only rules 1 and 3 fire for the given crisp input measurements, while rules 1, 2, and 3 fire for their fuzzified counterparts.

Step 5.   The most frequently used defuzzifications method in the simple fuzzy controller is the centroid method. If we accept it for our controller, we obtain our defuzzified values by (12.3), as exemplified in Fig. 12.11.

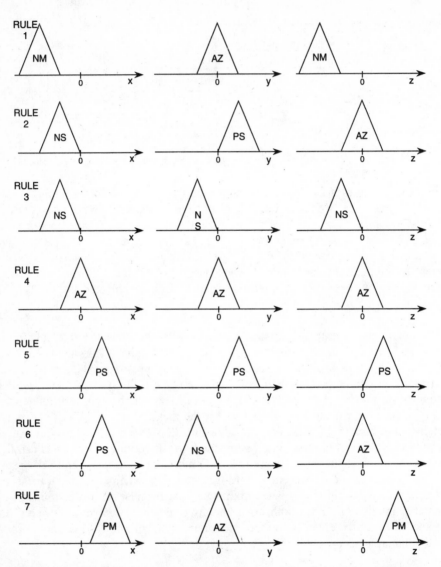

Figure 12.10 Fuzzy rule base of the described fuzzy controller designed for stabilizing an inverted pendulum.

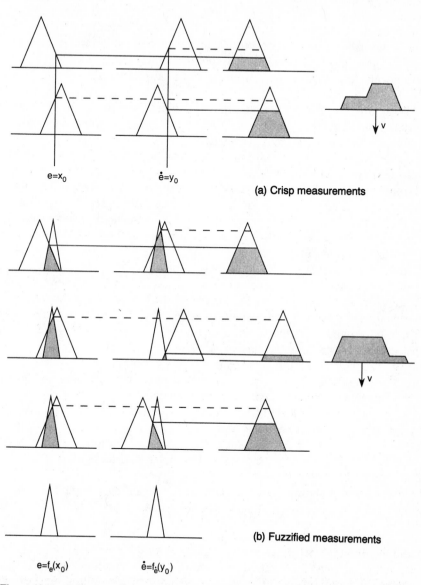

(a) Crisp measurements

$e = x_0$ $\dot{e} = y_0$

(b) Fuzzified measurements

$e = f_e(x_0)$ $\dot{e} = f_{\dot{e}}(y_0)$

Figure 12.11 Examples of fuzzy inference rules (of the fuzzy rule base specified in Fig. 11.10) that fire for given measurements of input variables: (a) crisp measurements; (b) fuzzified measurements.

12.4 FUZZY SYSTEMS AND NEURAL NETWORKS

It has increasingly been recognized that the areas of fuzzy systems and neural networks are strongly interconnected. For example, neural networks have already been proven very useful in numerous applications of fuzzy set theory for constructing membership functions of relevant fuzzy sets and other context-dependent entities from sample data (Sec. 10.7). They also show great promise as an efficient tool for solving fuzzy relation equations, which play a fundamental role in dealing with many practical problems involving fuzzy systems (Sec. 6.7).

In this section, we discuss the possibility of approximating a given fuzzy system by an appropriate neural network. The discussion is restricted to the classical multilayer neural networks, which are introduced in Appendix A.

The motivation for approximating fuzzy systems by neural networks is based upon the inherent capability of neural networks to perform massive parallel processing of information. This is important in those fuzzy controllers and, more generally, fuzzy expert systems, that are required to process large numbers of fuzzy inference rules in real time. When the neural network representing a given fuzzy expert system is implemented in hardware, all relevant fuzzy inference rules are processed in parallel. This results in high computational efficiency, which is crucial in many applications. Furthermore, the neural network representation is eminently fitted for introducing suitable adaptive capabilities into the system. This is due to the inherent learning capabilities of neural networks, which, in this context, can be utilized for modifying fuzzy inference rules of the system on the basis of experience.

An important connection between fuzzy expert systems and neural networks, which has been recognized and investigated since the early 1990s, is that they are both universal approximators of continuous functions of a rather general class. The term "universal approximator" has the following precise mathematical meaning.

Let X be a compact subset of $\mathbb{R}^n$ (i.e., a subset of $\mathbb{R}^n$ that is closed and bounded), and let $\mathbf{C}(X; n, m)$ denote the set of all continuous functions f of the form $f : X \to \mathbb{R}^m$. Then a *universal approximator*, $\mathbf{A}$, is a set of functions g of the form $g : X \to \mathbb{R}^m$ that satisfies the following: for any given function $f \in \mathbf{C}(X; n, m)$ and any real number $\varepsilon > 0$, there exists a function $g \in \mathbf{A}$ such that $|f(\mathbf{x}) - g(\mathbf{x})| < \varepsilon$ for all $\mathbf{x} \in X$. While $\mathbf{A}$ is usually a subset of $\mathbf{C}(X; n, m)$, the two sets may also be disjoint. The latter case takes place when functions in $\mathbf{A}$ are not continuous.

The following is a summary of the main results regarding computational equivalences between continuous functions, neural networks, and fuzzy expert systems (Note 12.4):

1. Feedforward neural networks with n inputs, m outputs ($n \geq 1, m \geq 1$), one hidden layer, and a continuous activation function (e.g., the sigmoid function) in each neuron are universal approximators. Comparable neural networks with more than one hidden layer are, of course, universal approximators as well.

2. Fuzzy expert systems based on multiconditional approximate reasoning (Sec. 11.4) can approximate feedforward neural networks with n inputs, m outputs, one or more hidden layers, and a continuous activation function in each neuron, provided that the range of the input variable is discretized into n values and the range of the output variable is discretized into m values.

3. It follows from (1) and (2) that fuzzy expert systems of the type described in (2) are also universal approximators.

4. Fuzzy input-output controllers, that is, fuzzy expert systems based on multiconditional approximate reasoning and a defuzzification of obtained conclusions, are universal approximators.

Most of these results, which are of considerable theoretical significance, are thus far of limited practical value. They are primarily existence results, which do not provide us with procedures for constructing practical approximators.

In the rest of this section, we describe an example proposed by Patrikar and Provence [1993] for approximating the inference engine of a simple fuzzy controller by a feedforward neural network with one hidden layer.

For convenience, let us consider a simple fuzzy controller of the type introduced in Sec. 12.2, but not necessarily its special application to the problem of stabilizing an inverted pendulum discussed in Sec. 12.3. The fuzzy controller has two input variables, e and $\dot{e}$, and one output variable, v, which have the same meaning as in Sec. 12.2. Seven linguistic states are distinguished for each variable, which are represented by triangular-shape fuzzy numbers equally spread over the range of values of the variable, as depicted in Fig. 12.4. Assume, for convenience, that the variables have the same range $[-6, 6]$. That is, the range $[-a, a]$ in Fig. 12.4 is interpreted for each variable as $[-6, 6]$. It is obvious that any given range can be normalized to this convenient range. Assume further that the 49 fuzzy rules specified in Fig. 12.6 are all included in the fuzzy rule base of our controller.

A possible structure of a feedforward neural network with one hidden layer by which the inference engine of our fuzzy controller can be approximated is sketched in Fig. 12.12. It is assumed that the sigmoid function is chosen as the activation function for each neuron, and the backpropagation algorithm (Appendix A) is employed for training the neural network to map a set of given input patterns into a set of desirable output patterns. We assume that the neural network has q neurons in the hidden layer. According to available heuristic rules (no definite formulas have been developed as yet), $q \geq 6$.

Inputs of the neural network are partitioned into two subsets that correspond to variables e and $\dot{e}$ as shown in Fig. 12.12. Each input is assigned to a fuzzy number that represents a particular linguistic state of the respective variable. Each output is allocated to one of thirteen equally distributed discrete points in the range $[-6, 6]$, which are the integers $-6, -5, -4, -3, -2, -1, 0, 1, 2, 3, 4, 5, 6$. Its value specifies, at the given discrete point in the range $[-6, 6]$, the membership grade of the fuzzy number that represents the output variable v.

Each fuzzy inference rule is represented in the neural network by an input vector, which specifies the linguistic states of the input variables e and $\dot{e}$, and an output vector, which defines (at 13 discrete points) the corresponding fuzzy number of the output variable v. For example, the fuzzy inference rule

If e is AZ and $\dot{e}$ is NS, then v is PS

is represented in the neural network by the input vector

$$\langle 0, 0, 0, 1, 0, 0, 0; 0, 0, 1, 0, 0, 0, 0 \rangle$$

and the output vector

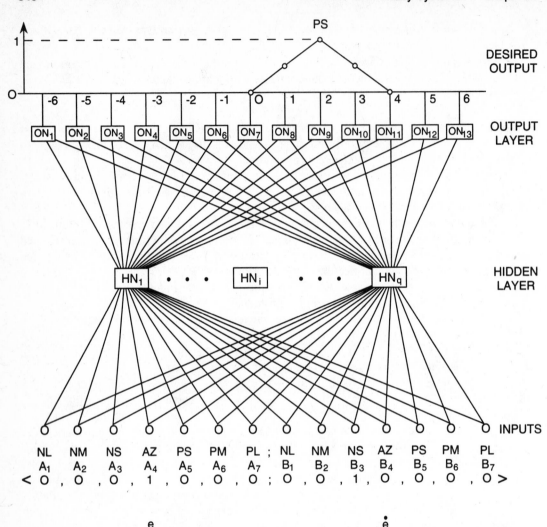

Figure 12.12 A neural network approximating a fuzzy inference engine.

$$\langle 0, 0, 0, 0, 0, 0, 0, .5, 1, .5, 0, 0, 0 \rangle,$$

as illustrated in Fig. 12.12. These two vectors represent, in this application of the neural network one input-output pair of a training set. The full training set consists of all 49 fuzzy inference rules specified in Fig. 12.6. When this training set is applied to the backpropagation algorithm (Appendix A), the neural network gradually learns to associate the proper fuzzy number at the output with each of the possible pairs of input linguistic states.

After training, the neural network responds correctly to each input vector in the training set. To utilize the network for producing appropriate control actions, it must be supplemented with fuzzification and defuzzification modules. The role of the fuzzification module is to feed appropriate input values into the neural network for any given measurements $e = x_0$ and

$\dot{e} = y_0$. For general fuzzification functions f_e and $f_{\dot{e}}$, these values form the input vector

$$\langle a_1, a_2, a_3, a_4, a_5, a_6, a_7; b_1, b_2, b_3, b_4, b_5, b_6, b_7 \rangle,$$

where a_j expresses the degree of compatibility of $f_e(x_0)$ with the antecedent $e = A_j$, and b_j expresses the degree of compatibility of $f_{\dot{e}}(y_0)$ with the antecedent $\dot{e} = B_j (j = 1, 2, \ldots, 7)$. Receiving an input vector of this form and meaning, the neural network produces an output vector

$$\langle c_{-6}, c_{-5}, c_{-4}, c_{-3}, c_{-2}, c_{-1}, c_0, c_1, c_2, c_3, c_4, c_5, c_6 \rangle,$$

by which a fuzzy set representing the conclusion of the inference is defined. This fuzzy set must be converted to a single real number by the defuzzification module.

Once trained, the neural network provides us with a blueprint for a hardware implementation. Its actual hardware implementation involves massive parallel processing of information; hence, it is computationally very efficient. If desirable, the output representation of the neural network can be made more refined by dividing the range of the output variable into more discrete values and increasing the number of output neurons as needed.

12.5   FUZZY NEURAL NETWORKS

As discussed in Sec. 12.4, neural networks are eminently suited for approximating fuzzy controllers and other types of fuzzy expert systems, as well as for implementing these approximations in appropriate hardware. Although classical neural networks can be employed for this purpose, attempts have been made to develop alternative neural networks, more attuned to the various procedures of approximate reasoning. These alternative neural networks are usually referred to as *fuzzy neural networks* .

The following features, or some of them, distinguish fuzzy neural networks from their classical counterparts:

1. inputs are fuzzy numbers;
2. outputs are fuzzy numbers;
3. weights are fuzzy numbers;
4. weighted inputs of each neuron are not aggregated by summation, but by some other aggregation operation (Chapter 3).

A deviation from classical neural networks in any of these features requires that a properly modified learning algorithm be developed. This, in some cases, is not an easy task.

Various types of fuzzy neural networks have been proposed in the literature. As an example, we describe basic characteristics of only one type. Some other types are listed, with relevant references, in Note 12.5.

Fuzzy neural networks to be described here were proposed by Hayashi, Buckley, and Czogala [1993]. They are obtained by directly fuzzifying the classical feedforward neural networks with one or more layers. The following are basic features of the resulting networks:

1. All real numbers that characterize a classical neural network become fuzzy numbers in its fuzzified counterpart. These are numbers that characterize inputs to the network,

outputs of neurons at hidden layers and the output layer, and weights at all layers. Consider, for example, all numbers relevant to a particular output neuron, ON_k, of a single-layer feedforward neural network, as depicted in Fig. 12.13. If ON_k is a fuzzy neuron, then the inputs $X_{k0}, X_{k1}, \ldots, X_{kn}$, the weights $W_0, W_1, \ldots, W_n$, and the output Y_k of this neuron are all fuzzy numbers.

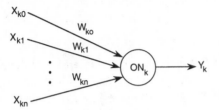

Figure 12.13 Fuzzy numbers characterizing a single fuzzy neuron.

2. The output of each neuron, exemplified here by the neuron characterized in Fig. 12.13, is defined by the formula

$$Y_k = S_\beta(\sum_{j=0}^{n} W_j X_{kj}),\qquad(12.12)$$

where S_β is a sigmoid function for some chosen value of the steepness parameter β (Appendix A). Since symbols W_j and X_{kj} in (12.12) designate fuzzy numbers, the sum

$$A_k = \sum_{j=0}^{n} W_j X_{kj}$$

must be calculated by fuzzy arithmetic. The output of the neuron,

$$Y_k = S_\beta(A_k),$$

is then determined by using the extension principle.

3. Error function E_p, employed in the backpropagation learning algorithm in a fuzzy neural network with m outputs for each training sample p is defined by the formula

$$E_p = \frac{1}{2}\sum (T_k^p - Y_k^p)^2,\qquad(12.13)$$

where T_k^p is the target output and Y_k^p is the actual output of output neuron ON_k for training sample p. Here, again, fuzzy arithmetic must be used to calculate E_p. Otherwise, this formula for E_p is exactly the same as its counterpart for classical neural networks (compare (12.13) with (A.4) in Appendix A).

4. The stopping criterion for fuzzy neural networks must also be properly fuzzified. Assume that $T_k^p = Y_k^p$ for all k, which represents a perfect match of the actual outputs with the target outputs. Then, assuming that the support of T_k^p (and, in this case, also of Y_k^p) is the interval $[t_{k_1}^p, t_{k_2}^p]$, the support of E_p is included in the interval $[-\lambda, \lambda]$, where

$$\lambda = \frac{1}{2}\sum_{k=1}^{n}(t_{k_2}^p - t_{k_1}^p)^2.$$

Choosing now some number $\varepsilon > 0$ as an acceptable deviation from the value of E_p

when $T_k^p = Y_k^p$ for all k, it is reasonable to stop the learning algorithm whenever E_p is included in the interval $[-\lambda - \varepsilon, \lambda + \varepsilon]$.

5. Finally, we need to fuzzify the backpropagation learning algorithm. One way, proposed by Hayashi *et al.* [1993], is to replace the real numbers in the standard formulas (Appendix A) with their fuzzy counterparts and apply fuzzy arithmetic to them.

12.6   FUZZY AUTOMATA

A *finite automaton* (also called a *finite-state machine* or *sequential machine*) is a dynamic system operating in discrete time that transforms sequences of input states (stimuli) received at the input of the system to sequences of output states (responses) produced at the output of the system. The sequences may be finite or countably infinite. The transformation is accomplished by the concept of a dynamically changing internal state. At each discrete time, the response of the system is determined on the basis of the received stimulus and the internal state of the system. At the same time, a new internal state is determined, which replaces its predecessor. The new internal state is stored in the system to be used the next time. An automaton is called a fuzzy automaton when its states are characterized by fuzzy sets, and the production of responses and next states is facilitated by appropriate fuzzy relations.

A *finite fuzzy automaton*, $\mathcal{A}$, is a fuzzy relational system defined by the quintuple

$$\mathcal{A} = \langle X, Y, Z, R, S \rangle,$$

where

- X is a nonempty finite set of input states (stimuli),
- Y is a nonempty finite set of output states (responses),
- Z is a nonempty finite set of internal states,
- R is a fuzzy relation on $Z \times Y$, and
- S is a fuzzy relation on $X \times Z \times Z$.

Assume that $X = \{x_1, x_2, \ldots, x_n\}, Y = \{y_1, y_2, \ldots, y_m\}, Z = \{z_1, z_2, \ldots, z_q\}$, and let A^t, B^t, C^t, E^t denote the fuzzy sets that characterize, respectively, the stimulus, response, current internal state, and emerging internal state (next state) of the automaton at time t.

The idea of a fuzzy automaton is depicted in Fig. 12.14. Given A^t and C^t at some time t, fuzzy relations R and S allow us to determine B^t and E^t. Clearly, $A^t \in \mathcal{F}(X), B^t \in \mathcal{F}(Y)$, and $C^t, E^t \in \mathcal{F}(Z)$. A fuzzy set C^1, which characterizes the *initial internal state*, must be given to make the fuzzy automaton operate. Then, $C^t = E^{t-1}$ for each time $t \in \mathbb{N} - \{1\}$. The equation $C^t = E^{t-1}$ is assumed to be implemented by the block called *storage* in Fig. 12.14. Its role is to store the produced fuzzy set E^t at each time t and release it the next time under the label C^t.

Given a sequence $A^1, A^2, \ldots,$ and an initial characterization C^1 of the internal state, fuzzy relations R and S allow us to generate the corresponding sequences $B^1, B^2, \ldots$ and $C^2 = E^1, C^3 = E^2, \ldots$. Due to the roles of relations R and S, it is reasonable to call R a *response relation* and S a *state-transition relation*.

Assuming the standard fuzzy set operations, the fuzzy automaton operates as follows.

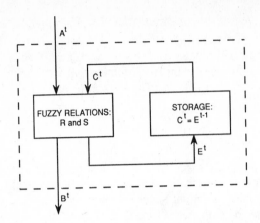

Figure 12.14   Basic scheme of fuzzy automata.

For any given fuzzy input state A^t, the ternary state-transition relation S is converted into a binary relation, S_{A^t}, on $Z \times Z$ by the formula

$$S_{A^t}(z_i, z_j) = \max_{k \in \mathbb{N}_n}(\min[A^t(x_k), S(x_k, z_i, z_j)]) \tag{12.14}$$

for all pairs $\langle z_i, z_j \rangle \in Z \times Z$. Then, assuming the present fuzzy state C^t is given, the fuzzy next state E^t and fuzzy output state B^t are determined by the max-min compositions

$$E^t = C^t \circ S_{A^t}, \tag{12.15}$$

$$B^t = C^t \circ R. \tag{12.16}$$

Equations (12.14)–(12.16) are sufficient for handling sequences of fuzzy states. Consider, for example, a sequence $A^1, A^2, \ldots, A^r$ of r fuzzy input states applied to a given initial fuzzy state C^1. Then, the fuzzy automaton produces the sequence of fuzzy internal states

$$E^1 = C^1 \circ S_{A^1},$$

$$E^2 = E^1 \circ S_{A^2},$$

$$\ldots \ldots \ldots \ldots \ldots$$

$$E^r = E^{r-1} \circ S_{A^r}$$

and the corresponding sequence of fuzzy output states

$$B^1 = C^1 \circ R,$$

$$B^2 = E^1 \circ R,$$

$$\ldots \ldots \ldots \ldots \ldots$$

$$B^r = E^{r-1} \circ R.$$

If we are interested only in the final internal state and the final output state, we can use the formulas

$$E^r = C^1 \circ S_{A^1} \circ S_{A^2} \circ \ldots \circ S_{A^r},$$

$$B^r = C^1 \circ S_{A^1} \circ S_{A^2} \circ \ldots \circ S_{A^{r-1}} \circ R.$$

Let us illustrate the concept of fuzzy automata by a simple example. Consider a fuzzy automaton with $X = \{x_1, x_2\}$, $Y = \{y_1, y_2, y_3\}$, $Z = \{z_1, z_2, z_3, z_4\}$ whose output relations R and state-transition relation S are defined, respectively, by the matrix

$$
R =
\begin{array}{c}
\\ z_1 \\ z_2 \\ z_3 \\ z_4
\end{array}
\begin{array}{c}
y_1 \quad y_2 \quad y_3 \\
\left[
\begin{array}{ccc}
1 & 0 & 0 \\
0 & 1 & 0 \\
0 & 0 & 1 \\
.5 & 1 & .3
\end{array}
\right]
\end{array}
$$

and the three-dimensional array

$$
S =
\begin{array}{c}
\\ z_1 \\ z_2 \\ z_3 \\ z_4
\end{array}
\left[
\begin{array}{c}
x_1 \\
\begin{array}{cccc}
z_1 & z_2 & z_3 & z_4 \\
0 & .4 & .2 & 1 \\
.3 & 1 & 0 & .2 \\
.5 & 0 & 0 & 1 \\
0 & 0 & 0 & 1
\end{array}
\end{array}
\begin{array}{c}
x_2 \\
\begin{array}{cccc}
z_1 & z_2 & z_3 & z_4 \\
0 & 0 & 1 & 0 \\
.2 & 0 & 0 & 1 \\
0 & 0 & 0 & 1 \\
1 & .3 & 0 & .6
\end{array}
\end{array}
\right].
$$

To describe how this fuzzy automaton operates, let fuzzy sets describing input, output, and internal states at any time t be defined by the vectors

$$\mathbf{A}^t = [A^t(x_1), A^t(x_2)],$$
$$\mathbf{B}^t = [B^t(y_1), B^t(y_2), B^t(y_3)],$$
$$\mathbf{C}^t = [C^t(z_1), C^t(z_2), C^t(z_3), C^t(z_4)].$$

Assume now that the initial fuzzy state of the automaton is $\mathbf{C}^1 = [1 \ .8 \ .6 \ .4]$ and its fuzzy input state is $\mathbf{A}^1 = [1 \ .4]$. Then, using (12.14),

$$
S_{A^1} =
\begin{array}{c}
\\ z_1 \\ z_2 \\ z_3 \\ z_4
\end{array}
\begin{array}{c}
z_1 \quad z_2 \quad z_3 \quad z_4 \\
\left[
\begin{array}{cccc}
0 & .4 & .4 & 1 \\
.3 & 1 & 0 & .4 \\
.5 & 0 & 0 & 1 \\
.4 & .3 & 0 & 1
\end{array}
\right].
\end{array}
$$

For example,

$$S_{A^1}(z_1, z_3) = \max(\min[A^t(x_1), S(x_1, z_1, z_3)], \min[A^t(x_2), S(x_2, z_1, z_3)])$$
$$= \max(\min[1, .2], \min[.4, 1])$$
$$= \max(.2, .4) = .4.$$

To calculate the fuzzy next state E^1 and the fuzzy output state B^1 of the automaton, we now use (12.15) and (12.16):

$$
E^1 = [1 \ .8 \ .6 \ .4] \circ
\left[
\begin{array}{cccc}
0 & .4 & .4 & 1 \\
.3 & 1 & 0 & .4 \\
.5 & 0 & 0 & 1 \\
.4 & .3 & 0 & 1
\end{array}
\right] = [.5 \ .8 \ .4 \ 1],
$$

$$B^1 = \begin{bmatrix} 1 & .8 & .6 & .4 \end{bmatrix} \circ \begin{bmatrix} 1 & 0 & 0 \\ 0 & 1 & 0 \\ 0 & 0 & 1 \\ .5 & 1 & .3 \end{bmatrix} = \begin{bmatrix} 1 & .8 & .6 \end{bmatrix}.$$

Assuming now that the next fuzzy input state is $A^2 = [0\ 1]$, we obtain

$$E^2 = E^1 \circ S_{A^2} = \begin{bmatrix} .5 & .8 & .4 & 1 \end{bmatrix} \circ \begin{bmatrix} 0 & 0 & 1 & 0 \\ .2 & 0 & 0 & 1 \\ 0 & 0 & 0 & 1 \\ 1 & .3 & 0 & .6 \end{bmatrix} = \begin{bmatrix} 1 & .3 & .5 & .8 \end{bmatrix},$$

$$B^2 = E^1 \circ R = \begin{bmatrix} .5 & .8 & .4 & 1 \end{bmatrix} \circ \begin{bmatrix} 1 & 0 & 0 \\ 0 & 1 & 0 \\ 0 & 0 & 1 \\ .5 & 1 & .3 \end{bmatrix} = \begin{bmatrix} .5 & 1 & .4 \end{bmatrix}.$$

Similarly, we can produce larger sequences of fuzzy internal and output states for any given sequence of fuzzy input states.

To define a meaningful fuzzy automaton, relations R and S cannot be arbitrary. For example, some next internal state and some output state must be assured for any given input state and present internal state. That is, for each pair $\langle x_k, z_i \rangle \in X \times Z$, we must require that $S(x_k, z_i, z_j) > 0$ for at least one $z_j \in Z$; similarly, for each $z_i \in Z$, we must require that $R(z_i, y_l) > 0$ for at least one $y_l \in Y$. These requirements may also be stated in a stronger form: for each pair $x_k, z_i \in X \times Z$, $S(x_k, z_i, z_j) = 1$ for at least one $z_j \in Z$; and for each $z_i \in Z$, $R(z_i, y_l) = 1$ for at least one $y_l \in Y$. When these requirements are satisfied, respectively, for exactly one $z_j \in Z$ and exactly one $y_l \in Y$, we call the relations *deterministic*.

When all states of a fuzzy automaton are defined as crisp sets and R, S are crisp relations, we obtain a crisp automaton, which, in general, is nondeterministic. When, in addition, all states are singletons taken from sets X, Y, Z and relations R, S are deterministic, we obtain the classical deterministic automaton of the Moore type.

The operations min and max employed in (12.14)–(12.16) may, of course, be replaced with other t-norms and t-conorms, respectively. For each replacement, we obtain an automaton of a different type. When min is replaced with the product and max is replaced with the algebraic sum, and we require, in addition, that input states are singletons and

$$\sum_{z_i \in Z} C^1(z_i) = 1,$$

$$\sum_{y_l \in Y} R(z_i, y_l) = 1 \text{ for each } z_i \in Z,$$

$$\sum_{z_j \in Z} S(x_k, z_i, z_j) = 1 \text{ for each } \langle x_k, z_i \rangle \in X \times Z,$$

we obtain a classical *probabilistic automaton* of the Moore type.

The concept of a fuzzy automaton is a broad one, which subsumes classical crisp automata (deterministic and nondeterministic) as well as classical probabilistic automata as special cases. This concept, whose further study is beyond the scope of this text, clearly extends the domain of applicability covered by the various classical types of finite automata.

12.7   FUZZY DYNAMIC SYSTEMS

Fuzzy dynamic systems, as the name suggests, are fuzzifications of classical (crisp) dynamic systems. However, there are different types of classical dynamics systems, and the issues involved in the fuzzification may be very different from one type to another. To discuss these issues, let us introduce the classical concept of a general dynamic system, under which all types of crisp dynamic systems are subsumed.

A *general dynamic system*, S, is a mathematical structure that is captured by the 8-tuple

$$S = \langle X, Y, Z, T, \leq_T, U, s, r, \rangle$$

where

- X, Y, Z are sets of input, output, and internal states of the system, respectively;
- T is a time set;
- $\leq_T$ is a total ordering of the time set T;
- U is a set of time functions, $u : T \to X$, which is required to be closed under a composition that is called a τ-concatenation and defined as follows: for any $u, v \in U$ and $\tau \in T$, the τ-concatenation, $u \circ_\tau v$, is the function

$$[u \circ_\tau v](t) = \begin{cases} u(t) & \text{when } t < \tau \\ v(t) & \text{when } t \geq \tau; \end{cases}$$

- s is a global state-transition function, $s : T \times T \times Z \times U \to Z$, which is required to have the following properties:

  (a) $s(t, t, z, u) = z$ (consistency);
  (b) $s(t_3, t_1, z, u) = s[t_3, t_2, s(t_2, t_1, z, u), u]$ for any $t_1 \leq t_2 < t_3$ (state-substitution property);
  (c) $s(t_2, t_1, z, u) = s(t_2, t_1, z, v)$ when $u(t) = v(t)$ for $t_1 \leq t < t_2$ (causality);

- r is a response function (or an output function), $r : T \times Z \times A \to B$.

Special types of dynamic systems are obtained when some properties of the eight components of S are modified or additional properties are required. When $T = \mathbb{N}$, for example, we obtain discrete-time dynamic systems. When, in addition, sets X, Y, Z are finite and the global state-transition function is replaced with a local state-transition function $s : Z \times X \to Z$ (i.e., the behavior of the system is time-invariant), we obtain classical finite automata. We explained in Sec. 12.6 how these special dynamic systems can be fuzzified.

When $T = \mathbb{R}$ (or $\mathbb{R}^+$), we obtain continuous-time dynamic systems. Then, in general, $X = \mathbb{R}^n, Y = \mathbb{R}^m, Z = \mathbb{R}^q$ for some integers $n, m, q \geq 1$. In this important class of dynamic systems, state-transition functions are expressed in terms of appropriate differential equations, which are, in general, time-varying and nonlinear. One way of fuzzifying these systems is to use linguistic approximation, as explained in Sec. 12.2 and 12.3. Another way is to apply the extension principle directly to the differential equations involved. This requires, in some sense, the development of a fuzzy differential calculus. Important work along this line has been pursued by Dubois and Prade [1982a], Puri and Ralescu [1983], and Kaleva [1987], but this topic is beyond the scope of this text.

NOTES

12.1. Uncertainty resulting from resolution limitations of measuring instruments is analyzed by Fridrich [1994a]. He introduces the concept of finite resolution, by which classical mathematical concepts such as crisp sets, additive measures, and classical integrals become fuzzy sets, fuzzy measures, and fuzzy integrals.

12.2. Several specialized books on fuzzy control are now available. Harris *et al.* [1993] wrote a comprehensive textbook with a strong emphasis on the connection between fuzzy logic and neural networks. A multiauthor book edited by Jamshidi *et al.* [1993] is also suitable as a text; it covers the theoretical foundations of fuzzy control, relevant software and hardware, and eleven application areas. Pedrycz [1989] wrote a more general book on fuzzy systems, in which fuzzy control is covered more thoroughly than other topics; the specialty of the book is its emphasis on the use of fuzzy relation equations in dealing with various problems involving fuzzy systems. The book edited by Sugeno [1985a] covers a broad spectrum of applications of fuzzy control and contains an excellent annotated bibliography on the subject. A handbook edited by White and Sofge [1992] covers the role of fuzzy logic and neural networks in intelligent control, with somewhat greater emphasis on neural networks.

12.3. Initial ideas of fuzzy systems were introduced by Zadeh [1965a, 1971a, 1973, 1974a, b]. In these papers, but more explicitly in [Zadeh, 1972b] and [Chang and Zadeh, 1972], the idea of applying fuzzy sets to control problems was presented for the first time. The actual research on fuzzy controllers was initiated by Mamdani and his students at Queen Mary College in London in the mid-1970s [Mamdani and Assilian, 1975; Mamdani, 1976]. Mamdani's work influenced other researchers to explore the applicability of fuzzy controllers to various control problems. Some of these efforts resulted in laboratory prototypes, and only one of them led eventually to the development of a commercially available fuzzy controller for cement kilns [Holmblad and Ostergaard, 1982]; according to the literature, this was the first commercially available fuzzy controller. Literature on fuzzy controllers in the period 1975–1985 is well overviewed by Tong [1985]. Another good overview of fuzzy controllers and other applications of fuzzy set theory was prepared by Maiers and Sherif [1985]; see also [Sugeno, 1985b; Tong, 1977, 1984]. In the late 1980s, the interest in fuzzy controllers increased very rapidly in Japan. This increased interest was likely an outcome of the first implementation of fuzzy control in a significant project, an automatic-drive fuzzy control system for subway trains in Sendai City. Although it took seven years to complete this project in 1987, the final product was extremely successful. It is generally praised as superior to other comparable systems based on classical control. The fuzzy controller achieves not only a higher precision in stopping at any designated point, but makes each stop more comfortable; in addition, it saves about 10% of energy. Many other industrial projects that employ fuzzy control have been completed in Japan since the opening of the subway system in Sendai City in 1987. A complete list would be too long. A few examples are chlorine control for water purification plants, elevator control systems, traffic control systems, control of bulldozers, air conditioning systems, and control systems for cement kilns. Fuzzy controllers have also been installed with great success in a broad variety of consumer products, including washing machines, refrigerators, video cameras, vacuum cleaners, automobiles (antiskid brake systems, automatic transmissions), TV sets, and many others. In the 1990s, some researchers began to explore the use of fuzzy controllers to solve certain control problems that are considered beyond the capabilities of classical control theory. One example is a fuzzy control system for an unmanned helicopter [Sugeno and Park, 1993], a project headed by Sugeno at the Tokyo Institute of Technology, which has already been completed and successfully tested. Another example is a fuzzy controller that can stabilize a triple inverted pendulum [Zhang *et al.*, 1993]. Research on fuzzy controllers in the 1990s is also characterized by exploring the integration of rule-based and model-based approaches in fuzzy control, as exemplified by the work of Filev [1991, 1992] and Sugeno and Yasakawa [1993], and by investigating connections between fuzzy controllers (and, in general, fuzzy systems) and neural networks (Notes 12.4 and 12.5).

12.4. Fuzzy systems and neural networks are now established as universal approximators, as originally recognized by Kosko [1992] and further investigated by Buckley [1993b], Buckley and Hayashi [1993a, b], and Buckley, Hayashi, and Czogala [1993]. This implies that fuzzy systems and neural networks can approximate each other. This leads to a symbiotic relationship, in which fuzzy systems provide a powerful framework for knowledge representation, while neural networks provide learning capabilities and exceptional suitability for computationally efficient hardware implementations. The literature regarding this symbiotic relationship is extensive. The following are a few representative papers: Berenji [1992], Berenji and Khedkar [1992], Jang [1992, 1993], Takagi and Hayashi [1991], and Wang and Mendel [1992b]. Various ways of implementating fuzzy controllers by neural networks were explored, in addition to the particular way proposed by Patricar and Provence [1993] and described in Sec. 12.4, by Yager [1992a, b, d], Keller, Yager, and Tahani [1992], and Keller and Tahani [1992].

12.5. Various fuzzifications of neural networks have been suggested, which attempt to extend their capabilities or make them more attuned to fuzzy systems for the purpose of hardware implementation. These efforts are exemplified by the following papers: Lee and Lee [1974, 1975], Keller and Hunt [1985], Gupta and Qi [1992], Hayashi, Buckley, and Czogala [1993], Carpenter *et al.* [1992], Pal and Mitra [1992], Simpson [1992, 1993], Horikawa, Furuhashi, and Uchikawa [1992], Yager [1992a, b, d], Pedrycz [1991b, 1993a], and Pedrycz and Rocha [1993].

12.6. An overview of defuzzification methods was prepared by Hellendoorn and Thomas [1993]. General classes of parametrized defuzzification methods, including the one described in Sec. 12.2, were explored by Filev and Yager [1991, 1993a] and Yager and Filev [1993a, b]. They also show how a proper defuzzification method can be determined by learning algorithms. An interesting strategy for dealing with the defuzzification problem, based on sensitivity analysis, was developed by Mabuchi [1993]. A defuzzification based upon the principle of uncertainty invariance was proposed by Klir [1991a]. Defuzzification of fuzzy intervals is addressed by Zhao and Govind [1991].

12.7. Fuzzy automata have been studied by Santos [1968, 1973, 1975], Santos and Wee [1968], Wee and Fu [1969], Mizumoto, Toyoda, and Tanaka [1969], Dal Cin [1975a, b], Gaines and Kohout [1975], Močkoř [1991], and Ray *et al.* [1991]. They are also covered in the books by Negoita and Ralescu [1975b], Wechler [1978], Kandel and Lee [1979], and Pal and Majumder [1986]. These writings not only cover theoretical aspects of fuzzy automata, but also explore their applicability in various areas, such as fault-tolerant design, learning, formal languages and grammars, or pattern recognition.

12.8. The notion of fuzzy dynamic systems emerged from a series of papers by Zadeh [1965a, 1971a, 1973, 1974a, b, 1982a]. Properties of various types of fuzzy dynamic systems were further investigated by Negoita and Ralescu [1975b], Kloeden [1982], De Glas [1983, 1984], Chen and

Tsao [1989], and Kang [1993a, b]. The role of fuzzification of dynamic systems that exhibit chaotic behavior has been investigated by Diamond [1992], Teodorescu [1992], Grim [1993], Diamond and Pokrovskii [1994], and Fridrich [1994b]. Fuzzy Petri nets, whose applications seem quite promising, are currently emerging as an important area of fuzzy systems. The contributions by Chen, Ke, and Chang [1990], Garg, Ahson, and Gupta [1991], and Scarpelli and Gomide [1993] are representative of this area. Iterated fuzzy systems were proposed by Cabrelli *et al.* [1992] and applied to the inverse problem for fractals.

12.9. Literature dealing with various issues regarding the construction of fuzzy models is quite extensive. The following are some representative publications on this subject: Gaines [1979a], Pedrycz [1984b, 1985a, b, 1989, 1990a, 1991c], Hirota and Pedrycz [1983], Higashi and Klir [1984b], Sugeno and Kang [1988], Sugeno and Tanaka [1991], Delgado and Gonzalez [1993], Yi and Chung [1993], Sugeno and Yasakawa [1993], and Yoshinari, Pedrycz, and Hirota [1993].

EXERCISES

12.1. Formulate reasonable fuzzy inference rules for an air-conditioning fuzzy control system.

12.2. Consider the fuzzy automaton employed in Sec. 12.6 as an example. Generate sequences of three fuzzy internal and output states under the following conditions:
   (a) the initial fuzzy state is $\mathbf{C}^1 = [1\ .8\ .6\ .4]$, the input fuzzy states are $\mathbf{A}^1 = [.2\ 1], \mathbf{A}^2 = [1\ 0], \mathbf{A}^3 = [1\ .4]$;
   (b) the initial fuzzy state is $\mathbf{C}^1 = [0\ .5\ 1\ 1]$, the input fuzzy states are $\mathbf{A}^1 = [1\ 0], \mathbf{A}^2 = [1\ 0], \mathbf{A}^3 = [1\ 1]$;
   (c) the initial fuzzy state is $\mathbf{C}^1 = [1\ 0\ 0\ 1]$, the input states are $\mathbf{A}^1 = [.2\ 1], \mathbf{A}^2 = [1\ 0], \mathbf{A}^3 = [1\ .4]$.

12.3. Modify the fuzzy automaton introduced in Sec. 12.6 by defining R as a fuzzy relation on $X \times Z \times Y$. Reformulate all equations for the modified automaton.

12.4. Repeat Exercise 12.2 for the fuzzy automaton formulated in Exercise 12.3 under the assumption that the fuzzy binary relation R employed in the example in Sec. 12.6 is replaced with the fuzzy ternary relation

$$R = 1/x_1 y_1 z_1 + 1/x_1 y_1 z_2 + 1/x_1 y_3 z_3 + .7/x_1 y_1 z_4 + 1/x_1 y_2 z_4$$

$$+ 1/x_2 y_3 z_1 + 1/x_2 y_1 z_2 + .5/x_2 y_3 z_2 + 1/x_2 y_2 z_3 + 1/x_2 y_2 z_4.$$

12.5. Discuss possible ways of fuzzifying the general dynamic system introduced in Sec. 12.7.

13

PATTERN RECOGNITION

13.1 INTRODUCTION

The capability of recognizing and classifying patterns is one of the most fundamental characteristics of human intelligence. It plays a key role in perception as well as at the various levels of cognition. As a field of study, pattern recognition has been evolving since the early 1950s, in close connection with the emergence and evolution of computer technology.

From a general point of view, *pattern recognition* may be defined as a process by which we search for structures in data and classify these structures into categories such that the degree of association is high among structures of the same category and low between structures of different categories. Relevant categories are usually characterized by prototypical structures derived from past experience. Each category may be characterized by more than one prototypical structure.

The classification of objects into categories is the subject of *cluster analysis*. Since cluster analysis plays a crucial role in pattern recognition, it is covered in this chapter. However, the applicability of cluster analysis is not restricted to pattern recognition. It is applicable, for example, to the construction of taxonomies in biology and other areas, classification of documents in information retrieval, and social groupings based on various criteria.

The utility of fuzzy set theory in pattern recognition and cluster analysis was already recognized in the mid-1960s, and the literature dealing with fuzzy pattern recognition and fuzzy clustering is now quite extensive. This is not surprising, since most categories we commonly encounter and employ have vague boundaries. Our aim in this chapter is to characterize the spirit of fuzzy clustering and fuzzy pattern recognition. In addition to our discussion of general issues of fuzzy pattern recognition, we also overview the area of fuzzy image processing, which may be viewed as a special branch of fuzzy pattern recognition.

There are three fundamental problems in pattern recognition. The first one is concerned with the representation of input data obtained by measurements on objects that are to be recognized. This is called a *sensing problem*. In general, each object is represented by a vector of measured values of r variables,

$$\mathbf{a} = [a_1 \ a_2 \ldots a_r],$$

where a_i (for each $i \in \mathbb{N}_r$) is a particular characteristic of the object of interest; this vector is usually called a *pattern vector*.

The second problem concerns the extraction of characteristic features from the input data in terms of which the dimensionality of pattern vectors can be reduced. This is referred to as a *feature extraction problem*. The features should be characterizing attributes by which the given pattern classes are well discriminated.

The third problem of pattern recognition involves the determination of optimal decision procedures for the classification of given patterns. This is usually done by defining an appropriate *discrimination function* for each class, which assigns a real number to each pattern vector. Individual pattern vectors are evaluated by these discrimination functions, and their classification is decided by the resulting values. Each pattern vector is classified to that class whose discrimination function yields the largest value.

Computer-based automatic pattern recognition systems have vast applicability. The following are examples of areas in which the use of these systems is well established: handwritten character and word recognition; automatic screening and classification of X-ray images; electrocardiograms, electroencephalograms, and other medical diagnostic tools; speech recognition and speaker identification; fingerprint recognition; classification of remotely sensed data; analysis and classification of chromosomes; image understanding; classification of seismic waves; target identification; and human face recognition. Many additional examples could be listed. It is obvious that we cannot describe the use of fuzzy set theory in all these application areas of pattern recognition. We can only examine a few representative examples. Similarly, we cannot cover all methodological nuances, but describe only a few typical methods of fuzzy pattern recognition.

13.2 FUZZY CLUSTERING

Clustering is one of the most fundamental issues in pattern recognition. It plays a key role in searching for structures in data. Given a finite set of data, X, the problem of clustering in X is to find several cluster centers that can properly characterize relevant classes of X. In classical cluster analysis, these classes are required to form a *partition* of X such that the degree of association is strong for data within blocks of the partition and weak for data in different blocks. However, this requirement is too strong in many practical applications, and it is thus desirable to replace it with a weaker requirement. When the requirement of a crisp partition of X is replaced with a weaker requirement of a *fuzzy partition* or a *fuzzy pseudopartition* on X, we refer to the emerging problem area as *fuzzy clustering*. Fuzzy pseudopartitions are often called *fuzzy c-partitions*, where c designates the number of fuzzy classes in the partition.

The reader should be aware of the difference between fuzzy pseudopartitions, as defined later in this section, and regular fuzzy partitions. Both of them are generalizations of classical partitions. However, the latter are obtained from associated fuzzy equivalence relations, while the former are not.

There are two basic methods of fuzzy clustering. One of them, which is based on fuzzy c-partitions, is called a *fuzzy c-means clustering method*. The other method, based on fuzzy equivalence relations, is called a *fuzzy equivalence relation-based hierarchical clustering method*. We describe basic characteristics of these methods and illustrate each of them by an example. Various modifications of the described methods can be found in the literature.

Fuzzy c-Means Clustering Method

Let $X = \{x_1, x_2, \ldots, x_n\}$ be a set of given data. A fuzzy pseudopartition or fuzzy c-partition of X is a family of fuzzy subsets of X, denoted by $\mathcal{P} = \{A_1, A_2, \ldots, A_c\}$, which satisfies

$$\sum_{i=1}^{c} A_i(x_k) = 1 \tag{13.1}$$

for all $k \in \mathbb{N}_n$ and

$$0 < \sum_{k=1}^{n} A_i(x_k) < n \tag{13.2}$$

for all $i \in \mathbb{N}_c$, where c is a positive integer.

For instance, given $X = \{x_1, x_2, x_3\}$ and

$$A_1 = .6/x_1 + 1/x_2 + .1/x_3,$$
$$A_2 = .4/x_1 + 0/x_2 + .9/x_3,$$

then $\{A_1, A_2\}$ is a fuzzy pseudopartition or fuzzy 2-partition of X. Fuzzy quantizations (or granulations) of variables in fuzzy systems are also examples of fuzzy pseudopartitions (see, e.g., Figs. 12.1 and 12.4).

Given a set of data $X = \{\mathbf{x}_1, \mathbf{x}_2, \ldots, \mathbf{x}_n\}$, where $\mathbf{x}_k$, in general, is a vector

$$\mathbf{x}_k = [x_{k1} \; x_{k2} \ldots x_{kp}] \in \mathbb{R}^p$$

for all $k \in \mathbb{N}_n$, the problem of fuzzy clustering is to find a fuzzy pseudopartition and the associated cluster centers by which the structure of the data is represented as best as possible. This requires some criterion expressing the general idea that associations (in the sense described by the criterion) be strong within clusters and weak between clusters. To solve the problem of fuzzy clustering, we need to formulate this criterion in terms of a *performance index*. Usually, the performance index is based upon cluster centers. Given a pseudopartition $\mathcal{P} = \{A_1, A_2, \ldots, A_c\}$, the c cluster centers, $\mathbf{v}_1, \mathbf{v}_2, \ldots, \mathbf{v}_c$ associated with the partition are calculated by the formula

$$\mathbf{v}_i = \frac{\sum_{k=1}^{n} [A_i(\mathbf{x}_k)]^m \mathbf{x}_k}{\sum_{k=1}^{n} [A_i(\mathbf{x}_k)]^m} \tag{13.3}$$

for all $i \in \mathbb{N}_c$, where $m > 1$ is a real number that governs the influence of membership grades. Observe that the vector $\mathbf{v}_i$ calculated by (13.3), which is viewed as the cluster center of the fuzzy class A_i, is actually the weighted average of data in A_i. The weight of a datum $\mathbf{x}_k$ is the mth power of the membership grade of $\mathbf{x}_k$ in the fuzzy set A_i.

The performance index of a fuzzy pseudopartition $\mathcal{P}$, $J_m(\mathcal{P})$, is then defined in terms of the cluster centers by the formula

$$J_m(\mathcal{P}) = \sum_{k=1}^{n} \sum_{i=1}^{c} [A_i(\mathbf{x}_k)]^m \|\mathbf{x}_k - \mathbf{v}_i\|^2, \tag{13.4}$$

where $\| \cdot \|$ is some inner product-induced norm in space $\mathbb{R}^p$ and $\|\mathbf{x}_k - \mathbf{v}_i\|^2$ represents the distance between $\mathbf{x}_k$ and $\mathbf{v}_i$. This performance index measures the weighted sum of distances between cluster centers and elements in the corresponding fuzzy clusters. Clearly, the smaller the value of $J_m(\mathcal{P})$, the better the fuzzy pseudopartition $\mathcal{P}$. Therefore, the goal of the fuzzy c-means clustering method is to find a fuzzy pseudopartition $\mathcal{P}$ that minimizes the performance index $J_m(\mathcal{P})$. That is, the clustering problem is an optimization problem. The following *fuzzy c-means algorithm* was developed by Bezdek [1981] for solving this optimization problem.

Fuzzy c-Means Algorithm

The algorithm is based on the assumption that the desired number of clusters c is given and, in addition, a particular distance, a real number $m \in (1, \infty)$, and a small positive number ε, serving as a stopping criterion, are chosen.

Step 1. Let $t = 0$. Select an initial fuzzy pseudopartition $\mathcal{P}^{(0)}$.

Step 2. Calculate the c cluster centers $\mathbf{v}_1^{(t)}, \ldots, \mathbf{v}_c^{(t)}$ by (13.3) for $\mathcal{P}^{(t)}$ and the chosen value of m.

Step 3. Update $\mathcal{P}^{(t+1)}$ by the following procedure: For each $\mathbf{x}_k \in X$, if $\|\mathbf{x}_k - \mathbf{v}_i^{(t)}\|^2 > 0$ for all $i \in \mathbb{N}_c$, then define

$$A_i^{(t+1)}(\mathbf{x}_k) = \left[\sum_{j=1}^{c} \left(\frac{\|\mathbf{x}_k - \mathbf{v}_i^{(t)}\|^2}{\|\mathbf{x}_k - \mathbf{v}_j^{(t)}\|^2} \right)^{\frac{1}{m-1}} \right]^{-1};$$

if $\|\mathbf{x}_k - \mathbf{v}_i^{(t)}\|^2 = 0$ for some $i \in I \subseteq \mathbb{N}_c$, then define $A_i^{(t+1)}(\mathbf{x}_k)$ for $i \in I$ by any nonnegative real numbers satisfying

$$\sum_{i \in I} A_i^{(t+1)}(\mathbf{x}_k) = 1,$$

and define $A_i^{(t+1)}(\mathbf{x}_k) = 0$ for $i \in \mathbb{N}_c - I$.

Step 4. Compare $\mathcal{P}^{(t)}$ and $\mathcal{P}^{(t+1)}$. If $|\mathcal{P}^{(t+1)} - \mathcal{P}^{(t)}| \le \varepsilon$, then stop; otherwise, increase t by one and return to **Step 2**.

In Step 4, $|\mathcal{P}^{(t+1)} - \mathcal{P}^{(t)}|$ denotes a distance between $\mathcal{P}^{(t+1)}$ and $\mathcal{P}^{(t)}$ in the space $\mathbb{R}^{n \times c}$. An example of this distance is

$$|\mathcal{P}^{(t+1)} - \mathcal{P}^{(t)}| = \max_{i \in \mathbb{N}_c, k \in \mathbb{N}_n} |A_i^{(t+1)}(\mathbf{x}_k) - A_i^{(t)}(\mathbf{x}_k)|. \tag{13.5}$$

In the algorithm, the parameter m is selected according to the problem under consideration. When $m \to 1$, the fuzzy c-means converges to a "generalized" classical c means. When $m \to \infty$, all cluster centers tend towards the centroid of the data set X. That is, the partition becomes fuzzier with increasing m. Currently, there is no theoretical basis for an optimal choice for the value of m. However, it is established that the algorithm converges for any $m \in (1, \infty)$.

Example 13.1   [Bezdek, 1981]

To illustrate the fuzzy c-means algorithm, let us consider a data set X that consists of the following 15 points in $\mathbb{R}^2$:

k	1	2	3	4	5	6	7	8	9	10	11	12	13	14	15
x_{k1}	0	0	0	1	1	1	2	3	4	5	5	5	6	6	6
x_{k2}	0	2	4	1	2	3	2	2	2	1	2	3	0	2	4

The data are also shown in Fig. 13.1a. Assume that we want to determine a fuzzy pseudopartition with two clusters (i.e., $c = 2$). Assume further that we choose $m = 1.25$, $\varepsilon = 0.01$; $\| \cdot \|$ is the Euclidean distance, and the initial fuzzy pseudopartition is $\mathcal{P}^{(0)} = \{A_1, A_2\}$ with

$$A_1 = .854/x_1 + .854/x_2 + \ldots + .854/x_{15},$$
$$A_2 = .146/x_1 + .146/x_2 + \ldots + .146/x_{15}.$$

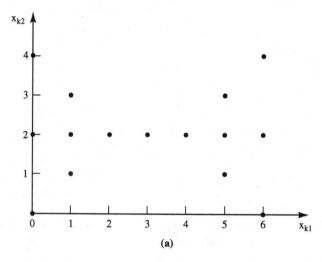

(a)

k	1	2	3	4	5	6	7	8	9	10	11	12	13	14	15
$A_1(\mathbf{x}_k)$	.99	1	.99	1	1	1	.99	.47	.01	0	0	0	.01	0	.01
$A_2(\mathbf{x}_k)$	.01	0	.01	0	0	0	.01	.53	.99	1	1	1	.99	1	.99

(b)

Figure 13.1   Illustration to Example 13.1: (a) data; (b) fuzzy pseudopartition $\mathcal{P}^{(6)} = \{A_1, A_2\}$.

Then, the algorithm stops for $t = 6$, and we obtain the fuzzy pseudopartition defined in Fig. 13.1b. The two cluster centers are

$$\mathbf{v}_1 = \langle 0.88, 2 \rangle \text{ and } \mathbf{v}_2 = \langle 5.14, 2 \rangle.$$

Clustering Methods Based Upon Fuzzy Equivalence Relations

The fuzzy c-means method requires that the desired number of clusters be specified. This is a disadvantage whenever the clustering problem does not specify any desired number of clusters. In such problems, the number of clusters should reflect, in a natural way, the structure of given data. Methods based on fuzzy equivalence relations work in this way.

As discussed in Sec. 5.5, every fuzzy equivalence relation (a relation that is reflexive, symmetric, and max-min transitive) induces a crisp partition in each of its α-cuts. The fuzzy clustering problem can thus be viewed as the problem of identifying an appropriate fuzzy equivalence relation on given data. Although this cannot usually be done directly, we can readily determine a fuzzy compatibility relation (reflexive and symmetric) in terms of an appropriate distance function applied to given data. Then, a meaningful fuzzy equivalence relation is defined as the transitive closure of this fuzzy compatibility relation.

Given a set of data X of the same form as defined earlier in this section (n p-tuples of $\mathbb{R}^p$), let a fuzzy compatibility relation, R, on X be defined in terms of an appropriate distance function of the Minkowski class by the formula

$$R(\mathbf{x}_i, \mathbf{x}_k) = 1 - \delta \left(\sum_{j=1}^p |x_{ij} - x_{kj}|^q \right)^{\frac{1}{q}} \tag{13.6}$$

for all pairs $\langle \mathbf{x}_i, \mathbf{x}_k \rangle \in X$, where $q \in \mathbb{R}^+$, and δ is a constant that ensures that $R(\mathbf{x}_i, \mathbf{x}_k) \in [0, 1]$. Clearly, δ is the inverse value of the largest distance in X.

In general, R defined by (13.6) is a fuzzy compatibility relation, but not necessarily a fuzzy equivalence relation. Hence, we usually need to determine the transitive closure of R. This can be done by the simple algorithm described in Sec. 5.4. However, since R is a compatibility relation, we can utilize the following theorem to formulate a more efficient algorithm.

Theorem 13.1. Let R be a fuzzy compatibility relation on a finite universal set X with $|X| = n$. Then, the max-min transitive closure of R is the relation $R^{(n-1)}$.

Proof: Left to the reader as an exercise. ■

The theorem suggests calculating the transitive closure, $R_T = R^{(n-1)}$, by calculating the sequence of relations

$$R^{(2)} = R \circ R,$$
$$R^{(4)} = R^{(2)} \circ R^{(2)},$$
$$\dots\dots\dots\dots\dots\dots$$
$$R^{(2^k)} = R^{(2^{k-1})} \circ R^{(2^{k-1})}$$

until no new relation is produced or $2^k \geq n - 1$. This algorithm, applicable only to fuzzy reflexive relations, is clearly computationally much more efficient than the more general algorithm in Sec. 5.4.

Example 13.2

To illustrate the clustering method based on fuzzy equivalence relations, let us use a small data set X consisting of the following five points in $\mathbb{R}^2$:

k	1	2	3	4	5
x_{k1}	0	1	2	3	4
x_{k2}	0	1	3	1	0

The data are also shown in Fig. 13.2a. To see the effect of the value of parameter q in (13.6) on the results, let us analyze the data for $q = 1, 2$.

As the first step, we perform the analysis for $q = 2$, which corresponds to the Euclidean distance. First, we need to determine the value of δ in (13.6). Since the largest Euclidean distance between any pair of the given data points is 4 (between x_1 and x_5), we have $\delta = 1/4 = 0.25$. Now, we can calculate membership grades of R by (13.6). For example,

$$R(x_1, x_3) = 1 - 0.25(2^2 + 3^2)^{0.5} = 0.1.$$

When determined, relation R may conveniently be represented by the matrix

$$\mathbf{R} = \begin{bmatrix} 1 & .65 & .1 & .21 & 0 \\ .65 & 1 & .44 & .5 & .21 \\ .1 & .44 & 1 & .44 & .1 \\ .21 & .5 & .44 & 1 & .65 \\ 0 & .21 & .1 & .65 & 1 \end{bmatrix},$$

This relation is not max-min transitive; its transitive closure is

$$\mathbf{R}_T = \begin{bmatrix} 1 & .65 & .44 & .5 & .5 \\ .65 & 1 & .44 & .5 & .5 \\ .44 & .44 & 1 & .44 & .44 \\ .5 & .5 & .44 & 1 & .65 \\ .5 & .5 & .44 & .65 & 1 \end{bmatrix}.$$

This relation induces four distinct partitions of its α-cuts:

$$\alpha \in [0, .44] : \{\{x_1, x_2, x_3, x_4, x_5\}\},$$

$$\alpha \in (.44, .5] : \{\{x_1, x_2, x_4, x_5\}, \{x_3\}\},$$

$$\alpha \in (.5, .65] : \{\{x_1, x_2\}, \{x_3\}, \{x_4, x_5\}\}$$

$$\alpha \in (.65, 1] : \{\{x_1\}, \{x_2\}, \{x_3\}, \{x_4\}, \{x_5\}\}.$$

This result agrees with our visual perception of geometric clusters in the data. This is undoubtedly due to the use of the Euclidean distance.

Let us now repeat the analysis for $q = 1$ in (13.6), which represents the Hamming distance. Since the largest Hamming distance in the data is 5 (between x_1 and x_3 and between x_3 and x_5), we have $\delta = 1/5 = 0.2$. The matrix form of relation R given by (13.6) is now

$$\mathbf{R} = \begin{bmatrix} 1 & .6 & 0 & .2 & .2 \\ .6 & 1 & .4 & .6 & .2 \\ 0 & .4 & 1 & .4 & 0 \\ .2 & .6 & .4 & 1 & .6 \\ .2 & .2 & 0 & .6 & 1 \end{bmatrix}.$$

and its transitive closure is

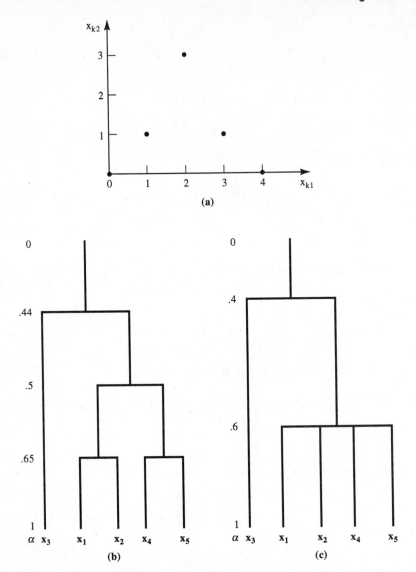

Figure 13.2 Illustration to Example 13.2: (a) data; (b) clustering tree for Euclidean distance; (c) clustering tree for Hamming distance.

$$R_T = \begin{bmatrix} 1 & .6 & .4 & .6 & .6 \\ .6 & 1 & .4 & .6 & .6 \\ .4 & .4 & 1 & .4 & .4 \\ .6 & .6 & .4 & 1 & .6 \\ .6 & .6 & .4 & .6 & 1 \end{bmatrix}$$

This relation yields the following partitions in its α-cuts:

$$\alpha \in [0, .4] : \{\{x_1, x_2, x_3, x_4, x_5\}\},$$

$$\alpha \in (.4, .6] \ : \ \{\{\mathbf{x}_1, \mathbf{x}_2, \mathbf{x}_4, \mathbf{x}_5\}, \{\mathbf{x}_3\}\},$$

$$\alpha \in (.6, 1] \ : \ \{\{\mathbf{x}_1\}, \{\mathbf{x}_2\}, \{\mathbf{x}_3\}, \{\mathbf{x}_4\}, \{\mathbf{x}_5\}\}.$$

This result again agrees with our visual perception, but it is less refined, since visually perceived clusters $\{\mathbf{x}_1, \mathbf{x}_2\}$ and $\{\mathbf{x}_4, \mathbf{x}_5\}$ are not distinguished. This is due to the coarseness of the Hamming distance. Both results are illustrated in Fig. 13.2 by their clustering trees, which are self-explanatory.

In the next example, adopted from [Tamura *et al.*, 1971], we want to illustrate some additional aspects of clustering methods based on fuzzy equivalence relations.

Example 13.3

Consider 16 portraits labelled by the integers in $\mathbb{N}_{16}$, which we know are portraits of members of three families. We also know that each family consists of four to seven numbers. Our aim is to cluster these portraits according to the families. First, a degree of similarity for each pair of portraits must be determined. This can only be done subjectively, by a group of people and some method by which their individual judgements are aggregated. Assume that the similarity degrees obtained, which may be viewed as membership grades of a fuzzy compatibility relation R on $\mathbb{N}_{16}$, are given in terms of the matrix in Table 13.1a. Since the matrix is symmetric, only its lower triangle is shown.

An interesting feature of this example is that similarities can be expected between parents and their children, but not between parents themselves. However, the connection between parents can be established through their similarities to children by converting R into its transitive closure R_T; the latter is shown in Table 13.1b. Applying the algorithm based on Theorem 13.1, we obtain $R_T = R^{(8)}$.

The clustering tree of R_T is shown in Fig. 13.3. We can see that none of the partitions fully satisfies the known constraints regarding the families: three families, each with four to seven members. However, the partition that least violates these constraints is the one for $\alpha = 0.6$:

$$^{.6}R_T = \{\{3\}, \{1, 6, 8, 13, 16\}, \{2, 5, 7, 11, 14\}, \{4, 9, 10, 12, 15\}\}.$$

The only violation of the constraints by this partition is that portrait 3 forms its own class. This must be rejected and the portrait left unclassified. This is reasonable, since this unclassifiable portrait may be a portrait of an adopted child or a child from a previous marriage.

Tamura *et al.* [1971] mention in their paper that they performed an experiment with 60 families divided into 20 groups, each consisting of three families. They report the overall rate of 75% correct classification, 13% misclassification, and 12% rejection (unclassifiability). These results are quite impressive, considering the extreme vagueness of information in this application and the full dependence on subjective judgment.

13.3   *FUZZY PATTERN RECOGNITION*

In this section, we overview two classes of methods of fuzzy pattern recognition. One of them consists of generalizations of classical membership-roster methods; the other one consists of generalizations of classical syntactic methods.

In classical membership-roster methods of pattern recognition, each pattern class is characterized by a set of patterns that are stored in the pattern recognition system. An

TABLE 13.1 FUZZY RELATIONS IN EXAMPLE 13.3

(a) Matrix of fuzzy compatibility relation $\mathbf{R}$ on $\mathbb{N}_{16}$.

Portrait Number	1	2	3	4	5	6	7	8	9	10	11	12	13	14	15	16
1	1															
2	0	1														
3	0	0	1													
4	0	0	0.4	1												
5	0	0.8	0	0	1											
6	0.5	0	0.2	0.2	0	1										
7	0	0.8	0	0	0.4	0	1									
8	0.4	0.2	0.2	0.5	0	0.8	0	1								
9	0	0.4	0	0.8	0.4	0.2	0.4	0	1							
10	0	0	0.2	0.2	0	0	0.2	0	0.2	1						
11	0	0.5	0.2	0.2	0	0	0.8	0	0.4	0.2	1					
12	0	0	0.2	0.8	0	0	0	0	0.4	0.8	0	1				
13	0.8	0	0.2	0.4	0	0.4	0	0.4	0	0	0	0	1			
14	0	0.8	0	0.2	0.4	0	0.8	0	0.2	0.2	0.6	0	0	1		
15	0	0	0.4	0.8	0	0.2	0	0	0.2	0	0	0.2	0.2	0	1	
16	0.6	0	0	0.2	0.2	0.8	0	0.4	0	0	0	0	0.4	0.2	0	1

(b) Matrix of the transitive closure $\mathbf{R_T}$ of $\mathbf{R}$.

Portrait Number	1	2	3	4	5	6	7	8	9	10	11	12	13	14	15	16
1	1															
2	0.4	1														
3	0.4	0.4	1													
4	0.5	0.4	0.4	1												
5	0.4	0.8	0.4	0.4	1											
6	0.6	0.4	0.4	0.5	0.4	1										
7	0.4	0.8	0.4	0.4	0.8	0.4	1									
8	0.6	0.4	0.4	0.5	0.4	0.8	0.4	1								
9	0.5	0.4	0.4	0.8	0.4	0.5	0.4	0.5	1							
10	0.5	0.4	0.4	0.8	0.4	0.5	0.4	0.5	0.8	1						
11	0.4	0.8	0.4	0.4	0.8	0.4	0.8	0.4	0.4	0.4	1					
12	0.5	0.4	0.4	0.8	0.4	0.5	0.4	0.5	0.8	0.8	0.4	1				
13	0.8	0.4	0.4	0.5	0.4	0.6	0.4	0.6	0.5	0.5	0.4	0.5	1			
14	0.4	0.8	0.4	0.4	0.8	0.4	0.8	0.4	0.4	0.4	0.8	0.4	0.4	1		
15	0.5	0.4	0.4	0.8	0.4	0.5	0.4	0.5	0.8	0.8	0.4	0.8	0.5	0.4	1	
16	0.6	0.4	0.4	0.5	0.4	0.8	0.4	0.8	0.5	0.5	0.4	0.5	0.6	0.4	0.5	1

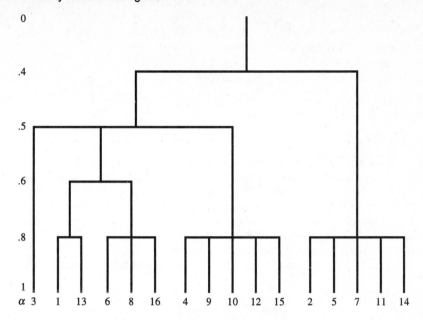

Figure 13.3   Clustering tree in Example 13.3.

unknown pattern to be classified is compared with the stored patterns one by one. The pattern is classified as a member of a pattern class if it matches one of the stored patterns in that class. For efficient pattern recognition, an appropriate set of patterns must be stored for each pattern class to capture its pattern variety. For example, letters of all relevant fonts must be stored in a printed character recognition system.

In classical syntactic methods of pattern recognition, a pattern is represented by a string of concatenated subpatterns called primitives. These primitives are viewed as the alphabet of a formal language. A pattern, then, is a sentence generated by some grammar. All patterns whose sentences are generated by the same grammar belong to the same pattern class. An unknown pattern is thus classified to a particular pattern class if it can be generated by the grammar corresponding to that class.

Fuzzy Membership-Roster Methods

In fuzzy membership-roster methods, contrary to their classical counterparts, we need to store only one standard pattern for each pattern class. For a given unknown pattern, we measure, in an appropriate way, its degree of compatibility with each standard pattern and then classify the pattern to a particular class according to some criteria.

Assume that n pattern classes are recognized, which are labelled by the integers in $\mathbb{N}_n$. Given a relevant pattern

$$\mathbf{u} = \langle u_1, u_2, \ldots, u_p \rangle,$$

where u_i is the measurement associated with the ith feature of the pattern ($i \in \mathbb{N}_p$), let $A_k(\mathbf{u})$ denote the degree of compatibility of $\mathbf{u}$ with the standard pattern representing class

$k(k \in \mathbb{N}_n)$. A given pattern is usually classified by the largest value of $A_k(\mathbf{u})$ for all $k \in \mathbb{N}_n$, but other classification criteria have also been suggested.

Specific methods for selecting pattern features, determining the degrees $A_k(\mathbf{u})$, and classifying given patterns according to these degrees have been developed for specific types of pattern recognition problems. We illustrate this class of fuzzy pattern recognition method by a particular example.

Example 13.4

Lee [1975] describes one straightforward method of examining the shape of chromosomes in order to classify them into the three categories pictured in Fig. 13.4. As can be seen from this figure, the classification scheme is based on the ratio of the length of the arms of the chromosome to its total body length. It is difficult to identify sharp boundaries between these three types. Therefore, Lee uses a method of fuzzy pattern recognition, which compares the angles and arm lengths of the chromosome with those labeled in the idealized skeleton in Fig. 13.5. His method belongs to the class of fuzzy membership-roster methods.

Each pattern $\mathbf{u}$ is characterized by 13 features (angles and distances), which are shown in Fig. 13.5. That is,

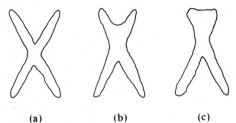

(a)   (b)   (c)

Figure 13.4 Chromosome images: (a) median; (b) submedian; (c) acrocentric.

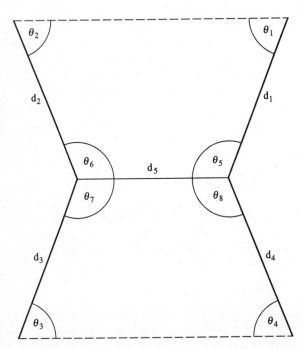

Figure 13.5 Idealized pattern for chromosome classification.

$$\mathbf{u} = \langle \theta_1, \theta_2, \ldots, \theta_8, d_1, d_2, \ldots, d_5 \rangle.$$

In order to determine membership grade functions corresponding to the three classes of chromosomes, a fuzzy set of symmetric chromosomes, S, is defined first. Fuzzy sets M, SM, and AC, corresponding, to median, submedian, and acrocentric chromosomes respectively, are then defined in terms of S.

The membership grade $S(\mathbf{u})$ of each chromosome characterized by pattern $\mathbf{u}$ in the fuzzy set of symmetric chromosomes is defined by the formula

$$S(\mathbf{u}) = 1 - \frac{1}{720^0} \sum_{i=1}^{4} |\theta_{2i-1} - \theta_{2i}|.$$

The three fuzzy sets of primary interest in this pattern recognition problem, M, SM, and AC, are defined in terms of S by the formulas

$$M(\mathbf{u}) = S(\mathbf{u}) \left[1 - \frac{|d_1 - d_4| + |d_2 - d_3|}{d_T} \right],$$

$$SM(\mathbf{u}) = S(\mathbf{u}) \left[1 - \frac{d_{SM}}{2d_T} \right],$$

$$AC(\mathbf{u}) = S(\mathbf{u}) \left[1 - \frac{d_{AC}}{4d_T} \right],$$

where

$$d_T = d_1 + d_2 + d_3 + d_4 + d_5,$$
$$d_{SM} = \min(|d_1 - 2d_4| + |d_2 - 2d_3|, |2d_1 - d_4| + |2d_2 - d_3|),$$
$$d_{AC} = \min(|d_1 - 4d_4| + |d_2 - 4d_3|, |4d_1 - d_4| + |4d_2 - d_3|).$$

Each chromosome can be classified as *approximately median, approximately submedian,* or *approximately acrocentric* by calculating each of the three membership grades in M, SM, and AC; the category in which the chromosome attains the maximum value is chosen if that value is sufficiently large. If the maximum value falls below some designated threshold, then the image is rejected from all three classes. If the maximum is not unique, then the classification is based on a priority defined on the three classes. As can be seen from this example, geometric similarity is conveniently represented in terms of membership grades in the interval [0, 1]. The further advantages of this type of shape-oriented classification scheme lie in the fact that the method is insensitive to rotation, translation, expansion, or contraction of the chromosome image; these factors do affect the way in which humans are able to classify images.

Fuzzy Syntactic Methods

Classical syntactic methods of pattern recognition are based on the theory of formal languages and grammars. In these methods, pattern classes are represented by languages, each of which is a set of strings of symbols from a vocabulary that are generated by the pattern grammar. These methods are suitable for recognizing patterns that are rich in structural information which cannot be easily expressed in numerical values.

Let V be a vocabulary, and let V^* denote the set of all strings formed by symbols from V, including the empty string. Then any subset of V^* is called a *language* based upon the vocabulary V. Some languages can be defined by grammars. A *grammar*, $\mathbf{G}$, is the quadruple

$$G = \langle V_N, V_T, P, s \rangle, \tag{13.7}$$

where

- V_N is a nonterminal vocabulary;
- V_T is a terminal vocabulary such that $V_T \cap V_N = \varnothing$;
- P is a finite set of production rules of the form $\mathbf{x} \to \mathbf{y}$, where $\mathbf{x}$ and $\mathbf{y}$ are strings of symbols from $V = V_N \cup V_T$ such that $\mathbf{x}$ contains at least one symbol of V_N; and
- s is the starting symbol ($s \in V_N$).

The language generated by grammar $\mathbf{G}$, denoted by $L(\mathbf{G})$, is the set of all strings formed by symbols in V_T that can be obtained by the production rules in P.

As an example of a grammar $\mathbf{G}$, let $V_N = \{s, n_1, n_2\}$ and $V_T = \{t_1, t_2\}$ and let P consist of the following eight production rules:

(1) $s \to n_2 t_1$	(5) $n_1 \to t_1$
(2) $s \to n_1 t_2$	(6) $n_2 \to s t_2$
(3) $n_1 \to s t_1$	(7) $n_2 \to n_2 n_2 t_1$
(4) $n_1 \to n_1 n_1 t_2$	(8) $n_2 \to t_2$

The following are examples of generating strings $\mathbf{x} \in V_T^*$ that belong to the language $L(\mathbf{G})$, defined by this grammar:

$$s \xrightarrow{(1)} n_2 t_1 \xrightarrow{(6)} s t_2 t_1 \xrightarrow{(2)} n_1 t_2 t_2 t_1 \xrightarrow{(5)} t_1 t_2 t_2 t_1 \in L(\mathbf{G})$$

$$s \xrightarrow{(2)} n_1 t_2 \xrightarrow{(4)} n_1 n_1 t_2 t_2 \xrightarrow{(4)} n_1 n_1 t_2 n_1 n_1 t_2 t_2 t_2 \xrightarrow{(5)} t_1 t_1 t_2 t_1 t_1 t_2 t_2 t_2 \in L(\mathbf{G})$$

$$s \xrightarrow{(1)} n_2 t_1 \xrightarrow{(7)} n_2 n_2 t_1 t_1 \xrightarrow{(8)} t_2 t_2 t_1 t_1 \in L(\mathbf{G})$$

In syntactic pattern recognition, features of patterns are represented by the elements of the terminal vocabulary V_T. They are usually called primitives. Each pattern is represented by a string of these primitives, and each pattern class is defined by a grammar that generates strings representing patterns in that class. For background in this area of classical pattern recognition, we recommend the book *Syntactic Methods in Pattern Recognition* by K. S. Fu (Academic Press, 1974).

In many applications, structural information is inherently vague. In such applications, it is desirable to increase the descriptive power of syntactic pattern recognition by fuzzifying the concepts of a grammar and the associated language. This can be done by fuzzifying the primitives involved (i.e., the primitives become labels of fuzzy sets) or by fuzzifying the production rules of the grammar and, consequently, also the language defined by the grammar (i.e., the language becomes a fuzzy set of strings formed by symbols from the terminal vocabulary).

A *fuzzy grammar*, $\mathbf{FG}$, is defined by the quintuple

$$\mathbf{FG} = \langle V_n, V_T, P, s, A \rangle, \tag{13.8}$$

where

- V_N is a nonterminal vocabulary as in (13.7);

- V_T is a terminal vocabulary as in (13.7);
- P is a finite set of production rules as in (13.7);
- s is the starting symbol ($s \in V_N$); and
- A is a fuzzy set defined on P.

Every fuzzy grammar defined by (13.8) has an associated crisp grammar defined by (13.7). The language generated by the fuzzy grammar is a fuzzy set, $L(\mathbf{FG})$, defined on the language generated by the associated crisp grammar. For each string $\mathbf{x} \in L(\mathbf{G})$,

$$L(\mathbf{FG})(\mathbf{x}) = \max_{1 \le k \le m} \min_{1 \le i \le n_k} A(p_i^k), \tag{13.9}$$

where m is the number of derivations of string $\mathbf{x}$ by grammar $\mathbf{FG}$, n_k is the length of the kth derivation chain, and p_i^k denotes the ith production rule used in the kth derivation chain ($i = 1, 2, \ldots, n_k$).

Fuzzy syntactic pattern recognition proceeds as follows. After determining significant features of patterns to be recognized, these features form a terminal vocabulary V_T. Appropriate fuzzy grammars are then defined for this vocabulary, each of which characterizes one of the pattern classes to be distinguished. Given an unknown pattern to be classified, whose features form a string $\mathbf{x} \in V_T^*$, its membership grades in languages generated by the various fuzzy grammars are calculated by (13.9). The pattern is then classified by the largest membership grade.

In classical syntactic pattern recognition, languages generated by grammars representing different pattern classes are required to be pair-wise disjoint. This requirement is too strong for many practical applications. The use of fuzzy grammars relaxes this requirement by allowing overlaps between the associated fuzzy languages.

To illustrate the basic ideas of fuzzy syntactic pattern recognition, we use the following example, adopted in a simplified form from [Pathak and Pal, 1986].

Example 13.5

Consider the problem of identifying the skeletal maturity of children from X-ray images. Nine stages of skeletal maturity are usually distinguished. Eight of the stages, expressed in terms of the radius of hand and wrist and labelled by the integers $2, 3, \ldots, 8$, are illustrated in Fig. 13.6 in terms of typical images of the radius of hand and wrist. The first stage (labelled by 1), during which the epiphysis is totally absent, is not shown in the figure. Given a particular image of this kind, the problem is to classify it into one of the nine classes on the basis of shapes of the epiphysis and metaphysis as well as palmar and dorsal surfaces. Fuzzy syntactic methods are suitable for dealing with this problem.

Since some stages are more difficult to distinguish from each other, a three-level hierarchical classification scheme (shown in Fig. 13.7) is employed, where the subscripted symbols $\mathbf{FG}$ designate the various fuzzy grammars involved in this pattern recognition process, and the symbols $C_1, C_2, \ldots$ are labels of the associated pattern classes. No grammar is assigned in this figure to stage 1 (class C_1) since epilepsies is totally absent in this stage; hence, C_1 is characterized by the empty string. In all fuzzy grammars in this example,

$$V_T = \{t_1, t_2, t_3, t_4\},$$

where t_1, t_2, t_3, t_4 denote a line segment of unit length, a clockwise curve, an anticlockwise curve, and a dot, respectively. The nonterminal vocabulary V_N consists of 13 symbols $n_1, n_2, \ldots, n_{13}$.

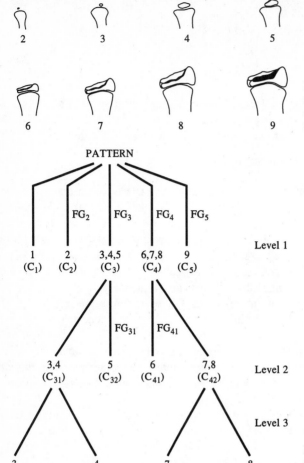

Figure 13.6 Different stages of skeletal maturity of radius (Stage 1, in which epiphysis is totally absent, is not shown here).

Figure 13.7 Three-level hierarchical classification procedure (Example 13.5).

Production rules of fuzzy grammars at the first classification level ($\mathbf{FG}_3, \mathbf{FG}_4, \mathbf{FG}_5$) are listed in Table 13.2, together with membership grades of the associated fuzzy sets A_3, A_4, A_5. Symbols SH, FA, and GE in this table denote fuzzy sets defined on the set of curves (both clockwise and anticlockwise) that represent the linguistic labels *sharp*, *fair*, and *gentle*, respectively. We can see, for example, that the fuzzy grammar $\mathbf{FG}_3$ consists of production rules 1, 7, 8, 9, 10, production rule 11 with the membership grade $FA(t_2)$, and production rule 12 with the membership grade $SH(t_2)$. Grammar $\mathbf{FG}_2$ is not included in Table 13.2 since it is trivial: class C_2 is characterized by a single string, string t_4, hence, grammar $\mathbf{FG}_2$ is actually crisp and consists of the single production rule $s \rightarrow t_4$.

Fuzzy sets SH, FA, and GE are defined in terms of another fuzzy set, denoted by ARC_β, whose membership function is defined for any given curve c by the formula

$$ARC_\beta(c) = \left(1 - \frac{a}{b}\right)^\beta, \tag{13.10}$$

where a is the length of the straight line segment joining the two extreme points of curve c, b is the length of the curve, and $\beta > 0$ is a parameter by which the definition can be adjusted as needed. The value $ARC_\beta(c)$ expresses the degree of archness of c; clearly, the lower the ration

TABLE 13.2 PRODUCTION RULES OF FUZZY GRAMMARS IN EXAMPLE 13.5

(a) Level 1

j	Production rules p_j	Membership $A_3(p_j)$	$A_4(p_j)$	Grades $A_5(p_j)$
1	$s \to n_1 n_1$	1	0	0
2	$s \to n_1 n_1 n_1$	0	1	0
3	$s \to n_1 n_3 n_1$	0	1	0
4	$s \to n_4 S$	0	1	0
5	$s \to s n_3$	0	1	0
6	$s \to n_{12} n_6 n_{13}$	0	0	1
7	$n_1 \to n_2 n_3$	1	1	0
8	$n_1 \to n_3$	1	0	0
9	$n_2 \to t_1 n_2$	1	1	1
10	$n_2 \to t_1$	1	1	1
11	$n_3 \to t_2$	$FA(t_2)$	$FA(t_2)$	1
12	$n_3 \to t_2$	$SH(t_2)$	$SH(t_2)$	1
13	$n_4 \to n_2 n_5$	0	1	1
14	$n_5 \to t_2$	0	$GE(t_2)$	$GE(t_2)$
15	$n_6 \to t_3 n_7 t_3$	0	0	1
16	$n_7 \to n_1 n_8 n_8$	0	0	1
17	$n_7 \to n_1 n_8 n_8 n_2$	0	0	1
18	$n_7 \to n_1 n_7$	0	0	1
19	$n_8 \to n_9 n_3$	0	0	1
20	$n_9 \to n_2$	0	0	1
21	$n_9 \to n_2 n_{11} n_2$	0	0	1
22	$n_9 \to n_{11} n_2$	0	0	1
23	$n_9 \to n_2 n_{11}$	0	0	1
24	$n_{11} \to t_3$	0	0	$GE(t_3)$
25	$n_{11} \to t_2$	0	0	$GE(t_2)$
26	$n_{12} \to n_9 n_3 n_9$	0	0	1
27	$n_{12} \to n_9 n_3$	0	0	1
28	$n_{12} \to n_9$	0	0	1
29	$n_{13} \to n_9 n_3 n_9$	0	0	1
30	$n_{13} \to n_3 n_9$	0	0	1
31	$n_{13} \to n_9$	0	0	1

(b) Level 2

j	Production rules p_j	Membership $A_{32}(p_j)$	Grades $A_{41}(p_j)$
1	$s \to n_1$	1	0
2	$s \to n_2 n_2$	0	1
3	$n_2 \to n_4 n_4$	1	1
4	$n_2 \to n_4 n_6 n_4$	0	$1 - GE(t_2)$
5	$n_4 \to n_5 t_2$	$1 - GE(t_2)$	$1 - GE(t_2)$
6	$n_4 \to t_2$	0	1
7	$n_5 \to n_8$	1	1
8	$n_5 \to n_8 n_{10} n_8$	1	1
9	$n_5 \to n_{10} n_5$	1	1
10	$n_5 \to n_8 n_{12}$	1	1
11	$n_5 \to n_8 n_{10} n_8 n_{12}$	1	1
12	$n_5 \to n_{10} n_5 n_{12}$	1	1
13	$n_5 \to n_{10}$	0	1
14	$n_6 \to t_3$	0	$1 - GE(t_3)$
15	$n_6 \to n_5 t_3$	0	$1 - GE(t_3)$
16	$n_8 \to t_1 n_8$	1	1
17	$n_8 \to t_1$	1	1
18	$n_{10} \to n_{11}$	1	1
19	$n_{10} \to n_{11} n_{11}$	1	1
20	$n_{10} \to n_{11} n_8 n_{11}$	1	1
21	$n_{11} \to t_3$	$GE(t_3)$	$GE(t_3)$
22	$n_{11} \to t_2$	$GE(t_2)$	$GE(t_2)$
23	$n_{12} \to n_{10}$	1	1
24	$n_{12} \to n_{10} n_{12}$	1	1

a/b, the higher the degree of archness. Now,

$$SH_\beta(c) = f(ARC_\beta(c)),$$

$$FA_\beta(c) = g(|ARC_\beta(x) - 0.5|),$$

$$GE_\beta(c) = h(ARC_\beta(c)),$$

where f is a monotonically increasing function on $[0, 1]$, and g and h are monotonically decreasing functions on $[0, 0.5]$ and $[0, 1]$, respectively.

Production rules of fuzzy grammars at the second classification level (FG_{32} and FG_{41}) are listed in Table 13.2b, together with membership grades of the associated fuzzy sets A_{32} and A_{41}.

The whole procedure of pattern classification in this example can now be summarized, in a simplified manner, as follows. Given an X-ray image to be classified, it is first converted into a string of symbols in V_T. If the string is empty, it is classified to C_1; if it is t_4, it is classified to C_2; otherwise, the string is classified in one of the classes C_3, C_4, and C_5 according to the largest membership grade in fuzzy languages generated by the associated fuzzy grammars FG_3, FG_4, and FG_5. If the string is classified in C_3 or C_4, we proceed to level 2, where fuzzy grammars FG_{31} and FG_{41} are employed for further classification. Classification at level 3 (Fig. 13.7) is based on specific measurements and crisp criteria.

Many additional details of this interesting example, omitted here for the sake of simplicity, are covered in the original paper by Pathak and Pal [1986] as well as in the book by Pal and Majumder [1986].

13.4 *FUZZY IMAGE PROCESSING*

Image processing is connected with pattern recognition in the sense that data in many pattern recognition problems are given in terms of digital images. Examples of such problems are printed and handwritten character recognition, automatic classification of X-ray images, fingerprints recognition, target identification, human face recognition, and classification of remotely sensed data. The role of image processing is to enhance a given image in an appropriate way to make the subsequent pattern recognition and classification easier.

For the sake of simplicity, let us consider only monochrome or grey-tone images. In general, a grey-tone image is a discrete approximation of a black and white picture, which is essential for computer processing. Such an approximation is conveniently represented by the $m \times n$ matrix

$$\mathbf{R} = \begin{bmatrix} r_{11} & r_{12} & \cdots & r_{1n} \\ r_{21} & r_{22} & \cdots & r_{2n} \\ \vdots & \vdots & \vdots & \vdots \\ r_{m1} & r_{m2} & \cdots & r_{mn} \end{bmatrix},$$

where r_{ij} expresses, for each $i \in \mathbb{N}_m$ and each $j \in \mathbb{N}_n$, the level of brightness at the spatial point whose position in a two-dimensional grid of discrete points is identified by the vertical index i and the horizontal index j. The ordering of entries in $\mathbf{R}$ is assumed to be the same as the ordering of points in the grid, and r_{ij} is assumed to be a value from a discrete set $\{b_1 = 0, b_2, \ldots, b_q = b_{max}\}$; we assume values b_k increase with increasing $k \in \mathbb{N}_{0,q}$. Each element of R is usually called a *pixel*.

There are basically two classes of methods for image processing, which are referred to as frequency domain methods and spatial domain methods. In *frequency domain methods*, the image is processed in terms of its Fourier transform; in *spatial domain methods*, the processing directly involves the pixels of matrix **R**. To illustrate the use of fuzzy sets in image processing, we consider only spatial domain methods. In some of these methods, each pixel is modified independent of other pixels, while in other methods, it is modified on the basis of pixels in its neighborhood.

In fuzzy image-processing methods, matrix $\mathbf{R} = [r_{ij}]$ of a given image is converted into its fuzzy counterpart, $\tilde{\mathbf{R}} = [\tilde{r}_{ij}]$, which is then manipulated by appropriate fuzzy operators. The conversion from **R** to $\tilde{\mathbf{R}}$ is usually done by the formula

$$\tilde{r}_{ij} = \left(1 + \frac{\hat{b} - r_{ij}}{\beta}\right)^{-\gamma} \tag{13.11}$$

for all $i \in \mathbb{N}_m$ and $j \in \mathbb{N}_n$, where $\hat{b} \in [0, b_{\max}]$ is a reference constant defining the degree of brightness for which $\tilde{r}_{ij} = 1$, and β, γ are positive parameters that affect the conversion formula and are determined from required properties of enhancement operations to be applied to a given image.

Two ways of manipulating images represented by fuzzy matrices are illustrated by a particular example adopted from [Pal and King, 1981].

Example 13.6

The image considered in this example is the discrete approximation of a picture of three handwritten letters, *Shu*, by a 96×96 spatial grid of points and 32 levels of brightness (grey levels), shown in Fig. 13.8a. The image is represented by a 96×96 matrix $\mathbf{R} = [r_{ij}]$, where $r_{ij} \in \{0, 1, \ldots, 31\}$ for all $i, j \in \mathbb{N}_{96}$. For converting **R** into $\tilde{\mathbf{R}}$, $\hat{b} = b_{\max} = 31$ is chosen in this example and, hence,

$$\tilde{r}_{ij} = \left(1 + \frac{31 - r_{ij}}{\beta}\right)^{-\gamma},$$

where appropriate values of parameters β and γ are selected on the basis of the requirements imposed upon the following *contrast intensification* operation, which is one of the operations intended to enhance the image for subsequent pattern recognition and classification. Observe that this conversion function is an *S*-shape function, since it is based on $\hat{b} = b_{\max} = 31$.

Any contrast intensification operation, INT, is a function of the form

$$\text{INT} : [0, 1] \to [0, 1]$$

such that

$$\text{INT}(a) > a \text{ when } a \in (0.5, 1),$$
$$\text{INT}(a) < a \text{ when } a \in (0, 0.5),$$
$$\text{INT}(a) = a \text{ when } a = 0, 0.5, 1.$$

When function INT is applied to entries of matrix $\tilde{\mathbf{R}}$, let $\text{INT}(\tilde{r}_{ij})$ be denoted by $\tilde{r}'_{ij}$.

The intensification operation employed in this example is defined by

$$\text{INT}(\tilde{r}_{ij}) = \begin{cases} 2\tilde{r}_{ij}^2 & \text{when } \tilde{r}_{ij} \in [0, 0.5] \\ 1 - 2(1 - \tilde{r}_{ij})^2 & \text{when } \tilde{r}_{ij} \in [0.5, 1] \end{cases}$$

(a) Original image

(b) Result of contrast stretching

(c) Result of smoothing

Figure 13.8 Image discussed in Example 13.6: (a) original image; (b) result of contrast stretching; (c) result of smoothing.

Observe that this operation can also be expressed by a sigmoid function (Appendix A).

The intensification operation INT requires selection of a suitable equilibrium point, b_c, of the conversion function to ensure that $\tilde{r}'_{ij} > \tilde{r}_{ij}$ for $\tilde{r}_{ij} > b_c$ and $\tilde{r}'_{ij} < \tilde{r}_{ij}$ for $\tilde{r}_{ij} < b_c$. By choosing a subinterval of $[0, b_{\max}]$ within which we want to apply the intensification operation, we can determine values of β and γ in the conversion function that satisfy this requirement. Assume, for example, that we want to apply the intensification operation within the subinterval $[x, x + 1]$ of $[0, b_{\max}]$. Then $b_c = x + 0.5$ and

$$\left(1 + \frac{31 - b_c}{\beta}\right)^{-\gamma} = 0.5.$$

Considering, for example, $x = 9$ and choosing $\gamma = 1$, we obtain

$$\left(1 + \frac{21.5}{\beta}\right)^{-1} = 0.5,$$

which yields $\beta = 21.5$. Similarly, choosing $\gamma = 2$, we obtain $\beta = 52$, and so on.

The intensification operator may be applied repeatedly. When it is applied twice to the image in Fig. 13.8a for $\beta = 43$ and $\gamma = 2$, we obtain the image in Fig. 13.8b.

The second operation on fuzzified images to be illustrated by this example is *smoothing*. The purpose of smoothing is to equalize the level of brightness of image points that are spatially close to each other. There are several known smoothing operations (or algorithms). One of them is based on averaging the brightness levels within neighbors. Assuming the use of the arithmetic average, the smoothing operation is defined by the formula

$$\tilde{r}''_{uv} = \frac{1}{4} \sum_{\langle i, j \rangle \in Q} \tilde{r}'_{ij} \tag{13.12}$$

for all $u \in \mathbb{N}_m$ and $v \in \mathbb{N}_n$, where $Q = \{\langle u, v + 1 \rangle, \langle u, v - 1 \rangle, \langle u + 1, v \rangle, \langle u - 1, v \rangle\}$ is the neighborhood of pixel $\langle u, v \rangle$. Applying this operation to the image in Fig. 13.8b, we obtain the smoother image in Fig. 13.8c.

Comparing the three images in Fig. 13.8, we can clearly see the effect of the two operations illustrated, contrast stretching (intensification) and smoothing (averaging). After the original image is processed by these two operations, it is undoubtedly more suitable for the subsequent pattern recognition and classification.

NOTES

13.1. Books by Bezdek [1981] and Kandel [1982] are classics in fuzzy pattern recognition. Both books also cover fuzzy clustering and various applications of fuzzy pattern recognition. Kandel's book contains a large bibliography (with 3,064 entries) of fuzzy set theory that focuses particularly on fuzzy pattern recognition. A more recent book on fuzzy pattern recognition [Pal and Majumder, 1986] has a broad coverage, including the use of fuzzy sets in image processing, fuzzy grammars and their use in syntactic pattern recognition, and numerous applications of the various types of pattern recognition problems. The role of fuzzy logic and neural networks in pattern recognition is also discussed in the book by Pao [1989].

13.2. A book edited by Bezdek and Pal [1992] is currently the main resource of information regarding the various aspects of fuzzy pattern recognition. It contains reprints of 51 key articles in this area, as well as thorough overviews of the whole area and four of its subareas: cluster analysis;

classifier design and feature analysis; image processing and machine vision; and fuzzy logic, neural networks and learning in pattern recognition. Each of these overviews contains a relevant bibliography.

EXERCISES

13.1. Describe differences between fuzzy pseudopartitions and regular fuzzy partitions resulting from fuzzy equivalence relations.

13.2. Repeat Example 13.1 (preferably by writing a computer program for the fuzzy c-means algorithm) for different initial fuzzy pseudopartitions; for example,

$$A_1 = .8/x_1 + \ldots + .8/x_8 + .2/x_9 + \ldots + .2/x_{15},$$
$$A_2 = .2/x_1 + \ldots + .2/x_8 + .8/x_9 + \ldots + .8/x_{15}.$$

13.3. Apply the fuzzy c-means algorithm to the data in Example 13.2 with $c = 2$ and $c = 3$.

13.4. Prove Theorem 13.1.

13.5. Apply the clustering method based on the transitive closure of fuzzy relation defined by (13.6) to the data in Example 13.1 for $q = 1, 2$.

14

FUZZY DATABASES AND
INFORMATION RETRIEVAL SYSTEMS

14.1 GENERAL DISCUSSION

Applications of fuzzy set theory and fuzzy logic within the field of computer science have been quite extensive, particularly in those endeavors concerned with the storage and manipulation of knowledge in a manner compatible with human thinking. This includes fuzzy databases, fuzzy information retrieval systems, and fuzzy expert systems. These three areas are not independent of one another. For example, each expert system contains a database as a subsystem. On the other hand, information retrieval may be handled by a specific database system.

The principal difference between expert systems and database systems is the capability of expert systems to make inferences. This capability is examined for fuzzy expert systems in Chapter 11. In this chapter, we focus on fuzzy database and information retrieval systems. Although information retrieval may be conceived in terms of a specific database system, the agendas of database systems and information retrieval systems are sufficiently different that it is preferable to discuss them as separate subjects.

The motivation for the application of fuzzy set theory to the design of databases and information storage and retrieval systems lies in the need to handle imprecise information. The database that can accommodate imprecise information can store and manipulate not only precise facts, but also subjective expert opinions, judgments, and values that can be specified in linguistic terms. This type of information can be quite useful when the database is to be used as a decision aid in areas such as medical diagnosis, employment, investment, and geological exploration, where "soft" subjective and imprecise data are not only common but quite valuable. In addition, it is also desirable to relieve the user of the constraint of having to formulate queries to the database in precise terms. Vague queries such as "Which employment candidates are highly educated and moderately experienced?", "Which industries are forecasted to experience significant growth by a substantial number of experts?" or "Which reasonably priced hotels are in close proximity to the city center?" often capture the relevant concerns of database users more accurately and easily than precise queries. It is important, however, that the database system which incorporates imprecision be able to appropriately propagate the level of uncertainty associated with the data to the level of uncertainty associated with answers or conclusions based on the data. Precise answers should not be generated from imprecise data.

The significance of fuzzy databases is well characterized by the following excerpt from a paper by Gaines [1979b]:

> The initial applications of computers were in the exact sciences and comparable commercial areas such as accountancy. Database theory and practice in developing from this, even though it allows for non-numerical data, still requires it to be precise and well-defined. As applications move out of the realms of the accountant and into the less quantitative areas of the firm so also does a requirement for high precision in specifying retrievals and updates of a database become increasingly unnatural. It is possible to argue that precision in itself is always a virtue—a reply to a request for a delivery data that says "soon" would be rated less satisfactory than one that says "in 3 days time"—the latter is more "businesslike".
>
> However, unwarranted precision can itself be highly misleading since actions may be taken based on it—"we will deliver 7 parcels each weighing 15.2 kilograms at the rear entrance of building 6A on 15th February at 0.03 p.m.", "we will deliver some heavy equipment to your site Saturday evening", and "see you with the goods over the weekend", may each refer to the same event but are clearly not interchangeable, i.e., each conveys an exact meaning that (presumably) properly represents what is to occur. If we prefer the precision of the first statement it is not for its own sake but because the tighter tolerances it implies on the actual situation allow us to plan ahead with greater accuracy and less use of resources. However, if the third statement really represents all that can be said it would be ridiculous to replace it with either of the previous ones. It would be equally ridiculous to say nothing, however, since even the least precise of the three statements does provide a basis for planning and action. A key aspect of executive action is planning under uncertainty and normal language provides a means for imprecision to be clearly and exactly expressed.
>
> In retrieving information from a database the requirement for artificial precision is at least irritating and at worst highly misleading, e.g. the request, "list the young salesmen who have a good selling record for household goods in the north of England", is perfectly comprehensible to a person. Translating it into, "list salesmen under 25 years old who have sold more than £20,000 of goods in the categories...to shops in the regions...", generates unnecessary work and makes no allowances for the whole spectrum of trade-offs possible, i.e., it will not list the chap of 26 who has made a real killing, or the one of 19 who sold £19,000, etc. The second request is more precise but the first represents far more accurately the actual *meaning* of the retrieval required.

One of the major concerns in the design of both fuzzy database and information retrieval systems is efficiency; these systems must be able to perform quickly enough to make interaction with human users feasible, despite large amounts of stored data with their degrees of membership. The implementation of these systems is thus strongly dependent on the availability of integrated circuits designed specifically to implement fuzzy logic (Sec. 16.5). In general, it is preferable to store fuzzy information in linguistic form and generate the implied membership functions as required or, alternatively, handle fuzzy information completely in its linguistic form.

14.2 FUZZY DATABASES

A database is a computer-based system the purpose of which is to store information regarding a set of entities and to provide users with the capability of organizing, manipulating, and retrieving the stored information as requested. Several models for representing information in databases have been proposed. One of these models, referred to as a *relational model*, has become predominant. Virtually all fuzzy databases described in the literature are conceived in terms of the relational model. To illustrate the issues involved in fuzzy databases, we describe one of several known approaches to fuzzy databases.

Buckles and Petry [1982, 1983] developed a model for a fuzzy relational database that contains, as a special case, the classical crisp model of a relational database. The model of a classical relational database consists of a set of multidimensional relations conceptualized as tables. The columns of these tables correspond to fields or attributes and are usually called domains. Each domain is defined on an appropriate domain base (or universal) set. The rows are elements of the relation; they correspond to records or entries, and are called tuples. Access to the database is accomplished through a relational algebra. This algebra consists of the procedural application of operations containing four basic elements: an operation name, the names of relations and the names of domains to be operated on, and an optional conditional expression. For instance, if our database contains a ternary relation STUDENT with domains NAME, ADDRESS, and MAJOR, we can obtain the names and addresses of all students whose major is computer science by constructing a new relation with domains NAME and ADDRESS as a projection of the original relation. The algebraic operation performing this task would be

Project (STUDENT: NAME, ADDRESS) where
MAJOR = "computer science."

The algebra also contains other relational operations, such as **Complement, Union, Intersection**, and **Join**, which perform the corresponding tasks on the relation and domains specified in order to produce the desired information.

The fuzzy relational database proposed by Buckles and Petry differs from this crisp model in two ways: first, elements of the tuples contained in the relations may be crisp subsets of the domain universal set, and second, a similarity relation is defined on each domain universal set. The first qualification allows the elements of tuples to consist of either singletons of the domain universal sets (as in the conventional relational database model) or crisp subsets of the domain universal sets, as in the relation MARKETS with the domains AREA, SIZE, and POTENTIAL represented by the table

RELATION: MARKETS		
AREA	**SIZE**	**POTENTIAL**
east	large	good
midwest	(large, medium)	(moderate, good)
south	small	(good, excellent)

Domain values that are not singletons may indicate, for instance, the merging of the opinions or judgments of several experts.

The second qualification is based on the assumption that in the classical database model, a crisp equivalence relation is defined on each domain universal set which groups together elements that are strictly equivalent. This equivalence is utilized, for example, when redundant tuples are to be eliminated or ignored. Most often, the equivalence classes generated by this relation are simply the singletons of the universal set. In the fuzzy database model, this equivalence relation is generalized to a fuzzy equivalence relation (or a similarity relation). This introduction of fuzziness provides an interesting element of flexibility, since the value or meaning structures of different individual database users may be reflected by modifying the domain equivalence relations appropriately. Moreover, as argued by Shenoi and Melton [1989, 1990], it is desirable to further generalize the model by allowing fuzzy compatibility (or proximity) relations in each domain rather than requiring fuzzy equivalence relations. By dropping transitivity, users of the fuzzy relational database are given more freedom to express their value structures.

The fuzzy relational algebra used to access this fuzzy database consists of the same four components as the conventional relational algebra and, in addition, allows for the specification of a threshold level defining the minimum acceptable degree of similarity between elements in some specified domain. In the special case of the conventional database, all threshold levels are implicitly assumed to be equal to 1, thus requiring strict equivalence for the merging or elimination of tuples. In the fuzzy database, tuples may be merged if they are considered sufficiently similar.

As an example of the use of this fuzzy database model and its associated fuzzy relational algebra, suppose our database contains the opinions of a group of experts on three policy options, $X, Y,$ and Z. Two relations are contained within the database: EXPERT, which has domains NAME and FIELD and associates the name and field of each expert; and ASSESSMENT, which has domains OPTION, NAME, and OPINION and associates the name of each expert with their expressed opinions on the policy options. These two relations are specified in Table 14.1. In addition, the following fuzzy compatibility relation is defined for the domain OPINION on the domain universal set (highly favorable (HF), favorable (F), slightly favorable (SF), slightly negative (SN), negative (N), and highly negative (HN)):

	HF	F	SF	SN	N	HN
HF	1	.8	.6	.2	0	0
F	.8	1	.8	.6	.2	0
SF	.6	.8	1	.8	.6	.2
SN	.2	.6	.8	1	.8	.6
N	0	.2	.6	.8	1	.8
HN	0	0	.2	.6	.8	1

Crisp equivalence relations in which equivalence classes are singletons are assumed to be defined on domains NAME, FIELD, and OPTION.

Suppose now that our query to this fuzzy database consists of the following question: "Which sociologists are in considerable agreement with Kass concerning policy option Y?" The first step is to retrieve the opinion of Kass concerning option Y. This is accomplished with the relational algebraic operation

TABLE 14.1   EXAMPLES OF RELATIONS IN RELATIONAL DATABASE

RELATION: EXPERT	
NAME	FIELD
Cohen	sociologist
Fadem	economist
Fee	attorney
Feldman	economist
Kass	physician
Osborn	sociologist
Schreiber	sociologist
Specterman	sociologist

RELATION: ASSESSMENT		
OPTION	NAME	OPINION
X	Osborn	favorable
X	Fee	negative
X	Fadem	slightly favorable
X	Feldman	highly favorable
Y	Cohen	slightly favorable
Y	Osborn	slightly favorable
Y	Fee	highly favorable
Y	Schreiber	favorable
Y	Kass	favorable
Y	Fadem	negative
Y	Specterman	highly favorable
Y	Feldman	slightly negative
Z	Osborn	negative
Z	Kass	slightly negative
Z	Fee	slightly favorable

(Project (Select ASSESSMENT where NAME = Kass and
OPTION = Y) over OPINION) giving R1.

The resulting temporary relation R1 on domain OPINION is given by

RELATION: R1
OPINION
favorable

The next step involves the selection of all sociologists from the table of experts. This is accomplished by the operation

(Project (Select EXPERT where FIELD = Sociologists)
over NAME) giving R2.

Here, R2 is a temporary relation on domain NAME listing only sociologists. It is equal to

RELATION: R2
NAME
Cohen
Osborn
Schreiber
Specterman

Next, temporary relation R3 must be constructed on domains NAME and OPINION, which lists the opinions of the sociologists in R2 about option Y. The algebraic expression accomplishing this is

(Project (Select (Join R2 and ASSESSMENT over NAME)
where OPTION = Y) over NAME, OPINION) giving R3.

The relation R3 that is produced is given by

RELATION: R3	
NAME	OPINION
Cohen	slightly negative
Osborn	slightly favorable
Schreiber	favorable
Specterman	highly favorable

Finally, we perform a join of relations R1 (giving the opinion of Kass) and R3 (giving the opinion of the sociologists) that specifies a threshold similarity level of .75 on the domain OPINION, which is chosen for this example to represent the condition of "considerable" agreement. The algebraic expression for this task is

(Join R3 and R1 over OPINION) with
THRES(OPINION) $\geq$ .75, and THRES(NAME) $\geq$ 0.

The specification of a zero similarity threshold level for NAME is necessary to allow the merging of names into sets, as shown in the result given by

NAME	OPINION
(Osborn, Schreiber, Specterman)	(slightly favorable, favorable, highly favorable)

Note that the response which results is less than precise and contains less information than a response of

NAME	OPINION
Osborn	slightly favorable
Schreiber	favorable
Specterman	highly favorable

In this way, the uncertainty contained in the specification of "considerable agreement" and in the similarity defined over the possible opinions is propagated to the response given.

The illustrated fuzzy database model developed by Buckles and Petry [1982, 1983] introduces fuzziness only by means of fuzzy equivalence relations or, more generally, fuzzy compatibility relations on individual domain universal sets. Fuzziness in data is not addressed by this model. However, other fuzzy database models have been proposed in which attribute values may be expressed in vague linguistic terms (Note 14.2).

14.3 FUZZY INFORMATION RETRIEVAL

Information retrieval may be defined, in general, as the problem of the selection of documentary information from storage in response to search questions. Each search question is a statement, in words or other symbols, which expresses the subject of interest of the inquirer. It is assumed that the subject of each document in the storage is characterized by a set of key words or other symbols. The problem of information retrieval is to match the words or other symbols of the inquiry with those characterizing the individual documents and make appropriate selections. The aim is to select, at minimal cost, documents that are of maximum relevance to the inquirer.

The term *fuzzy information retrieval* refers to methods of information retrieval that are based upon the theory of fuzzy sets. These methods are increasingly recognized as more realistic than the various classical methods of information retrieval. Among publications dealing with fuzzy information retrieval, as reviewed in Note 14.4, the only comprehensive treatment of this subject is covered in a monograph by Miyamoto [1990].

Our aim in this section is to characterize the role of fuzzy set theory in dealing with the problem of information retrieval. We do not attempt to describe specific methods of fuzzy information retrieval. Readers interested in this subject should consult the above-mentioned monograph.

The problem of information retrieval involves two finite crisp sets, a set of *recognized index terms*,

$$X = \{x_1, x_2, \ldots, x_n\},$$

and a set of *relevant documents*,

$$Y = \{y_1, y_2, \ldots, y_n\}.$$

Although these sets change whenever new documents are added to systems or new index terms are recognized (or, possibly, when some documents or index terms are discarded), they are fixed for each particular inquiry.

In fuzzy information retrieval, the relevance of index terms to individual documents is expressed by a fuzzy relation,

$$R : X \times Y \to [0, 1],$$

such that the membership value $R(x_i, y_i)$ specifies for each $x_i \in X$ and each $y_j \in Y$ the *grade of relevance* of index term x_i to document y_j. These grades are determined either subjectively, by authors of the documents, or objectively, by some algorithmic procedure. One way of determining the grades objectively is to define them in an appropriate way in terms of the numbers of occurrences of individual index terms in titles and/or abstracts of the documents involved. This can be combined with other criteria. One possible criterion is to discount the grade of relevance involving old documents or old index terms by some rate. Other possible criteria in defining the grades of relevance are to discriminate among different types of documents (journal articles, papers in conference proceedings, unpublished reports, etc.), to rank relevant journals, and so on. These and other criteria may be specified by the user.

Another important relation in fuzzy information retrieval is called a *fuzzy thesaurus*. This is a reflexive fuzzy relation, T, defined on X^2. For each pair of index terms $\langle x_i, x_k \rangle \in X^2$, $T(x_i, x_k)$ expresses the degree of association of x_i with x_k; that is, the degree to which the meaning of index term x_k is compatible with the meaning of the given index term x_i. The role of this relation is to deal with the problem of synonyms among index terms. The relation helps to identify relevant documents for a given inquiry that otherwise would not be identified. This happens whenever a document is characterized by an index term that is synonymous with an index term contained in the inquiry.

Various methods have been developed for constructing fuzzy thesauri. For example, experts in a given field of study are asked to identify, in a given set of index terms, pairs whose meanings they consider associated (or, possibly, to give degrees of association for each pair). Grades of membership in T are then determined by averaging the scores for each pair. Another way of obtaining these grades is to use statistical data obtained from the documents or such as frequencies of occurrence of pairs of index terms in the same document or frequencies of associations based on citations. When a fuzzy thesaurus is updated by introducing new index terms, old index terms are usually discounted at some rate.

In fuzzy information retrieval, an inquiry can be expressed by any fuzzy set defined on the set of index terms X. Let A denote the fuzzy set representing a particular inquiry. Then, by composing A with the fuzzy thesaurus T, we obtain a new fuzzy set on X (say, set B), which represents an *augmented inquiry* (i.e., augmented by associated index terms). That is,

$$A \circ T = B, \tag{14.1}$$

where $\circ$ is usually understood to be the max-min composition, so that

$$B(x_j) = \max_{x_i \in X} \min[A(x_i), T(x_i, x_j)]$$

for all $x_j \in X$. The retrieved documents, expressed by a fuzzy set D defined on Y, are then obtained by composing the augmented inquiry, expressed by fuzzy set B, with the relevance relation R. That is,

$$B \circ R = D. \tag{14.2}$$

Thus (14.1) and (14.2) represent the process of fuzzy information retrieval.

To illustrate this process, let us consider a very simple example, in which the inquiry involves only the following three index terms:

$x_1 = $ *fuzzy logic*,
$x_2 = $ *fuzzy relation equations*,
$x_3 = $ *fuzzy modus ponens*.

That is, $^{0+}A = \{x_1, x_2, x_3\}$ is the support of fuzzy set A expressing the inquiry. Assume that the vector representation of A is

$$\begin{array}{ccc} x_1 & x_2 & x_3 \end{array}$$
$$A = \begin{bmatrix} 1 & .4 & .1 \end{bmatrix}.$$

Assume further that the relevant part of fuzzy thesaurus (restricted to the support of A and nonzero columns) is given by the matrix

$$T = \begin{array}{c} \\ x_1 \\ x_2 \\ x_3 \end{array} \begin{array}{cc} \begin{array}{cccccc} x_1 & x_2 & x_3 & x_4 & x_5 & x_6 \end{array} \\ \left[\begin{array}{cccccc} 1 & .2 & 1 & 1 & .5 & 1 \\ .2 & 1 & .1 & .7 & .9 & 0 \\ 1 & .4 & 1 & .9 & .3 & 1 \end{array} \right], \end{array}$$

where

$x_4 =$ *approximate reasoning,*
$x_5 =$ *max-min composition,*
$x_6 =$ *fuzzy implication.*

Then, by (14.1), the composition $A \circ T$ results in fuzzy set B, which represents the augmented inquiry; its vector form is

$$B = \begin{array}{c} \begin{array}{cccccc} x_1 & x_2 & x_3 & x_4 & x_5 & x_6 \end{array} \\ \left[\begin{array}{cccccc} 1 & .4 & 1 & 1 & .5 & 1 \end{array} \right]. \end{array}$$

Assume now that the relevant part of the relevance relation (restricted to the support of B and nonzero columns) is given by the matrix

$$R = \begin{array}{c} \\ x_1 \\ x_2 \\ x_3 \\ x_4 \\ x_5 \\ x_6 \end{array} \begin{array}{c} \begin{array}{cccccccccc} y_1 & y_2 & y_3 & y_4 & y_5 & y_6 & y_7 & y_8 & y_9 & y_{10} \end{array} \\ \left[\begin{array}{cccccccccc} .2 & 0 & 1 & 0 & 0 & 0 & 1 & 0 & 0 & 0 \\ 1 & 0 & 0 & .3 & 0 & .4 & 0 & 0 & 1 & 0 \\ 0 & 0 & .8 & 0 & .4 & 0 & 1 & 0 & 0 & 0 \\ 0 & 1 & 0 & 0 & 0 & 0 & 0 & .9 & .7 & .5 \\ 1 & 0 & .5 & 0 & 0 & .6 & 0 & 0 & 0 & 0 \\ 0 & 1 & 0 & 0 & .2 & 0 & 1 & 0 & 0 & .5 \end{array} \right] \end{array}$$

where $y_1, y_2, \ldots, y_{10}$ are the only documents related to index terms $x_1, x_2, \ldots, x_6$. By (14.2), the composition $B \circ R$ results in fuzzy set D, which characterizes the retrieved documents; its vector form is

$$D = \begin{array}{c} \begin{array}{cccccccccc} y_1 & y_2 & y_3 & y_4 & y_5 & y_6 & y_7 & y_8 & y_9 & y_{10} \end{array} \\ \left[\begin{array}{cccccccccc} .5 & 1 & 1 & .3 & .4 & .5 & 1 & .9 & .7 & .5 \end{array} \right]. \end{array}$$

The user can now decide whether to inspect all documents captured by the support of D or to consider only documents captured by some α-cut of D.

The use of fuzzy set theory in information retrieval has at least the following advantages in comparison with classical methods: fuzzy relevance relations and fuzzy thesauri are more expressive than their crisp counterparts, and their construction is more realistic; the fuzzy set characterizing the retrieved documents establishes, by its α-cuts, layers of retrieved documents distinguished by their relevance (the value of α) and thus provide the user with a guideline regarding the order in which the documents should be inspected or which documents to neglect when the total number of retrieved documents is too large; and fuzzy inquiry provides the user with greater flexibility in expressing the subject area of interest.

The reader should be aware that our presentation of fuzzy information retrieval in this section is rather restricted. We ignore some important issues, such as the effect of the type of composition in (14.1) and (14.2) on the performance, the role of citations, or aspects of information retrieval with feedback. We also do not discuss the important role of fuzzy clustering (Sec. 13.2) in information retrieval, which is well covered by Miyamoto [1990].

NOTES

14.1. For background regarding classical relational database systems, we recommend the book *Principles of Database Systems* by J.D. Ullman (Computer Science Press, 1980).

14.2. In addition to the fuzzy database model developed by Buckles and Petry [1982, 1983] and generalized by Shenoi and Melton [1989, 1990], as described in Sec. 14.2, three alternative models were developed by Umano [1982], Prade and Testemale [1984], and Zemankova and Kandel [1985]. In each of these models, attribute values may be expressed in linguistic terms, which are represented by appropriate possibility distributions. The models differ in methods of data manipulation and retrieval. An attempt to develop a framework under which all these models can be integrated was made by Medina *et al.* [1994].

14.3. Research regarding theoretical issues pertaining to the design of fuzzy relational databases (fuzzy functional dependencies, fuzzy lossless join decompositions, etc.) has been pursued since the late 1980s by Raju and Majumdar [1987, 1988], Tripathy and Saxena [1990], and Shenoi, Melton, and Fan [1992]. An overview of these issues and other aspects of fuzzy relational databases is covered in a book by Li and Liu [1990], whose focus is on the use of fuzzy Prolog and a fuzzy relational query language, FSQL.

14.4. The principal source of information about fuzzy information retrieval is the previously mentioned book by Miyamoto [1990]. Various issues of fuzzy information retrieval have been investigated since the early 1970s by numerous authors, including Negoita [1973], Negoita and Flondor [1976], Radecki [1981, 1983], Kohout *et al.* [1984], Zenner *et al.* [1985], Bezdek *et al.* [1986], Boy and Kuss [1986], Tong [1986], Murai *et al.* [1988, 1989], López de Mántaras *et al.* [1990], Nomoto *et al.* [1990], Larsen and Yager [1990, 1993], and Ogawa *et al.* [1991].

EXERCISES

14.1. Repeat the example discussed in Sec. 14.2 with the following questions:

    (a) Which sociologists or economists are in considerable agreement with Feldman concerning option Y?"

    (b) "Which experts who are not sociologists are somewhat in agreement with Fee regarding option X?" (Assume that a threshold similarity of 0.5 represents the condition of "somewhat in agreement.")

    (c) "Which sociologists are in considerable agreement with any economists concerning option Y?"

14.2. Repeat the example discussed in Sec. 14.3 for the fuzzy inquiry

$$A = 1/x_1 + .7/x_2,$$

where $x_1 =$ fuzzy information retrieval and $x_2 =$ fuzzy databases. Assume that the relevant part of a fuzzy thesaurus is given by the matrix

$$
\mathbf{T} = \begin{array}{c} \\ x_1 \\ x_2 \end{array} \begin{array}{c} \begin{array}{cccccc} x_1 & x_2 & x_3 & x_4 & x_5 & x_6 \end{array} \\ \left[\begin{array}{cccccc} 1 & .7 & .8 & 1 & 1 & .3 \\ .7 & 1 & 0 & 0 & 1 & .9 \end{array} \right], \end{array}
$$

where $x_3 =$ fuzzy clustering, $x_4 =$ fuzzy thesaurus, $x_5 =$ fuzzy inquiry, and $x_6 =$ fuzzy relations. Assuming that the relevance relation R is the same as in Sec. 14.3, calculate the fuzzy set D that characterizes the retrieved documents.

15

FUZZY DECISION MAKING

15.1 GENERAL DISCUSSION

Making decisions is undoubtedly one of the most fundamental activities of human beings. We all are faced in our daily life with varieties of alternative actions available to us and, at least in some instances, we have to decide which of the available actions to take. The beginnings of decision making, as a subject of study, can be traced, presumably, to the late 18th century, when various studies were made in France regarding methods of election and social choice. Since these initial studies, decision making has evolved into a respectable and rich field of study. The current literature on decision making, based largely on theories and methods developed in this century, is enormous.

The subject of decision making is, as the name suggests, the study of how decisions are actually made and how they can be made better or more successfully. That is, the field is concerned, in general, with both descriptive theories and normative theories. Much of the focus in developing the field has been in the area of management, in which the decision-making process is of key importance for functions such as inventory control, investment, personnel actions, new-product development, and allocation of resources, as well as many others. Decision making itself, however, is broadly defined to include any choice or selection of alternatives, and is therefore of importance in many fields in both the "soft" social sciences and the "hard" disciplines of natural sciences and engineering.

Applications of fuzzy sets within the field of decision making have, for the most part, consisted of fuzzifications of the classical theories of decision making. While decision making under conditions of risk have been modeled by probabilistic decision theories and game theories, fuzzy decision theories attempt to deal with the vagueness and nonspecificity inherent in human formulation of preferences, constraints, and goals. In this chapter, we overview the applicability of fuzzy set theory to the main classes of decision-making problems.

Classical decision making generally deals with a set of alternative states of nature (outcomes, results), a set of alternative actions that are available to the decision maker, a relation indicating the state or outcome to be expected from each alternative action, and, finally, a utility or objective function, which orders the outcomes according to their desirability. A decision is said to be made under conditions of *certainty* when the outcome for each action can be determined and ordered precisely. In this case, the alternative that leads to the outcome yielding the highest utility is chosen. That is, the decision-making problem becomes an optimization problem, the problem of maximizing the utility function. A decision is made under conditions of *risk*, on the other hand, when the only available knowledge concerning the outcomes consists of their conditional probability distributions, one for each action. In this case, the decision-making problem becomes an optimization problem of maximizing the expected utility. When probabilities of the outcomes are not known, or may not even be relevant, and outcomes for each action are characterized only approximately, we say that decisions are made under *uncertainty*. This is the prime domain for fuzzy decision making.

Decision making under uncertainty is perhaps the most important category of decision-making problems, as well characterized by the British economist Shackle [1961]:

> In a predestinate world, decision would be *illusory*; in a world of perfect foreknowledge, *empty*; in a world without natural order, *powerless*. Our intuitive attitude to life implies non-illusory, non-empty, non-powerless decision. . . Since decision in this sense excludes both perfect foresight and anarchy in nature, it must be defined as choice in face of bounded uncertainty.

This indicates the importance of fuzzy set theory in decision making.

Several classes of decision-making problems are usually recognized. According to one criterion, decision problems are classified as those involving a single decision maker and those which involve several decision makers. These problem classes are referred to as *individual decision making* and *multiperson decision making*, respectively. According to another criterion, we distinguish decision problems that involve a *simple optimization* of a utility function, an *optimization under constraints*, or an *optimization under multiple objective criteria*. Furthermore, decision making can be done in *one stage*, or it can be done iteratively, in *several stages*. This chapter is structured, by and large, according to these classifications.

We do not attempt to cover fuzzy decision making comprehensively. This would require a large book fully specialized on this subject. Instead, we want to convey the spirit of fuzzy decision making, as applied to the various classes of decision problems.

15.2   INDIVIDUAL DECISION MAKING

Fuzziness can be introduced into the existing models of decision models in various ways. In the first paper on fuzzy decision making, Bellman and Zadeh [1970] suggest a fuzzy model of decision making in which relevant goals and constraints are expressed in terms of fuzzy sets, and a decision is determined by an appropriate aggregation of these fuzzy sets. A decision situation in this model is characterized by the following components:

- a set A of *possible actions*;
- a set of *goals* $G_i (i \in \mathbb{N}_n)$, each of which is expressed in terms of a fuzzy set defined on A;
- a set of *constraints* $C_j (j \in \mathbb{N}_m)$, each of which is also expressed by a fuzzy set defined on A.

It is common that the fuzzy sets expressing goals and constraints in this formulation are not defined directly on the set of actions, but indirectly, through other sets that characterize relevant states of nature. Let G_i' and C_j' be fuzzy sets defined on sets X_i and Y_j, respectively, where $i \in \mathbb{N}_n$ and $j \in \mathbb{N}_m$. Assume that these fuzzy sets represent goals and constraints expressed by the decision maker. Then, for each $i \in \mathbb{N}_n$ and each $j \in \mathbb{N}_m$, we describe the meanings of actions in set A in terms of sets X_i and Y_j by functions

$$g_i : A \to X_i,$$

$$c_j : A \to Y_j,$$

and express goals G_i and constraints C_j by the compositions of g_i with G_i' and the compositions of c_j and C_j'; that is,

$$G_i(a) = G_i'(g_i(a)), \tag{15.1}$$

$$C_j(a) = C_j'(c_j(a)) \tag{15.2}$$

for each $a \in A$.

Given a decision situation characterized by fuzzy sets A, $G_i(i \in \mathbb{N}_n)$, and $C_j(j \in \mathbb{N}_m)$, a *fuzzy decision*, D, is conceived as a fuzzy set on A that simultaneously satisfies the given goals G_i and constraints C_j. That is,

$$D(a) = \min[\inf_{i \in \mathbb{N}_n} G_i(a), \inf_{j \in \mathbb{N}_m} C_j(a)] \tag{15.3}$$

for all $a \in A$, provided that the standard operator of fuzzy intersection is employed.

Once a fuzzy decision has been arrived at, it may be necessary to choose the "best" single crisp alternative from this fuzzy set. This may be accomplished in a straightforward manner by choosing an alternative $\hat{a} \in A$ that attains the maximum membership grade in D. Since this method ignores information concerning any of the other alternatives, it may not be desirable in all situations. When A is defined on $\mathbb{R}$, it is preferable to determine $\hat{a}$ by an appropriate defuzzification method (Sec. 12.2).

Before discussing the various features of this fuzzy decision model and its possible modifications or extensions, let us illustrate how it works by two simple examples.

Example 15.1

Suppose that an individual needs to decide which of four possible jobs, a_1, a_2, a_3, a_4, to choose. His or her goal is to choose a job that offers a high salary under the constraints that the job is interesting and within close driving distance. In this case, $A = \{a_1, a_2, a_3, a_4\}$, and the fuzzy sets involved represent the concepts of *high salary*, *interesting job*, and *close driving distance*. These concepts are highly subjective and context-dependent, and must be defined by the individual in a given context. The goal is expressed in monetary terms, independent of the jobs available. Hence, according to our notation, we denote the fuzzy set expressing the goal by G'. A possible definition of G' is given in Fig. 15.1a, where we assume, for convenience, that the underlying universal set is $\mathbb{R}^+$. To express the goal in terms of set A, we need a function g: $A \to \mathbb{R}^+$, which assigns to each job the respective salary. Assume the following assignments:

$$g(a_1) = \$40,000,$$
$$g(a_2) = \$45,000,$$
$$g(a_3) = \$50,000,$$
$$g(a_4) = \$60,000.$$

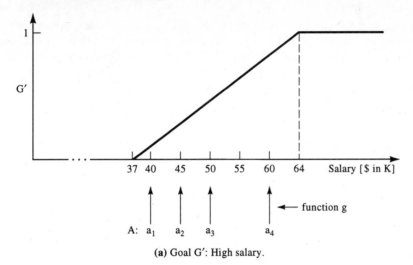

(a) Goal G': High salary.

(b) Constraint C_2': Close driving distance.

Figure 15.1   Fuzzy goal and constraint (Example 15.1): (a) goal G': high salary; (b) constraint C_2': close driving distance.

This assignment is also shown in Fig. 15.1a. Composing now functions g and G', according to (15.1), we obtain the fuzzy set

$$G = .11/a_1 + .3/a_2 + .48/a_3 + .8/a_4,$$

which expresses the goal in terms of the available jobs in set A.

The first constraint, requiring that the job be interesting, is expressed directly in terms of set A (i.e., c_1, in (15.2) is the identity function and $C_1 = C_1'$). Assume that the individual assigns to the four jobs in A the following membership grades in the fuzzy set of interesting jobs:

$$C_1 = .4/a_1 + .6/a_2 + .2/a_3 + .2/a_4.$$

The second constraint, requiring that the driving distance be close, is expressed in terms of the driving distance from home to work. Following our notation, we denote the fuzzy set expressing this constraint by C_2'. A possible definition of C_2' is given in Fig. 15.1b, where distances of the four jobs are also shown. Specifically,

$$c_2(a_1) = 27 \text{ miles,}$$

$$c_2(a_2) = 7.5 \text{ miles,}$$

$$c_2(a_3) = 12 \text{ miles,}$$

$$c_2(a_4) = 2.5 \text{ miles.}$$

By composing functions c_2 and C_2', according to (15.2), we obtain the fuzzy set

$$C_2 = .1/a_1 + .9/a_2 + .7/a_3 + 1/a_4,$$

which expresses the constraint in terms of the set A.

Applying now formula (15.3), we obtain the fuzzy set

$$D = .1/a_1 + .3/a_2 + .2/a_3 + .2/a_4,$$

which represents a fuzzy characterization of the concept of *desirable job*. The job to be chosen is $\hat{a} = a_2$; this is the most desirable job among the four available jobs under the given goal G and constraints C_1, C_2, provided that we aggregate the goal and constraints as expressed by (15.3).

Example 15.2

In this very simple example, adopted from Zimmermann [1987], we illustrate a case in which A is not a discrete set. The board of directors of a company needs to determine the optimal dividend to be paid to the shareholders. For financial reasons, the dividend should be *attractive* (goal G); for reasons of wage negotiations, it should be *modest* (constraint C). The set of actions, A, is the set of possible dividends, assumed here to be the interval $[0, a_{max}]$ of real numbers, where a_{max} denotes the largest acceptable dividend. The goal as well as the constraint are expressed directly as fuzzy sets on $A = [0, a_{max}]$. A possible scenario is shown in Fig. 15.2, which is self-explanatory.

The described fuzzy decision model allows the decision maker to frame the goals and constraints in vague, linguistic terms, which may more accurately reflect practical problem solving situations. The membership functions of fuzzy goals in this model serve much the same purpose as utility or objective functions in classical decision making that order the outcomes according to preferability. Unlike the classical theory of decision making under constraints, however, the symmetry between the goals and constraints under this fuzzy model allows them to be treated in exactly the same manner.

Formula (15.3), based upon the standard operator of fuzzy intersection, does not allow, however, for any interdependence, interaction, or trade-off between the goals and constraints under consideration. For many decision applications, this lack of compensation may not be appropriate; the full compensation or trade-off offered by the union operation that corresponds to the logical "or" (the max operator) may be inappropriate as well. Therefore, an alternative fuzzy set intersection or an averaging operator may be used to reflect a situation in which some degree of positive compensation exists among the goals and constraints.

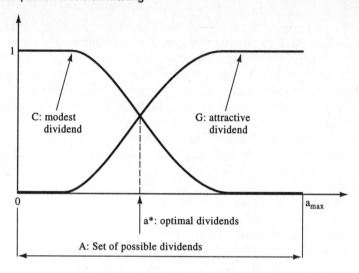

Figure 15.2   Illustration to Example 15.2.

This fuzzy model can be further extended to accommodate the relative importance of the various goals and constraints by the use of weighting coefficients. In this case, the fuzzy decision D can be arrived at by a convex combination of the n weighted goals and m weighted constraints of the form

$$D(a) = \sum_{i=1}^{n} u_i G_i(a) + \sum_{j=1}^{m} v_j C_j(a) \tag{15.4}$$

for all $a \in A$, where u_i and v_j are non-negative weights attached to each fuzzy goal $G_i (i \in \mathbb{N}_n)$ and each fuzzy constraint $C_j (j \in \mathbb{N}_m)$, respectively, such that

$$\sum_{i=1}^{n} u_i + \sum_{j=1}^{m} v_j = 1.$$

However, a direct extension of formula (15.3) may be used as well; that is,

$$D(a) = \min[\inf_{i \in \mathbb{N}_n} G_i^{u_i}(a), \inf_{j \in \mathbb{N}_m} C_j^{v_j}(a)], \tag{15.5}$$

where the weights u_i and v_j possess the above-specified properties.

15.3 MULTIPERSON DECISION MAKING

When decisions made by more than one person are modeled, two differences from the case of a single decision maker can be considered: first, the goals of the individual decision makers may differ such that each places a different ordering on the alternatives; second, the individual decision makers may have access to different information upon which to base their decision. Theories known as n-person game theories deal with both of these considerations, team theories of decision making deal only with the second, and group-decision theories deal only with the first.

A fuzzy model group decision was proposed by Blin [1974] and Blin and Whinston [1973]. Here, each member of a group of n individual decision makers is assumed to have a reflexive, antisymmetric, and transitive preference ordering $\mathbf{P}_k, k \in \mathbb{N}_n$, which totally or partially orders a set X of alternatives. A "social choice" function must then be found which, given the individual preference orderings, produces the most acceptable overall group preference ordering. Basically, this model allows for the individual decision makers to possess different aims and values while still assuming that the overall purpose is to reach a common, acceptable decision. In order to deal with the multiplicity of opinion evidenced in the group, the social preference S may be defined as a fuzzy binary relation with membership grade function

$$S : X \times X \rightarrow [0, 1],$$

which assigns the membership grade $S(x_i, x_j)$, indicating the degree of group preference of alternative x_i over x_j. The expression of this group preference requires some appropriate means of aggregating the individual preferences. One simple method computes the relative popularity of alternative x_i over x_j by dividing the number of persons preferring x_i to x_j, denoted by $N(x_i, x_j)$, by the total number of decision makers, n. This scheme corresponds to the simple majority vote. Thus,

$$S(x_i, x_j) = \frac{N(x_i, x_j)}{n}. \tag{15.6}$$

Other methods of aggregating the individual preferences may be used to accommodate different degrees of influence exercised by the individuals in the group. For instance, a dictatorial situation can be modeled by the group preference relation S for which

$$S(x_i, x_j) = \begin{cases} 1 & \text{if } x_i \overset{k}{>} x_j \text{ for some individual } k \\ 0 & \text{otherwise,} \end{cases}$$

where $\overset{k}{>}$ represents the preference ordering of the one individual k who exercises complete control over the group decision.

Once the fuzzy relationship S has been defined, the final nonfuzzy group preference can be determined by converting S into its resolution form

$$S = \bigcup_{\alpha \in [0,1]} \alpha^{\alpha}S,$$

which is the union of the crisp relations $^{\alpha}S$ comprising the α-cuts of the fuzzy relation S, each scaled by α. Each value α essentially represents the level of agreement between the individuals concerning the particular crisp ordering $^{\alpha}S$. One procedure that maximizes the final agreement level consists of intersecting the classes of crisp total orderings that are compatible with the pairs in the α-cuts $^{\alpha}S$ for increasingly smaller values of α until a single crisp total ordering is achieved. In this process, any pairs $\langle x_i, x_j \rangle$ that lead to an intransitivity are removed. The largest value α for which the unique compatible ordering on $X \times X$ is found represents the maximized agreement level of the group, and the crisp ordering itself represents the group decision. This procedure is illustrated in the following example.

Example 15.3

Assume that each individual of a group of eight decision makers has a total preference ordering $\mathbf{P}_i (i \in \mathbb{N}_8)$ on a set of alternatives $X = \{w, x, y, z\}$ as follows:

$$P_1 = \langle w, x, y, z \rangle$$

$$P_2 = P_5 = \langle z, y, x, w \rangle$$

$$P_3 = P_7 = \langle x, w, y, z \rangle$$

$$P_4 = P_8 = \langle w, z, x, y \rangle$$

$$P_6 = \langle z, w, x, y \rangle$$

Using the membership function given in (15.6) for the fuzzy group preference ordering relation S (where $n = 8$), we arrive at the following fuzzy social preference relation:

$$\mathbf{S} = \begin{array}{c} \\ w \\ x \\ y \\ z \end{array} \begin{array}{cccc} w & x & y & z \\ \left[\begin{array}{cccc} 0 & .5 & .75 & .625 \\ .5 & 0 & .75 & .375 \\ .25 & .25 & 0 & .375 \\ .375 & .625 & .625 & 0 \end{array} \right] \end{array}$$

The α-cuts of this fuzzy relation S are:

$${}^{1}S = \varnothing$$

$${}^{.75}S = \{\langle w, y \rangle, \langle x, y \rangle\}$$

$${}^{.625}S = \{\langle w, z \rangle, \langle z, x \rangle, \langle z, y \rangle, \langle w, y \rangle, \langle x, y \rangle\}$$

$${}^{.5}S = \{\langle x, w \rangle, \langle w, x \rangle, \langle w, z \rangle, \langle z, x \rangle, \langle z, y \rangle, \langle w, y \rangle, \langle x, y \rangle\}$$

$${}^{.375}S = \{\langle z, w \rangle, \langle x, z \rangle, \langle y, z \rangle, \langle x, w \rangle, \langle w, x \rangle, \langle w, z \rangle, \langle z, x \rangle, \langle z, y \rangle, \langle w, y \rangle, \langle x, y \rangle\}$$

$${}^{.25}S = \{\langle y, w \rangle, \langle y, x \rangle, \langle z, w \rangle, \langle x, z \rangle, \langle y, z \rangle, \langle x, w \rangle, \langle w, x \rangle, \langle w, z \rangle, \langle z, x \rangle, \langle z, y \rangle, \langle w, y \rangle, \langle x, y \rangle\}$$

We can now apply the procedure to arrive at the unique crisp ordering that constitutes the group choice. All total orderings on $X \times X$ are, of course, compatible with the empty set of ${}^{1}S$. The total orderings ${}^{.75}O$ that are compatible with the pairs in the crisp relations ${}^{.75}S$ are

$${}^{.75}O = \{\langle z, w, x, y \rangle, \langle w, x, y, z \rangle, \langle w, z, x, y \rangle, \langle w, x, z, y \rangle,$$

$$\langle z, x, w, y \rangle, \langle x, w, y, z \rangle, \langle x, z, w, y \rangle, \langle x, w, z, y \rangle\}.$$

Thus,

$${}^{1}O \cap {}^{.75}O = {}^{.75}O.$$

The orderings compatible with ${}^{.625}S$ are

$${}^{.625}O = \{\langle w, z, x, y \rangle, \langle w, z, y, x \rangle\}$$

and

$${}^{1}O \cap {}^{.75}O \cap {}^{.625}O = \{\langle w, z, x, y \rangle\}.$$

Thus, the value .625 represents the group level of agreement concerning the social choice denoted by the total ordering $\langle w, z, x, y \rangle$.

In the described procedure of group decision making, it is required that each group member can order the given set of alternatives. This requirement may be too strong in some cases. However, it is relatively easy for each individual to make pairwise comparisons between the given alternatives. A simple method proposed by Shimura [1973] is designed to construct an ordering of all given alternatives on the basis of their pairwise comparisons. In this method, $f(x_i, x_j)$, denotes the attractiveness grade given by the individual to x_i with respect to x_j. These primitive evaluations, which are expressed by positive numbers in a given range, are made by the individual for all pairs of alternatives in the given set X. They are then converted to relative preference grades, $F(x_i, x_j)$, by the formula

$$F(x_i, x_j) = \frac{f(x_i, x_j)}{\max[f(x_i, x_j), f(x_j, x_i)]}$$

$$= \min[1, f(x_i, x_j)/f(x_j, x_i)] \tag{15.7}$$

for each pair $\langle x_i, x_j \rangle \in X^2$. Clearly, $F(x_i, x_j) \in [0, 1]$ for all pairs $\langle x_i, x_j \rangle \in X^2$. When $F(x_i, x_j) = 1$, x_i is considered at least as attractive as x_j. Function F, which may be viewed as a membership function of a fuzzy relation on X, has for each pair $\langle x_i, y_j \rangle \in X^2$ the property

$$\max[F(x_i, x_j), F(x_j, x_i)] = 1.$$

The property means: for each pair of alternatives, at least one must be as attractive as the other.

For each $x_i \in X$, we can now calculate the overall relative preference grades, $p(x_i)$, of x_i with respect to all other alternatives in X by the formula

$$p(x_i) = \min_{x_j \in X} F(x_i, x_j). \tag{15.8}$$

The preference ordering of alternatives in X is then induced by the numerical ordering of these grades $p(x_i)$.

Example 15.4

To illustrate the described method, consider a group of people involved in a business partnership who intend to buy a common car for business purposes. To decide what car to buy is a multiperson decision problem. The method described in this section can be used, but each person in the group has to order the available alternatives first. To do that, the method based on the degrees of attractiveness can be used.

Assume, for the sake of simplicity, that only five car models are considered: Acclaim, Accord, Camry, Cutlass, and Sable. Assume further that, using the numbers suggested in Table 15.1a for specifying the attractiveness grades, the evaluation prepared by one person in the group is given in Table 15.1b. The corresponding relative preference grades (calculated by (15.7)) and the overall relative preference grades (calculated by (15.8)) are given in Table 15.1c. The latter induce the following preference ordering of the car models: Camry, Sable, Accord, Cutlass, Acclaim. Orderings expressing preference by the other members of the group can be determined in a similar way. Then, the method for multiperson decision making described in this section can be applied to these preference orderings to obtain a group decision.

TABLE 15.1   ILLUSTRATION TO EXAMPLE 15.4

(a) Suggested numbers for attractiveness grading

$f(x_i, x_j)$	Attractiveness of x_i with respect to x_j
1	Little attractive
3	Moderately attractive
5	Strongly attractive
7	Very strongly attractive
9	Extremely attractive
2, 4, 6, 8	Intermediate values between levels

(b) Given attractiveness grades

$f(x_i, x_j)$	Acclaim	Accord	Camry	Cutlass	Sable
Acclaim	1	7	9	3	8
Accord	3	1	3	2	4
Camry	1	1	1	3	5
Cutlass	2	7	7	1	7
Sable	2	6	8	3	1

(c) Relative preference grades and overall relative preference grades

$F(x_i, x_j)$	Acclaim	Accord	Camry	Cutlass	Sable	$p(x_i)$
Acclaim	1	0.43	0.11	0.67	0.25	0.11
Accord	1	1.00	0.33	1.00	1.00	0.33
Camry	1	1.00	1.00	1.00	1.00	1.00
Cutlass	1	0.29	0.43	1.00	0.43	0.29
Sable	1	0.66	0.625	1.00	1.00	0.63

15.4   MULTICRITERIA DECISION MAKING

In multicriteria decision problems, relevant alternatives are evaluated according to a number of criteria. Each criterion induces a particular ordering of the alternatives, and we need a procedure by which to construct one overall preference ordering. There is a visible similarity between these decision problems and problems of multiperson decision making. In both cases, multiple orderings of relevant alternatives are involved and have to be integrated into one global preference ordering. The difference is that the multiple orderings represent either preferences of different people or ratings based on different criteria.

The number of criteria in multicriteria decision making is virtually always assumed to be finite. In this section, we assume, in addition, that the number of considered alternatives is also finite. Decision situations with infinite sets of alternatives are considered in Sec. 15.7, which deals with fuzzy mathematical programming.

Let $X = \{x_1, x_2, \ldots, x_n\}$ and $C = \{c_1, c_2, \ldots, c_m\}$ be, a set of alternatives and a set of criteria characterizing a decision situation, respectively. Then, the basic information involved in multicriteria decision making can be expressed by the matrix

$$
\mathbf{R} = \begin{array}{c} \\ c_1 \\ c_2 \\ \vdots \\ c_m \end{array}
\overset{\begin{array}{cccc} x_1 & x_2 & \cdots & x_n \end{array}}
{\left[\begin{array}{cccc}
r_{11} & r_{12} & \cdots & r_{1n} \\
r_{21} & r_{22} & \cdots & r_{2n} \\
\vdots & \vdots & \vdots & \vdots \\
r_{m1} & r_{m2} & \cdots & r_{mn}
\end{array} \right]}.
$$

Assume first that all entries of this matrix are real numbers in $[0, 1]$, and each entry r_{ij} expresses the degree to which criterion c_i is satisfied by alternative x_j ($i \in \mathbb{N}_m$, $j \in \mathbb{N}_n$). Then $\mathbf{R}$ may be viewed as a matrix representation of a fuzzy relation on $C \times X$.

It may happen that, instead of matrix $\mathbf{R}$ with entries in $[0, 1]$, an alternative matrix $\mathbf{R}' = [r'_{ij}]$, whose entries are arbitrary real numbers, is initially given. In this case, $\mathbf{R}'$ can be converted to the desired matrix $\mathbf{R}$ by the formula

$$
r_{ij} = \frac{r'_{ij} - \min\limits_{j \in \mathbb{N}_n} r'_{ij}}{\max\limits_{j \in \mathbb{N}_n} r'_{ij} - \min\limits_{j \in \mathbb{N}_n} r'_{ij}} \tag{15.9}
$$

for all $i \in \mathbb{N}_m$ and $j \in \mathbb{N}_n$.

The most common approach to multicriteria decision problems is to convert them to single-criterion decision problems. This is done by finding a global criterion, $r_j = h(r_{1j}, r_{2j}, \ldots, r_{mj})$, that for each $x_j \in X$ is an adequate aggregate of values $r_{1j}, r_{2j}, \ldots, r_{mj}$ to which the individual criteria $c_1, c_2, \ldots, c_m$ are satisfied.

An example of multicriteria decision problem is the problem of recruiting and selecting personnel. In this particular problem, the selection of conditions from a given set of individuals, say $x_1, x_2, \ldots, x_n$, is guided by comparing candidates' profiles with a required profile in terms of given criteria $c_1, c_2, \ldots, c_m$. This results in matrix $\mathbf{R}$ (or in a matrix that can be converted to matrix $\mathbf{R}$ by (15.9)). The entries r_{ij} of $\mathbf{R}$ express, for each $i \in \mathbb{N}_m$ and $j \in \mathbb{N}_n$, the degree to which candidate x_j conforms to the required profile in terms of criterion c_i. Function h may be any of the aggregating operations examined in Chapter 3.

A frequently employed aggregating operator is the weighted average

$$
r_j = \frac{\sum\limits_{i=1}^{m} w_i r_{ij}}{\sum\limits_{i=1}^{m} w_i} \qquad (j \in \mathbb{N}_n), \tag{15.10}
$$

where $w_1, w_2, \ldots, w_m$ are weights that indicate the relative importance of criteria $c_1, c_2, \ldots, c_m$. A class of possible weighted aggregations is given by the formula

$$
r_j = h(r_{1j}^{w_1}, r_{2j}^{w_2}, \ldots, r_{mj}^{w_m}),
$$

where h is an aggregation operator and $w_1, w_2, \ldots, w_m$ are weights.

Consider now a more general situation in which the entries of matrix $\mathbf{R}$ are fuzzy numbers $\tilde{r}_{ij}$ on $\mathbb{R}^+$, and weights are specified in terms of fuzzy numbers $\tilde{w}_i$ on $[0, 1]$. Then, using the operations of fuzzy addition and fuzzy multiplication, we can calculate the weighted average $\tilde{r}_j$ by the formula

$$\tilde{r}_j = \sum_{i=1}^{m} \tilde{w}_i \tilde{r}_{ij}. \tag{15.11}$$

Since fuzzy numbers are not linearly ordered, a ranking method is needed to order the resulting fuzzy numbers $\tilde{r}_1, \tilde{r}_2, \ldots, \tilde{r}_n$. This issue is addressed in Sec. 15.6.

15.5 MULTISTAGE DECISION MAKING

Multistage decision making is a sort of dynamic process. A required goal is not achieved by solving a single decision problem, but by solving a sequence of decision-making problems. These decision-making problems, which represent stages in overall multistage decision making, are dependent on one another in the dynamic sense. Any task-oriented control, for example, is basically a multistage decision-making problem.

In general, theories of multistage decision making may be viewed as part of the theory of general dynamic systems (Sec. 12.7). The most important theory of multistage decision making, which is closely connected with dynamic systems, is that of *dynamic programming* [Bellman, 1957]. As can any mathematical theory, dynamic programming can be fuzzified. A fuzzification of dynamic programming extends its practical utility since it allows decision makers to express their goals, constraints, decisions, and so on in approximate, fuzzy terms, whenever desirable.

Fuzzy dynamic programming was formulated for the first time in the classical paper by Bellman and Zadeh [1970]. In this section, we explain basic ideas of this formulation, which is based on the concept of a finite-state fuzzy automaton introduced in Sec. 12.6. To see connections between the two sections, we adopt here the notation used in Sec. 12.6.

A decision problem conceived in terms of fuzzy dynamic programming is viewed as a decision problem regarding a fuzzy finite-state automaton. However, the automaton involved is a special version of the general fuzzy automaton examined in Sec. 12.6. One restriction of the automaton in dynamic programming is that the state-transition relation is crisp and, hence, characterized by the usual state-transition function of classical automata. Otherwise, the automaton operates with fuzzy input states and fuzzy internal states, and it is thus fuzzy in this sense. Another restriction is that no special output is needed. That is, the next internal state is also utilized as output and; consequently, the two need not be distinguished.

Under the mentioned restrictions, the automaton, $\mathcal{A}$, involved in fuzzy dynamic programming is defined by the triple

$$\mathcal{A} = \langle X, Z, f \rangle,$$

where X and Z are, respectively, the sets of input states and output states of $\mathcal{A}$, and

$$f : Z \times X \to Z$$

is the state-transition function of $\mathcal{A}$, whose meaning is to define, for each discrete time t ($t \in \mathbb{N}$), the next internal state, z^{t+1}, of the automaton in terms of its present internal state, z^t, and its present input state, x^t. That is,

$$z^{t+1} = f(z^t, x^t). \tag{15.12}$$

A scheme of the described automaton is shown in Fig. 15.3a. This type of automata are used

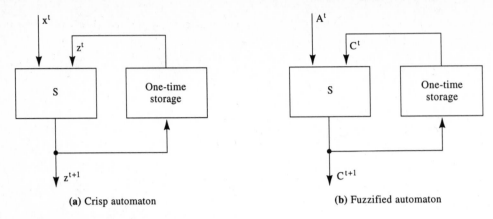

(a) Crisp automaton   **(b)** Fuzzified automaton

Figure 15.3 The automaton employed in crisp or fuzzy dynamic programming: (a) crisp automaton; (b) fuzzified automaton.

in classical dynamic programming. For fuzzy dynamic programming they must be fuzzified by using the extension principle. A scheme of the fuzzified version is shown in Fig. 15.3b, where A^t, C^t denote, respectively, the fuzzy input state and fuzzy internal state at time t, and C^{t+1} denotes the fuzzy internal state at time $t + 1$. Clearly, A^t is a fuzzy set on X, while C^t and C^{t+1} are fuzzy sets on Z.

Employing the fuzzified automaton depicted in Fig. 15.3b, we can now proceed to a description of fuzzy dynamic programming. In this conception of decision making, the desired goal is expressed in terms of a fuzzy set C^N (the fuzzy internal state of $\mathcal{A}$ at time N), where N is the time of termination of the decision process. The value of N, which defines the number of stages in the decision process, is assumed to be given. It is also assumed that the input of $\mathcal{A}$ is expressed at each time t by a fuzzy state A^t and that a particular crisp initial internal state z^0 is given.

Considering fuzzy input states $A^0, A^1, \ldots, A^{N-1}$ as constraints and fuzzy internal state C^N as fuzzy goal in a fuzzy decision making, we may conceive of a fuzzy decision (in the sense discussed in Sec. 15.2) as a fuzzy set on X^N defined by

$$D = \tilde{A}^0 \cap \tilde{A}^1 \cap \ldots \tilde{A}^{N-1} \cap \tilde{C}^N,$$

where $\tilde{A}^t$ is a cylindric extension of A^t from X to X^N for each $t = 0, 1, \ldots, N - 1$, and $\tilde{C}^N$ is the fuzzy set on X^N that induces C^N on Z. That is, for any sequence $x^0, x^1, \ldots, x^{N-1}$, viewed as a sequence of decisions, the membership grade of D is defined by

$$D(x^0, x^1, \ldots, x^{N-1}) = \min[A^0(x^0), A^1(x^1), \ldots, A^{N-1}(x^{N-1}), C^N(z^N)], \qquad (15.13)$$

where z^N is uniquely determined by $x^0, x^1, \ldots, x^{N-1}$ and z^0 via (15.12); this definition assumes, of course, that we use the standard operator of intersection. The decision problem is to find a sequence $\hat{x}^0, \hat{x}^1 \ldots \hat{x}^{N-1}$ of input states such that

$$D(\hat{x}^0, \hat{x}^1, \ldots, \hat{x}^{N-1}) = \max_{x^0, \ldots, x^{N-1}} D(x^0, x^1, \ldots, x^{N-1}). \qquad (15.14)$$

To solve this problem by fuzzy dynamic programming, we need to apply a principle known in dynamic programming as the *principle of optimality* [Bellman, 1957], which can be expressed as follows: An optimal decision sequence has the property that whatever the initial state and initial decision are, the remaining decisions must constitute an optimal policy with regard to the state resulting from the first decision.

Applying the principle of optimality and substituting for D from (15.13), we can write (15.14) in the form

$$D(\hat{x}^0, \hat{x}^1, \ldots, \hat{x}^{N-1}) = \max_{x^0, \ldots, x^{N-2}} \{ \max_{x^{N-1}} \min[A^0(x^0), A^1(x^1), \ldots, A^{N-1}(x^{N-1}),$$

$$C^N(f(z^{N-1}, x^{N-1}))]\}.$$

This equation can be rewritten as

$$D(\hat{x}^0, \hat{x}^1, \ldots, \hat{x}^{N-1}) = \max_{x^0, \ldots, x^{N-2}} \{ \min[A^0(x^0), A^1(x^1), \ldots, A^{N-2}(x^{N-2}),$$

$$\max_{x^{N-1}} \min[A^{N-1}(x^{N-1}), C^N(f(z^{N-1}, x^{N-1}))]]\}$$

$$= \max_{x^0, \ldots, x^{N-2}} \{ \min[A^0(x^0), A^1(x^1), \ldots, A^{N-2}(x^{N-2}),$$

$$\max_{x^{N-1}} \min[A^{N-1}(x^{N-1}), C^N(z^N)]]\}$$

$$= \max_{x^0, \ldots, x^{N-2}} \{ \min[A^0(x^0), A^1(x^1), \ldots, A^{N-2}(x^{N-2}),$$

$$C^{N-1}(z^{N-1})]\}$$

where

$$C^{N-1}(z^{N-1}) = \max_{x^{N-1}} \min[A^{N-1}(x^{N-1}), C^N(z^N)].$$

Repeating this *backward iteration*, we obtain the set of N recurrence equations

$$C^{N-k}(z^{N-k}) = \max_{x^{N-k}} \min[A^{N-k}(x^{N-k}), C^{N-k+1}(z^{N-k+1})] \tag{15.15}$$

for $k = 1, 2, \ldots, N$, where

$$z^{N-k+1} = f(z^{N-k}, x^{N-k}).$$

Hence, the optimal sequence $\hat{x}^0, \hat{x}^1, \ldots, \hat{x}^{N-1}$ of decisions can be obtained by successively maximizing values x^{N-k} in (15.15) for $k = 1, 2, \ldots, N$. This results successively in values $\hat{x}^{N-1}, \hat{x}^{N-2}, \ldots, \hat{x}^0$.

Example 15.5 [Bellman and Zadeh, 1970]

Let us consider an automaton with $X = \{x_1, x_2\}$, $Z = \{z_1, z_2, z_3\}$, and the state-transition function expressed by the matrix

$$\begin{array}{c} \\ z_1 \\ z_2 \\ z_3 \end{array} \begin{array}{cc} x_1 & x_2 \\ \left[\begin{array}{cc} z_1 & z_2 \\ z_3 & z_1 \\ z_1 & z_3 \end{array} \right] \end{array}$$

whose entries are next internal states for any given present internal and output states. Assume that $N = 2$, and the fuzzy goal at $t = 2$ is

$$C^2 = .3/z_1 + 1/z_2 + .8/z_3.$$

Assume further that the fuzzy constraints at input at times $t = 0$ and $t = 1$ are

$$A^0 = .7/x_1 + 1/x_2,$$
$$A^1 = 1/x_1 + .6/x_2.$$

To solve this decision problem, we need to find a sequence $\hat{x}^0, \hat{x}^1$ of input states for which the maximum,

$$\max_{x^0, x^1} \min[A^0(x^0), A^1(x^1), C^2(f(z^1, x^1))],$$

is obtained. Applying the first backward iteration for $t = 1$, we obtain

$$
\begin{aligned}
C^1(z_1) &= \max\{\min[A^1(x_1), C^2(f(z_1, x_1))], \min[A^1(x_2), C^2(f(z_1, x_2))]\} \\
&= \max\{\min[A^1(x_1), C^2(z_1)], \min[A^1(x_2), C^2(z_2)]\} \\
&= \max\{\min[1, .3], \min[.6, 1]\} \\
&= .6
\end{aligned}
$$

$$
\begin{aligned}
C^1(z_2) &= \max\{\min[A^1(x_1), C^2(f(z_2, x_1))], \min[A^1(x_2), C^2(f(z_2, x_2))]\} \\
&= \max\{\min[A^1(x_1), C^2(z_3)], \min[A^1(x_2), C^2(z_1)]\} \\
&= \max\{\min[1, .8], \min[.6, .3]\} \\
&= .8
\end{aligned}
$$

$$
\begin{aligned}
C^1(z_3) &= \max\{\min[A^1(x_1), C^2(f(z_3, x_1))], \min[A^1(x_2), C^2(f(z_3, x_2))]\} \\
&= \max\{\min[A^1(x_1), C^2(z_1)], \min[A^1(x_2), C^2(z_3)]\} \\
&= \max\{\min[1, .3], \min[.6, .8]\} \\
&= .6
\end{aligned}
$$

Hence,

$$C^1 = .6/z_1 + .8/z_2 + .6/z_3.$$

By maximizing the expression

$$\min[A^1(x^1), C^2(f(z^1, x^1))],$$

we find the following best decision $\hat{x}^1$ for each state $z^1 \in Z$ at time $t = 1$:

z^1	z_1	z_2	z_3
$\hat{x}^1$	x_2	x_1	x_2

Applying now the second backward iteration for $t = 0$, we obtain

$$
\begin{aligned}
C^0(z_1) &= \max\{\min[A^0(x_1), C^1(f(z_1, x_1))], \min[A^0(x_2), C^1(f(z_1, x_2))]\} \\
&= \max\{\min[A^0(x_1), C^1(z_1)], \min[A^0(x_2), C^1(z_2)]\} \\
&= \max\{\min[.7, .6], \min[1, .8]\} \\
&= .8
\end{aligned}
$$

$$
\begin{aligned}
C^0(z_2) &= \max\{\min[A^0(x_1), C^1(f(z_2, x_1))], \min[A^0(x_2), C^1(f(z_2, x_2))]\} \\
&= \max\{\min[A^0(x_1), C^1(z_3)], \min[A^0(x_2), C^1(z_1)]\} \\
&= \max\{\min[.7, .6], \min[1, .6]\} \\
&= .6
\end{aligned}
$$

$$C^0(z_3) = \max\{\min[A^0(x_1), C^1(f(z_3, x_1))], \min[A^0(x_2), C^1(f(z_3, x_2))]\}$$

$$= \max\{\min[A^0(x_1), C^1(z_1)], \min[A^0(x_2), C^1(z_3)]\}$$

$$= \max\{\min[.7, .6], \min[1, .6]\}$$

$$= .6$$

Hence,

$$C^0 = .8/z_1 + .6/z_2 + .6/z_3.$$

By maximizing the expression

$$\min[A^0(x^0), C^1(f(z^0, x^0))],$$

we find the following best decision $\hat{x}^0$ for each state $z^0 \in Z$ at time $t = 0$:

z^0	z_1	z_2	z_3
$\hat{x}^0$	x_2	x_1 or x_2	x_1 or x_2

The maximizing decisions for different initial states z^0 are summarized in Fig. 15.4. For example, when the initial state is z_1, the maximizing decision is to apply action x_2 followed by x_1. In this case, the goal is satisfied to the degree

$$C^0(z_1) = \min[A^0(x_2), C^1(z_2)]$$

$$= \min[A^0(x_2), \min[A^1(x_1), C^2(z_3)]]$$

$$= \min[A^0(x_2), A^1(x_1), C^2(z_3)]$$

$$= \min[1, 1, .8]$$

$$= .8.$$

That is, the degree to which the goal is satisfied is expressed in terms of $C^0(z_1)$, where z_1 is the initial state. When the initial state is z_2, we have two maximizing decisions (Fig. 15.4); hence, there are two ways of calculating $C^0(z_2)$:

$$C^0(z_2) = \min[A^0(x_1), A^1(x_2), C^2(z_3)]$$

$$= \min[.7, .6, .8] = .6$$

$$C^0(z_2) = \min[A^0(x_2), A^1(x_2), C^2(z_2)]$$

$$= \min[1, .6, 1] = .6.$$

That is, this goal is satisfied to the degree .6 when the initial state is z_2, regardless of which of the two maximizing decisions is used. We can easily find the same result for the initial state z_3.

15.6 FUZZY RANKING METHODS

In many fuzzy decision problems, the final scores of alternatives are represented in terms of fuzzy numbers. In order to express a crisp preference of alternatives, we need a method for constructing a crisp total ordering from fuzzy numbers. Unfortunately, the lattice of fuzzy numbers, $\langle \mathcal{R}, \text{MIN}, \text{MAX} \rangle$, is not linearly ordered, as discussed in Sec. 4.5. Thus, some fuzzy numbers are not directly comparable.

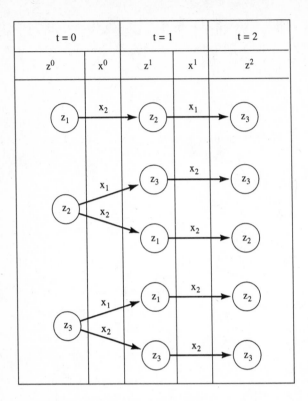

Figure 15.4 Maximizing decisions in Example 15.5 for different initial states z^0.

Numerous methods for total ordering of fuzzy numbers have been suggested in the literature. Each method appears to have some advantages as well as disadvantages. In the context of each application, some methods seem more appropriate than others. However, the issue of choosing a proper ordering method in a given context is still a subject of active research. To illustrate the problem of total ordering of fuzzy numbers, we describe three simple methods and illustrate them by examples.

The first method is based upon defining the *Hamming distance* on the set $\mathcal{R}$ of all fuzzy numbers. For any given fuzzy numbers A and B, the Hamming distance, $d(A, B)$, is defined by the formula

$$d(A, B) = \int_{\mathbb{R}} |A(x) - B(x)| dx. \tag{15.16}$$

For any given fuzzy numbers A and B, which we want to compare, we first determine their least upper bound, $\text{MAX}(A, B)$, in the lattice. Then, we calculate the Hamming distances $d(\text{MAX}(A, B), A)$ and $d(\text{MAX}(A, B), B)$, and define

$$A \preceq B \text{ if } d(\text{MAX}(A, B), A) \geq d(\text{MAX}(A, B), B).$$

If $A \preceq B$ (i.e., fuzzy numbers are directly comparable), then $\text{MAX}(A, B) = B$ and, hence, $A \leq B$. That is, the ordering defined by the Hamming distance is compatible with the ordering of comparable fuzzy numbers in $\mathcal{R}$. Observe that we can also define a similar ordering of fuzzy numbers A and B via the greatest lower bound $\text{MIN}(A, B)$.

The second method is based on α-cuts. In fact, a number of variations of this method have been suggested in the literature. A simple variation of this methods proceeds as follows. Given fuzzy numbers A and B to be compared, we select a particular value of $\alpha \in [0, 1]$ and determine the α-cuts ${}^{\alpha}A = [a_1, a_2]$ and ${}^{\alpha}B = [b_1, b_2]$. Then, we define

$$A \le B \text{ if } a_2 \le b_2.$$

This definition is, of course, dependent on the chosen value of α. It is usually required that $\alpha > 0.5$. More sophisticated methods based on α-cuts, such as the one developed by Mabuchi [1988], aggregate appropriately defined degrees expressing the dominance of one fuzzy number over the other one for all α-cuts.

The third method is based on the extension principle. This method can be employed for ordering several fuzzy numbers, say $A_1, A_2, \dots, A_n$. The basic idea is to construct a fuzzy set P on $\{A_1, A_2, \dots, A_n\}$, called a *priority set*, such as $P(A_i)$ is the degree to which A_i is ranked as the greatest fuzzy number. Using the extension principle, P is defined for each $i \in \mathbb{N}_n$ by the formula

$$P(A_i) = \sup \min_{k \in \mathbb{N}_n} A_k(r_k), \tag{15.17}$$

where the supremum is taken over all vectors $\langle r_1, r_2, \dots, r_n \rangle \in \mathbb{R}^n$ such that $r_i \ge r_j$ for all $j \in \mathbb{N}_n$.

Example 15.6

In this example, we illustrate and compare the three fuzzy ranking methods. Let A and B be fuzzy numbers whose triangular-type membership functions are given in Fig. 15.5a. Then, $\text{MAX}(A, B)$ is the fuzzy number whose membership function is indicated in the figure in bold. We can see that the Hamming distances $d(\text{MAX}(A, B), A)$ and $d(\text{MAX}(A, B), B)$ are expressed by the areas in the figure that are hatched horizontally and vertically, respectively. Using (15.16), we obtain

$$d(\text{MAX}(A, B), A) = \int_{1.5}^{2} [x - 1 - \frac{x}{3}]dx + \int_{2}^{2.25} [-x + 3 - \frac{x}{3}]dx$$

$$+ \int_{2.25}^{3} [\frac{x}{3} + x - 3]dx + \int_{3}^{4} [4 - x]dx$$

$$= \frac{1}{12} + \frac{1}{24} + \frac{3}{8} + \frac{1}{2} = 1$$

$$d(\text{MAX}(A, B), B) = \int_{0}^{1.5} \frac{x}{3}dx - \int_{1}^{1.5} [x - 1]dx$$

$$= \frac{3}{8} - \frac{1}{8} = 0.25.$$

Since $d(\text{MAX}(A, B), A) > d(\text{MAX}(A, B), B)$, we may conclude that, according to the first ranking method, $A \le B$. When applying the second method to the same example, we can easily find, from Fig. 15.5a, that $A \le B$ for any $\alpha \in [0, 1]$. According to the third method, we construct the priority fuzzy set P on $\{A, B\}$ as follows:

$$P(A) = \sup_{r_1 \ge r_2} \min[A(r_1), B(r_2)] = 0.75,$$

$$P(B) = \sup_{r_2 \ge r_1} \min[A(r_1), B(r_2)] = 1.$$

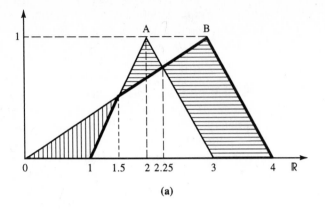

(a)

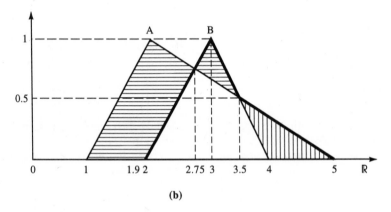

(b)

Figure 15.5   Ranking of fuzzy members (Example 15.6).

Hence, again, we conclude that $A \leq B$.

Consider now the fuzzy numbers A and B whose membership functions are given in Fig. 15.5b. The horizontally and vertically hatched areas have the same meaning as before. We can easily find that

$$d(\text{MAX}\,(A, B), A) = 1, d(\text{MAX}\,(A, B), B) = 0.25.$$

Hence, $A \leq B$ according to the first method. The second method gives the same result only for $\alpha > 0.5$. This shows that the method is inconsistent. According to the third method, we again obtain $P(A) = 0.75$ and $P(B) = 1$; hence, $A \leq B$.

15.7   FUZZY LINEAR PROGRAMMING

The *classical linear programming problem* is to find the minimum or maximum values of a linear function under constraints represented by linear inequalities or equations. The most typical linear programming problem is:

Minimize (or maximize) $c_1x_1 + c_2x_2 + \ldots + c_nx_n$

Subject to

$$a_{11}x_1 + a_{12}x_2 + \ldots + a_{1n}x_n \leq b_1$$

$$a_{21}x_1 + a_{22}x_2 + \ldots + a_{2n}x_n \leq b_2$$

$$\ldots\ldots\ldots\ldots\ldots\ldots\ldots\ldots\ldots\ldots$$

$$a_{m1}x_1 + a_{m2}x_2 + \ldots + a_{mn}x_n \leq b_m$$

$$x_1, x_2, \ldots, x_n \geq 0.$$

The function to be minimized (or maximized) is called an *objective function*; let us denote it by z. The numbers c_i ($i \in \mathbb{N}_n$) are called cost coefficients, and the vector $\mathbf{c} = \langle c_1, c_2, \ldots, c_n \rangle$ is called a *cost vector*. The matrix $\mathbf{A} = [a_{ij}]$, where $i \in \mathbb{N}_m$ and $j \in \mathbb{N}_n$, is called a *constraint matrix*, and the vector $\mathbf{b} = \langle b_1, b_2, \ldots, b_m \rangle^T$ is called a *right-hand-side vector*. Using this notation, the formulation of the problem can be simplified as

$$\text{Min} \quad z = \mathbf{cx}$$

$$\text{s.t.} \quad \mathbf{Ax} \leq \mathbf{b} \qquad\qquad (15.18)$$

$$\mathbf{x} \geq 0,$$

where $\mathbf{x} = \langle x_1, x_2, \ldots, x_n \rangle^T$ is a *vector of variables*, and s.t. stands for "subject to." The set of vectors $\mathbf{x}$ that satisfy all given constraints is called a *feasible set*. As is well known, many practical problems can be formulated as linear programming problems.

Example 15.7

To illustrate the spirit of classical linear programming, let us consider a simple example:

$$\text{Min} \quad z = x_1 - 2x_2$$

$$\text{s.t.} \quad 3x_1 - x_2 \geq 1$$

$$2x_1 + x_2 \leq 6$$

$$0 \leq x_2 \leq 2$$

$$0 \leq x_1$$

Using Fig. 15.6 as a guide, we can show graphically how the solution of this linear programming problem can be obtained. First, we need to determine the feasible set. Employing an obvious geometrical interpretation, the feasible set is obtained in Fig. 15.6 by drawing straight lines representing the equations $x_1 = 0$, $x_2 = 0$, $x_2 = 2$, $3x_1 - x_2 = 1$, and $2x_1 + x_2 = 6$. These straight lines, each of which constrains the whole plane into a half-plane, express the five inequalities in our example. When we take the intersection of the five-half planes, we obtain the shaded area in Fig. 15.6, which represents the feasible set. This area is always a convex polygon.

To find the minimum of the objective function z within the feasible set, we can draw a family of parallel straight lines representing the equation $x_1 - 2x_2 = p$, where p is a parameter, and observe the direction in which p decreases. Then, we can imagine a straight line parallel to the others moving in that direction until it touches either an edge or a vertex of the convex polygon. At that point, the value of parameter p is the minimum value of the objective function z. If the requirement were to maximize the objective function, we would move the line in the opposite direction, the direction in which p increases.

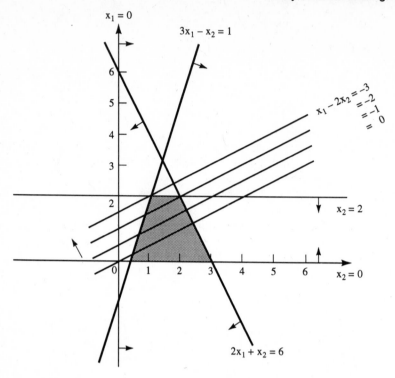

Figure 15.6 An example of a classical linear programming problem.

In many practical situations, it is not reasonable to require that the constraints or the objective function in linear programming problems be specified in precise, crisp terms. In such situations, it is desirable to use some type of fuzzy linear programming.

The most general type of fuzzy linear programming is formulated as follows:

$$\max \sum_{j=1}^{n} C_j X_j$$

$$\text{s.t.} \sum_{j=1}^{n} A_{ij} X_j \leq B_i \quad (i \in \mathbb{N}_m) \tag{15.19}$$

$$X_j \geq 0 \quad (j \in \mathbb{N}_n),$$

where A_{ij}, B_i, C_j are fuzzy numbers, and X_j are variables whose states are fuzzy numbers ($i \in \mathbb{N}_m, j \in \mathbb{N}_n$); the operations of addition and multiplication are operations of fuzzy arithmetic, and $\leq$ denotes the ordering of fuzzy numbers. Instead of discussing this general type, we exemplify the issues involved by two special cases of fuzzy linear programming problems.

Case 1. Fuzzy linear programming problems in which only the right-hand-side numbers B_i are fuzzy numbers:

$$\max \ \sum_{j=1}^{n} c_j x_j$$

$$\text{s.t.} \ \sum_{j=1}^{n} a_{ij} x_j \leq B_i \quad (i \in \mathbb{N}_m) \tag{15.20}$$

$$x_j \geq 0 \quad (j \in \mathbb{N}_n).$$

Case 2. Fuzzy linear programming problems in which the right-hand-side numbers B_i and the coefficients A_{ij} of the constraint matrix are fuzzy numbers:

$$\max \ \sum_{j=1}^{n} c_j x_j$$

$$\text{s.t.} \ \sum_{j=1}^{n} A_{ij} x_j \leq B_i \quad (i \in \mathbb{N}_m) \tag{15.21}$$

$$x_j \geq 0 \quad (j \in \mathbb{N}_n).$$

In general, fuzzy linear programming problems are first converted into equivalent crisp linear or nonlinear problems, which are then solved by standard methods. The final results of a fuzzy linear programming problem are thus real numbers, which represent a compromise in terms of the fuzzy numbers involved.

Let us discuss now fuzzy linear programming problems of type (15.20). In this case, fuzzy numbers $B_i (i \in \mathbb{N}_m)$ typically have the form

$$B_i(x) = \begin{cases} 1 & \text{when } x \leq b_i \\ \dfrac{b_i + p_i - x}{p_i} & \text{when } b_i < x < b_i + p_i \\ 0 & \text{when } b_i + p_i \leq x, \end{cases}$$

where $x \in \mathbb{R}$ (Fig. 15.7a). For each vector $\mathbf{x} = \langle x_1, x_2, \ldots, x_n \rangle$, we first calculate the degree, $D_i(\mathbf{x})$, to which $\mathbf{x}$ satisfies the ith constraint ($i \in \mathbb{N}_m$) by the formula

$$D_i(\mathbf{x}) = B_i(\sum_{j=1}^{n} a_{ij} x_j).$$

These degrees are fuzzy sets on $\mathbb{R}^n$, and their intersection, $\bigcap_{i=1}^{m} D_i$, is a *fuzzy feasible set*.

Next, we determine the fuzzy set of optimal values. This is done by calculating the lower and upper bounds of the optimal values first. The lower bound of the optimal values, z_l, is obtained by solving the standard linear programming problem:

$$\max \ z = \mathbf{cx}$$

$$\text{s.t.} \ \sum_{j=1}^{n} a_{ij} x_j \leq b_i \quad (i \in \mathbb{N}_m)$$

$$x_j \geq 0 \quad (j \in \mathbb{N}_n);$$

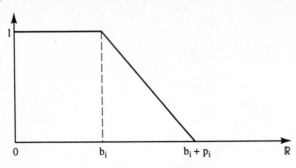

(a) Fuzzy numbers in (15.20).

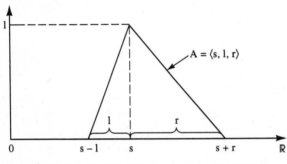

(b) Triangular fuzzy numbers employed in (15.21).

Figure 15.7 Types of fuzzy numbers employed in fuzzy linear programming problem: (a) fuzzy number in (15.20); (b) triangular fuzzy numbers employed in (15.21).

the upper bound of the optimal values, z_u, is obtained by a similar linear programming problem in which each b_i is replaced with $b_i + p_i$:

$$\max \quad z = \mathbf{cx}$$

$$\text{s.t.} \quad \sum_{j=1}^{n} a_{ij}x_j \le b_i + p_i \quad (i \in \mathbb{N}_m)$$

$$x_j \ge 0 \quad (j \in \mathbb{N}_n).$$

Then, the fuzzy set of optimal values, G, which is a fuzzy subset of $\mathbb{R}^n$, is defined by

$$G(\mathbf{x}) = \begin{cases} 1 & \text{when } z_u \le \mathbf{cx} \\ \dfrac{\mathbf{cx} - z_l}{z_u - z_l} & \text{when } z_l \le \mathbf{cx} \le z_u \\ 0 & \text{when } \mathbf{cx} \le z_l. \end{cases}$$

Now, the problem (15.20) becomes the following classical optimization problem:

$$\max \quad \lambda$$

$$\text{s.t.} \quad \lambda(z_u - z_l) - \mathbf{cx} \le -z_l$$

$$\lambda p_i + \sum_{i=1}^{n} a_{ij}x_j \le b_i + p_i \quad (i \in \mathbb{N}_m)$$

$$\lambda, x_j \ge 0 \quad (j \in \mathbb{N}_n).$$

The above problem is actually a problem of finding $\mathbf{x} \in \mathbb{R}^n$ such that

$$[(\bigcap_{i=1}^{m} D_i) \cap G](\mathbf{x})$$

reaches the maximum value; that is, a problem of finding a point which satisfies the constraints and goal with the maximum degree. As discussed in Sec. 15.2, this idea is due to Bellman and Zadeh [1970]. The method employed here is called a *symmetric method* (i.e., the constraints and the goal are treated symmetrically). There are also nonsymmetric methods. The following example illustrates the described method.

Example 15.8

Assume that a company makes two products. Product P_1 has a $0.40 per unit profit and product P_2 has a $0.30 per unit profit. Each unit of product P_1 requires twice as many labor hours as each product P_2. The total available labor hours are at least 500 hours per day, and may possibly be extended to 600 hours per day, due to special arrangements for overtime work. The supply of material is at least sufficient for 400 units of both products, P_1 and P_2, per day, but may possibly be extended to 500 units per day according to previous experience. The problem is, how many units of products P_1 and P_2 should be made per day to maximize the total profit?

Let x_1, x_2 denote the number of units of products P_1, P_2 made in one day, respectively. Then the problem can be formulated as the following fuzzy linear programming problem:

$$\max \quad z = .4x_1 + .3x_2 \text{ (profit)}$$
$$\text{s.t.} \quad x_1 + x_2 \leq B_1 \quad \text{(material)}$$
$$2x_1 + x_2 \leq B_2 \quad \text{(labor hours)}$$
$$x_1, x_2 \geq 0,$$

where B_1 is defined by

$$B_1(x) = \begin{cases} 1 & \text{when } x \leq 400 \\ \dfrac{500 - x}{100} & \text{when } 400 < x \leq 500 \\ 0 & \text{when } 500 < x, \end{cases}$$

and B_2 is defined by

$$B_2(x) = \begin{cases} 1 & \text{when } x \leq 500 \\ \dfrac{600 - x}{100} & \text{when } 500 < x \leq 600 \\ 0 & \text{when } 600 < x. \end{cases}$$

First we need to calculate the lower and upper bounds of the objective function. By solving the following two classical linear programming problems, we obtain $z_l = 130$ and $z_u = 160$.

$$(P_1) \quad \max \quad z = .4x_1 + .3x_2$$
$$\text{s.t.} \quad x_1 + x_2 \leq 400$$
$$2x_1 + x_2 \leq 500$$
$$x_1, x_2 \geq 0.$$
$$(P_2) \quad \max \quad z = .4x_1 + .3x_2$$
$$\text{s.t.} \quad x_1 + x_2 \leq 500$$
$$2x_1 + x_2 \leq 600$$
$$x_1, x_2 \geq 0.$$

Then, the fuzzy linear programming problem becomes:

$$\max \quad \lambda$$

$$\text{s.t.} \quad 30\lambda - (.4x_1 + .3x_2) \le -130$$

$$100\lambda + x_1 + x_2 \le 500$$

$$100\lambda + 2x_1 + x_2 \le 600$$

$$x_1, x_2, \lambda \ge 0.$$

Solving this classical optimization problem, we find that the maximum, $\lambda = 0.5$, is obtained for $\hat{x}_1 = 100, \hat{x}_2 = 350$. The maximum profit, $\hat{z}$, is then calculated by

$$\hat{z} = .4\hat{x}_1 + .3\hat{x}_2 = 145.$$

Let us consider now the more general problem of fuzzy linear programming defined by (15.21). In this case, we assume that all fuzzy numbers are triangular. Any triangular fuzzy number A can be represented by three real numbers, s, l, r, whose meanings are defined in Fig. 15.7b. Using this representation, we write $A = \langle s, l, r \rangle$. Problem (15.21) can then be rewritten as

$$\max \quad \sum_{j=1}^{n} c_j x_j$$

$$\text{s.t.} \quad \sum_{j=1}^{n} \langle s_{ij}, l_{ij}, r_j \rangle x_{ij} \le \langle t_i, u_i, v_i \rangle \quad (i \in \mathbb{N}_m)$$

$$x_j \ge 0 \quad (j \in \mathbb{N}_n),$$

where $A_{ij} = \langle s_{ij}, l_{ij}, r_{ij} \rangle$ and $B_i = \langle t_i, u_i, v_i \rangle$ are fuzzy numbers. Summation and multiplication are operations on fuzzy numbers, and the partial order $\le$ is defined by $A \le B$ iff $\text{MAX}(A, B) = B$. It is easy to prove that for any two triangular fuzzy numbers $A = \langle s_1, l_1, r_1 \rangle$ and $B = \langle s_2, l_2, r_2 \rangle$, $A \le B$ iff $s_1 \le s_2, s_1 - l_1 \le s_2 - l_2$ and $s_1 + r_1 \le s_2 + r_2$. Moreover, $\langle s_1, l_1, r_1 \rangle + \langle s_2, l_2, r_2 \rangle = \langle s_1 + s_2, l_1 + l_2, r_1 + r_2 \rangle$ and $\langle s_1, l_1, r_1 \rangle x = \langle s_1 x, l_1 x, r_1 x \rangle$ for any non-negative real number x. Then, the problem can be rewritten as

$$\max \quad \sum_{j=1}^{n} c_j x_j$$

$$\text{s.t.} \quad \sum_{j=1}^{n} s_{ij} x_j \le t_i$$

$$\sum_{j=1}^{n} (s_{ij} - l_{ij}) x_j \le t_i - u_i$$

$$\sum_{j=1}^{n} (s_{ij} + r_{ij}) x_j \le t_i + v_i \quad (i \in \mathbb{N}_m)$$

$$x_j \ge 0 \quad (j \in \mathbb{N}_n).$$

However, since all numbers involved are real numbers, this is a classical linear programming problem.

Example 15.9

Consider the following fuzzy linear programming problem:

$$\max \quad z = 5x_1 + 4x_2$$

$$\text{s.t.} \quad \langle 4, 2, 1 \rangle x_1 + \langle 5, 3, 1 \rangle x_2 \leq \langle 24, 5, 8 \rangle$$

$$\langle 4, 1, 2 \rangle x_1 + \langle 1, .5, 1 \rangle x_2 \leq \langle 12, 6, 3 \rangle$$

$$x_1, x_2 \geq 0.$$

We can rewrite it as

$$\max \quad z = 5x_1 + 4x_2$$

$$\text{s.t.} \quad 4x_1 + 5x_2 \leq 24$$

$$4x_1 + x_2 \leq 12$$

$$2x_1 + 2x_2 \leq 19$$

$$3x_1 + 0.5x_2 \leq 6$$

$$5x_1 + 6x_2 \leq 32$$

$$6x_1 + 2x_2 \leq 15$$

$$x_1, x_2 \geq 0.$$

Solving this problem, we obtain $\hat{x}_1 = 1.5, \hat{x}_2 = 3, \hat{z} = 19.5$.

Notice that if we defuzzified the fuzzy numbers in the constraints of the original problem by the maximum method, we would obtain another classical linear programming problem:

$$\max \quad z = 5x_1 + 4x_2$$

$$\text{s.t.} \quad 4x_1 + 5x_2 \leq 24$$

$$4x_1 + x_2 \leq 12$$

$$x_1, x_2 \geq 0.$$

We can see that this is a classical linear programming problem with a smaller number of constraints than the one converted from a fuzzy linear programming problem. Therefore, fuzziness in (15.21) results in stronger constraints, while fuzziness in (15.20) results in weaker constraints.

NOTES

15.1. The classical paper by Bellman and Zadeh [1970] is a rich source of ideas regarding fuzzy decision making and certainly worth reading; it is also reprinted in [Yager *et al.*, 1987]. An early book on fuzzy decision making was written by Kickert [1978]; although it is not fully up to date, this book is still pedagogically the best comprehensive introduction to the subject. A deeper and more up-to-date introduction to fuzzy decision making was written by Zimmermann [1987]. A rich source of information on various aspects of fuzzy decision making, which consists of 30 properly selected articles, was prepared by Zimmermann *et al.* [1984]. An approach to decision making (both fuzzy and crisp) based on binary relations that encode pairwise preferences is systematically investigated by Kitainik [1993].

15.2. For information on the various issues of multiperson fuzzy decision making, we recommend the book edited by Kacprzyk and Fedrizzi [1990].

15.3. Literature on multicriteria fuzzy decision making is extensive. Two important monographs on the subject, written by Hwang and Yoon [1981] and Chen and Hwang [1992], are now available. They cover the subject in great detail and provide the reader with a comprehensive overview of relevant literature. For a systematic study, they should be read in the given order. Another important source on the subject, focusing on the comparison between fuzzy and stochastic approaches, is the book edited by Slowinski and Teghem [1990].

15.4. Literature dealing with multistage fuzzy decision making is rather restricted. The book written by Kacprzyk [1983] is undoubtedly the most important source. Another notable reference is the paper by Baldwin and Pilsworth [1982].

15.5. The problem of fuzzy ranking or, more generally, ordering of fuzzy sets defined on $\mathbb{R}$ has been discussed in the literature quite extensively. The discussion is still ongoing. The following are some major representative references or this subject: Baas and Kwakernaak [1977], Efstathiou, and Tong [1982], Dubois and Prade [1983], Bortolan and Degani [1985], and Saade and Schwarzlander [1992]. A good overview of fuzzy ranking methods is in Chapter IV of the book by Chen and Hwang [1992].

15.6. Fuzzy linear programming is covered in the literature quite extensively. The book by Lai and Hwang [1992] is a comprehensive overview of this subject as well as relevant literature.

EXERCISES

15.1. Consider five travel packages a_1, a_2, a_3, a_4, a_5, from which we want to choose one. Their costs are $1,000, $3,000, $10,000, $5,000, and $7,000, respectively. Their travel times in hours are $15, 10, 28, 10$, and 15, respectively. Assume that they are viewed as interesting with the degrees $0.4, 0.3, 1, 0.6, 0.5$, respectively. Define your own fuzzy set of acceptable costs and your own fuzzy set of acceptable travel times. Then, determine the fuzzy set of interesting travel packages whose costs and travel times are acceptable, and use this set to choose one of the five travel packages.

15.2. Repeat Exercise 15.1 under the assumption that the importance of cost, travel time, and interest are expressed by the weights of .6, .1, and .3, respectively.

15.3. Assume that each individual of a group of five judges has a total preference ordering $\mathbf{P}_i (i \in \mathbb{N}_5)$ on four figure skaters a, b, c, d. The orderings are: $\mathbf{P}_1 = \langle a, b, d, c \rangle, \mathbf{P}_2 = \langle a, c, d, b \rangle, \mathbf{P}_3 = \langle b, a, c, d \rangle, \mathbf{P}_4 = \langle a, d, b, c \rangle$. Use fuzzy multiperson decision making to determine the group decision.

15.4. Employ the fuzzy multicriteria decision-making method described in Sec. 15.4 for solving Exercise 15.2.

15.5. Repeat Example 15.5 for the fuzzy goal

$$C^2 = .8/z_1 + 1/z_2 + .9/z_3$$

and the fuzzy constraints

$$A^0 = .8/x_1 + 1/x_2 \text{ and } A^1 = 1/x_1 + .7/x_2.$$

15.6. Let A be a symmetric trapezoidal-type fuzzy number with $^{0+}A = [0, 4]$ and $^1A = [1, 3]$, and let B, C be symmetric triangular-type fuzzy numbers with centers $c_B = 4$, $c_C = 5$, and spreads $s_B = s_C = 2$. Rank these fuzzy numbers by each of the three ranking methods described in Sec. 15.6.

15.7. Solve the following fuzzy linear programming problems.

(a)
$$\max \quad z = .5x_1 + .2x_2$$
$$\text{s.t.} \quad x_1 + x_2 \le B_1$$
$$2x_1 + x_2 \le B_2$$
$$x_1, x_2 \ge 0,$$

where

$$B_1(x) = \begin{cases} 1 & \text{for } x \le 300 \\ \dfrac{400 - x}{100} & \text{for } 300 < x \le 400 \\ 0 & \text{for } x > 400 \end{cases}$$

and

$$B_2(x) = \begin{cases} 1 & \text{for } x \le 400 \\ \dfrac{500 - x}{100} & \text{for } 400 < x \le 500 \\ 0 & \text{for } x > 500 \end{cases}.$$

(b)
$$\max \quad z = 6x_1 + 5x_2$$
$$\text{s.t.} \quad \langle 5, 3, 2 \rangle x_1 + \langle 6, 4, 2 \rangle x_2 \le \langle 25, 6, 9 \rangle$$
$$\langle 5, 2, 3 \rangle x_1 + \langle 2, 1.5, 1 \rangle x_2 \le \langle 13, 7, 4 \rangle$$
$$x_1, x_2 > 0.$$

16

ENGINEERING APPLICATIONS

16.1 INTRODUCTION

In applications of fuzzy set theory, fuzzy logic, and fuzzy measure theory, the field of engineering has undoubtedly been a leader. All engineering disciplines have already been affected, to various degrees, by the new methodological possibilities opened by fuzzy sets and fuzzy measures. The whole field of engineering is too broad to be covered here in a comprehensive way. Hence, we characterize only some typical and easily understandable engineering problems in the main engineering disciplines in which the use of fuzzy set theory has already proven useful. As always, further information regarding relevant literature is given in the Notes.

By developing fuzzy controllers, which are currently the most significant systems based on fuzzy set theory, electrical engineering was the first engineering discipline within which the utility of fuzzy sets and fuzzy logic was recognized. Since fuzzy controllers and other topics related to electrical engineering, such as fuzzy image processing, electronic circuits for fuzzy logic, or robotics, are covered elsewhere in this book, no special section on electrical engineering is included in this chapter. However, relevant literature is overviewed in Note 16.5.

Among other engineering disciplines, the utility of fuzzy set theory was recognized surprisingly early in civil engineering. Some initial ideas regarding the application of fuzzy sets in civil engineering emerged in the early 1970s and were endorsed by the civil engineering community quite enthusiastically. Since these beginnings, many civil engineers have become active in exploring the potential of fuzzy sets for dealing with a variety of specific problems in civil engineering. In Sec. 16.2, we examine a few representative problems in civil engineering in which the utility of fuzzy sets is now well established.

In mechanical engineering, the prospective role of fuzzy set theory was recognized only in the mid-1980s, and its full potential has not been fully realized as yet. Nevertheless, the number of publications dealing with applications of fuzzy sets in mechanical engineering has been steadily growing. The special nature of these applications is illustrated by a few typical examples in Sec. 16.3.

Since the mid-1980s, interest in fuzzy set theory has also been visible in industrial engineering. This interest is primarily connected with the use of fuzzy controllers in manufacturing, fuzzy expert systems for various special areas of industrial engineering, and virtually all types of fuzzy decision making, as well as fuzzy linear programming. The role of fuzzy set theory in industrial engineering is overviewed and illustrated by a few examples in Sec. 16.4.

Fuzzy set theory is also becoming important in computer engineering and knowledge engineering. Its role in computer engineering, which primarily involves the design of specialized hardware for fuzzy logic, is discussed in Sec. 16.5. Its role in knowledge engineering involves knowledge acquisition, knowledge representation, and human-machine interaction; some aspects of this role are implicitly covered in Chapters 10–14.

Other engineering disciplines, such as chemical, nuclear, or agricultural engineering, have not been much affected by fuzzy set theory as yet, but some successful examples of the use of fuzzy controllers in chemical engineering are described in the literature.

16.2   CIVIL ENGINEERING

Civil engineering, when compared with other engineering disciplines, is fundamentally different in the sense that available theories never fully fit the actual design problem. This is because each civil engineering project is, by and large, unique; hence, there is almost never a chance to test a prototype, as in other engineering disciplines. As a consequence, the uncertainty in applying theoretical solutions to civil engineering projects is large. How the designer deals with this uncertainty is crucial, because the standards of safety required by the general public regarding civil engineering constructions (such as bridges, buildings, dams, etc.) are extremely high. The designer has to make decisions in spite of the high uncertainty he or she faces.

The most fundamental knowledge of the civil engineer concerns the materials employed: how they are made, shaped, and assembled; how resistant they are to stress, weather, and use; and how they may fail. Before scientific knowledge regarding these aspects of materials was available, civil engineering was a craft. Design decisions (e.g., regarding the great cathedrals or elaborate mansions) were made by subjective judgments based on the experience of the designer and "rules of thumb" derived by accumulating design experience over the centuries. In spite of the scientific knowledge now available, great uncertainty concerning the application of the knowledge to actual design problems still remains, primarily due to the uniqueness of each design problem in civil engineering, and the use of subjective judgments and relevant "rules of thumb" is unavoidable. This seems to explain why civil engineers so quickly found a strong affinity with fuzzy set theory.

One important category of problems in civil engineering for which fuzzy set theory has already proven useful consists of problems of assessing or evaluating existing constructions. Typical examples of these problems are the assessment of fatigue in metal structure, the assessment of quality of highway pavements, and the assessment of damage in buildings after an earthquake. To illustrate the use of fuzzy set theory in these problems, we describe the problem of assessing the physical condition of bridges, as formulated by Tee *et al.* [1988].

With approximately 600,000 highway bridges in the United States, about one half of which were built before 1940, the problem of assessing their physical conditions is acute. The seriousness of the situation is magnified by the fact that many of these bridges, particularly the older ones, were designed for less traffic, lighter loads, and smaller speeds than required by current standards. Periodic assessment of bridges is thus essential for establishing priorities of funding for their rehabilitation or replacement.

All accumulated experience regarding the assessment of physical conditions of bridges is summarized in the *Bridge Inspector's Training Manual*, published by the U.S. Department of Transportation. The manual provides bridge inspectors with basic guidelines and procedures to perform their task. It specifies three components of each bridge, its deck, superstructure and substructure, which are further divided into 13, 16, and 20 subcomponents, respectively. The inspector is required to assess the condition of each subcomponent individually, to assess the relative structural importance of the subcomponents in the context of each particular bridge inspection, and to aggregate these individual assessments to obtain an overall assessment of the bridge.

Since each bridge inspection involves highly imprecise information, it is based to a large extent on the experience, intuition, and subjective judgment of the inspector. Human subjectivity and imprecision can be taken into account by using an appropriate fuzzy set to express the condition of each inspected component and, similarly, by using an appropriate fuzzy set to express the structural importance of each component. The latter fuzzy sets are obtained by surveying a group of engineers and inspectors regarding the dependence of structural importance on condition rating for each component and averaging their responses.

Once the two kinds of fuzzy sets are determined for all components (see the original paper for more details), the overall evaluation is obtained by calculating the weighted average for all components. Since numbers expressing conditions of the individual components and weights expressing the structural importance of these conditions are fuzzy numbers, the weighted average is a fuzzy number that is calculated by fuzzy arithmetic. Let C_i, W_i denote, respectively, the fuzzy number expressing the condition of component i and the fuzzy number expressing the structural significance of component i (weight of i), and let n denote the number of components that are assessed. Then, the fuzzy set expressing the overall evaluation, A, is defined by the formula

$$A = \frac{\sum_{i=1}^{n} W_i C_i}{\sum_{i=1}^{n} W_i}. \tag{16.1}$$

As a simple illustration of the described procedure, let us assume that only three components are to be assessed, which are referred to as *deck, beams*, and *piers* and labelled with $i = 1, 2, 3$, respectively. Assume further that each of these components is evaluated in linguistic terms as *poor, fair*, and *good*. The meaning of these linguistic terms is expressed by the fuzzy sets defined in Fig. 16.1 in terms of the interval [1, 5] of assumed condition ratings (the smaller the number, the worse the condition). For the sake of simplicity, we restrict our example to the integers 1, 2, 3, 4, 5 as the only accepted condition ratings. Then, the three linguistic terms are represented by the following fuzzy sets:

$$P = 0/1 + 1/2 + 0/3 + 0/4 + 0/5 \text{ for } poor,$$
$$F = 0/1 + 0/2 + 1/3 + .5/4 + 0/5 \text{ for } fair,$$
$$G = 0/1 + 0/2 + 0/3 + .5/4 + 1/5 \text{ for } good.$$

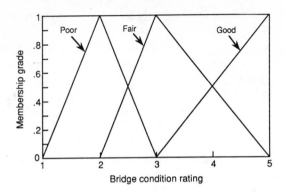

Figure 16.1 Membership functions in the example of bridge ratings.

Assume that it was found, during the bridge inspection, that the deck is in *good* condition, beams are in *fair* condition, and piers are in *poor* condition. Assume further that the fuzzy sets for structural importance are associated with the given condition assessments as follows:

$$IP = 0/1 + 0/2 + 1/3 + 0/4 \text{ for } poor,$$

$$IF = 0/1 + 0/2 + .5/3 + 1/4 \text{ for } fair,$$

$$IG = 0/1 + 1/2 + .5/3 + 0/4 \text{ for } good.$$

Using the labels $i = 1, 2, 3$, the symbols in (16.1) have the following meanings in this example:

$$C_1 = G, \quad W_1 = IG;$$

$$C_2 = F, \quad W_2 = IF;$$

$$C_3 = P, \quad W_3 = IP.$$

That is, (16.1) assumes the form

$$A = \frac{IG \cdot G + IF \cdot F + IP \cdot P}{IG + IF + IP}.$$

After evaluating this expression by fuzzy arithmetic, we obtain

$$A = 0/1 + 0/2 + 1/3 + .6/4 + 0/5$$

(details of the calculation are in the original paper).

To interpret the resulting fuzzy set A in terms of one of the three linguistic terms (*poor, fair, good*), we may calculate a distance A to each of the fuzzy sets P, F, G, and select that linguistic term whose fuzzy representation is closest to A. Employing, for example, the Euclidean distance, d, we have

$$d(A, P) = (\sum_{k=1}^{5}[A(k) - P(k)]^2)^{\frac{1}{2}}$$

$$= (0 + 1 + 1 + 0.36 + 0)^{\frac{1}{2}} = 1.536.$$

Similarly, we obtain $d(A, F) = 0.1$ and $d(A, G) = 1.418$. Since A is closest to F, we may conclude in this highly simplified example that the overall assessment of the inspected bridge is *fair*.

Several applied areas of fuzzy set theory have already been found to be of great utility in civil engineering. They include fuzzy decision making (often combined with fuzzy risk analysis), approximate reasoning (utilized in specialized expert systems), and fuzzy control (applied, e.g., to the control of traffic in cities). Since these applied areas are covered at other places in this book, we do not deem it necessary to discuss their specific utility in civil engineering. However, we describe an unorthodox application of fuzzy control to a transportation problem.

Consider a terminal where vehicles of different routes arrive and depart at fixed times. Assume that we want to design a schedule for which the transfer times from one route to another are minimized. This problem is called a *schedule coordination problem*. Three variations of the problem are possible, depending on which of the following objective criteria is chosen:

- to minimize the maximum transfer time;
- to minimize the average transfer time;
- to minimize the sum of all transfer times.

It is assumed that arrival and departure times of all vehicles and their routes are known, that the schedule is periodic with a given period (one day, one week, etc.), and that passengers transfer from a vehicle of one route to the next available vehicle of another route.

The schedule coordination problem is known to be computationally difficult. In terms of the classical theory of crisp algorithms, it belongs to the class of NP-complete problems. We describe an alternative approach to the problem, proposed by Kikuchi and Parameswaran [1993], which is based on the idea of fuzzy control.

Let a terminal be characterized by arriving and departing vehicles of n routes, and let t_{ik}^j denote the transfer time from the kth vehicle of route i to the next available vehicle of route j. Then,

$$m_i^j = \max_{k \in \mathbb{N}_{n_i}} t_{ik}^j$$

is the maximum time a passenger could wait during a transfer from route i to route j, and

$$\hat{m} = \max_{i,j \in \mathbb{N}_n} m_i^j$$

is the maximum possible transfer time for all pairs of routes.

Assume that the objective in this example is to minimize the maximum transfer combinations. That is, we want to minimize the sum of values m_i^j for all $i, j \in \mathbb{N}_n$. This objective is pursued by a fuzzy controller based upon four properly formulated fuzzy inference rules, which determine the amount by which the arrival times of route r are shifted towards the departure times of route s. The rules also specify whether the shift should be made in the positive or negative direction. To formulate the rules, let $m = m_r^s$ and let h_s denote the headway (the time interval between arrivals) on vehicles on route s. Using this notation, the rules are formulated as follows.

(a) $m \geq \dfrac{h_s}{2}$: If m is *high*, then make a *small negative shift*.

   If m is *low*, then make a *large negative shift*.

(b) $m < \dfrac{h_s}{2}$: If m is *high*, then make a *large positive shift*.

   If m is *low*, then make a *small positive shift*.

The linguistic terms *high*, *low*, *large positive* (or *negative*), and *small positive* (or *negative*) are represented by fuzzy sets whose membership functions are determined in the context of each particular problem. The membership functions employed in this example are defined in Fig. 16.2 (either rules (a) or rules (b) are applied at each time). Using the inference method described in Chapter 12, restricted in this example to one input variable, m, the rules are combined in the way illustrated for a particular value of m in Fig. 16.3. Output fuzzy sets for each inference are defuzzified in this example by the center-of-gravity method.

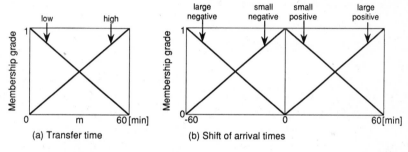

Figure 16.2 Membership functions of fuzzy sets representing the linguistic labels in the schedule coordination problem.

The described fuzzy inference rules are applied to a given initial schedule, $S^{(0)}$, according to the following algorithm:

1. Let $p = 0$ and let $S^{(p)}$ be a given schedule.
2. For all $i, j \in \mathbb{N}_n$, determine the maximum transfer times $m_i^j(p)$ in schedule $S^{(p)}$.
3. Identify a route pair r, s with the largest transfer time ($m_r^s = \hat{m}$).
4. Apply relevant inference rules to the route pair r, s (i.e., $m = m_r^s$). This results in a new schedule denoted by $S^{(p+1)}$.
5. For all $i, j \in \mathbb{N}_n$, determine the maximum transfer times $m_i^j(p + 1)$ in schedule $S^{(p+1)}$ and calculate the difference

$$D^{(p)} = \sum_{i,j \in \mathbb{N}_n} [m_i^j(p) - m_i^j(p + 1)].$$

6. If $D^{(p)} > 0$, increase p by one and go to (step 2).
7. If $D^{(p)} \leq 0$ and at least one route pair has not been examined yet, choose a route pair $r,$ s with the next largest transfer time; otherwise, terminate the algorithm.

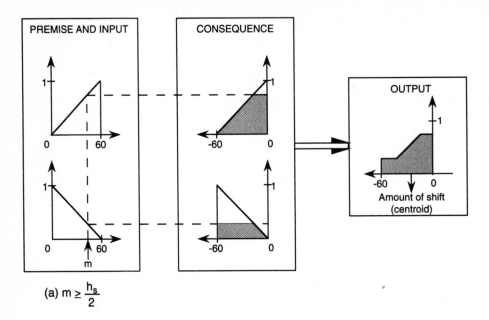

(a) $m \geq \dfrac{h_s}{2}$

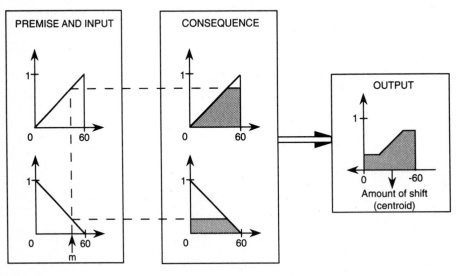

(b) $m < \dfrac{h_s}{2}$

Figure 16.3 Example of the use of the inference rules in the schedule coodination problem: (a) $m \geq \dfrac{h_s}{2}$; (b) $m < \dfrac{h_s}{2}$.

In Table 16.1, results obtained by the algorithm based on fuzzy inference rules are compared with results obtained by a crisp enumeration method for a given schedule with 25 routes. While the enumeration method improved the schedule by 3.3% in 500 seconds of CPU time, the fuzzy-based algorithm made an improvement of 21% in only 34.07 seconds of CPU time. The improvement produced by the two methods in time is expressed by the plots in Fig. 16.4a. Similar plots for a schedule with 50 routes are shown in Fig. 16.4b. We can see that the power of the fuzzy-based algorithm growth tremendously stronger with the increasing size of the scheduling problem.

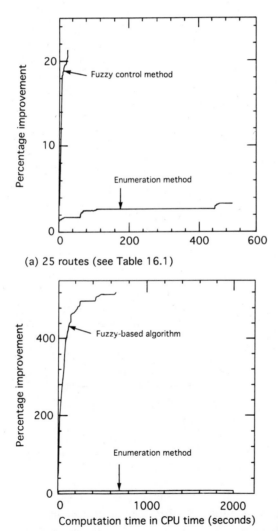

(a) 25 routes (see Table 16.1)

(b) 50 routes

Figure 16.4 Comparison of fuzzy control and enumeration for the scheduling problem: (a) 25 routes (see Table 16.1); (b) 50 routes.

TABLE 16.1 COMPARSION OF RESULTS OBTAINED
FOR THE SCHEDULING PROBLEM BY FUZZY-BASED ALGORITHM
AND ENUMERATION METHOD

			Departure Times (in min. after the hour)		
Route No.	Headway (min.)	Layover Time at Terminal (min.)	Initial Schedule	After Fuzzy Control	After Enumeration
1	20	8	5, 25, 45	3, 23, 43	5, 25, 45
2	60	6	5	5	5
3	60	12	0	17	0
4	30	23	0, 30	7, 37	0, 30
5	30	20	11, 41	11, 41	11, 41
6	60	13	5	23	5
7	30	10	25, 55	4, 34	25, 55
8	30	7	16, 46	7, 37	16, 46
9	60	9	25	6	25
10	60	16	35	8	35
11	60	12	55	20	55
12	15	4	10, 25, 40, 55	14, 29, 44, 59	10, 25, 40, 55
13	60	9	30	7	30
14	30	6	8, 38	8, 38	8, 38
15	15	13	6, 21, 36, 51	6, 21, 36, 51	6, 21, 36, 51
16	20	2	0, 20, 40	19, 39, 59	0, 20, 40
17	60	0	12	1	12
18	60	0	9	16	9
19	30	0	21, 51	0, 30	21, 51
20	60	0	34	16	29
21	20	0	19, 39, 59	19, 39, 59	9, 29, 49
22	15	0	13, 28, 43, 58	16, 31, 46	3, 18, 33, 48
23	30	0	15, 45	3, 33	0, 30
24	60	0	22	7	47
25	30	0	24, 54	1, 31	29, 59
Total Max. Transfer Time			15685 (min).	12630 (min.)	15255 (min.)
Percentage Improvement			-	21%	3.3%
Computation Time (CPU secs.)			-	34.07	500

16.3 MECHANICAL ENGINEERING

It has increasingly been recognized in engineering that the early stages in engineering design are more important than the later stages. This is a consequence of the fact that any early design decisions restrict the set of available design alternatives. If good alternatives in a design problem are eliminated by these decisions, they cannot be recovered in later stages of the design process. This means that every wrong early design decision is very costly. Unfortunately, if the early decisions are required to be precise, then it is virtually impossible to determine how good or bad each decision is in terms of the subsequent design steps and, eventually, in terms of the final design. Experienced designers recognize this difficulty and attempt to begin the design process with a complete but approximate, imprecise description of the desired artifact to be designed. As the design process advances from the formative stage to more detailed design and analysis, the degree of imprecision in describing the artifact is reduced. At the end of the design cycle, the imprecision is virtually eliminated, except for unavoidable tolerances resulting from imperfections in the manufacturing process.

Classical mathematics is not equipped to deal with imprecise descriptions. As a consequence, it has been difficult to provide the designer with computational tools for the early stages of the design process. It was realized around the mid-1980s, primarily in the context of mechanical engineering design, that fuzzy set theory is eminently suited to facilitate the whole design process, including the early stages. The basic idea is that fuzzy sets allow the designer to describe the designed artifact as approximately as desired at the early stages of the design process. This approximate description in terms of imprecise input parameters is employed to calculate the corresponding approximate characterization of relevant output parameters. The latter are compared with given performance criteria, and information obtained by this comparison is then utilized to determine appropriate values of input parameters.

To illustrate these general ideas pertaining to engineering design of any kind, we describe their more specific application to typical problems of mechanical engineering design, as developed by Wood and Antonsson [1989] and Otto *et al.* [1993a, b].

Variables involved in an engineering design are usually referred to as parameters. They are classified into input parameters (also called design parameters), output parameters, and performance parameters. An *input parameter* is any independent parameter whose value is determined during the design process. An *output parameter* involved in the design process is any parameter that is functionally dependent on the input parameters and, possibly, on some performance parameters, but is not subject to any specified functional requirement. A *performance parameter*, contrary to an output parameter, is subject to some functional requirement. The term *functional requirement* refers to a value, range of values, or fuzzy number that is specified for a performance parameter. Functional requirements, which are included in the formulation of each design problem, are independent of the design process. Performance achievable by the design is expressed in terms of the performance parameters.

After relevant parameters in a particular design problem are determined, the first step in applying fuzzy sets to this problem is to express *preferences* regarding values of input parameters by appropriate fuzzy sets. Given an input parameter v_i that takes values in set V_i, which is usually an interval of real numbers, let preferences for different values of v_i be expressed by a fuzzy set F_i on V_i. For each $x \in V_i$, the value $F_i(x)$ designates the *degree of desirability* of using the particular value x within the given set of values V_i. Set F_i may thus be referred to as the *set of desirable values* of parameter v_i (within the context of the given design problem), and $F_i(x)$ may be viewed as the *grade of membership* of value x in this set. Index i is used here to distinguish different input parameters in the same design problem. In general, we assume that $i \in \mathbb{N}_n$ for some positive integer n.

Membership grades $F_i(x)$, which are interpreted as representing the designer's desire to use the various values $v_i \in V_i$ for the input parameter v_i, are obtained either subjectively, by the designer, or objectively, by relevant engineering data. In subjective terms, the designer may express the various dimensions of the design artifact by appropriate fuzzy numbers representing linguistic descriptions such as *about 15* cm or *smaller than but close to 50* kg. Triangular fuzzy numbers seem most convenient for this purpose. Consider, for example, the linguistic description *about 15* cm pertaining to parameter v_i. Assume that there is a restriction on the dimension to be greater than 10 cm and that the designer wants to keep the dimension under 22 cm. Then, $F_i = \langle 15, 5, 7 \rangle$ is the corresponding triangular fuzzy number expressed by the triple $\langle s, l, r \rangle$, defined in Fig. 15.7b.

Membership functions of fuzzy sets representing objective preferences are determined by relevant physical, chemical, and other characteristics. For example, a wide range of materials might be used and the membership function expressed in terms of corrosion, thermal expansion, or some other measurable material property. A combination of several properties, including the cost of different materials, may also be used. An example of a membership function constructed from the cost data for certain steel alloys is shown in Fig. 16.5; it is based on the designer's preference for minimum cost [Wood and Antonsson, 1989].

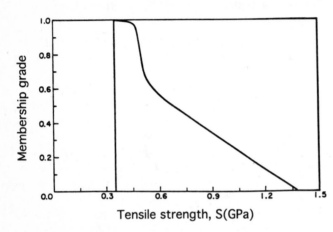

Figure 16.5 Preference function: steel alloy data.

Once the fuzzy sets expressing preferences of the designer are determined for all input parameters, they are employed for calculating the associated fuzzy sets for performance parameters. The latter fuzzy sets express the achievable performance of the design project. They are calculated on the basis of known functional dependencies of individual performance parameters on some or all of the input parameters by the extension principle. The calculation may conveniently be performed in approximate discrete fashion by using the following algorithm. It is assumed that fuzzy sets F_i expressing preferences for input parameters v_i ($i \in \mathbb{N}_n$) are given, and that these sets are normalized and convex (i.e., they are fuzzy numbers). It is also assumed that a single performance parameter p is involved, which takes values from set P, and which is expressed by a function

$$f : V_1 \times V_2 \times \ldots \times V_n \to P.$$

For each $a_i \in V_i$ ($i \in \mathbb{N}_n$),

$$b = f(a_1, a_2, \ldots, a_n)$$

is the value of the performance parameter p that corresponds to the values $a_1, a_2, \ldots, a_n$ of the input parameters $v_1, v_2, \ldots, v_n$, respectively ($b \in P$). The algorithm to determine a fuzzy set G that is induced on P by fuzzy sets F_i ($i \in \mathbb{N}_n$) through function f has the following steps:

1. Select appropriate values $\alpha_1, \alpha_2, \ldots, \alpha_r$ in $(0, 1]$, preferably equally spaced, such as $0.1, 0.2, \ldots, 1$. Let $k = 1$.

2. For each v_i, determine intervals of V_i that represent the α_k-cuts of fuzzy sets F_i ($i \in \mathbb{N}_n$).

3. Generate all 2^n combinations of the endpoints of the intervals representing the α_k-cuts of sets F_i ($i \in \mathbb{N}_n$); each combination is an n-tuple, $\langle e_1, e_2, \ldots, e_n \rangle$.

4. For each n-tuple generated in Step 3, determine

$$b_j = f(e_1, e_2, \ldots, e_n), j \in 1, 2, \ldots, 2^n.$$

Then,

$$^{\alpha_k}G = [\min b_j, \max b_j].$$

5. If $k < r$, increase k by one and return to Step 2; otherwise, stop.

While input parameters are subject to the designer's desires (preferences), target values of performance parameters are specified by functional requirements and do not directly express desires (preferences) of the designer. However, the fuzzy sets calculated for performance parameters from their counterparts defined for input parameters do express the designer's preferences, but in a somewhat different way than the input parameters. The output parameter value with preference (membership grade) 1 corresponds to the input values with preference 1. This follows the extension principle as well as fuzzy arithmetic. That is, if the designer's desires are fully met, then the performance is expressed by the output value with preference 1. If this output value satisfies the functional requirements, then the designer is justified to use the values of input parameters with preference 1. If it is necessary to use an off-peak value of a performance parameter to satisfy the functional requirements, then input values other than the most desirable must be used. For example, if it is necessary to use a value of a performance parameter whose performance is 0.7, then this implies that at least one input parameter must have a preference of 0.7 or less.

When only one performance parameter is involved, the method consists basically of two steps: a value of the performance parameter is determined that satisfies the functional requirements and has the highest performance; and suitable values of the input parameters are identified that are functionally connected with the value determined in the first step. After completing the two steps, the designer may decide to redefine the input preferences and repeat the procedure. In design problems with multiple performance parameters, a figure of merit must be introduced to combine the different performance parameter preferences.

To illustrate the procedure, we describe a simple example of mechanical engineering design that is adopted from the mentioned paper by Otto *et al.* [1993].

Consider the problem of designing a simple structural frame, depicted in Fig. 16.6, whose purpose is to support a weight w at a distance from a wall. Assuming that the configuration shown in Fig. 16.6 is required, the designer needs to express preferences regarding values of the various input parameters introduced in the figure, which are based on geometric constraints, customer requirements, and so forth. For the sake of simplicity, we assume that values of all these parameters, except v_1, v_2, are given. In particular, $d = 4$ m and $w = 20$ kN. We also assume that the designer specified the preferences for values of v_1 and v_2 (the width and thickness of the supporting beams) that are shown in Fig. 16.7a and b.

After expressing the preferences for the input parameters, the designer must rate different values of these parameters in terms of their effect on a performance parameter. In

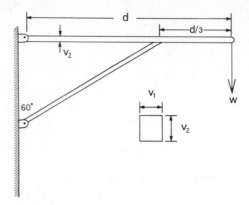

Figure 16.6 Design example.

this example, a typical performance parameter is the maximum bending stress, σ, in the horizontal beam, whose dependence on v_1 and v_2 is expressed by the formula

$$\sigma = \frac{2dw + \rho g v_1 v_2 d^2/3}{v_1 v_2^2},$$

where $g = 9.8 \text{ m/s}^2$ and $\rho = 7830 \text{ kg/m}^2$ are relevant physical constants. It must be ensured that the bending stress is not excessive. A specification of the range of bending stress (measured in gigapascals, GPa) that is *not excessive* is represented by a fuzzy set NE whose membership is specified in Fig. 16.7c.

Given the preferences for values of the input parameters v_1 and v_2, and the functional dependence of the performance parameter σ on the input parameters, the designer can now apply the extension principle to determine the induced fuzzy set G for the performance parameter σ. Applying the above-described algorithm based on discrete α-cuts, we obtain the membership function shown in Fig. 16.7d.

Comparing the value of σ for which the membership function G has its maximum with function NE, we can see that this value is almost 0.5; hence it does not satisfy the requirement that the bending stress not be excessive. Consequently, the values of input parameters with the highest preferences (i.e., ideal values) cannot be employed in the design. To obtain the optional value, σ^*, of the performance parameter, we need to find a value of σ that belongs to the intersection of sets G and NE with the highest membership grade. That is, σ^* is the value of σ for which

$$\sup_{\sigma \in \mathbb{R}} \min[G(\sigma), NE(\sigma)]$$

is obtained. This calculation, which is illustrated graphically in Fig. 16.7e, results in $\sigma^* = 0.298 \text{ [GPa]}$.

Once we obtain the optimal values σ^* of the performance parameter σ, it remains to determine the corresponding optimal values v_1^* and v_2^* of the input parameters v_1 and v_2. This can be done by determining the α-cuts

$$^\alpha F_1 = [e_{11}, e_{12}],$$

$$^\alpha F_2 = [e_{21}, e_{22}]$$

for $\alpha = G(\sigma^*)$ and calculating

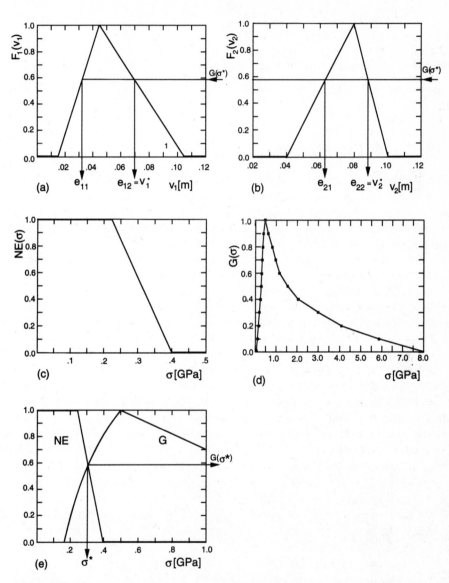

Figure 16.7 Fuzzy sets involved in the example of mechanical system design depicted in Fig. 16.6.

$$b_1 = f(e_{11}, e_{21}),$$

$$b_2 = f(e_{11}, e_{22}),$$

$$b_3 = f(e_{12}, e_{21}),$$

$$b_4 = f(e_{12}, e_{22})$$

for all combinations of the endpoints of $^{\alpha}F_1$ and $^{\alpha}F_2$. Then v_1^* and v_2^* are equal to the endpoints for which $\min\limits_{j \in \mathbb{N}_4} b_j$ is obtained. In our example, where $\sigma^* = 0.298$ [Gpa] and $G(\sigma^*) = 0.58$, the optimal values of the input parameters are $v_1^* = 0.07003$ [m] and $v_2^* = 0.08834$ [m] (see also Fig. 17.7a, b, and e).

16.4 INDUSTRIAL ENGINEERING

In general, industrial engineering is concerned with the design, operation, and control of systems whose components are human beings, machines, material, and money. Contrary to other engineering disciplines, industrial engineering deals not only with technical issues involving man-made systems, but also with behavioral, ergonomic, organizational, economic, and other issues. This implies that industrial engineering is a cross-disciplinary field. Subject areas covered by industrial engineering include manufacturing, project management, control of industrial processes, organizational design, financial management, quality control, human factors, risk analysis, ergonomics, inventory control, safety engineering, and others.

Although human beings play an important role in most problems of concern in industrial engineering, traditional techniques for dealing with these problems are adaptations of techniques developed for solving problems of mechanistic systems. Fuzzy set theory, which was motivated to a large extent by the need for a more expressive mathematical framework to deal with humanistic systems, has undoubtedly a great deal to offer to industrial engineering. Two well-developed applied areas of fuzzy set theory that are directly relevant to industrial engineering are fuzzy control (Chapter 12) and fuzzy decision making (Chapter 15). Numerous other applications of fuzzy set theory in industrial engineering have also been explored to various degrees. The main sources of information regarding these other applications are two books, a book edited by Karwowski and Mital [1986], which focuses on problems concerning human factors, and a broader book edited by Evans *et al.* [1989]. In this section, we illustrate the utility of fuzzy set theory in industrial engineering by a few examples borrowed primarily from these books.

Fuzzy sets are convenient for estimating the service life of a given piece of equipment for various conditions under which it operates. Some information about the estimated service life of the equipment is expected from its manufacturer. However, it is usually not reasonable to request a precise estimate. A realistic estimate of this kind is always only approximate, and a statement in natural language is often the best way to express it. A typical statement expressing the estimated service life might have the form: "Under normal operating conditions, the estimated service life of the equipment is around x years." The term *normal operating conditions* may conveniently be expressed by a collection of fuzzy sets, one for each operational characeric (variable) that is known to effect the service life of the equipment. The term *around x years* is expressed by a fuzzy number whose spread around its peak at x indicates the degree of nonspecificity in the estimate.

Considering the above statement regarding the estimated service life of equipment, let the fuzzy sets that express the individual normal operating conditions be denoted by $C_1, C_2, \ldots, C_n$, and let the fuzzy number expressing the estimated service life be denoted by L. Assume that fuzzy sets $C_1, C_2, \ldots, C_n$ are defined on universal sets $X_1, X_2, \ldots, X_n$, respectively, which are often appropriate subsets of real numbers. Assume further that the fuzzy number L is defined on a universal set Y, which is always a given subset of real numbers. Then, all normal operating conditions can be expressed by one fuzzy set, C, on $X = X_1 \times X_2 \times \ldots \times X_n$. Assuming that the conditions are mutually independent, set C is defined by the formula

$$C(x) = \min[C_1(x_1), C_2(x_2), \ldots, C_n(x_n)]$$

for all n-tuples $x = \langle x_1, x_2, \ldots, x_n \rangle \in X$. Clearly, C is the cylindric closure of $C_1, C_2, \ldots, C_n$.

Using set C, we can now define a fuzzy relation R on $X \times Y$ by the formula

$$R(x, y) = \min[C(x), L(y)]$$

for all $x \in X$ and $y \in Y$. This relation, which is a cylindric closure of C and L, is a convenient representation of the available information regarding the estimated service life of the equipment in question. It can readily be used for estimating the service life under operating conditions that deviate the normal operating conditions. We have

$$L' = C' \circ R,$$

where C' is a fuzzy set on X that expresses the actual operating conditions (not necessarily normal) and L' is a fuzzy number expressing the estimated service life of the given equipment under these conditions.

Let us proceed to another application of fuzzy sets in industrial environment, the problem of designing built-in tests for industrial systems. The term *built-in test* is loosely defined as a system's ability to evaluate its own state of repair and take appropriate action in the event of an anomaly. Consider, for example, an automobile with a temperature warning light. If the engine coolant temperature rises above a certain threshold, the warning light is illuminated. In this case, the automobile could be said to be performing a built-in test; its state of repair is evaluated using coolant temperature, and, if necessary, appropriate action is taken by illuminating the warning light rather than, say, turning the engine off. This example illustrates special built-in tests known as *range tests*.

Classically, we think of warning lights such as the one in the example above as being actuated by mechanical systems. Increasingly, however, tasks such as this are the responsibility of a computer, resident in an embedded control or monitoring system. In a range test, the computer must determine if a quantity is acceptable; typically, the quantity is a function of the values of one or more signals monitored by the system, for example, the signal above, the average of several signals, or the difference between two signals. The computer obtains data about the monitored quantity through an observation channel, which typically consists of some conditioning circuitry and a digital sampler. That is, the quantity is observed only at discrete instants of time at which samples are taken. This means that information regarding the quantity is limited by the resolution of the sampler. The computer, then, is really making an educated guess about the acceptability of the quantity with respect to a specified operating range.

If the quantity is determined to be unacceptable, an appropriate action must be taken quickly enough to allow the prevention of adverse effects, such as permanent damage of the machinery involved. To develop a procedure by which to decide when the action is needed, the linguistic terms *acceptable*, *unacceptable*, and *quickly enough* must be examined. The term *unacceptable* would frequently require the following definition:

> A quantity is unacceptable if its sample values violate the range of acceptable values to a *sufficiently high degree* and *often enough* to believe that the quantity itself *consistently* violates this range.

This definition takes into account the fact that the amount of noise introduced due to the physical characteristics of the electronics and/or the harshness of the operation environment is not always insignificant. It is recognized that an occasional violation of the range of acceptable values is not necessarily indicative of an unacceptable condition. In order to avoid failures due to noise or some other inexplicable fluke of nature, the idea of consistency is introduced into the definition of the term *unacceptable*.

Next, we must examine the linguistic term *quickly enough*. While it is evident from the above discussion that more than one sample value should be collected before declaring a failure, there is a limit to the amount of time that may be used to make the decision. In the boundary condition, where all sample values are definitely unacceptable, this limit is governed by the shortest amount of time required by the system to incur adverse effects. Thus, we need to make sure that in this case, the number of samples required to record a failure is large enough to provide sufficient noise intolerance and overall belief that the actual signal is indeed unacceptable, yet small enough that the associated execution time is safely less than the worst-case reaction time of the system. At the other boundary condition, as long as the sample values of the quantity are definitely acceptable, a failure should never be declared. In between these boundary conditions, the general "rule of thumb" is as follows:

> The *larger* the deviation of the quantity value from the required range, the *greater* the chances are of incurring adverse effects, and the *faster* a failure must be declared.

Using all these considerations, a meaningful procedure for constructing a range test is described as follows:

1. Define a universal set X consisting of all possible sample values of the given quantity, which are assumed to be discrete.
2. Define fuzzy sets A and U on X that characterize the set of acceptable sample values and the set of unacceptable sample values, respectively. Membership functions of these fuzzy sets may conveniently be defined by the trapezoidal shapes shown in Fig. 16.8.
3. Define an overall level of belief, b, that the actual behavior of the quantity is unacceptable as a function of the accumulation over time of the membership of the individual sample values in the sets A and U. In general,

$$b(x_k) = f[b(x_{k-1}), A(x_k), U(x_k)],$$

where k denotes the kth iteration of the built-in test logic and x_k denotes the kth sample of the quantity being evaluated. A reasonable specific function f is given by the formula:

$$b(x_k) = \max[0, b(x_{k-1}) + A(x_k) - U(x_k)].$$

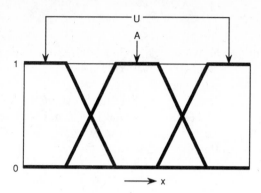

Figure 16.8 Fuzzy sets in the example of range built-in tests.

4. Define a threshold value, t, such that $b(x_k) \geq t$ is a necessary and sufficient condition to declare a failure, and such that the time required for $b(x_k) \geq t$ to occur is consistent with the needs of the boundary conditions discussed above.

A range built-in test using this procedure was applied to turbines, where the monitored quantity was the turbine blade temperature. This use of the fuzzy sets, upon which the procedure is based, showed a substantial improvement in carefully designed simulation experiments when compared with procedures based on crisp sets [Brown and Klir, 1993].

Some important problems pertaining to industrial engineering have been formulated in terms of networks of various kinds. In general, a network is a graph whose edges are associated with one or more numerical characteristics. In location problems, for example, vertices of a network represent places of demand for service, and edges are viewed as the routes that connect them. Each edge is described by the estimated travel time between the two places and, possibly, by other characteristics (safety, quality of the route, etc.). The objective is to find a point on the graph (at a vertex or along an edge) for which the maximum travel time to any place (vertex) is minimized, possibly under constraints specified in terms of the other characteristics. Such a point is called an *absolute center*.

It is easy to understand that the network for a location problem can be formulated more realistically if the estimated travel times and other characteristics are allowed to be expressed in terms of fuzzy numbers. The solution to the problem is a fuzzy set of points of the graph that is called a *fuzzy absolute center*.

The location problem is important, for example, in flexible manufacturing systems. These systems use automated guided vehicles that deliver materials to robotics workstations as required. A fuzzy absolute center is a very useful concept by which the resting area for these vehicles is efficiently characterized.

Other fuzzy networks are used for describing complex production processes consisting of many mutually dependent activities. In these networks, each edge is associated with a particular activity and is characterized by the approximate length of time of that activity. One problem regarding this kind of network is to determine critical paths in each given network (paths of maximal duration) and time floats of other paths.

To cover details of the many problems involving fuzzy networks of various types that are relevant to industrial engineering would require too much space. Readers interested in this topic are referred to [Evans *et al.*, 1989].

16.5 COMPUTER ENGINEERING

Since the mid-1980s, when the utility of fuzzy controllers became increasingly visible, the need for computer hardware to implement the various operations involved in fuzzy logic and approximate reasoning has been recognized. Initial attempts to develop hardware for fuzzy computing, at least those described in the literature, date from 1985. These developments intensified in the late 1980s and especially in the 1990s, and eventually resulted in commercially available hardware for certain types of fuzzy computing. The primary focus of these developments has been on the implementation of fuzzy rules of inference and defuzzification procedures for fuzzy controllers.

The principal reason for using specialized hardware for fuzzy computing is to increase operational speed via parallel processing. In principle, fuzzy computer hardware allows all inference rules of a complex fuzzy inference engine to be processed in parallel. This increases efficiency tremendously and, as a consequence, extends the scope of applicability of fuzzy controllers and, potentially, other fuzzy expert systems.

In general, computer hardware for fuzzy logic is implemented in either digital mode or analog mode. In *digital mode*, fuzzy sets are represented as vectors of numbers in $[0, 1]$. Operations on fuzzy sets are thus performed as operations on vectors. In *analog mode*, fuzzy sets are represented in terms of continuous electric signals (electric currents or voltages) by appropriate electric circuits. These circuits play a role similar to function generators in classical analog computers.

Either of the two modes of fuzzy computer hardware has some favorable features. Digital fuzzy hardware is characterized by flexible programmability and good compatibility with existing computers, which are predominantly digital; it is suitable for implementing complex schemes of multistage fuzzy inference. Analog fuzzy hardware, on the contrary, is characterized by high speed and good compatibility with sensors; it is thus particularly suitable for complex on-line fuzzy controllers.

As an illustration, we outline a few basic ideas regarding fuzzy computer hardware of the analog type that was developed by Yamakawa [1993]. Technical details, which are not covered here, can be found in the references mentioned in Note 16.4.

Yamakawa's hardware is designed for fuzzy controllers of the type discussed in Secs. 12.2 and 12.3. It consists of units that implement individual fuzzy inference rules (rule units), units that implement the Max operation needed for aggregating inferences made by multiple inference rules (Max units), and defuzzification units. Each rule unit is capable of implementing one fuzzy inference rule with three antecedents or less. Inputs for each antecedent are required to be crisp. One of seven linguistic labels can be chosen for each antecedent and each consequent: NL (negative large), NM (negative medium), NS (negative small), AZ (approximately zero), PS (positive small), PM (positive medium), or PL (positive large). Fuzzy sets representing these linguistic labels for antecedents may be expressed by membership functions of either triangular or trapezoidal shapes. The triangles or trapezoids can be positioned as desired by choosing appropriate values of voltage in the circuits, and their left and right slopes can be adjusted as desired by choosing appropriate resistance values of variable resistors in the circuits. For consequents, the shapes of membership functions may be arbitrary, as explained later.

A block diagram of the hardware implementation of a fuzzy controller with n fuzzy inference rules is shown in Fig. 16.9. For each $k \in \mathbb{N}_n$, the rule unit k is characterized by membership functions X_k, Y_k, Z_k, which represent the antecedents in fuzzy inference-rule k, and membership function C_k, which represents the associated consequent. Functions X_k, Y_k, Z_k have either triangular or trapezoidal shapes with required slopes. Crisp input signals x, y, z are applied to all rule units in parallel. The output of each rule unit, which represents the inference obtained by the associated fuzzy inference rule, is expressed in discrete form by a vector of 25 numbers in [0, 1] represented by appropriate voltages on 25 signal lines. All these outputs, denoted in Fig. 16.9 by symbols $C_1', C_2', \ldots, C_n'$, are fed to a unit that determines their component-wise maximum. The resulting membership function C, expressed again in discrete form, is then defuzzified by the unit referred to as the defuzzifier. The output is a single real number, $d(C)$, which represents the value of the control variable. The current defuzzifiers are based on the centroid method of defuzzification, but there is no reason why they could not be extended to a parametrized family of defuzzification methods.

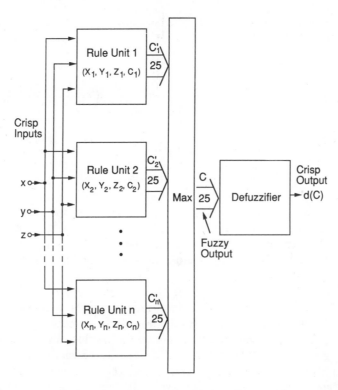

Figure 16.9   Hardware implementation of a fuzzy controller.

A block diagram of one rule unit (say, unit k) is shown in Fig. 1(unit are three *membership function circuits*, one for each antecedent. 1 circuits is to express, in analog mode, the membership function of or and to determine the degree of compatibility of the actual value of the with the antecedent. The membership function is defined by three inp first input specifies one of the seven linguistic labels and, in addition, no linguistic label is assigned (denoted by NA), which is needed for ir

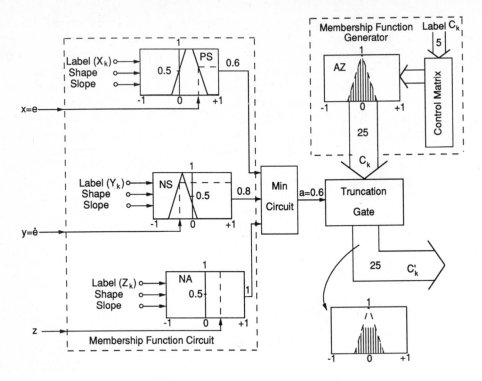

Figure 16.10   Block diagram of rule unit k.

rules that contain less than three antecedents. The second input specifies whether the shape of the membership function is triangular or trapezoidal. The third input specifies the left and right slopes of the membership function. The ranges of values of the three variables for which the various membership functions are defined are assumed here to be normalized to the interval $[-1, 1]$.

An example of the fuzzy inference rule "If $X_k(= e)$ is PS and Y_k $(= \dot{e})$ is NS, then C_k $(= v)$ is AZ," which conforms to the type of inference rules discussed in Secs. 12.2 and 12.3, is illustrated in Fig. 16.10. Since the rule has only two antecedents, no linguistic label is assigned to Z_k. The circuit for Z_k is thus not utilized in this case. This degenerate case, labelled by NA, is conveniently handled by defining Z_k as the whole interval $[-1, 1]$ and by setting the input z to any convenient constant in $[-1, 1]$. The output of the circuit is then equal to 1 and, consequently, does not have any effect on the output produced by the rule unit. In our example, X_k is of trapezoidal shape and Y_k is of triangular shape, as indicated in the figure.

According to the inference procedure, the outputs of the three membership function circuits are fed to a circuit that determines their minimum. The output of this circuit is then applied to a circuit called a *truncation gate*. The purpose of this circuit is to produce a truncated vector C'_k of 25 values that approximate the membership function the consequent C_k of the inference rule. In our example, C_k $(= v)$ is a triangular ership function representing the linguistic label AZ. This function is approximated te form by a circuit referred to as a *membership function generator*; its 25 outputs are fed to the truncation gate. The seven linguistic labels and the special label NA (not assigned) are specified by three binary digits, and two additional binary digits are used for defining four distinct shapes of the membership functions (triangular, trapezoidal, S-shaped, and Z-shaped). The decoding from the five-bit characterization to the 25-tuple of members in [0, 1] is done by a circuit called a *control matrix*.

We feel that this level of detail is sufficient for general understanding of one type of computer hardware for fuzzy logic. Further details, including diagrams of the various electric circuits, are covered in the mentioned article by Yamakawa [1993].

16.6 RELIABILITY THEORY

Reliability theory is a cross-disciplinary engineering discipline that studies the dependability of engineering products in behaving as required under specific operating conditions when put into service. The central concept of reliability theory, as the name suggests, is *reliability*. In a broad sense, reliability is a measure of the expected capability of an engineering product to operate without failures under specific conditions for a given period of time.

The classical reliability theory, which has been developed, by and large, since World War II, is based on two basic assumptions:

(a) *Assumption of dichotomous states*—At any given time, the engineering product is either in functioning state or in failed state.

(b) *Probability assumption*—The behavior of the engineering product with respect to the two critical states (functioning and failed) can adequately be characterized in terms of probability theory.

These assumptions, which in the classical reliability theory are taken for granted, are, under closer scrutiny, questionable in many practical situations. They make sense only when the mathematical ideal of crisp events is acceptable in a given experimental context, large collections of relevant data are available, and observed frequencies are indicators of the underlying physical process.

An alternative reliability theory, rooted in fuzzy sets and possibility theory, has been proposed, which is based on fundamentally different assumptions:

(a') *Assumption of fuzzy states*—At any given time, the engineering product may be in functioning state to some degree and in failed state to another degree.

(b') *Possibility assumption*—The behavior of the engineering product with respect to the two critical fuzzy states (fuzzy functioning state and fuzzy failed state) can adequately be characterized in terms of possibility theory.

By accepting either assumption (a) or assumption (a') and, similarly, either (b) or (b'), we can recognize four types of reliability theories. When (b) is combined with either (a) or (a'), we obtain two types of *probabilistic reliability theories*. The first one is the classical reliability theory; the second one is a probabilistic reliability theory based on fuzzy events. When (b') is combined with either (a) or (a'), we obtain two types of *possibilistic reliability theories*. The first one is based on classical set theory, while the second one is based on fuzzy set theory. All these reliability theories are meaningful and have been developed. Which of them to use depends on the context of each application. In general, possibilistic reliability theories are more meaningful than their probabilistic counterparts when only a small number of statistical samples is available, as is typical, for example in astronautics (reliability problems of space shuttles, space probes, etc.) and software engineering.

We do not deem it necessary to cover the new, nonclassical reliability theories here; to cover them adequately would require too much space. However, we provide readers interested in these theories with relevant references in Note 16.6.

16.7 ROBOTICS

Robotics is a cross-disciplinary subject area that is concerned with the design and construction of machines that are capable of human-like behavior. Such machines are referred to as *robots*. Although industries began interested in robots in the 1960s, the first commercial robots were produced only in the 1970s. These early robots, which are called *industrial robots*, were designed for repetitive actions of a typical production line. Advances in computer technology and in the area of artificial intelligence in the 1980s stimulated greater ambitions in robotics. Research in robotics became oriented primarily on robots with high intelligence.

Intelligent robots must be equipped with at least three types of functions: appropriate *perceptual functions* facilitated by visual, auditory, and other sensors to allow the robot to perceive its environment; intelligent *information-processing functions* that allow the robot to process the incoming information with respect to a given task; and *mechanical functions* with appropriate controls to allow the robot to move and act as desired.

To achieve human-like behavior, an intelligent robot must have some key capabilities that distinguish human beings from classical nonintelligent machines. They include the capability of common-sense reasoning in natural language that is based on incoming information as well as background knowledge, high-level capabilities of pattern recognition and image understanding, refined motor controls, and the capability of making decisions in the face of bounded uncertainty. It is clear that the use of fuzzy set theory is essential for all these capabilities.

The main subjects of fuzzy set theory that are relevant to robotics include approximate reasoning, fuzzy controllers and other kinds of fuzzy systems, fuzzy pattern recognition and image processing, fuzzy data bases, information retrieval systems, and fuzzy decision making. In robotics, all these subjects, and a host of others, are utilized as components integrated in the overall architecture of intelligent robots. To cover this important role of fuzzy set theory in the formidable task of designing intelligent robots would require the introduction of a prohibitively extensive background information. Readers interested in this area are given a few relevant references in Note 16.8.

NOTES

16.1. Existing and prospective applications of fuzzy set theory in civil engineering are overviewed in articles by Blockley [1982], Chameau *et al.* [1983], Brown *et al.* in [Bezdek 1987], and

Ayyub [1991]. Using fuzzy sets in architectural design is explored by Oguntade and Gero [1981]. The primary source of information regarding specific applications of fuzzy sets in civil engineering is the journal *Civil Engineering Systems*. Conference proceedings edited by Brown *et al.* [1985] and a book edited by Ayyub *et al.* [1992] are also valuable sources.

16.2. Applications of fuzzy set theory in mechanical engineering are discussed in articles by Otto *et al.* [1991, 1993 a, b] and by Wood *et al.* [1989, 1990, 1992].

16.3. In addition to the books mentioned in Sec. 16.4, a good overview of the utility of fuzzy sets in industrial engineering was written by Karwowski and Evans [1986]. Issues of dealing with fuzzified networks are discussed by Mareš and Horák [1983]. A thorough coverage of the role of fuzzy sets in risk analysis was prepared by Schmucker [1984]. The use of approximate reasoning and fuzzy Petri nets in flexible manufacturing systems is explored by Scarpelli and Gomide [1993].

16.4. Yamakawa's fuzzy logic hardware of analog mode is described in several papers by Yamakawa [1988, 1989, 1993], Yamakawa and Kaboo [1988], Yamakawa and Miki [1986], and Miki *et al.* [1993]. Other approaches to fuzzy logic hardware are described in Gupta and Yamakawa [1988a], Diamond *et al.* [1992], and proceedings of various conferences in the 1990s (particularly IFSA and IEEE). An important contribution to fuzzy logic hardware is a design and implementation of a fuzzy flip-flop by Hirota and Ozawa [1989]. This is a memory element that allows us to store one-digit fuzzy information. It is essential for implementing multistage procedures of fuzzy inference.

16.5. Electrical engineering has been affected by fuzzy set theory primarily through fuzzy controllers and fuzzy computer hardware. However, there are other areas of electrical engineering where methods based on fuzzy sets have been proven useful. The use of fuzzy adaptive filters to nonlinear channel equalization [Wang and Mendel, 1993], signal detection [Saade and Schwarzlander, 1994], and the use of fuzzy cognitive maps to qualitative circuit analysis [Styblinski and Meyer, 1991] are three examples.

16.6. The new, nonclassical reliability theories mentioned in Sec. 16.6 are covered in several papers by Cai *et al.* [1991 a–d, 1993], and also in books by Kaufmann and Gupta [1988] and Kerre [1991]. Additional contributions to these theories and their applications to specific problems can be found in many issues of *IEEE Trans. on Reliability, Microelectronics and Reliability* and *Reliability Engineering and System Safety* published in the 1980s and 1990s.

16.7. The name "robot" was coined by the Czech writer Karel Čapek in his play *Rossum's Universal Robots*, written in 1920.

16.8. No book or major survey paper describing the use of fuzzy set theory in robotics is currently available. Many specific applications of fuzzy set theory in robotics are described in short papers in proceedings of conferences oriented to either fuzzy systems or robotics, in particular IEEE Conferences and IFSA Congresses. The following are a few relevant journal articles: [Dodds, 1988; Palm, 1989, 1992; Hirota, Arai, and Hachisu, 1989; Nedungadi, 1993; Kim, Ko, and Chung, 1994].

EXERCISES

16.1. Repeat the example of bridge evaluation discussed in Sec. 16.2 by assuming that it was found during the bridge inspection that the deck is in poor condition, beams are in poor condition, and piers are in fair condition.

16.2. Repeat the example of mechanical design discussed in Sec. 16.3 by replacing F_1 and F_2 with symmetric triangular-type fuzzy numbers with centers 0.06 and 0.07, and spreads 0.45 and 0.3, respectively.

16.3. Using the procedure of estimating service life of a given equipment discussed in Sec. 16.4, consider the following fuzzy proposition regarding the estimated life of a furnace: "If the furnace is operated under normal temperature, its service life is estimated around 7 years." Assume that the linguistic terms *normal temperature* [in °C] and *around 7 years* are approximated, respectively, by the fuzzy sets

$$T = .4/780 + .8/800 + 1/820 + .8/840 + .4/860,$$

$$L = .5/6 + 1/7 + .5/8.$$

Assuming now that the actual operating temperature is characterized by the fuzzy set

$$T' = .4/840 + .8/860 + 1/880 + .8/900 + .4/920,$$

determine the estimated service life of the furnace under this operating condition.

17

MISCELLANEOUS APPLICATIONS

17.1 INTRODUCTION

The inventory of successful applications of fuzzy set theory has been growing steadily, particularly in the 1990s. Few areas of mathematics, science, and engineering remain that have not been affected by the theory. Some emerging applications were previously unsuspected, and the performance of many exceeds previous expectations.

Thus far, some areas of human endeavors have been particularly active in exploring the utility of fuzzy set theory and developing many diverse applications. These include information and knowledge-base systems, various areas of engineering, and virtually all problem areas of decision making. These have been covered in previous chapters. The purpose of this chapter is to overview applications of fuzzy set theory in other areas. We do not attempt to be fully comprehensive. The utility of fuzzy set theory in each area covered in this chapter has already been established, and future developments seem quite promising.

Scattered applications of fuzzy set theory in some additional areas can also be found in the literature. These areas include physics, chemistry, biology, ecology, political science, geology, meteorology, nuclear engineering, and many others. However, these applications are still rather isolated, unconvincing, or insufficiently developed. We mention some of them in the Notes.

The last section in the chapter is devoted to our speculations about prospective future applications of fuzzy set theory. We focus on applications that are generally recognized as very important, but appear to involve insurmountable difficulties. In these speculations, we attempt to look far into the future to stimulate imagination.

17.2 MEDICINE

As overviewed in Note 17.1, medicine is one field in which the applicability of fuzzy set theory was recognized quite early, in the mid-1970s. Within this field, it is the uncertainty found in the process of diagnosis of disease that has most frequently been the focus of applications of fuzzy set theory. In this section, we examine some basic issues of these applications.

With the increased volume of information available to physicians from new medical technologies, the process of classifying different sets of symptoms under a single name and determining appropriate therapeutic actions becomes increasingly difficult. A single disease may manifest itself quite differently in different patients and at different disease stages. Furthermore, a single symptom may be indicative of several different diseases, and the presence of several diseases in a single patient may disrupt the expected symptom pattern of any one of them. The best and most useful descriptions of disease entities often use linguistic terms that are irreducibly vague. For example, hepatitis is characterized by the statement:

"Total proteins are *usually normal*, albumin is *decreased*, α-globulins are *slightly decreased*, β-globulins are *slightly decreased*, and γ-globulins are *increased*,"

where the linguistic terms printed in italics are inherently vague. Although medical knowledge concerning the symptom-disease relationship constitutes one source of imprecision and uncertainty in the diagnostic process, the knowledge concerning the state of the patient constitutes another. The physician generally gathers knowledge about the patient from the past history, physical examination, laboratory test results, and other investigative procedures such as X-rays and ultrasonics. The knowledge provided by each of these sources carries with it varying degrees of uncertainty. The past history offered by the patient may be subjective, exaggerated, underestimated, or incomplete. Mistakes may be made in the physical examination, and symptoms may be overlooked. The measurements provided by laboratory tests are often of limited precision, and the exact borderline between normal and pathological is often unclear. X-rays and other similar procedures require correct interpretation of the results. Thus, the state and symptoms of the patient can be known by the physician with only a limited degree of precision. In the face of the uncertainty concerning the observed symptoms of the patient as well as the uncertainty concerning the relation of the symptoms to a disease entity, it is nevertheless crucial that the physician determine the diagnostic label that will entail the appropriate therapeutic regimen.

The desire to better understand and teach this difficult and important process of medical diagnosis has prompted attempts to model it with the use of fuzzy sets. These models vary in the degree to which they attempt to deal with different complicating aspects of medical diagnosis such as the relative importance of symptoms, the varied symptom patterns of different disease stages, relations between diseases themselves, and the stages of hypothesis formation, preliminary diagnosis, and final diagnosis within the diagnostic process itself. These models also form the basis for computerized medical expert systems, which are usually designed to aid the physician in the diagnosis of some specified category of diseases.

The fuzzy set framework has been utilized in several different approaches to modeling the diagnostic process. In the approach formulated by Sanchez [1979], the physician's medical knowledge is represented as a fuzzy relation between symptoms and diseases. Thus, given the fuzzy set A of the symptoms observed in the patient and the fuzzy relation R representing the medical knowledge that relates the symptoms in set S to the diseases in set D, then the fuzzy set B of the possible diseases of the patient can be inferred by means of the compositional rule of inference

$$B = A \circ R \tag{17.1}$$

or

$$B(d) = \max_{s \in S}[\min(A(s), R(s, d))]$$

for each $d \in D$. The membership grades of observed symptoms in fuzzy set A may represent the degree of possibility of the presence of the symptom or its severity. The membership grades in fuzzy set B denote the degree of possibility with which we can attach each relevant diagnostic label to the patient. The fuzzy relation R of medical knowledge should constitute the greatest relation such that given the fuzzy relation Q on the set P of patients and S of symptoms and the fuzzy relation T on the sets P of patients and D of diseases, then

$$T = Q \circ R. \tag{17.2}$$

Thus, relations Q and T may represent, respectively, the symptoms that were present and diagnoses consequently made for a number of known cases. Figure 17.1 summarizes the meanings and uses of fuzzy relations Q, T, and R and fuzzy sets A and B. By solving the fuzzy relation equation (17.2) for R, the accumulated medical experience can be used to specify the relation between symptoms and diseases that was evidenced in the previous diagnoses. The maximal solution to (17.2) must be chosen for R in order to avoid arriving at a relation that is more specific than our information warrants. However, this can lead to cases in which R shows more symptom-disease association than exists in reality. Therefore, it may be necessary to interpret the results of applying relation R to a specific set of symptoms as a diagnostic hypothesis rather than as a confirmed diagnosis. Adlassnig and Kolarz [1982] and Adlassnig [1986] elaborate on this relational model in the design of CADIAG-2, a computerized system for diagnosis assistance. We illustrate their approach with a somewhat simplified version of part of this design.

The model proposes two types of relations to exist between symptoms and diseases: an occurrence relation and a confirmability relation. The first provides knowledge about the tendency or frequency of appearance of a symptom when the specific disease is present; it corresponds to the question, "How often does symptom s occur with disease d?" The second relation describes the discriminating power of the symptom to confirm the presence of the disease; it corresponds to the question, "How strongly does symptom s confirm disease d?" The distinction between occurrence and confirmability is useful because a symptom may be quite likely to occur with a given disease but may also commonly occur with several other diseases, therefore limiting its power as a discriminating factor among them. Another symptom, on the other hand, may be relatively rare with a given disease, but its presence may nevertheless constitute almost certain confirmation of the presence of the disease.

For this example, let S denote the crisp universal set of all symptoms, D be the crisp universal set of all diseases, and P be the crisp universal set of all patients. Let us define a fuzzy relation R_S on the set $P \times S$ in which membership grades $R_S(p, s)$ (where $p \in P, s \in S$) indicate the degree to which the symptom s is present in patient p. For instance, if s represents the symptom of increased potassium level and the normal test result range is roughly 3.5 to 5.2, then a test result of 5.2 for patient p could lead to a membership grade $R_S(p, s) = .5$. Let us further define a fuzzy relation R_O on the universal set $S \times D$, where $R_O(s, d)$ ($s \in S, d \in D$) indicates the frequency of occurrence of symptom s with

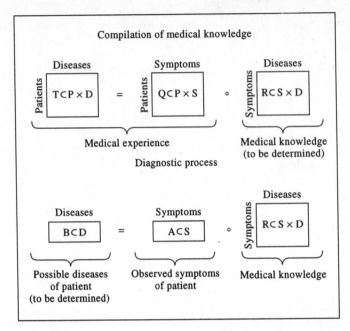

Figure 17.1 Fuzzy sets and fuzzy relations involved in medical diagnosis.

disease d. Let R_C also be a fuzzy relation on the same universal set, where $R_C(s, d)$ corresponds to the degree to which symptom s confirms the presence of disease d.

In this example, the fuzzy occurrence and confirmability relations are determined from expert medical documentation. Since this documentation usually takes the form of statements such as "Symptom s seldom occurs in disease d" or "Symptom s always indicates disease d," we assign membership grades of 1, .75, .5, .25, or 0 in fuzzy sets R_O and R_C for the linguistic terms *always, often, unspecific, seldom,* and *never,* respectively. We use a concentration operation to model the linguistic modifier *very* such that

$$A_{very}(x) = A^2(x).$$

Assume that the following medical documentation exists concerning the relations of symptoms s_1, s_2, and s_3 to diseases d_1 and d_2:

- Symptom s_1 occurs very seldom in patients with disease d_1.
- Symptom s_1 often occurs in patients with disease d_2 but seldom confirms the presence of disease d_2.
- Symptom s_2 always occurs with disease d_1 and always confirms the presence of disease d_1; s_2 never occurs with disease d_2, and (obviously) its presence never confirms disease d_2.
- Symptom s_3 very often occurs with disease d_2 and often confirms the presence of d_2.
- Symptom s_3 seldom occurs in patients with disease d_1.

All missing relational pairs of symptoms and diseases are assumed to be *unspecified* and are given a membership grade of .5. From our medical documentation we construct the following matrices of relations $R_O, R_C \in S \times D$ (the rows and columns of the matrices are ordered by subscripts of the corresponding symbols):

$$\mathbf{R_O} = \begin{bmatrix} .06 & .75 \\ 1 & 0 \\ .25 & .56 \end{bmatrix},$$

$$\mathbf{R_C} = \begin{bmatrix} .5 & .25 \\ 1 & 0 \\ .5 & .75 \end{bmatrix}.$$

Now assume that we are given a fuzzy relation R_s specifying the degree of presence of symptoms s_1, s_2, and s_3 for three patients p_1, p_2, and p_3 as follows:

$$\mathbf{R_S} = \begin{bmatrix} .4 & .8 & .7 \\ .6 & .9 & 0 \\ .9 & 0 & 1 \end{bmatrix}.$$

Using relations R_S, R_O, and R_C, we can now calculate four different indication relations defined on the set $P \times D$ of patients and diseases. The first is the occurrence indication R_1 defined as

$$R_1 = R_S \circ R_O.$$

For our example, R_1 is given by the following matrix:

$$\mathbf{R_1} = \begin{bmatrix} .8 & .56 \\ .9 & .6 \\ .25 & .75 \end{bmatrix}.$$

The confirmability indication relation R_2 is calculated by

$$R_2 = R_S \circ R_C;$$

this results in

$$\mathbf{R_2} = \begin{bmatrix} .8 & .7 \\ .9 & .25 \\ .5 & .75 \end{bmatrix}.$$

The nonoccurrence indication R_3 is defined as

$$R_3 = R_S \circ (1 - R_O)$$

and specified here by

$$\mathbf{R_3} = \begin{bmatrix} .7 & .8 \\ .6 & .9 \\ .9 & .44 \end{bmatrix}.$$

Finally, the nonsymptom indication R_4 is given by

$$R_4 = (1 - R_S) \circ R_O$$

and equals

$$\mathbf{R}_4 = \begin{bmatrix} .25 & .6 \\ .25 & .56 \\ 1 & .1 \end{bmatrix}.$$

From these four indication relations, we may draw different types of diagnostic conclusions. For instance, we may make a confirmed diagnosis of a disease d for patient p if $R_2(p, d) = 1$. Although this is not the case for any of our three patients, R_2 does seem to indicate, for instance, that disease d_1 is strongly confirmed for patient p_2. We may make an excluded diagnosis for a disease d in patient p if $R_3(p, d) = 1$ or $R_4(p, d) = 1$. In our example, we may exclude disease d_1 as a possible diagnosis for patient p_3. Finally, we may include in our set of diagnostic hypotheses for patient p any disease d such that the inequality

$$.5 < \max[R_1(p, d), R_2(p, d)]$$

is satisfied. In our example, both diseases d_1 and d_2 are suitable diagnostic hypotheses for patients p_1 and p_2, whereas the only acceptable diagnostic hypothesis for patient p_3 is disease d_2. Our three types of diagnostic results, therefore, seem to point to the presence of disease d_2 in patient p_3 and disease d_1 in patient p_2, whereas the symptoms of patient p_1 do not strongly resemble the symptom pattern of either disease d_1 or d_2 alone.

The actual CADIAG-2 system incorporates relations not only between symptoms and diseases but also between diseases themselves, between symptoms themselves, and between combinations of symptoms and diseases. Partial testing of the system on patients with rheumatological diseases produced an accuracy of 94.5% in achieving a correct diagnosis.

Another alternative approach to modeling the medical diagnostic process utilizes fuzzy cluster analysis. This type of technique is used by Fordon and Bezdek [1979] and Esogbue and Elder [1979, 1980, 1983]. Models of medical diagnosis that use cluster analysis usually perform a clustering algorithm on the set of patients by examining the similarity of the presence and severity of symptom patterns exhibited by each. (The severity of the symptoms present can be designated with degrees of membership in fuzzy sets representing each symptom category.) Often the similarity measure is computed between the symptoms of the patient in question and the symptoms of a patient possessing the prototypical symptom pattern for each possible disease. The patient to be diagnosed is then clustered to varying degrees with the prototypical patients whose symptoms are most similar. The most likely diagnostic candidates are those disease clusters in which the patient's degree of membership is the greatest. We describe a simplified adaptation of the method employed by Esogbue and Elder [1979, 1980, 1983] to illustrate this technique.

Let us assume that we are given a patient x who displays the symptoms s_1, s_2, s_3, and s_4 at the levels of severity given by the fuzzy set

$$A_x = .1/s_1 + .7/s_2 + .4/s_3 + .6/s_4,$$

where $A_x(s_i) \in [0, 1]$ denotes the grade of membership in the fuzzy set characterizing patient x and defined on the set $S = \{s_1, s_2, s_3, s_4\}$, which indicates the severity level of the symptom s_i for the patient. We must determine a diagnosis for this patient among three possible diseases d_1, d_2, and d_3. Each of these diseases is described by a matrix giving the upper and lower bounds of the normal range of severity of each of the four symptoms that can be expected in a patient with the disease. The diseases d_1, d_2, and d_3 are described in this way by the matrices

$$B_1 = \begin{matrix} \text{lower} \\ \text{upper} \end{matrix} \begin{bmatrix} 0 & .6 & .5 & 0 \\ .2 & 1 & .7 & 0 \end{bmatrix},$$

$$B_2 = \begin{matrix} \text{lower} \\ \text{upper} \end{matrix} \begin{bmatrix} 0 & .9 & .3 & .2 \\ 0 & 1 & 1 & .4 \end{bmatrix},$$

$$B_3 = \begin{matrix} \text{lower} \\ \text{upper} \end{matrix} \begin{bmatrix} 0 & 0 & .7 & 0 \\ .3 & 0 & .9 & 0 \end{bmatrix}.$$

For each $j = 1, 2, 3$, matrix B_j defines fuzzy sets B_{jl} and B_{ju}, where $B_{jl}(s_i)$ and $B_{ju}(s_i)$ denote, respectively, the lower and upper bounds of symptom s_i for disease d_j. We further define a fuzzy relation W on the set of symptoms and diseases that specifies the pertinence or importance of each symptom s_i in the diagnosis of the matrix of each disease d_j. The relation W of these weights of relevance is given by

$$W = \begin{matrix} s_1 \\ s_2 \\ s_3 \\ s_4 \end{matrix} \begin{bmatrix} .4 & .8 & 1 \\ .5 & .6 & .3 \\ .7 & .1 & .9 \\ .9 & .6 & .3 \end{bmatrix},$$

with columns labeled $d_1 \quad d_2 \quad d_3$

where $W(s_i, d_j)$ denotes the weight of symptom s_i for disease d_j. In order to diagnose patient x, we use a clustering technique to determine to which diagnostic cluster (as specified by matrices B_1, B_2, and B_3) the patient is most similar. This clustering is performed by computing a similarity measure between the patient's symptoms and those typical of each disease d_j. To compute this similarity, we use a distance measure based on the Minkowski distance that is appropriately modified; it is given by the formula

$$D_p(d_j, x) = \left[\sum_{i \in I_l} |W(s_i, d_j)(B_{jl}(s_i) - A_x(s_i))|^p \right.$$

$$\left. + \sum_{i \in I_u} |W(s_i, d_j)(B_{ju}(s_i) - A_x(s_i))|^p \right]^{1/p}, \tag{17.3}$$

where

$$I_l = \{i \in \mathbb{N}_m | A_x(s_i) < B_{jl}(s_i)\},$$

$$I_u = \{i \in \mathbb{N}_m | A_x(s_i) > B_{ju}(s_i)\},$$

and m denotes the total number of symptoms. Choosing, for example, the Euclidean distance, we use (17.3) with $p = 2$ to calculate the similarity between patient x and diseases d_1, d_2, and d_3 in our example as follows:

$$D_2(d_1, x) = [|(.7)(.5 - .4)|^2 + |(.9)(0 - .6)|^2]^{1/2} = .54;$$

$$D_2(d_2, x) = [|(.6)(.9 - .7)|^2 + |(.8)(0 - .1)|^2 + |(.6)(.4 - .6)|^2]^{1/2} = .19;$$

$$D_2(d_3, x) = [|(.9)(.7 - .4)|^2 + |(.3)(0 - .7)|^2 + |(.3)(0 - .6)|^2]^{1/2} = .39.$$

The most likely disease candidate is the one for which the similarity measure attains the minimum value; in this case, the patient's symptoms are most similar to those typical of disease d_2.

Applications of fuzzy set theory in medicine are by no means restricted to medical diagnosis. Other applications involve, for example, fuzzy controllers for various medical devices, fuzzy pattern recognition and image processing for analysis of X-ray images and other visual data, and fuzzy decision making for determining appropriate therapies. These types of applications are covered elsewhere in this book. Literature regarding applications of fuzzy sets in medicine is overviewed in Note 17.1.

17.3 ECONOMICS

What is economics? Most modern economists define economics as a social science that studies how societies deal with problems that result from relative scarcity. Observing the development of economics since the early 19th century, we can see at its core a sequence of axiomatic theories, which are increasingly more precise and more mathematically sophisticated. At the same time, however, we can see a persistent gap between economic reality and predictions derived from these ever more sophisticated theories.

Several reasons could easily be identified why economic theories have not been successful in modeling economic reality. One reason, directly connected with the subject of this book, is that these theories are formulated in terms of classical mathematics, based on classical set theory, two-valued logic, and classical theory of additive measures. This is not realistic in economics for at least two important reasons. First, human reasoning and decision making in natural language, which plays an essential role in economic phenomena, is based on genuine uncertainty embedded in natural language. Classical mathematics is not capable of expressing this kind of uncertainty. Moreover, human preferences for complex choices are not determined, in general, by the rules of additives measures. The second, less obvious reason is connected with the complexity of models. In order to capture the ever-increasing richness of economic and related phenomena, we need increasingly complex models. When the required complexity for obtaining realistic models becomes unmanageable, we must simplify. In every implication, unfortunately, we are doomed to lose something. When we insist that the simplified model give us certain and precise predictions, we are forced to simplify by reducing the scope of the model which in turn, results in a loss of relevance of these predictions to the real world. We can preserve relevance by allowing some uncertainty in the models. That is, we can trade certainty and precision for relevance under given limits of acceptable complexity.

Imprecise but highly relevant (and hence valuable) economic predictions are often expressed by experienced economists in linguistic terms, such as

"The price of oil is *not likely* to *increase substantially* in the *near future*."

Such predictions are determined by common sense, employing the economist's knowledge (distinct from accepted economic theories) and relevant information, which is often expressed in linguistic terms as well. The capability of fuzzy set theory to express and deal with propositions in natural language should facilitate the elicitation of this kind of economic knowledge from economists with a high success rate in making economic predictions.

It is well known that Zadeh's motivation for introducing the theory of fuzzy sets was to facilitate the modeling and analysis of humanistic systems. The following statement is his more recent reflection on this issue [Zadeh, 1982a]:

> During the past decade the focus of research in systems theory has shifted increasingly toward the analysis of large-scale systems in which human judgement, perception, and emotions play an important role. Such *humanistic systems* are typified by socioeconomic systems, transportation systems, environmental control systems, food production systems, education systems, health care-delivery systems, criminal justice systems, information dissemination systems, and the like ...Despite the widespread use of systems-theoretic methods in the modeling of large-scale systems, serious questions have been raised regarding the applicability of systems theory to the analysis of humanistic and, especially, socioeconomic systems...
>
> The systems theory of the future—the systems theory that will be applicable to the analysis of humanistic systems—is certain to be quite different in spirit as well as in substance from systems theory as we know it today. I will take the liberty of referring to it as *fuzzy systems theory* because I believe that its distinguishing characteristic will be a conceptual framework for dealing with a key aspect of humanistic systems—namely, the pervasive fuzziness of almost all phenomena that are associated with their external as well as internal behavior...A semantic point that is in need of clarification at this juncture is that fuzzy systems theory is not merely a theory of fuzzy systems. Rather, it is a theory that allows an assertion about a system to be a fuzzy proposition (e.g., "System *S* is slightly nonlinear"). In this sense, then, fuzzy systems theory is not so much a precise theory of fuzzy systems as it is a fuzzy theory of both fuzzy and nonfuzzy systems. What this implies is that an assertion in fuzzy systems theory is normally not a theorem but a proposition that has a high degree of truth, and in addition, is informative in relation to a stated question.

As a humanistic science, economics should thus have been one of the early prime targets for utilizing fuzzy set theory. However, the role of fuzzy set theory in economics was recognized in economics much later than in many other areas. One exception can be found in writings by the British economist Shackle. He has argued since the late 1940s that probability theory, which is accepted in economics as the only mathematical tool for expressing uncertainty, is not meaningful for capturing the nature of uncertainty in economics. To develop an alternative, more meaningful framework for uncertainty in economics, Shackle has argued that uncertainty associated with imagined actions whose outcomes are to some extent unknown should be expressed in terms of degrees of possibility rather than by probabilities. In his own words [Shackle, 1961]:

> It is the degree of surprise to which we expose ourselves, when we examine an imagined happening as to its possibility, in general or in the prevailing circumstances, and assess the obstacles, tensions and difficulties which arise in our mind when we try to imagine it occurring, that provides the indicator of degree of possibility. This is the surprise we *should* feel, if the given thing *did* happen; it is a *potential* surprise. ...Only potential surprise called up in the mind and assessed, in the moment when decision is made, is relevant for that decision, and alone can have any bearing or influence on it.

Shackle analyzed the concept of potential surprise at great length and formalized it in terms of nine axioms. It follows from this formalization that the concept of potential surprise is mathematically equivalent to the concept of necessity measure in possibility theory. Although

Shackle often refers to possibility degrees, in addition to degrees of potential surprise, he falls short of incorporating both these measures into one formal framework. Using possibility theory, which is now well developed, Shackle's ideas can be made fully operational in economics.

There is no doubt that many applications of fuzzy set theory that have been described in the literature since the theory emerged in 1965 are relevant to economics to various degrees. Included in this category are, for example, fuzzy preference theory, fuzzy games, fuzzified methods for some problems of operations research, and the various problem areas of fuzzy decision making. However, the potential of fuzzy set theory for reformulating the texture of economic theory to make it more realistic was recognized by economists only in the 1980s. Thus far, only a few economists, by and large French, have actively contributed to this major undertaking.

A pioneer who initiated the reformulation of economic theory by taking advantage of fuzzy set theory was undoubtedly the French economist Claude Ponsard (1927–1990). His contributions, as well as related work of other economists, are overviewed in a special issue of *Fuzzy Sets and Systems* that is dedicated to him (Vol. 49, No. 1, 1992). According to this overview, two streams of activities regarding the reformulation of classical economic theory are currently pursued. One of them focuses on the use of fuzzy set theory, the other on the use of fuzzy measure theory. While the acceptance of both these efforts among economists has so far been lukewarm at best, the acceptance of fuzzy measure theory seems to be growing more rapidly.

The principal source of information regarding the current status of the use of fuzzy set theory in economics is a book by Billot [1992]. The book is oriented to microeconomics, which is substantially reformulated via the conception of fuzzy preferences. Since fuzzy preferences introduce a great diversity of possible behaviors of economic subjects or agents to the theory of microeconomics, the theory becomes more realistic. After careful analysis of properties of fuzzy preferences, Billot investigates equilibria of fuzzy noncooperative and cooperative games, as well as fuzzy economic equilibria. He shows that the introduction of fuzzy preferences does not affect the existence of these equilibria, but results in some nonstandard equilibria.

General background regarding this application area is too extensive to be covered here. Interested readers with sufficient background in economics can find details regarding the role of fuzzy set theory in the above mentioned book by Billot and in other references suggested in Note 17.2.

17.4 *FUZZY SYSTEMS AND GENETIC ALGORITHMS*

The connection between fuzzy systems and genetic algorithms is bidirectional. In one direction, genetic algorithms are utilized to deal with various optimization problems involving fuzzy systems. One important problem for which genetic algorithms have proven very useful is the problem of optimizing fuzzy inference rules in fuzzy controllers. In the other direction, classical genetic algorithms can be fuzzified. The resulting *fuzzy genetic algorithms* tend to be more efficient and more suitable for some applications. In this section, we discuss how classical genetic algorithms (Appendix B) can be fuzzified; the use of genetic algorithms in the area of fuzzy systems is covered only by a few relevant references in Note 17.3.

There are basically two ways of fuzzifying classical genetic algorithms. One way is to fuzzify the gene pool and the associated coding of chromosomes; the other one is to fuzzify operations on chromosomes. These two ways may, of course, be combined.

In classical genetic algorithms, the set $\{0, 1\}$ is often used as the gene pool, and chromosomes are coded by binary numbers. These algorithms can be fuzzified by extending their gene pool to the whole unit interval $[0, 1]$. To illustrate this possibility, let us consider the example of determining the maximum of function $f(x) = 2x - x^2/16$ within the domain $[0, 31]$, which is discussed in Appendix B. By employing the gene pool $[0, 1]$, there is no need to discretize the domain $[0, 31]$. Numbers in this domain are represented by chromosomes whose components are numbers in $[0, 1]$. For example, the chromosome $\langle .1, .5, 0, 1, .9 \rangle$ represents the number

$$8.5 = .1 \times 2^4 + .5 \times 2^3 + 0 \times 2^2 + 1 \times 2^1 + .9 \times 2^0$$

in $[0, 31]$. It turns out that this reformulation of classical genetic algorithms tends to converge faster and is more reliable in obtaining the desired optimum. To employ it, however, we have to find an appropriate way of coding alternatives of each given problem by chromosomes formed from the gene pool $[0, 1]$. To illustrate this issue, let us consider a traveling salesman problem with four cities, c_1, c_2, c_3, and c_4. The alternative routes that can be taken by the salesman may be characterized by chromosomes $\langle x_1, x_2, x_3, x_4 \rangle$ in which x_i corresponds to city $c_i (i \in \mathbb{N}_4)$ and represents the degree to which the city should be visited early. Thus, for example, $\langle .1, .9, .8, 0 \rangle$ denotes the route c_2, c_3, c_1, c_4, c_2.

Although the extension of the gene pool from $\{0, 1\}$ to $[0, 1]$ may be viewed as a fuzzification of genetic algorithms, more genuine fuzzification requires that the operations on chromosomes also be fuzzified. In the following, we explain, as an example, a fuzzified crossover proposed by Sanchez [1993].

Consider chromosomes $\mathbf{x} = \langle x_1, x_2, \ldots, x_n \rangle$ and $\mathbf{y} = \langle y_1, y_2, \ldots, y_n \rangle$ whose components are taken from a given gene pool. Then, the simple crossover with the crossover position $i \in \mathbb{N}_{n-1}$ can be formulated in terms of a special n-tuple

$$\mathbf{t} = \langle t_j | t_j = 1 \text{ for } j \in \mathbb{N}_i \text{ and } t_j = 0 \text{ for } \mathbb{N}_{i+1,n} \rangle,$$

referred to as a *template*, by the formulas

$$\mathbf{x}' = (\mathbf{x} \wedge \mathbf{t}) \vee (\mathbf{y} \wedge \bar{\mathbf{t}}),$$

$$\mathbf{y}' = (\mathbf{x} \wedge \bar{\mathbf{t}}) \vee (\mathbf{y} \wedge \mathbf{t}),$$

where $\wedge$ and $\vee$ are min and max operations on tuples and $\bar{\mathbf{t}} = \langle \bar{t}_j | \bar{t}_j = 1 - t_j \rangle$.

We can see that the template $\mathbf{t}$ defines an abrupt change at the crossover position i. This is characteristic of the usual, crisp operation of simple crossover. The change can be made gradual by defining the crossover position approximately. This can be done by a *fuzzy template*,

$$\mathbf{f} = \langle f_i | i \in \mathbb{N}_n, f_1 = 1, f_n = 0, i < j \Rightarrow f_i \geq f_j \rangle.$$

For example, $\mathbf{f} = \langle 1, \ldots, 1, .8, .5, .2, 0, \ldots, 0 \rangle$ is a fuzzy template for some n.

Assume that chromosomes $\mathbf{x} = \langle x_1, x_2, \ldots, x_n \rangle$ and $y = \langle y_1, y_2, \ldots, y_n \rangle$ are given, whose components are, in general, numbers in $[0, 1]$. Assume further that a fuzzy template $\mathbf{f} = \langle f_1, f_2, \ldots, f_n \rangle$ is given. Then, the operation of *fuzzy simple crossover* of mates $\mathbf{x}$ and $\mathbf{y}$ produces offsprings $\mathbf{x}'$ and $\mathbf{y}'$ defined by the formulas

$$\mathbf{x}' = (\mathbf{x} \wedge \mathbf{f}) \vee (\mathbf{y} \wedge \bar{\mathbf{f}}),$$
$$\mathbf{y}' = (\mathbf{x} \wedge \bar{\mathbf{f}}) \vee (\mathbf{y} \wedge \mathbf{f}).$$

These formulas can be written, more specifically, as

$$\mathbf{x}' = \langle \max[\min(x_i, f_i), \min(y_i, \bar{f}_i)] | i \in \mathbb{N}_n \rangle,$$
$$\mathbf{y}' = \langle \max[\min(x_i, \bar{f}_i), \min(y_i, f_i)] | i \in \mathbb{N}_n \rangle.$$

The operation of a double crossover as well as the other operations on chromosomes can be fuzzified in a similar way. Experience with fuzzy genetic algorithms seems to indicate that they are efficient, robust, and better attuned to some applications than their classical, crisp counterparts.

17.5 *FUZZY REGRESSION*

Regression analysis is an area of statistics that deals with the investigation of the dependence of a variable upon one or more other variables. The dependence is usually assumed to have a particular mathematical form with one or more parameters. The aim of regression analysis is then to estimate the parameters on the basis of empirical data. The linear form

$$y = \gamma_0 + \gamma_1 x_1 + \ldots + \gamma_n x_n, \tag{17.4}$$

where y is an *output variable*, $x_1, x_2, \ldots, x_n$ are *input variables*, and $\gamma_0, \gamma_1, \ldots, \gamma_n$ are parameters, is the most frequent mathematical form in regression analysis. Problems of regression analysis formulated in terms of this linear form are called *linear regressions*.

Consider, as an example, a linear regression with one variable. Then, the assumed form

$$y = \gamma_0 + \gamma_1 x \tag{17.5}$$

represents a straight line. Given a set of observed data $\langle a_1, b_1 \rangle, \langle a_2, b_2 \rangle, \ldots, \langle a_m, b_m \rangle$ for the pair of variables $\langle x, y \rangle$, we want to find values of γ_0 and γ_1 for which the total error of the estimated points on the straight line with respect to the corresponding observed points is minimal. In the usual method of linear regression, based on the least square error, the total error is expressed by the formula

$$\sum_{i=1}^{m} [b_i - (\gamma_0 + \gamma_1 a_i)]^2.$$

The optimal values of γ_0 and γ_1 are given by the formulas

$$\gamma_1 = \frac{m \sum_{i=1}^{m} a_i b_i - \sum_{i=1}^{m} a_i \sum_{i=1}^{m} b_i}{m \sum_{i=1}^{m} a_i^2 - (\sum_{i=1}^{m} a_i)^2},$$

$$\gamma_0 = \frac{\sum_{i=1}^{m} b_i - \gamma_1 \sum_{i=1}^{m} a_i}{m},$$

which can be easily determined by solving the optimization problem.

There are two motivations for developing fuzzy regression analysis. The first motivation results from the realization that it is often not realistic to assume that a crisp function of a given form, such as (17.4), represents the relationship between the given variables. Fuzzy relation, even though less precise, seems intuitively more realistic. The second motivation results from the nature of data, which in some applications are inherently fuzzy.

These two distinct motivations lead to two types of fuzzy regression analysis. One involves fuzzy parameters and crisp data, while the other one involves crisp parameters and fuzzy data. In this section, we briefly explain these two types of linear fuzzy regression. While methods for fuzzy regression with both fuzzy parameters and fuzzy data have also been developed, they are too complicated to be covered here.

Linear Regression with Fuzzy Parameters

In this type of fuzzy regression, the dependence of an output variable on input variables is expressed by the form

$$Y = C_1 x_1 + C_2 x_2 + \ldots + C_n x_n, \tag{17.6}$$

where $C_1, C_2, \ldots, C_n$ are fuzzy numbers, and $x_1, x_2, \ldots, x_n$ are real-valued input variables; for each n-tuple of values of the input variables, the value of the output variable defined by (17.6) is a fuzzy number Y. Given a set of crisp data points $\langle \mathbf{a}_1, b_1 \rangle, \langle \mathbf{a}_2, b_2 \rangle, \ldots, \langle \mathbf{a}_m, b_m \rangle$, the aim of this regression problem is to find fuzzy parameters $C_1, C_2, \ldots, C_n$ for which (17.6) expresses the best fit to these data points, according to some criterion of goodness.

Assume that the parameters in (17.6) are symmetric triangular fuzzy numbers defined by

$$C_i(c) = \begin{cases} 1 - \dfrac{|c - c_i|}{s_i} & \text{when } c_i - s_i \leq c \leq c_i + s_i \\ 0 & \text{otherwise,} \end{cases} \tag{17.7}$$

where c_i is the point for which $C_i(c_i) = 1$ and $s_i > 0$ is the spread of C_i (a half of the length of the support set of C_i). Let C_i, which expresses the linguistic terms *approximately* c_i or *around* c_i, be denoted by $C_i = \langle c_i, s_i \rangle$ for all $i \in \mathbb{N}_n$. Then, it is easy to prove by the extension principle that Y in (17.6) is also a symmetric triangular fuzzy number given by

$$Y(y) = \begin{cases} 1 - \dfrac{|y - \mathbf{x}^T \mathbf{c}|}{\mathbf{s}^T |\mathbf{x}|} & \text{when } \mathbf{x} \neq 0 \\ 1 & \text{when } \mathbf{x} = 0, y \neq 0 \\ 0 & \text{when } \mathbf{x} = 0, y = 0 \end{cases} \tag{17.8}$$

for all $y \in \mathbb{R}$, where

$$\mathbf{x} = \begin{bmatrix} x_1 \\ x_2 \\ \vdots \\ x_n \end{bmatrix}, \quad \mathbf{c} = \begin{bmatrix} c_1 \\ c_2 \\ \vdots \\ c_n \end{bmatrix}, \quad \mathbf{s} = \begin{bmatrix} s_1 \\ s_2 \\ \vdots \\ s_n \end{bmatrix}, \quad |\mathbf{x}| = \begin{bmatrix} |x_1| \\ |x_2| \\ \vdots \\ |x_n| \end{bmatrix},$$

and T denotes the operation of transposition.

The original problem of finding the fuzzy parameters $C_1, C_2, \ldots, C_n$ can be converted to the problem of finding the vectors $\mathbf{c}$ and $\mathbf{s}$ such that $Y(y)$ given by (17.8) fits the given data as well as possible. Two criteria of goodness are usually employed in this problem. According to the first criterion, for each given datum $\langle \mathbf{a}_j, b_j \rangle$, where $\mathbf{a}_j$ is a vector of values of the input variables, b_j should belong to the corresponding fuzzy number Y_j with a grade that is greater than or equal to some given value $h \in [0, 1]$. That is, $Y_j(b_j) \geq h$ for each $j \in \mathbb{N}_m$, where Y_j is the fuzzy number defined by (17.8) for $\mathbf{x} = \mathbf{a}_j$. According to the second criterion, the total nonspecificity of the fuzzy parameters must be minimized. That is, we want to obtain the most specific expression (17.6) for sufficiently good fit (as specified by the value of h). The nonspecificity of each fuzzy parameter C_i given by (17.7) may be expressed by its spread s_i.

The described fuzzy regression problem can be formulated in terms of the following classical linear programming problem:

$$\text{minimize} \quad \sum_{i=1}^{n} s_i$$

$$\text{s.t.} \quad (1 - h)\mathbf{s}^T |\mathbf{a_j}| - |b_j - \mathbf{a_j}^T \mathbf{c}| \geq 0, \, j \in \mathbb{N}_m, \tag{17.9}$$

$$s_i \geq 0, \, i \in \mathbb{N}_n.$$

Example 17.1

Let $\langle 1, 1 \rangle, \langle 2, 2 \rangle, \langle 3, 2 \rangle, \langle 4, 3 \rangle$ be data representing the dependence of variable y on variable x. To illustrate linear fuzzy regression for these data, assume the form

$$Y = Cx,$$

where $C = \langle c, s \rangle$ is a fuzzy parameter expressed by a symmetric triangular fuzzy member. Then, the linear programming problem has the form:

$$\text{Minimize} \quad s$$

$$\text{s.t.} \quad (1 - h)s - |1 - c| \geq 0$$

$$2(1 - h)s - |2 - 2c| \geq 0$$

$$3(1 - h)s - |2 - 3c| \geq 0$$

$$4(1 - h)s - |3 - 4c| \geq 0$$

$$c \geq 0$$

$$h \in [0, 1] \text{ is a fixed number.}$$

This problem can be expressed in the following simpler form:

$$\text{Minimize} \quad s$$

$$\text{s.t.} \quad s \geq \frac{1}{1 - h} \max(|1 - c|, |\tfrac{2}{3} - c|, |\tfrac{3}{4} - c|)$$

$$h \in [0, 1] \text{ is a fixed number}$$

Solving this problem, we find the optimal values are

$$c^* = \frac{5}{6} \quad \text{and} \quad s^* = \frac{1}{6(1 - h)}.$$

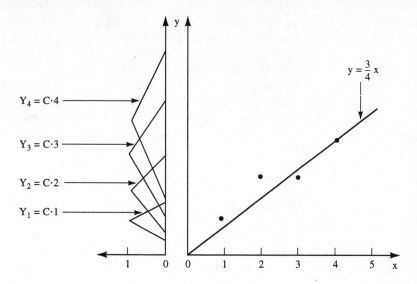

Figure 17.2 Illustration to Example 17.1.

Hence,

$$C = \left\langle \frac{5}{6}, \frac{1}{6(1-h)} \right\rangle.$$

Selecting, for example, $h = 2/3$, we obtain $C = \langle 5/6, 1/2 \rangle$. Fuzzy sets $Y_j = Ca_j$ for $a_1 = 1, a_2 = 2, a_3 = 3$, and $a_4 = 4$ are shown in Fig. 17.2. Also shown in the figure is the classical linear least-square fitting.

Linear Regression with Fuzzy Data

In this type of fuzzy regression, the dependence of an output variable on input variables is expressed by the form

$$Y = a_1 X_1 + a_2 X_2 + \ldots + a_n X_n, \tag{17.10}$$

where values of input and output variables are fuzzy numbers, assumed to be triangular and symmetric, and $a_1, a_2, \ldots, a_n$ are real-valued parameters. Let $X_i = \langle x_i, s_i \rangle$ for all $i \in \mathbb{N}_n$. Then,

$$Y(y) = \begin{cases} 1 - \dfrac{|y - \mathbf{a}^T \mathbf{x}|}{\mathbf{s}^T |\mathbf{a}|} & \text{when } \mathbf{a} \neq 0 \\ 1 & \text{when } \mathbf{a} = 0, y \neq 0 \\ 0 & \text{when } \mathbf{a} = 0, y = 0 \end{cases} \tag{17.11}$$

for all $y \in \mathbb{R}$, where

$$\mathbf{a} = \begin{bmatrix} a_1 \\ a_2 \\ \vdots \\ a_n \end{bmatrix}, \quad \mathbf{x} = \begin{bmatrix} x_1 \\ x_2 \\ \vdots \\ x_n \end{bmatrix}, \quad \mathbf{s} = \begin{bmatrix} s_1 \\ s_2 \\ \vdots \\ s_n \end{bmatrix}.$$

Data are given in terms of pairs $\langle \mathbf{X}^{(j)}, Y^{(j)} \rangle$, where $\mathbf{X}^{(j)}$ is an n-tuple of symmetric triangular fuzzy numbers, and $Y^{(j)}$ is a symmetric triangular fuzzy number for each $j \in \mathbb{N}_m$.

The aim of this regression problem is to find parameters $a_1, a_2, \ldots, a_n$ such that the fuzzy linear function (17.10) fits the given fuzzy data as best as possible. Two criteria of goodness are usually employed. According to the first criterion, the total difference between the areas of the actual fuzzy number $Y^{(j)}$ and the areas of the fuzzy numbers Y_j obtained for $\mathbf{X}^{(j)}$ by (17.10), where $j \in \mathbb{N}_m$, should be minimized. According to the second criterion, the fuzzy numbers $Y^{(j)}$ and Y_j should be compatible at least to some given degree $h \in [0, 1]$; the compatibility, com, is defined by

$$\mathrm{com}\,(Y^{(j)}, Y_j) = \sup_{y \in \mathbb{R}} \min[Y^{(j)}(y), Y_j(y)].$$

Using these two criteria, the described fuzzy regression problem can be formulated in terms of the following optimization problem:

$$\text{Minimize } \sum_{j=1}^{m} |\int_{\mathbb{R}} Y^{(j)}(y)dy - \int_{\mathbb{R}} Y_j(y)dy|$$

$$\text{s.t. } \min_{j \in \mathbb{N}_m} \mathrm{com}\,(Y^{(j)}, Y_j) \geq h. \qquad (17.12)$$

Let $X_i^{(j)} = \langle x_i^{(j)}, s_i^{(j)} \rangle$ for all $i \in \mathbb{N}_n$ and $Y^{(j)} = \langle y^{(j)}, s^{(j)} \rangle$. Then, the fuzzy regression problem of this type can also be formulated in the following form:

$$\text{Minimize } \sum_{j=1}^{m} |s^{(j)} - \sum_{i=1}^{n} |a_i| s_i^{(j)}|$$

$$\text{s.t. } -\sum_{i=1}^{n} |a_i| s_i^{(j)} + \sum_{i=1}^{n} a_i x_i^{(j)} \leq y^{(j)} - s^{(j)},$$

$$\sum_{i=1}^{n} |a_i| s_i^{(j)} + \sum_{i=1}^{n} a_i x_i^{(j)} \geq y^{(j)} - s^{(j)}, \qquad (17.13)$$

$$a_i \in \mathbb{R} \text{ for all } i \in \mathbb{N}_n \text{ and all } j \in \mathbb{N}_m.$$

Example 17.2

To illustrate the described method of linear regression with fuzzy data, let us consider the simple linear form

$$Y = aX$$

and the following data in terms of pairs of input/output fuzzy numbers:

$$\langle \langle 5/6, 1/2 \rangle, \langle 1, 0 \rangle \rangle,$$

$$\langle \langle 5/3, 1/2 \rangle, \langle 2, 1/2 \rangle \rangle,$$

$$\langle \langle 5/2, 1/2 \rangle, \langle 3, 1/2 \rangle \rangle,$$

$$\langle \langle 10/3, 1/2 \rangle, \langle 4, 0 \rangle \rangle.$$

Applying (17.13) to this example, we obtain:

$$\text{Minimize} \quad |a| + |1 - a|$$

$$\text{s.t.} \quad -\frac{|a|}{2} + \frac{5a}{6} \leq 1,$$

$$\frac{|a|}{2} + \frac{5a}{6} \geq 1,$$

$$-\frac{|a|}{2} + \frac{5a}{3} \leq 1.5,$$

$$\frac{|a|}{2} + \frac{5a}{3} \geq 1.5,$$

$$-\frac{|a|}{2} + \frac{5a}{2} \leq 2.5,$$

$$\frac{|a|}{2} + \frac{5a}{2} \geq 2.5,$$

$$-\frac{|a|}{2} + \frac{10a}{3} \leq 4,$$

$$\frac{|a|}{2} + \frac{10a}{3} \geq 4,$$

$$a \in \mathbb{R}.$$

This formulation can be simplified into

$$\text{Minimize} \quad |a| + |1 - a|$$

$$\text{s.t.} \quad a \in [6/8, 3],$$

$$a \in [9/13, 9/7],$$

$$a \in [5/6, 5/4],$$

$$a \in [24/23, 24/17].$$

Solving the problem, we find that the optimal value of the parameter a is $a^* = 24/23$. Hence, the form $Y = aX$ with the best fit (according to the chosen criteria) is $Y = 24X/23$.

17.6 INTERPERSONAL COMMUNICATION

The process of interpersonal communication consists of a vast array of different types of simultaneously communicated signals (words, voice tone, body posture, clothing, etc.), many of which conflict with each other. It is therefore difficult to determine the precise intention and meaning of the communication, because of both distortion from environmental noise and ambivalence on the part of the sender. Nevertheless, the receiver must respond appropriately in the face of this fuzzy or vague information. We outline here an approach suggested by Yager [1980b], which models this process and the vagueness associated with it through the use of fuzzy set theory.

Suppose that X constitutes the universal set of all possible signals x that may be communicated by the sender. Because of the distorting factors mentioned above, a clear, unique signal may not be available. Instead, the message received is a fuzzy subset M of

X, in which $M(x)$ denotes the degree of certainty of the receipt of the specific signal x. In order to determine whether an appropriate response can be chosen based on the message received or whether some error was involved in the communication, an assessment of the quality of the transmission must be made. Let the maximum value of membership that any $x \in X$ attains in the set M correspond to the *strength* of the transmission. If the set M has no unique maximum, then the message is called *ambiguous*. If the support of M is large, then M is considered to be *general*. The clarity of the message can be measured by the distance between the maximum membership grade attained in M and the next largest grade of any signal x in M. When the message received is strong, unambiguous, and clear, then the signal attaining the maximum membership grade in M can easily be selected as the most obvious intended communication. Difficulty occurs, however, when the message is weak, ambiguous, or unclear. In this case, the receiver must determine whether the problem in the communication lies in some environmental distortion (in which case a repetition of the signal may be requested) or in the sender of the message (in which case a response must be made that is, as far as possible, appropriate).

Usually, the receiver of the communication possesses some background information in the form of probabilities or possibilities of the signals that can be expected. If $p(x_1), p(x_2), \ldots, p(x_n)$ represent the probabilities associated with each of the signals $x_1, x_2, \ldots, x_n \in X$, then the probability of the fuzzy event of the receipt of message M is given by

$$p(M) = \sum_{x \in X} M(x)p(x).$$

The receiver can use this information to assess the consistency of the received message with his or her expectations. If the probability of the received message is high, then it can be assumed that little distortion was introduced by the environment. On the other hand, if the message is very clear and unambiguous, then an appropriate response can be made even if the probability of the signal was low.

Instead of the expectation or background information being given in probabilistic form, this information may be given in the form of a possibility distribution r on X. In this case, $r(x) \in [0, 1]$ indicates the receiver's belief in the possibility of signal x being sent. The total possibility of the fuzzy message M is calculated as

$$r(M) = \max_{x \in X}[\min(M(x), r(x))].$$

As in the case of probabilistic expectation, if the received message conflicts with the expected possibility of communication, then the receiver may attempt clarification by requesting a repetition of the transmission. Before this new transmission is sent, the receiver will probably have already modified his or her expectations based on the previous message. If r_0 indicates the initial possibilistic expectations of the receiver, and r_1 is the modified expectations subsequent to the receipt of message M, then

$$r_1(x) = \min[r_0^\alpha(x), M(x)]$$

for each $x \in X$, where α indicates the degree to which past messages are considered relevant in the modification of expectations. Our procedure for signal detection now consists of the following: a test of the consistency of M against the expectations and a test of the message M for strength and clarity. If both of these values are high, the signal attaining the maximum value in M can be comfortably assumed to be the intended signal. If both tests yield low values, the expectations are modified and a repetition is requested. If only one of these tests yields a satisfactory value, then either a new signal is requested or a response is made despite the presence of doubt.

An additional complications is introduced when we consider that the receiver may also introduce distortion in the message because of inconsistency with the expectations. Let

$$s(M, r) = \max_{x \in X}[\min(M(x), r(x))] \qquad (17.14)$$

correspond to the consistency of the received message with the possibilistic expectations. Then, let M' denote the message that the receiver actually hears, where

$$M'(x) = M^s(x) \qquad (17.15)$$

for each $x \in X$ where $s = s(M, r)$. The less consistent M is with the expectations, the less M' resembles M. Since the receiver will be modifying his or her expectations based on the message thought to have been received, the new possibilistic expectation structure is given by

$$r_1(x) = \min[r_0^{1-s}(x), M'(x)] \qquad (17.16)$$

for each $x \in X$.

Finally, once a determination has been made of the signal $x \in X$ that was sent, an appropriate response must be chosen. Let Y be the universal set of all responses, and let $R \subseteq Y \times X$ be a fuzzy binary relation in which $R(y, x)$ indicates the degree of appropriateness of response y given signal x. A fuzzy response set $A \in Y$ can be generated by composing the appropriateness relation R with the fuzzy message M,

$$A = R \circ M,$$

or

$$A(y) = \max_{x \in X}[\min(R(y, x), M(x))] \qquad (17.17)$$

for each $y \in Y$. The membership grade of each possible message y in fuzzy set A thus corresponds to the degree to which it is an appropriate response to the message M. A more interesting case occurs when the elements $y \in Y$ are not actual messages, but instead indicate characteristics or attributes that the appropriate message should possess. This allows for creativity in formulating the actual response. The following example illustrates the use of this model of interpersonal communication.

Suppose that a young man has just proposed marriage to a young woman and is now eagerly awaiting her response. Let us assume that her answer will be chosen from the set X of the following responses:

$x_1 =$ simple yes
$x_2 =$ simple no
$x_3 =$ request for time to think it over
$x_4 =$ request for the young man to ask permission of the young woman's parents
$x_5 =$ derisive laughter
$x_6 =$ joyful tears

Assume also that the young man has expectations of her response represented by the possibility distribution

$$\mathbf{r}_0 = \langle.9, .1, .7, .3, .1, .6\rangle.$$

We can see from this distribution that the young man expects a positive answer. Suppose, however, that the following message M_1 is received:

$$M_1 = .1/x_1 + .8/x_2 + .4x_3 + .1/x_5.$$

This message, although relatively strong, unambiguous, and clear, is rather inconsistent with the young man's expectations. As measured by (17.14), the consistency is

$$s(M_1, \mathbf{r}_0) = \max[.1, .1, .4, .1] = .4.$$

Because the message is contrary to the young man's expectations, let us assume that he introduces some distortion, as specified by (17.15), such that the message he hears is

$$M_1' = .4/x_1 + .9/x_2 + .7/x_3 + .4/x_5.$$

Based on this message, he modifies his expectations according to (17.16) such that

$$r_1(x) = \min[r_0^{.6}(x), M_1'(x)]$$

for each $x \in X$, or

$$r_1 = .4/x_1 + .25/x_2 + .7/x_3 + .25/x_5.$$

The young man has thus greatly diminished his expectation of a simple yes, somewhat increased his expectation of a simple no and of derisive laughter, and has given up all hope of the possibility of joyful tears. Suppose now that, in disbelief, he asks the young woman to repeat her answer and receives the following message:

$$M_2 = .9/x_2 + .4/x_5.$$

This message is stronger, clearer, and less general than the first answer. Its consistency with the young man's new expectations is

$$s(M_2, r_1) = .25.$$

Thus, the message is highly contrary even to the revised expectations of the young man, so let us suppose that he distorts the message such that he hears

$$M_2' = .97/x_2 + .8/x_5.$$

His surprise has thus diminished the clarity of the message heard and has led him to exaggerate the degree to which he believes that the young woman has responded with derisive laughter. Let us now suppose that the response which the young man makes will have characteristics chosen from the following set Y:

$$y_1 = \text{happiness} \qquad y_2 = \text{pain} \qquad y_3 = \text{surprise}$$
$$y_4 = \text{anger} \qquad y_5 = \text{patience} \qquad y_6 = \text{impatience}$$
$$y_7 = \text{affection}$$

Let the fuzzy relation $R \subseteq Y \times X$ represent the degree to which the young man plans to respond to a given signal x with a response having the attribute y. This relation is given by the following matrix (rows and columns are ordered by the subscripts of the symbols involved):

$$\begin{bmatrix} .9 & 0 & .2 & 0 & 0 & 1 \\ 0 & .9 & .1 & .2 & 1 & 0 \\ .1 & .9 & .2 & .9 & 1 & .3 \\ 0 & .5 & 0 & .6 & .7 & 0 \\ .1 & 0 & .9 & 0 & 0 & .5 \\ 0 & .3 & .2 & .3 & .4 & 0 \\ .9 & 0 & .9 & .3 & 0 & 1 \end{bmatrix}$$

Using (17.17), we can now calculate the response the young man will make to the message M_2':

$$A = R \circ M_2' = .9/y_2 + .9/y_3 + .7/y_4 + .4/y_6.$$

The young man's response, therefore, will have the characteristics of a great deal of pain and surprise, a large degree of anger, and some impatience.

17.7 OTHER APPLICATIONS

The purpose of this last section is to mention some additional application areas of fuzzy set theory, which are covered neither in previous sections of this chapter nor in previous chapters. These are areas in which applications of fuzzy set theory seem to have great potential, but are not well developed or have not even been tried as yet.

One area in which fuzzy set theory has a great potential is *psychology*. Although the interest of psychologists in fuzzy set theory has visibly been growing since the mid-1980s or so, the relevant literature is too dispersed at this time to indicate any general trends in this area. The principle sources consist of a book edited by Zétényi [1988] and two books by Smithson [1987, 1989].

Psychology is not only a field in which it is reasonable to anticipate profound applications of fuzzy set theory, but also one that is very important to the development of fuzzy set theory itself. In particular, the area of psycholinguistics is essential for studying the connection between the human use of linguistic terms in different contexts with the associated fuzzy sets and operations on fuzzy sets. To understand this connection is necessary for properly incorporating the notion of a context into the formalism of fuzzy set theory. This will undoubtedly help us, in the long run, to better understand human communication and design machines capable of communicating with people in a human-friendly way with natural language.

Applications of fuzzy set theory and fuzzy measure theory in *natural sciences* are relatively scarce. This may be explained by the fact that classical methods based on crisp sets and additive measures have worked quite well in these areas and, consequently, there have been no pressing needs to replace them with the more realistic methods based on fuzzy sets and fuzzy measures. One exception is *quantum mechanics*, where the need for nonclassical methods is acute. Based on some preliminary investigation by, for example, Dvurečenski and Riečan [1991], it is reasonable to expect that both fuzzy sets and fuzzy measures will play profound roles in quantum mechanics in the near future. Other areas of *physics* are likely to be affected by fuzzy sets and measures as well. Areas of physics in which the utility of fuzzy set theory has already been demonstrated include non-equilibrium thermodynamics [Singer, 1992] and dimensional analysis [Singer, 1994]. The concept of a *finite resolution limit* introduced by Fridrich [1994a], which is based on subadditive fuzzy measures that become additive on disjoint sets separated by more than a given finite resolution limit, is likely to influence physics in a major way by narrowing the gap between theoretical and experimental physics. Fuzzy sets and fuzzy measures are also likely to have a strong impact upon *chemistry*, as already indicated by Singer and Singer [1993].

Applications in *biology* have not been visible so far, which is somewhat surprising since the potential is enormous. Fuzzy sets will undoubtedly play an important role in narrowing down the large gap that currently exists between theoretical and experimental biology. It is reasonable to expect that some applications of fuzzy sets in biology will be profound. In the related area of *ecology*, a few applications have already been explored by Bosserman and Ragade [1982], Roberts [1989], and Salski [1992].

Let us close this book with a few speculations about some additional areas in which fuzzy set theory will likely play a major role sometime in the future. One such area is *soft computing*, which has already emerged and will likely play a profound role in computer technology in the not too distant future. In general, soft computing attempts to exploit the tolerance for uncertainty of various types to achieve tractability, low cost, and robustness. It is concerned with the effect of applying *approximate methods* to precisely or imprecisely formulated problems on computational complexity and cost. The primary aim of soft computing is to develop computational methods that produce acceptable approximate solutions at low cost. This aim is pursued by concerted efforts involving several areas, including *fuzzy set theory*, *neural networks*, *genetic algorithms*, *fuzzy measure theory*, and, perhaps, a few other areas. To facilitate soft computing, one important area is the development of *fuzzy hardware* (Sec. 16.5) and massively parallel computer architectures for approximate reasoning.

Fuzzy set theory and fuzzy logic will inevitably play an important role in any problem area that involves *natural language*. The capability of communicating with home computers or robots in natural language is likely to become available within a decade or so. A more difficult task will be to upgrade current systems of *machine translation* between natural languages to the level of experienced human translators. Another difficult task will be to develop the capability of machines to *understand images*, which will require studying the relationship between visual and linguistic information. An ultimate challenge involving natural language will be the development of machine capabilities to *summarize* literary creations.

One application area in which the use of fuzzy logic and the associated technology is essential is subsumed under the concept of an *intelligent car*. Fuzzy technology will help to solve various safety problems and facilitate automatic driving, optimal navigation by voice instructions in natural language, diagnosis and prevention of failures, automatic parking, and a host of other functions.

Fuzzy technology will likely be increasingly important for dealing with the various problem areas involved in health care. Its importance emanates from the nature of medical information, which is highly individualized, often imprecise (especially when expressed in natural language), context-sensitive, and often based on subjective judgment. To deal with this kind of information without fuzzy logic and approximate reasoning is virtually impossible. Expert systems for medical diagnosis and treatment planning that are based on approximate reasoning, which we touched upon in Sec. 17.2, represent just one facet of this very complex application area. Other facets include fuzzy control of various medical devices, comprehensive evaluation of patients' abnormal physiological conditions based not only on physiological data, but also on their appearance and behavior, artificial limbs, navigation systems aiding the visually handicapped, robots designed to assist patients, and other problem domains.

We may continue to speculate about other ways in which fuzzy thinking in its various forms is likely to affect our lifes in the future. We may speculate about its effects on education, social policy, law, art, and so on, but we prefer to leave it to the reader to use his or her own imagination and knowledge learned from this book to form a personal fuzzy vision of the future.

NOTES

17.1. The utility of fuzzy set theory in medical diagnosis was first demonstrated by Albin [1975]. Literature devoted to this topic is now quite large. Some relevant publications are mentioned in Sec. 17.1; a few additional references are [Soula and Sanchez, 1982; Kerre, 1982; Vila and Delgado, 1983; Umeyama, 1986; Sanchez, 1986; Degani and Bortolan, 1988]. Other applications within the area of medicine include the use of linguistic variables for questionnaires investigating the relation between social stresses, psychological factors, and the incidence of coronary disease [Saitta and Torasso, 1981], the incorporation of fuzziness in an expert system dealing with the treatment of diabetes [Buisson *et al.*, 1985], the use of linguistic descriptions of symptoms for the purpose of evaluating different treatment procedures [Oguntade and Beaumont, 1982], the use of fuzzy inference for evaluating orthodontic treatment [Yoshikawa *et al.*, 1994], and clinical monitoring with fuzzy automata [Steimann and Adlassnig, 1994]. Miscellaneous medical applications of fuzzy sets can also be found in books edited by Kohout and Bandler [1986] and Gupta and Sanchez [1982a]. A special journal, *Biomedical Fuzzy Systems Bulletin*, has been published by the Biomedical Fuzzy Systems Association in Japan since 1990 (in both Japanese and English).

17.2. The first major publication devoted to applications of fuzzy set theory in economics is a book edited by Ponsard and Fustier [1986]. This book and two papers by Ponsard [1981, 1988] contain sufficient information about Ponsard's pioneering contributions to fuzzy economics. A paper by Chen, Lee, and Yu [1983] is a readable overview of some issues of fuzzy economics. The concept of a fuzzy game was introduced by Butnariu [1978, 1985].

17.3. An application of genetic algorithms for altering membership functions of fuzzy controllers on-line was developed in the context of chemical engineering by Karr and Gentry [1993]. Advantages of genetic algorithms for optimizing various parameters in approximate reasoning are discussed by Park, Kandel, and Langholz [1994]. Numerous other applications of genetic algorithms in the area of fuzzy systems can be found in *Proceedings of the International Conference on Genetic Algorithms*, particularly in the 1990s.

17.4. The idea of fuzzifying genetic algorithms emerged in the early 1990s. Various forms of fuzzy genetic algorithms were proposed by Sanchez [1993], Xu and Vukovich [1993], and Buckley and Hayashi [1994b].

17.5. The two problems of fuzzy regression discussed in Sec. 17.5 were proposed in papers by Savic and Pedrycz [1991] and Wang and Li [1990]. The principal source on fuzzy regression analysis is a book edited by Kacprzyk and Fedrizzi [1992]. Among many papers on this subject, let us mention papers by Celmins [1987a, b], Diamond [1988], Heshmaty and Kandel [1985], and Tanaka [1987].

17.6. Among other areas connected with natural sciences, the use of fuzzy set theory has been observed in meteorology [Cao and Chen, 1983; Zhang and Chen, 1984] and earthquake research [Feng and Liu, 1986].

17.7. An interesting application of fuzzy set theory, which was studied by Bouchon [1981] and Akdag and Bouchon [1988], are fuzzy questionnaires. This application is quite important, since questionnaires are fundamental tools for analyzing structures of information.

EXERCISES

17.1. Explore other feasible scenarios involving the model of interpersonal communication introduced in Sec. 17.6.

17.2. Derive (17.8).

17.3. Repeat the examples of medical diagnosis in Sec. 17.2 for other numerical values.

17.4. Suppose that we are given the following data set in the two-dimensional space $\langle x, y \rangle$:

$$\{\langle 2, 14 \rangle\, , \langle 4, 11 \rangle, \langle 6, 17 \rangle, \langle 8, 15 \rangle, \langle 10, 19 \rangle, \ \langle 12, 22 \rangle, \langle 14, 18 \rangle, \langle 16, 30 \rangle\}.$$

Use the fuzzy linear regression method to estimate coefficients in (17.6) to obtain the best fitting of these data points.

17.5. Consider the following pairs of triangular fuzzy numbers in the two-dimensional space $\langle x, y \rangle$:

$$\langle \langle 1, 2 \rangle, \langle 6, 12 \rangle \rangle,$$

$$\langle \langle 1.5, 1 \rangle, \langle 9, 6 \rangle \rangle,$$

$$\langle \langle 2, 3 \rangle, \langle 12, 18 \rangle \rangle,$$

$$\langle \langle 3, 1 \rangle, \langle 18, 6 \rangle \rangle,$$

$$\langle \langle 4, 2 \rangle, \langle 24, 12 \rangle \rangle.$$

Use the regression method discussed in Sec. 17.5 to find the best-fitting function in the form of (17.10).

Appendix A

Artificial Neural Networks: An Overview

Although artificial neural networks are beyond the scope of this text, we want to make the reader aware of their important connections with fuzzy systems. While neural networks can effectively be used for learning membership functions, fuzzy inference rules, and other context-dependent patterns, fuzzification of neural networks extends their capabilities and applicability. The aim of this appendix is to provide the reader with a few basic ideas regarding neural networks to make some discussions involving neural networks in the text comprehensible.

An *artificial neural network* is a computational structure that is inspired by observed processes in natural networks of biological neurons in the brain. It consists of simple *computational units*, called *neurons*, that are highly interconnected. Each *interconnection* has a strength that is expressed by a number referred to as a *weight*.

The basic capability of neural networks is to learn patterns from examples. This is accomplished by adjusting the weights of given interconnections according to some *learning algorithm*. In general, the learning can be supervised or unsupervised. In a *supervised learning algorithm*, learning is guided by specifying, for each training input pattern, the class to which the pattern is supposed to belong. That is, the desired response of the network to each training input pattern and its comparison with the actual output of the network are used in the learning algorithm for appropriate adjustments of the weights. These adjustments, whose purpose is to minimize the difference between the desired and actual outputs, are made incrementally. That is, small adjustments in the weights are made in the desired direction for each training pair. This is essential for facilitating a *convergence* to a solution (specific values of the weights) in which patterns in the training set are recognized with high fidelity. Once a network converges to a solution, it is then capable of classifying each unknown input pattern with other patterns that are close to it in terms of the same distinguishing features.

In an *unsupervised learning algorithm*, the network forms its own classification of patterns. The classification is based on commonalities in certain features of input patterns. This requires that a neural network implementing an unsupervised learning algorithm be able to identify common features across the range of input patterns.

In this overview, we cover only supervised learning and special neural networks, usually called *multilayer feedforward networks* or *multilayer perceptrons*. Furthermore, we describe only one algorithm for supervised learning, the so-called *backpropagation learning algorithm*, which is the most common algorithm for applications of our interest.

The basic computational units of neural networks are artificial neurons. A single *neuron*, as depicted in Fig. A.1a, has *n* inputs $x_1, x_2, \ldots, x_n$, whose values are real numbers, and one *output y*. In addition, inputs of the neuron are associated with real numbers, $w_1, w_2, \ldots, w_n$, referred to as *weights*. The output depends on the *weighted sum of inputs*,

$$\sum_{i=1}^{n} w_i x_i,$$

in terms of a nonlinear function, which is called an *activation function* or *threshold function*. The most common activation functions are the *Heaviside function, h*, defined by

$$h(a) = \begin{cases} 1 & \text{when } a \geq 0 \\ 0 & \text{when } a < 0 \end{cases}$$

for all $a \in \mathbb{R}$, and the class of *sigmoid functions, s_β*, defined by the formula

$$s_\beta(a) = (1 + e^{-\beta a})^{-1}, \tag{A.1}$$

where β is a positive constant (so-called steepness parameter) whose value specifies a particular sigmoid function in this class. These functions are illustrated in Fig. A.2.

Since the Heaviside function is a special sigmoid function, obtained as $\beta \to \infty$, let us consider only the sigmoid functions. Then, the output of the neuron is defined by

$$y = s_\beta(\sum_{i=1}^{n} w_i x_i - \theta) \tag{A.2}$$

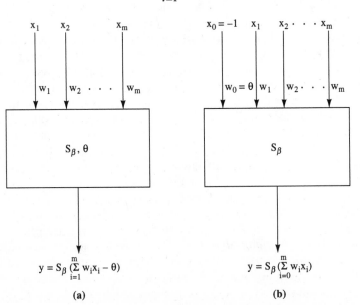

Figure A.1 Two equivalent representation of a neuron activated by a sigmoid function s_β with bias θ.

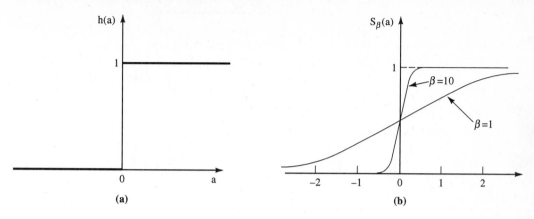

Figure A.2   Examples of activation functions: (a) Heaviside function h; (b) sigmoid functions s_β.

for some $\beta \in \mathbb{R}^+$ where θ is the so-called *bias* of the neuron. The bias defines the value of the weighted sum of inputs around which the output of the neuron is most sensitive to changes in the sum.

For convenience, the bias θ is usually represented by an extra input, $x_0 = -1$, and the associated weight $w_0 = \theta$. Then, (A.2) is replaced with the simpler formula

$$y = s_\beta(\sum_{i=0}^{n} w_i x_i). \tag{A.3}$$

In our further considerations, we employ this simpler characterization of the neuron, as depicted in Fig. A.1b.

We can now describe the structure of *layered feedforward neural networks*. Each of these networks consists of a set of inputs and one or more layers of parallel neurons. Inputs are connected only to neurons in the first layer with the exception of the special input x_0, representing the bias of each neuron, which is connected to all neurons in the network. Neurons in one layer are connected to all neurons in the next layer. No other connections exist in neural networks of this type. The last layer, which produces the output of the network, is called an *output layer*. Any layers that precede the output layer are called *hidden layers*.

The set of inputs is sometimes referred to as an input layer. We do not use this term, since inputs do not do any computation; their only role is to feed input patterns into the rest of the network.

It is established that three-layer feedforward neural networks are sufficient for approximating any function to a given accuracy, but it is not known, in general, how many neurons are necessary in the hidden layers. It is also known that two layers are sufficient to approximate any continuous function of n variables, provided that the hidden layer contains at least $2n + 1$ neurons.

Due to these theoretical results, we have to consider only networks with no more than three layers. The structure of feedforward neural networks with one, two, and three layers is shown in detail in Figs. A.3–A.5. For convenience, weights at each output layer are denoted by W with appropriate subscripts, while weights at each hidden layer are denoted by w with

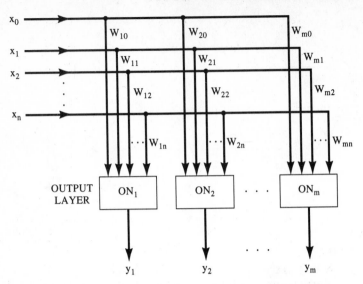

Figure A.3 Feedforward neural network with one layer (simple perceptron).

appropriate subscripts. When two hidden layers are employed, their weights are distinguished by the superscripts 1 and 2, as shown in Fig. A.5.

Before we proceed to formulating the backpropagation learning algorithm, which is applicable to neural networks with at least one hidden layer, let us describe a simple *gradient-descent learning algorithm* for networks with only one layer, the output layer (Fig. A.3).

As in any supervised learning, a *training set* of correct input-output pairs is given. Let $\langle \mathbf{X}_p, \mathbf{T}_p \rangle$ denote a particular input-output pair in the training set, where

$$\mathbf{X}_p = \langle x_1^p, x_2^p, \ldots, x_n^p \rangle,$$
$$\mathbf{T}_p = \langle t_1^p, t_2^p, \ldots, t_m^p \rangle.$$

The m-tuple $\mathbf{T}_p$ is usually called a *target output*; it is the desired output of the neural network for the input pattern $\mathbf{X}_p$. Let

$$\mathbf{Y}_p = \langle y_1^p, y_2^p, \ldots, y_m^p \rangle$$

denote the actual output of the neural network for the input pattern $\mathbf{X}_p$.

Given $\mathbf{X}_p$, $\mathbf{T}_p$, and $\mathbf{Y}_p$, the error of the neural network in responding to the input pattern $\mathbf{X}_p$ is usually expressed in terms of the *error function*

$$E_p = \frac{1}{2} \sum_{k=1}^{m} (t_k^p - y_k^p)^2 = \frac{1}{2} \sum_{k=1}^{m} [t_k^p - s_\beta (\sum_{i=0}^{n} W_{ki} x_i^p)]^2, \tag{A.4}$$

where the constant 1/2 is used solely for computational convenience. As previously explained, we define $x_0^p = -1$ in (A.4) to represent the bias of neuron k by the weight W_{k0}. Clearly, E_p is positive and converges to zero as the network approaches a solution for the training sample $\langle \mathbf{X}_p, \mathbf{T}_p \rangle$. The *cumulative cycle error*, E, associated with the whole training set is given by

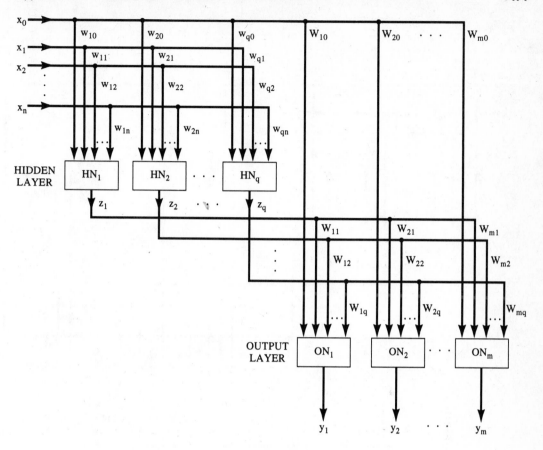

Figure A.4 Feedforward neural network with two layers.

$$E = \sum_p E_p. \tag{A.5}$$

For each given training pair $\langle \mathbf{X}_p, \mathbf{T}_p \rangle$, the error function depends on the weights involved in the neural network. According to the gradient descent algorithm, we can reduce the value E_p by changing each weight W_{ki} by an amount ΔW_{ki} proportional to the negative gradient of E_p at the present location. That is,

$$\Delta W_{ki} = -\eta \frac{\partial E_p}{\partial W_{ki}}, \tag{A.6}$$

where η is a positive constant referred to as the *learning rate*. The choice of η influences the accuracy of the final approximation as well as the speed of convergence. In general, a close approximation can be obtained if η is small but, then, the convergence is slow and less reliable.

To calculate the partial derivative in (A.6), let us rewrite (A.4) in a simpler form

$$E_p = \frac{1}{2} \sum_{k=1}^{m} [t_k^p - s_\beta(a_k^p)]^2,$$

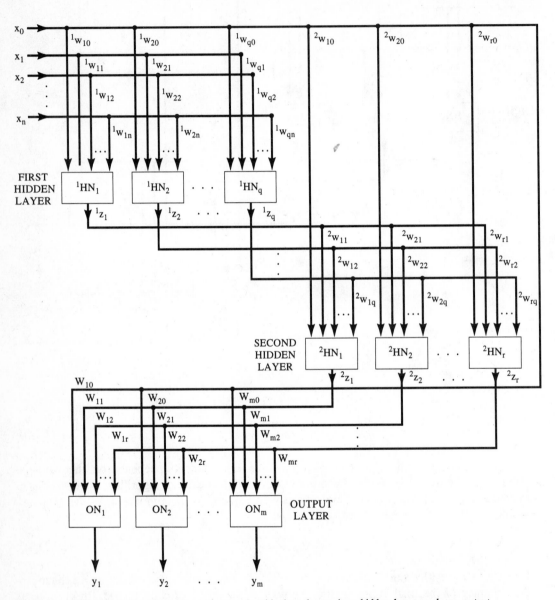

Figure A.5 Feedforward neural network with three layers (two hidden layers and one output layer).

where

$$a_k^p = \sum_{i=0}^{n} W_{ki} x_i^p.$$

Then,

$$\frac{\partial E_p}{\partial W_{ki}} = -[t_k^p - s_\beta(a_k^p)]s_\beta'(a_k^p)x_i^p$$
$$= -[t_k^p - y_k^p]s_\beta'(a_k^p)x_i^p,$$

where s_β' denotes the derivative of the sigmoid function, which can be written in the form

$$s_\beta'(a_k^p) = \beta s_\beta(a_k^p)[1 - s_\beta(a_k^p)]$$
$$= \beta y_k^p [1 - y_k^p]. \tag{A.7}$$

Introducing now the quantity

$$\delta_k^p = (t_k^p - y_k^p)s_\beta'(a_k^p)$$
$$= (t_k^p - y_k^p)\beta y_k^p(1 - y_k^p), \tag{A.8}$$

the gradient descent correction of the weights is given by the formula

$$\Delta W_{ki} = \eta \delta_k^p x_i^p \tag{A.9}$$

The whole algorithm proceeds in cycles. In each cycle, all input-output pairs in the given training set are applied to the network either in a predefined order or randomly. For each pair $\langle \mathbf{X}_p, \mathbf{T}_p \rangle$, we calculate the error E_p by (A.4) and update all weights in the network by the values ΔW_{ki} calculated by (A.9). During each cycle, we also calculate the cumulative cycle error E defined by (A.5). When a cycle is completed, E is compared with a maximum acceptable error $E_{\max}$ specified by the user. If $E \leq E_{\max}$, we obtain a solution (the network converged within the required accuracy) and the algorithm terminates. If $E > E_{\max}$, we initiate a new cycle, during which we calculate a new cumulative cycle error.

Let us describe now the backpropagation learning algorithm for feedforward neural networks with two layers, which is based on the gradient descent algorithm described for one-layer networks. We adopt all the symbols introduced in Fig. A.4, as well as relevant symbols introduced previously.

Given an input pattern $\mathbf{X}_p$, hidden neuron HN_j receives the total input

$$h_j^p = \sum_{i=0}^{n} w_{ji} x_i^p \tag{A.10}$$

and produces the total output

$$z_j^p = s_\beta(h_j^p) = s_\beta(\sum_{i=0}^{n} w_{ji} x_i^p). \tag{A.11}$$

Output neuron ON_k then receives the total input

$$o_k^p = \sum_{j=0}^{q} W_{kj} z_j^p = W_{k0} x_0^p + \sum_{j=1}^{q} W_{kj} s_\beta(\sum_{i=0}^{n} w_{ji} x_i^p), \tag{A.12}$$

where $z_0^p = x_0^p$ by convention (see Fig. A.4), and produces the output

$$y_k^p = s_\beta(o_k^p) = s_\beta(\sum_{j=0}^{q} W_{kj} z_j^p)$$

$$= s_\beta(W_{k0} x_0^p + \sum_{j=1}^{q} W_{kj} s_\beta(\sum_{i=0}^{n} w_{ji} x_i^p)).$$

(A.13)

Using this equation, we can now express the error function as

$$E_p = \frac{1}{2} \sum_{k=1}^{m} (t_k^p - y_k^p)^2 = \frac{1}{2} \sum_{k=1}^{m} (t_k^p - s_\beta(\sum_{j=0}^{q} W_{kj} z_j^p))$$

$$= \frac{1}{2} \sum_{k=1}^{m} [t_k^p - s_\beta(W_{k0} x_0^p + \sum_{j=1}^{q} W_{kj} s_\beta(\sum_{i=0}^{n} w_{ji} x_i^p))]^2,$$

(A.14)

and use the gradient descent algorithm to make appropriate adjustments of weights W_{kj} and w_{ji}. For weights W_{kj}, associated with the hidden-to-output connections, we obtain

$$\Delta W_{kj} = -\eta \frac{\partial E_p}{\partial W_{kj}} = \eta (t_k^p - y_k^p) s_\beta'(o_k^p) z_j^p$$

$$= \eta \delta_k^p z_j^p,$$

(A.15)

where

$$\delta_k^p = (t_k^p - y_k^p) s_\beta'(o_k^p).$$

(A.16)

Observe that (A.15) would become identical with (A.9) if z_j^p were viewed as inputs in a one-layer network. Using (A.7), δ_k^p can also be expressed as

$$\delta_k^p = \beta (t_k^p - y_k^p)(1 - y_k^p) y_k^p.$$

(A.17)

For weights w_{ji}, associated with the input-to-hidden connections, we must calculate the partial derivatives of E_p with respect to weights w_{ji}, which are more deeply embedded in the expression (A.14). We obtain

$$\Delta w_{ji} = -\eta \frac{\partial E_p}{\partial w_{ji}} = -\sum_{k=1}^{m} \eta \frac{\partial E_p}{\partial z_j^p} \frac{\partial z_j^p}{\partial w_{ji}}$$

$$= \sum_{k=1}^{m} \eta (t_k^p - y_k^p) s_\beta'(o_k^p) W_{kj} s_\beta'(h_j^p) x_i^p$$

$$= \sum_{k=1}^{m} \eta \delta_k^p W_{kj} s_\beta'(h_j^p) x_i^p$$

$$= \sum_{k=1}^{m} \eta \delta_j^p x_i^p,$$

(A.18)

where

$$\delta_j^p = s'_\beta(h_j^p)\delta_k^p W_{kj} \tag{A.19}$$

and δ_k^p is expressed by (A.16) or (A.17). Since $s'_\beta(a) = \beta[1 - s_\beta(a)]s_\beta(a)$ for the sigmoid function and $s_\beta(h_j^p) = z_j^p$, we may also express δ_j^p in the form

$$\delta_j^p = \delta_k^p W_{kj}\beta(1 - z_j^p)z_j^p. \tag{A.20}$$

The whole algorithm proceeds in cycles in a similar way as described for one-layer networks. In each cycle, we apply all input-output pairs in the given training set. For each training pair $\langle \mathbf{X}_p, \mathbf{T}_p \rangle$, we calculate the error E_p by (A.14) and update weights W_{kj} at the output layer by values ΔW_{kj} calculated by (A.15) as well as weights w_{ji} at the hidden layer by values Δw_{ji} calculated by (A.18). We also calculate the cumulative cycle error E by (A.5) during each cycle. At the end of the cycle, we compare E with a given maximum acceptable error $E_{\max}$. If $E \leq E_{\max}$, the algorithm terminates; otherwise, a new cycle is initiated.

The backpropagation learning algorithm described here for feedforward neural networks with two layers be extended to networks with three or more layers, but we do not deem it necessary to cover the general formulation in this overview. We also do not cover other types of learning algorithms, other types of neural networks, and various theoretical issues, such as the convergence of learning algorithms, the effect of the number of layers on performance, requisite numbers of neurons in hidden layers, and the like. This additional information can be found in numerous books that specialize on artificial neural networks. For the benefit of the reader, let us recommend a few of these books.

The only book that deals in depth with the connection between fuzzy systems and neural networks was written by Kosko [1992]. A simple overview of the area of artificial neural networks is covered in *Neural Computing* by R. Beale and T. Jackson (Adam Hilger, 1990). The following books are recommended for a deeper study of the field:

1. *Neurocomputing* by R. Hecht-Nielsen (Addison-Wesley, 1990).
2. *Introduction to the Theory of Neural Computation* by J. Hertz, A. Krogh, and R. G. Palmer (Addison-Wesley, 1991)
3. *Artificial Neural Systems* by J. M. Zurada (West Publishing Co., 1992).

In addition, we recommend a collection of classical papers dealing with theoretical foundations and analysis of neural networks, which is entitled *Neural Networks* (C. Lau, editor, IEEE Press, 1992).

APPENDIX B

GENETIC ALGORITHMS:
AN OVERVIEW

Genetic algorithms are unorthodox search or optimization algorithms, which were first suggested by John Holland in his book *Adaptation in Natural and Artificial Systems* (Univ. of Michigan Press, Ann Arbor, 1975). As the name suggests, genetic algorithms were inspired by the processes observed in natural evolution. They attempt to mimic these processes and utilize them for solving a wide range of optimization problems. In general, genetic algorithms perform directed random searches through a given set of alternatives with the aim of finding the best alternative with respect to given criteria of goodness. These criteria are required to be expressed in terms of an objective function, which is usually referred to as a *fitness function*.

Genetic algorithms require that the set of alternatives to be searched through be finite. If we want to apply them to an optimization problem where this requirement is not satisfied, we have to discretize the set involved and select an appropriate finite subset. It is further required that the alternatives be coded in strings of some specific finite length which consist of symbols from some finite alphabet. These strings are called *chromosomes*; the symbols that form them are called *genes*, and their set is called a *gene pool*.

Genetic algorithms search for the best alternative (in the sense of a given fitness function) through chromosomes' evolution. Basic steps in genetic algorithms are shown in Fig. B.1. First, an initial population of chromosomes is randomly selected. Then each of the chromosomes in the population is evaluated in terms of its fitness (expressed by the fitness function). Next, a new population of chromosomes is selected from the given population by giving a greater change to select chromosomes with high fitness. This is called *natural selection*. The new population may contain duplicates. If given stopping criteria (e.g., no change in the old and new population, specified computing time, etc.) are not met, some specific, genetic-like operations are performed on chromosomes of the new population. These operations produce new chromosomes, called *offsprings*. The same steps of this process, evaluation and natural selection, are then applied to chromosomes of the resulting population. The whole process is repeated until given stopping criteria are met. The solution is expressed by the best chromosome in the final population.

There are many variations on these basic ideas of genetic algorithms. To describe a particular type of genetic algorithm in greater detail, let G denote the gene pool, and let n

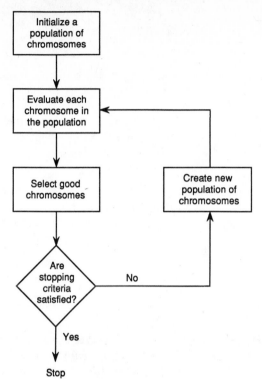

Figure B.1 High-level description of genetic algorithms.

denote the length of strings of genes that form chromosomes. That is, chromosomes are n-tuples in G^n. The size of the population of chromosomes is usually kept constant during the execution of a genetic algorithm. That is, when new members are added to the population, the corresponding number of old members are excluded. Let m denote this constant population size. Since each population may contain duplicates of chromosomes, we express populations by m-tuples whose elements are n-tuples from the set G^n. Finally, let f denote the fitness function employed in the algorithm.

The algorithm, which is iterative, consists of the following six steps:

1. *Select an initial population*, $\mathbf{p}^{(k)}$, *of a given size* m, *where* $k = 1$. This selection is made randomly from the set G^n. The choice of value m is important. If it is too large, the algorithm does not differ much from an exhaustive search; if it is too small, the algorithm may not reach the optimal solution.

2. *Evaluate each chromosome in population* $\mathbf{p}^{(k)}$ *in terms of its fitness*. This is done by determining for each chromosome $\mathbf{x}$ in the population the value of the fitness function, $f(\mathbf{x})$.

3. *Generate a new population*, $\mathbf{p}_n^{(k)}$, *from the given population* $\mathbf{p}^{(k)}$ *by some procedure of natural selection*. We describe only one possible procedure of natural selection, which is referred to as *deterministic sampling*. According to this procedure, we calculate the value $e(\mathbf{x}) = mg(\mathbf{x})$ for each $\mathbf{x}$ in $\mathbf{p}^{(k)}$, where $g(\mathbf{x})$ is a relative fitness defined by the formula

$$g(\mathbf{x}) = \frac{f(\mathbf{x})}{\sum\limits_{\mathbf{x} \in \mathbf{p}^{(k)}} f(\mathbf{x})}.$$

Then the number of copies of each chromosome $\mathbf{x}$ in $\mathbf{p}^{(k)}$ that is chosen for $\mathbf{p}_n^{(k)}$ is given by the integer part of $e(\mathbf{x})$. If the total number of chromosomes chosen in this way is smaller than m (the usual case), then we select the remaining chromosomes for $\mathbf{p}_n^{(k)}$ by the fractional parts of $e(\mathbf{x})$, from the highest values down. In general, the purpose of this procedure is to eliminate chromosomes with low fitness and duplicate those with high fitness.

4. If stopping criteria are not met, go to Step 5; otherwise, stop.

5. *Produce a population of new chromosomes,* $\mathbf{p}^{(k+1)}$, by operating on chromosomes in population $\mathbf{p}_n^{(k)}$. Operations that are involved in this step attempt to mimic genetic operations observed in biological systems. They include some or all of the following four operations:

- **Simple crossover**: Given two chromosomes

$$\mathbf{x} = \langle x_1, x_2, \ldots, x_n \rangle,$$
$$\mathbf{y} = \langle y_1, y_2, \ldots, y_n \rangle$$

and an integer $i \in \mathbb{N}_{n-1}$, which is called a *crossover position*, the operation of simple crossover applied to $\mathbf{x}$ and $\mathbf{y}$ replaces these chromosomes with their offsprings,

$$\mathbf{x}' = \langle x_1, \ldots, x_i, y_{i+1}, \ldots, y_n \rangle,$$
$$\mathbf{y}' = \langle y_1, \ldots, y_i, x_{i+1}, \ldots, x_n \rangle.$$

Chromosomes $\mathbf{x}$ and $\mathbf{y}$, to which this operation is applied, are called *mates*.

- **Double crossover**: Given the same chromosomes mates $\mathbf{x}$, $\mathbf{y}$ as in the simple crossover and two crossover positions $i, j \in \mathbb{N}_{n-1}(i < j)$, the operation of double crossover applied to $\mathbf{x}$ and $\mathbf{y}$ replaces these chromosomes with their offsprings,

$$\mathbf{x}' = \langle x_1, \ldots, x_i, y_{i+1}, \ldots, y_j, x_{j+1}, \ldots, x_n \rangle,$$
$$\mathbf{y}' = \langle y_1, \ldots, y_i, x_{i+1}, \ldots, x_j, y_{j+1}, \ldots, y_n \rangle$$

- **Mutation**: Given a chromosome $\mathbf{x} = \langle x_1, x_2, \ldots, x_n \rangle$ and an integer $i \in \mathbb{N}_n$, which is called a *mutation position*, the operation of mutation replaces $\mathbf{x}$ with

$$\mathbf{x}' = \langle x_1, \ldots, x_{i-1}, z, x_{i+1}, \ldots, x_n \rangle,$$

where z is a randomly chosen gene from the gene pool G.

- **Inversion**: Given a chromosome $\mathbf{x} = \langle x_1, x_2, \ldots, x_n \rangle$ and two integers $i, j \in \mathbb{N}_{n-1}(i < j)$, which are called *inversion positions*, the operation of inversion replaces $\mathbf{x}$ with

$$\mathbf{x}' = \langle x_1, \ldots, x_i, x_j, x_{j-1}, \ldots, x_{i+1}, x_{j+1}, \ldots, x_n \rangle.$$

6. *Replace population* $\mathbf{p}_n^{(k)}$ with population $\mathbf{p}^{(k+1)}$ produced in Step 4, increase k by one, and go to Step 2.

TABLE B.1   ILLUSTRATION TO EXAMPLE B.1

(a) $k = 1$: Steps 2 and 3

Chromosomes in $\mathbf{p}^{(1)}$	Integers	Fitness	$g(\mathbf{x})$	$4g(\mathbf{x})$	Number of selected copies
00010	2	3.75	0.068	0.272	0
01001	9	12.94	0.292	1.168	1
10011	19	15.44	0.350	1.400	2
11000	24	12.00	0.291	1.164	1

(b) $k = 1$: Step 5

Chromosomes in $\mathbf{p_n}^{(1)}$	Mate (randomly selected)	Crossover site (randomly selected)	Resulting chromosomes in $\mathbf{p}^{(2)}$
01001	10011	3	01011
10011	01001	3	10001
10011	11000	1	11000
11000	10011	1	10011

(c) $k = 2$: Steps 2 and 3

Chromosomes in $\mathbf{p}^{(2)}$	Integers	Fitness	$g(\mathbf{x})$	$4g(\mathbf{x})$	Number of copies selected
01011	11	14.44	0.250	0.100	0
10001	17	15.94	0.276	1.104	2
11000	24	12.00	0.207	0.828	1
10011	19	15.44	0.267	1.068	1

(d) $k = 2$: Step 5

Chromosomes in $\mathbf{p_n}^{(2)}$	Mate (randomly selected)	Crossover site (randomly selected)	Resulting chromosomes in $\mathbf{p}^{(3)}$
10001	3	2	10000
10001	4	3	10011
11000	1	2	11001
10011	2	3	10001

(e) $k = 3$: Steps 2 and 3

Chromosomes in $\mathbf{p}^{(3)}$	Integers	Fitness	$g(\mathbf{x})$	$4g(\mathbf{x})$	Number of selected copies
10000	16	16.00	0.274	1.096	1
10011	19	15.44	0.265	1.060	1
11001	25	10.94	0.188	0.752	1
10001	17	15.94	0.273	1.092	1

A crossover operation is employed in virtually all types of genetic algorithms, but the operations of mutation and inversion are sometimes omitted. Their role is to produce new chromosomes not on the basis of the fitness function, but for the purpose of avoiding a local minimum. This role is similar to the role of a disturbance employed in neural networks. If these operations are employed, they are usually chosen with small probabilities. The mates in the crossover operations and the crossover positions in the algorithm are selected randomly. When the algorithm terminates, the chromosome in $\mathbf{p}^{(k)}$ with the highest fitness represents the solution.

To illustrate a special version of the algorithm, in which we employ only the operation of simple crossover, we describe a very simple example of determining the maximum of a given algebraic function.

Example B.1

Let function $f(x) = 2x - x^2/16$ be defined on the interval $[0, 31]$. To illustrate the use of a genetic algorithm for determining the maximum of the function in the given interval, we approximate the interval by 32 interger points, $0, 1, \ldots, 31$, and code these points by the corresponding binary numbers. Then, $G = \{0, 1\}$, and all possible chromosomes are binary integers from 00000 through 11111. Assume that we choose $m = 4$ and $\mathbf{p}^{(1)} = \langle 00010, 01001, 10011, 11000 \rangle$ in Step 1 (Table B.1a). Using function f as the fitness function, we calculate the fitness of each chromosome in $\mathbf{p}^{(1)}$ (Step 2). Then, using the deterministic sampling in Step 3, we obtain the population $\mathbf{p}_n^{(1)} = \langle 01001, 10011, 10011, 11000 \rangle$, as shown in Table B.1b. If given stopping criteria in Step 4 are not met, we proceed to Step 5. Assuming that the condition $\mathbf{p}_n^{(k)} = \mathbf{p}^{(k)}$ was chosen as the stopping criterion in this example, the algorithm does not stop at this point and proceeds to Step 5. In this step, we assume that only simple crossovers are used, each of which produces one of the two possible offsprings. For each $\mathbf{x}$ in $\mathbf{p}_n^{(1)}$, a mate $\mathbf{y}$ in $\mathbf{p}_n^{(1)}$ and a crossover point are chosen randomly and, then, the offspring $\mathbf{x}'$ is produced (Table B.1b). Next, in Step 6, the old population $\mathbf{p}_n^{(1)}$, is replaced with the new population $\mathbf{p}^{(2)}$ of offsprings produced in Step 5, k is increased by one, and we proceed to Step 2. Steps 2 and 3 are now repeated for $k = 2$, and the results are shown in Table B.1c. The stopping criterion in Step 4 is again not satisfied; consequently, we proceed to Step 5. The result of this step is shown in Table B.1d. In Step 6, we replace $\mathbf{p}^{(2)}$ with $\mathbf{p}^{(3)}$, increase k by one, and proceed to Step 2. The application of Steps 2 and 3 for $k = 3$ results in $\mathbf{p}_n^{(3)}$, shown in Table B.1e. Now, the stopping criterion $\mathbf{p}_n^{(3)} = \mathbf{p}^{(3)}$ is satisfied in Step 4, and the algorithm terminates. The chromosome 10000, which has the highest fitness, represents the solution. This chromosome corresponds to the integer 16 which is, indeed, the point for which the function f reaches its maximum.

The only textbook on genetic algorithms, which is quite suitable as a self-study guide, is the book *Genetic Algorithms* by D. E. Goldberg (Addison-Wesley, 1989). For an overview of practical aspects and applications of genetic algorithms, we recommend *Handbook of Genetic Algorithms*, edited by L. Davis (Van Nostrand Reinhold, 1991). Important classical papers on genetic algorithms are collected in *Genetic Algorithms*, edited by B. P. Buckles and F. E. Petry (IEEE Computer Society Press, 1992).

APPENDIX C

FUZZY SETS
VERSUS ROUGH SETS

The primary feature of fuzzy sets is that their boundaries are not precise. There exists an alternative way to formulate sets with imprecise boundaries. Sets formulated in this way are called rough sets. A *rough set* is basically an approximate representation of a given crisp set in terms of two subsets of a crisp partition defined on the universal set involved. The two subsets are called a lower approximation and an upper approximation. The lower approximation consists of all blocks of the partition that are included in the represented set; the upper approximation consists of all blocks whose intersection with the set is not empty.

To define the concept of a rough set more precisely, let X denote a universal set, and let R be an equivalence relation on X. Moreover, let X/R denote the family of all equivalence classes induced on X by R (a quotient set), and let $[x]_R$ denote the equivalence class in X/R that contains $x \in X$.

A *rough set*, $R(A)$, is a representation of a given set $A \in \mathcal{P}(X)$ by two subsets of the quotient set X/R, $\underline{R}(A)$ and $\overline{R}(A)$, which approach A as closely as possible from inside and outside, respectively. That is,

$$R(A) = \langle \underline{R}(A), \overline{R}(A) \rangle,$$

where $\underline{R}(A)$ and $\overline{R}(A)$ are the *lower approximation* and the *upper approximation* of A, respectively, by equivalence classes in X/R. The lower approximation,

$$\underline{R}(A) = \cup\{[x]_R \mid [x]_R \subseteq A, x \in X\},$$

is the union of all equivalence classes in X/R that are contained in A. The upper approximation,

$$\overline{R}(A) = \cup\{[x]_R \mid [x]_R \cap A \neq \varnothing, x \in X\},$$

is the union of all equivalence classes in X/R that overlap with A. The set difference $\overline{R}(A) - \underline{R}(A)$ is a rough description of the boundary of A by granules of X/R.

Two examples of rough sets are shown in Fig. C.1. In the first one, designated as (a), X is a closed interval of real numbers, the quotient set X/R partitions X into 10 semiclosed intervals and one closed interval, and the set A to be approximated by elements of X/R is

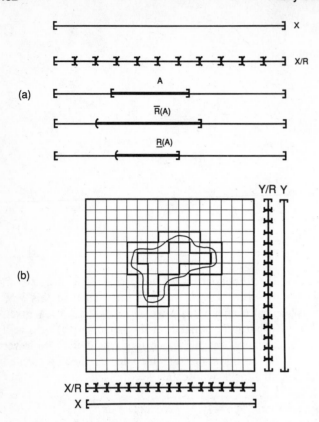

Figure C.1   Examples of rough sets.

the closed interval shown in this figure. The rough set approximation of A in this example consists of the two semiclosed intervals, $\underline{R}(A)$ and $\overline{R}(A)$, shown in the figure.

In the second example, labeled as (b), the universal set is $X \times Y$, and the quotient set on it, which is defined by the Cartesian product $(X/R) \times (Y/R)$, partitions the area $X \times Y$ into the small squares shown in the figure; it is obvious from X/R and Y/R which sides of each square are included in the corresponding equivalence class and which are not. The figure illustrates the rough set approximation of the shown subarea that does not match the equivalence classes.

Fuzzy sets and rough sets model different types of uncertainty. Since both types are relevant in some applications, it is useful to combine the two concepts. Rough sets based on fuzzy equivalence relations are usually called *fuzzy rough sets*, while rough set approximations of fuzzy sets in terms of given crisp equivalence relations are called *rough fuzzy sets*.

Given an arbitrary crisp subset A of X and a fuzzy equivalence relation R_F on X, the *fuzzy rough set* approximation of A in terms of R_F is represented at each α-cut of R_F by the rough set

$$^{\alpha}R_F(A) = \langle ^{\alpha}\underline{R}_F(A), {}^{\alpha}\overline{R}_F(A)\rangle.$$

Clearly, $\alpha \leq \beta$ implies $^{\alpha}\underline{R}_F(A) \subseteq {}^{\beta}\underline{R}_F(A)$ and $^{\alpha}\overline{R}_F(A) \supseteq {}^{\beta}\overline{R}_F(A)$.

On the other hand, given a fuzzy subset F of X and a crisp relation R on X, F is approximated by a *rough fuzzy set* whose α-cuts are rough sets

$$R(^{\alpha}F) = \langle \underline{R}(^{\alpha}F), \overline{R}(^{\alpha}F) \rangle.$$

In this case, $\alpha \leq \beta$ implies $\underline{R}(^{\alpha}F) \supseteq \underline{R}(^{\beta}F)$ and $\overline{R}(^{\alpha}F) \supseteq \overline{R}(^{\beta}F)$.

The concept of a rough set was introduced by Pawlak [1982]. The theory of rough sets and its various applications are well covered in the books by Pawlak [1991] and Slowinski [1992]. The two combinations of fuzzy sets and rough sets, which have distinct domains of applicability, have been investigated by Dubois and Prade [1990b, 1992a].

APPENDIX D

PROOFS OF SOME
MATHEMATICAL THEOREMS

D.1   THE PROOF OF THEOREM 3.7 (SEC. 3.2, p. 59)

(i) First, we prove the inverse implication $\Leftarrow$. Let g be a continuous function from $[0, 1]$ to $\mathbb{R}$ such that $g(0) = 0$ and g is strictly increasing. Then the pseudoinverse of g, denoted by $g^{(-1)}$, is a function from $\mathbb{R}$ to $[0,1]$ defined by

$$g^{(-1)}(a) = \begin{cases} 0 & \text{for } a \in (-\infty, 0) \\ g^{-1}(a) & \text{for } a \in [0, g(1)] \\ 1 & \text{for } a \in (g(1), \infty), \end{cases}$$

where g^{-1} is the ordinary inverse of g.

Let c be a function on $[0, 1]$ defined by (3.9). We now prove that c is a fuzzy complement. First, we show that c satisfies Axiom c2. For any $a, b \in [0, 1]$, if $a < b$, then $g(a) < g(b)$, since g is strictly increasing. Hence, $g(1) - g(a) > g(1) - g(b)$ and, consequently, $c(a) = g^{-1}[g(1) - g(a)] > g^{-1}[g(1) - g(b)] > c(b)$. Therefore, c satisfies Axiom c2. Second, we show that c is involutive. For any $a \in [0, 1]$, $c(c(a)) = g^{-1}[g(1) - g(c(a))] = g^{-1}[g(1) - g(g^{-1}(g(1) - g(a)))] = g^{-1}[g(1) - g(1) + g(a)] = g^{-1}(g(a)) = a$. Thus, c is involutive (i.e., c satisfies Axiom c4).

It follows from Theorem 3.1 that c also satisfies Axiom c2 and c3. Therefore, c is a fuzzy complement.

(ii) Now, we prove the direct implication $\Rightarrow$. Let c be a fuzzy complement satisfying Axioms c1–c4. We need to find a continuous, strictly increasing function g that satisfies (3.9) and $g(0) = 0$.

It follows from Theorem 3.4 that c must have a unique equilibrium, let us say e_c; that is, $c(e_c) = e_c$, where $e_c \in (0, 1)$. Let $h : [0, e_c] \rightarrow [0, b]$ be any continuous, strictly increasing bijection such that $h(0) = 0$ and $h(e_c) = b$, where b is any fixed positive real number. For example, function $h(a) = ba/e_c$ is one instance of this kind of function. Now we define a function $g : [0, 1] \rightarrow \mathbb{R}$ by

$$g(a) = \begin{cases} h(a) & a \in [0, e_c] \\ 2b - h(c(a)) & a \in (e_c, 1]. \end{cases}$$

Obviously, $g(0) = h(0) = 0$ and g is continuous as well as strictly increasing since h is continuous and strictly increasing. It is easy to show that the pseudoinverse of g is given by

$$g^{(-1)}(a) = \begin{cases} 0 & \text{for } a \in (-\infty, 0) \\ h^{-1}(a) & \text{for } a \in [0, b] \\ c(h^{-1}(2b - a)) & \text{for } a \in [b, 2b] \\ 1 & \text{for } a \in (2b, \infty]. \end{cases}$$

Now, we show that g satisfies (3.9). For any $a \in [0, 1]$, if $a \in [0, e_c]$, then $g^{-1}[g(1) - g(a)] = g^{-1}[g(1) - h(a)] = g^{-1}[2b - h(a)] = c(h^{-1}[2b - (2b - h(a))]) = c(a)$; if $a \in (e_c, 1]$, then $g^{-1}[g(1) - g(a)] = g^{-1}[2b - (2b - h(c(a)))] = g^{-1}[h(c(a))] = h^{-1}[h(c(a))] = c(a)$. Therefore, for any $a \in [0, 1]$, $c(a) = g^{-1}[g(1) - g(a)]$ (i.e., (3.9) holds). ∎

D.2   PROOF OF THEOREM 3.13 (SEC. 3.3, p. 75)

To prove that i^g is a t-norm, we need to show that i^g satisfies Axioms i1–i4 stated in Sec. 3.3.

For any $a \in [0, 1]$, $i^g(a, 1) = g^{(-1)}[i(g(a), g(1))] = g^{(-1)}[i(g(a), 1)] = g^{(-1)}[g(a)] = a$. Thus, i^g satisfies Axiom i1. It is also easy to show that i^g satisfies Axiom i2 and i3. In the following, we mainly show that i^g satisfies Axiom i4. For any $a, b, d \in [0, 1]$,

$$i^g(a, i^g(b, d)) = g^{(-1)}[i(g(a), g(g^{(-1)}[i(g(b), g(d))]))] \tag{D.1}$$

and

$$i^g(i^g(a, b), d) = g^{(-1)}[i(g(g^{(-1)}[i(g(a), g(b))]), g(d))]. \tag{D.2}$$

Now, we prove that $(D.1) = (D.2)$.

Let $a_0 = \lim_{x \to 0} g(x)$ and $b_0 = \lim_{x \to 1} g(x)$. Then we consider the following six cases of possible values of $i(g(a), g(b))$ and $i(g(b), g(d))$.

Case 1. $i(g(a), g(b)) \in [b_0, 1]$. Then, a and b must be 1. Hence $(D.1) = d = (D.2)$.

Case 2. $i(g(b), g(d)) \in [b_0, 1]$. By the same reason as in Case 1, $(D.1) = a = (D.2)$.

Case 3. $i(g(a), g(b)) \in (a_0, b_0)$ and $i(g(b), g(d)) \in (a_0, b_0)$. Then, $(D.1) = g^{(-1)}[i(g(a), i(g(b), g(d)))] = g^{(-1)}[i(i(g(a), g(b)), g(d))] = (D.2)$.

Case 4. $i(g(a), g(b)) \in (a_0, b_0)$ and $i(g(b), g(d)) \in [0, a_0]$. Then, $(D.1) = g^{(-1)}[i(g(a), 0)] = 0 = g^{(-1)}[i(g(b), g(d))] \geq g^{(-1)}[i(g(a), i(g(b), g(d)))] = g^{(-1)}[i(i(g(a), g(b)), g(d))] = (D.2) \geq 0$. Hence, $(D.1) = (D.2)$.

Case 5. $i(g(a), g(b)) \in [0, a_0]$ and $i(g(b), g(d)) \in (a_0, b_0)$. By the same reason as in Case 4 and Axiom i3, $(D.1) = (D.2)$.

Case 6. $i(g(a), g(b)) \in [0, a_0]$ and $i(g(b), g(d)) \in [0, a_0]$. Then, $(D.1) = g^{(-1)}[i(g(a), 0)] = 0 = g^{(-1)}[i(0, g(d))] = (D.2)$. ∎

D.3   PROOF OF THEOREM 3.28 (SEC. 3.6, p. 96).

Suppose that h is a continuous and idempotent norm operation. Then, h satisfies the properties of continunity, monotonicity, commutativity, associativity, and weak boundary conditions $(h(0, 0) = 0, h(1, 1) = 1,$ and $h(a, a) = a,$ for all $a \in [0, 1]$). Let $\lambda = h(0, 1) \in [0, 1]$. We show that this λ is what we need to find. First, we prove that h satisfies the following two properties:

$P1 : h(0, a) = a$ for all $a \in [0, \lambda]$,
$P2 : h(1, a) = a$ for all $a \in [\lambda, 1]$.

Let f_1 be a function defined by $f_1(x) = h(0, x)$ for all $x \in [0, 1]$. Then, $f_1(0) = 0, f_1(1) = \lambda$. Since f_1 is continuous and monotonically increasing for any $a \in [0, \lambda]$, there exists $x_0 \in [0, 1]$ such that $f_1(x_0) = a$. Then, $h(0, a) = h(0, f_1(x_0)) = h(0, h(0, x_0)) = h(h(0, 0), x_0) = h(0, x_0) = f_1(x_0) = a$. Hence, $P1$ is proved. It is similar to prove $P2$ by defining $f_2(x) = h(x, 1)$ for all $x \in [0, 1]$.

Now, we prove that h is actually a median as defined in the theorem. If $a, b \in [0, \lambda]$, then $a = h(a, 0) \le h(a, b)$ and $b = h(0, b) \le h(a, b)$. Thus, $\max(a, b) \le h(a, b)$. On the other hand, $h(a, b) \le h(\max(a, b), b) \le h(\max(a, b), \max(a, b)) = \max(a, b)$ (by idempotency). Therefore, $h(a, b) = \max(a, b)$.

If $a, b \in [\lambda, 1]$, then $h(a, b) \le h(a, 1) = a$ and $h(a, b) \le h(1, b) = b$. Thus, $h(a, b) \le \min(a, b)$. On the other hand, $\min(a, b) = h(\min(a, b), \min(a, b)) \le h(a, b)$. Therefore, $h(a, b) = \min(a, b)$. If $a \in [0, \lambda]$ and $b \in [\lambda, 1]$, then $\lambda = h(a, \lambda) \le h(a, b) \le h(\lambda, b) = \lambda$. Thus, $h(a, b) = \lambda$. If $a \in [\lambda, 1]$ and $b \in [0, \lambda]$, then $\lambda = h(\lambda, b) \le h(a, b) \le h(a, \lambda) = \lambda$. Thus, $h(a, b) = \lambda$. Therefore, for all $a, b \in [0, 1]$,

$$h(a, b) = \begin{cases} \max(a, b) & \text{when } a, b \in [0, \lambda] \\ \min(a, b) & \text{when } a, b \in [\lambda, 1] \\ \lambda & \text{otherwise.} \quad \blacksquare \end{cases}$$

APPENDIX E

GLOSSARY OF KEY CONCEPTS

Aggregation Operation for Fuzzy Sets

For n fuzzy sets ($n \geq 2$), a continuous function $h : [0, 1]^n \to [0, 1]$ that is monotonic increasing in all its arguments and for which $h(0, 0, \dots, 0) = 0$ and $h(1, 1, \dots, 1) = 1$.

Basic Probability Assignment

Function $m : \mathcal{P}(x) \to [0, 1]$ such that $m(\varnothing) = 0$ and $\sum_{A \in \mathcal{P}(X)} m(A) = 1$.

Belief Measure

Semicontinuous fuzzy measure that is superadditive and continuous from above.

Boolean Lattice of Crisp Power Set

The pair $\langle \mathcal{P}(X), \subseteq \rangle$, where $\mathcal{P}(X)$ denotes the crisp power set of X and the set inclusion $\subseteq$ defines a partial ordering on $\mathcal{P}(X)$, whose meet and join are the set operations $\cap$ and $\cup$, respectively.

Compatibility Relation

Binary relation on X that is reflexive and symmetric.

Convex Crisp Set A in $\mathbb{R}^n$

For every pair of points $\mathbf{r} = \langle r_i | i \in \mathbb{N}_n \rangle$ and $\mathbf{s} = \langle s_i | i \in \mathbb{N}_n \rangle$ in A and every real number $\lambda \in [0, 1]$, the point $\mathbf{t} = \langle \lambda r_i + (1 - \lambda)s_i | i \in \mathbb{N}_n \rangle$ is also in A.

Convex Fuzzy Set

Fuzzy set whose α-cuts are convex crisp sets for all $\alpha \in (0, 1]$.

De Morgan Lattice of Fuzzy Power Set

The pair $\langle \mathcal{F}(X), \subseteq \rangle$, where $\mathcal{F}(X)$ denotes the fuzzy power set of X and the fuzzy set inclusion $\subseteq$ defines a partial ordering on $\mathcal{F}(X)$, whose meet and join are the standard fuzzy set operations $\cap$ and $\cup$, respectively.

Equivalence Relation

Binary relation on X that is reflexive, symmetric, and transitive.

Fuzzy Cardinality of Fuzzy Subset A of Finite Set X

Fuzzy number $|\tilde{A}|$ defined on $\mathbb{N}$ by the formula $|\tilde{A}| (|^\alpha A|) = \alpha$ for all $\alpha \in \Lambda(A)$, where $\Lambda(A)$ denotes the level set of A.

Fuzzy Complement

A function $c : [0, 1] \to [0, 1]$ that is monotonic decreasing and satisfies $c(0) = 1$ and $c(1) = 0$; it is usually also continuous and such that $c(c(a)) = a$ for any $a \in [0, 1]$.

Fuzzy Implication

Function $\mathcal{J}$ of the form $[0, 1]^2 \to [0, 1]$ that for any truth values a, b of given fuzzy propositions p, q, respectively, defines the truth value, $\mathcal{J}(a, b)$, of the proposition "if p, then q."

Fuzzy Measure

Continuous or semicontinuous function $g : \mathcal{C} \to [0, 1]$, where $\mathcal{C} \subseteq \mathcal{P}(X)$, such $g(\varnothing) = 0$, $g(X) = 1$, and $A \subseteq B$ implies $g(A) \leq g(B)$ for all $A, B \in \mathcal{C}$.

Fuzzy Number

Normal fuzzy set on $\mathbb{R}$ whose support is bounded and whose α-cuts are closed intervals for all $\alpha \in (0, 1]$.

Fuzzy Partition

A family of crisp partitions induced by the α-cuts of a fuzzy equivalence relation.

Fuzzy Proposition

Sentence "$\mathcal{V}$ is F," where $\mathcal{V}$ is a variable that takes values from some universal set V and F is a fuzzy set on V.

Fuzzy Pseudopartition

Set of nonempty fuzzy sets $\{A_1, A_2, \ldots, A_n\}$ of X such that $\sum_{i=1}^{n} A_i(x) = 1$ for all $x \in X$.

Fuzzy Relation

Fuzzy subset of the Cartesian product of several crisp sets.

Fuzzy Set of Level 2

Fuzzy set whose membership function has the form $\mathcal{F}(X) \to [0, 1]$.

Fuzzy Set of Type 2

Fuzzy set whose membership function has the form $X \to \mathcal{F}([0, 1])$, where $\mathcal{F}([0, 1])$ denotes the set of ordinary fuzzy sets defined on $[0, 1]$.

Fuzzy System

System whose variables range over states that are fuzzy sets.

Interval-Valued Fuzzy Set

Fuzzy set whose membership function has the form $X \to \mathcal{E}([0, 1])$, where $\mathcal{E}([0, 1])$ denotes the family of closed intervals of real numbers in $[0, 1]$.

L-Fuzzy Set

Fuzzy set whose membership function has the form $X \to L$, where L is a lattice or, at least, a partially ordered set.

Linguistic Variable

A variable whose states are fuzzy numbers assigned to relevant linguistic terms.

Necessity Measure

Semicontinuous fuzzy measure, Nec, that is continuous from below and for which $\text{Nec} \left(\bigcap_{k \in K} A_k \right) = \inf_{k \in K} \text{Nec}(A_k)$ for any family $\{A_k | k \in K\}$ in $\mathcal{P}(X)$.

Nested Family of Crisp Sets

Family of sets $\{A_1, A_2, \ldots, A_n\}$ such that $A_i \subseteq A_{i+1}$ for all $i = 1, 2, \ldots, n - 1$.

Ordinary Fuzzy Set

Fuzzy set whose membership function has the form $X \rightarrow [0, 1]$.

Partial Ordering

A binary relation on X^2 that is reflexive, antisymmetric, and transitive.

Partition of X

A disjoint family $\{A_1, A_2, \ldots, A_n\}$ of nonempty subsets of X such that $\bigcup_{i=1}^{n} A_i = X$.

Plausibility Measure

Semicontinuous fuzzy measure that is subadditive and continuous from below.

Possibility Distribution Function

Function of the form $r : X \rightarrow [0, 1]$ such that $\text{Pos}(A) = \sup_{x \in A} r(x)$ for each $A \in \mathcal{P}(X)$.

Possibility Measure

Semicontinuous fuzzy measure, Pos that is continuous from below and for which $\text{Pos}\left(\bigcup_{k \in K} A_k\right) = \sup_{k \in K} \text{Pos}(A_k)$ for any family $\{A_k | k \in K\}$ in $\mathcal{P}(X)$.

Probability Measure

Continuous fuzzy measure that is additive.

Scalar Cardinality (Sigma Count) of Fuzzy Subset A of Finite Set X

The real number $|A| = \sum_{x \in X} A(x)$.

Standard Complement of Fuzzy Set A

Fuzzy set whose membership function is defined by $1 - A(x)$ for all $x \in X$.

Standard Intersection of Fuzzy Sets A and B

Fuzzy set whose membership function is defined by $\min[A(x), B(x)]$ for all $x \in X$.

Standard Union of Fuzzy Sets A and B

Fuzzy set whose membership function is defined by $\max[A(x), B(x)]$ for all $x \in X$.

Strong α-Cut of Fuzzy Set A

Crisp set $^{\alpha+}A = \{x | A(x) > \alpha\}$.

Subsethood Degree of Set A in Set B

The number $S(A, B) = |A \cap B| / |A|$, where $\cap$ denotes the standard fuzzy intersection and $|A \cap B|$ and $|A|$ are scalar cardinalities of the sets involved (A and B are defined on a finite X).

Transitive Closure of Fuzzy Relation R(X, X)

The smallest fuzzy relation that contains R and is transitive.

Triangular Conorm (t-Conorm)

A function $u : [0, 1]^2 \rightarrow [0, 1]$ such that for all $a, b, d \in [0, 1]$; $u(a, 0) = a$; $b \leq d$ implies $u(a, b) \leq u(a, d)$; $u(a, b) = u(b, a)$; $u(a, u(b, d)) = u(u(a, b), d)$. The function is usually also continuous and such that $u(a, a) \geq a$.

Triangular Norm (t-Norm)

A function $i : [0, 1]^2 \rightarrow [0, 1]$ such that for all $a, b, d \in [0, 1]$; $i(a, 1) = a$; $b \leq d$ implies $i(a, b) \leq i(a, d)$; $i(a, b) = i(b, a)$; $i(a, i(b, d)) = i(i(a, b), d)$. The function is usually also continuous and such that $i(a, a) \leq a$ for all $a \in [0, 1]$.

α-Cut of Fuzzy Set A

Crisp set $^{\alpha}A = \{x | A(x) \geq \alpha\}$.

Appendix F

Glossary of Main Symbols

General Symbols

$\{x, y, \ldots\}$	Set of elements $x, y, \ldots$
$\{x \mid p(x)\}$	Set determined by property p
$\langle x_1, x_2, \ldots, x_n \rangle$	n-tuple
$[x_{ij}]$	Matrix
$[x_1\ x_2 \ldots x_n]$	Vector
$[a, b]$	Closed interval of real numbers between a and b
$[a, b), (b, a]$	Interval of real numbers closed in a and open in b
(a, b)	Open interval of real numbers
$[a, \infty)$	Set of real numbers greater than or equal to a
$A, B, C, \ldots$	Arbitrary sets (crisp or fuzzy)
$x \in A$	Element x belongs to crisp set A
χ_A	Characteristic function of crisp set A
$A(x)$ or $\mu_A(x)$	Membership grade of x in fuzzy set A
$^{\alpha}A$	α-cut of fuzzy set A
$^{\alpha+}A$	Strong α-cut of fuzzy set A
$_{\alpha}A$	Fuzzy set $\alpha \cdot {}^{\alpha}A$
$A = B$	Set equality
$A \neq B$	Set inequality
$A - B$	Set difference
$A \subseteq B$	Set inclusion
$A \subset B$	Proper set inclusion ($A \subseteq B$ and $A \neq B$)
$S(A, B)$	Degree of subsethood of A in B
$\mathcal{P}(X)$	Set of all crisp subsets of X (power set)
$\mathcal{F}(X)$	Set of all fuzzy subsets of X (fuzzy power set)
$\lvert A \rvert$	Cardinality of crisp or fuzzy set A (sigma count)
$\lvert \tilde{A} \rvert$	Fuzzy cardinality of fuzzy set A

$h(A)$	Height of fuzzy set A
$\overline{A}$	Complement of set A
$A \cap B$	Set intersection
$A \cup B$	Set union
$A \times B$	Cartesian product of sets A and B
A^2	Cartesian product $A \times A$
$[a, b]^2$	Cartesian product $[a, b] \times [a, b]$
$X \rightarrow Y$	Function from X to Y
$R(X, Y)$	Relation on $X \times Y$
$R \circ Q$	Max-min composition of fuzzy relation R and Q
$R \overset{i}{\circ} Q$	Sup-i composition of fuzzy relations R and Q
$R \overset{\omega_i}{\circ} Q$	Inf-ω_i composition of fuzzy relations R and Q
$R * Q$	Join of fuzzy relations R and Q
R^{-1}	Inverse of a binary fuzzy relation
$[R \downarrow \mathcal{X}]$	Projection of relation R with respect to variables in set $\mathcal{X}$
$[R \uparrow \mathcal{X} - \mathcal{Y}]$	Cylindric extension of relation R with respect to variables in $\mathcal{X} - \mathcal{Y}$
$<$	Less than
$\leq$	Less than or equal to (also used for a partial ordering)
$\prec$	Subsequence (substate) relation or relation "sharper than"
$x \wedge y$	Meet (greatest lower bound) of x and y in a lattice or logic conjunction
$x \vee y$	Join (least upper bound) of x and y in a lattice or logic disjunction
$x\|y$	x given y
$x \Rightarrow y$	x implies y
$x \Leftrightarrow y$	x if and only if y
$\forall$	For all (universal quantifier)
$\exists$	There exists (existential quantifier)
$\sum$	Summation
$\prod$	Product
$\max(a_1, a_2, \ldots, a_n)$	Maximum of $a_1, a_2, \ldots, a_n$
$\min(a_1, a_2, \ldots, a_n)$	Minimum of $a_1, a_2, \ldots, a_n$
i, j, k	Arbitrary identifiers (indices)
I, J, K	General sets of identifiers
$\mathbb{N}$	Set of positive integers (natural numbers)
$\mathbb{N}_0$	Set of nonnegative integers
$\mathbb{N}_n$	Set $\{1, 2, \ldots, n\}$
$\mathbb{N}_{n,m}$	Set $\{n, n + 1, \ldots, m\}$
$\mathbb{R}$	Set of all real numbers
$\mathbb{R}^+$	Set of all nonnegative real numbers
$\mathbb{Z}$	Set of all integers
$\operatorname{dom} R$	Domain of fuzzy relation R
$\operatorname{ran} R$	Range of fuzzy relation R
R_T	Transitive max-min closure of fuzzy relation R
$R_{T(i)}$	i-transitive closure of fuzzy relation R
$R^{(n)}$	Sup-i composition of fuzzy relation R with itself, repeated $(n - 1)$-times
$\pi(A)$	Partition of A
$\Pi(A)$	Set of all partitions of A
$\pi(R)$	Partition corresponding to an equivalence relation R
$\mathbf{I}$	Identity matrix

Special Symbols

$\mathcal{A}$	A finite fuzzy automaton
Bel	Belief measure
c	Fuzzy complement
$C(m)$	Measure of confusion in evidence theory
$c(p, r)$	The degree of probability-possibility consistency
$\mathrm{Con}\,(A)$	Sum of individual conflicts of evidential claims with respect to a particular A in evidence theory
c_s	Standard fuzzy complement
c_w	Fuzzy complement of Yager class
c_λ	Fuzzy complement of Sugeno class
d_{CA}	Defuzzification function of center of gravity method
d_{CM}	Defuzzification function of center of maxima method
$D(m)$	Measure of discord in evidence theory
d_{MM}	Defuzzification function of mean of maxima method
d_p	A class of defuzzification functions defined by (12.10)
e_c	Equilibrium of fuzzy complement c
$E(m)$	Measure of dissonance
$\mathcal{E}([0, 1])$	The family of all closed intervals of real numbers in $[0, 1]$
$\mathcal{F}$	Set of focal elements in evidence theory
f_e	Fuzzification function
$F(m)$	Total degree of fuzziness of a body of evidence
$\langle \mathcal{F}, m \rangle$	Body of evidence
$\langle \mathcal{F}_X, m_X \rangle$	Marginal body of evidence
H	Linguistic hedge
$H(m)$	Shannon entropy
h_w	Ordered weighted averaging operation
h_α	Generalized means
h_λ	λ-average
i	Fuzzy intersection or t-norm
$i_{\min}$	Drastic fuzzy intersection
$\langle i, u, c \rangle$	Dual triple of fuzzy intersection i and fuzzy union u with respect to fuzzy complement c
i_w	Fuzzy intersection of Yager class
$\mathcal{J}$	Fuzzy implication operator
$L_1(L_{\aleph_1})$	Standard Lukasiewicz logic
L_A	Lower bound of interval-valued fuzzy set A
L_n	n-valued Lukasiewicz logic
m	Basic probability assignment in evidence theory
$\mathbf{m}$	Basic distribution of a possibility measure
MAX	Lattice operation maximum of fuzzy numbers
MIN	Lattice operation minimum of fuzzy numbers
m_X, m_Y	Marginal basic probability assignments
Nec	Necessity measure
Nec_F	Necessity measure corresponding to Pos_F
$N(m)$	U-uncertainty in evidence theory
$^n\mathcal{R}$	The set of all ordered possibility distributions of length n
$\langle ^n\mathcal{R}, \le \rangle$	Lattice of possibility distributions of length n

NS (m)	Total uncertainty in evidence theory
$\mathcal{P}$	A fuzzy pseudopartition
$\hat{\mathbf{p}}$	Maximal solution of (6.9)
$\check{\mathbf{p}}$	Minimal solution of (6.9)
$\hat{P}$	The greatest solution for (6.16) with unknown P
$\tilde{P}$	An approximate solution for (6.18) with unknown P
Pl	Plausibility measure
Pos	Possibility measure
Pos_F	Possibility measure associated with a proposition "$\mathcal{V}$ is F"
Pro	Probability measure
$\mathbf{p}_X, \mathbf{p}_Y$	Marginal probability distributions
$\mathbf{p}_{X|Y}, \mathbf{p}_{Y|X}$	Conditional probability distributions
$\check{Q}$	The smallest solution for (6.16) with unknown Q
$\mathbf{r}$	Possibility distribution
$\mathcal{R}$	The set of all fuzzy numbers or the set of all ordered possibility distributions
$\check{\mathbf{r}}_n$	The smallest possibility distribution with n components
$\hat{\mathbf{r}}_n$	The largest possibility distribution with n components
$\mathbf{r}_X, \mathbf{r}_Y$	Marginal possibility distributions
$\mathbf{r}_{X|Y}, \mathbf{r}_{Y|X}$	Conditional possibility distributions
$\mathcal{S}$	A general dynamic system
$\langle s, l, r \rangle$	A triangular fuzzy number shown in Fig. 15.7b
$S(m)$	Measure of strife in evidence theory
$S(\mathbf{r})$	Measure of strife of a possibility distribution $\mathbf{r}$
T_n	The set of truth values of an n-valued logic
$T(p)$	The degree of truth of a fuzzy proposition p
$T(X, Y)$	Information transmission
u	Fuzzy union or t-conorm
U_A	Upper bound of interval-valued fuzzy set A
$U(A)$	U-uncertainty, nonspecifity of set A, Hartley function
u_{max}	Drastic fuzzy union
u_w	Fuzzy union of Yager class
$U(X, Y)$	Joint U-uncertainty
$U(X|Y)$	Conditional U-uncertainty
$\mathcal{V}$	Linguistic variable
X	Universal set (universe of discourse)
$\varnothing$	Empty set
ω_i	Residuation operation with respect to a continuous fuzzy intersection i

Bibliography

1. Abdelnour, G. M., C. H. Chang, F. H. Huang and J. Y. Cheung [1991], "Design of a fuzzy controller using input and output mapping factors." *IEEE Trans. on Systems, Man, and Cybernetics*, **21**(5), pp. 925–960.

2. Abuhaiba, I. S. I. and P. Ahmed [1993], "A fuzzy graph theoretic approach to recognize the totally unconstrained handwritten numericals." *Pattern Recognition*, **26**(9), pp. 1335–1350.

3. Aczél, J. [**1966**], *Lectures on Functional Equations and Their Applications*. Academic Press, New York.

4. Aczél, J. and Z. Daróczy [**1975**], *On Measures of Information and Their Characterizations*. Academic Press, New York.

5. Adamatzky, A. I. [1994], "Hierarchy of fuzzy cellular automata." *Fuzzy Sets and Systems*, **62**(2), pp. 167–174.

6. Adamo, J. M. [1980a], "L.P.L.—a fuzzy programming language: 1. Symbolical aspects." *Fuzzy Sets and Systems*, **3**(2), pp. 151–179.

7. Adamo, J. M. [1980b], "L.P.L.—a fuzzy programming language: 2. Semantic aspects." *Fuzzy Sets and Systems*, **3**(3), pp. 261–289.

8. Adamo, J. M. [1980c], "Fuzzy decision trees." *Fuzzy Sets and Systems*, **4**(3), pp. 207–219.

9. Adamopoulos, G. I. and C. P. Pappis [1993], "Some results on the resolution of fuzzy relation equations." *Fuzzy Sets and Systems*, **60**(1), pp. 83–88.

10. Adeli, H. and S. L. Hung [1993], "Fuzzy neural network learning model for image recognition." *Integrated Computer-Aided Engineering*, **1**(1), pp. 43–55.

11. Adlassnig, K. P. [1982], "A survey on medical diagnosis and fuzzy subsets." In: Gupta, M. M. and E. Sanchez, eds., *Approximate Reasoning in Decision Analysis*. North-Holland, New York, pp. 203–217.

12. Adlassnig, K. P. [1986], "Fuzzy set theory in medical diagnosis." *IEEE Trans. on Systems, Man, and Cybernetics*, **16**(2), pp. 260–265.

13. Adlassnig, K. P. and G. Kolarz [1982], "CADIAG-2: Computer–assisted medical diagnosis using fuzzy subsets." In: Gupta, M. M. and E. Sanchez, eds., *Approximate Reasoning in Decision Analysis*. North-Holland, New York, pp. 219–247.

14. Agusti, J., F. Esteva, P. Garcia, L. Godo, R. López de Mántaras and C. Sierra [1994], "Local multi-valued logics in modular expert systems." *J. of Experimental & Theoretical Artificial Intelligence*, **6**(3), pp. 303–321.

15. Ahlquist, J. E. [1987], "Application of fuzzy implication to probe nonsymmetric relations: Part I." *Fuzzy Sets and Systems*, **22**(3), pp. 229–244.

16. Ajmal, N. and K. V. Thomas [1994], "Fuzzy lattices." *Information Sciences*, **79**(3–4), pp. 271–291.

17. Akdag, H. and B. Bouchon [1988], "Using fuzzy set theory in the analysis of structures of information." *Fuzzy Sets and Systems*, **28**(3), pp. 263–271.

18. Albert, P. [1978], "The algebra of fuzzy logic." *Fuzzy Sets and Systems.*, **1**(3), pp. 203–230.

19. Albin, M. A. [**1975**], *Fuzzy Sets and Their Application to Medical Diagnosis and Patterns Recognition*. (Ph. D. Dissertation) University of California, Berkeley.

20. Albrecht, M. [1992], "Approximation of functional relationships to fuzzy observations." *Fuzzy Sets and Systems*, **49**(3), pp. 301–305.

21. Alexeyev, A. V. and A. N. Borisov [1987], "A linguistic approach to decision-making problems." *Fuzzy Sets and Systems*, **22**(1), pp. 25–41.

22. Aliev, R. A., F. T. Aliev and M. D. Babaev [1992], "The synthesis of a fuzzy coordinate-parametric automatic control system for an oil-refinery unit." *Fuzzy Sets and Systems*, **47**(2), pp. 157–162.

23. Aliev, R. A. and G. A. Mamedova [1990], "Analysis of fuzzy models of industrial processes." *Fuzzy Sets and Systems*, **37**(1), pp. 13–21.

24. Aliev, R., F. Aliev and M. Babaev [**1991**], *Fuzzy Process Control and Knowledge Engineering in Petrochemical and Robotic Manufacturing*. Verlag TÜV Rheinland, Köln.

25. Alim, S. and D. L. Smith [1989], "Fuzzy set-theoretic models for interpretation of seismic design codes." *Fuzzy Sets and Systems*, **29**(3), pp. 277–291.

26. Alsina, C. [1988], "On a functional equation characterizing two binary operations on the space of membership functions." *Fuzzy Sets and Systems*, **27**(1), pp. 5–9.

27. Alsina, C., G. Mayor, M. S. Tomas and J. Torrens [1993], "A characterization of a class of aggregation functions." *Fuzzy Sets and Systems*, **53**(1), pp. 33–38.

28. Alsina, C. and E. Trillas [1993], "On uniformly close fuzzy preorders." *Fuzzy Sets and Systems*, **53**(3), pp. 343–346.

29. Alsina, C., E. Trillas and L. Valverde [1983], "On some logical connectives for fuzzy set theory." *J. of Math. Analysis and Applications*, **93**(1), pp. 15–26.

30. Al-Sultan, K. S. and S. Z. Selim [1993], "A globe algorithm for the fuzzy clustering problem." *Pattern Recognition*, **26**(9), pp. 1357–1361.

31. Altrock, C. v., H. O. Arend, B. Krause, C. Steffens and E. Behrens–Römmler [1994], "Adaptive fuzzy control applied to home heating system." *Fuzzy Sets and Systems*, **61**(1), pp. 29–36.

32. Altrock, C. v., B. Krause and H. J. Zimmermann [1992], "Advanced fuzzy logic control of a model car in extreme situations." *Fuzzy Sets and Systems*, **48**(2), pp. 41–52.

33. Andersson, L. [1986], "A new method based on the theory of fuzzy sets for obtaining an indication of risk." *Civil Engineering Systems*, **3**(3), pp. 164–174.

34. Angelov, P. [1994], "A generalized approach to fuzzy optimization." *Intern. J. of Intelligent Systems*, **9**(3), pp. 261–268.

35. Angelov, P. and N. Zamdjiev [1994], "An approach to fuzzy optimal control via parameterized conjunction and defuzzification." *Fuzzy Systems & A. I.*, **2**(1), pp. 53–57.

36. Arbib, M. A. and E. G. Manes [1975], "A category-theoretic approach to systems in a fuzzy world." *Synthese*, **30**(1), pp. 381–406.

37. Archer, K. P. and S. Wang [1991], "Fuzzy set representation of neural network classification." *IEEE Trans. on Systems, Man, and Cybernetics*, **21**(4), pp. 735–742.

38. Arnould, T. and S. Tano [1994a], "A rule-based method to calculate exactly the widest solution sets of a max-min fuzzy relational inequality." *Fuzzy Sets and Systems*, **64**(1), pp. 39–58.

39. Arnould, T. and S. Tano [1994b], "A rule-based method to calculate the widest solution sets of a max-min fuzzy relational equation." *Intern. J. of Uncertainty, Fuzziness and Knowledge–Based Systems*, **2**(3), pp. 247–256.

40. Atanassov, K. T. [1986], "Intuitionistic fuzzy sets." *Fuzzy Sets and Systems*, **20**(1), pp. 87–96.

41. Atanassov, K. T. [1993], "New operations defined over the intuitionistic fuzzy sets." *Fuzzy Sets and Systems*, **61**(2), pp. 137–142.

42. Atanassov, K. T. [1994], "Operators over interval valued intuitionistic fuzzy sets." *Fuzzy Sets and Systems*, **64**(2), pp. 159–174.

43. Atanassov, K. T. and G. Gargov [1989], "Interval valued intuitionistic fuzzy sets." *Fuzzy Sets and Systems*, **31**(3), pp. 343–349.

44. Athalye, A., D. Edwards, V. S. Manoranjan and A. d. S. Lazaro [1993], "On designing a fuzzy control system using an optimization algorithm." *Fuzzy Sets and Systems*, **56**(3), pp. 281–290.

45. Aubrun, C., D. Sauter, H. Noura and M. Robert [1993], "Fault diagnosis and reconfiguration of systems using fuzzy logic: application to a thermal plant." *Intern. J. of Systems Science*, **24**(10), pp. 1945–1954.

46. Ayyub, B. M. [1991], "Systems framework for fuzzy sets in civil engineering." *Fuzzy Sets and Systems*, **40**(3), pp. 491–508.

47. Ayyub, B. M., M. M. Gupta and L. N. Kanal, eds. [**1992**], *Analysis and Management of Uncertainty: Theory and Applications*. North-Holland, New York.

48. Ayyub, B. M. and M. H. M. Hassan [1992], "Control of construction activities." *Civil Engineering Systems*, **9**, pp. 123–146, 179–204.

49. Azmi, Z. A. [1993], "New fuzzy approaches by using statistical and mathematical methodologies in operations research." *J. of Fuzzy Mathematics*, **1**(1), pp. 69–87.

50. Baas, S. M. and H. Kwakernak [1977], "Rating and ranking of multiple aspect alternatives using fuzzy sets." *Automatica*, **13**(1), pp. 47–58.

51. Baboshin, N. P. and D. G. Naryshkin [1990], "On identification of multidimensional fuzzy systems." *Fuzzy Sets and Systems*, **35**(3), pp. 325–331.

52. Babu, G. P. and M. N. Murty [1994], "Clustering with evolution strategies." *Pattern Recognition*, **27**(2), pp. 321–329.

53. Bahrami, A. [1994], "Design by fuzzy association of needs-to-functions-to-structures." *J. of Intelligent & Fuzzy Systems*, **2**(2), pp. 179–189.

54. Balazinski, M., M. Bellerose and E. Czogala [1994], "Application of fuzzy logic techniques to the selection of cutting parameters in machining processes." *Fuzzy Sets and Systems*, **63**(3), pp. 307–317.

55. Balazinski, M., E. Czogala and T. Sadowski [1993], "Modelling of neural controllers with application to the control of a machining process." *Fuzzy Sets and Systems*, **56**(3), pp. 273–280.

56. Baldwin, J. F. [1979a], "A new approach to approximate reasoning using a fuzzy logic." *Fuzzy Sets and Systems*, **2**(4), pp. 309–325.

57. Baldwin, J. F. [1979b], "Fuzzy logic and fuzzy reasoning." *Intern. J. of Man-Machine Studies*, **11**(4), pp. 465–480.

58. Baldwin, J. F. [1979c], "A model of fuzzy reasoning through multi-valued logic and set theory." *Intern. J. of Man-Machine Studies*, **11**(3), pp. 351–380.

59. Baldwin, J. F. [1985], "Fuzzy sets and expert systems." *Information Sciences*, **36**(1–2), pp. 123–156.

60. Baldwin, J. F. [1987], "Evidential support logic programming." *Fuzzy Sets and Systems*, **24**(1), pp. 1–26.

61. Baldwin, J. F. [1993a], "Fuzzy reasoning in FRIL for fuzzy control and other knowledge-based applications." *Asia-Pacific Engineering J.*, **3**(1–2), pp. 59–82.

62. Baldwin, J. F. [1993b], "Evidential support logic, FRIL and case based reasoning." *Intern. J. of Intelligent Systems*, **8**(9), pp. 939–960.

63. Baldwin, J. F. and N. C. F. Guild [1980a], "Feasible algorithms for approximate reasoning using fuzzy logic." *Fuzzy Sets and Systems*, **3**(3), pp. 225–251.

64. Baldwin, J. F. and N. C. F. Guild [1980b], "The resolution of two paradoxes by approximate reasoning using a fuzzy logic." *Synthese*, **44**(3), pp. 397–420.

65. Baldwin, J. F. and N. C. F. Guild [1980c], "Modelling controllers using fuzzy relations." *Kybernetes*, **9**(3), pp. 223–229.

66. Baldwin, J. F. and F. E. Petry [1983], "Information-theoretical characterization of fuzzy relational databases." *IEEE Trans. on Systems, Man, and Cybernetics*, **13**(1), pp. 74–77.

67. Baldwin, J. F. and B. W. Pilsworth [1979], "A model of fuzzy reasoning through multi-valued logic and set theory." *Intern. J. of Man-Machine Studies*, **11**(3), pp. 351–380.

68. Baldwin, J. F. and B. W. Pilsworth [1980], "Axiomatic approach to implication for approximate reasoning with fuzzy logic." *Fuzzy Sets and Systems*, **3**(2), pp. 193–219.

69. Baldwin, J. F. and B. W. Pilsworth [1982], "Dynamic programming for fuzzy systems with fuzzy environment." *J. of Math. Analysis and Applications*, **85**(1), pp. 1–23.

70. Baldwin, J. F. and S. Q. Zhou [1984], "Fuzzy relational inference language." *Fuzzy Sets and Systems*, **14**(2), pp. 155–174.

71. Ballmer, T. T. and M. Pinkal, eds. [**1983**], *Approaching Vagueness*. North-Holland, New York.

72. Ban, J. [1991], "Sequences of random fuzzy sets." *Intern. J. of General Systems*, **20**(1), pp. 17–22.

73. Bandemer, H. [1987], "From fuzzy data to functional relationships." *Mathematical Modelling*, **9**(6), pp. 419–426.

74. Bandemer, H. and W. Näther [**1992**], *Fuzzy Data Analysis*. Kluwer, Boston.

75. Bandler, W. and L. J. Kohout [1980a], "Fuzzy power sets and fuzzy implication operators." *Fuzzy Sets and Systems*, **4**(1), pp. 13–30.

76. Bandler, W. and L. J. Kohout [1980b], "Semantics of implication operators and fuzzy relational products." *Intern. J. of Man-Machine Studies*, **12**(1), pp. 89–116.

77. Bandler, W. and L. J. Kohout [1985], "Probabilistic versus fuzzy production rules in expert systems." *Intern. J. of Man-Machine Studies*, **22**(3), pp. 347–353.

78. Bandler, W. and L. J. Kohout [1986a], "On new types of homomorphisms and congruences for partial algebraic structures and *n*-ary relations." *Intern. J. of General Systems*, **12**(2), pp. 149–157.

79. Bandler, W. and L. J. Kohout [1986b], "On the general theory of relational morphisms." *Intern. J. of General Systems*, **13**(1), pp. 47–68.

80. Bandler, W. and L. J. Kohout [1988], "Special properties, closures and interiors of crisp and fuzzy relations." *Fuzzy Sets and Systems*, **26**(3), pp. 317–331.

81. Banon, G. [1981], "Distinction between several subsets of fuzzy measures." *Fuzzy Sets and Systems*, **5**(3), pp. 219–305.

82. Bárdossy, A. [1990], "Note on fuzzy regression." *Fuzzy Sets and Systems*, **37**(1), pp. 65–76.

83. Bárdossy, A., I. Bogardi and W. Kelly [1990], "Fuzzy regression in hydrology." *Water Resources Research*, **26**(7), pp. 1497–1508.

84. Bárdossy, A., L. Duckstein and I. Bogardi [1993], "Combination of fuzzy numbers representing expert opinions." *Fuzzy Sets and Systems*, **57**(2), pp. 173–181.

85. Barro, S., R. Maríe, J. Mira and A. R. Patón [1993], "A model and a language for the fuzzy

representation and handing of time." *Fuzzy Sets and Systems*, **61**(2), pp. 153–176.

86. Basu, A. and A. Dutta [1989], "Reasoning with imprecise knowledge to enhance intelligent decision support." *IEEE Trans. on Systems, Man, and Cybernetics*, **19**(4), pp. 756–770.

87. Batyrshin, I. Z. [1990], "On fuzziness measures of entropy on Kleene algebras." *Fuzzy Sets and Systems*, **34**(1), pp. 47–60.

88. Baumont, C. [1989], "Theory of possibility as a basis for analyzing business experience process." *Fuzzy Sets and Systems*, **31**(1), pp. 1–12.

89. Bellman, R. **[1957]**, *Dynamic Programming*. Princeton University Press, Princeton, NJ.

90. Bellman, R. E. and L. A. Zadeh [1970], "Decision-making in a fuzzy environment." *Management Science*, **17**(4), pp. 141–164.

91. Bellman, R. E. and L. A. Zadeh [1977], "Local and fuzzy logics." In: Dunn, J. M. and G. Epstein, eds., *Modern Uses of Multiple-Valued Logic*. D. Reidel, Boston, pp. 105–165.

92. Bellman, R., R. Kalaba and L. A. Zadeh [1966], "Abstraction and pattern classification." *J. of Math. Analysis and Applications*, **13**(1), pp. 1–7.

93. Bellman, R. and M. Giertz [1973], "On the analytic formalism of the theory of fuzzy sets." *Information Sciences*, **5**, pp. 149–156.

94. Belmonte–Serrano, M., C. Sierra and R. López de Mántaras [1994], "RENOIR: An expert system using fuzzy logic for rheumatology diagnosis." *Intern. J. of Intelligent Systems*, **9**(11), pp. 985–1000.

95. Berenji, H. R. [1992], "A reinforcement learning-based architecture for fuzzy logic control." *Intern. J. of Approximate Reasoning*, **6**(2), pp. 267–292.

96. Berenji, H. R. and P. Khedkar [1992], "Learning and tuning fuzzy logic controllers through reinforcements." *IEEE Trans. on Neural Networks*, **3**(5), pp. 724–740.

97. Bernard, J. A. [1988], "Use of rule-based system for process control." *IEEE Control Systems Magazine*, **8**(5), pp. 3–13.

98. Bertram, T. [1993], "Design of a fuzzy controller for a rotating oscillator." *Intern. J. of Systems Science*, **24**(10), pp. 1923–1934.

99. Bezdek, J. C. [1974], "Cluster validity with fuzzy sets." *J. of Cybernetics*, **3**(3), pp. 58–73.

100. Bezdek, J. C. [1976], "A physical interpretation of fuzzy ISODATA." *IEEE Trans. on Systems, Man, and Cybernetics*, **6**(5), pp. 387–390.

101. Bezdek, J. C. **[1981]**, *Pattern Recognition with Fuzzy Objective Function Algorithms*. Plenum Press, New York.

102. Bezdek, J. C., ed. **[1987]**, *Analysis of Fuzzy Information*. CRC Press, Boca Raton, FL (3 volumes).

103. Bezdek, J. C. [1993], "A review of probabilistic, fuzzy, and neural models for pattern recognition." *J. of Intelligent & Fuzzy Systems*, **1**(1), pp. 1–25.

104. Bezdek, J. C., G. Biswas and L. Huang [1986], "Transitive closures of fuzzy thesauri for information-retrieval systems." *Intern. J. of Man-Machine Studies*, **25**(3), pp. 343–356.

105. Bezdek, J. C. and J. D. Harris [1979], "Convex decompositions of fuzzy partitions." *J. of Math. Analysis and Applications*, **67**(2), pp. 490–512.

106. Bezdek, J. C. and R. J. Hathaway [1987], "Clustering with relational *c*-means partitions from pairwise distance data." *Mathematical Modelling*, **9**(6), pp. 435–439.

107. Bezdek, J. C. and R. J. Hathaway [1990], "Dual object-relation clustering models." *Intern. J. of General Systems*, **16**(4), pp. 385–396.

108. Bezdek, J. C., R. J. Hathaway, M. J. Sabin and W. T. Tucker [1987], "Convergence theory for fuzzy *c*-means: counterexamples and repairs." *IEEE Trans. on Systems, Man, and Cybernetics*, **17**(5), pp. 873–877.

109. Bezdek, J. C. and S. K. Pal, eds. **[1992]**, *Fuzzy Models for Pattern Recognition: Methods that Search for Patterns in Data*. IEEE Press, New York.

110. Bhakat, S. K. and P. Das [1992], "On the definition of a fuzzy subgroup." *Fuzzy Sets and Systems*, **51**(2), pp. 235–241.

111. Bhandarkar, S. M. [1994], "A fuzzy probabilistic model for the generalized Hough transform." *IEEE Trans. on Systems, Man, and Cybernetics*, **24**(5), pp. 745–759.

112. Bharathi Devi, B. and V. V. S. Sarma [1985], "Estimation of fuzzy memberships from histograms." *Information Sciences*, **35**(1), pp. 43–59.

113. Bhattacharya, U., J. R. Rao and R. N. Tiwari [1992], "Fuzzy multi-criteria facility location problem." *Fuzzy Sets and Systems*, **51**(3), pp. 277–287.

114. Biacino, L. and M. R. Simonelli [1992], "The internal rate of return of fuzzy cash flows." *Stochastica*, **8**(1), pp. 13–22.

115. Bien, Z. and M. G. Chun [1994], "An inference network for bidirectional approximate reasoning based on an equality measure." *IEEE Trans. on Fuzzy Systems*, **2**(2), pp. 177–180.

116. Bigham, J. [1988], "The inductive inference of pattern recognition rules which are capable of a linguistic interpretation." *Computers and Mathematics with Applications*, **15**(10), pp. 839–862.

117. Billot, A. [1991], "Aggregation of preferences: the fuzzy case." *Theory and Decision*, **30**(1), pp. 51–93.

118. Billot, A. **[1992]**, *Economic Theory of Fuzzy Equilibria: An Axiomatic Analysis*. Springer-Verlag, New York.

119. Birkhoff, G. [**1967**], *Lattice Theory*. American Mathematical Society, Providence, RI.

120. Biswal, M. P. [1992], "Fuzzy programming technique to solve multi-objective geometric programming problems." *Fuzzy Sets and Systems*, **51**(1), pp. 67–72.

121. Biswas, G., R. Abramczyk and M. Oliff [1987], "OASES: an expert system for operations analysis: the system for cause analysis." *IEEE Trans. on Systems, Man, and Cybernetics*, **17**(2), pp. 133–145.

122. Biswas, P. and A. K. Majumdar [1981], "A multistage fuzzy classifier for recognition of handprinted characters." *IEEE Trans. on Systems, Man, and Cybernetics*, **11**(12), pp. 834–838.

123. Bit, A. K., M. P. Biswal and S. S. Alam [1992], "Fuzzy programming approach to multicriteria decision-making transportation problem." *Fuzzy Sets and Systems*, **50**(2), pp. 135–141.

124. Black, M. [1937], "Vagueness: an exercise in logical analysis." *Philosophy of Science*, **4**(4), pp. 427–455. (Reprinted in *Intern. J. of General Systems*, **17** (2–3), 1990, pp. 107–128).

125. Blanco, A. and M. Delgado [1993], "A direct fuzzy inference procedure by neural networks." *Fuzzy Sets and Systems*, **58**(2), pp. 133–141.

126. Blin, J. M. [1974], "Fuzzy relations in group decision theory." *J. of Cybernetics*, **4**(2), pp. 12–22.

127. Blin, J. M. and A. B. Whinston [1973], "Fuzzy sets and social choice." *J. of Cybernetics*, **3**(4), pp. 28–36.

128. Blockley, D. [1982], "Fuzzy systems in civil engineering." In: Gupta, M. M. and E. Sanchez, eds., *Approximate Reasoning in Decision Processes*. North-Holland, New York, pp. 103–115.

129. Bobrowski, L. and J. C. Bezdek [1991], "C-means clustering with the l_1 and l_∞." *IEEE Trans. on Systems, Man, and Cybernetics*, **21**(3), pp. 545–554.

130. Bocklish, S., S. Orlovski, M. Peschel and Y. Nishiwaki, eds. [**1986**], *Fuzzy Sets Applications, Methodological Approaches, and Results*. Akademie-Verlag, Berlin.

131. Bodjanová, S. [1993], "Some binary relations and operations on the set of fuzzy partitions." *Fuzzy Sets and Systems*, **53**(3), pp. 305–317.

132. Bodjanová, S. [1994], "Complement of fuzzy *k*-partitions." *Fuzzy Sets and Systems*, **62**(2), pp. 175–184.

133. Bogler, P. [1987], "Shafer–Dempster reasoning with applications to multisensor target identification systems." *IEEE Trans. on Systems, Man, and Cybernetics*, **17**(6), pp. 968–977.

134. Bonissone P. P., S. Dutta and N. C. Wood [1994], "Merging strategic and tactical planning in dynamic and uncertain environments." *IEEE Trans. on Systems, Man, and Cybernetics*, **24**(6), pp. 841–862.

135. Bortolan, G. and R. Degani [1985], "A review of some methods for ranking fuzzy subsets." *Fuzzy Sets and Systems*, **15**(1), pp. 1–19.

136. Bosc, P., M. Galibourg and G. Hamon [1988], "Fuzzy querying with SQL: Extensions and implementation aspects." *Fuzzy Sets and Systems*, **28**(3), pp. 333–349.

137. Bosc, P., O. Pivert and K. Farqugar [1994], "Integrating fuzzy queries into an existing database management system: An example." *Intern. J. of Intelligent Systems*, **9**(5), pp. 475–492.

138. Bosserman, R. W. and R. K. Ragade [1982], "Ecosystem analysis using fuzzy set theory." *Ecological Modelling*, **16**(2–4), pp. 191–208.

139. Bouchon, B. [1981], "Fuzzy questionnaires." *Fuzzy Sets and Systems*, **6**(1), pp. 1–9.

140. Bouchon, B. [1987], "Fuzzy inferences and conditional possibility distributions." *Fuzzy Sets and Systems*, **23**(1), pp. 33–41.

141. Bouchon, B., G. Cohen and P. Frankl [1982], "Metrical properties of fuzzy relations." *Problems of Control and Information Theory*, **11**(5), pp. 389–396.

142. Bouchon, B., L. Saitta and R. R. Yager, eds. [**1988**], *Uncertainty and Intelligent Systems*. Springer-Verlag, New York.

143. Bouchon, B. and R. R. Yager, eds. [**1987**], *Uncertainty in Knowledge–Based Systems*. Springer-Verlag, New York.

144. Bouchon–Meunier, B. and J. Yao [1992], "Linguistic modifiers and imprecise categories." *Intern. J. of Intelligent Systems*, **7**(1), pp. 25–36.

145. Bouslama, F. and A. Ichikawa [1992a], "Fuzzy control rules and their natural control laws." *Fuzzy Sets and Systems*, **48**(1), pp. 65–86.

146. Bouslama, F. and A. Ichikawa [1992b], "Application of limit fuzzy controllers to stability analysis." *Fuzzy Sets and Systems*, **49**(2), pp. 103–120.

147. Bouyssou, D. [1992], "A note on the sum of differences choice function for fuzzy preference relations." *Fuzzy Sets and Systems*, **47**(2), pp. 197–202.

148. Boy, G. A. and P. M. Kuss [1986], "A fuzzy method for the modeling of human-computer interaction in information retrieval tasks." In: Karwowski, W. and A. Mital, eds., *Applications of Fuzzy Set Theory in Human Factors*. Elsevier, New York, pp. 117–133.

149. Braae, M. and D. A. Rutherford [1979a], "Selection of parameters for a fuzzy logic controller." *Fuzzy Sets and Systems*, **2**(3), pp. 185–199.

150. Braae, M. and D. A. Rutherford [1979b], "Theoretical and linguistic aspects of the fuzzy logic controller." *Automatica*, **15**(5), pp. 553–577.

151. Bremerman, H. J. [1962], "Optimization through evolution and recombination." In: Yovits, M. C., G.

T. Jacobi and G. D. Goldstein, eds., *Self-Organizing Systems*. Spartan Books, Washington, pp. 93–106.

152. Brown, C. B., J. L. Chameau, R. Palmer and J. T. P. Yao, eds. [**1985**], *Proc. of NSF Workshop on Civil Engineering Applications of Fuzzy Sets*. Purdue University, West Lafayette.

153. Brown, J. D. and G. J. Klir [1993], "Range tests made fuzzy." *Proc. Second IEEE Intern. Conf. on Fuzzy Systems*, II, pp. 1214–1219.

154. Brown, J. G. [1971], "A note on fuzzy sets." *Information and Control*, **18**(1), pp. 32–39.

155. Brown, M. and C. Harris [**1994**], *Neurofuzzy Adaptive Modelling and Control*. Prentice Hall, Englewood Cliffs, NJ.

156. Buckles, B. P. and F. E. Petry [1982], "A fuzzy representation of data for relational databases." *Fuzzy Sets and Systems*, **7**(3), pp. 213–226.

157. Buckles, B. P. and F. E. Petry [1983], "Information-theoretical characterization of fuzzy relational databases." *IEEE Trans. on Systems, Man, and Cybernetics*, **13**(1), pp. 74–77.

158. Buckles, B. P. and F. E. Petry, eds. [**1992**], *Genetic Algorithms*. IEEE Computer Society, Los Alamitos, CA.

159. Buckley, J. J. [1984], "The multiple judge, multiple criteria ranking problem: a fuzzy set approach." *Fuzzy Sets and Systems*, **13**(1), pp. 25–37.

160. Buckley, J. J. [1985], "Fuzzy decision making with data: applications to statistics." *Fuzzy Sets and Systems*, **16**(2), pp. 139–147.

161. Buckley, J. J. [1987], "The fuzzy mathematics of finance." *Fuzzy Sets and Systems*, **21**(3), pp. 257–273.

162. Buckley, J. J. [1989], "Fuzzy vs. non-fuzzy controllers." *Control and Cybernetics*, **18**(2), pp. 127–130.

163. Buckley, J. J. [1990], "Belief updating in a fuzzy expert systems." *Intern. J. of Intelligent Systems*, **5**(3), pp. 265–275.

164. Buckley, J. J. [1992a], "Theory of fuzzy controller: a brief survey." In: Negoita, C. V., ed., *Cybernetics and Applied Systems*. Marcel Dekker, New York, pp. 293–307.

165. Buckley, J. J. [1992b], "Solving fuzzy equations in economics and finance." *Fuzzy Sets and Systems*, **48**(3), pp. 289–296.

166. Buckley, J. J. [1992c], "A general theory of uncertainty based on t-conorms." *Fuzzy Sets and Systems*, **49**(3), pp. 261–269.

167. Buckley, J. J. [1992d], "Solving fuzzy equations." *Fuzzy Sets and Systems*, **50**(1), pp. 1–14.

168. Buckley, J. J. [1992e], "Universal fuzzy controllers." *Automatica*, **28**(6), pp. 1245–1248.

169. Buckley, J. J. [1992f], "Theory of the fuzzy controller: an introduction." *Fuzzy Sets and Systems*, **51**(3), pp. 249–258.

170. Buckley, J. J. [1993a], "Controllable processes and the fuzzy controller." *Fuzzy Sets and Systems*, **53**(1), pp. 27–31.

171. Buckley, J. J. [1993b], "Sugeno type controllers are universal controllers." *Fuzzy Sets and Systems*, **53**(3), pp. 299–303.

172. Buckley, J. J. and Y. Hayashi [1993a], "Fuzzy input-output controllers are universal approximators." *Fuzzy Sets and Systems*, **58**(3), pp. 273–278.

173. Buckley, J. J. and Y. Hayashi [1993b], "Numerical relationship between neural networks, continuous functions, and fuzzy systems." *Fuzzy Sets and Systems*, **60**(1), pp. 1–8.

174. Buckley, J. J. and Y. Hayashi [1993c], "Hybrid neural nets can be fuzzy controllers and fuzzy expert systems." *Fuzzy Sets and Systems*, **60**(2), pp. 135–142.

175. Buckley, J. J. and Y. Hayashi [1994a], "Can fuzzy neural nets approximate continuous fuzzy functions?" *Fuzzy Sets and Systems*, **61**(1), pp. 43–52.

176. Buckley, J. J. and Y. Hayashi [1994b], "Fuzzy genetic algorithm and applications." *Fuzzy Sets and Systems*, **61**(2), pp. 129–136.

177. Buckley, J. J. and Y. Hayashi [1994c], "Can approximate reasoning be consistent?" *Fuzzy Sets and Systems*, **65**(1), pp. 13–18.

178. Buckley, J. J. and Y. Hayashi [1994d], "Fuzzy neural networks: a survey." *Fuzzy Sets and Systems*, **66**(1), pp. 1–13.

179. Buckley, J. J., Y. Hayashi and E. Czogala [1993], "On the equivalence of neural nets and fuzzy expert systems." *Fuzzy Sets and Systems*, **53**(2), pp. 129–134.

180. Buckley, J. J. and Y. Qu [1990], "Solving linear and quadratic fuzzy equations." *Fuzzy Sets and Systems*, **38**(1), pp. 43–59.

181. Buckley, J. J. and D. Tucker [1987], "Extended fuzzy relations: application to fuzzy expert systems." *Intern. J. of Approximate Reasoning*, **1**(2), pp. 177–195.

182. Buckley, J. J. and D. Tucker [1988], "The utility of information and risk-taking fuzzy expert systems." *Intern. J. of Intelligent Systems*, **3**(2), pp. 179–197.

183. Buell, D. A. [1982], "An analysis of some fuzzy subset applications to informational retrieval systems." *Fuzzy Sets and Systems*, **7**(1), pp. 35–42.

184. Bugarín, A. J. and S. Barro [1994], "Fuzzy reasoning supported by Petri nets." *IEEE Trans. on Fuzzy Systems*, **2**(2), pp. 135–150.

185. Bugarín, A. J., S. Barro and R. Ruiz [1994], "Fuzzy

control architectures." *J. of Intelligent & Fuzzy Systems*, **2**(2), pp. 125–146.

186. Buisson, J. C., H. Farrey and H. Prade [1985], "The development of a medical expert system and the treatment of imprecision in the framework of possibility theory." *Information Sciences*, **37**(1–3), pp. 211–226.

187. Buoncristiani, J. F. [1983], "Probability on fuzzy sets." *J. of Math. Analysis and Applications*, **96**(1), pp. 24–41.

188. Burdzy, K. and J. B. Kiszka [1983], "The reproducibility property of fuzzy control systems." *Fuzzy Sets and Systems*, **9**(2), pp. 161–177.

189. Butnariu, D. [1978], "Fuzzy games: a description of the concept." *Fuzzy Sets and Systems*, **1**(3), pp. 181–192.

190. Butnariu, D. [1985], "Non-atomic fuzzy measures and games." *Fuzzy Sets and Systems*, **17**(1), pp. 53–65.

191. Buxton, R. [1989], "Modelling uncertainty in expert systems." *Intern. J. of Man-Machine Studies*, **31**(4), pp. 415–476.

192. Bye, B. V., S. D. Biscoe and J. C. Henessey [1985], "A fuzzy algorithmic approach to the construction of composite indices: an application to a functional limitation index." *Intern. J. of General Systems*, **11**(2), pp. 163–172.

193. Cabrelli, C. A., B. Forte, U. M. Molter and E. R. Vrscay [1992], "Iterated fuzzy set systems: a new approach to the inverse problem for fractals and other sets." *J. of Math. Analysis and Applications*, **171**(1), pp. 79–100.

194. Cai, K. Y. [1993], "Parameter estimations of normal fuzzy variables." *Fuzzy Sets and Systems*, **55**(2), pp. 179–185.

195. Cai, K. Y. [1994], "Q-scale measures of fuzzy sets." *Fuzzy Sets and Systems*, **66**(1), pp. 59–81.

196. Cai, K. Y., C. Y. Wen and M. L. Zhang [1991a], "A critical review on software reliability modeling." *Reliability Eng. and System Safety*, **32**, pp. 357–371.

197. Cai, K. Y., C. Y. Wen and M. L. Zhang [1991b], "Fuzzy reliability modeling of gracefully degradable computing systems." *Reliability Eng. and System Safety*, **33**, pp. 141–157.

198. Cai, K. Y., C. Y. Wen and M. L. Zhang [1991c], "Fuzzy variables as a basis for a theory of fuzzy reliability in the possibility context." *Fuzzy Sets and Systems*, **42**(2), pp. 145–172.

199. Cai, K. Y., C. Y. Wen and M. L. Zhang [1991d], "Posbist reliability behavior of typical systems with two types of failure." *Fuzzy Sets and Systems*, **43**(1), pp. 17–32.

200. Cai, K. Y., C. Y. Wen and M. L. Zhang [1993], "Fuzzy states as a basis for a theory of fuzzy reliability." *Microelectronics and Reliability*, **33**(15), pp. 2253–2263.

201. Caianiello, E. R. and A. G. S. Ventre [1985], "A model of *C*-calculus." *Intern. J. of General Systems*, **11**(2), pp. 153–161.

202. Cao, B. [1993a], "Fuzzy geometric programming (I)." *Fuzzy Sets and Systems*, **53**(2), pp. 135–153.

203. Cao, B. [1993b], "Input-output mathematical model with *T*-fuzzy data." *Fuzzy Sets and Systems*, **59**(1), pp. 15–23.

204. Cao, H. and G. Chen [1983], "Some applications of fuzzy sets to meteorological forecasting." *Fuzzy Sets and Systems*, **9**(1), pp. 1–12.

205. Cao, Z. and A. Kandel [1989], "Applicability of some fuzzy implication operators." *Fuzzy Sets and Systems*, **31**(2), pp. 151–186.

206. Cao, Z., A. Kandel and L. Li [1990], "A new model of fuzzy reasoning." *Fuzzy Sets and Systems*, **36**(3), pp. 311–325.

207. Capocelli, R. M. and A. De Luca [1973], "Fuzzy sets and decision theory." *Information and Control*, **23**(5), pp. 446–473.

208. Carlsson, C. [1983], "An approach to handling fuzzy problem structures." *Cybernetics and Systems*, **14**(1), pp. 33–54.

209. Carlsson, C. [1984], "Fuzzy systems: basis for a modeling methodology?" *Cybernetics and Systems*, **15**(3–4), pp. 361–379.

210. Carlsson, C. [**1990**], *Fuzzy Set Theory for Management Decision*. Verlag TÜV Rheinland, Köln.

211. Carlsson, C. and R. Fuller [1994], "Interdependence in fuzzy multiple objective programming." *Fuzzy Sets and Systems*, **65**(1), pp. 19–29.

212. Carpenter, G. A., S. Grossberg, N. Markuzon, J. H. Reynolds and D. B. Rosen [1992], "Fuzzy ARTMAP: a neural network architecture for incremental supervised learning of analog multidimensional maps." *IEEE Trans. on Neural Networks*, **3**(5), pp. 698–713.

213. Castro, J. L. [1994], "Fuzzy logics as families of bivaluated logics." *Fuzzy Sets and Systems*, **64**(3), pp. 321–332.

214. Castro, J. L., M. Delgado and E. Trillas [1994], "Inducing implication relations." *Intern. J. of Approximate Reasoning*, **10**(3), pp. 235–250.

215. Castro, J. L., F. Herrera and J. L. Verdegay [1994], "Knowledge-based systems and fuzzy Boolean programming." *Intern. J. of Intelligent Systems*, **9**(2), pp. 211–225.

216. Cat Ho, N. and W. Wechler [1990], "Hedge algebras: An algebraic approach to structure of sets of linguistic truth values." *Fuzzy Sets and Systems*, **35**(3), pp. 281–293.

217. Catania, V., A. Puliafito, M. Russo and L. Vita [1994], "A VLSI fuzzy inference processor based

on a discrete analog approach." *IEEE Trans. on Fuzzy Systems*, **2**(2), pp. 93–106.

218. Cavallo, R. E. and G. J. Klir [1982], "Reconstruction of possibilistic behavior systems." *Fuzzy Sets and Systems*, **8**(2), pp. 175–197.

219. Celmins, A. [1987a], "Least squares model fitting to fuzzy vector data." *Fuzzy Sets and Systems*, **22**(3), pp. 245–270.

220. Celmins, A. [1987b], "Multidimensional least-squares fitting of fuzzy model." *Mathematical Modelling*, **9**(6), pp. 669–690.

221. Černý, M. [1991], "Fuzzy approach to vector optimization." *Intern. J. of General Systems*, **20**(1), pp. 23–29.

222. Chakravarty, S. R. and T. Roy [1985], "Measurement of fuzziness: a general approach." *Theory and Decision*, **19**(2), pp. 163–169.

223. Chameau, J. L., A. Alteschaeffl, H. L. Michael and J. T. P. Yao [1983], "Potential applications of fuzzy sets in civil engineering." *Intern. J. of Man-Machine Studies*, **19**(1), pp. 9–18.

224. Chameau, J. L. and J. C. Santamarina [1987], "Membership functions I, II." *Intern. J. of Approximate Reasoning*, **1**(3), pp. 287–301, 303–317.

225. Chan, K. P. and Y. S. Cheung [1992], "Fuzzy-attribute graph with application to Chinese character recognition." *IEEE Trans. on Systems, Man, and Cybernetics*, **22**(1), pp. 153–160.

226. Chanas, S. [1983], "The use of parametric programming in fuzzy linear programming." *Fuzzy Sets and Systems*, **11**(3), pp. 243–251.

227. Chang, C. C. [1958], "Algebraic analysis of many valued logic." *Trans. Am. Math. Soc.*, **88**, pp. 467–490.

228. Chang, C. C. [1959], "A new proof of the completeness of Lukasiewicz axioms." *Trans. Am. Math. Soc.*, **93**, pp. 74–80.

229. Chang, C. L. [1968], "Fuzzy topological spaces." *J. of Math. Analysis and Applications*, **24**(1), pp. 182–190.

230. Chang, P. L. and Y. C. Chen [1994], "A fuzzy multi-criteria decision making method for technology transfer strategy selection in biotechnology." *Fuzzy Sets and Systems*, **63**(2), pp. 131–139.

231. Chang, R. L. P. and T. Pavlidis [1977], "Fuzzy decision tree algorithms." *IEEE Trans. on Systems, Man, and Cybernetics*, **7**(1), pp. 28–34.

232. Chang, R. L. P. and T. Pavlidis [1979], "Applications of fuzzy sets in curve fitting." *Fuzzy Sets and Systems*, **2**(1), pp. 67–74.

233. Chang, S. S. L. and L. A. Zadeh [1972], "On fuzzy mapping and control." *IEEE Trans. on Systems, Man, and Cybernetics*, **2**(1), pp. 30–34.

234. Chaudhuri, B. B. and D. D. Majumder [1982], "On membership evaluation in fuzzy sets." In: Gupta, M. M. and E. Sanchez, eds., *Approximate Reasoning in Decision Analysis*. North-Holland, New York, pp. 3–11.

235. Chen, C. L. and W. C. Chen [1994], "Fuzzy controller design by using neural network techniques." *IEEE Trans. on Fuzzy Systems*, **2**(3), pp. 235–244.

236. Chen, G. Q., E. E. Kerre and J. Vandenbulcke [1994], "A computational algorithm for the FFD transitive closure and a complete axiomatization of fuzzy functional dependence (FFD)." *Intern. J. of Intelligent Systems*, **9**(5), pp. 421–439.

237. Chen, G. Q., S. C. Lee and E. S. H. Yu [1983], "Application of fuzzy set theory to economics." In: Wang, P. P., ed., *Advances in Fuzzy Sets, Possibility Theory, and Applications*. Plenum Press, New York, pp. 277–305.

238. Chen, J. Q. and L. J. Chen [1993], "Study on stability of fuzzy closed–loop control systems." *Fuzzy Sets and Systems*, **57**(2), pp. 159–168.

239. Chen, J. Q., J. H. Lu and L. J. Chen [1994], "An on-line identification algorithm for fuzzy systems." *Fuzzy Sets and Systems*, **64**(1), pp. 63–72.

240. Chen, L., H. D. Cheng and J. Zhang [1994], "Fuzzy subfiber and its application to seismic lithology classification." *Information Sciences: Applications*, **1**(2), pp. 77–95.

241. Chen, S. J. and C. L. Hwang [**1992**], *Fuzzy Multiple Attribute Decision Making: Methods and Applications*. Springer–Verlag, New York.

242. Chen, S. M. [1988], "A new approach to handling fuzzy decision making problems." *IEEE Trans. on Systems, Man, and Cybernetics*, **18**(6), pp. 1012–1016.

243. Chen, S. M. [1992], "An improved algorithm for inexact reasoning based on extended fuzzy production rules." *Cybernetics and Systems*, **23**(5), pp. 463–481.

244. Chen, S. M. [1994a], "A new method for handling multicriteria fuzzy decision-making problems." *Cybernetics and Systems*, **25**(5), pp. 409–420.

245. Chen, S. M. [1994b], "Fuzzy system reliability analysis using fuzzy number arithmetic operations." *Fuzzy Sets and Systems*, **64**(1), pp. 31–38.

246. Chen, S. M., J. S. Ke and J. F. Chang [1990], "Knowledge representation using fuzzy Petri nets." *IEEE Trans. Knowledge and Data Engineering*, **2**(3), pp. 311–319.

247. Chen, S. Q. [1988], "Analysis for multiple fuzzy regression." *Fuzzy Sets and Systems*, **25**(1), pp. 59–65.

248. Chen, Y. Y. and T. C. Tsao [1989], "A description of the dynamical behavior of fuzzy systems." *IEEE*

Trans. on Systems, Man and Cybernetics, **19**(4), pp. 745–755.

249. Cheng, F. H., W. H. Hsu and C. A. Chen [1989], "Fuzzy approach to solve the recognition problem of handwritten Chinese characters." *Pattern Recognition,* **22**(2), pp. 133–141.

250. Cheng, Y. Y. M. and B. McInnis [1980], "An algorithm for multiple attribute, multiple alternative decision problems based on fuzzy sets with application to medical diagnosis." *IEEE Trans. on Systems, Man, and Cybernetics,* **10**(10), pp. 645–650.

251. Chiu, C., A. F. Norcio and C. I. Hsu [1994], "Reasoning on domain knowledge level in human-computer interaction." *Information Sciences: Applications,* **1**(1), pp. 31–46.

252. Chiu, S. and M. Togai [1988], "A fuzzy logic programming environment for real-time control." *Intern. J. of Approximate Reasoning,* **2**(2), pp. 163–176.

253. Cho, K. B. and K. C. Lee [1994], "An adaptive fuzzy current controller with neural network for a field–oriented controller induction machine." *Intern. J. of Approximate Reasoning,* **10**(1), pp. 45–61.

254. Cho, S. and O. K. Ersoy [1992], "An algorithm to compute the degree of match in fuzzy systems." *Fuzzy Sets and Systems,* **49**(3), pp. 285–299.

255. Cho, S. and M. R. Lehto [1992], "A fuzzy scheme with application to expert classification systems for computing the degree of match between a rule and an assertion." *Cybernetics and Systems,* **23**(1), pp. 1–27.

256. Choobineh, F. and H. S. Li [1993], "An index for ordering fuzzy numbers." *Fuzzy Sets and Systems,* **54**(3), pp. 287–294.

257. Choquet, G. [1953–54], "Theory of capacities." *Annales de L'Institut Fourier,* **5**, pp. 131–295.

258. Chu, A. T. W., R. E. Kalaba and J. Spingarn [1979], "A comparison of two methods for determining the weights of belonging to fuzzy sets." *J. of Optimization Theory and Applications,* **27**(4), pp. 531–538.

259. Chu, C. K. P. and J. M. Mendel [1994], "First break refraction event picking using fuzzy logic systems." *IEEE Trans. on Fuzzy Systems,* **2**(4), pp. 255–266.

260. Chun, M. and Z. Bien [1993], "Neurocomputational approach to solve a convexly combined fuzzy relational equation with generalized connectives." *Fuzzy Sets and Systems,* **57**(3), pp. 321–333.

261. Chung, B. and J. Oh [1993], "Control of dynamic systems using fuzzy learning algorithm." *Fuzzy Sets and Systems,* **59**(1), pp. 1–14.

262. Chung, F. L. and T. Lee [1994], "Fuzzy competitive learning." *Neural Networks,* **7**(3), pp. 539–551.

263. Civanlar, M. R. and H. J. Trussell [1986], "Constructing membership functions using statistical data." *Fuzzy Sets and Systems,* **18**(1), pp. 1–13.

264. Cox, E. [**1994**], *The Fuzzy Systems Handbook.* Academic Press, Cambridge, MA.

265. Cross, V. [1994], "Fuzzy information retrieval." *J. of Intelligent Information Systems,* **3**(1), pp. 29–56.

266. Cross, V. and T. Sudkamp [1994], "Patterns of fuzzy rule-based inference." *Intern. J. of Approximate Reasoning,* **11**(3), pp. 235–255.

267. Cubero, J. C. and M. A. Vila [1994], "A new definition of fuzzy functional dependency in fuzzy relational databases." *Intern. J. of Intelligent Systems,* **9**(5), pp. 441–448.

268. Cucka, P. and A. Rosenfeld [1993], "Evidence-based pattern-matching relaxation." *Pattern Recognition,* **26**(9), pp. 1417–1428.

269. Cumani, A. [1982], "On a possibilistic approach to the analysis of fuzzy feedback systems." *IEEE Trans. on Systems, Man, and Cybernetics,* **12**(3), pp. 417–422.

270. Cutello, V. and J. Montero [1994], "Hierarchies of aggregation operators." *Intern. J. of Intelligent Systems,* **9**(11), pp. 1025–1045.

271. Cutsem, B. V. and I. Gath [1992], "Detection of outliers and robust estimation using fuzzy clustering." *Computational Statistics and Data Analysis,* **15**, pp. 47–61.

272. Czogala, E. [**1984**], *Probabilistic Sets in Decision Making and Control.* Verlag TÜV Rheinland, Köln.

273. Czogala, E. and K. Hirota [**1986**], *Probabilistic Sets: Fuzzy and Stochastic Approach to Decision, Control and Recognition Processes.* Verlag TÜV Rheinland, Köln.

274. Czogala, E. and W. Pedrycz [1981a], "Some problems concerning the construction of algorithms of decision-making in fuzzy systems." *Intern. J. of Man-Machine Studies,* **15**(2), pp. 201–221.

275. Czogala, E. and W. Pedrycz [1981b], "On identification in fuzzy systems and its applications in control problems." *Fuzzy Sets and Systems,* **6**(1), pp. 73–83.

276. Czogala, E. and W. Pedrycz [1982a], "Control problems in fuzzy systems." *Fuzzy Sets and Systems,* **7**(3), pp. 257–274.

277. Czogala, E. and W. Pedrycz [1982b], "Fuzzy rule generation for fuzzy control." *Cybernetics and Systems,* **13**(3), pp. 275–293.

278. Czogala, E. and T. Rawlik [1989], "Modelling of a fuzzy controller with application to the control of biological processes." *Fuzzy Sets and Systems,* **31**(1), pp. 13–22.

279. Da, R., E. E. Kerre, G. De Cooman, B. Cappelle and F. Vanmassenhove [1990], "Influence of the fuzzy implication operator on the method-of-cases

inference rule." *Intern. J. of Approximate Reasoning*, **4**(4), pp. 307–318.

280. Dal Cin, M. [1975a], "Fuzzy state automata: Their stability and fault tolerance." *Intern. J. of Computer and Information Sciences*, **4**(1), pp. 63–80.

281. Dal Cin, M. [1975b], "Modification tolerance of fuzzy state automata." *Intern. J. of Computer and Information Sciences*, **4**(1), pp. 81–93.

282. Dalton, R. E. [1994], "Towards a theory of fuzzy causality for diagnosis." *Information Sciences*, **80**(3–4), pp. 195–211.

283. D'ambrosio, B. [**1989**], *Qualitative Process Theory Using Linguistic Variables*. Springer–Verlag, New York.

284. Dave, R. N. [1990], "Fuzzy shell-clustering and applications to circle detection in digital images." *Intern. J. of General Systems*, **16**(4), pp. 343–355.

285. Dave, R. N. and T. X. Fu [1994], "Robust shape detection using fuzzy clustering: Practical application." *Fuzzy Sets and Systems*, **65**(2–3), pp. 161–185.

286. Davidson, J., W. Pedrycz and I. Goulter [1993], "A fuzzy decision model for the design of rural natural gas networks." *Fuzzy Sets and Systems*, **53**(3), pp. 241–252.

287. Davis, L. [**1991**], *Handbook of Genetic Algorithms*. Van Nostrand Reinhold, New York.

288. De Baets, B. and E. E. Kerre [1993], "Fuzzy relational compositions." *Fuzzy Sets and Systems*, **60**(1), pp. 109–120.

289. De Baets, B. and E. E. Kerre [1994a], "The cutting of compositions." *Fuzzy Sets and Systems*, **62**(3), pp. 295–309.

290. De Baets, B. and E. E. Kerre [1994b], "A primer on solving fuzzy relational equations on the unit interval." *Intern. J. of Uncertainty, Fuzziness and Knowledge–Based Systems*, **2**(2), pp. 205–225.

291. De Campos, L. M. and A. González [1993], "A fuzzy inference model based on an uncertainty forward propagation approach." *Intern. J. of Approximate Reasoning*, **9**(2), pp. 139–164.

292. De Campos, L. M., J. F. Huete and S. Moral [1994], "Probability intervals: A tool for uncertain reasoning." *Intern. J. of Uncertainty, Fuzziness and Knowledge–Based Systems*, **2**(2), pp. 167–196.

293. De Campos, L. M., M. T. Lamata and S. Moral [1990], "The concept of conditional fuzzy measure." *Intern. J. of Intelligent Systems*, **5**(3), pp. 237–246.

294. De Cooman, G., E. E. Kerre, B. Cappelle and R. Da [1990], "On the extension of classical propositional logic by means of a triangular norm." *Intern. J. of Intelligent Systems*, **5**(3), pp. 307–322.

295. De Glas, M. [1983], "Theory of fuzzy systems." *Fuzzy Sets and Systems*, **10**(1), pp. 65–77.

296. De Glas, M. [1984], "Invariance and stability of fuzzy systems." *J. of Math. Analysis and Applications*, **99**, pp. 299–319.

297. De, K. [1975], "A bibliography on fuzzy sets." *J. of Computational and Applied Mathematics*, **1**(3), pp. 205–212.

298. De Luca, A. and S. Termini [1972a], "A definition of a nonprobabilistic entropy in the setting of fuzzy sets theory." *Information and Control*, **20**(4), pp. 301–312.

299. De Luca, A. and S. Termini [1972b], "Algebraic properties of fuzzy sets." *J. of Math. Analysis and Applications*, **40**(2), pp. 373–386.

300. De Mori, R. [**1983**], *Computer Models of Speech Using Fuzzy Algorithms*. Plenum Press, New York.

301. De Neyer, M. and R. Gorez [1993], "Fuzzy and quantitative model-based control systems for robotic manipulators." *Intern. J. of Systems Science*, **24**(10), pp. 1863–1884.

302. De Silva, C. W. [1994], "A criterion for knowledge base decoupling in fuzzy-logic control systems." *IEEE Trans. on Systems, Man, and Cybernetics*, **24**(10), pp. 1548–1552.

303. Degani, R. and G. Bortolan [1988], "The problem of linguistic approximation in clinical decision making." *Intern. J. of Approximate Reasoning*, **2**(2), pp. 143–162.

304. Delgado, M. and A. Gonzalez [1993], "An inductive learning procedure to identify fuzzy systems." *Fuzzy Sets and Systems*, **55**(2), pp. 121–132.

305. Delgado, M. and S. Moral [1987], "On the concept of possibility–probability consistency." *Fuzzy Sets and Systems*, **21**(3), pp. 311–318.

306. Delgado, M., J. L. Verdegay and M. A. Vila [1990a], "Relating different approaches to solve linear programming problems with imprecise costs." *Fuzzy Sets and Systems*, **37**(1), pp. 33–42.

307. Delgado, M., J. Verdegay and M. A. Vila [1990b], "On valuation and optimization problems in fuzzy graphs: a general approach and some particular cases." *ORSA J. on Computing*, **2**(1), pp. 74–83.

308. Dempster, A. P. [1967], "Upper and lower probabilities induced by a multivalued mapping." *Annals Mathematical Statistics*, **38**, pp. 325–339.

309. Denneberg, D. [**1994**], *Non-additive Measure and Integral*. Boston, Kluwer.

310. Deutsch, S. J. and C. J. Malborg [1985], "A fuzzy set approach to data set evaluation for decision support." *IEEE Trans. on Systems, Man, and Cybernetics*, **15**(6), pp. 777–783.

311. Devi, B. B. and V. V. S. Sarma [1985], "Estimation of fuzzy memberships from histograms." *Information Sciences*, **35**(1), pp. 43–59.

312. Devi, B. B. and V. V. S. Sarma [1986], "A fuzzy approximation scheme for sequential learning in

pattern recognition." *IEEE Trans. on Systems, Man, and Cybernetics,* **16**(5), pp. 668–679.

313. Di Nola, A., W. Kolodziejczyk and S. Sessa [1993], "On reduction of transitive fuzzy matrices and its applications." *Intern. J. of Approximate Reasoning,* **9**(3), pp. 249–261.

314. Di Nola, A., W. Pedrycz and S. Sessa [1989], "An aspect of discrepancy in the implementation of modus ponens in the presence of fuzzy quantities." *Intern. J. of Approximate Reasoning,* **3**(3), pp. 259–265.

315. Di Nola, A., W. Pedrycz and S. Sessa [1993], "Models of matching of fuzzy sets." *Kybernetes,* **22**(3), pp. 41–46.

316. Di Nola, A., W. Pedrycz, S. Sessa and E. Sanchez [1991], "Fuzzy relation equations theory as a basis of fuzzy modelling: an overview." *Fuzzy Sets and Systems,* **40**(3), pp. 415–429.

317. Di Nola, A., W. Pedrycz, S. Sessa and P. Z. Wang [1984], "Fuzzy relation equation under a class of triangular norms: A survey and new results." *Stochastica,* **8**(2), pp. 99–145.

318. Di Nola, A. and S. Sessa [1983], "On the set of solutions of composite fuzzy relation equations." *Fuzzy Sets and Systems,* **9**(3), pp. 275–285.

319. Di Nola, A., S. Sessa and W. Pedrycz [1985], "Decomposition problem of fuzzy relations." *Intern. J. of General Systems,* **10**(2–3), pp. 123–133.

320. Di Nola, A., S. Sessa and W. Pedrycz [1990a], "Modus ponens for fuzzy data realized via equations with equality operators." *Intern. J. of Intelligent Systems,* **5**(1), pp. 1–14.

321. Di Nola, A., S. Sessa and W. Pedrycz [1990b], "On some finite fuzzy relation equations." *Information Sciences,* **50**(1), pp. 93–109.

322. Di Nola, A., S. Sessa and W. Pedrycz [1994], "Fuzzy information in knowledge representation and processing for frame-based structures." *IEEE Trans. on Systems, Man, and Cybernetics,* **24**(6), pp. 918–925.

323. Di Nola, A., S. Sessa, W. Pedrycz and M. Higashi [1985], "Minimal and maximal solutions of a decomposition problem of fuzzy relations." *Intern. J. of General Systems,* **11**(2), pp. 103–116.

324. Di Nola, A., S. Sessa, W. Pedrycz and E. Sanches [**1989**], *Fuzzy Relation Equations and Their Applications to Knowledge Engineering.* Kluwer, Boston.

325. Di Nola, A. and A. G. S. Ventre, eds. [**1986**], *The Mathematics of Fuzzy Systems.* Verlag TÜV Rheinland, Köln.

326. Diamond, J., R. D. McLeod and W. Pedrycz [1992], "A fuzzy cognitive structure: foundations, applications and VLSI implementation." *Fuzzy Sets and Systems,* **47**(1), pp. 49–64.

327. Diamond, P. [1988], "Fuzzy least squares." *Information Sciences,* **46**(3), pp. 141–157.

328. Diamond, P. [1992], "Chaos and fuzzy representation of dynamical systems." In: *Proc. Second Intern. Conf. on Fuzzy Logic and Neural Networks, Iizuka, Japan,* pp. 51–58.

329. Diamond, P. and A. Ramer [1993], "Approximation of knowledge and fuzzy sets." *Cybernetics and Systems,* **24**(5), pp. 407–417.

330. Diamond, P. and P. Kloeden [**1994**], *Metric Spaces of Fuzzy Sets: Theory and Application.* World Scientific, Singapore.

331. Diamond, P. and A. Pokrovskii [1994], "Chaos, entropy and a generalized extension principle." *Fuzzy Sets and Systems,* **61**(3), pp. 277–283.

332. Dishkant, H. [1981], "About membership function estimation." *Fuzzy Sets and Systems,* **5**(2), pp. 141–147.

333. Dockery, J. T. [1982], "Fuzzy design of military information systems." *Intern. J. of Man-Machine Studies,* **16**(1), pp. 1–38.

334. Dockery, J. T. and E. Murray [1987], "A fuzzy approach to aggregating military assessments." *Intern. J. of Approximate Reasoning,* **1**(3), pp. 251–271.

335. Dodds, D. R. [1988], "Fuzziness in knowledge-based robotics systems." *Fuzzy Sets and Systems,* **26**(2), pp. 179–193.

336. Doherty, P., D. Driankov and H. Hellendoorn [1993], "Fuzzy if-then-unless rules and their implementation." *Intern. J. of Uncertainty, Fuzziness and Knowledge–Based Systems,* **1**(2), pp. 167–182.

337. Dombi, J. [1982], "A general class of fuzzy operators, the De Morgan class of fuzzy operators and fuzziness measures induced by fuzzy operators." *Fuzzy Sets and Systems,* **8**(2), pp. 149–163.

338. Dombi, J. [1990], "Membership function as an evaluation." *Fuzzy Sets and Systems,* **35**(1), pp. 1–21.

339. Dompere, K. K. [1993a], "The theory of fuzzy decisions, cost distribution principle in social choice and optimal tax distribution." *Fuzzy Sets and Systems,* **53**(3), pp. 253–273.

340. Dompere, K. K. [1993b], "A fuzzy-decision theory of optimal social discount rate: Collective-choice-theoretic." *Fuzzy Sets and Systems,* **58**(3), pp. 279–302.

341. Dong, W. M. and F. S. Wong [1987], "Fuzzy weighted averages and implementation of the extension principle." *Fuzzy Sets and Systems,* **21**(2), pp. 183–199.

342. Driankov, D. [1987], "Inference with a single fuzzy conditional proposition." *Fuzzy Sets and Systems,* **24**(1), pp. 51–63.

343. Drossos, C. and G. Markakis [1993], "Boolean representation of fuzzy sets." *Kybernetes*, **22**(3), pp. 35–40.

344. Dubois, D. [1987], "An application of fuzzy arithmetic to the optimization of industrial machining processes." *Mathematical Modelling*, **9**(6), pp. 461–475.

345. Dubois, D. and H. Prade [1979a], "Fuzzy real algebra: Some results." *Fuzzy Sets and Systems*, **2**(4), pp. 327–348.

346. Dubois, D. and H. Prade [1979b], "Operations in a fuzzy-valued logic." *Information and Control*, **43**(2), pp. 224–240.

347. Dubois, D. and H. Prade [**1980**], *Fuzzy Sets and Systems: Theory and Applications*. Academic Press, New York.

348. Dubois, D. and H. Prade [1982a], "Towards fuzzy differential calculus." *Fuzzy Sets and Systems*, **8**(1), pp. 1–17; **8**(2), pp.105–116; **8**(3), pp. 225–233.

349. Dubois, D. and H. Prade [1982b], "A class of fuzzy measures based on triangular norms." *Intern. J. of General Systems*, **8**(1), pp. 43–61.

350. Dubois, D. and H. Prade [1983], "Ranking fuzzy numbers in the setting of possibility theory." *Information Sciences*, **30**, pp. 183–224.

351. Dubois, D. and H. Prade [1984a], "Fuzzy logics and the generalized modus ponens revisited." *Cybernetics and Systems*, **15**(3–4), pp. 293–331.

352. Dubois, D. and H. Prade [1984b], "A theorem on implication functions defined from triangular norms." *Stochastica*, **8**(3), pp. 267–279.

353. Dubois, D. and H. Prade [1985a], "Evidence measures based on fuzzy information." *Automatica*, **21**(5), pp. 547–562.

354. Dubois, D. and H. Prade [1985b], "A note on measures of specificity for fuzzy sets." *Intern. J. of General Systems*, **10**(4), pp. 279–283.

355. Dubois, D. and H. Prade [1985c], "Unfair coins and necessity measures: towards a possibilistic interpretation of histograms." *Fuzzy Sets and Systems*, **10**(1), pp. 15–20.

356. Dubois, D. and H. Prade [1985d], "The generalized modus ponens under sup-min composition: a theoretical study." In: Gupta, M. M., A. Kandel, W. Bandler and J. B. Kiszka, eds., *Approximate Reasoning in Expert Systems*. North-Holland, New York, pp. 217–232.

357. Dubois, D. and H. Prade [1985e], "A review of fuzzy set aggregation connectives." *Information Sciences*, **36**(1–2), pp. 85–121.

358. Dubois, D. and H. Prade [1986a], "Fuzzy sets and statistical data." *European J. of Operational Research*, **25**(3), pp. 345–356.

359. Dubois, D. and H. Prade [1986b], "Possibilistic inference under matrix form." In: Prade, H. and C. V. Negoita, eds., *Fuzzy Logic in Knowledge Engineering*. Verlag TÜV Rheinland, Köln, pp. 112–126.

360. Dubois, D. and H. Prade [1986c], "A set-theoretic view of belief function: Logical operations and approximations of fuzzy sets." *Intern. J. of General Systems*, **12**(3), pp. 193–226.

361. Dubois, D. and H. Prade [1987a], "Two–fold fuzzy sets and rough sets: Some issues in knowledge representation." *Fuzzy Sets and Systems*, **23**(1), pp. 3–18.

362. Dubois, D. and H. Prade [1987b], "Properties of measures of information in evidence and possibility theories." *Fuzzy Sets and Systems*, **24**(2), pp. 161–182.

363. Dubois, D. and H. Prade [1987c], "The mean value of a fuzzy number." *Fuzzy Sets and Systems*, **24**(3), pp. 279–300.

364. Dubois, D. and H. Prade [1987d], "Fuzzy numbers: an overview." In: Bezdek, J. C., ed., *Analysis of Fuzzy Information–Vol. 1: Mathematics and Logic*. CRC Press, Boca Raton, FL, pp. 3–39.

365. Dubois, D. and H. Prade [1987e], "Necessity measures and the resolution principle." *IEEE Trans. on Systems, Man, and Cybernetics*, **17**(3), pp. 474–478.

366. Dubois, D. and H. Prade [**1988a**], *Possibility Theory*. Plenum Press, New York.

367. Dubois, D. and H. Prade [1988b], "On the combination of uncertain or imprecise pieces of information in rule-based systems: A discussion in the framework of possibility theory." *Intern. J. of Approximate Reasoning*, **2**(1), pp. 65–87.

368. Dubois, D. and H. Prade [1988c], "The treatment of uncertainty in knowledge-based systems using fuzzy sets and possibility theory." *Intern. J. of Intelligent Systems*, **3**(2), pp. 141–165.

369. Dubois, D. and H. Prade [1989a], "Processing fuzzy temporal knowledge." *IEEE Trans. on Systems, Man, and Cybernetics*, **19**(4), pp. 729–744.

370. Dubois, D. and H. Prade [1989b], "Fuzzy sets, probability and measurement." *European J. of Operational Research*, **40**(2), pp. 135–154.

371. Dubois, D. and H. Prade [1990a], "The logical view of conditioning and its application to possibility and evidence theories." *Intern. J. of Approximate Reasoning*, **4**(1), pp. 23–46.

372. Dubois, D. and H. Prade [1990b], "Rough fuzzy sets and fuzzy rough sets." *Intern. J. of General Systems*, **17**(2–3), pp. 191–209.

373. Dubois, D. and H. Prade [1990c], "Resolution principles in possibilistic logic." *Intern. J. of Approximate Reasoning*, **4**(1), pp. 1–22.

374. Dubois, D. and H. Prade [1991a], "Fuzzy sets in approximate reasoning, Part 1: Inference with

possibility distributions." *Fuzzy Sets and Systems,* **40**(1), pp. 143–202.

375. Dubois, D. and H. Prade [1991b], "Fuzzy sets in approximate reasoning, Part 2: Logical approaches." *Fuzzy Sets and Systems,* **40**(1), pp. 202–244.

376. Dubois, D. and H. Prade [1991c], "Epistemic entrenchment and possibilistic logic." *Artificial Intelligence,* **50**(1), pp. 223–239.

377. Dubois, D. and H. Prade [1991d], "Fuzzy labels, imprecision and contextual dependency: Comments on Zeleny's 'Cogitive equilibrium: A knowledge-based theory of fuzzy sets'." *Intern. J. of General Systems,* **19**(4), pp. 383–386.

378. Dubois, D. and H. Prade [1991e], "Measuring and updating information." *Information Sciences,* **57–58**, pp. 181–195.

379. Dubois, D. and H. Prade [1992a], "Putting rough sets and fuzzy sets together." In: Slowinski, R., eds., *Intelligent Decision Support.* Kluwer, Boston, pp. 203–232.

380. Dubois, D. and H. Prade [1992b], "Gradual inference rules in approximate reasoning." *Information Sciences,* **61**(1–2), pp. 103–122.

381. Dubois, D. and H. Prade [1992c], "On the combination of evidence in various mathematical frameworks." In: Flamm, J. and T. Luisi, eds., *Reliability Data Collection and Analysis.* Kluwer, Boston, pp. 213–241.

382. Dubois, D. and H. Prade, eds. **[1993a]**, *Readings in Fuzzy Sets for Intelligent Systems.* Morgan Kaufmann, San Mateo, CA.

383. Dubois, D. and H. Prade [1993b], "Fuzzy sets and probability: Misunderstanding, bridges and gaps." *Proc. Second IEEE Intern. Conf. on Fuzzy Systems, San Francisco,* pp. 1059–1068.

384. Dubois, D. and H. Prade [1994], "A survey of belief revision and updating rules in various uncertainty models." *Intern. J. of Intelligent Systems,* **9**(1), pp. 61–100.

385. Dubois, D., H. Prade and C. Testemale [1988], "Weighted fuzzy pattern matching." *Fuzzy Sets and Systems,* **28**(3), pp. 313–331.

386. Dumitrescu, D. [1992], "Fuzzy partitions with the connectives T_∞, S_∞." *Fuzzy Sets and Systems,* **47**(2), pp. 193–195.

387. Dumitrescu, D. [1993], "Entropy of a fuzzy process." *Fuzzy Sets and Systems,* **55**(2), pp. 169–177.

388. Dumitrescu, D. and D. Tatar [1994], "Normal forms of fuzzy formulas and their minimization." *Fuzzy Sets and Systems,* **64**(1), pp. 113–117.

389. Dunn, J. C. [1973], "A fuzzy relative of the ISODATA process and its use in detecting compact well-separated clusters." *J. of Cybernetics,* **3**(3), pp. 32–57.

390. Dunn, J. C. [1974], "A graph theoretic analysis of pattern classification via Tamura's fuzzy relation."

IEEE Trans. on Systems, Man, and Cybernetics, **4**(3), pp. 310–313.

391. Dutta, D., J. R. Rao and R. N. Tiwari [1993], "Effect of tolerance in fuzzy linear fractional programming." *Fuzzy Sets and Systems,* **55**(2), pp. 133–142.

392. Dutta, D., R. N. Tiwari and R. Rao [1992], "Multiple objective linear fractional programming: a fuzzy set theoretic approach." *Fuzzy Sets and Systems,* **52**(1), pp. 39–45.

393. Dutta, S. [1991a], "Approximate spatial reasoning: Integrating qualitative and quantitative constraints." *Intern. J. of Approximate Reasoning,* **5**(3), pp. 307–330.

394. Dutta, S. [1991b], "Approximate reasoning by analogy to answer null queries." *Intern. J. of Approximate Reasoning,* **5**(4), pp. 373–398.

395. Dutta, S. and P. P. Bonissone [1993], "Integrating case- and rule-based reasoning." *Intern. J. of Approximate Reasoning,* **8**(3), pp. 163–204.

396. Dvurečenski, A. and S. Riečan [1991], "Fuzzy quantum models." *Intern. J. of General Systems,* **20**(1), pp. 383–386.

397. Dyckhoff, H. and W. Pedrycz [1984], "Generalized means as a model of compensative connectives." *Fuzzy Sets and Systems,* **14**(2), pp. 143–154.

398. Ebert, C. [1994], "Rule-based fuzzy classification for software quality control." *Fuzzy Sets and Systems,* **63**(3), pp. 349–358.

399. Edmons, E. A. [1980], "Lattice fuzzy logic." *Intern. J. of Man-Machine Studies,* **13**(4), pp. 455–465.

400. Efstathiou, J. and V. Rajkovic [1979], "Multiattribute decision making using a fuzzy heuristic approach." *IEEE Trans. on Systems, Man, and Cybernetics,* **9**(6), pp. 326–333.

401. Efstathiou, J. and R. M. Tong [1982], "Ranking fuzzy sets: A decision theoretic approach." *IEEE Trans. on Systems, Man, and Cybernetics,* **12**(5), pp. 655–659.

402. Eick, C. F. and N. N. Mehta [1993], "Decision making involving imperfect knowledge." *IEEE Trans. on Systems, Man, and Cybernetics,* **23**(3), pp. 840–851.

403. Eklund, P., J. Forsström, A. Holm, M. Nyström and G. Selén [1994], "Rule generation as an alternative to knowledge acquisition: A systems architecture for medical informatics." *Fuzzy Sets and Systems,* **66**(2), pp. 195–205.

404. El Hajjaji, A. and A. Rachid [1994], "Explicit formulas for fuzzy controller." *Fuzzy Sets and Systems,* **62**(2), pp. 135–141.

405. El Rayes, A. B. and N. N. Morsi [1994], "Generalized possibility measures." *Information Sciences,* **79**(3–4), pp. 201–222.

406. Elms, D. [1984], "Use of fuzzy sets in developing code risk factors." *Civil Engineering Systems*, **1**(4), pp. 178–184.

407. Esogbue, A. O. [1983], "Dynamic programming, fuzzy sets, and the modeling of R&D management control systems." *IEEE Trans. on Systems, Man, and Cybernetics*, **13**(1), pp. 18–29.

408. Esogbue, A. O. and R. C. Elder [1979], "Fuzzy sets and the modelling of physician decision processes: Part I: The initial interview–information gathering process." *Fuzzy Sets and Systems*, **2**, pp. 279–291.

409. Esogbue, A. O. and R. C. Elder [1980], "Fuzzy sets and the modelling of physician decision processes: Part II: Fuzzy diagnosis decision models." *Fuzzy Sets and Systems*, **3**(1), pp. 1–9.

410. Esogbue, A. O. and R. C. Elder [1983], "Measurement and valuation of a fuzzy mathematical model for medical diagnosis." *Fuzzy Sets and Systems*, **10**, pp. 223–242.

411. Esogbue, A. O., M. Theologidu and K. Guo [1992], "On the application of fuzzy set theory to the optimal flood control problem arising in water resources systems." *Fuzzy Sets and Systems*, **48**(2), pp. 155–172.

412. Estep, M. L. [1993], "On the law of excluded middle and arguments for multivalued logics in systems inquiry." *Cybernetics and Systems*, **24**(3), pp. 243–254.

413. Esteva, F., P. Garcia–Calvés and L. Godo [1994], "Relating and extending semantical approaches to possibilistic reasoning." *Intern. J. of Approximate Reasoning*, **10**(4), pp. 311–344.

414. Esteva, F., E. Trillas and X. Domingo [1981], "Weak and strong negation function for fuzzy set theory." *Proc. Eleventh IEEE Intern. Symp. on Multi-Valued Logic, Norman, Oklahoma*, pp. 23–27.

415. Eswar, P., C. C. Sekhar and B. Yegnanarayana [1992], "Use of fuzzy mathematical concepts in character spotting for automatic recognition of continuous speech in Hindi." *Fuzzy Sets and Systems*, **46**(1), pp. 1–9.

416. Evans, G., W. Karwowski and M. Wilhelm, eds. [**1989**], *Applications of Fuzzy Methodologies in Industrial Engineering*. Elsevier, New York.

417. Ezhkova, I. V. [1989], "Knowledge formation through context formalization." *Computers and Artificial Intelligence*, **8**(4), pp. 305–322.

418. Fang, N., H. P. Wang and M. C. Cheng [1993], "A fuzzy target recognition system with homomorphic invariant feature extraction." *Intern. J. of Systems Science*, **24**(11), pp. 1955–1971.

419. Farinwata, S. S. [**1993**], *Performance Assessment of Fuzzy Logic Control Systems via Stability and Robustness Measures*. (Ph. D. dissertation) Georgia Institute of Technology, Atlanda, GA.

420. Farreny, H. and H. Prade [1986], "Default and inexact reasoning with possibility degrees." *IEEE Trans. on Systems, Man, and Cybernetics*, **16**(2), pp. 270–276.

421. Fathi–Torbaghan, M., L. Hildebrand and K. Becker [1994], "Using fuzzy logic to increase the performance of FEM modules." *Cybernetics and Systems*, **25**(2), pp. 207–215.

422. Faurous, P. and J. P. Fillard [1993], "A new approach to the similarity in the fuzzy set theory." *Information Sciences*, **75**(3), pp. 213–221.

423. Fedrizzi, M., J. Kacprzyk and M. Roubens, eds. [**1991**], *Interactive Fuzzy Optimization*. Springer-Verlag, New York.

424. Feldman, D. D. [1993], "Fuzzy network synthesis with genetic algorithms." *Proc. Fifth Intern. Conf. on Genetic Algorithms*, pp. 312–317.

425. Feng, C. [1990], "Quantitative evaluation of university teaching quality – An application of fuzzy set and approximate reasoning." *Fuzzy Sets and Systems*, **37**(1), pp. 1–11.

426. Feng, D. Y. and X. H. Liu [**1986**], *Fuzzy Mathematics in Earthquake Researches*. Seismological Press, Beijing (2 volumes).

427. Feng, D. Y., M. Z. Lin and C. Jiang [1990], "Application of fuzzy decision-making in earthquake research." *Fuzzy Sets and Systems*, **36**(1), pp. 15–26.

428. Fernandez, M. J., F. Suarez and P. Gil [1992], "Equations of fuzzy relations defined on fuzzy subsets." *Fuzzy Sets and Systems*, **52**(3), pp. 319–336.

429. Filev, D. P. [1991], "Fuzzy modeling of complex systems." *Intern. J. of Approximate Reasoning*, **5**(3), pp. 281–290.

430. Filev, D. P. [1992], "System approach to dynamic fuzzy models." *Intern. J. of General Systems*, **21**(3), pp. 311–337.

431. Filev, D. P. and P. Angelov [1992], "Fuzzy optimal control." *Fuzzy Sets and Systems*, **47**(2), pp. 151–156.

432. Filev, D. P., M. Kishimoto, S. Sengupta, T. Yoshida and H. Taguchi [1985], "Application of fuzzy theory to simulation of batch fermentation." *J. of Fermentation Technology*, **63**, pp. 545–553.

433. Filev, D. P. and R. R. Yager [1991], "A generalized defuzzification method via bad distributions." *Intern. J. of Intelligent Systems*, **6**(7), pp. 687–697.

434. Filev, D. P. and R. R. Yager [1993a], "An adaptive approach to defuzzification based on level sets." *Fuzzy Sets and Systems*, **54**(3), pp. 355–360.

435. Filev, D. P. and R. R. Yager [1993b], "Three models of fuzzy logic controllers." *Cybernetics and Systems*, **24**(2), pp. 91–114.

436. Fishwick, P. A. [1991], "Fuzzy simulation:

Specifying and identifying qualitative models." *Intern. J. of General Systems*, **19**(3), pp. 295–316.

437. Fodor, J. C. [1991a], "A remark on constructing *t*-norms." *Fuzzy Sets and Systems*, **41**(2), pp. 195–199.

438. Fodor, J. C. [1991b], "On fuzzy implication operators." *Fuzzy Sets and Systems*, **42**(3), pp. 293–300.

439. Fodor, J. C. [1992a], "Traces of fuzzy binary relations." *Fuzzy Sets and Systems*, **50**(3), pp. 331–341.

440. Fodor, J. C. [1992b], "An axiomatic approach to fuzzy preference modelling." *Fuzzy Sets and Systems*, **52**(1), pp. 47–52.

441. Fodor, J. C. [1993], "A new look at fuzzy connectives." *Fuzzy Sets and Systems*, **57**(2), pp. 141–148.

442. Fodor, J. C. and T. Keresztfalvi [1994], "A characterization of the Hamacher family of *t*-norms." *Fuzzy Sets and Systems*, **65**(1), pp. 51–58.

443. Fordon, W. A. and J. C. Bezdek [1979], "The application of fuzzy set theory to medical diagnosis." In: Gupta, M. M., R. K. Ragade and R. R. Yager, eds., *Advances in Fuzzy Set Theory and Applications*. North-Holland, New York, pp. 445–461.

444. Frank, M. J. [1979], "On the simultaneous associativity of $F(x, y)$ and $x + y − F(x, y)$." *Aequationes Mathematicae*, **19**(2–3), pp. 194–226.

445. Frank, P. M. and N. Kiupel [1993], "Fuzzy supervision and application to lean production." *Intern. J. of Systems Science*, **24**(10), pp. 1935–1944.

446. Freeling, A. N. S. [1980], "Fuzzy sets and decision analysis." *IEEE Trans. on Systems, Man, and Cybernetics*, **10**(7), pp. 341–354.

447. Fridrich, J. [1994a], "Fuzzy mathematics in dynamical systems: Is there a place for it?" *Intern. J. of General Systems*, **22**(4), pp. 381–389.

448. Fridrich, J. [1994b], "On chaotic systems: Fuzzified logistic mapping." *Intern. J. of General Systems*, **22**(4), pp. 369–380.

449. Frühwirth–Schnatter, S. [1992], "On statistical inference for fuzzy data with applications to descriptive statistics." *Fuzzy Sets and Systems*, **50**(2), pp. 143–165.

450. Frühwirth–Schnatter, S. [1993], "On fuzzy Bayesian inference." *Fuzzy Sets and Systems*, **60**(1), pp. 41–58.

451. Fu, G. Y. [1992], "An algorithm for computing the transitive closure of a fuzzy similarity matrix." *Fuzzy Sets and Systems*, **51**(2), pp. 189–194.

452. Fu, L. M. [1994], "Rule generation from neural networks." *IEEE Trans. on Systems, Man, and Cybernetics*, **24**(8), pp. 1114–1124.

453. Fuhrmann, G. Y. [1988], "Fuzziness of concepts and concepts of fuzziness." *Synthese*, **75**, pp. 349–372.

454. Fuhrmann, G. Y. [1991], "Note on the integration of prototype theory and fuzzy-set theory." *Synthese*, **86**(1), pp. 1–27.

455. Fukami, S., M. Mizumoto and K. Tanaka [1980], "Some consideration of fuzzy conditional inference." *Fuzzy Sets and Systems*, **4**(3), pp. 243–273.

456. Fullér, R. and H. J. Zimmermann [1992], "On computation of the compositional rule of inference under triangular norms." *Fuzzy Sets and Systems*, **51**(3), pp. 267–275.

457. Fung, L. W. and K. S. Fu [1975], "An axiomatic approach to rational decision making in a fuzzy environment." In: Zadeh, L. A., K. S. Fu, K. Tanaka and M. Shimura, eds., *Fuzzy Sets and Their Applications to Cognitive and Decision Processes*. Academic Press, New York

458. Furuta, H. [1993], "Comprehensive analysis for structural damage based upon fuzzy set theory." *J. of Intelligent & Fuzzy Systems*, **1**(1), pp. 55–61.

459. Gähler, S. and W. Gähler [1994], "Fuzzy real numbers." *Fuzzy Sets and Systems*, **66**(2), pp. 137–158.

460. Gaines, B. R. [1976], "Foundations of fuzzy reasoning." *Intern. J. of Man-Machine Studies*, **8**(6), pp. 623–668. 9

461. Gaines, B. R. [1978], "Fuzzy and probability uncertainty logics." *Information and Control*, **38**(2), pp. 154–169.

462. Gaines, B. R. [1979a], "Sequential fuzzy system identification." *Fuzzy Sets and Systems*, **2**(1), pp. 15–24.

463. Gaines, B. R. [1979b], "Logical foundations for database systems." *Intern. J. of Man-Machine Studies*, **11**(4), pp. 481–500.

464. Gaines, B. R. [1983], "Precise past, fuzzy future." *Intern. J. of Man-Machine Studies*, **19**(1), pp. 117–134.

465. Gaines, B. R. [1993], "Modeling practical reasoning." *Intern. J. of Intelligent Systems*, **8**(1), pp. 51–70.

466. Gaines, B. R. and L. J. Kohout [1975], "The logic of automata." *Intern. J. of General Systems*, **2**(4), pp. 191–208.

467. Gaines, B. R. and L. J. Kohout [1977], "The fuzzy decade: A bibliography of fuzzy systems and closely related topics." *Intern. J. of Man-Machine Studies*, **9**(1), pp. 1–68.

468. Gaines, B. R. and M. L. G. Shaw [1985], "From fuzzy logic to expert systems." *Information Sciences*, **36**(1–2), pp. 5–16.

469. Gale, S. [1972], "Inexactness, fuzzy sets, and the foundation of behavioral geography." *Geographical Analysis*, **4**(4), pp. 337–349.

470. Garg, M. L., S. I. Ahson and P. V. Gupta [1991], "A fuzzy Petri net for knowledge representation and

reasoning." *Information Processing Letters*, **39**(3), pp. 165–171.

471. Gau, W. and D. J. Buehrer [1993], "Vague sets." *IEEE Trans. on Systems, Man, and Cybernetics*, **23**(2), pp. 610–614.

472. Gazdik, I. [1983], "Fuzzy network planning – FNET." *IEEE Trans. on Reliability*, **32**(3), pp. 304–313.

473. Gazdik, I. [1985], "Fault diagnosis and prevention by fuzzy sets." *IEEE. Trans. on Reliability*, **34**(4), pp. 382–388.

474. Gebhardt, J. and R. Kruse [1993], "The context model: An integrating view of vagueness and uncertainty." *Intern. J. of Approximate Reasoning*, **9**(3), pp. 283–314.

475. Geer, J. F. and G. J. Klir [1991], "Discord in possibility theory." *Intern. J. of General Systems*, **19**(2), pp. 119–132.

476. Geer, J. F. and G. J. Klir [1992], "A mathematical analysis of information-processing transformation between probabilistic and possibilistic formulations of uncertainty." *Intern. J. of General Systems*, **20**(2), pp. 143–176.

477. Gegov, A. [1994], "Multilevel intelligent fuzzy control of oversaturated urban traffic networks." *Intern. J. of Systems Science*, **25**(6), pp. 967–978.

478. Gelenbe, E. [1991], "Distributed associative memory and the computation of membership functions." *Information Sciences*, **57–58**, pp. 171–180.

479. Gharpuray, M., H. Tanaka, L. Fan and F. Lai [1986], "Fuzzy linear regression analysis of cellulose hydrolysis." *Chem. Eng. Commun.*, **41**, pp. 299–314.

480. Ghosh, A., N. R. Pal and S. K. Pal [1993], "Self-organization for object extraction using a multilayer neural network and fuzziness measures." *IEEE Trans on Fuzzy Systems*, **1**(1), pp. 54–68.

481. Gil, M. A. [1987], "Fuzziness and loss of information in statistical problems." *IEEE Trans. on Systems, Man, and Cybernetics*, **17**(6), pp. 1016–1025.

482. Giles, R. [1977], "Lukasiewicz logic and fuzzy set theory." *Intern. J. of Man-Machine Studies*, **8**(3), pp. 313–327.

483. Giles, R. [1982], "Semantics for fuzzy reasoning." *Intern. J. of Man-Machine Studies*, **17**(4), pp. 401–415.

484. Giles, R. [1988a], "The concept of grade of membership." *Fuzzy Sets and Systems*, **25**(3), pp. 297–323.

485. Giles, R. [1988b], "A utility-valued logic for decision making." *Intern. J. of Approximate Reasoning*, **2**(2), pp. 113–142.

486. Gisolfi, A. and G. Nunez [1993], "An algebraic approximation to the classification with fuzzy attributes." *Intern. J. of Approximate Reasoning*, **9**(1), pp. 75–95.

487. Giuntini, R. [1992], "Semantic alternatives in Brouwer–Zadeh logics–Part 1: Quantum logics." *Intern. J. of Theoretical Physics*, **31**(9), pp. 1653–1667.

488. Givone, D. D., M. E. Liebler and R. P. Roesser [1971], "A method of solution of multiple-valued logic expressions." *IEEE Trans. on Computers*, **20**(4), pp. 464–467.

489. Goguen, J. A. [1967], "*L*-fuzzy sets." *J. of Math. Analysis and Applications*, **18**(1), pp. 145–174.

490. Goguen, J. A. [1968–69], "The logic of inexact concepts." *Synthese*, **19**, pp. 325–373.

491. Goguen, J. A. [1974], "Concept representation in natural and artificial languages: Axioms, extensions and applications for fuzzy sets." *Intern. J. of Man-Machine Studies*, **6**(5), pp. 513–561.

492. Goldberg, D. E. [**1989**], *Genetic Algorithms in Search, Optimization & Machine Learning*. Addison–Wesley, New York.

493. Goodman, I. R. [1991], "Evaluation of combinations of conditioned information: A history." *Information Sciences*, **57–58**, pp. 79–110.

494. Goodman, I. R., M. M. Gupta, H. T. Nguyen and G. S. Rogers, eds. [**1991**], *Conditional Logic in Expert Systems*. North-Holland, New York.

495. Goodman, I. R. and H. T. Nguyen [**1985**], *Uncertainty Models for Knowledge–Based Systems*. North-Holland, New York.

496. Goodman, I. R. and H. T. Nguyen [1991], "Foundations for an algebraic theory of conditioning." *Fuzzy Sets and Systems*, **42**(1), pp. 103–117.

497. Goodman, I. R., H. T. Nguyen and E. A. Walker [**1991**], *Conditional Inference and Logic for Intelligent Systems: A Theory of Measure-Free Conditioning*. North-Holland, New York.

498. Gorzalczany, M. B. [1987], "A method of inference in approximate reasoning based on interval-valued fuzzy sets." *Fuzzy Sets and Systems*, **21**(1), pp. 1–17.

499. Gorzalczany, M. B. [1989a], "Interval-valued fuzzy inference involving uncertain (inconsistent) conditional propositions." *Fuzzy Sets and Systems*, **29**(2), pp. 235–240.

500. Gorzalczany, M. B. [1989b], "An interval-valued fuzzy inference method: Some basic properties." *Fuzzy Sets and Systems*, **31**(2), pp. 243–251.

501. Gottwald, S. [1979], "Set theory for fuzzy sets of higher level." *Fuzzy Sets and Systems*, **2**(2), pp. 125–151.

502. Gottwald, S. [1980], "Fuzzy propositional logics." *Fuzzy Sets and Systems*, **3**(2), pp. 181–192.

503. Gottwald, S. [1985], "Generalized solvability criteria for fuzzy equations." *Fuzzy Sets and Systems*, **17**(3), pp. 285–296.

504. Gottwald, S. [**1993**], *Fuzzy Sets and Fuzzy Logic.* Verlag Vieweg, Wiesbaden (Germany).

505. Gottwald, S. [1994], "Approximately solving fuzzy relation equations: Some mathematical results and some heuristic proposals." *Fuzzy Sets and Systems*, **66**(2), pp. 175–193.

506. Gottwald, S. and W. Pedrycz [1986], "Solvability of fuzzy relational equations and manipulation of fuzzy data." *Fuzzy Sets and Systems*, **18**(1), pp. 45–65.

507. Grabisch, M., T. Murofushi and M. Sugeno [1992], "Fuzzy measure of fuzzy events defined by fuzzy integrals." *Fuzzy Sets and Systems*, **50**(3), pp. 293–313.

508. Grabisch, M. and J. M. Nicolas [1994], "Classification by fuzzy integral: Performance and tests." *Fuzzy Sets and Systems*, **65**(2–3), pp. 255–271.

509. Grabot, B. [1993], "A decision support system for variable–routings management in manufacturing systems." *Fuzzy Sets and Systems*, **58**(1), pp. 87–104.

510. Graham, B. P. and R. B. Newell [1988], "Fuzzy identification and control of a liquid level rig." *Fuzzy Sets and Systems*, **26**(3), pp. 255–273.

511. Graham, B. P. and R. B. Newell [1989], "Fuzzy adaptive control of a first-order process." *Fuzzy Sets and Systems*, **31**(1), pp. 47–65.

512. Greco, G. and A. F. Rocha [1987], "The fuzzy logic of text understanding." *Fuzzy Sets and Systems*, **23**(3), pp. 347–360.

513. Grim, P. [1993], "Self-reference and chaos in fuzzy logic." *IEEE Trans. on Fuzzy Systems*, **1**(4), pp. 237–253.

514. Grzymala–Busse, J. W. [**1991**], *Managing Uncertainty in Expert Systems.* Kluwer, Boston.

515. Gu, W. X. and T. Lu [1992], "Fuzzy linear spaces." *Fuzzy Sets and Systems*, **49**(3), pp. 377–380.

516. Guan, J. W. and D. A. Bell [**1991**], *Evidence Theory and Its Applications, Vol. 1.* North-Holland, New York.

517. Guan, J. W. and D. A. Bell [**1992**], *Evidence Theory and Its Applications, Vol. 2.* North-Holland, New York.

518. Guely, F. and P. Siarry [1994], "A centered formulation of Takagi–Sugeno rules for improved learning efficiency." *Fuzzy Sets and Systems*, **62**(3), pp. 277–285.

519. Guiasu, S. [1994], "Fuzzy sets with inner interdependence." *Information Sciences*, **79**(3–4), pp. 315–338.

520. Guillemin, P. [1994], "Universal motor control with fuzzy logic." *Fuzzy Sets and Systems*, **63**(3), pp. 339–348.

521. Gunaratne, M., J. L. Chameau and A. G. Alteschaeffl [1985], "Fuzzy multi-attribute decision making in pavement management." *Civil Engineering Systems*, **2**(3), pp. 166–170.

522. Gunaratne, M., J. L. Chameau and A. G. Alteschaeffl [1988], "A successive fuzzification technique and its application to pavement evaluation." *Civil Engineering Systems*, **5**(2), pp. 77–88.

523. Gunderson, R. W. and R. Canfield [1990], "Piece-wise multilinear prediction from FCV disjoint principal component models." *Intern. J. of General Systems*, **16**(4), pp. 373–383.

524. Guo, G. R., W. X. Yu and W. Zhang [1990], "An intelligence recognition method of ship targets." *Fuzzy Sets and Systems*, **36**(1), pp. 27–36.

525. Gupta, C. P. [1993], "A note on the transformation of possibilistic information into probabilistic information for investment decisions." *Fuzzy Sets and Systems*, **56**(2), pp. 175–182.

526. Gupta, M. M., A. Kandel, W. Bandler and J. B. Kiszka, eds. [**1985**], *Approximate Reasoning in Expert Systems.* North-Holland, New York.

527. Gupta, M. M., J. B. Kiszka and G. M. Trojan [1986], "Multivariable structure of fuzzy control systems." *IEEE Trans. on Systems, Man, and Cybernetics*, **16**(5), pp. 638–656.

528. Gupta, M. M. and J. Qi [1991a], "Theory of T-norms and fuzzy inference methods." *Fuzzy Sets and Systems*, **40**(3), pp. 431–450.

529. Gupta, M. M. and J. Qi [1991b], "Design of fuzzy logic controllers based on generalized T-operators." *Fuzzy Sets and Systems*, **40**(3), pp. 473–489.

530. Gupta, M. M. and J. Qi [1992], "On fuzzy neuron models." In: Zadeh, L. A. and J. Kacprzyk, eds., *Fuzzy Logic for the Management of Uncertainty.* John Wiley, New York, pp. 479–491.

531. Gupta, M. M., R. K. Ragade and R. R. Yager, eds. [**1978**], *Advances in Fuzzy Set Theory and Applications.* North-Holland, New York.

532. Gupta, M. M. and D. H. Rao [1994], "On the principles of fuzzy neural networks." *Fuzzy Sets and Systems*, **61**(1), pp. 1–18.

533. Gupta, M. M. and E. Sanchez, eds. [**1982a**], *Approximate Reasoning in Decision Analysis.* North-Holland, New York.

534. Gupta, M. M. and E. Sanchez, eds. [**1982b**], *Fuzzy Information and Decision Processes.* North-Holland, New York.

535. Gupta, M. M., G. N. Saridis and B. R. Gaines, eds. [**1977**], *Fuzzy Automata and Decision Processes.* North-Holland, New York.

536. Gupta, M. M., G. M. Trojan and J. B. Kiszka [1986], "Controllability of fuzzy control systems." *IEEE Trans. on Systems, Man, and Cybernetics*, **16**(4), pp. 576–582.

537. Gupta, M. M. and T. Yamakawa, eds. **[1988a]**, *Fuzzy Computing: Theory, Hardware, and Applications.* North-Holland, New York.

538. Gupta, M. M. and T. Yamakawa, eds. **[1988b]**, *Fuzzy Logic in Knowledge Based Systems, Decision and Control.* North-Holland, New York.

539. Hájek, P., T. Havránek and **[1992]**, *Uncertain Information Processing in Expert Systems.* CRC Press, Boca Raton, FL.

540. Halgamuge, S. K. and M. Glesner [1994], "Neural networks in designing fuzzy systems for real world." *Fuzzy Sets and Systems*, **65**(1), pp. 1–12.

541. Hall, L. O., M. Friedman and A. Kandel [1988], "On the validation and testing of fuzzy expert systems." *IEEE Trans. on Systems, Man, and Cybernetics*, **18**(6), pp. 1023–1027.

542. Hall, L. O. and A. Kandel **[1986]**, *Designing Fuzzy Expert Systems.* Verlag TÜV Rheinland, Köln.

543. Hall, L. O., S. Szabo and A. Kandel [1986], "On the derivation of memberships for fuzzy sets in expert systems." *Information Sciences*, **40**(1), pp. 39–52.

544. Han, J. Y. and V. McMurray [1993], "Two–layer multiple–variable fuzzy logic controller." *IEEE Trans. on Systems, Man, and Cybernetics*, **23**(1), pp. 277–285.

545. Hang, H. Q., H. Yao and J. D. Jones [1993], "Calculating functions of fuzzy numbers." *Fuzzy Sets and Systems*, **55**(3), pp. 273–284.

546. Harmanec, D. and P. Hájek [1994], "A qualitative belief logic." *Intern. J. of Uncertainty, Fuzziness and Knowledge–Based Systems*, **2**(2), pp. 227–236.

547. Harmanec, D. and G. J. Klir [1994], "Measuring total uncertainty in Dempster–Shafer theory: A novel approach." *Intern. J. of General Systems*, **22**(4), pp. 405–419.

548. Harmanec, D., G. J. Klir and G. Resconi [1994], "On modal logic interpretation of Dempster–Shafer theory of evidence." *Intern. J. of Intelligent Systems*, **9**(10), pp. 941–951.

549. Harris, C. J., C. G. Moore and M. Brown **[1993]**, *Intelligent Control: Aspects of Fuzzy Logic and Neural Nets.* World Scientific, Singapore.

550. Hartley, R. V. L. [1928], "Transmission of information." *The Bell System Technical J.*, **7**, pp. 535–563.

551. Hathaway, R. J. and J. C. Bezdek [1993], "Switching regression models and fuzzy clustering." *IEEE Trans. on Fuzzy Systems*, **1**(3), pp. 195–204.

552. Hathaway, R. J. and J. C. Bezdek [1994], "NERF *c*-means: Non-Euclidean relational fuzzy clustering." *Pattern Recognition*, **27**(3), pp. 429–437.

553. Hau, H. Y. [1993], "Decomposition of belief function in hierarchical hypotheses space." *Intern. J. of Pattern Recognition and Artificial Intelligence*, **7**(3), pp. 459–474.

554. Hawkes, L. W., S. J. Derry and E. A. Rundensteiner [1990], "Individualized tutoring using an intelligent fuzzy temporal relational database." *Intern. J. of Man-Machine Studies*, **33**(4), pp. 409–429.

555. Hayashi, I., H. Nomura, H. Yamasaki and N. Wakaori [1992], "Construction of fuzzy inference rules by NDF and NDFL." *Intern. J. of Approximate Reasoning*, **6**(2), pp. 241–266.

556. Hayashi, Y. [1994], "Neural expert system using fuzzy teaching input and its application to medical diagnosis." *Information Sciences: Applications*, **1**(1), pp. 47–58.

557. Hayashi, Y. and J. J. Buckley [1994], "Approximations between fuzzy expert systems and neural networks." *Intern. J. of Approximate Reasoning*, **10**(1), pp. 63–73.

558. Hayashi, Y., J. J. Buckley and E. Czogala [1993], "Fuzzy neural network with fuzzy signals and weights." *Intern. J. of Intelligent Systems*, **8**(4), pp. 527–537.

559. He, S. Z., S. H. Tan, C. C. Hang and P. Z. Wang [1993], "Control of dynamical processes using an on-line rule-adaptive fuzzy control system." *Fuzzy Sets and Systems*, **54**(1), pp. 11–22.

560. Heilpern, S. [1993], "Fuzzy subsets of the space of probability measures and expected value of fuzzy variable." *Fuzzy Sets and Systems*, **54**(3), pp. 301–309.

561. Hellendoorn, H. [1990], "Closure properties of the compositional rule of inference." *Fuzzy Sets and Systems*, **35**(2), pp. 163–183.

562. Hellendoorn, H. [1992], "The generalized modus ponens considered as a fuzzy relation." *Fuzzy Sets and Systems*, **46**(1), pp. 29–48.

563. Hellendoorn, H. and R. Palm [1994], "Fuzzy system technologies at Siemens R&D." *Fuzzy Sets and Systems*, **63**(3), pp. 245–269.

564. Hellendoorn, H. and C. Thomas [1993], "Defuzzification in fuzzy controllers." *J. of Intelligent & Fuzzy Systems*, **1**(2), pp. 109–123.

565. Henkind, S. J. and M. C. Harriron [1988], "An analysis of four uncertainty calculi." *IEEE Trans. on Systems, Man, and Cybernetics*, **18**(5), pp. 700–714.

566. Herrera, F., J. L. Verdegay and H. J. Zimmermann [1993], "Boolean programming problems with fuzzy constraints." *Fuzzy Sets and Systems*, **55**(3), pp. 285–294.

567. Heshmaty, B. and A. Kandel [1985], "Fuzzy linear regression and its applications to forecasting in

uncertain environment." *Fuzzy Sets and Systems*, **15**(2), pp. 159–191.

568. Higashi, M., A. Di Nola, S. Sessa and W. Pedrycz [1984], "Ordering fuzzy sets by consensus concept and fuzzy relation equations." *Intern. J. of General Systems*, **10**(1), pp. 47–56.

569. Higashi, M. and G. J. Klir [1982], "On measure of fuzziness and fuzzy complements." *Intern. J. of General Systems*, **8**(3), pp. 169–180.

570. Higashi, M. and G. J. Klir [1983a], "Measures of uncertainty and information based on possibility distributions." *Intern. J. of General Systems*, **9**(1), pp. 43–58.

571. Higashi, M. and G. J. Klir [1983b], "On the notion of distance representing information closeness: Possibility and probability distributions." *Intern. J. of General Systems*, **9**(2), pp. 103–115.

572. Higashi, M. and G. J. Klir [1984a], "Resolution of finite fuzzy relation equations." *Fuzzy Sets and Systems*, **13**(1), pp. 65–82.

573. Higashi, M. and G. J. Klir [1984b], "Identification of fuzzy relation systems." *IEEE Trans. on Systems, Man, and Cybernetics*, **14**(2), pp. 349–355.

574. Hinde, C. J. [1983], "Inference of fuzzy relational tableaux from fuzzy exemplifications." *Fuzzy Sets and Systems*, **11**(1), pp. 91–101.

575. Hinde, C. J. [1986], "Fuzzy Prolog." *Intern. J. of Man-Machine Studies*, **24**(6), pp. 569–595.

576. Hirota, K., ed. [1993], *Industrial Applications of Fuzzy Technology*. Springer–Verlag, New York.

577. Hirota, K., Y. Arai and S. Hachisu [1989], "Fuzzy controlled robot arm playing two-dimensional ping–pong game." *Fuzzy Sets and Systems*, **32**(2), pp. 149–159.

578. Hirota, K. and K. Ozawa [1989], "The concept of fuzzy flip-flop." *IEEE Trans. on Systems, Man, and Cybernetics*, **19**(5), pp. 980–997.

579. Hirota, K. and W. Pedrycz [1983], "Analysis and synthesis of fuzzy systems by the use of fuzzy sets." *Fuzzy Sets and Systems*, **10**(1), pp. 1–14.

580. Hirota, K. and W. Pedrycz [1994], "OR/AND neuron in modeling fuzzy set connectives." *IEEE Trans. on Fuzzy Systems*, **2**(2), pp. 151–162.

581. Hisdal, E. [1978], "Conditional possibilities, independence and noninteraction." *Fuzzy Sets and Systems*, **1**(4), pp. 283–297.

582. Hisdal, E. [1988], "Are grades of membership probabilities?" *Fuzzy Sets and Systems*, **25**(3), pp. 349–356.

583. Höhle, U. [1987], "Fuzzy real numbers as Dedekind cuts with respect to a multiple-valued logic." *Fuzzy Sets and Systems*, **24**(3), pp. 263–278.

584. Höhle, U. [1988], "Quotients with respect to similarity relations." *Fuzzy Sets and Systems*, **27**(1), pp. 31–44.

585. Höhle, U. and E. P. Klement **[1994]**, *Non-Classical Logics and Their Applications – A Handbook*. Kluwer, Boston.

586. Höhle, U. and L. N. Stout [1991], "Foundations of fuzzy sets." *Fuzzy Sets and Systems*, **40**(2), pp. 257–296.

587. Holmblad, L. P. and J. J. Ostergaard [1982], "Control of a cement kiln by fuzzy logic." In: Gupta, M. M. and E. Sanchez, eds., *Fuzzy Information and Decision Processes*. North-Holland, New York, pp. 389–399.

588. Homaifar, A., B. Sayyarrodsari and J. E. Hogans IV [1994], "Fuzzy controller robot arm trajectory." *Information Sciences: Applications*, **2**(2), pp. 69–83.

589. Hong, D. H. and S. Y. Hwang [1994a], "On the convergence of T-sum of L-R fuzzy numbers." *Fuzzy Sets and Systems*, **63**(2), pp. 175–180.

590. Hong, D. H. and S. Y. Hwang [1994b], "On the compositional rule of inference under triangular norms." *Fuzzy Sets and Systems*, **66**(1), pp. 25–38.

591. Horikawa, S., T. Furuhashi and Y. Uchikawa [1992], "On fuzzy modeling using fuzzy neural networks with the back-propagation algorithm." *IEEE Trans. on Neural Networks*, **3**(5), pp. 801–806.

592. Hossain, A., A. R. Marudarajan and M. A. Manzoul [1991], "Fuzzy replacement algorithm for cache memory." *Cybernetics and Systems*, **22**(6), pp. 733–746.

593. Hsu, Y. and C. Cheng [1993], "A fuzzy controller for generator excitation control." *IEEE Trans. on Systems, Man, and Cybernetics*, **23**(2), pp. 532–539.

594. Hu, Q. and D. B. Hertz [1994], "Fuzzy logic controlled neural network learning." *Information Sciences: Applications*, **2**(1), pp. 15–33.

595. Huang, L. J. and M. Tomizuka [1990], "A self-paced fuzzy tracking controller for two-dimensional motion control." *IEEE Trans. on Systems, Man, and Cybernetics*, **20**(5), pp. 1115–1124.

596. Hudson, D. L., M. E. Cohen and M. F. Anderson [1992], "Approximate reasoning with IF–THEN–UNLESS rule in a medical expert system." *Intern. J. of Intelligent Systems*, **7**(1), pp. 71–79.

597. Hunt, R. M. and W. B. Rouse [1984], "A fuzzy rule-based model of human problem solving." *IEEE Trans. on Systems, Man, and Cybernetics*, **14**(1), pp. 112–120.

598. Hwang, C. and K. Yoon **[1981]**, *Multiple Attribute Decision Making: Methods and Applications*. Springer–Verlag, New York.

599. Hwang, G. C. and S. C. Lin [1992], "A stability approach to fuzzy control design for nonlinear systems." *Fuzzy Sets and Systems*, **48**(3), pp. 279–287.

600. Hwang, Y. R. and M. Tomizuka [1994], "Fuzzy smoothing algorithms for variable structure systems." *IEEE Trans. on Fuzzy Systems*, **2**(4), pp. 277–284.

601. Hyung, L. K., Y. S. Song and K. M. Lee [1994], "Similarity measure between fuzzy sets and between elements." *Fuzzy Sets and Systems*, **62**(3), pp. 291–293.

602. Ichihashi, H. and I. B. Turksen [1993], "A neuro-fuzzy approach to data analysis of pairwise comparisons." *Intern. J. of Approximate Reasoning*, **9**(3), pp. 227–248.

603. Ikejima, K. and D. M. Frangopol [1987], "Risk assessment for gas pipelines using fuzzy sets." *Civil Engineering Systems*, **4**(3), pp. 147–152.

604. Inuiguchi, M., H. Ichihashi and Y. Kume [1992], "Relationships between modality constrained programming problems and various fuzzy mathematical programming problems." *Fuzzy Sets and Systems*, **49**(3), pp. 243–259.

605. Isaka, S. and A. V. Sebald [1992], "An optimization approach for fuzzy controller design." *IEEE Trans. on Systems, Man, and Cybernetics*, **22**(6), pp. 1469–1473.

606. Ishibuchi, H., R. Fujioka and H. Tanaka [1992], "Possibility and necessity pattern classification using neural network." *Fuzzy Sets and Systems*, **48**(3), pp. 331–340.

607. Ishibuchi, H., R. Fujioka and H. Tanaka [1993], "Neural networks that learn from fuzzy if-then rules." *IEEE Trans. on Fuzzy Systems*, **1**(2), pp. 85–97.

608. Ishibuchi, H., H. Tanaka and H. Okada [1994], "Interpolation of fuzzy If–Then rules by neural networks." *Intern. J. of Approximate Reasoning*, **10**(1), pp. 3–27.

609. Ishibuchi, H., K. Nozaki and H. Tanaka [1992], "Distributed representation of fuzzy rules and its application to pattern classification." *Fuzzy Sets and Systems*, **52**(1), pp. 21–32.

610. Ishibuchi, H., K. Nozaki, H. Tanaka, Y. Hosaka and M. Matsuda [1994], "Empirical study on learning in fuzzy systems by rice taste analysis." *Fuzzy Sets and Systems*, **64**(2), pp. 129–144.

611. Ishibuchi, H., K. Nozaki and N. Yamamoto [1993], "Selecting fuzzy rules by genetic algorithm for classification problems." *Proc. Second IEEE Intern. Conf. on Fuzzy Systems, San Francisco.*, II, pp. 1119–1124

612. Ishibuchi, H., K. Nozaki, N. Yamamoto and H. Tanaka [1994], "Construction of fuzzy classification systems with rectangular fuzzy rules using genetic algorithms." *Fuzzy Sets and Systems*, **65**(2–3), pp. 237–253.

613. Ishibuchi, H. and H. Tanaka [1992], "Fuzzy regression analysis using neural networks." *Fuzzy Sets and Systems*, **50**(3), pp. 257–265.

614. Ishibuchi, H., H. Tanaka and O. Okada [1993], "An architecture of neural networks with interval weights and its application to fuzzy regression analysis." *Fuzzy Sets and Systems*, **57**(1), pp. 27–39.

615. Itzkovich, I. and L. W. Hawkes [1994], "Fuzzy extension of inheritance hierarchies." *Fuzzy Sets and Systems*, **62**(2), pp. 143–153.

616. Ivánek, J. [1991], "Representation of expert knowledge as a fuzzy axiomatic theory." *Intern. J. of General Systems*, **20**(1), pp. 55–58.

617. Jain, R. [1976], "Decisionmaking in the presence of fuzzy variables." *IEEE Trans. on Systems, Man, and Cybernetics*, **6**(10), pp. 698–702.

618. Jain, R. [1977], "A procedure for multi-aspect decision-making using fuzzy sets." *Intern, J. of Systems Science*, **8**(1), pp. 1–7.

619. Jamshidi, M., N. Vadiee and T. J. Ross, eds. [**1993**], *Fuzzy Logic and Control*. Prentice Hall, Englewood Cliffs, NJ.

620. Jang, J. R. [1992], "Self-learning fuzzy controllers based on temporal back propagation." *IEEE Trans. on Neural Networks*, **3**(5), pp. 714–723.

621. Jang, J. R. [1993], "ANFIS: Adaptive-network-based fuzzy inference system." *IEEE Trans. on Systems, Man, and Cybernetics*, **23**(3), pp. 665–685.

622. Janko, W. H., M. Roubens and H. J. Zimmermann, eds. [**1990**], *Progress in Fuzzy Sets and Systems*. Kluwer, Boston.

623. Janowitz, M. F. and R. C. Powers [1992], "A duality between fuzzy and percentile clustering." *Fuzzy Sets and Systems*, **50**(1), pp. 51–58.

624. Jayabharathi, R. and M. A. Manzoul [1993], "Fuzzy logic for standard cell placement." *Cybernetics and Systems*, **24**(3), pp. 197–215.

625. Jia, L. M. and X. D. Zhang [1994], "Distributed intelligent railway traffic control based on fuzzy decisionmaking." *Fuzzy Sets and Systems*, **62**(3), pp. 255–265.

626. Johansen, T. A. [1994], "Fuzzy model based control: Stability, robustness, and performance issues." *IEEE Trans. on Fuzzy Systems*, **2**(3), pp. 221–234.

627. Johnston, D. M. and R. N. Palmer [1988], "Application of fuzzy decision making: An evaluation." *Civil Engineering Systems*, **5**(2), pp. 87–92.

628. Jones, A., A. Kaufmann and H. J. Zimmermann, eds. [**1986**], *Fuzzy Sets Theory and Applications*. D. Reidel, Boston.

629. Joyce, D. T. [1994], "Examining the potential of fuzzy software requirements specifications." *Information Sciences: Applications*, **2**(2), pp. 85–102.

630. Juang, C. H., J. L. Burati and S. N. Kalidindi [1987], "A fuzzy system for bid proposal evaluation using microcomputers." *Civil Engineering Systems*, **4**(3), pp. 124–130.

631. Juang, C. H. and D. J. Elton [1986], "Fuzzy logic for estimation of earthquake intensity based on building damage records." *Civil Engineering Systems*, **3**(4), pp. 187–191.

632. Julien, B. [1994], "An extension to possibilistic linear programming." *Fuzzy Sets and Systems*, **64**(2), pp. 195–206.

633. Jumarie, G. [1987], "Observation with information invariance: Introduction to a new modeling of fuzzy arithmetic." *Cybernetics and Systems*, **18**(5), pp. 407–424.

634. Jumarie, G. [1993], "Expert systems and fuzzy systems: A new approach via possibility–probability conversion." *Kybernetes*, **22**(8), pp. 21–36.

635. Jumarie, G. [1994], "Possibility–probability transformation: A new result via information theory of deterministic functions." *Kybernetes*, **23**(5), pp. 56–59.

636. Jung, J. S., Y. J. Cho and J. K. Kim [1993], "Minimization theorems for fixed point theorems in fuzzy metric space and applications." *Fuzzy Sets and Systems*, **61**(2), pp. 199–208.

637. Jung, S. W., S. W. Bae and G. T. Park [1994], "A design scheme for a hierarchical fuzzy pattern matching classifier and its application to the tire tread pattern recognition." *Fuzzy Sets and Systems*, **65**(2–3), pp. 311–322.

638. Kacprzyk, J. [**1983**], *Multistage Decision-Making under Fuzziness*. Verlag TÜV Rheinland, Köln.

639. Kacprzyk, J. [1985a], "Group decision-making with a fuzzy majority via linguistic quantifiers. Part I: A consensory–like pooling." *Cybernetics and Systems*, **16**(2–3), pp. 119–129.

640. Kacprzyk, J. [1985b], "Group decision-making with a fuzzy majority via linguistic quantifiers. Part II: A competitive-like pooling." *Cybernetics and Systems*, **16**(2–3), pp. 131–144.

641. Kacprzyk, J. [1994], "On measuring the specificity of IF–THEN rules." *Intern. J. of Approximate Reasoning*, **11**(1), pp. 29–53.

642. Kacprzyk, J. and M. Fedrizzi, eds. [**1988**], *Combining Fuzzy Imprecision with Probabilistic Uncertainty in Decision Making*. Springer–Verlag, New York.

643. Kacprzyk, J. and M. Fedrizzi, eds. [**1990**], *Multiperson Decision Making Models Using Fuzzy Sets and Possibility Theory*. Kluwer, Boston.

644. Kacprzyk, J. and M. Fedrizzi, eds. [**1992**], *Fuzzy Regression Analysis*. Omnitech Press, Warsaw.

645. Kacprzyk, J. and S. A. Orlovski, eds. [**1987**], *Optimization Models Using Fuzzy Sets and Possibility Theory*. Kluwer, Boston.

646. Kacprzyk, J. and M. Roubens, eds. [**1988**], *Non-Conventional Preference Relations in Decision Making*. Springer–Verlag, New York.

647. Kacprzyk, J. and R. R. Yager, eds. [**1985**], *Management Decision-Support Systems Using Fuzzy Sets and Possibility Theory*. Verlag TÜV Rheinland, Köln.

648. Kacprzyk, J. and A. Ziolkowski [1986], "Database queries with fuzzy linguistic qualifiers." *IEEE Trans. on Systems, Man, and Cybernetics*, **16**(3), pp. 474–479.

649. Kaleva, O. [1987], "Fuzzy differential equations." *Fuzzy Sets and Systems*, **24**(3), pp. 301–317.

650. Kaleva, O. [1994], "Interpolation of fuzzy data." *Fuzzy Sets and Systems*, **61**(1), pp. 63–70.

651. Kaleva, O. and S. Seikkala [1984], "On fuzzy metric spaces." *Fuzzy Sets and Systems*, **12**(3), pp. 215–229.

652. Kamel, M. S. and S. Z. Selim [1993], "A relaxation approach to the fuzzy clustering problem." *Fuzzy Sets and Systems*, **61**(2), pp. 177–188.

653. Kamel, M. S. and S. Z. Selim [1994], "New algorithms for solving the fuzzy clustering problem." *Pattern Recognition*, **27**(3), pp. 421–428.

654. Kanagawa, A. and H. Ohta [1990], "Fuzzy design for fixed–number life tests." *IEEE Trans. on Reliability*, **39**(3), pp. 394–398.

655. Kandel, A. [1978a], "On fuzzy statistics." In: Gupta, M. M., R. K. Ragade and R. R. Yager, eds., *Advances in Fuzzy Set Theory and Applications*. North-Holland, New York, pp. 181–199.

656. Kandel, A. [1978b], "Fuzzy statistics and forecast evaluation." *IEEE Trans. on Systems, Man, and Cybernetics*, **8**(5), pp. 396–400.

657. Kandel, A. [**1982**], *A Fuzzy Techniques in Pattern Recognition*. John Wiley, New York.

658. Kandel, A. [**1986**], *Fuzzy Mathematical Techniques with Applications*. Addison–Wesley, Reading, MA.

659. Kandel, A., ed. [**1991**], *Fuzzy Expert Systems*. CRC Press, Boca Raton, FL.

660. Kandel, A. and W. J. Byatt [1978], "Fuzzy sets, fuzzy algebra, and fuzzy statistics." *Proc. IEEE*, **66**(12), pp. 1619–1639.

661. Kandel, A. and W. J. Byatt [1980], "Fuzzy processes." *Fuzzy Sets and Systems*, **4**(2), pp. 117–152.

662. Kandel, A. and G. Langholz, eds. [**1994**], *Fuzzy Control Systems*. CRC Press, Boca Raton, FL.

663. Kandel, A. and C. S. Lee [**1979**], *Fuzzy Switching and Automata: Theory and Applications*. Crane & Russak, New York.

664. Kandel, A., L. H. Li and Z. Q. Cao [1992], "Fuzzy inference and its applicability to control systems." *Fuzzy Sets and Systems*, **48**(1), pp. 99–111.

665. Kandel, A. and L. Yelowitz [1974], "Fuzzy chain." *IEEE Trans. on Systems, Man, and Cybernetics*, **4**(5), pp. 472–475.

666. Kang, H. [1993a], "Stability of fuzzy dynamic control systems via cell-state transitions in fuzzy hypercubes." *Asia-Pacific Engineering J.*, **3**(1–2), pp. 33–58.

667. Kang, H. [1993b], "Stability and control of fuzzy dynamic systems via cell-state transitions in fuzzy hypercubes." *IEEE Trans. on Fuzzy Systems*, **1**(4), pp. 267–279.

668. Kang, H. B. and E. L. Walker [1994], "Characterizing and controlling approximation in hierarchical perceptual grouping." *Fuzzy Sets and Systems*, **65**(2–3), pp. 187–223.

669. Karr, C. [1991a], "Genetic algorithms for fuzzy controllers." *AI Expert*, **6**(2), pp. 26–33.

670. Karr, C. [1991b], "Applying Genetics." *AI Expert*, **6**(3), pp. 38–43.

671. Karr, C. [1991c], "Design of an adaptive fuzzy logic controller using a genetic algorithm." *Proc. Fourth Intern. Conf. on Genetic Algorithms, San Mateo, CA*, pp. 450–457.

672. Karr, C. L. and E. J. Gentry [1993], "Fuzzy control of pH using genetic algorithms." *IEEE Trans. on Fuzzy Systems*, **1**(1), pp. 46–53.

673. Karwowski, W. and G. W. Evans [1986], "Fuzzy concepts in production management research: A review." *Intern. J. of Production Research*, **24**(1), pp. 129–147.

674. Karwowski, W. and A. Mital, eds. [**1986**], *Applications of Fuzzy Set Theory in Human Factors*. Elsevier, New York.

675. Karwowski, W., N. O. Mulholland and T. L. Ward [1987], "A fuzzy knowledge base of an expert system for analysis of manual lifting tasks (case studies and applications contribution)." *Fuzzy Sets and Systems*, **21**(3), pp. 363–374.

676. Kaufmann, A. [**1975**], *Introduction to the Theory of Fuzzy Subsets*. Academic Press, New York.

677. Kaufmann, A. and M. M. Gupta [**1985**], *Introduction to Fuzzy Arithmetic: Theory and Applications*. Van Nostrand, New York.

678. Kaufmann, A. and M. M. Gupta [**1988**], *Fuzzy Mathematical Models in Engineering and Management Sciences*. North-Holland, New York.

679. Kawamura, H. [1993], "Fuzzy network for decision support systems." *Fuzzy sets and Systems*, **58**(1), pp. 59–72.

680. Kean, A. [1993], "The approximation of implicates and explanations." *Intern. J. of Approximate Reasoning*, **9**(2), pp. 97–128.

681. Kelemen, M. [1981], "Fuzziness and structural stability." *Kybernetes*, **10**(1), pp. 67–69.

682. Keller, J. M., P. Gader, H. Tahani, J. H. Chiang and M. Mohamed [1994], "Advances in fuzzy integration for pattern recognition." *Fuzzy Sets and Systems*, **65**(2–3), pp. 273–283.

683. Keller, J. M., M. R. Gray and J. A. Givens [1985], "A fuzzy *k*-nearest neighbor algorithm." *IEEE Trans. on Systems, Man, and Cybernetics*, **15**(4), pp. 580–585.

684. Keller, J. M., G. Hobson, J. Wootton, A. Nafarieh and K. Luetkemeyer [1987], "Fuzzy confidence measure in midlevel vision." *IEEE Trans. on Systems, Man, and Cybernetics*, **17**(4), pp. 676–683.

685. Keller, J. M. and D. J. Hunt [1985], "Incorporating fuzzy membership functions into the perceptron algorithm." *IEEE Trans. on Pattern Analysis and Machine Intelligence*, **7**(6), pp. 693–699.

686. Keller, J. M., R. Krishnapuram, Z. H. Chen and O. Nasraoui [1994], "Fuzzy additive hybrid operators for network-based decision making." *Intern. J. of Intelligent Systems*, **9**(11), pp. 1001–1023.

687. Keller, J. M., R. Krishnapuram and F. C. Rhee [1992], "Evidence aggregation networks for fuzzy logic inference." *IEEE Trans. on Neural Networks*, **3**(5), pp. 761–769.

688. Keller, J. M., D. Subhangkasen, K. Unklesbay and N. Unklesbay [1990], "An approximate reasoning technique for recognition in color images of beef steaks." *Intern. J. of General Systems*, **16**(4), pp. 331–342.

689. Keller, J. M. and H. Tahani [1992], "Implementation of conjunctive and disjunctive fuzzy logic rules with neural networks." *Intern. J. of Approximate Reasoning*, **6**(2), pp. 221–240.

690. Keller, J. M., R. R. Yager and H. Tahani [1992], "Neural network implementation of fuzzy logic." *Fuzzy Sets and Systems*, **45**(1), pp. 1–12.

691. Kenarangui, R. [1991], "Event-tree analysis by fuzzy probability." *IEEE Trans. on Reliability*, **40**(1), pp. 120–124.

692. Kerre, E. E. [1982], "The use of fuzzy set theory in electrocardiological diagnostics." In: Gupta, M. M. and S. Sanchez, eds., *Approximate Reasoning in Decision Analysis*, pp. 277–282.

693. Kerre, E. E., ed. [**1991**], *Introduction to the Basic Principles of Fuzzy Set Theory and Some of Its Applications*. Communication & Cognition, Gent, Belgium.

694. Kesavan, H. K. and J. N. Kapur [1989], "The generalized maximum entropy principle." *IEEE Trans. on Systems, Man, and Cybernetics*, **19**(5), pp. 1042–1052.

695. Khalili, S. [1979], "Independent fuzzy events." *J. of Math. Analysis and Applications*, **67**(2), pp. 412–420.

696. Kickert, W. J. M. [**1978**], *Fuzzy Theories on Decision-Making.* Martinus Nijhoff, Boston.

697. Kickert, W. J. M. [1979], "Towards an analysis of linguistic modeling." *Fuzzy Sets and Systems,* **2**(4), pp. 293–307.

698. Kickert, W. J. M. and H. Koppelaar [1976], "Application of fuzzy set theory to syntactic pattern recognition of handwritten capitals." *IEEE Trans. on Systems, Man, and Cybernetics,* **6**(2), pp. 148–150.

699. Kickert, W. J. M. and E. H. Mamdani [1978], "Analysis of a fuzzy logic controller." *Fuzzy Sets and Systems,* **1**(1), pp. 29–44.

700. Kickert, W. J. M. and H. R. Van Nauta Lemke [1976], "Application of a fuzzy controller in a warm water plant." *Automatica,* **12**(4), pp. 301–308.

701. Kikuchi, S. and P. Chakroborty [1993], "Car-following model based on fuzzy inference system." *Transportation Research Record,* No. 1365, pp. 82–91.

702. Kikuchi, S. and J. Parameswaran [1993], "Use of fuzzy control for designing transportation schedules." *Proc. NAFIPS Meeting, Allentown, PA,* pp. 169–173.

703. Kikuchi, S., V. Perincherry, P. Chakroborty and H. Takahashi [1993], "Modeling of driver anxiety during signal change intervals." *Transportation Research Record,* No. 1399, pp. 27–35.

704. Kikuchi, S. and J. R. Riegner [1993], "Methodology to analysis drive decision environment during signal change intervals: Application of fuzzy set theory." *Transportation Research Record,* No. 1368, pp. 49–57.

705. Kikuchi, S. and N. Vukadinovic [1994], "Grouping trips by fuzzy similarity for scheduling of demand-responsive transportation vehicles." *Transportation Planning and Technology,* **18**(1), pp. 65–80.

706. Kikuchi, S., N. Vukadinovic and S. M. Easa [1991], "Characteristics of the fuzzy LP transportation problem for civil engineering application." *Civil Engineering Systems,* **8**, pp. 134–144.

707. Kim, J. S. and H. S. Cho [1994], "A fuzzy logic and neural network approach to boundary detection for noisy imagery." *Fuzzy Sets and Systems,* **65**(2–3), pp. 141–159.

708. Kim, K. H. and W. Roush [1980], "Generalized fuzzy matrices." *Fuzzy Sets and Systems,* **4**(3), pp. 293–315.

709. Kim, S. J., W. D. Kim and N. S. Goo [1994], "Identification of nonlinear membership function for failure of structural material and its application to structural optimization." *Fuzzy Sets and Systems,* **66**(1), pp. 15–23.

710. Kim, W. J., J. H. Ko and M. J. Chung [1994], "Uncertain robot environment modelling using fuzzy numbers." *Fuzzy Sets and Systems,* **61**(1), pp. 53–62.

711. Kim, Y. S. and S. Mitra [1994], "An adaptive integrated fuzzy clustering model for pattern recognition." *Fuzzy Sets and Systems,* **65**(2–3), pp. 297–310.

712. King, P. J. and E. H. Mamdani [1977], "The application of fuzzy control systems to industrial processes." *Automatica,* **13**(3), pp. 235–242.

713. Kiszka, J. B., M. M. Gupta and P. N. Nikiforuk [1985], "Energetistic stability of fuzzy dynamic systems." *IEEE Trans. on Systems, Man, and Cybernetics,* **15**(6), pp. 783–792.

714. Kitainik, L. [**1993**], *Fuzzy Decision Procedures With Binary Relations: Towards a Unified Theory.* Kluwer, Boston.

715. Kitainik, L., S. Orlovski and M. Roubens [1993], "Expert assistant FICCKAS: fuzzy information cluster, choice and knowledge acquisition systems." *Fuzzy Sets and Systems,* **58**(1), pp. 105–118.

716. Kiupel, N. and P. M. Frank [1993], "Fuzzy control of steam turbines." *Intern. J. of Systems Science,* **24**(10), pp. 1905–1914.

717. Kiupel, N., P. M. Frank and O. Bux [1994], "Fuzzy control of steam turbines." *Fuzzy Sets and Systems,* **63**(3), pp. 319–327.

718. Klawonn, F. [1994], "Fuzzy sets and vague environments." *Fuzzy Sets and Systems,* **66**(2), pp. 207–221.

719. Klawonn, F. and R. Kruse [1993], "Equality relations as a basis for fuzzy control." *Fuzzy Sets and Systems,* **54**(2), pp. 147–156.

720. Klement, E. P. and W. Slany, eds. [**1993**], *Fuzzy Logic in Artificial Intelligence.* Springer-Verlag, New York.

721. Kleyle, R. and A. de Korvin [1994], "Object identification when imprecise information is available from multiple sources of unequal reliability." *J. of Intelligent & Fuzzy Systems,* **2**(2), pp. 191–199.

722. Klir, G. J. [**1985**], *Architecture of Systems Problem Solving.* Plenum Press, New York.

723. Klir, G. J. [1987], "Where do we stand on measures of uncertainty, ambiguity, fuzziness, and the like?" *Fuzzy Sets and Systems,* **24**(2), pp. 141–160.

724. Klir, G. J. [1989], "Is there more to uncertainty than some probability theorist might have us believe?" *Intern. J. of General Systems,* **15**(4), pp. 347–378.

725. Klir, G. J. [1990a], "Dynamic aspects in reconstructability analysis: The role of minimum uncertainty principles." *Revue Internationale de Systemique,* **4**(1), pp. 33–43.

726. Klir, G. J. [1990b], "A principle of uncertainty and information invariance." *Intern. J. of General Systems,* **17**(2–3), pp. 249–275.

727. Klir, G. J. [1991a], "Some applications of the principle of uncertainty invariance." *Proc. Intern. Fuzzy Eng. Symp., Yokohama, Japan*, pp. 15–26.

728. Klir, G. J. [1991b], "Generalized information theory." *Fuzzy Sets and Systems*, **40**(1), pp. 127–142.

729. Klir, G. J. [1992], "Probabilistic versus possibilistic conceptualization of uncertainty." In: Ayyub, B. M., M. M. Gupta and L. N. Kanal, eds., *Analysis and Mangement of Uncertainty*. Elsevier, New York, pp. 13–25.

730. Klir, G. J. [1993], "Developments in uncertainty-based information." In: Yovits, M. C., ed., *Advances in Computers*. Academic Press, San Diego, pp. 255–332.

731. Klir, G. J. [1994], "Multivalued logics versus modal logics: Alternative frameworks for uncertainty modelling." In: Wang, P. P., ed., *Advances in Fuzzy Theory and Technology, Vol. II*. Duke Univ., Durham, NC

732. Klir, G. J. and T. Folger [**1988**], *Fuzzy Sets, Uncertainty, and Information*. Prentice Hall, Englewood Cliffs, NJ.

733. Klir, G. J. and D. Harmanec [1994], "On modal logic interpretation of possibility theory." *Intern. J. of Uncertainty, Fuzziness and Knowledge–Based Systems*, **2**(2), pp. 237–245.

734. Klir, G. J. and M. Mariano [1987], "On the uniqueness of possibilistic measure of uncertainty and information." *Fuzzy Sets and Systems*, **24**(2), pp. 197–219.

735. Klir, G. J. and B. Parviz [1992a], "A note on the measure of discord." *Proc. Eighth Conference on Artificial Intelligence, San Mateo, California*, pp. 138–141.

736. Klir, G. J. and B. Parviz [1992b], "Probability-possibility transformations: A comparison." *Intern. J. of General Systems*, **21**(3), pp. 291–310.

737. Klir, G. J., B. Parviz and M. Higashi [1986], "Relationship between true and estimated possibilistic systems and their reconstruction." *Intern. J. of General Systems*, **12**(4), pp. 319–331.

738. Klir, G. J. and A. Ramer [1990], "Uncertainty in the Dempster–Shafer theory : A critical re-examination." *Intern. J. of General Systems*, **18**(2), pp. 155–166.

739. Kloeden, P. E. [1982], "Fuzzy dynamic systems." *Fuzzy Sets and Systems*, **7**(3), pp. 275–296.

740. Kloeden, P. E. [1991], "Chaotic iterations of fuzzy sets." *Fuzzy Sets and Systems*, **42**(1), pp. 37–42.

741. Koczy, L. T. and K. Hirota [1993], "Approximate reasoning by linear rule interpolation and general approximation." *Intern. J. of Approximate Reasoning*, **9**(3), pp. 197–225.

742. Kohlas, J. and P. A. Monney [1991], "Propagating belief functions through constraint systems." *Intern. J. of Approximate Reasoning*, **5**(5), pp. 433–462.

743. Kohout, L. J. [1988], "Theories of possibility: Meta-axiomatics and semantics." *Fuzzy Sets and Systems*, **25**(3), pp. 357–367.

744. Kohout, L. J. [1991], "Quo vadis fuzzy systems: A critical evaluation of recent methodological trends." *Intern. J. of General Systems*, **19**(4), pp. 395–424.

745. Kohout, L. J., J. Anderson, W. Bandler, A. Behrooz, G. Song and C. Trayner [1991], "Activity structure based architectures for knowledge-based systems, Part 1: Dynamics of localized fuzzy inference and its interaction with planning." *Fuzzy Sets and Systems*, **44**(3), pp. 405–420.

746. Kohout, L. J. and W. Bandler [1985], "Relational-product architectures for information processing." *Information Sciences*, **37**(1–3), pp. 25–37.

747. Kohout, L. J. and W. Bandler, eds. [**1986**], *Knowledge Representation in Medicine and Clinical Behavioural Science*. Abacus Press, Tunbridge Wells, Kent.

748. Kohout, L. J., E. Keravnou and W. Bandler [1984], "Automatic documentary information retrieval by means of fuzzy relational products." In: Zimmermann, H. J., L. A. Zadeh and B. R. Gaines, eds., *Fuzzy Sets and Decision Analysis*. North-Holland, New York, pp. 383–404.

749. Kolodziejczyk, W. [1987], "Canonical form of a strongly transitive fuzzy matrix." *Fuzzy Sets and Systems*, **22**(3), pp. 297–302.

750. Kolodziejczyk, W. [1988], "Decomposition problem of fuzzy relations: Further results." *Intern. J. of General Systems*, **14**(4), pp. 307–315.

751. Kolodziejczyk, W. [1990], "On transitive solutions of sigma-fuzzy relation equations describing fuzzy systems." *Intern. J. of General Systems*, **17**(2–3), pp. 277–288.

752. Kong, S. G. and B. Kosko [1992], "Adaptive fuzzy systems for backing up a truck and trailer." *IEEE Trans. on Neural Networks*, **3**(3), pp. 211–223.

753. Koo, J. T. K. [1994], "Analysis of a class of fuzzy controllers." *Intern. J. of Uncertainty, Fuzziness and Knowledge–Based Systems*, **2**(3), pp. 257–264.

754. Kosko, B. [1988], "Hidden patterns in combined and adaptive knowledge." *Intern. J. of Approximate Reasoning*, **2**(4), pp. 377–394.

755. Kosko, B. [1990], "Fuzziness vs. probability." *Intern. J. of General Systems*, **17**(2–3), pp. 211–240.

756. Kosko, B. [**1991**], *Neural Networks and Fuzzy Systems*. Prentice Hall, Englewood, NJ.

757. Kosko, B. [1992], "Fuzzy systems as universal approximators." *Proc. First IEEE Intern. Conf. on Fuzzy Systems, San Diego*, pp. 1153–1162.

758. Kosko, B. [**1993a**], *Fuzzy Thinking: The New Science of Fuzzy Logic*. Hyperion, New York.

759. Kosko, B. [1993b], "Addition as fuzzy mutual entropy." *Information Sciences*, **73**(3), pp. 273–284.

760. Kovalerchuk, B. and V. Taliansky [1992], "Comparison of empirical and computed values of fuzzy conjunction." *Fuzzy Sets and Systems*, **46**(1), pp. 49–53.

761. Kraft, D. H. and D. A. Buell [1983], "Fuzzy sets and generalized Boolean retrieval systems." *Intern. J. of Man-Machine Studies*, **19**(1), pp. 45–56.

762. Kramosil, I. [1992a], "An alternative approach to rough sets." *Kybernetika*, **28**(1), pp. 1–25.

763. Kramosil, I. [1992b], "From an alternative model of rough sets to fuzzy sets." *Kybernetika*, **28**(Supplement), pp. 12–16.

764. Kramosil, I. and J. Michálek [1975], "Fuzzy metrics and statistical metric spaces." *Kybernetika*, **11**(5), pp. 336–344.

765. Krause, B., C. v. Altrock, K. Limper and W. Schäfers [1994], "A neuro-fuzzy adaptive control strategy for refuse incineration plants." *Fuzzy Sets and Systems*, **63**(3), pp. 329–337.

766. Krishnapuram, R. and J. M. Keller [1993], "A possibilistic approach to clustering." *IEEE Trans. on Fuzzy Systems*, **1**(2), pp. 98–110.

767. Krishnapuram, R., J. M. Keller and Y. Ma [1993], "Quantitative analysis of properties and spatial relations of fuzzy image regions." *IEEE Trans. on Fuzzy Systems*, **1**(3), pp. 222–233.

768. Kruse, R. [1982], "The strong law of large numbers for fuzzy random variables." *Information Sciences*, **28**(3), pp. 233–241.

769. Kruse, R., R. Buck–Emden and R. Cordes [1987], "Processor power considerations – An application of fuzzy Markov chains." *Fuzzy Sets and Systems*, **21**(3), pp. 289–299.

770. Kruse, R. and K. D. Meyer [**1987**], *Statistics with Vague Data*. D. Reidel, Boston.

771. Kruse, R. and E. Schwecke [1990], "Fuzzy reasoning in a multidimensional space of hypotheses." *Intern. J. of Approximate Reasoning*, **4**(1), pp. 47–68.

772. Kruse, R., E. Schwecke and J. Heinsohn [**1991**], *Uncertainty and Vagueness in Knowledge Based Systems: Numerical Methods*. Springer–Verlag, New York.

773. Kruse, R. and P. Siegel, eds. [**1991**], *Symbolic and Quantitative Approaches to Uncertainty*. Springer–Verlag, New York.

774. Kulka, J. and V. Novák [1984], "Have fuzzy operations a psychological correspondence?" *Studia Psychologica*, **26**, pp. 131–141.

775. Kuncheva, L. I. [1992], "Fuzzy rough sets: Application to feature selection." *Fuzzy Sets and Systems*, **51**(2), pp. 147–153.

776. Kuncheva, L. I. [1994], "Pattern recognition with a model of fuzzy neuron using degree of consensus." *Fuzzy Sets and Systems*, **66**(2), pp. 241–250.

777. Kung, Y. S. and C. M. Liaw [1994], "A fuzzy controller improving a linear model following controller for motor drives." *IEEE Trans. on Fuzzy Systems*, **2**(3), pp. 194–202.

778. Kuo, Y. H., C. I. Kao and J. J. Chen [1993], "A fuzzy neural network model and its hardware implementation." *IEEE Trans. on Fuzzy Systems*, **1**(3), pp. 171–183.

779. Kuz'min, V. B. [1981], "A parametric approach to description of linguistic values of variables and hedges." *Fuzzy Sets and Systems*, **6**(1), pp. 27–41.

780. Kwan, H. K. and Y. Cai [1994], "A fuzzy neural network and its applications to pattern recognition." *IEEE Trans. on Fuzzy Systems*, **2**(3), pp. 185–193.

781. Lai, Y. J. and A. I. Chang [1994], "A fuzzy approach for multiresponse optimization: An off–line quality engineering problem." *Fuzzy Sets and Systems*, **63**(2), pp. 117–129.

782. Lai, Y. and C. Hwang [**1992**], *Fuzzy Mathematical Programming*. Springer–Verlag, New York.

783. Lai, Y. and C. Hwang [1993], "Possibilistic linear programming for managing interest rate risk." *Fuzzy Sets and Systems*, **54**(2), pp. 135–146.

784. Lakoff, G. [1973], "Hedges: A study in meaning criteria and the logic of fuzzy concepts." *J. of Philosophical Logic*, **2**, pp. 458–508.

785. Lakoff, G. [**1987**], *Women, Fire, and Dangerous Things*. University of Chicago Press, Chicago.

786. Lamata, M. T. and S. Moral [1988], "Measures of entropy in the theory of evidence." *Intern. J. of General Systems*, **14**(4), pp. 297–305.

787. Lambert, J. M. [1992], "The fuzzy set membership problem using the hierarchy decision method." *Fuzzy Sets and Systems*, **48**(3), pp. 323–330.

788. Lano, K. [1992a], "Fuzzy sets and residuated logic." *Fuzzy Sets and Systems*, **47**(2), pp. 203–220.

789. Lano, K. [1992b], "Formal frameworks for approximate reasoning." *Fuzzy Sets and Systems*, **51**(2), pp. 131–146.

790. Larsen, H. L. and R. R. Yager [1990], "An approach to customized end–user views in multi-user information retrieval systems." In: Kacprzyk, J. and M. Fedrizzi, eds., *Multiperson Decision Making Models Using Fuzzy Sets and Possibility Theory*. Kluwer, Boston, pp. 128–139.

791. Larsen, H. L. and R. R. Yager [1993], "The use of fuzzy relational thesauri for classificatory problem solving in information retrieval and expert systems." *IEEE Trans. on Systems, Man, and Cybernetics*, **23**(1), pp. 31–41.

792. Lasek, M. [1992], "Hierarchical structures of fuzzy ratings in the analysis of strategic goals of enterprises." *Fuzzy Sets and Systems*, **50**(2), pp. 127–134.

793. Lasker, G. E., ed. **[1981]**, *Applied Systems and Cybernetics. Vol. VI: Fuzzy Sets and Systems, Possibility Theory, and Special Topics in Systems Research.* Pergamon Press, New York.

794. Laviolette, M. and J. W. Seaman [1992], "Evaluating fuzzy representations of uncertainty." *Mathematical Sciences,* **17**(1), pp. 26–41.

795. Lee, C. C. [1979a], "Section of parameters for a fuzzy logic controller." *Fuzzy Sets and Systems,* **2**(3), pp. 185–199.

796. Lee, C. C. [1979b], "Theoretical and linguistic aspects of the fuzzy logic controller." *Automatica,* **15**(5), pp. 553–577.

797. Lee, C. C. [1990], "Fuzzy logic in control systems: fuzzy logic controller, Part I, II." *IEEE Trans. on Systems, Man, and Cybernetics,* **20**(2), pp. 404–418, 419–432.

798. Lee, C. C. [1991], "A self-learning rule-based controller employing approximate reasoning and neural net concepts." *Intern. J. of Intelligent Systems,* **6**(1), pp. 71–93.

799. Lee, E. S. and R. J. Li [1993], "Fuzzy multiple objective programming and compromise programming with Pareto optimum." *Fuzzy Sets and Systems,* **53**(3), pp. 275–288.

800. Lee, E. T. [1975], "Shape oriented chromosome classification." *IEEE Trans. on Systems, Man, and Cybernetics,* **5**(6), pp. 629–632.

801. Lee, E. T. [1993], "Fuzzy symmetric functions with don't-care conditions and applications." *Kybernetes,* **22**(4), pp. 54–68.

802. Lee, E. T. and L. A. Zadeh [1969], "Note on fuzzy languages." *Information Sciences,* **1**(4), pp. 421–434.

803. Lee, H. M. and W. T. Wang [1994], "A neural network architecture for classification of fuzzy inputs." *Fuzzy Sets and Systems,* **63**(2), pp. 159–173.

804. Lee, J. [1993], "On methods for improving performance of PI-type fuzzy logic controllers." *IEEE Trans. on Fuzzy Systems,* **1**(4), pp. 298–301.

805. Lee, K. M., C. H. Cho and H. Lee–Kwang [1994], "Ranking fuzzy values with satisfaction function." *Fuzzy Sets and Systems,* **64**(3), pp. 295–309.

806. Lee, K. M., D. D. Kwang and H. L. Wang [1994], "A fuzzy neural network model for fuzzy inference and rule tuning." *Intern. J. of Uncertainty, Fuzziness and Knowledge–Based Systems,* **2**(3), pp. 265–277.

807. Lee, M., S. Y. Lee and C. H. Park [1994], "A new neuro-fuzzy identification model of nonlinear dynamic systems." *Intern. J. of Approximate Reasoning,* **10**(1), pp. 29–44.

808. Lee, N. S., Y. L. Grize and K. Dehnad [1987], "Quantitative models for reasoning under uncertainty in knowledge-based expert systems." *Intern. J. of Intelligent Systems,* **2**(1), pp. 15–38.

809. Lee, R. C. T. [1972], "Fuzzy logic and the resolution principle." *J. of ACM,* **19**(1), pp. 109–119.

810. Lee, R. C. T. and C. L. Chang [1971], "Some properties of fuzzy logic." *Information and Control,* **19**(5), pp. 417–431.

811. Lee, S. C. and E. T. Lee [1974], "Fuzzy sets and neural networks." *J. of Cybernetics,* **4**(2), pp. 83–103.

812. Lee, S. C. and E. T. Lee [1975], "Fuzzy neural networks." *Mathematical Bioscience,* **23**(1–2), pp. 151–177.

813. Lee, Y. C., C. Hwang and Y. P. Shih [1994], "A combined approach to fuzzy model identification." *IEEE Trans. on Systems, Man, and Cybernetics,* **24**(5), pp. 736–744.

814. Lenart, C. [1993], "Defining separability of two fuzzy clusters by a fuzzy decision hyperplane." *Pattern Recognition,* **26**(9), pp. 1351–1356.

815. Lesmo, L. and R. Torasso [1987], "Prototypical knowledge for interpreting fuzzy concepts and quantifiers." *Fuzzy Sets and Systems,* **23**(3), pp. 361–370.

816. Leung, K. S. and Y. T. So [1993], "Consistency checking for fuzzy expert systems." *Intern. J. of Approximate Reasoning,* **9**(3), pp. 263–282.

817. Leung, Y. **[1988]**, *Spacial Analysis and Planning under Imprecision.* North-Holland, New York.

818. Li, B. W. [1990], "Weighted and graded fuzzy clustering." *Fuzzy Sets and Systems,* **36**(1), pp. 37–43.

819. Li, C. J. and J. C. Tzou [1992], "A new learning fuzzy controller based on the P–integrator concept." *Fuzzy Sets and Systems,* **48**(3), pp. 297–303.

820. Li, D. Y. and D. B. Liu **[1990]**, *A Fuzzy Prolog Database System.* John Wiley, New York.

821. Li, H. and H. S. Yang [1989], "Fast and reliable image enhancement using fuzzy relaxation techniques." *IEEE Trans. on Systems, Man, and Cybernetics,* **19**(5), pp. 1276–1281.

822. Li, J. X. [1992], "An upper bound on indices of finite fuzzy relations." *Fuzzy Sets and Systems,* **49**(3), pp. 317–321.

823. Li, J. X. [1994], "Convergence of powers of controllable fuzzy matrices." *Fuzzy Sets and Systems,* **62**(1), pp. 83–88.

824. Li, Y. F. and C. C. Lau [1989], "Development of fuzzy algorithms for servo systems." *IEEE Control Systems Magazine,* **9**(3), pp. 65–72.

825. Li, Z. F. [1990], "The problem reduction method under uncertainty and decomposition of functions." *Fuzzy Sets and Systems,* **36**(1), pp. 45–53.

826. Li, Z. Y., Z. P. Chen and J. T. Li [1988], "A model of weather forecast by fuzzy grade statistics." *Fuzzy Sets and Systems*, **26**(3), pp. 275–281.

827. Liang, G. S. and M. J. J. Wang [1993], "Evaluating human reliability using fuzzy relation." *Microelectronics and Reliability*, **33**(1), pp. 63–80.

828. Liau, C. J. and B. I. Lin [1993], "Proof methods for reasoning about possibility and necessity." *Intern. J. of Approximate Reasoning*, **9**(4), pp. 327–364.

829. Liaw, C. M. and J. B. Wang [1991], "Design and implementation of a fuzzy controller for a high performance motor drive." *IEEE Trans. on Systems, Man, and Cybernetics*, **21**(4), pp. 921–929.

830. Lim, M. H. and T. Takefuji [1990], "Implementing fuzzy rule-based systems on silicon chips." *IEEE Expert*, **5**(1), pp. 31–45.

831. Lin, C. T. [**1994**], *Neural Fuzzy Control Systems With Structure And Parameter Learning*. World Scientific, Singapore.

832. Lin, C. T. and C. S. G. Lee [1991], "Neural-network-based fuzzy logic control and decision system." *IEEE Trans. on Computers*, **40**(12), pp. 1320–1336.

833. Lin, K. and M. Chern [1993], "The fuzzy shortest path problem and its most vital arcs." *Fuzzy Sets and Systems*, **58**(3), pp. 343–353.

834. Lin, Y. [1991], "On fuzzy stability of *L*-fuzzy systems." *Cybernetics and Systems*, **22**(6), pp. 761–772.

835. Ling, C. H. [1965], "Representation of associative functions." *Publ. Math. Debrecen*, **12**, pp. 189–212.

836. Ling, C. and T. F. Edgar [1993a], "The tuning of fuzzy heuristic controllers." *Asia-Pacific Engineering J.*, **3**(1–2), pp. 83–104.

837. Ling, C. and T. F. Edgar [1993b], "A new fuzzy scheduling algorithm for process control." *Asia-Pacific Engineering J.*, **3**(1–2), pp. 129–142.

838. Liou, T. S. and M. J. J. Wang [1994], "Subjective assessment of mental workload: A fuzzy multi-criteria approach." *Fuzzy Sets and Systems*, **62**(2), pp. 155–165.

839. Liou, T. and M. J. Wang [1992a], "Fuzzy weighed average: An improved algorithm." *Fuzzy Sets and Systems*, **49**(3), pp. 307–315.

840. Liou, T. and M. J. Wang [1992b], "Ranking fuzzy numbers with integral value." *Fuzzy Sets and Systems*, **50**(3), pp. 247–255.

841. Lipski, W. [1979], "On semantic issues connected with incomplete–information data bases." *ACM Trans. on Database Systems*, **4**(3), pp. 262–296.

842. Lipski, W. [1981], "On databases with incomplete information." *J. of ACM*, **28**(1), pp. 41–47.

843. Liu, M. H. and S. Wienand [1994], "Applications of fuzzy logic in automated robotic deburring." *Fuzzy Sets and Systems*, **63**(3), pp. 293–305.

844. Liu, T. S. and J. C. Wu [1993], "A model for rider–motorcycle system using fuzzy control." *IEEE Trans. on Systems, Man, and Cybernetics*, **23**(1), pp. 267–276.

845. Liu, W. [1992], "The reduction of the fuzzy data domain and fuzzy consistent join." *Fuzzy Sets and Systems*, **50**(1), pp. 89–96.

846. Liu, W., J. Hong, M. F. McTear and J. G. Hughes [1993], "An extended framework for evidential reasoning systems." *Intern. J. of Pattern Recognition and Artificial Intelligence*, **7**(3), pp. 441–458.

847. Liu, X., S. Tan, V. Srinivasan, S. H. Ong and W. Xie [1994], "Fuzzy pyramid-based invariant object recognition." *Pattern Recognition*, **27**(5), pp. 741–756.

848. Liu, Y. M. [1985], "Some properties of convex fuzzy sets." *J. of Math. Analysis and Applications*, **111**(1), pp. 119–129.

849. Liu, Z. R. and C. F. Huang [1990], "Information distribution method relevant in fuzzy information analysis." *Fuzzy Sets and Systems*, **36**(1), pp. 67–76.

850. Loo, S. G. [1978], "Fuzzy relations in the social and behavioral sciences." *J. of Cybernetics*, **8**(1), pp. 1–16.

851. Looney, C. G. [1988], "Fuzzy Petri nets for rule-based decisionmaking." *IEEE Trans. on Systems, Man, and Cybernetics*, **18**(1), pp. 178–183.

852. López de Mántaras, R. [**1990**], *Approximate Reasoning Models*. Ellis Horwood, Chichester.

853. López de Mántaras, R., U. Cortés, J. Manero and E. Plaza [1990], "Knowledge engineering for a document retrieval system." *Fuzzy Sets and Systems*, **38**(2), pp. 223–240.

854. López de Mántaras, R. and L. Valverde [1988], "New results in fuzzy clustering based on the concept of indistinguishability relation." *IEEE Trans. on Pattern Analysis and Machine Intelligence*, **10**(5), pp. 754–757.

855. Lowen, R. [1976], "Fuzzy topological spaces and fuzzy compactness." *J. of Math. Analysis and Applications*, **56**(3), pp. 621–633.

856. Lowen, R. [1978], "On fuzzy complements." *Information Sciences*, **14**(2), pp. 107–113.

857. Lowen, R. [1980], "Convex fuzzy sets." *Fuzzy Sets and Systems*, **3**(3), pp. 291–310.

858. Lowen, R. [**1985**], *On the Existence of Natural Non-Topological Fuzzy Topological Spaces*. Heldermann Verlag, Berlin.

859. Lowen, R. [1991], "Comments on Zeleny's paper concerning cognitive equilibria." *Intern. J. of General Systems*, **19**(4), pp. 387–393.

860. Luhandjula, M. K. [1987], "Multiple objective programming problems with possibilistic coefficients." *Fuzzy Sets and Systems*, **21**(2), pp. 135–145.

861. Lui, H. C. [1994], "Adaptive truth valued flow inference." *Intern. J. of Uncertainty, Fuzziness and Knowledge–Based Systems*, **2**(3), pp. 279–286.

862. Luo, C. Z. [1984], "Reliable solution set of a fuzzy relation equation." *J. of Math. Analysis and Applications*, **2**(2), pp. 524–532.

863. Luo, C. Z. and Z. P. Wang [1990], "Representation of compositional relations in fuzzy reasoning." *Fuzzy Sets and Systems*, **36**(1), pp. 77–81.

864. Mabuchi, S. [1988], "An approach to the comparison of fuzzy subsets with an α-cut dependent index." *IEEE Trans. on Systems, Man, and Cybernetics*, **18**(2), pp. 264–272.

865. Mabuchi, S. [1993], "A proposal for a defuzzification strategy by the concept of sensitivity analysis." *Fuzzy Sets and Systems*, **55**(1), pp. 1–14.

866. Macvicar–Whelan, P. J. [1978], "Fuzzy sets, the concept of height, and the hedge VERY." *IEEE Trans. on Systems, Man, and Cybernetics*, **8**(6), pp. 507–511.

867. Maeda, M. and S. Murakami [1992], "A self-tuning fuzzy controller." *Fuzzy Sets and Systems*, **51**(1), pp. 29–40.

868. Maeda, Y. and H. Ichihashi [1993], "An uncertainty measure with monotonicity under the random set inclusion." *Intern. J. of General Systems*, **21**(4), pp. 379–392.

869. Maeda, Y., H. T. Nguyen and H. Ichihashi [1993], "Maximum entropy algorithms for uncertainty measures." *Intern. J. of Uncertainty, Fuzziness and Knowledge–Based Systems*, **1**(1), pp. 69–93.

870. Magrez, P. and P. Smets [1989a], "Epistemic necessity, possibility, and truth: Tools for dealing with imprecision and uncertainty in fuzzy knowledge-based systems." *Intern. J. of Approximate Reasoning*, **3**(1), pp. 35–58.

871. Magrez, P. and P. Smets [1989b], "Fuzzy modus ponens: A new model suitable for applications in knowledge-based systems." *Intern. J. of Intelligent Systems*, **4**(2), pp. 181–200.

872. Maiers, J. and Y. S. Sherif [1985], "Applications of fuzzy set theory." *IEEE Trans. on Systems, Man, and Cybernetics*, **15**(1), pp. 175–189.

873. Malki, H. A., H. Li and G. Chen [1994], "New design and stability analysis of fuzzy proportional-derivative control systems." *IEEE Trans. on Fuzzy Systems*, **2**(4), pp. 245–254.

874. Mamdani, E. H. [1976], "Advances in the linguistic synthesis of fuzzy controllers." *Intern. J. of Man-Machine Studies*, **8**(6), pp. 669–678.

875. Mamdani, E. H. [1977], "Applications of fuzzy logic to approximate reasoning using linguistic systems." *IEEE Trans. on Systems, Man, and Cybernetics*, **26**(12), pp. 1182–1191.

876. Mamdani, E. H. and S. Assilian [1975], "An experiment in linguistic synthesis with a fuzzy logic controller." *Intern. J. of Man-Machine Studies*, **7**(1), pp. 1–13.

877. Mamdani, E. H. and B. R. Gaines, eds. [**1981**], *Fuzzy Reasoning and its Applications*. Academic Press, London.

878. Mandal, D. P., C. A. Murthy and S. K. Pal [1992], "Determining a pattern class from its prototypes." *Intern. J. of General Systems*, **20**(4), pp. 307–339.

879. Mandal, D. P., C. A. Murthy and S. K. Pal [1994], "A remote sensing application of a fuzzy classifier." *Intern. J. of Uncertainty, Fuzziness and Knowledge–Based Systems*, **2**(3), pp. 287–295.

880. Manes, E. G. [1982], "A class of fuzzy theories." *J. of Math. Analysis and Applications*, **85**(2), pp. 409–451.

881. Manzoul, M. A. and S. Tayal [1990], "Systolic VLSI array for multi-variable fuzzy control systems." *Cybernetics and Systems*, **21**(1), pp. 27–42.

882. Mareš, M. [1991], "Algebra of fuzzy quantities." *Intern. J. of General Systems*, **20**(1), pp. 59–65.

883. Mareš, M. [1992], "Multiplication of fuzzy quantities." *Kybernetika*, **28**(5), pp. 337–356.

884. Mareš, M. [1993a], "Algebraic equivalencies over fuzzy quantities." *Kybernetika*, **29**(2), pp. 121–132.

885. Mareš, M. [1993b], "Remarks on fuzzy quantities with finite support." *Kybernetika*, **29**(2), pp. 133–143.

886. Mareš, M. [**1994**], *Computation Over Fuzzy Quantities*. CRC Press, Boca Raton, Florida.

887. Mareš, M. [1994], "Analysis of data with fuzzy noise." *Fuzzy Sets and Systems*, **64**(3), pp. 353–360.

888. Mareš, M. and J. Horák [1983], "Fuzzy quantities in networks." *Fuzzy Sets and Systems*, **10**(2), pp. 123–134.

889. Marín, R., S. Barro, A. Bosch and J. Mira [1994], "Modeling the representation of time from a fuzzy perspective." *Cybernetics and Systems*, **25**(2), pp. 217–231.

890. Markechová, D. [1992], "The entropy of fuzzy dynamical systems and generators." *Fuzzy Sets and Systems*, **48**(3), pp. 351–363.

891. Markechová, D. [1994], "A note to the Kolmogorov-Sinaj entropy of fuzzy dynamical systems." *Fuzzy Sets and Systems*, **64**(1), pp. 87–90.

892. Marks II, R. J., ed. [**1994**], *Fuzzy Logic Technology and Applications*. IEEE Press, New York.

893. Matia, F., A. Jimenez, R. Galan and R. Sanz [1992], "Fuzzy controllers: Lifting the linear–nonlinear frontier." *Fuzzy Sets and Systems*, **52**(2), pp. 113–128.

894. McAllister, M. N. [1987], "Availability, production and competition: a model." *Mathematical Modelling*, **9**(6), pp. 477–490.

895. McAllister, M. N. [1988], "Fuzzy intersection graphs." *Computers and Mathematics with Applications,* **15**(10), pp. 871–886.

896. McAllister, M. N. [1990], "A computationally simple model to represent and manipulate linguistic imprecision." *Intern. J. of General Systems,* **16**(3), pp. 265–289.

897. McCahon, C. S. and E. S. Lee [1988], "Project network analysis with fuzzy activity times." *Computers and Mathematics with Applications,* **15**(10), pp. 829–838.

898. McCahon, C. S. and E. S. Lee [1990], "Comparing fuzzy numbers: The proportion of the optimum method." *Intern. J. of Approximate Reasoning,* **4**(3), pp. 159–182.

899. McCain, R. A. [1987], "Fuzzy confidence intervals in a theory of economic rationality." *Fuzzy Sets and Systems,* **23**(2), pp. 205–218.

900. McLeish, M., ed. [**1988**], *An Inquiry into Computer Understanding.* Debate Section of *Computational Intellegence,* **4**(1), pp. 57–142.

901. McNeill, D. and P. Freiberger [**1993**], *Fuzzy Logic: The Discovery of a Revolutionary Computer Technology—and How It Is Changing Our World.* Simon & Schuster, New York.

902. McNeill, F. M. and E. Thro [**1994**], *Fuzzy Logic: A Practical Approach.* AP Professional, New York.

903. Medina, J. M., O. Pons and M. A. Vila [1994], "GEFRED: A general model of fuzzy relational databases." *Information Sciences: Informatics and Computer Sciences,* **76**(1–2), pp. 87–109.

904. Meier, W., R. Weber and H. J. Zimmermann [1994], "Fuzzy data analysis: Methods and industrial applications." *Fuzzy Sets and Systems,* **61**(1), pp. 19–28.

905. Melton, A. and S. Shenoi [1991], "Fuzzy relations and fuzzy relational databases." *Computers and Mathematics with Applications,* **21**(11–12), pp. 129–138.

906. Meng, H. K. and W. L. Chiang [1994], "Application of identification of fuzzy model in structural mechanics." *Intern. J. of Uncertainty, Fuzziness and Knowledge–Based Systems,* **2**(3), pp. 297–304.

907. Menger, K. [1942], "Statistical metrics." *Proc. Nat. Acad. Sci.,* **28**, pp. 535–537.

908. Mesiar, R. [1991], "Bayes principle and the entropy of fuzzy probability spaces." *Intern. J. of General Systems,* **20**(1), pp. 67–71.

909. Mesiar, R. [1993], "Fuzzy measurable functions." *Fuzzy Sets and Systems,* **59**(1), pp. 35–41.

910. Miki, T., H. Matsumoto, K. Ohto and T. Yamakawa [1993], "Silicon implementation for a novel high–speed fuzzy inference engine: Mega-FLIPS analog fuzzy processor." *J. of Intelligent & Fuzzy Systems,* **1**(1), pp. 27–42.

911. Mili, H. and R. Rada [1990], "Inheritance generalized to fuzzy regularity." *IEEE Trans. on Systems, Man, and Cybernetics,* **20**(5), pp. 1184–1198.

912. Misra, K. B. and G. G. Weber [1989], "A new method for fuzzy fault tree analysis." *Microelectronics and Reliability,* **29**(2), pp. 195–216.

913. Mitchell, K. C., M. A. Woodbury and A. F. Norcio [1994], "Individualizing user interfaces: Application of the grade of membership (GoM) model for development of fuzzy user classes." *Information Sciences: Applications,* **1**(1), pp. 9–29.

914. Mitra, S. [1994], "Fuzzy MLP based expert system for medical diagnosis." *Fuzzy Sets and Systems,* **65**(2–3), pp. 285–296.

915. Mitra, S. and S. K. Pal [1994a], "Self-organizing neural network as a fuzzy classifier." *IEEE Trans. on Systems, Man, and Cybernetics,* **24**(3), pp. 385–399.

916. Mitra, S. and S. K. Pal [1994b], "Logical operation based fuzzy MLP for classification and rule generation." *Neural Networks,* **7**(2), pp. 353–373.

917. Miyajina, K. and A. Ralescu [1994], "Spatial organization in 2D segmented images: Representation and recognition of primitive spatial relations." *Fuzzy Sets and Systems,* **65**(2–3), pp. 225–236.

918. Miyakawa, M., K. Nakamura, J. Ramík and I. G. Rosenberg [1993], "Joint canonical fuzzy numbers." *Fuzzy Sets and Systems,* **53**(1), pp. 39–47.

919. Miyakoshi, M. and M. Shimbo [1985], "Solutions of composite fuzzy relational equations with triangular norms." *Fuzzy Sets and Systems,* **16**(1), pp. 53–63.

920. Miyamoto, S. [1989], "Two approaches for information retrieval through fuzzy associations." *IEEE Trans. on Systems, Man, and Cybernetics,* **19**(1), pp. 123–130.

921. Miyamoto, S. [**1990**], *Fuzzy Sets in Information Retrieval and Cluster Analysis.* Kluwer, Boston.

922. Miyamoto, S., T. Miyake and K. Nakayama [1983], "Generation of a pseudothesaurus for information retrieval based on cooccurrences and fuzzy set operations." *IEEE Trans. on Systems, Man, and Cybernetics,* **13**(1), pp. 62–70.

923. Miyamoto, S. and K. Nakayama [1986], "Fuzzy information retrieval based on a fuzzy pseudothesarus." *IEEE Trans. on Systems, Man, and Cybernetics,* **16**(2), pp. 278–282.

924. Mizraji, E. [1992], "Vector logics: The matrix–vector representation of logical calculus." *Fuzzy Sets and Systems,* **50**(2), pp. 179–185.

925. Mizumoto, M. [1981], "Note on the arithmetic rule by Zadeh for fuzzy conditional inference." *Cybernetics and Systems,* **12**(3), pp. 247–306.

926. Mizumoto, M. [1982a], "Fuzzy inference using max-$\wedge$ composition in the compositional rule of inference." In: Gupta, M. M. and E. Sanchez, eds.,

Approximate Reasoning in Decision Analysis. North-Holland, New York, pp. 67–76.

927. Mizumoto, M. [1982b], "Fuzzy conditional inference under max-⊙ composition." *Information Sciences,* **27**(3), pp. 183–209.

928. Mizumoto, M. [1989], "Pictorial representations of fuzzy connectives, Part I: Cases of *t*-norms, *t*-conorms and averaging operators." *Fuzzy Sets and Systems,* **31**(2), pp. 217–242.

929. Mizumoto, M. [1994], "Fuzzy controls by product-sum-gravity method dealing with fuzzy rules of emphatic and suppressive types." *Intern. J. of Uncertainty, Fuzziness and Knowledge-Based Systems,* **2**(3), pp. 305–319.

930. Mizumoto, M., S. Fukami and K. Tanaka [1979], "Some methods of fuzzy reasoning." In: Gupta, M. M., R. K. Ragade and R. R. Yager, eds., *Advances in Fuzzy Set Theory and Applications.* North-Holland, New York, pp. 253–283.

931. Mizumoto, M. and K. Tanaka [1976], "Some properties of fuzzy sets of type 2." *Information and Control,* **31**(4), pp. 312–340.

932. Mizumoto, M. and K. Tanaka [1981a], "Fuzzy sets and their operations." *Information and Control,* **48**(1), pp. 30–48.

933. Mizumoto, M. and K. Tanaka [1981b], "Fuzzy sets of type 2 under algebraic product and algebraic sum." *Fuzzy Sets and Systems,* **5**(3), pp. 277–290.

934. Mizumoto, M., J. Toyoda and K. Tanaka [1969], "Some considerations on fuzzy automata." *J. of Computer and System Sciences,* **3**(4), pp. 409–422.

935. Mizumoto, M., J. Toyoda and K. Tanaka [1972], "General formulation of formal grammars." *Information Sciences,* **4**, pp. 87–100.

936. Mizumoto, M., J. Toyoda and K. Tanaka [1973], "*N*-fold fuzzy grammars." *Information Sciences,* **5**(1), pp. 25–43.

937. Mizumoto, M. and H. J. Zimmermann [1982], "Comparison of fuzzy reasoning methods." *Fuzzy Sets and Systems,* **8**(3), pp. 253–283.

938. Močkoř, J. [1991], "A category of fuzzy automata." *Intern. J. of General Systems,* **20**(1), pp. 73–82.

939. Mogre, A., R. W. McLaren, J. M. Keller and R. Krishnapuram [1994], "Uncertainty management for rule-based systems with applications to image analysis." *IEEE Trans. on Systems, Man, and Cybernetics,* **24**(3), pp. 470–481.

940. Mohamed, R. H. [1992], "A chance–constrained fuzzy goal program." *Fuzzy Sets and Systems,* **47**(2), pp. 183–186.

941. Mohanty, B. K. and N. Singh [1994], "Fuzzy relational equations in analytical hierarchy process." *Fuzzy Sets and Systems,* **63**(1), pp. 11–19.

942. Moisil, G. C. [**1975**], *Lectures on the Logic of Fuzzy Reasoning.* Scientific Editions, Bucharest.

943. Mon, D. L. and C. H. Cheng [1994], "Fuzzy system reliability analysis for components with different membership functions." *Fuzzy Sets and Systems,* **64**(2), pp. 145–157.

944. Mon, D. L., C. H. Cheng and J. C. Lin [1994], "Evaluating weapon system using fuzzy analytic hierarchy process based on entropy weight." *Fuzzy Sets and Systems,* **62**(2), pp. 127–134.

945. Montero, J. [1994], "Rational aggregation rules." *Fuzzy Sets and Systems,* **62**(3), pp. 267–276.

946. Moore, R. E. [**1966**], *Interval Analysis.* Prentice Hall, Englewood Cliffs, NJ.

947. Moore, R. E. [**1979**], *Methods and Applications of Interval Analysis.* SIAM, Philadelphia.

948. Mordeson, J. and C. S. Peng [1994], "Operations on fuzzy graphs." *Information Sciences,* **79**(3–4), pp. 159–170.

949. Morikawa, O. [1994], "A sequential formulation of a logic based on fuzzy modalities." *Fuzzy Sets and Systems,* **63**(2), pp. 181–185.

950. Moskowitz, H. and K. Kim [1993], "On assessing the H value in fuzzy linear regression." *Fuzzy Sets and Systems,* **58**(3), pp. 303–328.

951. Mouaddib, N. [1994], "Fuzzy identification in fuzzy databases: The nuanced relational division." *Intern. J. of Intelligent Systems,* **9**(5), pp. 461–473.

952. Mukaidono, M., Z. Shen and L. Ding [1989], "Fundamentals of fuzzy Prolog." *Intern. J. of Approximate Reasoning,* **3**(2), pp. 179–194.

953. Murai, T., M. Miakoshi and M. Shimbo [1988], "A model of search oriented thesaurus use based on multivalued logical inference." *Information Sciences,* **45**(2), pp. 185–215.

954. Murai, T., M. Miyakoshi and M. Shimbo [1989], "A fuzzy document retrieval method based on two-valued indexing." *Fuzzy Sets and Systems,* **30**(2), pp. 103–120.

955. Murofushi, T., M. Sugeno and M. Machida [1994], "Non-monotonic fuzzy measures and the Choquet integral." *Fuzzy Sets and Systems,* **64**(1), pp. 73–86.

956. Murthy, C. A., D. D. Majumder and S. K. Pal [1987], "Representation of fuzzy operators using ordinary sets." *IEEE Trans. on Systems, Man, and Cybernetics,* **17**(5), pp. 840–847.

957. Murthy, S. V. and A. Kandel [1990], "Fuzzy sets and typicality theory." *Information Sciences,* **51**(1), pp. 61–93.

958. Nafarieh, A. and J. M. Keller [1991], "A fuzzy logic rule-based automatic target recognizer." *Intern. J. of Intelligent Systems,* **6**(3), pp. 295–312.

959. Nakamori, Y. and M. Ryoke [1994], "Identification of fuzzy prediction models through hyperellipsoidal clustering." *IEEE Trans. on Systems, Man, and Cybernetics,* **24**(8), pp. 1153–1173.

960. Nakamura, A. and J. M. Gao [1991], "A logic for fuzzy data analysis." *Fuzzy Sets and Systems*, **39**(2), pp. 127–132.

961. Nakamura, K. [1990], "Canonical fuzzy numbers." *Information Sciences*, **50**(1), pp. 1–22.

962. Nakamura, K. and S. Iwai [1982], "Topological fuzzy sets as a quantitative description of analogical inference and its application to question-answering systems for information retrieval." *IEEE Trans. on Systems, Man, and Cybernetics*, **12**(2), pp. 193–203.

963. Nakanishi, H., I. B. Turksen and M. Sugeno [1993], "A review and comparison of six reasoning methods." *Fuzzy Sets and Systems*, **57**(3), pp. 257–294.

964. Nakanishi, S. [1989], "Some properties of many valued sets." *Fuzzy Sets and Systems*, **30**(2), pp. 193–204.

965. Narasimhan, R. [1979], "A fuzzy subset characterization of a site–selection problem." *Decision Sciences*, **10**(4), pp. 618–628.

966. Narazaki, H. and A. L. Ralescu [1993], "An improved synthesis method for multilayered neural networks using qualitative knowledge." *IEEE Trans. on Fuzzy Systems*, **1**(2), pp. 125–137.

967. Narazaki, H. and A. L. Ralescu [1994], "An alternative method for inducing a membership function of a category." *Intern. J. of Approximate Reasoning*, **11**(1), pp. 1–27.

968. Nasution, S. H. [1994], "Fuzzy critical path method." *IEEE Trans. on Systems, Man, and Cybernetics*, **24**(1), pp. 48–57.

969. Nedungadi, A. [1993], "A fuzzy logic-based robot controller." *J. of Intelligent & Fuzzy Systems*, **1**(3), pp. 243–251.

970. Negoita, C. V. [1973], "On the application of the fuzzy sets separation theorem for automatic classification in information retrieval systems." *Information Sciences*, **5**(1), pp. 279–286.

971. Negoita, C. V. [**1979**], *Management Applications of Systems Theory*. Birkhäuser Verlag, Basel and Stuttgart.

972. Negoita, C. V. [**1981**], *Fuzzy Systems*. Abacus Press, Tunbridge Wells, UK.

973. Negoita, C. V. [**1985**], *Expert Systems and Fuzzy Systems*. Benjamin/Cummings, Menlo Park, CA.

974. Negoita, C. V. and P. Flondor [1976], "On fuzziness in information retrieval." *Intern. J. of Man-Machine Studies*, **8**(6), pp. 711–716.

975. Negoita, C. V. and D. A. Ralescu [1975a], "Representation theorems for fuzzy concepts." *Kybernetes*, **4**(3), pp. 169–174.

976. Negoita, C. V. and D. A. Ralescu [**1975b**], *Applications of Fuzzy Sets to Systems Analysis*. Birkhäuser, Basel and Stuttgart, and Halsted Press, New York.

977. Negoita, C. V. and D. A. Ralescu [**1987**], *Simulation, Knowledge–Based Computing and Fuzzy Statistics*. Van Nostrand Reinhold, New York.

978. Negoita, G. M. and V. V. Canciu [1992], "Fuzzy identification of systems: a new cybernetic method." *Kybernetics*, **21**(4), pp. 67–79.

979. Ngo, C. Y. and V. O. K. Li [1994], "Freeway traffic control using fuzzy logic controllers." *Information Sciences: Applications*, **1**(2), pp. 59–76.

980. Nguyen, H. T. [1978a], "A note on the extension principle for fuzzy sets." *J. of Math. Analysis and Applications*, **64**(2), pp. 369–380.

981. Nguyen, H. T. [1978b], "Random sets and belief functions." *J. of Math. Analysis and Applications*, **65**(3), pp. 531–542.

982. Nguyen, H. T. [1978c], "On conditional possibility distributions." *Fuzzy Sets and Systems*, **1**(4), pp. 299–309.

983. Nguyen, H. T. [1984], "On modeling of linguistic information using random sets." *Information Sciences*, **34**(3), pp. 265–274.

984. Nie, J. and D. A. Linkens [1993], "Learning control using fuzzified self-organizing radial basis function network." *IEEE Trans. on Fuzzy Systems*, **1**(4), pp. 280–287.

985. Nie, J. and D. A. Linkens [**1994**], *Fuzzy Neural Control: Principles, Algorithms and Applications*. Prentice Hall, Englewood Cliffs, NJ.

986. Nishizaki, I. and M. Sakawa [1992a], "A solution concept based on fuzzy decisions in *n*-person cooperative games." *Japanese J. of Fuzzy Theory and Systems*, **4**(2), pp. 183–194.

987. Nishizaki, I. and M. Sakawa [1992b], "Two–person zero–sum games with multiple fuzzy goal." *Japanese J. of Fuzzy Theory and Systems*, **4**(3), pp. 289–300.

988. Niskanen, V. A. [1993], "Metric truth as a basis for fuzzy linguistic reasoning." *Fuzzy Sets and Systems*, **57**(1), pp. 1–25.

989. Nomoto, K., S. Wakayama, T. Kirimoto, Y. Ohashi and M. Kondo [1990], "A document retrieval system based on citations using fuzzy graphs." *Fuzzy Sets and Systems*, **38**(2), pp. 207–222.

990. Nomura, H., I. Hayashi and N. Wakami [1992], "A self-tuning method of fuzzy reasoning by genetic algorithm." *Proc. Intern. Fuzzy Systems and Intelligent Control Conf., Louisville, KY*, pp. 236–245.

991. Noor, M. A. [1994], "Fuzzy preinvex functions." *Fuzzy Sets and Systems*, **64**(1), pp. 95–104.

992. Norwich, A. M. and I. B. Turksen [1984], "A model for the measurement of membership and the consequences of its empirical implementation." *Fuzzy Sets and Systems*, **12**(1), pp. 1–25.

993. Novák, V. [**1989**], *Fuzzy Sets and Their Applications*. Adam Hilger, Bristol.

994. Novák, V. [1990], "On the syntactico–semantical completeness of first-order fuzzy logic. Part I, II." *Kybernetika*, **26**(1), pp. 47–66, **26**(2), pp.134–154.

995. Novák, V. [1991], "Fuzzy logic, fuzzy sets, and natural languages." *Intern. J. of General Systems*, **20**(1), pp. 83–97.

996. Novák, V. [**1992**], *The Alternative Mathematical Model of Linguistic Semantics and Pragmatic*. Plenum Press, New York.

997. Novák, V. [1994], "Fuzzy control from the logical point of view." *Fuzzy Sets and Systems*, **66**(2), pp. 159–173.

998. Novák, V. and W. Pedrycz [1988], "Fuzzy sets and *t*-norms in the light of fuzzy logic." *Intern. J. of Man-Machine Studies*, **29**, pp. 113–127.

999. Novák, V. and J. Ramík [1991], "Mathematical theory of vagueness in Czechoslovakia: A historical survey and bibliography." *Intern. J. of General Systems*, **20**(1), pp. 5–15.

1000. Novák, V., J. Ramík, M., Mareš, M. Černý and J. Nekola, eds. [**1992**], *Fuzzy Approach to Reasoning and Decision-Making*. Kluwer, Boston.

1001. Nowakowska, M. [1977], "Methodological problems of measurement of fuzzy concepts in the social science." *Behavioral Science*, **22**(2), pp. 107–115.

1002. Nowakowska, M. [1979], "Fuzzy concepts: Their structure and problems of measurement." In: Gupta, M. M., R. K. Ragade and R. R. Yager, eds., *Advances in Fuzzy Set Theory and Applications*. North-Holland, New York, pp. 361–387.

1003. Nowakowska, M. [1990], "Cluster analysis, graphs, and branching processes as new methodologies for intelligent systems on example of bibliometric and social network data." *Intern. J. of Intelligent Systems*, **5**(3), pp. 247–264.

1004. Oblow, E. M. [1987a], "O-theory: A hybrid uncertainty theory." *Intern. J. of General Systems*, **13**(2), pp. 95–106.

1005. Oblow, E. M. [1987b], "A probabilistic–propositional framework for the O-theory intersection rule." *Intern. J. of General Systems*, **13**(3), pp. 187–201.

1006. Oblow, E. M. [1988], "Foundations of O-theory: Measurements and relation to fuzzy set theory." *Intern. J. of General Systems*, **14**(4), pp. 357–378.

1007. Ogawa, Y., T. Morita and K. Kobayashi [1991], "A fuzzy document retrieval system using the keyword connection matrix and a learning method." *Fuzzy Sets and Systems*, **39**(2), pp. 163–179.

1008. Oguntade, O. O. and P. E. Beaumont [1982], "Ophthalmological prognosis via fuzzy subsets." *Fuzzy Sets and Systems*, **7**(2), pp. 123–138.

1009. Oguntade, O. O. and J. S. Gero [1981], "Evaluation of architectural design profiles using fuzzy sets." *Fuzzy Sets and Systems*, **5**(3), pp. 221–234.

1010. Oh, K. W. and W. Bandler [1987], "Properties of fuzzy implication operators." *Intern. J. of Approximate Reasoning*, **1**(3), pp. 273–285.

1011. Ohsato, A. and T. Sekiguchi [1988], "Convexly combined fuzzy relational equations and several aspects of their application to fuzzy information processing." *Information Sciences*, **45**(2), pp. 275–313.

1012. Ohtani, Y. and T. Yoshimura [1994], "Fuzzy control of a manipulator using the switching motion of brakes." *Intern. J. of Systems Science*, **25**(6), pp. 979–989.

1013. Oliveira, J. V. d. [1993], "Neuron inspired learning rules for fuzzy relational structures." *Fuzzy Sets and Systems*, **57**(1), pp. 41–53.

1014. Ollero, A. and A. J. García–Cerezo [1989], "Direct digital control, auto-tuning and supervision using fuzzy logic." *Fuzzy Sets and Systems*, **30**(2), pp. 135–153.

1015. Onisawa, T. [1988], "An approach to human reliability in man-machine systems using error possibility." *Fuzzy Sets and Systems*, **27**(2), pp. 87–103.

1016. Onisawa, T. [1990], "An application of fuzzy concepts to modelling of reliability analysis." *Fuzzy Sets and Systems*, **37**(3), pp. 267–286.

1017. Onisawa, T. [1991], "Fuzzy reliability assessment considering the influence of many factors on reliability." *Intern. J. of Approximate Reasoning*, **5**(3), pp. 265–280.

1018. Onisawa, T. and Y. Nishiwaki [1988], "Fuzzy human reliability analysis on the Chernobyl accident." *Fuzzy Sets and Systems*, **28**(2), pp. 115–127.

1019. Orlovsky, S. A. [1978], "Decision-making with a fuzzy preference relation." *Fuzzy Sets and Systems*, **1**(3), pp. 155–167.

1020. Orlowska, E. [1988], "Representation of vague information." *Information Systems*, **13**(2), pp. 167–174.

1021. Osgood, C. E., G. J. Suci and P. H. Tannenbaum [**1957**], *The Measurement of Meaning*. University of Illinois Press, Urbana.

1022. Ostaszewski, K. [**1993**], *An Investigation into Possible Applications of Fuzzy Set Methods in Actuarial Science*. Society of Actuaries, Schaumburg, Illinois.

1023. Östermark, R. [1988], "Profit apportionment in concerns with mutual ownership – An application of fuzzy inequalities." *Fuzzy Sets and Systems*, **26**(3), pp. 283–297.

1024. Ostertag, E. and M. J. Carvalho–Ostertag [1993], "Fuzzy control of an inverted pendulum with fuzzy compensation of friction forces." *Intern. J. of Systems Science*, **24**(10), pp. 1915–1922.

1025. Otto, K. N. and E. K. Antonsson [1991], "Trade-off strategies in engineering design." *Research in Engineering Design*, **3**(2), pp. 87–104.

1026. Otto, K. N. and E. K. Antonsson [1993a], "Extensions to the Taguchi method of product design." *ASME J. of Mechanical Design*, **115**(1), pp. 5–13.

1027. Otto, K. N. and E. K. Antonsson [1993b], "Tuning parameters in engineering design." *ASME J. of Mechanical Design*, **115**(1), pp. 14–19.

1028. Otto, K. N., D. Lewis and E. K. Antonsson [1993a], "Determining optimal points of membership with dependent variables." *Fuzzy Sets and Systems*, **60**(1), pp. 19–24.

1029. Otto, K. N., D. Lewis and E. K. Antonsson [1993b], "Approximating α-cuts with the vertex method." *Fuzzy Sets and Systems*, **55**(1), pp. 43–50.

1030. Otto, M. and R. R. Yager [1992], "An application of approximate reasoning to chemical knowledge." *Revue Intern. de Systémique*, **6**(5), pp. 465–481.

1031. Ouyang, M. and Z. F. Su [1985], "An application of possibility theory: the evaluation of availability of acupuncture anesthesia." *Fuzzy Sets and Systems*, **16**(2), pp. 115–121.

1032. Ovchinnikov, S. V. [1981a], "Structure of fuzzy binary relations." *Fuzzy Sets and Systems*, **6**(2), pp. 169–195.

1033. Ovchinnikov, S. V. [1981b], "Innovations in fuzzy set theory." *Proc. Eleventh IEEE Intern. Symp. on Multi-Valued Logic, Norman, Oklahoma*, pp. 226–227.

1034. Ovchinnikov, S. V. [1983], "General negations in fuzzy set theory." *J. of Math. Analysis and Applications*, **92**(1), pp. 234–239.

1035. Ovchinnikov, S. V. [1984], "Representations of transitive fuzzy relations." In: Skala, H. J., S. Termini and E. Trillas, eds., *Aspects of Vagueness*. D. Reidel, Boston, pp. 105–118.

1036. Ovchinnikov, S. V. [1989], "Transitive fuzzy orderings of fuzzy numbers." *Fuzzy Sets and Systems*, **30**(3), pp. 283–295.

1037. Ovchinnikov, S. V. [1991a], "Similarity relations, fuzzy partitions, and fuzzy orderings." *Fuzzy Sets and Systems*, **40**(1), pp. 107–126.

1038. Ovchinnikov, S. V. [1991b], "The duality principle in fuzzy set theory." *Fuzzy Sets and Systems*, **42**(1), pp. 133–144.

1039. Ovchinnikov, S. V. and M. Migdal [1987], "On ranking fuzzy sets." *Fuzzy Sets and Systems*, **24**(1), pp. 113–116.

1040. Paass, G. [1992], "Probabilistic reasoning and probabilistic neural networks." *Intern. J. of Intelligent Systems*, **7**(1), pp. 47–59.

1041. Pal, S. K. and D. Bhandari [1994], "Genetic algorithms with fuzzy fitness function for object extraction using cellular networks." *Fuzzy Sets and Systems*, **65**(2–3), pp. 129–139.

1042. Pal, S. K. and B. Chakraborty [1986], "Fuzzy set theoretic measure for automatic feature evaluation." *IEEE Trans. on Systems, Man, and Cybernetics*, **16**(5), pp. 754–760.

1043. Pal, S. K. and A. Ghosh [1992], "Fuzzy geometry in image analysis." *Fuzzy Sets and Systems*, **48**(1), pp. 23–40.

1044. Pal, S. K. and R. A. King [1981], "Image enhancement using smoothing with fuzzy sets." *IEEE Trans. on Systems, Man, and Cybernetics*, **11**(7), pp. 494–501.

1045. Pal, S. K. and D. K. D. Majumder [**1986**], *Fuzzy Mathematical Approach to Pattern Recognition*. John Wiley, New York.

1046. Pal, S. K. and S. Mitra [1992], "Multilayer perceptron, fuzzy sets, and classification." *IEEE Trans. on Neural Networks*, **3**(5), pp. 683–697.

1047. Pal, S. K. and S. Mitra [1994], "Fuzzy version of Kohonen's net and MLP-based classification: Performance evaluation for certain nonconvex decision regions." *Information Sciences: Intelligent Systems*, **76**(3–4), pp. 297–337.

1048. Palm, R. [1989], "Fuzzy controller for a sensor–guided robot manipulator." *Fuzzy Sets and Systems*, **31**(2), pp. 133–149.

1049. Palm, R. [1992], "Control of a redundant manipulator using fuzzy rules." *Fuzzy Sets and Systems*, **45**(3), pp. 279–298.

1050. Pao, Y. [**1989**], *Adaptive Pattern Recognition and Neural Networks*. Addison–Wesley, Reading, Mass.

1051. Pap, E. [1994], "The range of null-additive fuzzy and non-fuzzy measures." *Fuzzy Sets and Systems*, **65**(1), pp. 105–115.

1052. Pappis, C. P. and E. H. Mamdani [1977], "A fuzzy logic controller for a traffic junction." *IEEE Trans. on Systems, Man, and Cybernetics*, **7**(10), pp. 707–717.

1053. Pardo, L. [1985], "Information energy of a fuzzy event and a partition of fuzzy events." *IEEE Trans. on Systems, Man, and Cybernetics*, **15**(1), pp. 139–144.

1054. Park, D., Z. Cao and A. Kandel [1992], "Investigations on the applicability of fuzzy inference." *Fuzzy Sets and Systems*, **49**(2), pp. 151–169.

1055. Park, D., A. Kandel and G. Langholz [1994], "Genetic-based new fuzzy reasoning models with application to fuzzy control." *IEEE Trans. on Systems, Man, and Cybernetics*, **24**(1), pp. 39–47.

1056. Park, K. S. [1987], "Fuzzy set theoretic interpretation of economic order quantity." *IEEE Trans. on Systems, Man, and Cybernetics*, **17**(6), pp. 1082–1084.

1057. Park, K. S. and J. S. Kim [1990], "Fuzzy weighted–checklist with linguistic variables." *IEEE Trans. on Reliability*, **39**(3), pp. 389–393.

1058. Parkinson, W. J., P. D. Shalek, K. H. Duerre, G. F. Luger and M. Jamshidi [1993], "Two intelligent control systems for silicon carbide whisker production." *J. of Intelligent & Fuzzy Systems*, **1**(3), pp. 199–214.

1059. Pathak, A. and S. K. Pal [1986], "Fuzzy grammars in syntactic recognition of skeletal maturity from X–rays." *IEEE Trans. on Systems, Man, and Cybernetics*, **16**(5), pp. 657–667.

1060. Patrikar, A. and J. Provence [1993], "Control of dynamic systems using fuzzy logic and neural networks." *Intern. J. of Intelligent Systems*, **8**(6), pp. 727–748.

1061. Pavelka, J. [1979], "On fuzzy logic I, II, III." *Zeitschrift für Math. Logik und Grundlagen der Mathematik*, **25**(1), pp. 45–52, **25**(2), pp.119–134, **25**(5), pp. 447–464.

1062. Pawlak, Z. [1982], "Rough sets." *Intern. J. of Computer and Information Sciences*, **11**(5), pp. 341–356.

1063. Pawlak, Z. **[1991]**, *Rough Sets: Theoretical Aspects of Reasoning About Data*. Kluwer, Boston.

1064. Pedrycz, W. [1981], "An approach to the analysis of fuzzy systems." *Intern. J. of Control*, **34**(3), pp. 403–421.

1065. Pedrycz, W. [1983a], "Some applicational aspects of fuzzy relational equations in systems analysis." *Intern. J. of General Systems*, **9**(3), pp. 125–132.

1066. Pedrycz, W. [1983b], "Fuzzy relational equations with generalized connectives and their applications." *Fuzzy Sets and Systems*, **10**(2), pp. 185–201.

1067. Pedrycz, W. [1983c], "Numerical and applicational aspects of fuzzy relational equations." *Fuzzy Sets and Systems*, **11**(1), pp. 1–18.

1068. Pedrycz, W. [1984a], "An identification algorithm in fuzzy relational systems." *Fuzzy Sets and Systems*, **13**(2), pp. 153–167.

1069. Pedrycz, W. [1984b], "Identification in fuzzy systems." *IEEE Trans. on Systems, Man, and Cybernetics*, **14**(2), pp. 361–366.

1070. Pedrycz, W. [1985a], "Structured fuzzy models." *Cybernetics and Systems*, **16**(1), pp. 103–117.

1071. Pedrycz, W. [1985b], "Applications of fuzzy relational equations for methods of reasoning in presence of fuzzy data." *Fuzzy Sets and Systems*, **16**(2), pp. 163–175.

1072. Pedrycz, W. [1987], "Fuzzy models and relational equations." *Mathematical Modelling*, **9**(6), pp. 427–434.

1073. Pedrycz, W. [1988], "Approximate solutions of fuzzy relational equations." *Fuzzy Sets and Systems*, **28**(2), pp. 183–202.

1074. Pedrycz, W. **[1989]**, *Fuzzy Control and Fuzzy Systems*. John Wiley, New York.

1075. Pedrycz, W. [1990a], "Fuzzy systems: Analysis and synthesis from theory to applications." *Intern. J. of General Systems*, **17**(2–3), pp. 135–156.

1076. Pedrycz, W. [1990b], "Fuzzy sets in pattern recognition methodology and methods." *Pattern Recognition*, **23**(1–2), pp. 121–146.

1077. Pedrycz, W. [1990c], "Inverse problem in fuzzy relational equations." *Fuzzy Sets and Systems*, **36**(2), pp. 277–291.

1078. Pedrycz, W. [1990d], "Fuzzy set framework for development of a perception perspective." *Fuzzy Sets and Systems*, **37**(2), pp. 123–137.

1079. Pedrycz, W. [1991a], "Fuzzy logic in development of fundamentals of pattern recognition." *Intern. J. of Approximate Reasoning*, **5**(3), pp. 251–264.

1080. Pedrycz, W. [1991b], "Neurocomputations in relational systems." *IEEE Trans. on Pattern Analysis and Machine Intelligence*, **13**(3), pp. 289–297.

1081. Pedrycz, W. [1991c], "Processing in relational structures: Fuzzy relational equations." *Fuzzy Sets and Systems*, **40**(1), pp. 77–106.

1082. Pedrycz, W. [1992a], "Fuzzy neural networks with reference neurons as pattern classifiers." *IEEE Trans. on Neural Networks*, **3**(5), pp. 770–775.

1083. Pedrycz, W. [1992b], "Associations of fuzzy sets." *IEEE Trans. on Systems, Man, and Cybernetics*, **22**(6), pp. 1483–1488.

1084. Pedrycz, W. [1993a], "Fuzzy neural networks and neurocomputations." *Fuzzy Sets and Systems*, **56**(1), pp. 1–28.

1085. Pedrycz, W. [1993b], "Fuzzy controllers: Principles and architectures." *Asia-Pacific Engineering J.*, **3**(1–2), pp. 1–32.

1086. Pedrycz, W. [1994a], "Why triangular membership functions?" *Fuzzy Sets and Systems*, **64**(1), pp. 21–30.

1087. Pedrycz, W. [1994b], "Neural structures of fuzzy decision-making." *J. of Intelligent & Fuzzy Systems*, **2**(2), pp. 161–178.

1088. Pedrycz, W., G. Bortolan and R. Degani [1991], "Classification of electrocardiographic signals: A fuzzy pattern matching approach." *Artificial Intelligence in Medicine*, **3**(4), pp. 211–226.

1089. Pedrycz, W. and F. Gomide [1994], "A generalized fuzzy Petri net model." *IEEE Trans. on Fuzzy Systems*, **2**(4), pp. 295–301.

1090. Pedrycz, W. and A. F. Rocha [1993], "Fuzzy–set based models of neurons and knowledge-based networks." *IEEE Trans. on Fuzzy Systems*, **1**(4), pp. 254–266.

1091. Peeva, K. [1991], "Fuzzy acceptors for syntactic pattern recognition." *Intern. J. of Approximate Reasoning*, **5**(3), pp. 291–306.

1092. Peng, X. T. [1990], "Generating rules for fuzzy logic controllers by functions." *Fuzzy Sets and Systems*, **36**(1), pp. 83–89.

1093. Peng, X. T., A. Kandel and P. Z. Wang [1991], "Concepts, rules, and fuzzy reasoning: A factor space approach." *IEEE Trans. on Systems, Man, and Cybernetics*, **21**(1), pp. 194–205.

1094. Peres, A. [1992], "Emergence of local realism in fuzzy observations of correlated quantum systems." *Found. Physis.*, **22**(6), pp. 819–828.

1095. Peters, G. [1994], "Fuzzy linear regression with fuzzy intervals." *Fuzzy Sets and Systems*, **63**(1), pp. 45–55.

1096. Petry, F. E., P. J. Chang, J. R. Adams–Webber and K. M. Ford [1991], "An approach to knowledge acquisition based on the structure of personal construct systems." *IEEE Trans. on Knowledge and Data Engineering*, **3**(1), pp. 78–88.

1097. Pham, D. T. and E. J. Bayro–Corrochano [1994], "Self-organizing neural-network-based pattern clustering method with fuzzy outputs." *Pattern Recognition*, **27**(8), pp. 1103–1110.

1098. Pham, T. D. and S. Valliappan [1994], "A least squares model for fuzzy rules of inference." *Fuzzy Sets and Systems*, **64**(2), pp. 207–212.

1099. Pienkowski, A. E. K. [**1989**], *Artificial Colour Perception Using Fuzzy Techniques in Digital Image Processing*. Verlag TÜV Rheinland, Köln.

1100. Pin, F. G. [1993], "Steps toward sensor-based vehicle navigation in outdoor environments using a fuzzy behaviorist approach." *J. of Intelligent & Fuzzy Systems*, **1**(2), pp. 95–107.

1101. Pinkava, V. [1976], "Fuzzification of binary and finite multivalued logic calculi." *Intern. J. of Man-Machine Studies*, **8**(6), pp. 717–730.

1102. Piskunov, A. [1992], "Fuzzy implication in fuzzy systems control." *Fuzzy Sets and Systems*, **45**(1), pp. 25–35.

1103. Ponsard, C. [1981], "An application of fuzzy subsets theory to the analysis of consumer's spatial preferences." *Fuzzy Sets and Systems*, **5**(3), pp. 235–244.

1104. Ponsard, C. [1988], "Fuzzy mathematical models in economics." *Fuzzy Sets and Systems*, **28**(3), pp. 273–283.

1105. Ponsard, C. and B. Fustier, eds. [**1986**], *Fuzzy Economics and Spatial Analysis*. Librairie de L'Université, Dijon, France.

1106. Popchrb, I. and V. Peneva [1993], "An algorithm for comparison of fuzzy sets." *Fuzzy Sets and Systems*, **60**(1), pp. 59–65.

1107. Prade, H. [1980], "Operations research with fuzzy data." In: Wang, P. P. and S. K. Chang, eds., *Fuzzy Sets: Theory and Applications to Policy Analysis and Information Systems*. Plenum Press, New York, pp. 155–170.

1108. Prade, H. [1983], "Fuzzy programming: why and how? Some hints and examples." In: Wang, P. P., ed., *Advances in Fuzzy Sets, Possibility Theory, and Applications*. Plenum Press, New York, pp. 237–251.

1109. Prade, H. [1984], "Lipski's approach to incomplete-information data bases, restated and generalized in the setting of Zadeh's possibility theory." *Information Systems*, **9**(1), pp. 27–42.

1110. Prade, H. [1985], "A computational approach to approximate and plausible reasoning with applications to expert systems." *IEEE Trans. on Pattern Analysis and Machine Intelligence*, **7**(3), pp. 260–283.

1111. Prade, H. and D. Dubois [1988a], "The treatment of uncertainty in knowledge-based systems using fuzzy sets and possibility theory." *Intern. J. of Intelligent Systems*, **3**(2), pp. 141–165.

1112. Prade, H. and D. Dubois [1988b], "Default reasoning and possibility theory." *Artificial Intelligence*, **35**(2), pp. 243–257.

1113. Prade, H. and D. Dubois [1988c], "Representation and combination of uncertainty with belief functions and possibility measures." *Comput. Intell.*, **4**, pp. 244–264.

1114. Prade, H. and H. Farreny [1985], "A possibility theory-based approach to default and inexact reasoning." *Computers and Artificial Intelligence*, **4**, pp. 125–136.

1115. Prade, H. and C. V. Negoita, eds. [**1986**], *Fuzzy Logic in Knowledge Engineering*. Verlag TÜV Rheinland, Köln.

1116. Prade, H. and C. Testemale [1984], "Generalizing database relational algebra for the treatment of incomplete or uncertain information and vague queries." *Information Sciences*, **34**(2), pp. 115–143.

1117. Prevot, M. [1981], "Algorithm for the solution of fuzzy relations." *Fuzzy Sets and Systems*, **5**(3), pp. 319–322.

1118. Procyk, T. J. and E. H. Mamdani [1979], "A linguistic self-organizing process controller." *Automatica*, **15**(1), pp. 15–30.

1119. Puri, M. L. and D. A. Ralescu [1983], "Differentials for fuzzy functions." *J. of Math. Analysis and Applications*, **91**(2), pp. 552–558.

1120. Puri, M. L. and D. A. Ralescu [1986], "Fuzzy random variables." *J. of Math. Analysis and Applications*, **114**(2), pp. 409–422.

1121. Pykacz, J. [1992], "Fuzzy set ideas in quantum logics—Part 1: Quantum logics." *Intern. J. of Theoretical Physics*, **31**(9), pp. 1767–1783.

1122. Qian, D. Q. [1992], "Representation and use of

imprecise temporal knowledge in dynamic systems." *Fuzzy Sets and Systems*, **50**(1), pp. 59–77.

1123. Qiao, Z., Y. Zhang and G. Y. Wang [1994], "On fuzzy random linear programming." *Fuzzy Sets and Systems*, **65**(1), pp. 31–49.

1124. Radecki, T. [1981], "Outline of a fuzzy logic approach to information retrieval." *Intern. J. of Man-Machine Studies*, **14**(2), pp. 169–178.

1125. Radecki, T. [1983], "A theoretical background for applying fuzzy set theory in information retrieval." *Fuzzy Sets and Systems*, **10**(2), pp. 169–183.

1126. Ragot, R. and M. Lamotte [1993], "Fuzzy logic control." *Intern. J. of Systems Science*, **24**(10), pp. 1825–1848.

1127. Raha, S. and K. S. Ray [1992], "Analogy between approximate reasoning and the method of interpolation." *Fuzzy Sets and Systems*, **51**(3), pp. 259–266.

1128. Raha, S. and K. S. Ray [1993], "Approximate reasoning based on generalized disjunctive syllogism." *Fuzzy Sets and Systems*, **61**(2), pp. 143–152.

1129. Raju, G. V. S. and J. Zhou [1993], "Adaptive hierarchical fuzzy controller." *IEEE Trans. on Systems, Man, and Cybernetics*, **23**(4), pp. 973–980.

1130. Raju, K. V. and A. K. Majumdar [1987], "The study of joins in fuzzy relational databases." *Fuzzy Sets and Systems*, **21**(1), pp. 19–34.

1131. Raju, K. V. and A. K. Majumdar [1988], "Fuzzy functional dependencies and lossless join decomposition of fuzzy relational database systems." *ACM Trans. on Database Systems*, **13**, pp. 129–166.

1132. Ralescu, D. [1982], "Toward a general theory of fuzzy variables." *J. of Math. Analysis and Applications*, **86**(1), pp. 176–193.

1133. Ramer, A. [1987], "Uniqueness of information measure in the theory of evidence." *Fuzzy Sets and Systems*, **24**(2), pp. 183–196.

1134. Ramer, A. [1989], "Conditional possibility measures." *Cybernetics and Systems*, **20**(3), pp. 233–247.

1135. Ramer, A. and G. J. Klir [1993], "Measures of discord in the Dempster–Shafer theory." *Information Sciences*, **67**(1–2), pp. 35–50.

1136. Ramer, A. and L. Lander [1987], "Classification of possibilistic uncertainty and information functions." *Fuzzy Sets and Systems*, **24**(2), pp. 221–230.

1137. Ramesh, J. [1976], "Tolerance analysis using fuzzy sets." *Intern. J. of Systems Science*, **7**(12), pp. 1393–1401.

1138. Ramík, J. [1991], "Vaguely interrelated coefficients in PL as bicriterial optimization problem." *Intern. J. of General Systems*, **20**(1), pp. 99–114.

1139. Ramík, J. and K. Nakamura [1993], "Canonical fuzzy numbers of dimension two." *Fuzzy Sets and Systems*, **54**(2), pp. 167–180.

1140. Ramík, J. and J. Římánek [1985], "Inequality relation between fuzzy numbers and its use in fuzzy optimization." *Fuzzy Sets and Systems*, **16**(2), pp. 123–138.

1141. Rao, G. P. and D. A. Rutherford [1981], "Approximate reconstruction of mapping functions from linguistic descriptions in problems of fuzzy logic applied to system control." *Cybernetics and Systems*, **12**(3), pp. 225–236.

1142. Rapoport, A., T. S. Wallsten and J. A. Cox [1987], "Direct and indirect scaling of membership functions of probability phrases." *Mathematical Modelling*, **9**(6), pp. 397–417.

1143. Rasiowa, H. [1994], "Axiomatization and completeness of uncountably valued approximate logic." *Studia Logica*, **53**, pp. 137–160.

1144. Ray, A. K., B. Chatterjee and A. K. Majumdar [1991], "A formal power series approach to the construction of minimal fuzzy automata." *Information Sciences*, **55**(1–3), pp. 189–207.

1145. Ray, K. S. and D. Dutta Majumder [1984], "Application of circle criteria for stability analysis of linear SISO and MIMO systems associated with fuzzy logic controller." *IEEE Trans. on Systems, Man, and Cybernetics.*, **14**(2), pp. 345–349.

1146. Ray, K. S. and D. Dutta Majumder [1985], "Fuzzy logic control of a nonlinear multivariable steam generating unit using decoupling theory." *IEEE Trans. on Systems, Man, and Cybernetics*, **15**(4), pp. 539–558.

1147. Redden, D. T. and W. H. Woodall [1994], "Properties of certain fuzzy linear regression methods." *Fuzzy Sets and Systems*, **64**(3), pp. 361–375.

1148. Reddy, P. V. S. and M. S. Babu [1992], "Some methods of reasoning for fuzzy conditional propositions." *Fuzzy Sets and Systems*, **52**(3), pp. 229–250.

1149. Ren, P. [1990], "Generalized fuzzy sets and representation of incomplete knowledge." *Fuzzy Sets and Systems*, **36**(1), pp. 91–96.

1150. Rényi, A. **[1970]**, *Probability Theory*. North-Holland, New York.

1151. Requena, I., M. Delgado and J. L. Verdegay [1994], "Automatic ranking of fuzzy numbers with the criterion of a decision-maker learnt by an artificial neural network." *Fuzzy Sets and Systems*, **64**(1), pp. 1–19.

1152. Rescher, N. **[1969]**, *Many-Valued Logic*. McGraw-Hill, New York.

1153. Resconi, G., G. J. Klir and U. St.Clair [1992], "Hierarchical uncertainty metatheory based upon modal logic." *Intern. J. of General Systems*, **21**(1), pp. 23–50.

1154. Resconi, G., G. J. Klir, U. St. Clair and D. Harmanec [1993], "On the integration of uncertainty theories." *Intern. J. of Uncertainty, Fuzziness, and Knowledge–Based Systems*, **1**(1), pp. 1–18.

1155. Rhee, F. C. H. and R. Krishnapuram [1993], "Fuzzy rule generation methods for high–level computer vision." *Fuzzy Sets and Systems*, **60**(3), pp. 245–258.

1156. Roberts, D. W. [1989], "Analysis of forest succession with fuzzy graph theory." *Ecological Modelling*, **45**(4), pp. 261–274.

1157. Roberts, F. S. [**1979**], *Measurement Theory*. Addison–Wesley, Reading, MA.

1158. Rodabaugh, S., E. P. Klement and Y. Höhle, eds. [**1992**], *Applications of Category Theory to Fuzzy Subsets*. Kluwer, Boston.

1159. Rolland–May, C. [1991], "Automatical knowledge learning in an expert system for space management and planning." *Fuzzy Sets and Systems*, **44**(3), pp. 341–355.

1160. Rosenfeld, A. [1971], "Fuzzy groups." *J. of Math. Analysis and Applications*, **35**(3), pp. 512–517.

1161. Rosenfeld, A. [1975], "Fuzzy graphs." In: Zadeh, L. A., K. S. Fu, K. Tanaka and M. Shimura, eds., *Fuzzy Sets and Their Applications to Cognitive and Decision Processes*. Academic Press, New York, pp. 77–96.

1162. Rosenfeld, A. [1979], "Fuzzy digital topology." *Information and Control*, **40**(1), pp. 76–87.

1163. Rosenfeld, A. [1984], "The fuzzy geometry of image subsets." *Pattern Recognition Letters*, **2**, pp. 311–317.

1164. Ross, T. J., T. K. Hasselman, J. D. Chrostowski and S. J. Verzi [1993], "Fuzzy set methods for assessing uncertainty in the modeling and control of space structures." *J. of Intelligent & Fuzzy Systems*, **1**(2), pp. 135–155.

1165. Roubens, M. [1989], "Some properties of choice functions based on valued binary relations." *European J. of Operational Research*, **40**(3), pp. 309–321.

1166. Ruan, D., P. D'hondt, P. Govaerts and E. E. Kerre, eds. [**1994**], *Fuzzy Logic and Intelligent Technologies in Nuclear Science*. World Scientific, Singapore.

1167. Ruan, D. and E. E. Kerre [1993], "Fuzzy implication operators and generalized fuzzy method of cases." *Fuzzy Sets and Systems*, **54**(1), pp. 23–37.

1168. Rudeanu, S. [1993], "On Lukasiewicz–Moisil algebras of fuzzy sets." *Studia Logica*, **52**(1), pp. 95–111.

1169. Rundensteiner, E. A., L. W. Hawkes and W. Bandler [1989], "On nearness measures in fuzzy relational data models." *Intern. J. of Approximate Reasoning*, **3**(3), pp. 267–297.

1170. Ruspini, E. H. [1969], "A new approach to clustering." *Information and Control*, **15**(1), pp. 22–32.

1171. Ruspini, E. H. [1970], "Numerical methods for fuzzy clustering." *Information Sciences*, **2**(3), pp. 319–350.

1172. Ruspini, E. H. [1989], "The semantics of vague knowledge." *Revue Internationale de Systemique*, **3**(4), pp. 387–420.

1173. Ruspini, E. H. [1991a], "Approximate reasoning: Past, present, future." *Information Sciences*, **57–58**, pp. 297–317.

1174. Ruspini, E. H. [1991b], "On the semantics of fuzzy logic." *Intern. J. of Approximate Reasoning*, **5**(1), pp. 45–88.

1175. Ruspini, E. H., J. D. Lowrance and T. M. Strat [1992], "Understanding evidential reasoning." *Intern. J. of Approximate Reasoning*, **6**(3), pp. 401–424.

1176. Rutherford, D. A. and G. C. Bloore [1976], "The implementation of fuzzy algorithms for control." *Proc. IEEE*, **64**(4), pp. 572–573.

1177. Saade, J. J. [1994a], "Extension of fuzzy hypothesis testing with hybrid data." *Fuzzy Sets and Systems*, **63**(1), pp. 57–71.

1178. Saade, J. J. [1994b], "Towards intelligent radar systems." *Fuzzy Sets and Systems*, **63**(2), pp. 141–157.

1179. Saade, J. J. and H. Schwarzlander [1990], "Fuzzy hypothesis testing with hybrid data." *Fuzzy Sets and Systems*, **35**(2), pp. 197–212.

1180. Saade, J. J. and H. Schwarzlander [1992], "Ordering fuzzy sets over the real line: An approach based on decision making under uncertainty." *Fuzzy Sets and Systems*, **50**(3), pp. 237–246.

1181. Saade, J. J. and H. Schwarzlander [1994], "Application of fuzzy hypothesis testing to signal detection under uncertainty." *Fuzzy Sets and Systems*, **62**(1), pp. 9–19.

1182. Saaty, T. L. [1974], "Measuring of fuzziness of sets." *J. of Cybernetics*, **4**, pp. 53–61.

1183. Saaty, T. L. [1977], "A scaling method for priorities in hierarchical structures." *J. of Mathematical Psychology*, **15**(3), pp. 234–281.

1184. Saaty, T. L. [1978], "Exploring the interface between hierarchies, multiple objectives and fuzzy sets." *Fuzzy Sets and Systems*, **1**(1), pp. 57–68.

1185. Saaty, T. L. [1986], "Scaling the membership function." *European J. of Operational Research*, **25**(3), pp. 320–329.

1186. Saitta, L. and P. Torasso [1981], "Fuzzy characterization of coronary disease." *Fuzzy Sets and Systems*, **5**(3), pp. 245–258.

1187. Sakawa, M. [**1993**], *Fuzzy Sets and Interactive Multiobjective Optimization*. Plenum Press, New York.

1188. Sakawa, M. and H. Yano [1985a], "Interactive decision making for multiobjective linear fractional programming problems with fuzzy parameters." *Cybernetics and Systems*, **16**(4), pp. 377–394.

1189. Sakawa, M. and H. Yano [1985b], "An interactive fuzzy satisfying method using augmented minimax problems and its application to environmental systems." *IEEE Trans. on Systems, Man, and Cybernetics*, **15**(6), pp. 720–729.

1190. Sakawa, M. and H. Yano [1985c], "Interactive fuzzy decision-making for multi-objective non-linear programming using reference membership intervals." *Intern. J. of Man-Machine Studies*, **23**(4), pp. 407–421.

1191. Sakawa, M. and H. Yano [1991], "Feasibility and Pareto optimality for multiobjective nonlinear programming problems with fuzzy parameters." *Fuzzy Sets and Systems*, **43**(1), pp. 1–15.

1192. Sakawa, M. and H. Yano [1992], "Multiobjective fuzzy linear regression analysis for fuzzy input-output data." *Fuzzy Sets and Systems*, **47**(2), pp. 173–182.

1193. Sakawa, M., H. Yano and T. Yumine [1987], "An interactive fuzzy satisfying method for multiobjective linear-programming problems and its application." *IEEE Trans. on Systems, Man, and Cybernetics*, **17**(4), pp. 654–661.

1194. Salski, A. [1992], "Fuzzy knowledge-based models in ecological research." *Ecological Modelling*, **63**(1–4), pp. 103–112.

1195. Sanchez, E. [1976], "Resolution in composite fuzzy relation equations." *Information and Control*, **30**(1), pp. 38–48.

1196. Sanchez, E. [1977], "Solutions in composite fuzzy relation equations." In: Gupta, M. M., G. N. Saridis and B. R. Gaines, eds., *Fuzzy Automata and Decision Processes*. North-Holland, New York, pp. 221–234.

1197. Sanchez, E. [1979], "Medical diagnosis and composite fuzzy relations." In: Gupta, M. M., R. K. Ragade and R. R. Yager, eds., *Advances in Fuzzy Set Theory and Applications*. North-Holland, New York, pp. 437–444.

1198. Sanchez, E., ed. [**1984a**], *Fuzzy Information, Knowledge Representation and Decision Analysis*. Pergamon Press, Oxford.

1199. Sanchez, E. [1984b], "Solution of fuzzy equations with extended operations." *Fuzzy Sets and Systems*, **12**(3), pp. 237–248.

1200. Sanchez, E. [1986], "Medical applications with fuzzy sets." In: Jones, A., A. Kaufmann and H. J. Zimmermann, eds., *Fuzzy Sets Theory and Applications*. D. Reidel, Boston, pp. 331–347.

1201. Sanchez, E. [1993], "Fuzzy genetic algorithms in soft computing environment." *Proc. Fifth IFSA World Congress, Seoul*, Vol. I, pp. XLIV–L.

1202. Sanchez, E. and L. A. Zadeh, eds. [**1987**], *Approximate Reasoning in Intelligent Systems, Decision and Control*. Pergamon Press, Oxford, U. K.

1203. Santos, E. S. [1968], "Maximin automata." *Information and Control*, **13**(4), pp. 363–377.

1204. Santos, E. S. [1973], "Fuzzy sequential functions." *J. of Cybernetics*, **3**(3), pp. 15–31.

1205. Santos, E. S. [1975], "Realization of fuzzy languages by probabilistic, max-product and maximum automata." *Information Sciences*, **8**(1), pp. 39–53.

1206. Santos, E. S. and W. G. Wee [1968], "General information of sequential machines." *Information and Control*, **12**(1), pp. 5–10.

1207. Sarma, R. D. and N. Ajmal [1992], "Fuzzy nets and their application." *Fuzzy Sets and Systems*, **51**(1), pp. 41–52.

1208. Sarma, V. V. S. and S. Raju [1991], "Multisensor data fusion and decision support for airborne target identification." *IEEE Trans. on Systems, Man, and Cybernetics*, **21**(5), pp. 1224–1230.

1209. Sasaki, M. [1993], "Fuzzy functions." *Fuzzy Sets and Systems*, **55**(3), pp. 295–302.

1210. Sasaki, T. and T. Akiyama [1988], "Traffic control process of expressway by fuzzy logic." *Fuzzy Sets and Systems*, **26**(2), pp. 165–178.

1211. Sastri, V. N., R. N. Tiwari and K. Guo [1992], "Solution of optimal control problems with lumped parameters having single or multiple goal objectives in fuzzy environment." *Fuzzy Sets and Systems*, **48**(2), pp. 173–183.

1212. Sastry, N. V., K. S. Sastry and R. N. Tiwari [1993], "Spline membership function and its application in multiple objective fuzzy control problem." *Fuzzy Sets and Systems*, **55**(2), pp. 143–156.

1213. Sato, M. and Y. Sato [1994], "On a multicriteria fuzzy clustering method for 3–way data." *Intern. J. of Uncertainty, Fuzziness and Knowledge–Based Systems*, **2**(2), pp. 127–142.

1214. Savic, D. A. and W. Pedrycz [1991], "Evaluation of fuzzy linear regression models." *Fuzzy Sets and Systems*, **39**(1), pp. 51–64.

1215. Savinov, A. A. [1993], "Fuzzy propositional logic." *Fuzzy Sets and Systems*, **60**(1), pp. 9–17.

1216. Scarpelli, H. and F. Gomide [1993], "Fuzzy reasoning and fuzzy Petri nets in manufacturing systems modeling." *J. of Intelligent & Fuzzy Systems*, **1**(3), pp. 225–242.

1217. Scarpelli, H. and F. Gomide [1994], "A high level net approach for discovering potential inconsistencies in fuzzy knowledge bases." *Fuzzy Sets and Systems*, **64**(2), pp. 175–193.

1218. Schmucker, K. J. **[1984]**, *Fuzzy Sets, Natural Language Computations, and Risk Analysis*. Computer Science Press, Rockville, MD.

1219. Schneider, M. [1994], "On uncertainty management in fuzzy inference procedures." *Information Sciences*, **79**(3–4), pp. 181–190.

1220. Schneider, M., H. Lim and W. Shoaff [1992], "The utilization of fuzzy sets in the recognition of imperfect strings." *Fuzzy Sets and Systems*, **49**(3), pp. 331–337.

1221. Schneider, M. and A. Kandel **[1988]**, *Cooperative Fuzzy Expert Systems: Their Design and Applications in Intelligent Recognition*. Verlag TÜV Rheinland, Köln.

1222. Schneider, M. and A. Kandel [1988], "Properties of the fuzzy expected value and the fuzzy expected interval." *Fuzzy Sets and Systems*, **26**(3), pp. 373–385.

1223. Schödel, H. [1994], "Utilization of fuzzy techniques in intelligent sensors." *Fuzzy Sets and Systems*, **63**(3), pp. 271–292.

1224. Schott, B. and T. Whalen [1994], "Fuzzy uncertainty in imperfect competition." *Information Sciences: Intelligent Systems*, **76**(3–4), pp. 339–354.

1225. Schwartz, D. G. [1987], "Axioms for a theory of semantic equivalence." *Fuzzy Sets and Systems*, **21**(3), pp. 319–349.

1226. Schwartz, D. G. [1989], "Fuzzy inference in a formal theory of semantic equivalence." *Fuzzy Sets and Systems*, **31**(2), pp. 205–216.

1227. Schwartz, D. G. [1991], "A system for reasoning with imprecise linguistic information." *Intern. J. of Approximate Reasoning*, **5**(5), pp. 463–488.

1228. Schwartz, D. G. and G. J. Klir [1992], "Fuzzy logic flowers in Japan." *IEEE Spectrum*, **19**(2), pp. 32–35.

1229. Schweizer, B. and A. Sklar [1960], "Statistical metric spaces." *Pacific J. of Mathematics*, **10**, pp. 313–334.

1230. Schweizer, B. and A. Sklar [1961], "Associative functions and statistical triangle inequalities." *Publ. Math. Debrecen*, **8**, pp. 169–186.

1231. Schweizer, B. and A. Sklar [1963], "Associative functions and abstract semigroups." *Publ. Math. Debrecen*, **10**, pp. 69–81.

1232. Schweizer, B. and A. Sklar **[1983]**, *Probabilistic Metric Spaces*. North-Holland, New York.

1233. Selim, S. Z. and M. S. Kamel [1992], "On the mathematical and numerical properties of the fuzzy c-means algorithm." *Fuzzy Sets and Systems*, **49**(2), pp. 181–191.

1234. Seo, F. and I. Nishizaki [1992], "On construction of a cooperative fuzzy game in international fuzzy decision environment: A possibilistic approach." *Control and Cybernetics*, **21**(1), pp. 277–294.

1235. Seo, F. and M. Sakawa [1985], "Fuzzy multiattribute utility analysis for collective choice." *IEEE Trans. on Systems, Man, and Cybernetics*, **15**(1), pp. 45–53.

1236. Seselja, B. and A. Tepavcevic [1994], "Representation of lattices by fuzzy sets." *Information Sciences*, **79**(3–4), pp. 171–180.

1237. Sessa, S. [1984], "Some results in the setting of fuzzy relation equations theory." *Fuzzy Sets and Systems*, **14**(3), pp. 281–297.

1238. Sessa, S. [1989], "Finite fuzzy relation equations with unique solution in complete Brouwerian lattices." *Fuzzy Sets and Systems*, **29**(1), pp. 103–113.

1239. Shackle, G. L. S. **[1961]**, *Decision, Order and Time in Human Affairs*. Cambridge University Press, New York and Cambridge, U. K.

1240. Shafer, G. **[1976]**, *A Mathematical Theory of Evidence*. Princeton University Press, Princeton.

1241. Shafer, G. [1978], "Non-additive probabilities in the work of Bernoulli and Lambert." *Archive of History of Exact Sciences*, **19**(4), pp. 309–370.

1242. Shafer, G. [1981], "Jeffrey's rule of conditioning." *Philosophy of Science*, **48**(3), pp. 337–362.

1243. Shafer, G. [1987], "Belief functions and possibility measures." In: Bezdek, J. C., ed., *Analysis of Fuzzy Information (Vol. 1: Mathematics and Logic)*. CRC Press, Boca Raton, FL, pp. 51–84.

1244. Shan, S. M. and R. Horvath [1994], "A hardware digital fuzzy inference engine using standard integrated circuits." *Information Sciences: Applications*, **1**(1), pp. 1–7.

1245. Shannon, C. E. [1948], "The mathematical theory of communication." *The Bell System Technical J.*, **27**, pp. 379–423, 623–656.

1246. Shannon, C. E. and W. Weaver **[1964]**, *The Mathematical Theory of Communication*. University of Illinois Press, Urbana, Ill.

1247. Shao, S. H. [1988], "Fuzzy self-organizing controller and its application for dynamic processes." *Fuzzy Sets and Systems*, **26**(2), pp. 151–164.

1248. Shao, S. Y. and W. M. Wu [1990], "A method of graph and fuzzy techniques for Chinese character recognition." *Fuzzy Sets and Systems*, **36**(1), pp. 97–102.

1249. Sharpe, R. N., M. Chow, S. Briggs and L. Windingland [1994], "A methodology using fuzzy logic to optimize feedforward artificial neural network configurations." *IEEE Trans. on Systems, Man, and Cybernetics*, **24**(5), pp. 760–768.

1250. Shashi, M., K. Raju and P. S. Avadhani [1994], "Reasoning with fuzzy censors." *IEEE Trans. on Systems, Man, and Cybernetics*, **24**(7), pp. 1061–1064.

1251. Shaw, I. S. and J. J. Krüger [1992], "New fuzzy learning model with recursive estimation for dynamic systems." *Fuzzy Sets and Systems*, **48**(2), pp. 217–229.

1252. Shen, Q. and R. Leitch [1993], "Fuzzy qualitative simulation." *IEEE Trans. on Systems, Man, and Cybernetics*, **23**(4), pp. 1038–1061.

1253. Shen, Z. L., H. C. Lui and L. Y. Ding [1994], "Approximate case-based reasoning on neural networks." *Intern. J. of Approximate Reasoning*, **10**(1), pp. 75–98.

1254. Shenoi, S. and A. Melton [1989], "Proximity relations in the fuzzy relational database model." *Fuzzy Sets and Systems*, **31**(3), pp. 285–296.

1255. Shenoi, S. and A. Melton [1990], "An extended version of the fuzzy relational database model." *Information Sciences*, **52**(1), pp. 35–52.

1256. Shenoi, S., A. Melton and L. T. Fan [1990], "An equivalence classes model of fuzzy relational databases." *Fuzzy Sets and Systems*, **38**(2), pp. 153–170.

1257. Shenoi, S., A. Melton and L. T. Fan [1992], "Functional dependencies and normal forms in the fuzzy relational database model." *Information Sciences*, **60**(1), pp. 1–28.

1258. Shenoy, P. P. [1989], "A valuation-based language for expert systems." *Intern. J. of Approximate Reasoning*, **3**(5), pp. 383–412.

1259. Shenoy, P. P. [1992], "Using possibility theory in expert systems." *Fuzzy Sets and Systems*, **52**(2), pp. 129–142.

1260. Shenoy, P. P. [1994a], "Conditional independence in valuation-based systems." *Intern. J. of Approximate Reasoning*, **10**(3), pp. 203–234.

1261. Shenoy, P. P. [1994b], "Representing conditional independence relation by valuation networks." *Intern. J. of Uncertainty, Fuzziness and Knowledge-Based Systems*, **2**(2), pp. 143–165.

1262. Shih, F. Y. and G. P. Chen [1994], "Classification of Landsat remote sensing images by a fuzzy unsupervised clustering algorithm." *Information Sciences: Applications*, **1**(2), pp. 97–116.

1263. Shimura, M. [1973], "Fuzzy sets concept in rank-ordering objects." *J. of Math. Analysis and Applications*, **43**(3), pp. 717–733.

1264. Shiraishi, N., H. Furuta, M. Umano and K. Kawakami [1991], "An expert system for damage assessment of a reinforced concrete bridge deck." *Fuzzy Sets and Systems*, **44**(3), pp. 449–457.

1265. Shnaider, E. and A. Kandel [1989], "The use of fuzzy set theory for forecasting corporate tax revenues." *Fuzzy Sets and Systems*, **31**(2), pp. 187–204.

1266. Shnaider, E., T. Lynch and W. Bandler [1993], "Implication operators versus regression analysis: Application to time series data." *Intern. J. of Intelligent Systems*, **8**(9), pp. 895–920.

1267. Shoureshi, R. and K. Rahmani [1992], "Derivation and application of an expert fuzzy optimal control system." *Fuzzy Sets and Systems*, **49**(2), pp. 93–101.

1268. Silverman, B. G. [1987], "Distributed inference and fusion algorithms for real-time supervisory controller positions." *IEEE Trans. on Systems, Man, and Cybernetics*, **17**(2), pp. 230–239.

1269. Silvert, W. [1979], "Symmetric summation: A class of operations on fuzzy sets." *IEEE Trans. on Systems, Man, and Cybernetics*, **9**(10), pp. 657–659.

1270. Silvert, W. [1981], "The formulation and evaluation of predictions." *Intern. J. of General Systems*, **7**(3), pp. 189–205.

1271. Sim, J. R. and Z. Wang [1990], "Fuzzy measures and fuzzy integrals: An overview." *Intern. J. of General Systems*, **17**(2–3), pp. 321–405.

1272. Simpson, P. K. [1992], "Fuzzy min-max neural networks, Part 1: Classification." *IEEE Trans. on Neural Networks*, **3**(5), pp. 776–786.

1273. Simpson, P. K. [1993], "Fuzzy min-max neural networks. Part 2: Clustering." *IEEE Trans. on Fuzzy Systems*, **1**(1), pp. 32–45.

1274. Singer, D. [1992], "A fuzzy set approach to non-equilibrium thermodynamics." *Fuzzy Sets and Systems*, **47**(1), pp. 39–48.

1275. Singer, D. [1994], "A possibilistic approach to dimensional analysis methods." *Fuzzy Sets and Systems*, **61**(3), pp. 285–296.

1276. Singer, D. and P. G. Singer [1993], "Fuzzy chemicals kinetics: An algorithmic approach." *Intern. J. of Systems Science*, **24**(7), pp. 1363–1376.

1277. Sinha, D. and E. R. Dougherty [1993], "Fuzzification of set inclusion: Theory and applications." *Fuzzy Sets and Systems*, **55**(1), pp. 15–42.

1278. Siy, P. and C. S. Chen [1974], "Fuzzy logic for handwritten numeral character recognition." *IEEE Trans. on Systems, Man, and Cybernetics*, **4**(6), pp. 570–575.

1279. Skala, H. J. [1978], "On many-valued logics, fuzzy sets, fuzzy logics and their applications." *Fuzzy Sets and Systems*, **1**(2), pp. 129–149.

1280. Skala, H. J., S. Termini and E. Trillas, eds. [1984], *Aspects of Vagueness*. D. Reidel, Boston.

1281. Slowinski, R., ed. [1992], *Intelligent Decision Support: Handbook of Applications and Advances of the Rough Sets Theory*. Kluwer, Boston.

1282. Slowinski, R. and J. Teghem [1988], "Fuzzy versus stochastic approaches to multicriteria linear programming under uncertainty." *Naval Research Logistics*, **35**(6), pp. 673–695.

1283. Slowinski, R. and J. Teghem, eds. **[1990]**, *Stochastic Versus Fuzzy Approaches to Multiobjective Mathematical Programming under Uncertainty*. Kluwer, Boston.

1284. Smets, P. [1981a], "The degree of belief in a fuzzy event." *Information Sciences*, **25**(1), pp. 1–19.

1285. Smets, P. [1981b], "Medical diagnosis: Fuzzy sets and degrees of belief." *Fuzzy Sets and Systems*, **5**(3), pp. 259–266.

1286. Smets, P. [1983], "Information content of an evidence." *Intern. J. of Man-Machine Studies*, **19**(1), pp. 33–43.

1287. Smets, P. [1991], "Varieties of ignorance and the need for well-founded theories." *Information Sciences*, **57–58**, pp. 135–144.

1288. Smets, P. and P. Magrez [1987], "Implication in fuzzy logic." *Intern. J. of Approximate Reasoning*, **1**(4), pp. 327–347.

1289. Smets, P. and P. Magrez [1988], "The measure of the degree of truth and the grade of membership." *Fuzzy Sets and Systems*, **25**(1), pp. 67–72.

1290. Smets, P., E. H. Mamdani, D. Dubois and H. Prade, eds. **[1988]**, *Non-Standard Logics for Automated Reasoning*. Academic Press, New York.

1291. Smithson, M. [1982a], "Applications of fuzzy set concepts to behavioral sciences." *J. of Mathematical Social Sciences*, **2**, pp. 257–274.

1292. Smithson, M. [1982b], "Models for fuzzy nominal data." *Theory and Decision*, **14**(1), pp. 51–74.

1293. Smithson, M. **[1987]**, *Fuzzy Sets Analysis for Behavioral and Social Sciences*. Springer–Verlag, New York.

1294. Smithson, M. [1988], "Fuzzy set theory and the social sciences: The scope for applications." *Fuzzy Sets and Systems*, **26**(1), pp. 1–21.

1295. Smithson, M. **[1989]**, *Ignorance and Uncertainty: Emerging Paradigms*. Springer–Verlag, New York.

1296. Smithson, M. [1991], "A comment on Milan Zeleny's 'cognitive equilibrium'." *Intern. J. of General Systems*, **19**(4), pp. 425–433.

1297. Soman, K. P. and K. B. Misra [1993], "Fuzzy fault tree analysis using resolution identity." *J. of Fuzzy Mathematics*, **1**(1), pp. 193–212.

1298. Son, J. C., I. Song, S. Kim and S. I. Park [1993], "An application of generalized Neyman–Pearson fuzzy test to stochastic–signal detection." *IEEE Trans. on Systems, Man, and Cybernetics*, **23**(5), pp. 1474–1481.

1299. Song, J. J. and S. Park [1993], "A fuzzy dynamic learning controller for chemical process control." *Fuzzy Sets and Systems*, **54**(2), pp. 121–133.

1300. Song, Q. and G. Bortolan [1994], "Some properties of defuzzification neural networks." *Fuzzy Sets and Systems*, **61**(1), pp. 83–90.

1301. Song, Q. and B. S. Chissom [1993], "Forecasting enrollments with fuzzy time series – Part I." *Fuzzy Sets and Systems*, **54**(1), pp. 1–9.

1302. Song, Q. and B. S. Chissom [1994], "Forecasting enrollments with fuzzy time series – Part II." *Fuzzy Sets and Systems*, **62**(1), pp. 1–8.

1303. Sosnowski, Z. A. [1991], "Data structures for representing and processing of fuzzy information in LISP." *Computers and Artificial Intelligence*, **10**(6), pp. 561–571.

1304. Soula, G. and E. Sanchez [1982], "Soft deduction rules in medical diagnostic processes." In: Gupta, M. M. and E. Sanchez, eds., *Approximate Reasoning in Decision Analysis*. North-Holland, New York, pp. 77–88.

1305. Squillante, M. and A. G. S. Ventre [1992a], "On the analytic setting of *C*-calculus." *J. of Math. Analysis and Applications*, **165**(2), pp. 539–549.

1306. Squillante, M. and A. G. S. Ventre [1992b], "Generating fuzzy measures." *J. of Math. Analysis and Applications*, **165**(2), pp. 550–555.

1307. Steimann, F. and K. P. Adlassnig [1994], "Clinical monitoring with fuzzy automata." *Fuzzy Sets and Systems*, **61**(1), pp. 37–42.

1308. Stellakis, H. M. and K. P. Valavanis [1991], "Fuzzy logic-based formulation of the organizer of intelligent robotic systems." *J. of Intelligent and Robotic Systems*, **4**(1), pp. 1–24.

1309. Stephanou, H. E. and A. P. Sage [1987], "Perspectives on imperfect information." *IEEE Trans. on Systems, Man, and Cybernetics*, **17**(5), pp. 780–798.

1310. Steyn, W. H. [1994], "Fuzzy control for a non-linear MIMO plant sublect to control constraints." *IEEE Trans. on Systems, Man, and Cybernetics*, **24**(10), pp. 1565–1571.

1311. Stojakovic, M. [1992], "Fuzzy conditional expectation." *Fuzzy Sets and Systems*, **52**(1), pp. 53–60.

1312. Stojakovic, M. [1994], "Fuzzy valued measures." *Fuzzy Sets and Systems*, **65**(1), pp. 95–104.

1313. Strat, T. M. and Lowrance J. D. [1989], "Explaining evidential analyses." *Intern. J. of Approximate Reasoning*, **3**(4), pp. 299–353.

1314. Styblinski, M. A. and B. D. Meyer [1991], "Signal flow graphs vs. fuzzy cognitive maps in application to qualitative circuit analysis." *Intern. J. of Man-Machine Studies*, **35**(2), pp. 175–186.

1315. Su, C. Y. and Y. Stepanenko [1994], "Adaptive control of a class of nonlinear systems with fuzzy logic." *IEEE Trans. on Fuzzy Systems*, **2**(4), pp. 285–294.

1316. Subrahmanyam, P. V. and S. K. Sudarsanam [1994a], "On some fuzzy functional equations." *Fuzzy Sets and Systems*, **64**(3), pp. 333–338.

1317. Subrahmanyam, P. V. and S. K. Sudarsanam [1994b], "On the fuzzy functional equation $x(t) = a(t)h(t, x(t)) + y(t)$." *Intern. J. of Uncertainty, Fuzziness and Knowledge–Based Systems*, **2**(2), pp. 197–204.

1318. Sudkamp, T. [1992], "On probability–possibility transformations." *Fuzzy Sets and Systems*, **51**(1), pp. 73–82.

1319. Sudkamp, T. [1993a], "Similarity, interpolation, and fuzzy rule construction." *Fuzzy Sets and Systems*, **58**(1), pp. 73–86.

1320. Sudkamp, T. [1993b], "Geometric measures of possibilistic uncertainty." *Intern. J. of General Systems*, **22**(1), pp. 7–23.

1321. Sugeno, M. **[1974]**, *Theory of Fuzzy Integrals and its Applications*. (Ph. D. dissertation). Tokyo Institute of Technology, Tokyo, Japan.

1322. Sugeno, M. [1977], "Fuzzy measures and fuzzy integrals : A survey." In: Gupta, M. M., G. N. Saridis and B. R. Gaines, eds., *Fuzzy Automata and Decision Processes*. North-Holland, Amsterdam and New York, pp. 89–102.

1323. Sugeno, M., ed. **[1985a]**, *Industrial Applications of Fuzzy Control*. North-Holland, New York.

1324. Sugeno, M. [1985b], "An introductory survey of fuzzy control." *Information Sciences*, **36**(1–2), pp. 59–83.

1325. Sugeno, M. and G. T. Kang [1986], "Fuzzy modelling and control of multilayer incinerator." *Fuzzy Sets and Systems*, **18**(3), pp. 329–346.

1326. Sugeno, M. and G. T. Kang [1988], "Structure identification of fuzzy model." *Fuzzy Sets and Systems*, **28**(1), pp. 15–33.

1327. Sugeno, M. and M. Nishida [1985], "Fuzzy control of model car." *Fuzzy Sets and Systems*, **16**(2), pp. 103–113.

1328. Sugeno, M. and G. K. Park [1993], "An approach to linguistic instruction based learning." *Intern. J. of Uncertainty, Fuzziness and Knowledge–Based Systems*, **1**(1), pp. 19–56.

1329. Sugeno, M. and T. Takagi [1983a], "A new approach to design of fuzzy controller." In: Wang, P. P., ed., *Advances in Fuzzy Sets, Possibility Theory and Applications*. Plenum Press, New York, pp. 325–334.

1330. Sugeno, M. and T. Takagi [1983b], "Multi-dimensional fuzzy reasoning." *Fuzzy Sets and Systems*, **9**(3), pp. 313–325.

1331. Sugeno, M. and K. Tanaka [1991], "Successive identification of a fuzzy model and its applications to prediction of a complex system." *Fuzzy Sets and Systems*, **42**(3), pp. 315–334.

1332. Sugeno, M. and T. Terano [1977], "A model of learning based on fuzzy information." *Kybernetes*, **6**(3), pp. 157–166.

1333. Sugeno, M. and T. Yasukawa [1993], "A fuzzy-logic-based approach to qualitative modeling." *IEEE Trans. on Fuzzy Systems*, **1**(1), pp. 7–31.

1334. Suh, I. H. and T. W. Kim [1994], "Fuzzy membership function based neural networks with applications to the visual servoing of robot manipulators." *IEEE Trans. on Fuzzy Systems*, **2**(3), pp. 203–220.

1335. Sullivan, J. and W. H. Woodall [1994], "A comparison of fuzzy forecasting and Markov modelling." *Fuzzy Sets and Systems*, **64**(3), pp. 279–293.

1336. Suzuki, H. and S. Arimoto [1994], "Embedment of a fuzzy logic system into a Boolean lattice for satisfying a complementary law." *Information Sciences*, **78**(3–4), pp. 257–268.

1337. Suzuki, H. [1993], "Fuzzy sets and membership functions." *Fuzzy Sets and Systems*, **58**(2), pp. 123–132.

1338. Tahani, H. and J. M. Keller [1990], "Information fusion in computer vision using the fuzzy integral." *IEEE Trans. on Systems, Man, and Cybernetics*, **20**(3), pp. 733–741.

1339. Takagi, H. and I. Hayashi [1991], "NN–driven fuzzy reasoning." *Intern. J. of Approximate Reasoning*, **5**(3), pp. 191–212.

1340. Takagi, T. and M. Sugeno [1985], "Fuzzy identification of systems and its applications to modeling and control." *IEEE Trans. on Systems, Man, and Cybernetics*, **15**(1), pp. 116–132.

1341. Takeuti, G. and S. Titani [1992], "Fuzzy logic and fuzzy set theory." *Arch. Math. Logic*, **32**, pp. 1–32.

1342. Tamura, S., S. Higuchi and K. Tanaka [1971], "Pattern classification based on fuzzy relations." *IEEE Trans. on Systems, Man, and Cybernetics*, **1**(1), pp. 61–66.

1343. Tamura, S. and K. Tanaka [1973], "Learning of fuzzy formal language." *IEEE Trans. on Systems, Man, and Cybernetics*, **3**(1), pp. 98–102.

1344. Tan, S. H., Y. Lin, P. Z. Wang and S. Z. He [1994], "Objective–centered formulation of an adaptive fuzzy control scheme." *Intern. J. of Uncertainty, Fuzziness and Knowledge–Based Systems*, **2**(3), pp. 321–331.

1345. Tan, S. K., P. Z. Wang and E. S. Lee [1993], "Fuzzy set operations based on the theory of falling shadows." *J. of Math. Analysis and Applications*, **174**(1), pp. 242–255.

1346. Tan, S. K., P. Z. Wang and X. Z. Zhang [1993], "Fuzzy inference relation based on the theory of falling shadows." *Fuzzy Sets and Systems*, **53**(2), pp. 179–188.

1347. Tanaka, H. [1987], "Fuzzy data analysis by possibilistic linear models." *Fuzzy Sets and Systems*, **24**(3), pp. 363–375.

1348. Tanaka, H. and K. Asai [1984], "Fuzzy solution in fuzzy linear programming problems." *IEEE Trans. on Systems, Man, and Cybernetics*, **14**(2), pp. 325–328.

1349. Tanaka, H., I. Hayashi and J. Watada [1989], "Possibilistic linear regression analysis for fuzzy data." *European J. of Operational Research*, **40**(3), pp. 389–396.

1350. Tanaka, H. and H. Ishibuchi [1993], "Evidence theory of exponential possibility distributions." *Intern. J. of Approximate Reasoning*, **8**(2), pp. 123–140.

1351. Tanaka, H., H. Ishibuchi and I. Hayashi [1993], "Identification method of possibility distributions and its applications to discriminat analysis." *Fuzzy Sets and Systems*, **58**(1), pp. 41–50.

1352. Tanaka, H., S. Uejima and K. Asai [1982], "Linear regression analysis with fuzzy model." *IEEE Trans. on Systems, Man, and Cybernetics*, **12**(6), pp. 903–907.

1353. Tanaka, H. and J. Watada [1988], "Possibilistic linear systems and their application to the linear regression model." *Fuzzy Sets and Systems*, **27**(3), pp. 275–289.

1354. Tanaka, K. and M. Sano [1994], "A robust stabilization problem of fuzzy control systems and its application to backing up control of a truck-trailer." *IEEE Trans. on Fuzzy Systems*, **2**(2), pp. 107–118.

1355. Tanaka, K. and M. Sugeno [1991], "A study on subjective evaluations of printed color images." *Intern. J. of Approximate Reasoning*, **5**(3), pp. 213–222.

1356. Tanaka, K. and M. Sugeno [1992], "Stability analysis and design of fuzzy control systems." *Fuzzy Sets and Systems*, **45**(2), pp. 135–156.

1357. Tang, K. L. and R. J. Mulholland [1987], "Comparing fuzzy logic with classical controller designs." *IEEE Trans. on Systems, Man, and Cybernetics*, **17**(6), pp. 1085–1087.

1358. Tanscheit, R. and E. M. Scharf [1988], "Experiments with the use of rule-based self-organizing controller for robotics applications." *Fuzzy Sets and Systems*, **26**(2), pp. 195–214.

1359. Tazaki, E. and M. Amagasa [1979], "Heuristic structure synthesis in a class of systems using a fuzzy automation." *IEEE Trans. on Systems, Man, and Cybernetics*, **9**(2), pp. 73–78.

1360. Tee, A. B., M. D. Bowman and K. C. Sinha [1988], "A fuzzy mathematical approach for bridge condition evaluation." *Civil Engineering Systems*, **5**(1), pp. 17–24.

1361. Teodorescu, H. N. [1992], "Chaos in fuzzy systems and signals." *Proc. Second Intern. Conf. on Fuzzy Logic and Neural Networks, Iizuka, Japan*, pp. 21–50.

1362. Teodorescu, H. N., T. Yamakawa and A. Rascanu [**1991**], *Fuzzy Systems and Artificial Intelligence*. Iasi University Publ. House, Iasi, Romania.

1363. Terano, T., K. Asai and M. Sugeno [**1992**], *Fuzzy Systems Theory and its Applications*. Academic Press, New York.

1364. Terano, T., K. Asai and M. Sugeno [**1994**], *Applied Fuzzy Systems*. AP Professional, New York.

1365. Thole, U., H. J. Zimmermann and P. Zysno [1979], "On the suitability of minimum and product operators for the intersection of fuzzy sets." *Fuzzy Sets and Systems*, **2**(2), pp. 167–180.

1366. Thomason, M. G. [1973], "Finite fuzzy automata, regular fuzzy languages and pattern recognition." *Pattern Recognition*, **5**(4), pp. 383–390.

1367. Thomason, M. G. and P. N. Marinos [1974], "Deterministic acceptors of regular fuzzy languages." *IEEE Trans. on Systems, Man, and Cybernetics*, **4**(2), pp. 228–230.

1368. Thornber, K. K. [1993a], "A key to fuzzy logic inference." *Intern. J. of Approximate Reasoning*, **8**(2), pp. 105–121.

1369. Thornber, K. K. [1993b], "The fidelity of fuzzy-logic inference." *IEEE Trans. on Fuzzy Systems*, **1**(4), pp. 288–297.

1370. Thrift, P. [1991], "Fuzzy logic synthesis with genetic algorithms." *Proc. Fourth Intern. Conf. on Genetic Algorithms, San Matreo, CA*, pp. 509–513.

1371. Tian, Y. and I. B. Turksen [1993], "Combination of rules or their consequences in fuzzy expert systems." *Fuzzy Sets and Systems*, **58**(1), pp. 3–40.

1372. Tilli, T. [1994], "High performance software implementations of fuzzy logic algorithms." *Fuzzy Sets and Systems*, **66**(2), pp. 233–240.

1373. Tobi, T. and T. Hanafusa [1991], "A practical application of fuzzy control for an air–conditioning system." *Intern. J. of Approximate Reasoning*, **5**(3), pp. 331–348.

1374. Tobi, T., T. Hanafusa, S. Ito and N. Kashiwagi [1992], "The application of fuzzy control to a coke oven gas cooling plant." *Fuzzy Sets and Systems*, **46**(3), pp. 373–381.

1375. Togai, M. and H. Watanabe [1986], "A VLSI implementation of a fuzzy-inference engine: Toward an expert systems on a chip." *Information Sciences*, **38**(2), pp. 147–163.

1376. Tong, R. M. [1976], "Analysis of fuzzy control algorithms using the relation matrix." *Intern. J. of Man-Machine Studies*, **8**(6), pp. 679–686.

1377. Tong, R. M. [1977], "A control engineering review of fuzzy systems." *Automatica*, **13**(6), pp. 559–569.

1378. Tong, R. M. [1978], "Synthesis of fuzzy models for individual processes: Some recent results." *Intern. J. of General Systems*, **4**(3), pp. 143–162.

1379. Tong, R. M. [1980a], "Some properties of fuzzy feedback systems." *IEEE Trans. on Systems, Man, and Cybernetics*, **10**(6), pp. 327–331.

1380. Tong, R. M. [1980b], "The evaluation of fuzzy models derived from experimental data." *Fuzzy Sets and Systems*, **4**(1), pp. 1–12.

1381. Tong, R. M. [1984], "A retrospective view of fuzzy control systems." *Fuzzy Sets and Systems*, **14**(3), pp. 199–210.

1382. Tong, R. M. [1985], "An annotated bibliography of fuzzy control." In: Sugeno, M., ed., *Industrial Applications of Fuzzy Control*. North-Holland, New York, pp. 249–269.

1383. Tong, R. M. [1986], "The representation of uncertainty in an expert system for information retrieval." In: Prade, H. and C. V. Negoita, eds., *Fuzzy Logic in Knowledge Engineering*. Verlag TÜV Rheinland, Köln, pp. 58–72.

1384. Tong, R. M., M. B. Beck and A. Latten [1980], "Fuzzy control of the activated sludge wastewater treatment process." *Automatica*, **16**(6), pp. 695–701.

1385. Tong, R. M. and P. Bonissone [1980], "A linguistic approach to decision-making with fuzzy sets." *IEEE Trans. on Systems, Man, and Cybernetics*, **10**(11), pp. 116–223.

1386. Tönshoff, H. K. and A. Walter [1994], "Self-tuning fuzzy-controller for process control in internal grinding." *Fuzzy Sets and Systems*, **63**(3), pp. 359–373.

1387. Torasso, P. [1991], "Supervising the heuristic learning in a diagnostic expert system." *Fuzzy Sets and Systems*, **44**(3), pp. 357–372.

1388. Torasso, P. and L. Console [1989], "Approximate reasoning and prototypical knowledge." *Intern. J. of Approximate Reasoning*, **3**(2), pp. 157–178.

1389. Toth, H. [1992], "Reconstruction possibilities for fuzzy sets: Towards a new level of understanding?" *Fuzzy Sets and Systems*, **52**(3), pp. 283–303.

1390. Trappey, C. V. and A. J. C. Trappey [1993], "Planning merchandise investments using fuzzy optimization." *J. of Intelligent & Fuzzy Systems*, **1**(3), pp. 189–197.

1391. Trauwaert, E. [1988], "On the meaning of Dunn's partition coefficient for fuzzy clusters." *Fuzzy Sets and Systems*, **25**(2), pp. 217–242.

1392. Trauwaert, E., L. Kaufman and P. Rousseeuw [1991], "Fuzzy clustering algorithms based on the maximum likelihood principle." *Fuzzy Sets and Systems*, **42**(2), pp. 213–227.

1393. Triantaphyllou, E. [1993], "A quadratic programming approach in estimating similarity relations." *IEEE Trans. on Fuzzy Systems*, **1**(2), pp. 138–145.

1394. Triantaphyllou, E., P. M. Pardalos and S. H. Mann [1990], "The problem of determining membership values in fuzzy sets in real world situations." In: Brown, D. E. and C. C. White, eds., *Operations Research and Artificial Intelligence: The Integration of Problem-Solving Strategies*. Kluwer, Boston, pp. 197–214.

1395. Triantaphyllou, E. and S. H. Mann [1990], "An evaluation of the eigenvalue approach for determining the membership values of fuzzy sets." *Fuzzy Sets and Systems*, **35**(3), pp. 295–301.

1396. Trillas, E. [1993], "On logic and fuzzy logic." *Intern. J. of Uncertainty, Fuzziness and Knowledge-Based Systems*, **1**(2), pp. 107–137.

1397. Trillas, E. and C. Alsina [1992], "Some remarks on approximate entailment." *Intern. J. of Approximate Reasoning*, **6**(4), pp. 525–534.

1398. Trillas, E. and C. Alsina [1993], "Logic: Going farther from Tarski?" *Fuzzy Sets and Systems*, **53**(1), pp. 1–13.

1399. Trillas, E. and T. Riera [1978], "Entropies in finite fuzzy sets." *Information Sciences*, **15**(2), pp. 159–168.

1400. Trillas, E. and L. Valverde [1985], "On mode and implications in approximate reasoning." In: Gupta, M. M., A. Kandel, W. Bandler and J. B. Kiszka, eds., *Approximate Reasoning in Expert Systems*. North-Holland, New York, pp. 157–166.

1401. Tripathy, R. C. and P. A. Saxena [1990], "Multivalued dependencies in fuzzy relational databases." *Fuzzy Sets and Systems*, **38**(3), pp. 267–279.

1402. Trivedi, M. M. and J. C. Bezdek [1986], "Low-level segmentation of aerial images with fuzzy clustering." *IEEE Trans. on Systems, Man, and Cybernetics*, **16**(4), pp. 589–598.

1403. Tsao, E. C. K., J. C. Bezdek and N. R. Pal [1994], "Fuzzy Kohonen clustering networks." *Pattern Recognition*, **27**(5), pp. 757–764.

1404. Turksen, I. B. [1986], "Interval valued fuzzy sets based on normal forms." *Fuzzy Sets and Systems*, **20**(2), pp. 191–210.

1405. Turksen, I. B. [1988], "Approximate reasoning for production planning." *Fuzzy Sets and Systems*, **26**(1), pp. 23–37.

1406. Turksen, I. B. [1989], "Four methods of approximate reasoning with interval-valued fuzzy sets." *Intern. J. of Approximate Reasoning*, **3**(2), pp. 121–142.

1407. Turksen, I. B. [1991], "Measurement of membership functions and their acquisition." *Fuzzy Sets and Systems*, **40**(1), pp. 5–38.

1408. Turksen, I. B. [1992a], "Fuzzy expert systems for IE/OR/MS." *Fuzzy Sets and Systems*, **51**(1), pp. 1–28.

1409. Turksen, I. B. [1992b], "Interval-valued fuzzy sets

and compensatory AND." *Fuzzy Sets and Systems,* **51**(3), pp. 295–307.

1410. Turksen, I. B. [1994], "Fuzzy systems modeling." *Fuzzy Systems & A. I.,* **2**(2), pp. 3–34.

1411. Turksen, I. B. and M. Berg [1991], "An expert system prototype for inventory capacity planning: An approximate reasoning approach." *Intern. J. of Approximate Reasoning,* **5**(3), pp. 223–250.

1412. Turksen, I. B. and Y. Tian [1992], "Interval-valued fuzzy sets representation on multiple antecedent fuzzy *S*-implications and reasoning." *Fuzzy Sets and Systems,* **52**(2), pp. 143–167.

1413. Turksen, I. B., D. Ulguary and Q. Wang [1992], "Hierarchical scheduling based on approximate reasoning – A comparison with ISIS." *Fuzzy Sets and Systems,* **46**(3), pp. 349–371.

1414. Turksen, I. B. and Z. Zhong [1988], "An approximate analogical reasoning approach based on similarity measures." *IEEE Trans. on Systems, Man, and Cybernetics,* **18**(6), pp. 1049–1056.

1415. Turksen, I. B. and Z. Zhong [1990], "An approximate analogical reasoning schema based on similarity measures and interval-valued fuzzy sets." *Fuzzy Sets and Systems,* **34**(3), pp. 323–346.

1416. Turksen, I. B. and S. Jiang [1993], "Rule base reorganization and search with a fuzzy cluster analysis." *Intern. J. of Approximate Reasoning,* **9**(3), pp. 167–196.

1417. Turksen, I. B. and D. D. W. Yao [1984], "Representations of connectives in fuzzy reasoning: The view through normal form." *IEEE Trans. on Systems, Man, and Cybernetics,* **14**(1), pp. 146–151.

1418. Turksen, I. B. and H. Zhao [1993], "An equivalence between inductive learning and pseudo-boolean logic simplification: A rule generation and reduction scheme." *IEEE Trans. on Systems, Man, and Cybernetics,* **23**(3), pp. 907–917.

1419. Turunen, E. [1992], "Algebraic structures in fuzzy logic." *Fuzzy Sets and Systems,* **52**(2), pp. 181–188.

1420. Uchino, E., T. Yamakawa, T. Miki and S. Nakamura [1993], "Fuzzy rule-based simple interpolation algorithm for discrete signal." *Fuzzy Sets and Systems,* **59**(3), pp. 259–270.

1421. Uehara, K. and M. Fujise [1993a], "Fuzzy inference based on families of alpha-level sets." *IEEE Trans. on Fuzzy Systems,* **1**(2), pp. 111–124.

1422. Uehara, K. and M. Fujise [1993b], "Multistage fuzzy inference formulated as linguistic-truth-value propagation and its learning algorithm based on back-propagating error information." *IEEE Trans. on Fuzzy Systems,* **1**(3), pp. 205–221.

1423. Uemura, Y. [1993a], "A simple decision rule on fuzzy events." *Cybernetics and Systems,* **24**(5), pp. 509–521.

1424. Uemura, Y. [1993b], "A decision rule on fuzzy events under an observation." *J. of Fuzzy Mathematics,* **1**(1), pp. 39–52.

1425. Ulieru, M. and R. Isermann [1993], "Design of a fuzzy-logic based diagnostic model for technical processes." *Fuzzy Sets and Systems,* **58**(3), pp. 249–272.

1426. Umano, M. [1982], "FREEDOM-O: A fuzzy database system." In: Gupta, M. M. and E. Sanchez, eds., *Fuzzy Information and Decision Processes.* North-Holland, New York, pp. 339–347.

1427. Umano, M. [1984], "Retrieval from fuzzy database by fuzzy relational algebra." In: Sanchez, S., ed., *Fuzzy Information Knowledge Representation and Decision Analysis.* Pergamon Press, Oxford. U. K., pp. 1–6.

1428. Umano, M. and S. Fukami [1994], "Fuzzy relational algebra for possibility-distribution-fuzzy-relational model of fuzzy data." *J. of Intelligent Information Systems,* **3**(1), pp. 7–27.

1429. Umbers, I. G. and P. J. King [1980], "An analysis of human decision-making in cement kiln control and the implications for automation." *Intern. J. of Man-Machine Studies,* **12**(1), pp. 11–23.

1430. Umeyama, S. [1986], "The complementary process of fuzzy medical diagnosis and its properties." *Information Sciences,* **38**(3), pp. 229–242.

1431. Uragami, A., M. Mizumoto and K. Tanaka [1976], "Fuzzy robot controls." *J. of Cybernetics,* **6**(1–2), pp. 39–64.

1432. Utkin, L. V. [1994], "Redundancy optimization by fuzzy reliability and cost of system components." *Microelectronics and Reliability,* **34**(1), pp. 53–59.

1433. Valente de Oliveira, J. [1993], "Neuron inspired learning rules for fuzzy relational structures." *Fuzzy Sets and Systems,* **57**(1), pp. 41–53.

1434. Valenzuela–Rendón, M. [1991], "The fuzzy classifier system: A classifier system for continuously varying variables." *Proc. Fourth Intern. Conf. on Genetic Algorithms, San Mateo, CA,* pp. 340–353.

1435. Van de Walle, B., D. Ruan and E. E. Kerre [1994], "Applications of fuzzy reasoning in nuclear decision aiding systems." *Fuzzy Systems & A. I.,* **2**(2), pp. 35–46.

1436. Van der Gang, L. C. [1989], "A conceptual model for inexact reasoning in rule-based systems." *Intern. J. of Approximate Reasoning,* **3**(3), pp. 239–258.

1437. Van Laarhoven, P. J. M. and W. Pedrycz [1983], "A fuzzy extension of Saaty's priority theory." *Fuzzy Sets and Systems,* **11**(3), pp. 229–241.

1438. Vasko, F. J., F. E. Wolf and K. L. Stott [1989], "A practical solution to a fuzzy two-dimensional cutting stock problem." *Fuzzy Sets and Systems,* **29**(3), pp. 259–275.

1439. Vejnarová, J. and G. J. Klir [1994], "Measure of strife in Dempster–Shafer theory." *Intern. J. of General Systems*, **22**(1), pp. 25–42.

1440. Verdegay, J. and M. Delgado **[1989]**, *The Interface between Artificial Intelligence and Operations Research in Fuzzy Environment*. Verlag TÜV Rheinland, Köln.

1441. Verdegay, J. L. and M. Delgado, eds. **[1990]**, *Approximate Reasoning Tools for Artificial Intelligence*. Verlag TÜV Rheinland, Köln.

1442. Viertl, R. and H. Hule [1991], "On Bayes' theorem for fuzzy data." *Statistical Papers*, **32**, pp. 115–122.

1443. Vila, M. A., J. C. Cubero, J. M. Medina and O. Pons [1994], "A logic approach to fuzzy relational databases." *Intern. J. of Intelligent Systems*, **9**(5), pp. 449–460.

1444. Vila, M. A. and M. Delgado [1983], "On medical diagnosis using possibility measures." *Fuzzy Sets and Systems*, **10**(3), pp. 211–222.

1445. Vopěnka P. [1979], *Mathematics in the Alternative Set Theory*. Teubner, Leipzig.

1446. Vopěnka P. and P. Hájek **[1972]**, *The Theory of Semisets*. North-Holland, Amsterdam.

1447. Voxman, W. and R. Goetschel [1983], "A note on the characterization of the max and min operators." *Information Sciences*, **30**(1), pp. 5–10.

1448. Vrba, J. [1992a], "Peak-pattern concept and max-min inverse problem in fuzzy control modelling." *Fuzzy Sets and Systems*, **47**(1), pp. 1–11.

1449. Vrba, J. [1992b], "A note on inverses in arithmetic with fuzzy numbers." *Fuzzy Sets and Systems*, **50**(3), pp. 267–278.

1450. Vrba, J. [1993], "General decomposition problem of fuzzy relations." *Fuzzy Sets and Systems*, **54**(1), pp. 69–79.

1451. Vuorimaa, P. [1994], "Fuzzy self-organizing map." *Fuzzy Sets and Systems*, **66**(2), pp. 223–231.

1452. Wagenknecht, M. [1991], "On pseudo-transitive approximations of fuzzy relations." *Fuzzy Sets and Systems*, **44**(1), pp. 45–55.

1453. Wagman, D., M. Schneider and E. Shnaider [1994], "On the use of interval mathematics in fuzzy expert systems." *Intern. J. of Intelligent Systems*, **9**(2), pp. 241–259.

1454. Wagner, W. [1981], "A fuzzy model of concept representation in memory." *Fuzzy Sets and Systems*, **6**(1), pp. 11–26.

1455. Walley, P. **[1991]**, *Statistical Reasoning With Imprecise Probabilities*. Chapman and Hall, London.

1456. Walley, P. and T. L. Fine [1979], "Varieties of model (classificatory) and comparative probability." *Synthese*, **41**(3), pp. 321–374.

1457. Wang, G. Y. and J. P. Ou [1990], "Theory of fuzzy random vibration with fuzzy parameters." *Fuzzy Sets and Systems*, **36**(1), pp. 103–112.

1458. Wang, G. Y. and Z. Qiao [1994], "Convergence of sequences of fuzzy random variables and its application." *Fuzzy Sets and Systems*, **63**(2), pp. 187–199.

1459. Wang, G. Y. and Y. Zheng [1992], "The theory of fuzzy stochastic processes." *Fuzzy Sets and Systems*, **51**(2), pp. 161–178.

1460. Wang, H. F. [1993], "Numerical analysis on fuzzy relation equations with various operators." *Fuzzy Sets and Systems*, **53**(2), pp. 155–166.

1461. Wang, H. F. and H. M. Hsu [1991], "Sensitivity analysis of fuzzy relation equations." *Intern. J. of General Systems*, **19**(2), pp. 155–169.

1462. Wang, H. F. and H. M. Hsu [1992], "An alternative approach to the resolution of fuzzy relation equations." *Fuzzy Sets and Systems*, **45**(2), pp. 203–213.

1463. Wang, H. F., C. Wang and G. Y. Wu [1994], "Bi-criteria fuzzy *c*-means analysis." *Fuzzy Sets and Systems*, **64**(3), pp. 311–319.

1464. Wang, L. X. [1993a], "Stable adaptive fuzzy control of nonlinear systems." *IEEE Trans on Fuzzy Systems*, **1**(2), pp. 146–155.

1465. Wang, L. X. [1993b], "Solving fuzzy relational equations through network training." *Proc. Second IEEE Intern. Conf. on Fuzzy Systems, San Francisco*, pp. 956–960.

1466. Wang, L. X. **[1994]**, *Adaptive Fuzzy Systems and Control: Design and Stability Analysis*. Prentice Hall, Englewood Cliffs, NJ.

1467. Wang, L. X. and J. M. Mendel [1991], "Three-dimensional structured networks for matrix equation solving." *IEEE Trans. on Computers*, **40**(12), pp. 1337–1346.

1468. Wang, L. X. and J. M. Mendel [1992a], "Fuzzy basis function, universal approximation, and orthogonal least-squares learning." *IEEE Trans. on Neural Networks*, **3**(5), pp. 807–814.

1469. Wang, L. X. and J. M. Mendel [1992b], "Generating fuzzy rules by learning through examples." *IEEE Trans. on Systems, Man, and Cybernetics*, **22**(6), pp. 1414–1427.

1470. Wang, L. X. and J. M. Mendel [1992c], "Back-propagation fuzzy system as nonlinear dynamic system identifiers." *Proc. First IEEE Intern. Conf. on Fuzzy Systems, San Diego*, pp. 1409–1416.

1471. Wang, L. X. and J. M. Mendel [1992d], "Parallel structured networks for solving a wide variety of matrix algebra problems." *J. of Parallel and Distributed Computing*, **14**(3), pp. 236–247.

1472. Wang, L. X. and J. M. Mendel [1993], "Fuzzy adaptive filters, with application to nonlinear channel equalization." *IEEE Trans. on Fuzzy Systems*, **1**(3), pp. 161–170.

1473. Wang, P. P., ed. **[1983]**, *Advances in Fuzzy Sets, Possibility Theory, and Applications*. Plenum Press, New York.

1474. Wang, P. P., ed. **[1993]**, *Advances in Fuzzy Theory and Technology, Vol. I*. Bookwrights Press, Durham, NC.

1475. Wang, P. P. and S. K. Chang, eds. **[1980]**, *Fuzzy Sets: Theory and Applications to Policy Analysis and Information Systems*. Plenum Press, New York.

1476. Wang, P. Z. [1990], "A factor spaces approach to knowledge representation." *Fuzzy Sets and Systems*, **36**(1), pp. 113–124.

1477. Wang, P. Z. and K. F. Loe, eds. **[1993]**, *Between Mind and Computer: Fuzzy Science and Engineering*. World Scientific, Singapore.

1478. Wang, P. Z. and D. Z. Zhang [1992], "The netlike inference process and stability analysis." *Intern. J. of Intelligent Systems*, **7**(4), pp. 361–372.

1479. Wang, P. Z., H. M. Zhang and W. Xu [1990], "Pad-analysis of fuzzy control stability." *Fuzzy Sets and Systems*, **38**(1), pp. 27–42.

1480. Wang, S. [1994], "Generating fuzzy membership functions: A monotonic neural network model." *Fuzzy Sets and Systems*, **61**(1), pp. 71–82.

1481. Wang, X. and M. Ha [1992], "Fuzzy linear regression analysis." *Fuzzy Sets and Systems*, **51**(2), pp. 179–188.

1482. Wang, Z. [1990], "Structural characteristics of fuzzy measures on S-compact space." *Intern. J. of General Systems*, **17**(2–3), pp. 157–189.

1483. Wang, Z. and G. J. Klir **[1992]**, *Fuzzy Measure Theory*. Plenum Press, New York.

1484. Wang, Z. and S. Li [1990], "Fuzzy linear regression analysis of fuzzy valued variables." *Fuzzy Sets and Systems*, **36**(1), pp. 125–136.

1485. Warmerdam, J. M. and T. L. Jacobs [1994], "Fuzzy set approach to routing and siting hazardous waste operations." *Information Sciences: Applications*, **2**(1), pp. 1–14.

1486. Watanabe, H., W. J. Yakowenko, Y. M. Kim, J. Anbe and T. Tobi [1994], "Application of a fuzzy discrimination analysis for diagnosis of valvular heart disease." *IEEE Trans. on Fuzzy Systems*, **2**(4), pp. 267–276.

1487. Watanabe, N. and T. Imaizumi [1993], "A fuzzy statistical test of fuzzy hypotheses." *Fuzzy Sets and Systems*, **53**(2), pp. 167–178.

1488. Watanable, S. [1978], "A generalized fuzzy-set theory." *IEEE Trans. on Systems, Man, and Cybernetics*, **8**(10), pp. 756–759.

1489. Watson, S. R., J. J. Weiss and M. L. Donnell [1979], "Fuzzy decision analysis." *IEEE Trans. on Systems, Man, and Cybernetics*, **9**(1), pp. 1–9.

1490. Weaver, W. [1948], "Science and complexity." *American Scientist*, **36**(4), pp. 536–544.

1491. Weber, S. [1983], "A general concept of fuzzy connectives, negations and implications based on t-norms and t-conorms." *Fuzzy Sets and Systems*, **11**(2), pp. 115–134.

1492. Weber, S. [1984], "Measures of fuzzy sets and measures of fuzziness." *Fuzzy Sets and Systems*, **13**(3), pp. 247–271.

1493. Weber, S. [1988], "Conditional measures based on Archimedean semigroups." *Fuzzy Sets and Systems*, **27**(1), pp. 63–72.

1494. Wechler, W. **[1978]**, *The Concept of Fuzziness in Automata and Language Theory*. Academic–Verlag, Berlin.

1495. Wee, W. G. and K. S. Fu [1969], "A formulation of fuzzy automata and its application as a model of learning system." *IEEE Trans. on Systems, Man, and Cybernetics*, **5**(3), pp. 215–223.

1496. Wenstop, F. [1976], "Fuzzy set simulation models in a systems dynamics perspective." *Kybernetes*, **6**(3), pp. 209–218.

1497. Werbos, P. J. [1992], "Neurocontrol and fuzzy logic: Connections and designs." *Intern. J. of Approximate Reasoning*, **6**(2), pp. 185–220.

1498. Whalen, T. [1984], "Decision making under uncertainty with various assumptions about available information." *IEEE Trans. on Systems, Man, and Cybernetics*, **14**(6), pp. 888–900.

1499. Whalen, T. and B. Schott [1985a], "Goal-directed approximate reasoning in a fuzzy production system." In: Gupta, M. M., A. Kandel, W. Bandler and J. B. Kiszka, eds., *Approximate Reasoning in Expert Systems*. North-Holland, New York, pp. 505–517.

1500. Whalen, T. and B. Schott [1985b], "Alternative logics for approximate reasoning in expert systems: A comparative study." *Intern. J. of Man-Machine Studies*, **22**(3), pp. 327–346.

1501. Whalen, T. and B. Schott [1986], "Financial ratio analysis." In: Prade, H. and C. V. Negoita, eds., *Fuzzy Logic in Knowledge Engineering*. Verlag TÜV Rheinland, Köln, pp. 58–72.

1502. Whalen, T. and B. Schott [1989], "Presumption and prejudice in logical inference." *Intern. J. of Approximate Reasoning*, **3**(5), pp. 359–382.

1503. Whalen, T. and B. Schott [1992], "Usuality, regularity, and fuzzy set logic." *Intern. J. of Approximate Reasoning*, **6**(4), pp. 481–504.

1504. White, D. A. and D. A. Sofge, eds. **[1992]**, *Handbook of Intelligent Control: Neuro-Fuzzy and Adaptive Approaches*. Van Nostrand, New York.

1505. White, R. B. [1979], "The consistency of the axiom of comprehension in the infinite-valued predicate logic of Lukasiewicz." *J. of Philosophical Logic*, **8**(4), pp. 509–534.

1506. Wierzchon, S. T. [1983], "An algorithm for identification of fuzzy measure." *Fuzzy Sets and Systems*, **9**(1), pp. 69–78.

1507. Wierzchon, S. T. [1987], "Linear programming with fuzzy sets: A general approach." *Mathematical Modelling*, **9**(6), pp. 447–459.

1508. Willaeys, D. and N. Malvache [1981], "The use of fuzzy sets for the treatment of fuzzy information by computer." *Fuzzy Sets and Systems*, **5**(3), pp. 323–328.

1509. Willmott, R. [1980], "Two fuzzier implication operators in the theory of fuzzy power sets." *Fuzzy Sets and Systems*, **4**(1), pp. 31–36.

1510. Willmott, R. [1985], "A probabilistic interpretation of a case of inference involving." *Fuzzy Sets and Systems*, **16**(2), pp. 149–162.

1511. Winslow, D. N. and D. Shi [1988], "Automatic image segmentation using fuzzy probability." *Civil Engineering Systems*, **5**(2), pp. 104–108.

1512. Wolf, R. G. [1977], "A survey of many-valued logic (1966–1974)." In: Dunn, J. M. and G. Epstein, eds., *Modern Uses of Multiple-Valued Logic*. D. Reidel, Boston, pp. 167–323.

1513. Wong, C. K. [1975], "Fuzzy topology." In: Zadeh, L. A., K. S. Fu, K. Tanaka and M. Shimura, eds., *Fuzzy Sets and Their Applications to Cognitive and Decision Processes*. Academic Press, New York, pp. 171–190.

1514. Wong, C., C. Chou and D. Mon [1993], "Studies on the output of fuzzy controller with multiple inputs." *Fuzzy Sets and Systems*, **57**(2), pp. 149–158.

1515. Wong, S. K. M., P. Bollmann and Y. Y. Yao [1991], "Information retrieval based on axiomatic decision theory." *Intern. J. of General Systems*, **19**(2), pp. 107–117.

1516. Wong, S. K. M., Y. Y. Yao, P. Bollmann and H. C. Burger [1991], "Axiomatization of qualitative belief structure." *IEEE Trans. on Systems, Man, and Cybernetics*, **21**(4), pp. 726–734.

1517. Wong, S. K. M., Y. Y. Yao and P. Lingras [1993], "Comparative beliefs and their measurements." *Intern. J. of General Systems*, **22**(1), pp. 69–89.

1518. Wonneberger, S. [1994], "Generalization of an invertible mapping between probability and possibility." *Fuzzy Sets and Systems*, **64**(2), pp. 229–240.

1519. Wood, K. L. and E. K. Antonsson [1987], "A fuzzy sets approach to computational tools for preliminary engineering design." In: Rao, S. S., ed., *Design Methods, Computer Graphics, and Expert Systems*. ASME, New York, pp. 263–271.

1520. Wood, K. L. and E. K. Antonsson [1989], "Computations with imprecise parameters in engineering design: Background and theory." *ASME J. of Mechanisms, Transmissions, and Automation in Design*, **111**(4), pp. 616–625.

1521. Wood, K. L. and E. K. Antonsson [1990], "Modeling imprecision and uncertainty in preliminary engineering design." *Mechanism and Machine Theory*, **25**(3), pp. 305–324.

1522. Wood, K. L., E. K. Antonsson and J. L. Beck [1990], "Representing imprecision in engineering design: Comparing fuzzy and probability calculus." *Research in Engineering Design*, **1**(3–4), pp. 187–203.

1523. Wood, K. L., K. N. Otto and E. K. Antonsson [1990], "A formal method for representing uncertainties in engineering design." In: Fitzhorn, P., ed., *First Intern. Workshop on Formal Methods in Engineering Design, Fort Collins, Colorado*, pp. 202–246.

1524. Wood, K. L., K. N. Otto and E. K. Antonsson [1992], "Engineering design calculations with fuzzy parameters." *Fuzzy Sets and Systems*, **52**(1), pp. 1–20.

1525. Woodbury, M. A., K. G. Manton and H. D. Tolley [1994], "A general model for statistical analysis using fuzzy sets: Sufficient conditions for identifiability and statistical properties." *Information Sciences: Applications*, **1**(3), pp. 149–180.

1526. Woodyatt, L. R., K. L. Stott, F. E. Wolf and F. J. Vasko [1993], "An application combining set covering and fuzzy sets to optimally assign metallurgical grades to customer orders." *Fuzzy Sets and Systems*, **53**(1), pp. 15–25.

1527. Wu, W. M. [1986], "Fuzzy reasoning and fuzzy relational equations." *Fuzzy Sets and Systems*, **20**(1), pp. 67–78.

1528. Wu, W. M. [1988], "A multivalued logic systems with respect to T-norms." In: Gupta, M. M. and T. Yamakawa, eds., *Fuzzy Computing: Theory, Hardware, and Applications*. North-Holland, New York, pp. 101–118.

1529. Wu, W. M. [1994], "Commutative implications on complete lattices." *Intern. J. of Uncertainty, Fuzziness and Knowledge-Based Systems*, **2**(3), pp. 333–341.

1530. Wu, Z. Q. [1990], "The application of fuzzy control theory to an oil-fueled annealing furnace." *Fuzzy Sets and Systems*, **36**(1), pp. 145–156.

1531. Wygralak, M. [1993], "Generalized cardinal numbers and operations on them." *Fuzzy Sets and Systems*, **53**(1), pp. 49–85.

1532. Xie, W. X. and S. D. Bedrosian [1984], "An information measure for fuzzy sets." *IEEE Trans. on Systems, Man, and Cybernetics*, **14**(1), pp. 151–156.

1533. Xie, W. X. and J. Z. Liu [1994], "Fuzzy *c*-means clustering algorithm with two layers and its application to image segmentation based on two-dimensional histogram." *Intern. J. of Uncertainty, Fuzziness and Knowledge–Based Systems*, **2**(3), pp. 343–350.

1534. Xu, C. W. [1989], "Decoupling fuzzy relational systems: an output feedback approach." *IEEE Trans. on Systems, Man, and Cybernetics*, **19**(2), pp. 414–418.

1535. Xu, C. W. [1990], "Analysis and feedback/feedforward control of fuzzy relational systems." *Fuzzy Sets and Systems*, **35**(1), pp. 105–113.

1536. Xu, C. W. and Y. Z. Lu [1987], "Fuzzy model identification and self-learning for dynamic systems." *IEEE Trans. on Systems, Man, and Cybernetics*, **17**(4), pp. 683–689.

1537. Xu, C. W. and Y. Z. Lu [1989], "Decoupling in fuzzy systems: A cascade compensation approach." *Fuzzy Sets and Systems*, **29**(2), pp. 177–185.

1538. Xu, H. Y. and G. Vukovich [1993], "A fuzzy genetic algorithm with effective search and optimization." *Proc. Intern. Joint Conf. on Neural Networks*, pp. 2967–2970.

1539. Xu, R. N. and X. Y. Zhai [1992], "Extensions of the analytic hierarchy process in fuzzy environment." *Fuzzy Sets and Systems*, **52**(3), pp. 251–257.

1540. Yager, R. R. [1977], "Multiple objective decision-making using fuzzy sets." *Intern. J. of Man-Machine Studies*, **9**(4), pp. 375–382.

1541. Yager, R. R. [1978], "Fuzzy decision making including unequal objectives." *Fuzzy Sets and Systems*, **1**(2), pp. 87–95.

1542. Yager, R. R. [1979a], "A measurement-informational discussion of fuzzy union and intersection." *Intern. J. of Man-Machine Studies*, **11**(2), pp. 189–200.

1543. Yager, R. R. [1979b], "On the measure of fuzziness and negation. Part I: Membership in the unit interval." *Intern. J. of General Systems*, **5**(4), pp. 221–229.

1544. Yager, R. R. [1979c], "Possibilistic decisionmaking." *IEEE Trans. on Systems, Man, and Cybernetics*, **9**(7), pp. 388–392.

1545. Yager, R. R. [1980a], "Satisfaction and fuzzy decision functions." In: Wang, P. P. and S. K. Chang, eds., *Fuzzy Sets: Theory and Applications to Policy Analysis and Information Systems*. Plenum Press, New York, pp. 171–194.

1546. Yager, R. R. [1980b], "On modeling interpersonal communication." In: Wang, P. P. and S. K. Chang, eds., *Fuzzy Sets: Theory and Applications to Policy Analysis and Information Systems*. Plenum Press, New York, pp. 309–320.

1547. Yager, R. R. [1980c], "Fuzzy sets, probabilitics, and decision." *J. of Cybernetics*, **10**(1–3), pp. 1–18.

1548. Yager, R. R. [1980d], "Fuzzy subsets of type II in decisions." *J. of Cybernetics*, **10**(1–3), pp. 137–159.

1549. Yager, R. R. [1980e], "A foundation for a theory of possibility." *J. of Cybernetics*, **10**(1–3), pp. 177–204.

1550. Yager, R. R. [1980f], "On a general class of fuzzy connectives." *Fuzzy Sets and Systems*, **4**(3), pp. 235–242.

1551. Yager, R. R. [1980g], "On the measure of fuzziness and negation. Part II: Lattices." *Information and Control*, **44**(3), pp. 236–260.

1552. Yager, R. R. [1980h], "Aspects of possibilistic uncertainty." *Intern. J. of Man-Machine Studies*, **12**(3), pp. 283–298.

1553. Yager, R. R. [1980i], "Fuzzy thinking as quick and efficient." *Cybernetica*, **23**(4), pp. 265–298.

1554. Yager, R. R. [1980j], "A logical on-line bibliographic searcher: An application of fuzzy sets." *IEEE Trans. on Systems, Man, and Cybernetics*, **10**(1), pp. 51–53.

1555. Yager, R. R. [1981a], "Some properties of fuzzy relationships." *Cybernetics and Systems*, **12**(1–2), pp. 123–140.

1556. Yager, R. R. [1981b], "A new methodology for ordinal multiobjective decision based on fuzzy sets." *Decision Sciences*, **12**(4), pp. 589–600.

1557. Yager, R. R. [1982a], "Fuzzy prediction based on regression models." *Information Sciences*, **26**(1), pp. 45–63.

1558. Yager, R. R. [1982b], "A new approach to the summarization of data." *Information Sciences*, **28**(1), pp. 69–86.

1559. Yager, R. R. [1982c], "Some procedures for selecting fuzzy set-theoretic operations." *Intern. J. of General Systems*, **8**(2), pp. 115–124.

1560. Yager, R. R. [1982d], "Measuring tranquillity and anxiety in decision making: An application of fuzzy sets." *Intern. J. of General Systems*, **8**(3), pp. 139–146.

1561. Yager, R. R. [1982e], "Measures of fuzziness based on t-norms." *Stochastica*, **6**(1), pp. 207–229.

1562. Yager, R. R., ed. [**1982f**], *Fuzzy Set and Possibility Theory: Recent Developments*. Pergamon Press, New York.

1563. Yager, R. R. [1982g], "Linguistic hedge: Their relation to context and their experimental realization." *Cybernetics and Systems*, **13**(4), pp. 357–374.

1564. Yager, R. R. [1983a], "Quantifiers in the formulation of multiple objective decision functions." *Information Sciences*, **31**(2), pp. 107–139.

1565. Yager, R. R. [1983b], "On the implication operator in fuzzy logic." *Information Sciences*, **31**(2), pp. 141–164.

1566. Yager, R. R. [1983c], "Some relationships between possibility, truth and certainty." *Fuzzy Sets and Systems*, **11**(2), pp. 151–156.

1567. Yager, R. R. [1983d], "Entropy and specificity in a mathematical theory of evidence." *Intern. J. of General Systems*, **9**(4), pp. 249–260.

1568. Yager, R. R. [1983e], "Membership in compound fuzzy subset." *Cybernetics and Systems*, **14**(2–3), pp. 173–184.

1569. Yager, R. R. [1984a], "On different classes of linguistic variables defined via fuzzy subsets." *Kybernetes*, **13**(2), pp. 103–110.

1570. Yager, R. R. [1984b], "Fuzzy subsets with uncertain membership grades." *IEEE Trans. on Systems, Man, and Cybernetics*, **14**(2), pp. 271–275.

1571. Yager, R. R. [1984c], "Probabilities from fuzzy observations." *Information Sciences*, **32**(1), pp. 1–31.

1572. Yager, R. R. [1984d], "Linguistic representation of default values in frames." *IEEE Trans. on Systems, Man, and Cybernetics*, **14**(4), pp. 630–633.

1573. Yager, R. R. [1985a], "On the relationship of methods of aggregating evidence in expert systems." *Cybernetics and Systems*, **16**(1), pp. 1–21.

1574. Yager, R. R. [1985b], "Strong truth and rules of inference in fuzzy logic and approximate reasoning." *Cybernetics and Systems*, **16**(1), pp. 23–63.

1575. Yager, R. R. [1985c], "On truth functional modification." *Intern. J. of General Systems*, **10**(2–3), pp. 105–121.

1576. Yager, R. R. [1985d], "Inference in a multivalued logic systems." *Intern. J. of Man-Machine Studies*, **23**(1), pp. 27–44.

1577. Yager, R. R. [1985e], "Q-projections on possibility distributions." *IEEE Trans. on Systems, Man, and Cybernetics*, **15**(6), pp. 775–777.

1578. Yager, R. R. [1986a], "A characterization of the extension principle." *Fuzzy Sets and Systems*, **18**(3), pp. 205–217.

1579. Yager, R. R. [1986b], "On the theory of bags." *Intern. J. of General Systems*, **13**(1), pp. 23–37.

1580. Yager, R. R. [1987a], "On the knowledge structure of multi-solution variable, including quantified statements." *Intern. J. of Approximate Reasoning*, **1**(1), pp. 23–70.

1581. Yager, R. R. [1987b], "Using approximate reasoning to represent default knowledge." *Artificial Intelligence*, **31**(1), pp. 99–112.

1582. Yager, R. R. [1987c], "On the representation of transition matrices by possibility probability granules." *IEEE Trans. on Systems, Man, and Cybernetics*, **17**(5), pp. 851–857.

1583. Yager, R. R. [1987d], "Cardinality of fuzzy sets via bags." *Mathematical Modelling*, **9**(6), pp. 441–446.

1584. Yager, R. R. [1987e], "Toward a theory of conjunctive variables." *Intern. J. of General Systems*, **13**(3), pp. 203–227.

1585. Yager, R. R. [1988a], "Reasoning with conjunctive knowledge." *Fuzzy Sets and Systems*, **28**(1), pp. 69–83.

1586. Yager, R. R. [1988b], "On ordered weighted averaging aggregation operators in multicriteria decisionmaking." *IEEE Trans. on Systems, Man, and Cybernetics*, **18**(1), pp. 183–190.

1587. Yager, R. R. [1988c], "Nonmonotonic inheritance systems." *IEEE Trans. on Systems, Man, and Cybernetics*, **18**(6), pp. 1028–1034.

1588. Yager, R. R. [1989a], "On usual values in commonsense reasoning." *Fuzzy Sets and Systems*, **30**(3), pp. 239–255.

1589. Yager, R. R. [1989b], "On the representation of commonsense knowledge by possibilistic reasoning." *Intern. J. of Man-Machine Studies*, **31**(5), pp. 587–610.

1590. Yager, R. R. [1990a], "On a generalization of variable precision logic." *IEEE Trans. on Systems, Man, and Cybernetics*, **20**(1), pp. 248–252.

1591. Yager, R. R. [1990b], "A model of participatory learning." *IEEE Trans. on Systems, Man, and Cybernetics*, **20**(5), pp. 1229–1234.

1592. Yager, R. R. [1990c], "Ordinal measures of specificity." *Intern. J. of General Systems*, **17**(1), pp. 57–72.

1593. Yager, R. R. [1991], "Similarity based specificity measures." *Intern. J. of General Systems*, **19**(2), pp. 91–105.

1594. Yager, R. R. [1992a], "Adaptive models for the defuzzification process." *Proc. Second Intern. Conf. on Fuzzy Logic and Neural Networks, Iizuka, Japan*, pp. 65–71.

1595. Yager, R. R. [1992b], "Implementing fuzzy logic controllers using a neural network framework." *Fuzzy Sets and Systems*, **48**(1), pp. 53–64.

1596. Yager, R. R. [1992c], "On the specificity of a possibility distribution." *Fuzzy Sets and Systems*, **50**(3), pp. 279–292.

1597. Yager, R. R. [1992d], "On a semantics for neural networks based on fuzzy quantifiers." *Intern. J. of Intelligent Systems*, **7**(8), pp. 765–786.

1598. Yager, R. R. [1992e], "On considerations of credibility of evidence." *Intern. J. of Approximate Reasoning*, **7**(1–2), pp. 45–72.

1599. Yager, R. R. [1992f], "Entropy measures under similarity relations." *Intern. J. of General Systems*, **20**(4), pp. 341–356.

1600. Yager, R. R. [1992g], "A general approach to rule aggregation in fuzzy logic control." *Applied Intelligence*, **2**(4), pp. 335–351.

1601. Yager, R. R. [1993a], "Generalized fuzzy and matrix associative holographic memories." *J. of Intelligent & Fuzzy Systems*, **1**(1), pp. 43–53.

1602. Yager, R. R. [1993b], "Aggregating fuzzy sets represented by belief structures." *J. of Intelligent & Fuzzy Systems*, **1**(3), pp. 215–224.

1603. Yager, R. R. [1993c], "Counting the number of classes in a fuzzy set." *IEEE Trans. on Systems, Man, and Cybernetics*, **23**(1), pp. 257–264.

1604. Yager, R. R. [1993d], "Element selection from a fuzzy subset using the fuzzy integral." *IEEE Trans. on Systems, Man, and Cybernetics*, **23**(2), pp. 467–477.

1605. Yager, R. R. [1993e], "On a hierarchical structure for fuzzy modeling and control." *IEEE Trans. on Systems, Man, and Cybernetics*, **23**(4), pp. 1189–1197.

1606. Yager, R. R. [1993f], "On the completion of qualitative possibility measures." *IEEE Trans. on Fuzzy Systems*, **1**(3), pp. 184–194.

1607. Yager, R. R. [1993g], "Families of OWA operators." *Fuzzy Sets and Systems*, **59**(2), pp. 125–148.

1608. Yager, R. R. [1994], "On the RAGE aggregation method with applications to neural networks and decision making." *Intern. J. of Approximate Reasoning*, **11**(3), pp. 175–204.

1609. Yager, R. R., M. Fedrizzi and J. Kacprzyk, eds. **[1994]**, *Advances in the Dempster–Shafer Theory of Evidence*. John Wiley, New York.

1610. Yager, R. R. and D. P. Filev [1993a], "SLIDE: A simple adaptive defuzzification method." *IEEE Trans. on Fuzzy Systems*, **1**(1), pp. 69–78.

1611. Yager, R. R. and D. P. Filev [1993b], "On the issue of defuzzification and selection based on a fuzzy sets." *Fuzzy Sets and Systems*, **55**(3), pp. 255–272.

1612. Yager, R. R. and D. P. Filev [1993c], "Unified structure and parameter identification of fuzzy model." *IEEE Trans. on Systems, Man, and Cybernetics*, **23**(4), pp. 1198–1205.

1613. Yager, R. R. and D. P. Filev **[1994a]**, *Essentials of Fuzzy Modeling and Control*. John Wiley, New York.

1614. Yager, R. R. and D. P. Filev [1994b], "Defuzzification under constraints and forbidden zones." *Kybernetes*, **23**(2), pp. 43–57.

1615. Yager, R. R. and D. P. Filev [1994c], "Approximate clustering via the mountain method." *IEEE Trans. on Systems, Man, and Cybernetics*, **24**(8), pp. 1279–1284.

1616. Yager, R. R., D. P. Filev and T. Sadeghi [1994], "Analysis of flexible structured fuzzy logic controllers." *IEEE Trans. on Systems, Man, and Cybernetics*, **24**(7), pp. 1035–1043.

1617. Yager, R. R. and H. L. Larsen [1991], "On discovering potential inconsistencies in validating uncertainty knowledge bases by reflecting on the input." *IEEE Trans. on Systems, Man, and Cybernetics*, **21**(4), pp. 790–801.

1618. Yager, R. R., S. Ovchinnikov, R. M. Tong and H. T. Nguyen, eds. **[1987]**, *Fuzzy Sets and Applications: Selected Papers by L. A. Zadeh*. John Wiley, New York.

1619. Yager, R. R. and L. A. Zadeh, eds. **[1992]**, *An Introduction to Fuzzy Logic Applications in Intelligent Systems*. Kluwer, Boston.

1620. Yager, R. R. and L. A. Zadeh, eds. **[1994]**, *Fuzzy Sets, Neural Networks, and Soft Computing*. Van Nostrand Reinhold, New York.

1621. Yager, R. R. and D. Zhang [1993], "On quasi-monotonic measures." *Intern. J. of General Systems*, **22**(1), pp. 43–54.

1622. Yamakawa, T. [1988], "High–speed fuzzy controller hardware system." *Information Sciences*, **45**(2), pp. 113–128.

1623. Yamakawa, T. [1989], "Stabilization of an inverted pendulum by a high–speed logic controller hardware system." *Fuzzy Sets and Systems*, **32**(2), pp. 161–180.

1624. Yamakawa, T. [1993], "A fuzzy inference engine in nonlinear analog mode and its application to a fuzzy logic control." *IEEE Trans. on Neural Networks*, **4**(3), pp. 496–522.

1625. Yamakawa, T. and H. Kaboo [1988], "A programmable fuzzifier integrated circuit-synthesis, design, and fabrication." *Information Sciences*, **45**(1), pp. 75–112.

1626. Yamakawa, T. and T. Miki [1986], "The current mode fuzzy logic integrated circuits fabricated by the standard CMOS process." *IEEE Trans. on Computers*, **35**(2), pp. 161–167.

1627. Yamashita, H., E. Tsuda and Y. Katsumata [1991], "Instruction and cognition analysis applying fuzzy graphs." *Intern. J. of Approximate Reasoning*, **5**(3), pp. 349–372.

1628. Yamashita, Y., S. Matsumoto and M. Suzuki [1988], "Start-up of a catalytic reactor by fuzzy controller." *J. of Chemical Eng. of Japan*, **21**(3), pp. 277–282.

1629. Yan, B. [1993], "Seminormed possibility integrals for application oriented modelling." *Fuzzy Sets and Systems*, **61**(2), pp. 189–198.

1630. Yan, J., M. Ryan and J. Power **[1994]**, *Using Fuzzy Logic: Towards Intelligent Systems*. Prentice Hall, Englewood Cliffs, NJ.

1631. Yanaru, T., T. Hirotja and N. Kimura [1994], "An emotion-processing system based on fuzzy inference and its subjective observations." *Intern. J. of Approximate Reasoning*, **10**(1), pp. 99–122.

1632. Yang, J. D. [1994], "A uniform framework for deductive processing of fuzzy information." *Fuzzy Sets and Systems*, **64**(3), pp. 377–385.

1633. Yang, X. M. [1993], "A note on convex fuzzy sets." *Fuzzy Sets and Systems*, **53**(1), pp. 117–118.

1634. Yao, Y. Y. and S. K. M. Wong [1992], "A decision theoretic framework for approximating concepts." *Intern. J. of Man-Machine Studies*, **37**(6), pp. 793–809.

1635. Yeh, E. C. and S. H. Lu [1994], "Hysteresis characterization by a fuzzy learning algorithm." *Intern. J. of Uncertainty, Fuzziness and Knowledge-Based Systems*, **2**(3), pp. 351–360.

1636. Yeh, R. T. and S. Y. Bang [1975], "Fuzzy relations, fuzzy graphs, and their applications." In: Zadeh, L., K. S. Fu, K. Tanaka and M. Shimura, eds., *Fuzzy Sets and their Applications to Cognitive and Decision Processes*. Academic Press, New York, pp. 125–149.

1637. Yeh, Z. M. [1994], "A performance approach to fuzzy control design for nonlinear systems." *Fuzzy Sets and Systems*, **64**(3), pp. 339–352.

1638. Yen, J. [1990], "Generalizing the Dempster–Shafer theory to fuzzy sets." *IEEE Trans. on Systems, Man, and Cybernetics.*, **20**(3), pp. 559–570.

1639. Yen, J. and R. Langari [**1994**], *Industrial Applications of Fuzzy Logic and Intelligent Systems*. IEEE Press, New York.

1640. Yi, L. [1990], "The concept of fuzzy systems." *Kybernetes*, **19**(3), pp. 45–51.

1641. Yi, S. and S. Park [1993], "A new fast fuzzy algorithm." *Fuzzy Sets and Systems*, **60**(1), pp. 33–40.

1642. Yi, S. Y. and M. J. Chung [1993], "Identification of fuzzy relational model and its application to control." *Fuzzy Sets and Systems*, **59**(1), pp. 25–33.

1643. Ying, H. [1994], "Analytical structure of a two-input two-output fuzzy controller and its relation to PI and multilevel relay controllers." *Fuzzy Sets and Systems*, **63**(1), pp. 21–33.

1644. Ying, M. S. [1988a], "Some notes on multidimensional fuzzy reasoning." *Cybernetics and Systems*, **19**(4), pp. 281–293.

1645. Ying, M. S. [1988b], "On standard models of fuzzy modal logics." *Fuzzy Sets and Systems*, **26**(3), pp. 357–363.

1646. Ying, M. S. [1990], "Reasonableness of the compositional rule of fuzzy inference." *Fuzzy Sets and Systems*, **36**(2), pp. 305–310.

1647. Yoon, B., D. J. Holmes, G. Langholz and A. Kandel [1994], "Efficient genetic algorithms for training layered feedforward neural networks." *Information Sciences: Informatics and Computer Sciences*, **76**(1–2), pp. 67–85.

1648. Yoshida, Y. [1994], "Markov chains with a transition possibility measure and fuzzy dynamic programming." *Fuzzy Sets and Systems*, **66**(1), pp. 39–57.

1649. Yoshida, Y., M. Yasuda, J. Nakagami and M. Kurano [1994], "A potential of fuzzy relations with a linear structure: The unbounded case." *Fuzzy Sets and Systems*, **66**(1), pp. 83–95.

1650. Yoshikawa, Y. and T. Deguchi [1994], "Evaluation of orthodontic results with fuzzy inference." *Intern. J. of Intelligent Systems*, **9**(2), pp. 227–240.

1651. Yoshinari, Y., W. Pedrycz and K. Hirota [1993], "Construction of fuzzy models through clustering techniques." *Fuzzy Sets and Systems*, **54**(2), pp. 157–165.

1652. Yu, C. [1993], "Correlation of fuzzy numbers." *Fuzzy Sets and Systems*, **55**(3), pp. 303–308.

1653. Yu, C., Z. Cao and A. Kandel [1990], "Application of fuzzy reasoning to the control of an activated sludge plant." *Fuzzy Sets and Systems*, **38**(1), pp. 1–14.

1654. Yu, W. and Z. Bien [1994], "Design of fuzzy logic controller with inconsistent rule base." *J. of Intelligent & Fuzzy Systems*, **2**(2), pp. 147–159.

1655. Yu, Y. D. [1985], "Triangular norms and TNF-sigma-algebras." *Fuzzy Sets and Systems*, **16**(3), pp. 251–264.

1656. Yuan, B. and G. J. Klir [1993], "On approximate solutions of fuzzy relation equations." *Proc. NAFIPS Meeting, Allentown, PA.*, pp. 237–241.

1657. Yuan, B. and Y. Pan [1993], "Generalized fuzzy method-of-cases." *Intern. J. of Approximate Reasoning*, **9**(2), pp. 129–138.

1658. Yuan, B. and W. Wu [1990], "Fuzzy ideals on a distributive lattice." *Fuzzy Sets and Systems*, **35**(2), pp. 231–240.

1659. Zadeh, L. A. [1962], "From circuit theory to systems theory." *IRE Proc.*, **50**, pp. 856–865.

1660. Zadeh, L. A. [1965a], "Fuzzy sets and systems." In: Fox, J., ed., *System Theory*. Polytechnic Press, Brooklyn, NY, pp. 29–37.

1661. Zadeh, L. A. [1965b], "Fuzzy sets." *Information and Control*, **8**(3), pp. 338–353.

1662. Zadeh, L. A. [1968a], "Probability measures and fuzzy events." *J. of Math. Analysis and Applications*, **23**(2), pp. 421–427.

1663. Zadeh, L. A. [1968b], "Fuzzy algorithms." *Information and Control*, **12**(2), pp. 94–102.

1664. Zadeh, L. A. [1971a], "Towards a theory of fuzzy systems." In: Kalman, R. E. and R. N. De Clairis, eds., *Aspects of Networks and Systems Theory*. Holt, Rinehart & Winston, New York, pp. 469–490.

1665. Zadeh, L. A. [1971b], "Quantitative fuzzy semantics." *Information Sciences*, **3**(2), pp. 159–176.

1666. Zadeh, L. A. [1971c], "Similarity relations and fuzzy orderings." *Information Sciences*, **3**(2), pp. 177–200.

1667. Zadeh, L. A. [1972a], "A rationale for fuzzy control." *J. of Dynamical Systems, Measurement, and Control (Trans. ASME. Ser. G)*, **94**(1), pp. 3–4.

1668. Zadeh, L. A. [1972b], "A fuzzy set interpretation of linguistic hedges." *J. of Cybernetics*, **2**(3), pp. 4–34.

1669. Zadeh, L. A. [1973], "Outline of a new approach to the analysis of complex systems and decision processes." *IEEE Trans. on Systems, Man, and Cybernetics*, **1**(1), pp. 28–44.

1670. Zadeh, L. A. [1974a], "A new approach to system analysis." In: Marois, M., ed., *Man and Computer*. North-Holland, New York, pp. 55–94.

1671. Zadeh, L. A. [1974b], "On the analysis of large scale systems." In: Gottinger, H., ed., *Systems Approaches and Environment Problems*. Vandenhoeck and Ruprecht, Gottingen, pp. 23–37.

1672. Zadeh, L. A. [1975a], "Fuzzy logic and approximate reasoning." *Synthese*, **30**(1), pp. 407–428.

1673. Zadeh, L. A. [1975b], "The concept of a linguistic variable and its application to approximate reasoning I, II, III." *Information Sciences*, **8**, pp. 199–251, 301–357; **9**, pp. 43–80.

1674. Zadeh, L. A. [1975c], "Calculus of fuzzy restrictions." In: Zadeh, L. A., K. S. Fu, K. Tanaka and M. Shimura, eds., *Fuzzy Sets and Their Applications to Cognitive and Decision Processes*. Academic Press, New York, pp. 1–39.

1675. Zadeh, L. A. [1976a], "A fuzzy-algorithmic approach to the definition of complex or imprecise concepts." *Intern. J. of Man-Machine Studies*, **8**(3), pp. 249–291.

1676. Zadeh, L. A. [1976b], "The linguistic approach and its application to decision analysis." In: Ho, Y. C. and S. K. Mitter, eds., *Directions in Large Scale Systems*. Plenum Press, New York, pp. 339–370.

1677. Zadeh, L. A. [1977], "Linguistic characterization of preference relations as a basis for choice in social systems." *Erkenntnis*, **11**(3), pp. 383–410.

1678. Zadeh, L. A. [1978a], "PRUF—A meaning representation language for nature languages." *Intern. J. of Man-Machine Studies*, **10**(4), pp. 395–460.

1679. Zadeh, L. A. [1978b], "Fuzzy sets as a basis for a theory of possibility." *Fuzzy Sets and Systems*, **1**(1), pp. 3–28.

1680. Zadeh, L. A. [1979a], "Fuzzy sets and information granularity." In: Gupta, M. M., R. K. Ragade and R. R. Yager, eds., *Advances in Fuzzy Set Theory and Applications*. North-Holland, New York, pp. 3–18.

1681. Zadeh, L. A. [1979b], "A theory of approximate reasoning." In: Hayes, J., D. Michie and L. I. Mikulich, eds., *Machine Intelligence, Vol. 9*. Halstead Press, New York, pp. 149–194.

1682. Zadeh, L. A. [1981], "Possibility theory and soft data analysis." In: Cobb, L. and R. M. Thrall, Eds., *Mathematical Frontiers of the Social and Policy Sciences*. Westview Press, Boulder, Colorado, pp. 69–129.

1683. Zadeh, L. A. [1982a], "Fuzzy systems theory: A framework for the analysis of humanistic systems." In: Cavallo, R. E., Ed., *Systems Methodology in Social Science Research*. Kluwer, Boston, pp. 25–41.

1684. Zadeh, L. A. [1982b], "Test-score semantics for natural languages and meaning representation via PRUF." In: Reiger, B., ed., *Empirical Semantics*. Brockmeyer, Bochum, Germany, pp. 281–349.

1685. Zadeh, L. A. [1982c], "A note on prototype theory and fuzzy sets." *Cognition*, **12**(3), pp. 291–297.

1686. Zadeh, L. A. [1983a], "A computational approach to fuzzy quantifiers in natural languages." *Computers and Mathematics with Applications*, **9**(1), pp. 149–184.

1687. Zadeh, L. A. [1983b], "A fuzzy-set theoretic approach to the compositionality of meaning: Propositions, dispositions and canonical forms." *J. of Semantics*, **3**, pp. 253–272.

1688. Zadeh, L. A. [1983c], "Linguistic variables, approximate reasoning and dispositions." *Medical Information*, **8**, pp. 173–186.

1689. Zadeh, L. A. [1983d], "The role of fuzzy logic in the management of uncertainty in expert systems." *Fuzzy Sets and Systems*, **11**(3), pp. 199–228.

1690. Zadeh, L. A. [1984], "Precisiation of meaning via translation into PRUF." In: Vaina, L. and J. Hintikka, eds., *Cognitive Constraints on Communication*. D. Reidel, Boston, pp. 373–402.

1691. Zadeh, L. A. [1985], "Syllogistic reasoning in fuzzy logic and its application to usuality and reasoning with dispositions." *IEEE Trans. on Systems, Man, and Cybernetics*, **15**(6), pp. 754–765.

1692. Zadeh, L. A. [1987], "A computational theory of dispositions." *Intern. J. of Intelligent Systems*, **2**(1), pp. 39–63.

1693. Zadeh, L. A. [1989], "Knowledge representation in fuzzy logic." *IEEE Trans. on Knowledge and Data Engineering*, **1**(1), pp. 89–100.

1694. Zadeh, L. A. [1990], "The birth and evolution of fuzzy logic." *Intern. J. of General Systems*, **17**(2–3), pp. 95–105.

1695. Zadeh, L. A., R. E. Bellman and R. Kalaba [1966], "Abstraction and pattern classification." *J. of Math. Analysis and Applications*, **13**(1), pp. 1–7.

1696. Zadeh, L. A., K. S. Fu, K. Tanaka and M. Shimura, eds. **[1975]**, *Fuzzy Sets and Their Applications to Cognitive and Decision Processes*. Academic Press, New York.

1697. Zadeh, L. A. and J. Kacprzyk, eds. **[1992]**, *Fuzzy Logic for the Management of Uncertainty*. John Wiley, New York.

1698. Zadeh, L. A. and E. T. Lee [1969], "Note on fuzzy languages." *Information Sciences*, **1**(4), pp. 421–434.

1699. Zeising, G., M. Wagenknecht and K. Hartmann [1984], "Synthesis of distillation trains with heat integration by a combined fuzzy and graphical approach." *Fuzzy Sets and Systems*, 12(2), pp. 103–115.

1700. Zeleny, M. [1991a], "Cognitive equilibrium: A knowledge-based theory of fuzziness and fuzzy sets." *Intern. J. of General Systems*, 19(4), pp. 359–381.

1701. Zeleny, M. [1991b], "Fuzzifying the 'precise' is more relevant than modeling the fuzzy 'crisply' (rejoiner)." *Intern. J. of General Systems*, 19(4), pp. 435–440.

1702. Zemankova, M. [1989], "FILIP: A fuzzy intelligent information system with learning capabilities." *Information Systems*, 14(6), pp. 473–486.

1703. Zemankova, M. and A. Kandel [1985], "Implementing imprecision in information systems." *Information Sciences*, 37(1–3), pp. 107–141.

1704. Zemankova–Leech, M. and A. Kandel [**1984**], *Fuzzy Relational Data Bases: A Key to Expert Systems*. Verlag TÜV Rheinland, Köln.

1705. Zeng, X. J. and M. G. Singh [1994], "Approximation theory of fuzzy systems: SISO case." *IEEE Trans. on Fuzzy Systems*, 2(2), pp. 162–176.

1706. Zenner, R. B. R., R. M. M. DeCaluwe and E. E. Kerre [1985], "A new approach to information retrieval systems using fuzzy expressions." *Fuzzy Sets and Systems*, 17(1), pp. 9–22.

1707. Zétényi, T., ed. [**1988**], *Fuzzy Sets in Psychology*. North-Holland, New York.

1708. Zhang, D. L. and Z. X. Wang [1993], "Fuzzy integrals of fuzzy-valued functions." *Fuzzy Sets and Systems*, 54(1), pp. 63–67.

1709. Zhang, D., P. L. Yu and P. Z. Wang [1992], "State-dependent weights in multicriteria value functions." *J. of Optimization Theory and Applications*, 74(1), pp. 1–21.

1710. Zhang, G. Q. [1992], "Fuzzy number-valued fuzzy measure and fuzzy number-valued fuzzy integral on the fuzzy set." *Fuzzy Sets and Systems*, 49(3), pp. 357–376.

1711. Zhang, H. and L. Chen [1991], "A technique for handling fuzzy decision-making problems concerning two kinds of uncertainty." *Cybernetics and Systems*, 22(6), pp. 681–698.

1712. Zhang, H., X. W. Ma, W. Xu and P. Z. Wang [1993], "Design fuzzy controllers for complex systems with an application to 3–stage inverted pendulum." *Information Sciences*, 72(3), pp. 271–284.

1713. Zhang, J. W. [1993], "Applications of fuzzy logic control in autonomous robot systems." *Intern. J. of Systems Science*, 24(10), pp. 1885–1904.

1714. Zhang, W. and Y. Chen [1984], "Mathematical models of multifactorial decisions and weather forecast." In: Sanchez, E., ed., *Fuzzy Information, Knowledge Representation and Decision Analysis*. Pergamon Press, Oxford, U. K., pp. 265–269.

1715. Zhang, W. R., S. S. Chen and J. C. Bezdek [1989], "Pool 2: A genetic system for cognitive map development and decision analysis." *IEEE Trans. on Systems, Man, and Cybernetics*, 19(1), pp. 31–39.

1716. Zhang, Z. [1993], "An approximate reasoning system: Design and implementation." *Intern. J. of Approximate Reasoning*, 9(4), pp. 315–326.

1717. Zhao, Q. and B. Li [1993], "M: An approximate reasoning system." *Intern. J. of Pattern Recognition and Artificial Intelligence*, 7(3), pp. 431–440.

1718. Zhao, R. and R. Govind [1991], "Defuzzification of fuzzy intervals." *Fuzzy Sets and Systems*, 43(1), pp. 45–55.

1719. Zhao, R., R. Govind and G. Fan [1992], "The complete decision set of the generalized symmetrical fuzzy linear programming problems." *Fuzzy Sets and Systems*, 51(1), pp. 53–66.

1720. Zhong, Q. and G. Y. Wang [1993], "On solution and distribution problems of the linear programming with fuzzy random variable coefficients." *Fuzzy Sets and Systems*, 58(2), pp. 155–170.

1721. Zimmermann, H. J. [1975], "Description and optimization of fuzzy systems." *Intern. J. of General Systems*, 2(4), pp. 209–215.

1722. Zimmermann, H. J. [1978a], "Results of empirical studies in fuzzy set theory." In: Klir, G. J., ed., *Applied General Systems Research*. Plenum Press, New York, pp. 303–312.

1723. Zimmermann, H. J. [1978b], "Fuzzy programming and linear programming with several objective functions." *Fuzzy Sets and Systems*, 1(1), pp. 45–55.

1724. Zimmermann, H. J. [1985a], "Applications of fuzzy set theory to mathematical programming." *Information Sciences*, 36(1), pp. 29–58.

1725. Zimmermann, H. J. [**1985b**], *Fuzzy Set Theory and Its Applications*. Kluwer, Boston.

1726. Zimmermann, H. J. [**1987**], *Fuzzy Sets, Decision Making, and Expert Systems*. Kluwer, Boston.

1727. Zimmermann, H. J., L. A. Zadeh and B. R. Gaines, eds. [**1984**], *Fuzzy Sets and Decision Analysis*. North-Holland, New York.

1728. Zimmermann, H. J. and P. Zysno [1980], "Latent connectives in human decision making." *Fuzzy Sets and Systems*, 4(1), pp. 37–51.

1729. Zimmermann, K. [1991], "Fuzzy set covering problem." *Intern. J. of General Systems*, 20(1), pp. 127–131.

1730. Zurada, J. M., R. J. Marks II and C. J. Robinson, eds. [**1994**], *Computational Intelligence: Imitating Life*. IEEE Press, New York.

1731. Zwick, R., E. Carlstein and D. V. Budescu [1987], "Measures of similarity among fuzzy concepts: A comparative analysis." *Intern. J. of Approximate Reasoning*, 1(2), pp. 221–242.

Bibliographical Index

Name Index

SUBJECT INDEX

α-cut, 19, 21, 22, 24, 35–42, 102, 103, 250, 396, 489
α-compatibility, 135
α-cover, complete, 135, 136
λ-average, 93
ε-reflexivity, 130
Absolute complement, 7, 8
Absolute quantifier, 229
Additivity, 179
  axiom, 200
Aggregation operation, 51, 88–95, 487
Algebra:
  Boolean, 8, 214, 215
  De Morgan, 25
Algebraic product, 63
Algebraic sum, 78
Algorithm:
  fuzzy c-means, 360–362
  genetic, 304, 452, 464, 476–480
  learning:
    backpropagation, 296, 348, 349, 468, 473–475
    gradient-descent, 470
    supervised, 467
    unsupervised, 467
Algorithmic information, 246
Alternative set theory, 33
Ambiguity, 268
Ampliative reasoning, 271
Analysis:
  cluster, 357, 448
  dimensional, 464
  fuzzy regression, 455
  interval, 97, 103
Analog fuzzy hardware, 436

Antireflexive relation, 128, 131
  fuzzy, 130, 141
Antisymmetric relation, 128, 131
  fuzzy, 130, 138, 140, 141
Antisymmetry, 137
Antitransitive, relation, 129
  fuzzy, 130
Approximate reasoning, 304, 323, 325, 335, 465
  interval-valued, 323, 324
  multiconditional, 317
Approximate solution, 166–171, 173, 322
  greatest, 168
Approximation:
  lower, 481
  upper, 481
Approximator, universal, 344, 345, 355
Archimedean t-conorm, 77, 78
  strict, 77
Archimedean t-norm, 63, 65, 68
  strict, 63
Arithmetic, fuzzy, 97–118, 348, 349, 420
Arithmetic mean, 90
Arithmetic, interval, 117
Array, n-dimensional, 120
Assignment:
  marginal basic, 183
  basic probability, 181, 182, 187, 201, 487
Associativity, 62, 77
Associative averaging operation, 93
Asymmetric relation, 128
  fuzzy, 130

Asymmetry, 137
Augmented inquiry, 386, 387
Automaton:
  fuzzy, 349–352, 355, 401
  probabilistic, 352
Automorphism, 142
Average:
  λ-, 93
  weighted, 92
  weighted quasi-, 92
Averaging operation, 51, 89, 93
  associative, 93
  ordered weighted, 90
Axiom:
  of additivity, 200
  of fuzzy implications, 308

Backpropagation learning algorithm, 296, 348, 349, 468, 473–475
Backward chaining, 303
Base:
  fuzzy rule, 331, 342
  data, 302, 303, 379, 380
  knowledge, 302, 303
  metaknowledge, 303, 304
Basic distribution, 192
Basic probability assignment, 181, 182, 187, 201, 487
  marginal, 183
Bell-shaped membership function, 98, 292, 293
Belief measure, 180, 182, 187, 200, 201, 203, 267, 487
Bias, 469
Biology, 464